MISCELLANEOUS

THEOLOGICAL WORKS

OF

EMANUEL SWEDENBORG,

Servant of the Lord Jesus Christ.

THE NEW JERUSALEM AND ITS HEAVENLY DOCTRINE;
BRIEF EXPOSITION;
THE INTERCOURSE BETWEEN THE SOUL AND THE BODY;
THE WHITE HORSE MENTIONED IN THE APOCALYPSE, CHAP. XIX.;
AN APPENDIX TO THE TREATISE ON THE WHITE HORSE;
ON THE EARTHS IN THE UNIVERSE;
THE LAST JUDGMENT;
A CONTINUATION CONCERNING THE LAST JUDGMENT.

NEW YORK:
AMERICAN SWEDENBORG PRINTING AND PUBLISHING SOCIETY.
1871.

Published by THE AMERICAN SWEDENBORG PRINTING AND PUBLISHING SOCIETY, *organized for the purpose of Stereotyping, Printing, and Publishing Uniform Editions of the Theological Writings of* EMANUEL SWEDENBORG, *and incorporated in the State of New York*, A. D. 1850.

GENERAL INDEX.

☞ The *pages* are numbered at bottom; the figures at top referring to the *section* numbers of each treatise.

THE NEW JERUSALEM, AND ITS HEAVENLY DOCTRINE,

ACCORDING TO

WHAT HAS BEEN HEARD FROM HEAVEN·

TO WHICH IS PREFIXED

INFORMATION RESPECTING THE NEW HEAVEN AND THE NEW EARTH.

From the Latin of

EMANUEL SWEDENBORG

Servant of the Lord Jesus Christ.

BEING A TRANSLATION OF HIS WORK ENTITLED

"De Nova Hierosolyma et ejus Doctrina Cœlesti: ex auditis e Cœlo. Quibus præmittitur aliquid de Novo Cœlo et Nova Terra." Londini, 1758

NEW YORK:

AMERICAN SWEDENBORG PRINTING AND PUBLISHING SOCIETY

MATTHEW vi. 33.

Seek ye first the Kingdom of GOD, and all things shall be added unto you.

CONTENTS.

ON

THE NEW JERUSALEM,

AND ITS

HEAVENLY DOCTRINE.

OF THE NEW HEAVEN AND NEW EARTH, AND WHAT IS MEANT BY THE NEW JERUSALEM.

1. It is written in the Revelation, "I saw a new heaven and a new earth; for the first heaven and the first earth had passed away. And I John saw the holy city, New Jerusalem, coming down from God out of heaven, prepared as a bride adorned for her husband. The city had a wall, great and high, which had twelve gates, and at the gates twelve angels, and names written thereon, which are the names of the twelve tribes of the children of Israel. And the wall of the city had twelve foundations, and in them the names of the twelve Apostles of the Lamb. And the city lieth four-square, and the length is as great as the breadth. And he measured the city with the reed, twelve thousand furlongs; the length and the breadth and the height of it were equal. And he measured the wall thereof, a hundred and forty and four cubits, the measure of a man, that is, of the angel. And the wall of it was of jasper; and the city was pure gold, like unto pure glass; and the foundations of the wall of the city were garnished with all manner of precious stones. And the twelve gates were twelve pearls. And the street of the city was pure gold, as it were transparent glass. The glory of God did lighten it, and the Lamb is the light thereof. And the nations of them which are saved shall walk in the light of it; and the kings of the earth shall bring their glory and honor into it." Chap. xxi. 1, 2, 12—24.

When a man reads these words, he understands them only according to their literal sense, and concludes that the visible heaven and earth will be dissolved, and a new heaven be created, and that the holy city Jerusalem, answering to the measures above described, will descend upon the new earth; but the angels understand these things altogether differently; that is to say, what man understands naturally, they understand spiritually; and what they understand is the true signification; and this is the internal or spiritual sense of the Word. According to this internal or spiritual sense, a new heaven and a new earth mean a new church, both in the heavens and on the earth, which will be more particularly spoken of hereafter. The city Jerusalem descending from God out of heaven, signifies the heavenly doctrine of that church; the length, the breadth, and the height thereof, which are equal, signify all the varieties of good and truth belonging to that doctrine in the aggregate. The wall of the city means the truths which protect it; the measure of the wall, which is a hundred and forty and four cubits, which is the measure of a man, that is, of the angel, signifies all those defending truths in the aggregate, and their quality. The twelve gates of pearl mean all introductory truths; and the twelve angels at the gates signify the same. The foundations of the wall, which are of every precious stone, mean the knowledges on which that doctrine is founded. The twelve tribes of Israel, and the twelve Apostles, mean all things belonging to the church in general and in particular. The city and its streets being of gold like unto pure glass, signifies the good of love, giving brightness and transparency to the doctrine and its truths. The nations who are saved, and the kings of the earth who bring glory and honor into the city, mean all the members of that church who are in goodness and in truth. God and the Lamb mean the Lord as to the Essential Divinity and the Divine Humanity. Such is the spiritual sense of the Word, to which the natural sense, which is that of the letter, serves as a basis; but still these two senses, the spiritual and the natural, form a one by correspondences.

It is not the design of the present work to prove that such a spiritual meaning is involved in the afore-mentioned passages, but the proof of it may be seen in the ARCANA CŒLESTIA, in the following places. That the term, LAND, when used in the Word, means the church, particularly when it is applied to signify the Land of Canaan, n. 662, 1066, 1067, 1413, 1607, 2928, 3355, 4447, 4535, 5577, 8011, 9325, 9643. Because earth, or land, in a spiritual sense, signifies the nation dwelling therein, and its worship, n. 1262. That the people of the land signify those who belong to the spiritual church, n. 2928. That a new heaven and a new earth signify something new in the heavens and on earth, with respect to good and truth, thus respecting those things that relate to the church in each, n. 1733, 1850, 2117, 2118, 3358, 4535, 10,373. What is to be understood by the first heaven and the first earth which passed away, may be seen in the work ON THE LAST JUDGMENT AND THE DESTRUCTION OF BABYLON throughout, but particularly from n. 65 to 72. That JERUSALEM signifies the church with respect to doctrine, n. 402, 3654, 9166. That cities signify doctrines which belong to the church, and to religion, n. 402, 2450, 2712, 2943, 3216, 4492, 4493. That the WALL of a city signifies the defensive truth of doctrine, n. 6419. That the GATES of a city signify such truths as are introductory to doctrine, and thereby to the church, n. 2943, 4478, 4492, 4493. That the TWELVE TRIBES OF ISRAEL represented, and thence signified, all the varieties of the truth and good of the church, in general and in particular, thus all things relative to faith and love, n. 3858, 3926, 4060, 6335. That the same is signified by the Lord's TWELVE APOSTLES, n. 2129, 2329, 3354, 3488, 3858, 6397. That when it is said of the Apostles, *that they shall sit upon twelve thrones, and judge the twelve tribes of Israel*, the meaning is, that all are to be judged according to the good and truth of the church, consequently, by the Lord, from whom that truth and good proceed, n. 2129, 6397. That TWELVE signifies all things in the aggregate, n. 577, 2089, 2129, 2130, 3272, 3858, 3913. Also, a hundred and forty-four, because that number is the product of twelve multiplied by itself, n. 7973. That twelve thousand has also the same signication, n. 7973. That all numbers in the Word signify things, n. 482, 487, 647, 648, 755, 813, 1963, 1988, 2075, 2252, 3252, 4264, 6175, 9488, 9659, 10,217, 10,253. That the products arising from numbers multiplied into each other have the same signification as the simple numbers, n. 5291, 5335, 5708, 7973. That MEASURE signifies the quality of a thing with respect to truth and good, n. 3104, 9603, 10,262. That the FOUNDATIONS of a wall signify the knowledges of truth on which doctrine is founded, n. 9642. That a QUADRANGULAR figure or SQUARE, signifies what is perfect, n. 9717, 9861. That LENGTH signifies good and its extension, and BREADTH, truth and its extension, n. 1613, 9487. That PRECIOUS STONES signify truths from good, n. 114, 9863, 9865. What the precious stones in the Urim and Thummim signify, both in general and in particular, n. 3862, 9864, 9866, 9905, 9891, 9895. What the JASPER of which the wall was built signifies, n. 9872. That the STREET of the city signifies the truth of doctrine from good, n. 2336. That GOLD signifies the good of love, n. 113, 1551, 1552, 5658, 6914, 6917, 9510, 9874, 9881. That GLORY signifies Divine Truth, such as it is in heaven, with the intelligence and wisdom thence derived, n. 4809, 5292, 5922, 8267, 8427, 9429, 10,574. That NATIONS signify those in the church who are in good, and, in an abstract sense, the good of the church, n. 1059, 1159, 1258, 1260, 1288, 1416, 1849, 4574, 7830, 9255, 9256. That KINGS mean those in the church who are in truth, and, in an abstract sense, the truth of the church, n. 4675, 5044. That the rites and ceremonies observed at the coronation of kings, involve such things as are derived from Divine

Truth, but that the knowledge of these things is at this day lost, n. 4581, 4966.

2. Before the New Jerusalem and its doctrine are treated of, it may be expedient to give some account of the new heaven and the new earth. What is to be understood by the first heaven and the first earth, which passed away, is shown in the small work ON THE LAST JUDGMENT AND THE DESTRUCTION OF BABYLON. Immediately after that event, that is, when the last judgment was completed, a new heaven was created or formed by the Lord; which heaven was composed of all those persons who, from the coming of the Lord to the present time, had lived in faith and charity; for such persons alone are capable of being assimilated to the form of heaven. For the form of heaven, according to which all consociations and communications therein are effected, is the form of Divine Truth, grounded in Divine Good, proceeding from the Lord; and this form man, as to his spirit, acquires by a life according to Divine Truth. That the form of heaven is thence derived may be seen in the work on HEAVEN AND HELL, n. 200 to 212, and that all the angels are forms of heaven, n. 51 to 58, and 73 to 77. Hence it may be clearly seen, who they are of whom the new heaven consists; and thereby what its quality is, namely, that it is altogether unanimous. He who lives in faith and charity, loves others as himself, and by love conjoins them with himself, the effect of which is reciprocal: for, in the spiritual world, love is conjunction. Wherefore, when all act thus, then from many, yea from innumerable individuals, consociated according to the form of heaven, unanimity exists, and they become as one; for then nothing separates and divides, but everything conjoins and unites.

3. Since this heaven was formed of all those who had been of such a quality from the coming of the Lord until the present time, it follows that it is composed both of Christians and of Gentiles, but chiefly of infants from all parts of the world, who have died since the Lord's coming: for all these were received by the Lord, and educated in heaven, and instructed by the angels, and reserved, that they, together with the others, might constitute a new heaven; whence it may be concluded how vast that heaven is. That all who die in infancy are educated in heaven, and become angels, may be seen in the work on HEAVEN AND HELL, n. 329 to 345. And that heaven is formed of Gentiles as well as of Christians, n. 318 to 328.

4. Moreover, with respect to this new heaven, it is to be observed, that it is distinct from the ancient heavens which were formed before the coming of the Lord; at the same time there is such an orderly connexion established between them, that, together they form but one heaven. The reason why this new heaven is distinct from the ancient heavens, is, that in the

ancient churches there was no other doctrine than the doctrine of love and charity; and that at that time they were unacquainted with any doctrine of faith separated from those principles. Hence, also, it is, that the ancient heavens constitute superior expanses, while the new heaven constitutes an expanse beneath them; for the heavens are expanses one above another. In the highest expanse those dwell who are called celestial angels, many of whom were of the Most Ancient Church; they are so named from celestial love, which is love to the Lord. In the expanse beneath them are those who are called spiritual angels, many of whom were of the Ancient Church; they are called spiritual angels, from spiritual love, which is charity towards our neighbor. Below these are the angels who are in the good of faith: these are they who have lived a life of faith: for a man to live a life of faith, is to live according to the doctrine of his particular church; and to live is to will and to do. All these heavens, however, form a one, by mediate and immediate influx from the Lord. A more full idea of these heavens may be obtained from what is said of them in the work on HEAVEN AND HELL, and particularly in the article which treats of the two kingdoms into which the heavens in general are divided, n. 20 to 28; and in the article concerning the three heavens, n. 29 to 40: concerning mediate and immediate influx, in the extracts from the ARCANA CŒLESTIA, after n. 603; and concerning the Ancient and Most Ancient Churches, in the small work ON THE LAST JUDGMENT AND THE DESTRUCTION OF BABYLON, n. 46.

5. It may be sufficient to state thus much concerning the new heaven; something shall now be said concerning the new earth. By the new earth is understood a new church upon earth; for when a former church ceases to exist, then a new one is established by the Lord. It is provided by the Lord that there should always be a church on earth, since by means of the church there is a conjunction of the Lord with mankind, and of heaven with the world; there the Lord is known, and therein are divine truths by which man is conjoined to him. That a new church is at this time being established, may be seen in the small work ON THE LAST JUDGMENT AND THE DESTRUCTION OF BABYLON, n. 74. The reason why a new church is signified by a new earth arises from the spiritual sense of the Word; for in that sense, by the word earth or land, no particular country is meant, but the nation dwelling there, and its divine worship; this, in the spiritual sense, being what answers to earth in the natural sense. Moreover, by earth or land, in the Word, when there is no name of any particular country affixed to the term, is signified the land of Canaan; and in that land a church had existed from the earliest ages; in consequence of which, all the places therein, and in the adja-

cent countries, with the mountains and rivers, as mentioned in the Word, became representative and significative of those things which compose the internals of the church, and which are called its spiritual things. Hence it is, as was observed, that earth or land, in the Word, as meaning the land of Canaan, signifies the church; it is therefore usual in the church to speak of the heavenly Canaan, by which is understood heaven itself. Thus, also, by the new earth is here meant a new church. That the land of Canaan, in the spiritual sense of the Word, signifies the church, is shown in the ARCANA CŒLESTIA, in various places, of which the following are here adduced. That the Most Ancient Church, which was before the flood, and the Ancient Church, which was after the flood, were in the land of Canaan, n. 567, 3686, 4447, 4454, 4516, 4517, 5136, 6516, 9327. That then all places in that land became representative of such things as are in the kingdom of the Lord, and in the church, n. 1505, 3686, 4447, 5136. That therefore Abraham was commanded to go thither, to the intent that amongst his posterity, the children of Israel, a representative church might be established, and that the Word might be written, the ultimate of which should consist of representatives existing in that land, n. 3686, 4447, 5136, 6516. Hence it is, that earth or land, and the land of Canaan, when they are mentioned in the Word, signify the church, n. 3038, 3481, 3705, 4447, 4517, 5757, 10,658.

6. What is understood by Jerusalem in the spiritual sense of the Word shall also be briefly described. Jerusalem means the church with respect to doctrine, because at Jerusalem, in the land of Canaan, and in no other place, were the temple, the altar, the sacrifices, and, consequently, all that pertained to divine worship. On this account, also, three festivals were celebrated there every year, to which every male throughout the whole land was commanded to go. This, then, is the reason why Jerusalem, in the spiritual sense, signifies the church with respect to worship, or, what is the same thing, with respect to doctrine; for worship is prescribed by doctrine, and is performed according to it. The reason why it is said, *The holy city, New Jerusalem, descending from God out of heaven*, is, because, in the spiritual sense of the Word, a city signifies doctrine, and a holy city the doctrine of Divine Truth, since Divine Truth is what is called holy in the Word. It is called the New Jerusalem for the same reason that the earth is called a new earth, because, as was observed above, earth or land signifies the church, and Jerusalem, the church with respect to doctrine; and it is said to descend from God out of heaven, because all Divine Truth, whence doctrine is derived, descends out of heaven from the Lord. That Jerusalem does not mean a city, although it was seen *as* a city, manifestly appears from its being said

that *its height was*, as its length and breadth, *twelve thousand furlongs* (ver. 16); and that the measure of its wall, which was *a hundred and forty-four cubits*, was the measure of a man, that is, of the angel (ver. 17); and also from its being said to be *prepared as a bride adorned for her husband* (ver. 2); and that afterwards *the angel said, Come hither, I will show thee the bride, the Lamb's wife: and he showed me that great city, the holy Jerusalem* (ver. 9, 10). The church is called in the Word the bride and the wife of the Lord; she is called the bride before conjunction, and the wife after conjunction. As may be seen in the ARCANA CŒLESTIA, n. 3103, 3105, 3164, 3165, 3207, 7022, 9182.

7. To add a few words respecting the doctrine which is delivered in the following pages. This, also, is from heaven, being from the spiritual sense of the Word, which is the same with the doctrine that is in heaven; for there is a church in heaven as well as on earth. In heaven there are the Word, and the doctrine from the Word; there are places of worship there, and sermons delivered in them; there are also both ecclesiastical and civil governments there: in a word, the only difference between the things which are in heaven, and those which are on earth, is, that in heaven all things exist in a state of greater perfection, since those who dwell there are spiritual, and spiritual things immensely exceed in perfection those that are natural. That such things exist in heaven may be seen in the work concerning HEAVEN AND HELL throughout, particularly in the article concerning governments in heaven, n. 213 to 220; and also in the article on divine worship in heaven, n. 221 to 227. Hence may evidently appear what is meant by the holy city, New Jerusalem, being seen to descend from God out of heaven. But I proceed to the doctrine itself, which is for the NEW CHURCH, and which is called, HEAVENLY DOCTRINE, because it was revealed to me out of heaven;—to deliver this doctrine is the design of the present work.

INTRODUCTION TO THE DOCTRINE.

8. WHEN there is no faith in consequence of there being no charity, the church is at an end. See this shown in the small work on the LAST JUDGMENT AND THE DESTRUCTION OF BABYLON, n. 33 to 39. The churches throughout the whole Christian world having made their differences to depend upon points of faith, when yet there can be no faith where there is no charity, I will, by way of introduction to the doctrine which follows, make some observations concerning the doctrine of charity as held by the ancients. When I use the phrase, "the churches

in the CHRISTIAN WORLD," I mean Protestant churches, and not the Popish or Roman Catholic church, since that is not a Christian church; for, wherever the church exists, the Lord is worshiped, and the Word is read; whereas, among Roman Catholics, they worship themselves instead of the Lord; forbid the Word to be read by the people; and affirm the Pope's decree to be equal, yea, even superior to it.

9. The doctrine of charity, which is the doctrine of life, was the essential doctrine in the ancient churches. Concerning these churches the reader may see more in the ARCANA CŒLESTIA, n. 1238, 2385. And that doctrine conjoined all churches, and thereby formed one church out of many. For they acknowledged all those as members of the church who lived in the good of charity, and called them brethren, however they might differ respecting truths, which at this day are called matters of faith. In these they instructed one another, which employment was among their works of charity; nor were they offended if one did not accede to the opinion of another, knowing that every one receives truth in proportion to the degree in which he is in good. Such being the character of the ancient churches, the members composing them were interior men; and because they were interior men they excelled in wisdom. For they who are in the good of love and charity, are, as to the internal man, in heaven, and belong to an angelic society in which the same good prevails. Hence they enjoy an elevation of mind towards interior things, and, consequently, they are in possession of wisdom; for wisdom can come from no other source than from heaven, that is, through heaven from the Lord; and in heaven there is wisdom, because its inhabitants are principled in good. Wisdom consists in seeing truth from the light of truth; and the light of truth is the light which shines in heaven. But in process of time that ancient wisdom decreased; for as mankind removed themselves from the good of love towards the Lord, and of love towards the neighbor, which latter is called charity, they removed themselves in the same proportion from wisdom, because, in the same proportion, they removed themselves from heaven. Hence it was that man, from being internal, became external, and this successively; and when he became external, he became also worldly and corporeal. When such is his quality, he cares but little for the things of heaven; for the delights of earthly loves, and the evils which, from those loves, are delightful to him, then possess him entirely. In this state the things which he hears concerning a life after death, concerning heaven and hell, and concerning spiritual subjects in general, are regarded by him as matters altogether foreign or extraneous to him, and not as things in which he has the most intimate concern; as, nevertheless, they ought to be. Hence also it is, that the doc-

trine of charity, which amongst the ancients was held in such estimation, is, at this day, with other excellent things, altogether lost. For who, at this day, is aware what charity is, in the genuine sense of the term, and what, in the same sense, is meant by our neighbor? whereas, that doctrine not only teaches this, but innumerable things beside, of which not a thousandth part is known at this day. The whole sacred Scripture is nothing else than the doctrine of love and charity, which the Lord also teaches, when he says: *Thou shalt love the Lord thy God with all thy heart, and with all thy soul, and with all thy mind; this is the first and great commandment: and the second is like unto it, thou shalt love thy neighbor as thyself: on these two commandments hang all the law and the prophets.* Matt. xxii. 37, 38, 39. The law and the prophets are the Word, in general and in particular.

10. In the following doctrine we will annex to each section extracts from the ARCANA CŒLESTIA, because in these the same things are more fully explained.

OF GOOD AND TRUTH.

11. ALL things in the universe, which are according to Divine order, have relation to good and truth. There is nothing either in heaven or on earth which has not relation to these two; the reason is, because both good and truth proceed from the Divine Being Who is the First Cause of all.

12. Hence it appears that there is nothing more necessary for man to know than what good and truth are; how the one has respect to the other; and how they become mutually conjoined. But such knowledge is especially necessary for every member of the church; for as all things of heaven have relation to good and truth, so also have all things of the church, because the good and truth of heaven are also the good and truth of the church. It is on this account that, in delivering the doctrine of the New Jerusalem, we commence with this subject.

13. It is in agreement with Divine order, that good and truth should be conjoined, and not separated; thus, that they should be a one, and not two; for they proceed in conjunction from the Divine Being, and continue so in heaven, and therefore they ought of necessity to remain conjoined in the church. The conjunction of good and truth is called, in heaven, the heavenly marriage, for all there are the subjects of this marriage; and hence it is, that, in the Word, heaven is compared to a marriage, and that the Lord is called the bridegroom and husband, whilst heaven, and also the church, are called the bride and wife. The

reason why heaven and the church are so styled, is, that all therein receive the Divine Good in truths.

14. All the intelligence and wisdom which the angels possess is derived from this marriage of good and truth, but not any of it from good separate from truth, nor from truth separate from good. So also it is with the members of the church.

15. Since therefore the conjunction of good and truth resembles a marriage, it is evident that there exist between them a mutual love, and a mutual desire to be conjoined. That member of the church, then, who does not possess such love and desire, is not the subject of the heavenly marriage; consequently, as yet, the church is not in him; for it is the conjunction of good and truth which constitutes the church.

16. There are numerous kinds of good, all, however, being comprehended under the general distinction of spiritual and natural good, which are conjoined in genuine moral good. As there are many kinds of good, so also there are various kinds of truth; for all truth pertains to good, and is, indeed, its form.

17. What has been said respecting good and truth, may, in a contrary sense, be affirmed of evil and falsity: for as all things in the universe which exist according to Divine order, have relation to good and truth, so also all things which exist in contrariety to Divine order, have relation to evil and falsity. Again, as there exist between good and truth a mutual love and desire to be conjoined, so do there exist a similar love and desire between evil and falsity. In fine, as all intelligence and wisdom are produced from the conjunction of good and truth, so all insanity and folly spring from the conjunction of evil and falsity. This latter conjunction is called the infernal marriage.

18. Now since evil and falsity are opposed to good and truth, it is plain that truth cannot be conjoined with evil, nor good with the falsity of evil; for if truth be adjoined to evil, it is no longer truth, but falsity, because it is falsified; and if good be adjoined to the falsity of evil, it is no longer good, but evil, as it is adulterated. Nevertheless, the falsity which is not grounded in evil, admits of being conjoined with good.

19. No one who, from confirmation and life, is principled in evil, and thence in falsity, can know what good and truth are, for he believes his own evil to be good, and his falsity to be truth; but every one who, from the same grounds, is principled in good and thence in truth, is capable of knowing what evil and falsity are. The reason of this is, because all good, with its truth, is, in its essence, celestial, and such as is not celestial in its essence, is still from a celestial origin; but all evil, with its falsity, is, in its essence, infernal, and such as is not infernal in its essence, has, nevertheless, its origin thence; and all that is celestial is in light, but all that is infernal is in darkness.

FROM THE ARCANA CŒLESTIA.

20. THAT all and singular things in the universe have relation to good and truth, or to evil and the false; those things which exist and are wrought agreeably to Divine order, to good and truth; and those which are opposite to Divine order, to evil and the false, n. 2451, 3166, 4390, 4409, 5232, 7256, 10,122. Consequently every thing in man has reference to the will and understanding, inasmuch as his understanding is the recipient of truth, or of the false; and his will the recipient of good, or of evil, n. 10,122. That at this day it is known by few what truth in its genuine essence is, by reason that it is little known what good is, when nevertheless all truth is from good, and all good is by truths, n. 2507, 3603, 4136, 9186, 9995.

That there are four kinds of men: 1. Those who are in falses from evil; and those who are in falses not from evil. 2. Those who are in truths without good. 3. Those who are in truths, and by them look and tend to good. 4. Those who are in truths from good. But each of these shall be spoken of in particular.

21. *Of those who are in falses from evil, and of those who are in falses not from evil: consequently of falses from evil, and of falses not from evil.* That there are innumerable kinds of the false, namely, as many as there are evils; and that the origins of evils, and thence of falses, are many, n. 1188, 1212, 4729, 4822, 7574. That there is a false from evil, or a false of evil; and that there is an evil from the false, or an evil of the false, and again a false thence derived, and thus in succession, n. 1679, 2243. That from one false, especially if it is in the place of a principle, there flow falses in a continual series, n. 1510, 1511, 4717, 4721. That there is a false from the cupidities of the love of self and of the world; and that there is a false from the fallacies of the senses, n. 1295, 4729. That there are falses of religion, and that there are falses of ignorance, n. 4729, 8318, 9258. That there is a false in which is good, and a false in which is no good, n. 2863, 9304, 10,109, 10,302. That there is what is falsified, n. 7318, 7319, 10,648. That all evil has a false with it, n. 7577, 8094. That the false from the cupidities of the love of self is the very false of evil; and that the worst kinds of falses are thence, n. 4729.

That evil is heavy, and has in itself a tendency to fall into hell, but not so the false, unless derived from evil, n. 8279, 8298. That good is changed into evil, and truth into the false, when it descends from heaven into hell, because into a gross and impure atmosphere, n. 3607. That the falses of evil appear as mists and foul waters over the hells, n. 8217, 8138, 8146. That they who are in the hells speak falses from evil, n. 1695, 7351, 7352, 7357, 7392, 7698. That they who are in evil cannot but think what is false, when they think from themselves, n. 7437. More is said concerning the evil of the false, n. 2408, 4818, 7272, 8266, 8279; and concerning the false of evil, n. 6359, 7272, 9304, 10,302.

That every false may be confirmed, and when confirmed appears as truth, n. 5033, 6865, 8521, 8780. That therefore every thing should be examined to see whether it is truth or not before it is confirmed, n. 4741, 7012, 7680, 7950, 8521. That care should be taken that the falses of religion be not confirmed, because a persuasion of what is false arises from thence, which adheres to man after death, n. 845, 8780. How pernicious the persuasion of the false is, n. 794, 806, 5096, 7686.

That good cannot flow into truths, so long as man is in evil, n. 2434. That goods and truths are so far removed from man as he is in evil, and thereby in falses, n. 3402. That great care is taken by the Lord lest truth be conjoined to evil, and the false of evil to good, n. 3110, 3116, 4416, 5217. That profanation arises from such mixture, n. 6348. That truths exterminate falses, and falses truths, n. 5207. That truths cannot be fully received so long as incredulity reigns, n. 3399.

How truths may be falsified, from examples, n. 7318. That the evil are permitted to falsify truths, with the reason thereof, n. 7332. That truths are falsified by the evil, by being applied, and thus turned aside, to evil, n. 8094, 8149. That truth is said to be falsified when it is applied to evil, which is principally done by fallacies and appearances in externals, n. 7334, 8602. That the evil are allowed to assault truth, but not good, because they can falsify truth by various interpretations and applications, n. 6677. That truth falsified from evil, is contrary to truth and good, n. 8602. That truth falsified from evil stinks grievously in the other life, n. 7319. More is said concerning the falsification of truth, at n. 7318, 7319, 10,648.

That there are falses of religion which agree with good, and others which disagree, n. 9258. That falses of religion, if they do not disagree with good, do not produce evil, except with those who are in evil, n. 8318. That falses of religion are not imputed to those who are in good, but to those who are in evil, n. 8051, 8149. That truths not genuine, and also falses, may be consociated with genuine truths with those who are in good, but not with those who are in evil, n. 3470, 3471, 4551, 4552, 7344, 8149, 9298. That falses and truths are consociated by appearances from the literal sense of the Word, n. 7344. That falses are made true by good, and grow soft when they are applied and turned to good, and evil is removed, n. 8149. That falses of religion with those who are in good, are received by the Lord as truths, n. 4736, 8149. That good whose quality is from the false of religion, is accepted by the Lord, if there is ignorance, and therein innocence, and a good end, n. 7887. That truths with man are appearances of truth and good imbued with fallacies; but that nevertheless the Lord adapts them to genuine truths with the man who lives in good, n. 2053. That falses in which is good, have place with those who are without the church, and thence in ignorance of truth; also with those who are within the church where are falses of doctrine, n. 2589 to 2604, 2861, 2863, 3263, 3778, 4189, 4190, 4197, 6700, 9256. That falses in which is no good are more grievous with those who are within the church, than with those who are without the church, n. 7688. That truths and goods are taken away from the evil in the other life, and given to the good, agreeably to the words of the Lord, *To him that hath shall be given that he may abound; and from him who hath not shall be taken away that which he hath*, n. 7770.

22. *Of those who are in truths, and not in good; consequently of truths without good.* That truths without good are not in themselves truths because they have no life, for all the life of truths is from good, n. 3603. Thus that they are as a body without a soul, n. 3180, 9454. That the knowledges of truth and good which are only in the memory and not in the life, are believed by them to be truths, n. 5276. That the truths are not appropriated to man, nor become his own, which he only knows and acknowledges from causes which proceed from the love of self and the world, n. 3402, 3824. But that those are appropriated, which he acknowledges for the sake of truth and good, n. 3849. That truths without good are not accepted by the Lord, n. 4368; neither do they save, n. 2261. That they who are in truths without good, are not of the church, n. 3963. That neither can they be regenerated, n. 10,637. That the Lord does not flow into truths except by good, n. 10,367.

Of the separation of truth from good, n. 5008, 5009, 5022, 5028. The quality of truth without good, and its quality from good, n. 1949, 1950, 1964, 5951; from comparisons, n. 5830. That truth without good is morose, n. 1949, 1950, 1951, 1964. That in the spiritual world it appears hard, n. 6359, 7068; and pointed, n. 2799. That truth without good is as the light of winter, in which all things of the earth are torpid, and nothing is produced; but that truth from good is as the light of spring and summer, in which all things flourish and are produced, n. 2231, 3146, 3412, 3413. That such a wintry light is turned into thick darkness when light flows in from heaven; and that then they who are in those truths come into blindness and stupidity, n. 3412, 3413.

That they who separate truths from good are in darkness, and in ignorance of truth and in falses, n. 9186. That from falses they cast themselves into evils, n. 3325, 8094. The errors and falses into which they cast themselves, n. 4721, 4730, 4776, 4783, 4925, 7779, 8313, 8765, 9221. That the Word is shut to them, n. 3773, 4783, 8780. That they do not see and attend to all those things which the Lord spake concerning love and charity, thus concerning good, n. 3051, 3416. That they know not what good is, nor what heavenly love and charity are, n. 2507, 3603, 4136, 9995. That they who know the truths of faith, and live evilly, in the other life abuse truths to domineer thereby, n. 4802. Concerning their quality and lot in another life, n. 4802.

That Divine Truth condemns to hell, but that Divine Good elevates to heaven, n. 7258. That Divine Truth terrifies, not so Divine Good, n. 4180. What it is to be judged from truth, and to be judged from good, n. 2335.

23. *Of those who are in truths, and thereby look and tend to good: consequently of truths by which come good.* That what man loves, this he wills, and what man loves or wills, this he thinks, and confirms in various ways: what man loves or wills, this he calls good, and what man thence thinks and confirms in various ways, this he calls truth, n. 4070. Hence it is, that truth becomes good, when it becomes of the love or will, or when man loves and wills it, n. 5526, 7835, 10,367.

And forasmuch as the love or the will is the very life of man, that truth does not live with man when he only knows it and thinks it, but when he loves and wills it, and from love and will does it, n. 5595, 9284. That thence truths receive life, consequently from good, n. 2434, 3111, 2607, 6077. Thus that the life of truths is from good, and that they have no life but from good, n. 1589, 1947, 1997, 2579, 3180, 4070, 4096, 4097, 4736, 4757, 4884, 5147, 5928, 9154, 9667, 9841, 10,729; illustrated, n. 9454. When truths may be said to have acquired life, n. 1928. That truth when it is conjoined to good, is appropriated to man because it becomes of his life, n. 3108, 3161. That truth may be conjoined to good, there must be a consent from the understanding and will; when the will also consents that then there is conjunction, n. 3157, 3158, 3161.

That when man is regenerated, truths enter with the delight of affection, because he loves to do them, and that they are reproduced with the same affection because the two cohere, n. 2484, 2487, 3040, 3066, 3074, 3336, 4018, 5893, 7967. That the affection which is of love always adjoins itself to truths according to uses of life, and that that affection is reproduced with the truths, and the truths are reproduced with the affection, n. 3336, 3824, 3849, 4205, 5893, 7967. That good acknowledges nothing else for truth than what accords with the affection which is of love, n. 3161. That truths are introduced by delights and pleasantnesses that agree therewith, n. 3502, 3512. That all genuine affection of truth is from good, and according to it, n. 4373, 8349, 8356. That thus there is an insinuation and influx of good into truths, and conjunction, n. 4301. And that thus truths have life, n. 7917, 7967.

Forasmuch as the affection which is of love always adjoins itself to truths according to uses of life, that therefore good acknowledges its own truth, and truth its own good, n. 2429, 3101, 3102, 3161, 3179, 3180, 4358, 5407, 5835, 9637. That thence is a conjunction of truth and good, concerning which, n. 3834, 4096, 4097, 4301, 4345, 4353, 4364, 4368, 5365, 7623 to 7627, 7752 to 7762, 8530, 9258, 10,555. That truths do also acknowledge each other, and are mutually consociated, n. 9079. And that this is from the influx of heaven, n. 9079.

That good is the esse of life, and truth the existere of life thence; and that thus good has its existere of life in truth, and truth its esse of life in good, n. 3049, 3180, 4574, 5002, 9144. Hence that every good has its own truth, and every truth its own good, because good without truth has no existence, and truth without good has no being [*non est*], n. 9637. That good has also its form and quality from truths, and that truth is the form and quality of good, n. 3049, 4574, 6951, 9454. And of consequence, that truth and good ought to be conjoined in order that they may be somewhat, n. 10,555. That hence good is in a perpetual endeavor and desire of conjoining truths unto itself, n. 9206, 9495; illustrated at n. 9207. And truths in like manner with good, n. 9206. That the conjunction is reciprocal, of good with truth, and of truth with good, n. 5365, 8516. That good acts, and truth re-acts, but from good, n. 3155, 4380, 4757, 5928, 10,729. That truths regard their own good, as beginning and end, n. 4353.

That the conjunction of truth with good is as the progression of man's life from infancy, as he first imbibes truths scientifically, then rationally, and at length applies them to life, n. 3025, 3665, 3690. It is also as with offspring, in that it is conceived, exists in the womb, is born, grows up, and becomes wise, n. 3298, 3299, 3308, 3665, 3690. It answers also to the case of seeds and ground, n. 3671. And to the case of water with bread, n. 4976. That the first affection of truth is not genuine, but that as man is perfected it is purified, n. 3040, 3089. That nevertheless goods and truths, not genuine, serve for the introducing goods and truths that are genuine, and that afterwards the former are relinquished, n. 3665, 3690, 3974, 3982, 3986, 4145.

Moreover, that a man is led to good by truths, and not without truths, n. 10,124, 10,367. If man does not learn or receive truths, that good cannot flow-in, thus that man cannot become spiritual, n. 3387. That the conjunction of good and truth takes place according to the increase of knowledges, n. 3141. That truths are received by every one according to his capacity, n. 3385.

That the truths of the natural man are scientifics, n. 3293, 3309, 3310. That scientifics and knowledges are as vessels, n. 6004, 6023, 6052, 6071, 6077. That truths are vessels of good, because they are recipients, n. 1946, 1900, 2063, 2261, 2269, 3318, 3368, 3365.

That good flows into man by an internal way, or that of the soul, but truths by an external way, or that of hearing and sight; and that they are conjoined in his interiors by the Lord, n. 3030, 3098. That truths are elevated out of the natural man, and implanted in good in the spiritual man; and that thus truths become spiritual, n. 3085, 3086. And that afterwards they flow thence into the natural man, spiritual good flowing immediately into the good of the natural, but mediately into the truth of the natural, n. 3314, 3573, 4563; illustrated at n. 3314, 3616, 3576, 3969, 3995. In a word, that truths are conjoined to good with man, so far and in such manner as man is in good as to life, n. 3834, 3843. That conjunction is accomplished in one manner with the celestial, and in another with the spiritual, n. 10,124. Further particulars relative to the conjunction of good and truth, and the manner in which it is effected, may be seen, n. 3090, 3203, 3308, 4096, 4097, 4345, 4353, 5365, 7623, to 7627. And in what manner spiritual good is formed by truths, at n. 3470, 3570.

24. *Of those who are in truths from good, consequently of truths from good.* Of the difference between truth that leads to good, and truth which proceeds from good, n. 1063. That truth is not essentially truth, any further than as it proceeds from good, n. 4736, 10,619; because truth has its esse from good, n. 3049, 3180, 4574, 5002, 9144; and its life, n. 3111, 2434, 6077; and because truth is the form or quality of good, n. 3049, 4574, 6951, 9454. That truth is altogether as good with man, in the same ratio and degree, n. 2429. In order that truth may be really truth, it must derive its essence from the good of charity and innocence, n. 3111, 6013. That the truths which are from good are spiritual truths, n. 5951.

That truth makes one with good when it proceeds from good, so completely that both together are one good, n. 4332, 7835, 10,252, 10,266. That the understanding and will make one mind and one life, when the understanding proceeds from the will, because the understanding is the recipient of truth, and the will, of good, but not when man thinks and speaks otherwise than he wills, n. 3623. That truth from good is truth in will and act, n. 4337, 4353, 4385, 4390. That when truth proceeds from good, good has its image in truth, n. 3180.

That in the universal heaven and world, and in the singulars thereof, there is a resemblance of marriage, n. 54, 718, 749, 917, 1432, 2173, 2516, 5194. Particularly between truth and good, n. 1094, 2173, 2503. By reason that all things in the universe have relation to truth and good, in order that they may be any thing, and to their conjunction, in order that any thing may be produced, n. 2451, 3166, 4390, 4409, 5232, 7256, 10,122, 10,555. That the ancients also instituted a marriage between truth and good, n. 1904. That the law of marriage is, that two be one, according to the words of the Lord, n. 10,130, 10,168, 10,169. That love truly conjugial descends and exists from heaven, from the marriage of truth and good, n. 2728, 2729.

That man is so far wise, as he is in good and thence in truths, but not so far as he knows truths and is not in good, n. 3182, 3190, 4884. That man who is in truths from good, is actually elevated from the light of the world into the light of heaven, consequently from what is obscure into what is clear; but on the other hand, that he is in the light of the world, and in what is obscure, so long as he knows truths and is not in good, n. 3190, 3191. That man does not know what good is, before he is in it, and has his perceptions from it, n. 3325, 3330, 3336. That truths increase immensely when they proceed from good, n. 2846, 2847, 5345. Of which increase, n. 5355. That this increase is as fructification from a tree, and multiplication from seeds from which whole gardens are produced, n. 1873, 2846, 2847 That wisdom increases in a like degree, and that to eternity, n. 3200, 3314, 4220, 4221, 5527, 5859, 6303. That the man who is in truths from good is in a like degree enlightened, and that he is so far in illustration when he reads the Word, n. 9382, 10,548, 10,549, 10,550, 10,691, 10,694. That the good of love is as fire, and truth thence as light from that fire, n. 3195, 3222, 5400, 8644, 9399, 9548, 9684. That in heaven truths from good shine, n.5219. That truths from good, by which is wisdom, increase according to the quality and quantity of the love of good; and on the other hand, falses from evil, according to the quality and quantity of the love of evil, n. 4099. That the man who is in truths from good comes into angelic intelligence and wisdom, and that they lie hid in his interiors so long as he lives in the world, but that they are opened in the other life, n. 2494. That man, who is in truths from good, becomes an angel after death, n. 8747.

That truths from good are as generations, n. 9079. That they are disposed in series, n. 5339, 5343, 5530, 7408, 10,303, 10,308. The ordination of truths from good compared with the fibres and blood-vessels in the body; and thence with their textures and forms, according to the uses of life, n. 3470, 3570, 3579, 9454. That truths from good form as it were a city, and this from the influx of heaven, n. 3584. That the truths which are of the principal love are in the middle; and that the rest are more or less remote from thence according to their degrees of disagreement, n. 3993, 4551, 4552, 5530, 6028. That a like arrangement exists in the evil, with respect to their principles, n. 4551, 4552. That truths when they proceed from good are disposed into the form of heaven, n. 4302, 4704, 5339, 5343, 6028, 10,303. And this according to the order in which are the angelic societies, n. 10,303. That all truths when they proceed from good are conjoined to one another by a certain affinity, and that they are as derivations of families from one father, n. 2863. That all truth has a sphere of extension into heaven, according to the quality and quantity of the good from which it is, n. 8063. That the marriage of good and truth is the church and heaven with man, n. 2231, 7752, 7753, 9224, 9795, 10,122. Of the delight and happiness of those with whom good is in truths, n. 1470.

That truths from good, in conjunction, present an image of man, n. 8370. That man is nothing else than his own good, and truth thence derived; or evil, and false thence derived, n. 10,298.

The sum is:—That faith is by truths, n. 4353, 4997, 7178, 10,367. That charity towards the neighbor is by truths, n. 4368, 7623, 7624, 8034. That love to the Lord is by truths, n. 10,143, 10,153, 10,310, 10,578, 10,648. That conscience is by truths, n. 1077, 2053, 9113. That innocence is by truths, n. 3183, 3495, 6013. That purification from evils is by truths, n. 2799, 5954, 7044, 7918, 9089, 10,229, 10,237. That regeneration is by truths, n. 1555, 1904, 2046, 2189, 9088, 9959, 10,028. That intelligence and wisdom are by truths, n. 3182, 3190, 3387, 10,064. That the beauty of angels, and also of men, as to the interiors which are their spirits, is by truths, n. 553, 3080, 4983, 5199. That power against evils and falses is by truths, n. 3091, 4015, 10,485. That order, such as is in heaven, is by truths, n. 3316, 3417, 3570, 4704, 5339, 5343, 6028, 10,303. That the church is by truths, n. 1798, 1799, 3963, 4468, 4672. That heaven is with man by truths, n. 1690, 9832, 9931, 10,303. That man becomes man by truths, n. 3175, 3387, 8370, 10,298. But nevertheless that all these things are by truths from good, and not by truths without good; and that good is from the Lord, n. 2434, 4070, 4736, 5147. That all good is from the Lord, n. 1614, 2016, 2904, 4151, 9981.

25. *That all good and truth is from the Lord.*—That the Lord is good itself and truth itself, n. 2011, 4151, 10,336, 10,619. That the Lord, both with respect to the Divine and the Human, is the Divine Good of Divine Love; and that from Him proceeds Divine Truth, n. 3704, 3712, 4180, 4577. That Divine Truth proceeds from the Divine Good of the Lord, comparatively as light from the sun, n. 3704, 3712, 4180, 4577. That the Divine Truth proceeding from the Lord appears in the heavens as light, and forms all the light of heaven, n. 3195, 3222, 5400, 8694, 9399, 9548, 9684. That the light of heaven, which is Divine Truth united to Divine Good, illuminates both the sight and understanding of angels and spirits, n. 2776, 3138. That heaven is in light and heat, because it is in truth and good, for Divine Truth is light there, and Divine Good is heat there, n. 3643, 9399, 9401; and in the work on HEAVEN AND HELL, n. 126 to 140. That Divine Truth proceeding from the Divine Good of the Lord, forms the angelic heaven and arranges it in order, n. 3038, 9408, 9613,

10,716, 10,717. That Divine Good united to Divine Truth, which is in the heavens, is called Divine Truth, n. 10,196.

That the Divine Truth proceeding from the Lord is the only reality, n. 6880, 7004, 8200. That by Divine Truth all things were made and created, n. 2803, 2884, 5272, 7835. That all power belongs to Divine Truth, n. 8200.

That man from himself can do nothing that is good, and think nothing that is true, n. 874, 875, 876. That the rational [principle] of man cannot perceive Divine Truth from itself, n. 2196, 2203, 2209. That truths which are not from the Lord, are from the proprium of man, and that they are not truths, but only appear as truths, r 8868.

That all good and truth is from the Lord, and nothing from man, n. 1614, 2016, 2904, 4151, 9981. That goods and truths are so far goods and truths, as they have the Lord in them, n. 2904, 3051, 8478. Of the Divine Truth proceeding immediately from the Lord, and of Divine Truth proceeding mediately through the angels, and of their influx with man, n. 7055, 7056, 7058. That the Lord flows into good with man, and by good into truths, n. 10,153. That He flows by good into truths of every kind, and particularly into genuine truths, n. 2531, 2554. That the Lord does not flow into truths separate from good, and that no parallelism exists between the Lord and man, with respect to them, but with respect to good, n. 1831, 1832, 3514, 3564.

That to do good and truth for the sake of good and truth is to love the Lord, and to love the neighbor, n. 10,336. That they who are in the internal of the Word, of the church, and of worship, love to do good and truth for the sake of good and truth; but that they who are in the external of these, without the internal, love to do good and truth for the sake of themselves and the world, n. 10,662. What it is to do good and truth for the sake of good and truth, illustrated by examples, n. 10,682.

26. *Of the various kinds of goods and truths.* That variety is infinite, and one thing is never exactly the same as another, n. 7236, 9002. That there is also an infinite variety in the heavens, n. 684, 690, 3744, 5598, 7236. That varieties in the heavens are varieties of good, and that thence is the distinction of all therein, n. 3519, 3744, 3804, 3986, 4005, 4067, 4149, 4263, 7236, 7833, 7836, 9002. That these varieties are from truths, which are manifold, by which every one has good, n. 3470, 3519, 3804, 4149, 6917, 7236. That thence all the angelic societies in the heavens, and every angel in a society are distinguished from each other, n. 690, 3241, 3519, 3804, 3986, 4067, 4149, 4263, 7236, 7833, 7836. But that they all act in unity by love from the Lord, and thereby regard one end, n. 457, 3986. That in general, goods and truths are distinguished according to degrees, into natural, spiritual, and celestial, n. 2069, 3240. That in general, there are three degrees of good, and consequently of truth, according to the three heavens, n. 4154, 9873, 10,296. That the goods and thence the truths in the internal man, are of a threefold kind, and so also in the external, n. 4154. That there is natural good, civil good, and moral good, n. 3768. That natural good, into which some are born, is not good in the other life, unless made spiritual good, n. 2463, 2464 2468

3408, 3469, 3470, 3508, 3518, 7761. Of natural spiritual good; and of that which is not spiritual, n. 4988, 4992, 5032. That there is intellectual truth, and scientific truth, n. 1904, 1911, 2503.

27. *That wisdom is from good by truths.*—In what manner the rational [principle] is conceived and born in man, n. 2094, 2574, 2557, 3030, 5126. That this is effected by an influx of the Lord through heaven into the knowledges and sciences which are with man, and a consequent elevation, n. 1895, 1896, 1900, 1901. That elevation is according to uses, and the love of them, n. 3074, 3085, 3086. That the rational [principle] is born by truths, hence such as they are, such is the rational, n. 2094, 2524, 2557. That the rational [principle] is opened and formed by truths from good; and that it is shut and destroyed by falses from evil, n. 3108, 5126. That man is not rational by virtue of an ability of reasoning on any subject; but by virtue of an ability to see and perceive whether a thing be true or not, n. 1944. That man is not born into any truth, because not born into good; but that he is to learn and imbibe both, n. 3175. That it is with difficulty that man can receive genuine truths, and thence become wise, on account of the fallacies of the senses, the persuasions of the false, and the doubts and reasonings thence, n. 3175. That man first begins to be wise, when he begins to be averse to reasonings against truths, and to reject doubts, n. 3175. That the unenlightened human rational laughs at interior truths,—from examples, n. 2654. That truths with man are called interior when they are implanted in his life, and not in consequence of his knowing them, although they may be truths of an interior kind, n. 10,199.

That in good there is a faculty of becoming wise, whence those who have lived in good in the world come into angelic wisdom after their departure out of the world, n. 5527, 5859, 8321. That there are innumerable things in every good, n. 4005. That innumerable things may be known from good, n. 3612. Concerning the multiplication of truth from good, n. 5345, 5355, 5912. That the good of infancy by truths, and by a life according to them, becomes the good of wisdom, n. 3504.

That there is an affection of truth, and an affection of good, n. 1904, 1997. What is the quality of those who are in the affection of truth, and what is the quality of those who are in the affection of good, n. 2422, 2430. Who are able to come into the affection of truth, and who are not able, n. 2689. That all truths are arranged in order under a common affection, n. 9094. That the affection of truth and the affection of good in the natural man are as brother and sister; but in the spiritual man, as husband and wife, n. 3160. That pure truths do not exist with man, nor even with angels, but only with the Lord, n. 3207, 7902. That truths with man are appearances of truth, n. 2053, 2519. That the first truths with man are appearances of truth from the fallacies of the senses, which nevertheless are successively put off, as he is perfected with respect to wisdom, n. 3131. That appearances of truth with the man who is in good are received by the Lord for truths, n. 2053, 3207. What, and of what quality the appearances of truth are, n. 3207, 3357 to 3362 3368, 3404, 3405, 3417. That the sense of the letter of the Word in many places is according to appearances, n. 1838. That the same truths with one man are more true, with another less so, and with another false, because falsified, n. 2439. That truths are also truths according to the correspondence between the natural and the spiritual man, n. 3128, 3138. That truths differ according to the various ideas and perceptions concerning them, n. 3470, 3804, 6017.

That truth when it is conjoined to good, vanishes out of the memory because it then becomes of the life, n. 3108. That truths cannot be conjoined to good except in a free state, n. 3158. That truths are conjoined to good by temptations, n. 3318, 4572, 7122. That there is in good a continual endeavor of arranging truths in order, and of restoring its state thereby, n. 3610. That truths appear undelightful when the communication with good is intercepted, n. 8352. That man can hardly distinguish between truth and good, because he can hardly distinguish between thinking and willing, n. 9995. That good is called in the Word the brother of truth, n. 4267. That also in a certain respect good is called lord, and truth, servant, n. 3409, 4267.

OF THE WILL AND THE UNDERSTANDING.

28. Man is endowed with two faculties which constitute his life: one is called the Will, and the other the Understanding. These faculties are distinct from each other, but are so created as to form a one; and when they are thus united they are called the Mind. Of these, then, the human mind consists; and in them resides the whole life of man.

29. As all things in the universe, which are according to divine order, have relation to good and truth, so all things in man have relation to the will and the understanding; for good in man pertains to his will, and truth in him pertains to his understanding: these two faculties, or these two lives, in man, are respectively their receptacles and subjects; the will being the receptacle and subject of all things relating to good, and the understanding the receptacle and subject of all things relating to truth. Goods and truths have no other residence with man; so neither, for the same reason, have love and faith; for love pertains to good, and good to love; and faith pertains to truth, and truth to faith.

30. Since, then, all things in the universe have relation to good and truth, and all things belonging to the church to the good of love and the truth of faith; and since it is from the possession of the faculties of will and understanding that man is man; they are treated of in this doctrine; for otherwise man could have no distinct idea of them, to form a basis for his thoughts.

31. The will and the understanding constitute also the spirit

of man; for in these his wisdom and intelligence, and his life in general, reside, the body being only their passive organ:

32. Nothing is of more importance to be known, than in what manner the will and the understanding make one mind. This they do as good and truth form a one; for between the will and the understanding there is a marriage, similar to that which takes place between good and truth. What the nature of this marriage is, may fully appear from what has been adduced above, in the section on Good and Truth; namely, that as good is the very *esse* of a thing, and truth its *existere* derived from that *esse*, so the will in man is the very *esse* of his life, and the understanding is the *existere* of his life thence derived: for good, which belongs to the will, assumes to itself a form in the understanding, and thus renders itself visible.

33. They who are principled in good and truth have will and understanding, but they who are principled in evil and in falsity have no will and understanding properly considered; but instead of will they have cupidity, and instead of understanding they have mere science. The human will, when truly such, is the receptacle of good, and the understanding is the receptacle of truth; for which reason will cannot be predicated of evil, nor can understanding be predicated of falsity, because they are opposites, and opposites destroy each other. Hence it is, that the man who is principled in evil and thence in falsity, cannot be called rational, wise, and intelligent, properly speaking. With the evil, also, the interiors of the mind, in which the will and the understanding principally reside, are closed. It is supposed, however, that the evil, as well as the good, have will and understanding, because they say that they will, and that they understand: but their volition is only the exercise of their cupidity, and their intellection is nothing more than science.

FROM THE ARCANA CŒLESTIA.

34. Spiritual truths cannot be comprehended, unless the following universals be known: I. That all things in the universe have relation to good and truth, and to the conjunction of both, in order to their being any thing; consequently to love and faith, and their conjunction. II. That with man there is will and understanding, and that the will is the receptacle of good, and the understanding the receptacle of truth, and that all things with man have relation to those two [principles], and to their conjunction, as all things relate to good and truth, and their conjunction. III. That there is an internal man and an external, and that they are distinct one from the other like heaven and the world, and nevertheless that they ought to make one, in order to man's being truly man. IV. That the light of heaven is

that in which the internal man is, and the light of the world that in which the external is; and that the light of heaven is Divine Truth itself, from which proceeds all intelligence. V. That there is a correspondence between the things which are in the internal, and those which are in the external man; and that consequently they appear in each under a different form, so that they can only be discerned by the science of correspondences. Unless these and many other things are known, it is impossible to form any ideas concerning spiritual and celestial things, but such as are incongruous; and thus the scientifics and knowledges, which are of the external man, without these universals, can produce but little to the understanding and improvement of the rational man. Hence it appears, how necessary scientifics are. Concerning those universals, much is said in the ARCANA CŒLESTIA.

35. That man has two faculties, one which is called will, and the other understanding, n. 35, 641, 3623, 3939, 10,122. That those two faculties constitute the real man, n. 10,076, 10,109, 10,110, 10,264, 10,284. That the quality of man is according to those two faculties with him, n. 7342, 8885, 9282, 10,264, 10,284. That by them also man is distinguished from beasts, by reason that the understanding of man may be elevated by the Lord, and see Divine Truths, and in like manner his will may be elevated and perceive Divine Goods; and thus man may be conjoined to the Lord by those two faculties which are his constituent principles; but that the case is otherwise with beasts, n. 4525, 5302, 5114, 6323, 9231. And since man may thus be conjoined to the Lord, that he cannot die as to his interiors, which are his spirit, but that he lives for ever, n. 5302. That man is not man by virtue of his form, but by virtue of good and truth, which are of his will and understanding, n. 4051, 5302.

That as all things in the universe relate to good and truth, so do all things in man to the will and the understanding, n. 803, 10,122. For the will is the receptacle of good, and the understanding is the receptacle of truth, n. 3332, 3623, 5332, 6065, 6125, 7503, 9300, 9930. It amounts to the same, whether you say truth or faith, for faith is of truth, and truth is of faith; and it amounts to the same whether you say good or love, for love is of good, and good is of love; for what a man believes, that he calls true; and what he loves, that he calls good, n. 4353, 4997, 7178, 10,122, 10,367. Hence it follows that the understanding is the recipient of faith, and the will the recipient of love; and that faith and love are in man, when they are in his understanding and will, for the life of man resides therein, n. 7178, 10,122, 10,367. And since the understanding of man is capable of receiving faith towards the Lord, and the will of receiving love to the Lord, that by faith and love he may be conjoined to the Lord, and whoever is capable of conjunction with the Lord by faith and love, cannot die to eternity, n. 4525, 6323, 9231. That love is conjunction in the spiritual world, n. 1594, 2057, 3939, 4018, 5807, 6195, 6196, 7081 to 7086, 7501, 10,130.

That the will of man is the very esse of his life, inasmuch as it is the receptacle of good, and that the understanding is the existere of life thence derived, inasmuch as it is the receptacle of truth, n. 3619, 5002, 9282. Consequently that the life of the will is the principal life of man, and that the life of the understanding proceeds therefrom,

n. 585, 590, 3619, 7342, 8885, 9282, 10,076, 10,109, 10,110; comparatively as light proceeds from fire or flame, n. 6032, 6314. That whatever things enter into the understanding, and at the same time into the will, are appropriated to man, but not those which are received in the understanding alone, n. 9009, 9069, 9071, 9129, 9182, 9386, 9393, 10,076, 10,109, 10,110. That those things become of the life of man, which are received in the will, and thence in the understanding, n. 8911, 9069, 9071, 10,076, 10,109, 10,110. Every man also is loved and esteemed by others according to the good of his will and thence of his understanding; for he who wills well and understands well, is loved and esteemed, and he who understands well and does not will well, is rejected and regarded as vile, n. 8911, 10,076. That man after death remains such as his will and its understanding are, n. 9069, 9071, 9386, 10,153. And that those things which are of the understanding, and not at the same time of the will, then vanish, because they are not in the spirit of man, n. 9282; or, which amounts to the same, that man after death remains as his love and its faith are, or as his good and its truth are; and that the things which are of faith and not at the same time of love, or the things which are of truth and not at the same time of good, vanish, inasmuch as they are not in the man, consequently not of the man, n. 553, 2364, 10,153. That man is capable of comprehending with the understanding what he does not practise from the will, or that he may understand what he does not will, because it is against his love, n. 3539.

That the will and the understanding constitute one mind, n. 35, 3623, 5832, 10,122. That those two faculties of life ought to act in unity, in order to man's being man, n. 3623, 4832, 5969, 9300. How perverted a state they are in, whose understanding and will do not act in unity, n. 9075. That such is the state of hypocrites, of the deceitful, of flatterers, and of simulators, n. 4326, 3573, 4799, 8250. That the will and the understanding are reduced to one in another life, and that there it is not allowable to have a divided mind, n. 8250.

That every doctrinal of the church has ideas peculiar to itself, by which its quality is perceived, n. 3310. That the understanding of the doctrinal is according to those ideas, and that without an intellectual idea, man would only have an idea of words, and none of things, n. 3825. That the ideas of the understanding extend themselves widely into the societies of spirits and angels round about, n. 6598, 6600 to 6605, 6609, 6613. That the ideas of man's understanding are opened in another life, and appear to the life in their true quality, n. 1869, 3310, 5510. Of what quality the ideas of some appear, n. 6201, 8885.

That all will of good and understanding of truth is from the Lord, but not so the understanding of truth separate from the will of good, n. 1831, 3514, 5483, 5649, 6027, 8685, 8701, 10,153. That it is the understanding which is enlightened by the Lord, n. 6222, 6608, 10,659. That the Lord grants to those who are enlightened, to see and understand truth, n. 9382, 10,659. That the enlightening of the understanding is various, according to the states of man's life, n. 5221, 7012, 7233. That the understanding is enlightened in pro portion as man receives truth in the will, that is, in proportion as he wills to act according thereto, n. 3619. That they have their understanding enlightened, who read the Word from the love of truth and from the love of the uses of life, but not they who read it from the love of fame, honor, or gain, n. 9382, 10,548, 10,549, 10,550. That illustration is an actual elevation of the mind into the light of heaven, n. 10,330; from experience, n. 1526, 6608. That light from heaven is illustration to the understanding, as light from the world is to the sight, n. 1524, 5114, 6608, 9128. That the light of heaven is Divine Truth, from which is derived all wisdom and intelligence, n. 3195, 3222, 5400, 8644, 9399, 9548, 9684. That it is the understanding of man which is enlightened by that light, n. 1524, 3138, 3167, 4408, 6608, 8707, 9126, 9399, 10,569.

That the understanding is of such a quality as are the truths from good, of which it is formed, n. 10,064. That that is understanding which is formed by truths from good, but not what is formed by falses from evil, n. 10,675. That understanding consists in seeing truths, the causes of things, their connections, and consequences in regular order, from those things which are of experience and science, n. 6125. That understanding consists in seeing and perceiving whether a thing be true, before it is confirmed, but not in being able to confirm every thing, n. 4741, 7012, 7680, 7950, 8521, 8780. That the light of confirmation without a previous perception of truth, is natural light, and may be possessed even by those who are not wise, n. 8780. That to see and perceive whether a thing be true before confirmation, is only given with those who are affected with truth for the sake of truth, consequently who are in spiritual light, n. 8780. That every tenet, however false, may be confirmed, even so as to appear true, n. 2482, 2490, 5033, 6865, 7950.

How the rational is conceived and born with man, n. 2024, 2574, 2557, 3030, 5126. That it is from the influx of the light of heaven from the Lord through the internal man into knowledges and sciences, which are in the external, and an elevation thence, n. 1895, 1896, 1900, 1901, 1902. That the rational is born by truths, and not by falses; consequently according to the quality of the truths, such is the rational, n. 2094, 2524, 2557. That the rational is opened and formed by truths from good, and that it is shut and destroyed by falses from evil, n. 3108, 5126. That a man is not rational who is in falses from evil; and consequently a man is not rational from being able to reason upon every subject, n. 1944.

That man hardly knows how to distinguish between understanding and will, because he hardly knows how to distinguish between thinking and willing, n. 9991.

Many more things concerning the will and understanding may be known and concluded from what has just been adduced concerning good and truth, provided will be perceived instead of good, and understanding instead of truth, for the will is of good, and the understanding is of truth.

OF THE INTERNAL AND EXTERNAL MAN.

36. MAN is so created as to be in the spiritual and in the natural world at the same time. The spiritual world is that which is the abode of angels, and the natural world is that which is the abode of men. As man is so created, he is endowed both with an internal and an external; that by means of his internal he may be present in the spiritual world, and by means of his external, in the natural world. His internal is what is called the internal man, and his external is what is called the external man.

37. Every man is possessed of both an internal and an external; but these widely differ with the good and the evil. With the good, the internal is in heaven, and in its light, and the external is in the world, and in its light; and, with them, this latter light is illuminated by the light of heaven, so that their internal and external act in unity, or form a one, like cause and effect, or like what is prior and what is posterior. But, with the evil, the internal is in the world, and in its light; as is also the external; for which reason they see nothing from the light of heaven, but only from the light of the world, which they call the light of nature. Hence it is that, to them, the things of heaven are immersed in darkness, whilst the things of the world appear in light. Hence it is manifest, that the good have both an internal and an external man, but that the evil have not an internal man, but only an external.

38. The internal man is called the SPIRITUAL MAN, because it is in the light of heaven, which light is spiritual: and the external man is called the NATURAL MAN, because it is in the light of the world, which light is natural. The man whose internal is in the light of heaven, and whose external is in the light of the world, is a spiritual man as to both; but the man whose internal is not in the light of heaven, but only in the light of the world, in which is his external also, is a natural man as to both. The spiritual man is said in the Word to be ALIVE, but the natural man to be DEAD.

39. The man whose internal is in the light of heaven, and his external in the light of the world, thinks both spiritually and naturally; but when he thinks naturally, his spiritual thought flows into his natural thought, and is there perceived. But the man who has both his internal and external in the light of the world, does not think spiritually, but materially: for he thinks from such things as are within nature as it belongs to the world, all which are material. To think spiritually, is to think of things as they essentially are, to see truths in the light of truth, and to perceive goods from the love of good; also, to see the qualities of things, and to perceive their affections, abstractedly from matter. But to think materially of

things, is to think, to see, and perceive them together with matter, and in matter, thus in a gross and obscure manner respectively.

40. The internal spiritual man, simply considered, is an angel of heaven; and during his life in the body, although not conscious of the fact, is also in society with angels, amongst whom he is introduced after his separation from the body. But the merely natural man, as to his internal or soul, is a spirit, but not an angel: he also, during his life in the body, is in society with spirits, but with those who are in hell; and amongst these he is introduced after his separation from the body.

41. The interiors of the mind of those who are spiritual men, are also actually elevated towards heaven, for heaven is the primary object of their regard; but with those who are merely natural, the interiors are directed towards the world, because this is the primary object of regard with them. Indeed, the interiors of every man's mind are directed towards that which he loves supremely; and his exteriors take the same direction.

42. They who entertain only a general idea concerning the internal and external man, believe that it is the internal man which thinks and wills, and that it is the external which speaks and acts; because to think and to will relate to what is internal, and to speak and act to what is external. But it is to be observed, that, when man thinks intelligently, and wills wisely, he thinks and wills from a spiritual internal; but when he does not thus think and will, he thinks and wills from a natural internal. Hence, when man thinks well concerning the Lord, and those things which are the Lord's, and concerning the neighbor, and the things which are the neighbor's, and wills well towards them, he then thinks and wills from a spiritual internal, because from the faith of truth and from the love of good, consequently, from heaven. But when man is ill affected towards them, both in thought and in will, he thinks and wills from a natural internal, because from the faith of what is false and the love of what is evil, consequently, from hell. In short, so far as man is principled in love to the Lord, he is in the spiritual internal, whence he both thinks and wills, and also speaks and acts; but so far as he is in the love of self and in the love of the world, he is in the natural internal, from which he thinks and wills, and also speaks and acts.

43. It is so provided and ordered by the Lord, that in proportion as man thinks and wills from heaven, his internal spiritual man is opened and formed: it is opened into heaven even to the Lord; and it is formed according to those things which belong to heaven. But on the contrary, in proportion as man does not think and will from heaven, but from the world, his internal spiritual man is closed, and his external is opened; and

it is opened into the world, and is formed according to those things which belong to the world.

44. They who have the internal spiritual man opened into heaven to the Lord, are in the light of heaven, and in illumination from the Lord, and are thence in intelligence and wisdom; they see truth in the light of truth, and perceive good from the love of good. But they whose internal spiritual man is closed, do not so much as know that there is an internal man; much less do they know what the internal man is; neither do they believe that there is a Divine Being, nor that there is a life after death; consequently, neither do they believe in any thing belonging to heaven and the church. And since such persons are only in the light of the world, and in illumination thence, they believe in nature as the Divine Being; they see falsity as truth, and perceive evil as good.

45. The man whose internal is so far external that he believes in nothing but what he can see with his eyes, and touch with his hands, is called a sensual man. The sensual man is one who is in the lowest degree natural; and he is in fallacies concerning all things belonging to faith and the church.

46. The internal and external which have been treated of, are the internal and external of the spirit of man; his body being merely an additional external, within which the former exist; for the body does nothing of itself, but is solely actuated by the spirit which is in it. And here it is to be observed, that the spirit of man, after its separation from the body, thinks, and wills, and speaks, and acts, as it did when in the body: to think and to will constitute its internal, and to speak and to act, its external: concerning which see the work ON HEAVEN AND HELL, n. 234 to 245, 265—272, 432, 444, 458—484

FROM THE ARCANA CŒLESTIA.

47. OF *the internal and external with man.* That it is known in the Christian world, that man has an internal and an external, or an internal man and an external man; but that it is little known what is the quality of the one and of the other, n. 1889, 1940. That the internal man is spiritual, and the external is natural, n. 978, 1015, 4459, 6309, 9701 to 9708. How the internal man, which is spiritual, is formed after the image of heaven; and the external, which is natural, after the image of the world; and that man was therefore called by the ancients a microcosm, n. 3628, 4523, 4524, 6057, 6314, 9706, 10,156, 10,472. That thus in man the spiritual and natural worlds are conjoined, n. 6057, 10,472. That consequently man is of such a quality, that he can look up towards heaven, and down towards the world, n. 7601, 7604, 7607. That when he looks upwards, he is in the light of heaven and sees thence; but when he

looks downwards, he is in the light of the world and sees thence, n. 3167, 10,134. That there is given with man a descent from the spiritual world into the natural, n. 3702, 4042.

That the internal man, which is spiritual, and the external man, which is natural, are altogether distinct, n. 1999, 2018, 3691, 4459. That the distinction is such as exists between cause and effect, and between prior and posterior, and that there in no continuity, n. 3691, 4145, 5146, 5711, 6275, 6284, 6299, 6326, 6465, 8603, 10,076, 10,099, 10,181. Consequently that the distinction is like that between heaven and the world, or between what is spiritual and what is natural, n. 4292, 5132, 8610. That the interiors and exteriors of man are not continuous, but distinct according to degrees, each degree having its own termination, n. 3691, 4145, 5114, 6326, 6465, 8603, 10,099. That he who does not perceive the distinctions of the interiors and exteriors of man according to degrees, and understands not the quality of those degrees, cannot comprehend the internal and external of man, n. 5146, 6465, 10,099, 10,181. That the things of a superior degree are more perfect than those of an inferior degree, n. 3405. That there are three degrees in man answering to the three heavens, n. 4154. That the exteriors are more remote from the Divine with man, and that therefore they are respectively obscure, and of a common or general nature, n. 6451. And that they are also respectively not in order, n. 996, 3855. That the interiors are more perfect, as being nearer to the Divine, n. 5146, 5147. That in the internal there are thousands and thousands of things, which in the external appear as one general thing, n. 5707. That consequently, thought and per ception is clearer in proportion as it is interior, n. 5920. That hence it follows, that man ought to be in internals, n. 1175, 4464.

That the interiors of the mind, with the man who is in love and charity, are actually elevated by the Lord, and that otherwise they would look downwards, n. 6952, 6954, 10,330. That influx and illustration from heaven with man, is an actual elevation of the interiors by the Lord, n. 7816, 10,330. That man is elevated when he advances to spiritual things, n. 2922. That in proportion as man is elevated from externals towards interiors, in the same proportion he comes into light, consequently into intelligence; and that this is what is meant by being withdrawn from sensual things, according to the saying of the ancients, n. 6183, 6313. That elevation from the external to the interiors, is like that from mist into light, n. 4958.

That influx from the Lord is through the internal man into the external, n. 1940, 5119. That interiors can flow into exteriors, but not the contrary; consequently that influx is spiritual and not physical,—from the spiritual man into the natural, and not from the natural man into the spiritual, n. 3219, 5119, 5259, 5427, 5428, 5477, 6322, 9110, 9111. That the Lord from the internal, wherein all is peace, governs the externals, wherein all is confusion, n. 5396.

That the internal can see all things in the external, but not the contrary, n. 1914, 1953, 5427, 5428, 5477. That when man lives in the world, he thinks from the internal in the external, consequently that his spiritual thought flows into his natural, and there subsists naturally, n. 3679. That when man thinks well, it is from the internal or spiritual in the external or natural, n. 9704, 9705, 9707 That the external man thinks and wills according to conjunction with the internal, n. 9702, 9703. That there is an interior and an exterior thought; the quality of the one and the other, n. 2515, 2552, 5127, 5141, 5168, 6007. That the thought and affection in the internal is not perceived by man during his life in the world, but only that which is in the external derived therefrom, n. 10,236, 10,240. But that in another life externals are taken away, and man is then let into his own internals, n. 8870. That it then becomes manifest what is the quality of his internals, n. 1806, 1807.

That the internal produces the external, n. 994, 995. And that the internal then invests itself with such things as enable it to produce its effects in the external, n. 6275, 6284, 6299. And by which it may live in the external, n. 1175, 6275. That the Lord conjoins the internal or spiritual man to the external or natural man, when He regenerates him, n. 1577, 1594, 1904, 1999. That the external or natural man is then reduced into order through the internal or spiritual man, and that it is brought into subordination, n. 9708.

That the external must be subordinate and subject to the internal, n. 5077, 5125, 5128, 5786, 5947, 10,272. That the external is so created, that it may serve the internal, n. 5947. That the internal must be lord [or master], and the external its minister, and in a certain respect its servant, n. 10,471.

That the external ought to be in correspondence with the internal, that there may be conjunction, n. 5427, 5428, 5477. What the quality of the external is when it corresponds with the internal, and what when it does not correspond, n. 3493, 5422, 5423, 5427, 5428, 5477, 5512. That in the external man there are things which correspond and agree with the internal, and that there are things which do not correspond and agree, n. 1563, 1568.

That the external takes its quality from the internal, n. 9912, 9921, 9922. How great the beauty of the external man is, when it is conjoined with the internal, n. 1590. And how great its deformity is, when not conjoined therewith, n. 1598. That love to the Lord, and charity towards the neighbor, conjoin the external man with the internal, n. 1594. That, unless the internal man be conjoined with the external, there is no fructification, n. 3987.

That the interiors successively flow into the exteriors, even into the extreme or ultimate, and that they there exist and subsist together, n. 634, 6239, 9216, 9217. That they not only flow in successively, but also exist in the ultimate in a simultaneous form, and in what order, n. 5897, 6451, 8603, 10,099. That all the interiors are held in connection from the first, by means of the ultimate, n. 9828. That thence also in the ultimates are strength and power, n. 9836. And that therefore responses and revelations were made from the ultimates, n. 9905, 10,548. That thence also the ultimate is holy above the interiors, n. 9824. That hence also in the Word, first and last signify all and every particular, consequently the whole, n. 10,044, 10,329, 10,335.

That the internal man is open to him who is in Divine order, but shut to him who is not in Divine order, n 8513. That there is no conjunction of heaven with the external man without the internal, n. 9380. That evils and the falses of evil shut the internal man, and cause man to be only in externals, n. 1587, 10,492. Especially evils from the love of self, n. 1594. That the interiors are shut even to the sensual, which is the ultimate, if the Divine be denied, n. 6564. That with the intelligent and learned of the world, who from the sciences confirm themselves against the things of heaven and the church, the internal is shut more than with the simple, n. 10,492.

Inasmuch as the internal man is in the light of heaven, and the external in the light of the world, that therefore they who are in the external without the internal, that is, they with whom the internal is shut, do not care for the internal things of heaven and the church, n. 4464, 4946. That in another life they cannot at all endure internal things, n. 10,694, 10,701, 10,707. That they believe nothing, n. 10,396, 10,400, 10,411, 10,429. That they love themselves and the world above all things, n. 10,407, 10,412, 10,422. That their interiors, or the things which are of their thought and affection, are vile, filthy, and profane, however they may appear in externals, n. 1182, 7046, 9705, 9707. That the ideas of their thought are material, and not at all spiritual, n. 10,582. The quality further described of those whose internal, that looks heavenward, is shut, n. 4459, 9709, 10,284, 10,286, 10,429, 10,472, 10,492, 10,602, 10,682.

That so far as the internal, which is spiritual, is opened, so far truths and goods are multiplied; and that so far as the internal, which is spiritual, is shut, so far truths and goods vanish, n. 4099. That the church is in the internal spiritual man, inasmuch as that is in heaven, and not in the external without it, n. 10,698. Consequently that the external church with man is nothing without the internal church, n. 1795. That external worship without internal worship is no worship, n. 1094, 1175. Concerning those who are in the internal of the church, of worship, and of the Word; of those who are in the external wherein is the internal; and of those who are in the external without the internal, n. 10,682. That the external without the internal is hard, n. 10,682.

That the merely natural man is in hell, unless he be made spiritual by regeneration, n. 10,156. That all, who are in the external, without the internal, or with whom the spiritual internal is shut, are in hell, n. 9128, 10,483, 10,489.

That the interiors of man are actually turned according to his loves, n. 10,702. That in all and every particular there must be an internal and an external, in order to its subsistence, n. 9473.

That above and high, in the Word, signifies internal, n. 1725, 2148, 4210, 4599. Consequently that in the Word superior is interior, and inferior is exterior, n. 3084.

48. *Of the natural and the spiritual* [*principles*]. How perverse it is, in the world at this day, to attribute so much to nature, and so little to the Divine, n. 3483. Why it is so, n. 5116. When nevertheless all and every particular in nature not only received its existence, but likewise continually subsists from the Divine, and through the spiritual world, n. 775, 8211. That Divine, celestial, and spiritual things terminate in nature, n. 4240, 4939. That nature is the ultimate plane whereon they stand, n. 4240, 5051, 6275, 6284, 6299, 9216. That celestial, spiritual, and natural things follow and succeed each other in order; so do Divine things with them, inasmuch as

they are from the Divine, n. 880, 4938, 4939, 9992, 10,005, 10,017, 10,068. That celestial things are the head, spiritual things the body, and natural things the feet, n. 4938, 4939. That they also flow in an order similar to that wherein they follow and succeed each other, n. 4938, 4939. That the good of the inmost or third heaven is called celestial, the good of the middle or second heaven is called spiritual, and the good of the ultimate or first heaven is called spiritual natural, whence it may be known what is the celestial, spiritual, and natural, n. 4279, 4286, 4938, 4939, 9992, 10,005, 10,017, 10,068; and in the work ON HEAVEN AND HELL, n. 20 to 28, and 29 to 40.

That all things of the natural world are from the Divine through the spiritual world, n. 5013. Consequently that there is a spiritual principle in every thing natural, just as the efficient cause is in the effect, n. 3562, 5711; or as effort is in motion, n. 5173, and as the internal is in the external, n. 3562, 5711, 5326. And since the cause is the essential in the effect, as effort is in motion, and the internal in the external; hence it follows, that the spiritual, and consequently the Divine, is the very essential in the natural, n. 2987 to 3002, 9701 to 9709. That spiritual things are fixed and manifested in what is natural, and that the things manifested are representatives and correspondences, n. 1632, 2987 to 3002. That hence all nature is a theatre representative of the spiritual world, that is, of heaven, n. 2758, 2999, 3000, 4939, 8848, 9280. That all things in nature are disposed in order and series according to ends, n. 4104. That this is from the spiritual world, or from heaven, because ends, which are uses, reign there, n. 454, 696, 1103, 3645, 4054, 7038. That man is so created that Divine things descending according to order into nature, may be perceived in him, n. 3702.

That with every man, who is in Divine Order, there is an internal and an external, his internal is called the spiritual, or the spiritual man, and his external is called the natural, or the natural man, n. 978, 1015, 4459, 6309, 9701 to 9709. That the spiritual man is in the light of heaven, and the natural man in the light of the world, n. 5965. That the natural man can discern nothing from himself, but from the spiritual, n. 5286. That the natural is like a face in which the interiors see themselves, and that thus man thinks, n. 5165. That the spiritual man thinks in the natural, consequently naturally, so far as he comes to the sensual perception of the latter, n. 3679, 5165, 6284, 6299. That the natural is the plane, in which the spiritual terminates, n. 5651, 6275, 6284, 6299, 9216. That the spiritual sees nothing, unless the natural be in correspondence, n. 3493, 3620, 3623. That the spiritual or internal man can see what is transacting in the natural or external, but not the contrary, because the spiritual flows into the natural, and not the natural into the spiritual, n. 3219, 4667, 5119, 5259, 5427, 5428, 5477, 6322, 9110, 9111. That the natural man from his own light, which is called the light [*lumen*] of nature, knows nothing concerning God, nor concerning heaven, nor concerning a life after death; neither does he believe, if he hears of such things, unless spiritual light, which is light from heaven, flows into that natural light [*lumen*], n. 8444.

That the natural man of himself, by birth, is opposite to the spiritual man, n. 3913, 3928. That therefore as long as they are in opposition to each other, man feels it grievous to think of spiritual and celestial things, but delightsome to think of natural and corporeal things, n. 4096. That he utterly nauseates the things of heaven, and even the bare mention of any thing spiritual,—from experience, n. 5006, 9109. That merely natural men regard spiritual good and truth as a servant, n. 5013, 5025. When nevertheless the natural man ought to be subordinate to the spiritual man, and serve him, n. 3019, 5168. The spiritual man is said to serve the natural, when the latter from the intellectual principle seeks arguments to confirm the objects of his concupiscence, particularly from the Word, n. 3019, 5013, 5025, 5168. In what manner merely natural men appear in another life, and what is the quality of their state and lot there, n. 4630, 4633, 4940 to 4951, 5032, 5571.

That the truths, which are in the natural man, are called scientifics and knowledges, n. 3293. That the imagination of the natural man, when viewed in himself, is material, and that his affections are like those of beasts, n. 3020. But that there is a genuine thinking and imaginative principle from the internal or spiritual man, when the natural man sees, acts, and lives therefrom, n. 3493, 5422, 5423, 5427, 5428, 5477, 5512.

That the things which are in the natural man, respectively to those which are in the spiritual man, are common [or general], n. 3513, 5707; and consequently obscure, n. 6686.

That there is an interior and an exterior natural with man, n 3293, 3294, 3793, 5118, 5126, 5497, 5649. That there is also a medium between them, n. 4570, 9216. That the discharges [*exonerationes*] of the spiritual man are made into the natural, and by it, n. 9572.

That they who do good merely from a natural disposition, and not from religion, are not received in heaven, n. 8002, 8772.

49. *Of the light of heaven in which the spiritual man is.* That there is great light in the heavens, n. 1117, 1521, 1533, 1619 to 1632. That the light in the heavens exceeds the meridian light on earth by many degrees, n. 1117, 1521, 4527, 5400, 8644. That that light has been often seen by me, n. 1522, 4527, 7174. That the light which the angels of the inmost or third heaven enjoy is as the light from the sun, but the light which the angels of the second heaven enjoy is as the light from the moon, n. 1529, 1530. That the light in the inmost heaven is of a flame color, but in the second heaven it is white, n. 9570.

That all light in the heavens is from the Lord as a sun, n. 1053, 1521, 3195, 3341, 3636, 3643, 4415, 9548, 9684, 10,809. That the Lord is the sun of the angelic heaven, and that his Divine Love is that sun, n. 1521, 1529, 1530, 1531, 1837, 4321, 4696, 7078, 7171, 7173. That the Divine Truth proceeding from the Lord in the heavens appears as light, and constitutes all the light of heaven; and that consequently that light is spiritual light, n. 3195, 3322, 5400, 8644, 9399, 9548, 9684. That therefore the Lord in the Word is called light, n. 3195. That, inasmuch as that light is the Divine Truth, there is in it Divine Wisdom and intelligence, n. 3395, 3485, 3636, 3643, 3993, 4302, 4413, 4415, 9548, 9684. In what manner light from the Lord flows into the heavens, illustrated by the circles of rays round the sun, n. 9407 Tha the Lord is a sun to the heavens, and that from Him is all the light there, may be seen in the work ON HEAVEN AND HELL, n. 116 to 125. And that the light from that sun is the Divine Truth, and the heat from it the Divine Good of Divine Love, n. 126 to 140.

That the light of heaven illuminates both the sight and understanding of angels and spirits, n. 2776, 3138. That the light there is according to their understanding and wisdom, n. 1524, 3339. Proved from the Word, n. 1529, 1530. That there are as many differences of light in the heavens as there are angelic societies, n. 4414. Inasmuch as there are perpetual varieties in the heavens with respect to good and truth, so likewise there are with respect to wisdom and intelligence, n. 684, 690, 3241, 3744, 3745, 5598, 7236, 7833, 7836. That heaven's being in light and heat signifies its being in wisdom and in love, n. 3643, 9399, 9401.

That the light of heaven illuminates the understanding of man, n. 1524, 3138, 3167, 4408, 6608, 8707, 9126, 9399, 10,569. That man, when he is elevated from the sensual comes into a milder light [*lumen*], and at length into celestial light [*lux*], n. 6313, 6315, 9407. That there is elevation into the light of heaven when man comes into intelligence, n. 3190. What great light was perceived, when I have been withdrawn from worldly ideas, n. 1526, 6608. That the sight of the internal man is in the light of heaven, and that by reason thereof man is able to think analytically and rationally, n. 1532. That the light of heaven from the Lord is always present with man, but that it only so far flows in, as he is in truths from good, n. 4060, 4213. That that light is according to truth from good, n. 3094. That truths shine in the spiritual world, n. 5219. That spiritual heat and spiritual light make the true life of man, n. 6032.

That the light of the world is for the external man, and the light of heaven for the internal, n. 3222, 3223, 3337. That the light of heaven flows into natural light [*lumen*], and that the natural man is so far wise as he receives that light, n. 4302, 4408. That there is a correspondence between those lights, n. 3225. That the things which are in the light of heaven cannot be seen from the light of the world with man, which is called his natural light [*lumen*]; but the things in the light of the world may be seen from the light of heaven, n. 9574. Whence it follows, that they who are only in the light of the world, which is called natural light [*lumen*], do not perceive those things which are of the light of heaven, n. 3108. That to those who are in falses from evil, the light of heaven is black, n. 1783, 3337, 3413, 4060, 6907, 8197. That the light of the world shines with a fiery redness [*rutilet*] with the evil, and that so far as it so shines, so far the things which are of the light of heaven are dark to them, n. 6907. That the light of the world does not appear to the angels, n. 1521, 1783, 1880.

That in the heavens all light is from the Lord, and all shade from the ignorance and proprium of the angels and spirits; hence the modifications and variegations of light and shade, which are colors there, n. 3391. Concerning the variegations of light by urim and thummim, n. 3862.

That the light of those who are in faith separate from charity is snowy, and that it is like the light of winter, n. 3412, 3413. That that light is turned into mere darkness on the influx of light from heaven, n. 3412. Of the light of those who are in a persuasive faith, and in a life of evil, n. 4416. Of what quality the light appears with those who are in intelligence from proprium, and what with those who are in intelligence from the Lord, n. 4419.

That there is light [*lumen*] in the hells, but not real [*fatuum*], n. 1528, 3940, 4213, 4418, 4531. That this light is as light from a coal-fire, n. 1528, 4418, 4531. That they who are in the hells appear to themselves in their own light as men, but in the light of heaven as devils and monsters, n. 4532, 4533, 4674, 5057, 5058, 6605, 6626. That all things in the light of heaven appear according to their true quality, n. 4674. That the hells are said to be in blackness and darkness, because they are in falses from evil, n. 3340, 4418, 4531. That darkness signifies falses, and blackness the false of evil, n. 1839, 1860, 7688, 7711.

50. *Of the sensual man, who is the lowest natural, spoken of in the doctrine above*, n. 45. That the sensual [principle] is the ultimate of the life of man, adhering to and inhering in his corporeal [part], n. 5077, 5767, 9212, 9216, 9331, 9730. That he who judges and determines every thing from the bodily senses, and who believes nothing but what he can see with his eyes and touch with his hands, saying that these are real, and rejecting all things else as not real, is a sensual man, n. 5094, 7693. That such a man thinks in ultimates, and not interiorly in himself, n. 5089, 5094, 6564, 7693. That his interiors are shut, so that he sees nothing of truth therein, n. 6564, 6844, 6845. In a word, that he is in gross natural light, and of course perceives nothing which is from the light of heaven, n. 6201, 6310, 6564, 6844, 6845, 6598, 6612, 6614, 6622, 6624. That consequently he is interiorly against the things which are of heaven and the church, n. 6201, 6316, 6844, 6845, 6948, 6949. That the learned, who have confirmed themselves against the truths of the church, are sensual, n. 6316.

That sensual men reason sharply and shrewdly, because their thought is so near their speech as to be almost in it, and because they place all intelligence in discourse from mere memory, n. 195, 196, 5700, 10,236. But that they reason from the fallacies of the senses, with which the vulgar are captivated, n. 5084, 6948, 6949, 7693.

That sensual men are more crafty and malicious than others, n. 7693, 10,236. That the avaricious, adulterers, the voluptuous, and the deceitful, are in an especial manner sensual, n. 6310. That their interiors are foul and filthy, n. 6201. That by means thereof they communicate with the hells, n. 6311. That they who are in the hells are sensual in proportion to the depth of their respective situations therein, n. 4623, 6311. That the sphere of infernal spirits conjoins itself with man's sensual [principle] behind [*a tergo*], n. 6312. That they who reasoned from the sensual [principle], and thereby against the truths of faith, were called by the ancients serpents of the tree of science, n. 195, 196, 197, 6398, 6949, 10,313.

The sensual [principle] of man, and the sensual man himself, is further described, n. 10,236. And the extension of the sensual [principle] with man, n. 9731.

That sensual things ought to be in the last place, not in the first; and that with a wise and intelligent man they are in the last place, and subject to the interiors; but that with an unwise man they are in the first place, and have dominion; these are they who are properly called sensual, n. 5077, 5125, 5128, 7645. That if sensual things are in the last place, and are subject to the interiors, a way is opened through them to the understanding, and truths are refined by a kind of extraction, n. 5580.

That the sensual things of man stand proximate to the world, and admit things that flow from the world, and as it were sift them, n. 9726. That the external or natural man communicates with the world by means of those sensuals, and with heaven by means of rationals, n. 4009. That thus sensual things furnish what is subservient to the interiors of man, n. 5077, 5081. That there are sensual things ministering to the intellectual part, and likewise to the will part, n. 5077.

That unless the thought is elevated from sensual things, man possesses but little wisdom, n. 5089. That a wise man thinks above the sensual [principle], n. 5089, 5094. That man, when his thought is elevated above sensual things, comes into a clearer light [*lumen*], and at length into heavenly light [*lux*], n. 6183, 6313, 6315, 9407, 9730, 9922. That elevation above sensual things, and withdrawal from them, was known to the ancients, n. 6313. That man with his spirit may see the things which are in the spiritual world, if he can be withdrawn from the sensual things of the body, and elevated by the Lord into the light of heaven, n. 4622. The reason is, because the body has no perception, but the spirit in the body; and so far as the spirit perceives in the body, so far is the perception gross and obscure, consequently in darkness; but so far as not in the body, so far is the perception clear and in the light, n. 4622, 6614, 6622.

That the ultimate of the understanding is the sensual scientific [principle], and the ultimate of the will the sensual pleasurable [principle], concerning which see n. 9996. What is the difference between the sensual things that are common with beasts, and those that are not common with them, n. 10,236. That there are sensual men who are not evil, inasmuch as their interiors are not so much closed; concerning whose state in another life, see n. 6311.

51. *Of sciences and knowledges, by which the internal spiritual man is opened.* That those things are called scientifics, which are in the external or natural man, and its memory, but not those which are in the internal or spiritual man, n. 3019, 3020, 3293, 3309, 4967, 9918, 9922. That scientifics, as belonging to the external or natural man, are respectively instruments of service, inasmuch as the external or natural man is made to serve the internal or spiritual man, just as the world is made to be subservient to heaven, n. 5077, 5125, 5128, 5786, 5947, 10,272, 10,471. That the external man is respectively the world, because the laws of Divine order existing in the world are inscribed therein; and that the internal man is respectively heaven, because the laws of Divine order existing in heaven are inscribed therein, n. 4523, 4524, 5368, 6013, 6057, 9278, 9279, 9283, 9709, 10,156, 10,472; and in the work ON HEAVEN AND HELL, n. 51 to 58.

That there are some scientifics which concern natural things some which relate to the civil state and life, some which relate to the moral state and life, and some which relate to the spiritual state and life, n. 5934. But that, for distinction's sake, those which relate to the spiritual state and life, are called knowledges, consisting principally of doctrinals, n. 9945.

That man ought to be imbued with sciences and knowledges, since by these he learns to think, then to understand what is true and good, n. 129, 1450, 1451, 1453, 1548, 1802. That scientifics and knowledges are the first things, on which is built and founded the civil, moral, and spiritual life of man; but that they are to be learned for the sake of the use of life as their end, n. 1489, 3310. That knowledges open the way to the internal man, and then conjoin it with the external according to uses, n. 1563, 1616. That the rational [principle] is born by sciences and knowledges, n. 1895, 1900, 3086. Yet not by sciences and knowledges themselves, but by the affection of uses from them, and according to such affection, n. 1895. That the internal man is opened and successively perfected by sciences and knowledges, provided man has some good use for an end, particularly a use that regards eternal life, n. 3086. That in this case, spiritual things from the celestial and spiritual man meet the scientifics and knowledges which are in the natural man, and adopt those which agree, n. 1495. That uses of heavenly life are then extracted, refined, and elevated by the Lord, through the internal man, from the scientifics and knowledges which are in the natural man, n. 1895, 1896, 1900, 1901, 1902, 5871, 5874, 5901. And that the scientifics which are incongruous and adverse are rejected to the sides and exterminated, n. 5871, 5886, 5889. That the sight of the internal man calls nothing forth from the scientifics and knowledges of the external man, but such as are of its love, n. 9394. That scientifics and knowledges are disposed in fascicles or bundles [*fasciculatim*], and conjoined according to the loves which introduced them, n. 5811. That then, in the sight of the internal man, those which are of the love are in the middle and in clearness, but those which are not of the love are at the sides and in obscurity, n. 6068, 6085. That scientifics and knowledges with man are successively implanted in his loves, and dwell in them, n. 6325. That man would be born into every science, and thereby into intelligence, if he were born into love to the Lord, and love towards the neighbor; but since he is born into the love of self and the world, that therefore he is born in total ignorance, n. 6323, 6325. That science, intelligence, and wisdom are the sons of love to the Lord and of love towards the neighbor, n. 1226, 2049, 2116.

That scientifics and knowledges, inasmuch as they are of the external or natural man, are in the light of the world; but truths, which are become truths of love and faith, and have thus obtained life, are in the light of heaven, n. 5212. That nevertheless the truths, which have thus obtained life, are comprehended by man through natural ideas, n. 5510. That spiritual influx is through the internal man into the scientifics and knowledges which are in the external, n. 1940, 8005. That scientifics and knowledges are the receptacles and as it were the vessels of the truth and good of the interna man, n. 1469, 1496, 3068, 5489, 6004, 6023, 6052, 6071, 6077, 7770, 9922. That therefore vessels in the Word, in the spiritual sense, signifies scientifics and knowledges, n. 3068, 3069, 3079, 9394, 9544, 9723, 9724. That scientifics are as it were mirrors, in which the truths and goods of the internal man appear, and are perceived as in an image, n. 5201. That those truths and goods are together in scientifics as in their ultimate, n. 5373, 5874, 5886, 5901, 6004, 6023, 6052, 6071, 6077. That scientifics, as being in the light of the world, are perplexed [*implexa*], and obscure, respectively to those things which are in the light of heaven; consequently the things which are in the external man [are likewise perplexed and obscure], respectively to those in the internal, n. 2831. For which reason also by what is perplexed [*implexum*] in the Word is signified what is scientific, n. 2831. So also by the obscurity of a cloud, n. 8443, 10,551.

That every principle is to be drawn from truths of doctrine derived from the Word, which are first to be acknowledged, and that then it is allowable to consult scientifics in order to confirm those truths, and that thus they are corroborated, n. 6047. Consequently, that it is allowable for those who are in an affirmative [principle] concerning the truths of faith, intellectually to confirm them by scientifics, but not for those who are in a negative [principle], because a preceding affirmative draws all to favor its side, and a preceding negative has a like effect, n. 2568, 2588, 3913, 4760, 6047. That there is an affirmative [principle] of doubt, and a negative [principle] of doubt, the former with some who are good, and the latter with the evil, n. 2568. That to enter from the truths of faith into scientifics, is agreeable to order; but on the other hand, to enter from scientifics into the truths of faith, is contrary to order, n. 10,236. Inasmuch as influx is spiritual, and not physical or natural, consequently from the truths of faith, because these are spiritual, into scientifics, because these are natural, n. 3219, 5119, 5259, 5427, 5428, 5478, 6322, 9110, 9111.

That whoever is in a negative [principle] of doubt, which in itself is a negative, and says that he will not believe till he is persuaded by scientifics, will never believe, n. 2094, 2830. That they who do so, become mad with respect to those things which are of the church and heaven, n. 128, 129, 130. That they fall into the falses of evil, n. 232, 233, 6047. And that, in another life, when they think about spiritual things, they are like drunken persons, n. 1072. A further description of them, n. 196. Examples to illustrate that spiritual things cannot be comprehended, if the order of entering into them be inverted, n. 233, 2094, 2196, 2203, 2209. That many of the learned are more insane in spiritual things, than the simple, by reason that they are in a negative [principle], and have abundance of scientifics, by which they confirm the negative, n. 4760. An example of a learned man, who could understand nothing concerning spiritual life, n. 8629. That they who reason from scientifics against the truths of faith, reason sharply, inasmuch as they do it from the fallacies of the senses, which are captivating and persuasive, for it is with difficulty these can be shaken off, n. 5700. That they who understand nothing of truth, and they also who are in evil, can reason concerning tne truths and goods of faith, and yet be in no illustration, n. 4213. That only to confirm a dogma, is not the part of an intelligent man, because the false can be as easily confirmed as the true, n. 1017, 2482, 2490, 4741, 5033, 6865, 7012, 7680, 7950, 8521, 8780. That they who reason concerning the truths of the church, whether a thing be so or not, are evidently in obscurity respecting truths, and not yet in spiritual light, n. 215, 1385, 3033, 3428.

That there are scientifics which admit Divine Truths, and others which do not, n. 5213. That vain scientifics ought to be destroyed n. 1489, 1492, 1499, 1500. That those are vain scientifics which regard for their end and confirm the loves of self and the world, and which withdraw from love to the Lord and love towards the neighbor because such scientifics shut up the internal man, so that he is not then capable of receiving anything from heaven, n. 1563, 1600. That scientifics are the means of becoming wise, and the means of becoming insane; and that by them the internal man is either opened or shut; and thus the rational faculty is either improved or destroyed, n. 4156, 8628, 9922.

That sciences after death are of no account, but only those things which man has imbibed in his understanding and life by means of sciences, n. 2480. That nevertheless all scientifics abide after death, but that they are quiescent, n. 2476 to 2479, 2481 to 2486.

That the same scientifics which with evil men are false because applied to evils, are with good men true because applied to goods, n. 6917. That scientific truths with the evil are not truths, however they may appear such when spoken, because within them there is evil, and consequently they are falsified; and that the science of those men by no means deserves to be called science, inasmuch as it is destitute of life, n. 10,331.

That it is one thing to be wise, another to understand, another to know, and another to do; but that still, with those who are in spiritual life, they follow in order, and correspond, and are together in action or in works, n. 10,331. That it is also one thing to know, another to acknowledge, and another to have faith, n. 896.

What is the quality of the desire of knowing, which spirits possess, shown by an example, n. 1973. That angels have an immense desire of knowing and of becoming wise, inasmuch as science, intelligence, and wisdom, are spiritual food, n. 3114, 4459, 4792, 4976, 5147, 5293, 5340, 5342, 5410, 5426, 5576, 5582, 5588, 5656, 6277, 8562, 9003.

That the chief science among the ancients was the science of correspondences, but that at this day it is lost, n. 3021, 3419, 4280, 4344, 4964, 4965, 6004, 7729, 10,252. That the science of correspondences flourished among the eastern nations and in Egypt, n. 5702, 6692, 7097, 7779, 9391, 10,407. That thence came their hieroglyphics, n. 6692, 7097. That the ancients by the science of correspondences introduced themselves into the knowledges of spiritual things, n. 4844, 4749, 4965. That the Word is written by mere correspondences, whence its internal or spiritual sense, the existence of which cannot be known without the science of correspondences, nor can the quality of the Word, n. 3131, 3472 to 3485, 8615, 10,687. How much the science of correspondences excels other sciences n. 4280

52. *Of the natural memory, which is that of the external man, and of the spiritual memory, which is that of the internal man.* That man has two memories, an exterior and an interior memory, or a natural and a spiritual memory, n. 2469 to 2494. That man does not know that he has an interior memory, n. 2470, 2471. How much the interior memory excels the exterior memory, n. 2473. That the things in the exterior memory are in natural light, but the things in the interior memory, in spiritual light, n. 5212. That it is from the interior memory that man is able to think and speak intellectually and rationally, n. 9394. That all and every particular which man has thought, spoken, and done, and all that he has heard and seen, are inscribed on his interior memory, n. 2474, 7398. That that memory is man's book of life, n. 2474, 9386, 9841, 10,505. That in the interior memory are treasured up the truths which are become of faith, and the goods which are become of love, n. 5212, 8067. That the things which are rendered habitual, and have become of the life, are in the interior memory, n. 9394, 9723, 9841. That scientifics and knowledges are of the exterior memory, n. 5212, 9922. That they are very obscure and confused respectively to those things which are of the interior memory, n. 2831. That the languages which man speaks in the world, are from the exterior memory, n. 2472, 2476. That spirits and angels speak from the interior memory, and consequently their language is universal, being such that all can converse together, of whatever earth they may be, n. 2472, 2476, 2490, 2493; concerning which language, see the work ON HEAVEN AND HELL, n. 234 to 245; and concerning the wonders of the interior memory, see n. 463 of the same work.

53. *Of the fallacies of the senses, in which merely natural and sensual men are, mentioned above in this doctrine*, n. 45. That merely natural and sensual men think and reason from the fallacies of the senses, n. 5084, 5700, 6948, 6949, 7693. Of what quality the fallacies of the senses are, n. 5084, 5094, 6400, 6948. To which the following particulars shall be added. There are fallacies of the senses in things natural, civil, moral, and spiritual, and many in each of them; but here I design to recite some of the fallacies in spiritual things. He who thinks from the fallacies of the senses, cannot understand,—1. That man after death can appear as a man; nor that he can enjoy his senses as before; nor consequently that angels have such a capacity. 2. They think that the soul is only a vital something, purely etherial, of which no idea can be formed. 3. That it is the body alone which feels, sees, and hears. 4. That man is like a beast, with this difference only, that he can express his thoughts by speech. 5. That nature is all, and the first source from which all things proceed. 6. That man habituates and teaches himself to think by an influx of interior nature and its order. 7. That there is no spiritual [principle], and if there be, that it is a purer natural. 8. That man cannot enjoy any blessedness, if divested of the delights of the love of glory, honor, or gain. 9. That conscience is only a disease of the mind, proceeding from the infirmity of the body and from misfortunes. 10. That the Divine Love of the Lord is the love of glory. 11. That there is no providence, but that all things come to pass from self-derived prudence and intelli-

gence. 12. That honors and riches are real blessings bestowed by God :—not to mention many other things of a similar nature. Such are the fallacies of the senses in spiritual things. Hence it may appear, that heavenly things cannot be comprehended by those who are merely natural and sensual ;—by those, namely, whose internal spiritual man is shut, and whose natural man only is open.

OF LOVE IN GENERAL.

54. The very life of man is his love, and according to the quality of that love, such is his life, yea, such is the whole man ; it is, however, the ruling or reigning love, which constitutes the man. This love is accompanied by numerous other loves, which are derived from it, and are in subordination to it. These present themselves to view under other forms, but still they are all comprehended in the ruling love, and form, with it, one kingdom. The ruling love is, as it were, their king and head ; it directs all their movements, and by them, as mediate ends, it regards and designs its own end, which is the primary and ultimate end of all ; and this is done both directly and indirectly. The object of the ruling love is that which is loved supremely.

55. Whatever a man loves supremely is continually present in his thoughts and in his will, and constitutes the veriest essence of his life. As, for example, the man who loves wealth above all other things, whether in money or possessions, is continually revolving in his mind how he may attain it ; the possession of it affords him his highest joy, and the loss of it fills him with the deepest sorrow ; for his wealth absorbs his whole heart. So, also, the man who loves himself above all other objects, regards himself in all that he does ; he thinks of himself, speaks of himself, and acts entirely for the sake of himself ; for his life is the life of self.

56. That which a man loves supremely, forms the end which he always has in view ; he regards it in the whole of his conduct, even in the most minute particulars. It lurks in his will, and, like the latent current of a river, draws and bears him away, even when he is employed in other affairs ; for it constitutes his animating principle. Such is the nature of this love, that one man tries to discover it in another, and when he has found it, he either entirely leads him by it, or regulates all his intercourse with him according to it.

57. Man is entirely of such a character as is the ruling principle of his life. It is this which distinguishes one man from another ; and to this the heaven of each individual is adapted, if he is a good man, and his hell, if he is a wicked

man. It is this which constitutes his very will, his proper self, and his peculiar nature; for it is the very *esse* of his life. This cannot be changed after death, for it is the man himself.

58. All the delight, pleasure, and happiness which any one enjoys, are derived from his ruling love, and are in perfect accordance with it; for that which man loves, he calls delightful, because he feels it to be so: he may, indeed, also call that delightful which is an object of thought with him, but which he does not love; but this is not the delight of his life. That which is delightful to man's love is what he esteems good; and that which is disagreeable to it he considers evil.

59. There are two distinct loves, from which, as their fountains, all the varieties of good and of truth exist; and there are two distinct loves, from which all the varieties of evil and of falsity exist. The two loves, from which the varieties of good and truth are derived, are love to the Lord and love towards the neighbor; and the two loves, whence spring all the varieties of evil and of falsity, are the love of self and the love of the world. The two latter are in direct opposition to the two former.

60. The two loves from which all the varieties of good and truth are derived, and which, as has just been stated, are love to the Lord and love towards the neighbor, constitute heaven in man, and therefore they reign in heaven: and since they constitute heaven in man, they also constitute the church in him. The two loves, whence all the varieties of evil and of falsity proceed, and which, as has just been said, are the love of self and the love of the world, constitute hell in man; wherefore, also, they are the loves which reign in hell.

61. The two loves whence all the varieties of good and of truth are derived, and which, as already observed, are the loves of heaven, open and form the internal spiritual man, because it is in this that they have their residence. But the two loves whence originate all the varieties of evil and of falsity, when they obtain the ascendancy, shut up and destroy the internal spiritual man, and render man natural and sensual, in proportion to the extent and quality of their dominion.

FROM THE ARCANA CŒLESTIA.

62. THAT love is the esse of man's life, n. 5002. That man, spirit, and angel, are altogether as their love is, n. 6872, 10,177, 10,284. That man has what he loves for an end, n. 3796. That what man loves and has for an end reigns universally with him, that is, in all things and singulars, n. 3796, 5130, 5949. That love is spiritual heat, and the very vital principle of man, n. 1589, 2146, 3338, 4906, 7081 to 7086, 9954, 10,740. That all the interiors with man, which

are of his will and understanding, are disposed in a form according to his ruling love, n. 2024, 3189, 6690. That love is spiritual conjunction, n. 1594, 2057, 3939, 4018, 5807, 6195, 6196, 7081 to 7086, 7501, 10,130. Hence that all in the spiritual world are consociated according to their loves, *ibid.* That affection is love in continuity, n. 3938. That all delight, pleasure, happiness, and joy of heart, are of love; and their quality according to the quality of the love, n. 994, 995, 2204. That there are as many genera and species of delights and pleasures as there are of the affections which are of the love, n. 994, 995, 2204. That the delight of the love is more vile in proportion as it is more external, n. 996. That man enters into a state of life hereafter agreeing with the quality of his love, n. 2364.

63. Further particulars respecting love and its essence and quality, may be known from what has been said and shown above, concerning good and truth; also from what has been said and shown concerning the will and understanding; and also from what has been said and shown concerning the internal and external man; because all things which are of the love are referable either to goods or evils; and so also all things which are of the will: and forasmuch as the two loves of heaven open and form the internal spiritual man, and the two loves of hell close and destroy it, hence applications may be made and conclusions drawn respecting the quality of love in general and particular.

64. Love is also treated of in the work On Heaven and Hell; in which it is shown, that the Divine [principle] of the Lord in the heavens is love to Him and love towards the neighbor, n. 13 to 19. That all who are in the hells are in evils, and thence in falses, originating in the loves of self and of the world, n. 551 to 565. That the delights of every love are changed in the other life into their correspondences, n. 485 to 490. That spiritual heat in its essence is love, n. 133 to 140.

OF THE LOVE OF SELF, AND THE LOVE OF THE WORLD.

65. The love of self consists in wishing well to ourselves alone, and not to others, unless it be for the sake of ourselves, not even to the church, to our country, to society, or to a fellow-citizen. This love, it is true, may confer benefits on these several relations, when its own reputation, honor, and glory are concerned; but unless it sees that these will be secured by thus acting, its language is, "To what purpose is it? Why should I do this? Of what advantage will it be to me?" And thus it omits it. Hence it is evident that the man who is influenced by self-love, does not, in reality, love either the church, or his country, or his fellow-citizen, or society, or anything good, but himself alone.

66. Man is under the dominion of self-love, when, in his

houghts and actions, he has no regard to the neighbor, consequently, none for the public, still less for the Lord, but for himself alone and his connexions. Thus, whilst every thing which he does is for the sake of himself and his connexions, should he even do anything for his neighbor and for the public, it is done merely for the sake of appearance.

67. We have said, himself and his connexions; for the man who loves himself, loves those also who are connected with him. These are, in particular, his children and his other near relations, and, in general, all who co-operate with him, and whom he calls his friends. Still, however, his love for these is only self-love, for he regards them, as it were, in himself, and himself in them. Amongst those whom such a man denominates his friends, are all they who flatter him, honor him, and pay their court to him.

68. He also is under the influence of self-love, who thinks contemptuously of the neighbor in comparison with himself, and esteems him as an enemy unless he show him marks of favor, respect him, and treat him with great courtesy. But still more is he actuated by the love of self, who, for such reasons, hates and persecutes the neighbor; and more so still the man who burns with revenge against him, and desires his destruction. Such persons at length come to delight in savage cruelty.

69. The true nature of self-love may be clearly discerned from comparing it with heavenly love. Heavenly love consists in loving, for its own sake, the use or the good which a man ought to perform to the church, to his country, to society, and to his fellow-citizens; but he who loves these for his own sake, loves them no otherwise than he loves his domestics, that is, because they are serviceable to him. Hence it follows, that he who is immersed in self-love, would desire to have the church, his country, society, and his fellow-citizens, to be his servants, rather than that he should serve them; he exalts himself above them, and abases them beneath himself.

70. Moreover, in proportion as any one is influenced by celestial love, which consists in loving offices of usefulness, delighting in the performance of good deeds, and in being affected with joy of heart in thus acting, he is led by the Lord, for in this love the Lord himself is, and from Him it has its origin. But on the contrary, so far as any one is influenced by self-love, he is led by himself; and as far as he is so led, he is guided by his own selfhood, which is nothing but evil, being that hereditary evil which disposes man to love himself in preference to God, and the world in preference to heaven.

71. Such also is the nature of self-love, that in proportion as the reins are given to it, that is, so far as external restraints are removed, such as the fear of the law and its penalties, the

loss of reputation, of honor, of gain, of office, or of life, it rushes on with such unlimited desire as to grasp at universal dominion, not only over this world, but also over heaven, yea, over God himself; for its aim is boundless. This propensity lurks in the heart of every man who is governed by self-love, although it may not be visible to the eyes of the world, in consequence of the checks and restraints before-mentioned. Besides, when such a character encounters an insuperable obstacle, he waits till it is removed; and hence it is that even he himself is not aware that such a mad and unbounded cupidity lies latent within him. That this, however, is really the case, any one may see who observes the conduct of potentates and kings, who are not subject to such checks, restraints, and insuperable obstacles, and who so long as success attends their enterprises, rush on, and subjugate provinces and kingdoms, panting after unlimited power and glory. This is still more apparent in the case of those who endeavor to extend their dominion into heaven, transferring to themselves the Divine power of the Lord, and thirsting after something beyond even that.

72. There are two general kinds of dominion, one originating in love towards the neighbor, the other in the love of self; and these are, in essence, directly opposed to each other. He who exercises dominion from the influence of love towards the neighbor, is desirous of promoting the welfare of all, and has no higher delight than that which arises from the performance of works of real utility: this is his love, and the very delight of his heart. The higher such a person is exalted in dignity, the greater is his joy; not, indeed, on account of the dignity itself, but because the sphere of his usefulness is thus enlarged in extent, and rendered more excellent in degree. Such is the dominion that prevails in the heavens. But he who rules under the influence of self-love, has no desire to promote the welfare of any beyond himself and his own connexions. The works of utility which he performs are done for the advancement of his own honor and glory, which he considers as the only objects worthy of his pursuit. Hence, when he serves others, it is only that he may himself be served, honored, and intrusted with dominion; he desires preferment, not for the sake of extending his means of doing good, but that he may obtain pre-eminence and glory, and thus enjoy the delight of his heart.

73. The love of dominion remains also with man after the termination of his life in this world. They who have exercised it from love towards the neighbor, are then intrusted with dominion in the heavens; still, however, it is not they who rule, but the useful offices which they perform, and the goods which they love; and when these rule, the Lord rules. Those,

on the contrary, who, during their abode in the world, have exercised dominion from the influence of self-love, have their abode in hell, where they are vile slaves.

74. From what has been said, it may easily be perceived who they are that are influenced by the love of self. Nor is it of any consequence how they appear externally, whether haughty or humble; for the qualities which have been specified exist in the internal man, which the generality of mankind study to conceal, whilst they teach the external to assume the contrary appearance of love for the public good, and for the welfare of the neighbor. This also they do for the sake of self; for they well know that such love has the power of interiorly moving the affections of all men, and that they will be loved and esteemed in proportion as they appear to be under its influence. The reason why that love is possessed of such power is, because heaven enters into it by influx.

75. The evils which predominate in those whose ruling principle is self-love, are, in general, contempt of others, envy, enmity towards those who do not favor their designs, with hostility on that account; also hatreds of various kinds, revenge, cunning, deceit, unmercifulness, and cruelty. Where such evils exist, there is also a contempt of God, and of Divine things, that is, of all the good and truth belonging to the church; or if there be any respect shown to these by such persons, it is in words only, and not from the heart. And as such evils result from the love of self, it is also attended by corresponding falsities from the same source; for falsities are derived from evils.

76. The love of the world consists in desiring to appropriate to ourselves, by every available artifice, the wealth of others; also, in setting the heart on riches, and suffering the world to withdraw our affections from spiritual love, which is love towards the neighbor, consequently, from heaven. They are influenced by the love of the world, who are desirous of appropriating to themselves the property of others by various artifices; they particularly who have recourse to cunning and deceit, esteeming the welfare of the neighbor as of no account whatever. Such persons greedily covet the goods of others; and, when not restrained by the fear of the laws and the loss of reputation, which they regard only for the sake of gain, they deprive others of their possessions, nay, rob and plunder them.

77. The love of the world is not opposed to heavenly love in the same degree that the love of self is, because the evils contained in it are not so great. The love of the world is manifold. There is the love of riches as the means of exaltation to honors; there is the love of honors and dignities as the means of obtaining wealth; there is the love of wealth for various uses with which men are delighted in the world; there is

also the love of wealth merely for its own sake, which is the love of misers; and so in other instances. The end for which wealth is desired is called its use, and from the end or use the love derives its quality. The nature of all love is determined by the use to which it is directed; other things serve but as means to promote the end.

78. In short, the love of self and the love of the world are in direct opposition to love of the Lord and love towards the neighbor; wherefore the loves of self and the world are infernal and reign in hell, and constitute hell in man: but love to the Lord and love towards the neighbor are of heavenly origin, and reign in heaven, and constitute heaven in man.

79. From what has now been said it may be clearly seen, that all evils are contained in these loves, and are derived from them; for the evils which were enumerated at n. 75, are common or general in their nature; and the others, which were not enumerated there, because they are particular evils, are derived and flow from them. Hence it appears that, since man is born into the love of self and of the world, he is born into evils of every description.

80. In order that man may know what evils are, he ought to know their origin; and unless he know what evils are, he cannot know what good is, consequently neither can he know of what quality he himself is; and for this reason these two origins of evil have been here treated of.

FROM THE ARCANA CŒLESTIA.

81. Of *the loves of self and of the world.* As love to the Lord and love towards the neighbor, or charity, constitute heaven, so the love of self and the love of the world, where they reign, constitute hell; and therefore these loves are opposites, n. 2041, 3610, 4225, 4776, 6210, 7366, 7369, 7480, 7490, 8232, 8678, 10,455, 10,741, 10,742, 10,743, 10,745. That all evils proceed from the loves of self and of the world, n. 1307, 1308, 1321, 1594, 1691, 3413, 7255, 7376, 7480, 7488, 8318, 9335, 9348, 10,038, 10,742. That from the same origin proceed contempt of others, enmity, hatred, revenge, cruelty, and deceit, consequently all evil and all wickedness, n. 6667, 7372, 7373, 7374, 9348, 10,038, 10,742. That these loves rush on in proportion as the reins are given them, and that self-love aspires to the throne of God, n. 7375, 8678. That self-love and the love of the world are destructive of human society and of heavenly order, n. 2045, 2057. That for the sake of being preserved from the disorders occasioned by these loves, mankind have been obliged to form governments, and subject themselves to the powers thereof, n. 7364, 10,160, 10,814. That where these loves reign, the good of love and the truth of faith are either rejected, suffocated

or perverted, n. 2041, 7491, 7492, 7643, 8487, 10,455, 10,743. That in these loves there is not life, but spiritual death, n. 7494, 10,731, 10,741. The quality of these loves described, n. 1505, 2219, 2363 2364, 2444, 4221, 4227, 4947, 4949, 5721, 7366 to 7377, 8678. That all cupidity and concupiscence proceed from the love of self and of the world, n. 1668, 8910.

That the loves of self and of the world may serve as means, but not for an end, n. 7377, 7819, 7820. That when man is reformed, those loves are inverted, and serve as means, and not as ends, thus that they are as the soles of the feet, and not as the head, n 8995, 9210. That with those who are in the loves of self and of the world, there is no internal, but only an external, because the internal is shut towards heaven, but the external is open towards the world, n. 10,396, 10,400, 10,409, 10,412, 10,422, 10,424. That they who are in the loves of self and of the world do not know what charity is, what conscience is, and what the life of heaven is, n. 7490. That so far as a man is in the love of self and of the world, so far he does not receive the good and truth of faith which continually flows in with man from the Lord, n. 7491.

That they who are in the loves of self and the world are not bound by internal, but external restraints; and that on the removal thereof they rush into every wickedness, n. 10,744, 10,745, 10,746. That all in the spiritual world turn themselves according to their loves; they who are in love to the Lord and in love towards the neighbor, to the Lord, but those who are in the love of self and in the love of the world, turn their backs on the Lord, n. 10,130, 10,189, 10,420, 10,742. The quality of the worship in which the love of self prevails, n. 1304, 1306, 1307, 1308, 1321, 1322. That the Lord governs the world by means of the evil, in leading them by their peculiar loves, which have relation to self and the world, n. 6481, 6495. That the evil as well as the good can discharge the duties of offices, and perform uses and goods, because they regard honors and gain as their rewards, for the sake of which they act in an external form like the good, n. 6481, 6495.

That all who are in the hells are in evils and in falses thence derived, originating in self-love and the love of the world, see the work On Heaven and Hell, n. 551 to 565.

82. *Of the proprium of man, spoken of above, at* n. 70, *showing that it is the love of self and of the world.* That the proprium of man is nothing but dense evil, n. 210, 215, 731, 874, 875, 876, 987, 1047, 2307, 2318, 3518, 3701, 3812, 8480, 8550, 10,283, 10,284, 10,286, 10,731. That the proprium of man is his will [principle], n. 4328. That the proprium of man consists in loving himself more than God, and the world more than heaven, and in making his neighbor of no account respectively to himself,—consequently that it is the love of self and of the world, n. 694, 731, 4317, 5660. That not only every evil, but also every false, springs from the proprium of man, and that this false is the false of evil, n. 1047, 10,283, 10,284, 10,286. That the proprium of man is hell with him, n. 694, 8480. And therefore that he who is led by his proprium cannot be saved, n. 10,731. That the good which man does from proprium is

not good, but that in itself it is evil, because done for the sake of self and for the sake of the world, n. 8478.

That the proprium of man must be separated, in order that the Lord may be able to be present with him, n. 1023, 1044. And that it is actually separated when man is reformed, n. 9334, 9335, 9336, 9452, 9453, 9454, 9938. That this is done by the Lord alone, n 9445. That man by regeneration receives a heavenly proprium, n. 1937, 1947, 2882, 2883, 2891. That this appears to man as his own proprium, but that it is not his, but the Lord's with him, n. 8497. That they who are in this proprium are in liberty itself, because liberty consists in being led by the Lord, and by his proprium, n. 892, 905, 2872, 2886, 2890, 2891, 2892, 4096, 9586, 9587, 9589, 9590, 9591. That all liberty is from proprium, and its quality according thereto, n. 2880. What is the quality of the heavenly proprium, n. 164, 5660, 8480. How the heavenly proprium is implanted, n. 1712, 1937, 1947.

83. *Of the hereditary [principle] of man, spoken of above*, n. 70 to 79, *showing that it is the love of self and of the world.* That all men are born into evils of every kind, insomuch that their proprium is nothing but evil, n. 210, 215, 731, 874, 875, 876, 987, 1047, 2307, 2308, 3701, 3812, 8480, 8550, 10,283, 10,284, 10,286, 10,731. That it is on this account that man is to be born again, that is, regenerated, in order that he may receive a new life from the Lord, n. 3701.

That hereditary evils are derived, increased, and accumulated from parents and ancestors in a long backward series, and not from the first man's eating of the tree of knowledge, according to the general belief, n. 313, 494, 2910, 3469, 3701, 4317, 8550. That therefore hereditary evils are at this day more malignant than formerly, n. 2122. That infants who die such, and are brought up in heaven, are from their hereditary [principle], nothing but evils, n. 2307, 2308, 4563. That hence they are of various dispositions and inclinations, n. 2300. That every man's interior evils are from the father, and the exterior from the mother, n. 3701.

That man superadds of himself new evils to such as are hereditary, and that these are called actual evils, n. 8551. That no one suffers punishment in the other life for hereditary evils, but for actual evils, which return, n. 966, 2308. That the more malignant hells are kept separate lest they should operate on the hereditary evils with men and spirits, n. 1667, 8806.

That hereditary evils are those of the loves of self and the world, which consist in man's loving himself more than God, and the world more than heaven, and in making his neighbor of no account, n. 994, 4317, 5660. And forasmuch as these evils are contrary to the goods of heaven and to Divine order, that man cannot but be born into mere ignorance, n. 1050, 1902, 1992, 3175. That natural good is connate with some, but that nevertheless it is not good, because prone to all evils and falses; and that that good is not accepted in heaven unless it be made spiritual good, n. 2463, 2464, 2468, 3304, 3408, 3469, 3470, 3508, 3518, 7761.

OF LOVE TOWARDS THE NEIGHBOR, OR CHARITY.

84. HERE it shall first be shown what is meant by the term, NEIGHBOR; as it is the neighbor who is to be loved, and towards whom charity is to be exercised. Unless this point be clearly understood, charity may be exercised indiscriminately towards the evil and the good, and thus become no charity at all; for the evil, from the benefactions they receive, do evil to the neighbor, but the good do good.

85. It is a prevailing opinion at the present day; that every man is to be considered as being equally the neighbor, and that acts of beneficence are to be performed towards every one who needs our assistance. But it is the province of Christian prudence thoroughly to scrutinize the quality of a man's life, and to exercise charity towards him accordingly. The man who is a member of the internal church, exercises his charity in this manner; but he who is of the external church, because he cannot so easily discern things, acts without discrimination.

86. The distinctions of neighbor, which the member of the church ought well to understand, depend on the degree of good which each man possesses. And since all good proceeds from the Lord, the Lord himself is neighbor in the supreme sense of the word, and in the super-eminent degree, and from Him is the origin of this relationship. Hence it follows, that as far as the Lord is resident with any one, so far that man is the neighbor; and because no one receives the Lord, that is, receives good from Him, in exactly the same manner as another does, no one can be the neighbor in the same manner as another is; for all who are in the heavens, and all the good who are on earth, differ from each other as to the degree of their goodness. No two persons ever receive a divine gift that is in all respects one and the same: such gifts must be various, that each may subsist by itself. But all these varieties, consequently all the distinctions which exist in the relationship of neighbor, which depend on the reception of the Lord, that is, on the reception of good from Him, can never be known by any man, nor indeed by any angel, except in a general manner, or with respect to their kinds and species; neither does the Lord require any thing more from the members of His church, than that each should live according to what he knows.

87. Since every one possesses good in a different degree, it follows, that the quality of that good determines in what degree, and in what proportion, any man is to be considered as our neighbor. That this is the case is plain from the Lord's parable concerning the man who fell among thieves, whom, when half dead, the priest, and also the Levite, passed by; but whom the Samaritan, after pouring oil and wine into his

wounds, and binding them up, took upon his own beast, brought to an inn, and gave orders that care should be taken of him. This man, because he did good from a principle of genuine charity, is called his neighbor, (Luke x. 29—37); whence it may be known that they who are influenced by good are neighbors; for the oil and wine which the Samaritan poured into the wounds, signifies good and its truth.

88. From what has now been said, it is evident that good, in the universal sense of the word, is the neighbor, because man is the neighbor only according to the quality of the good which he receives from the Lord. And because good itself is the neighbor, so also is love, for all good is from love; consequently, every man is the neighbor according to the quality of the love which he possesses from the Lord.

89. That it is love which constitutes any one the neighbor, and that every man is the neighbor according to the quality of his love, manifestly appears ftom the case of those who are influenced by the love of self. Snch persons acknowledge as neighbor those who love them most, that is, they regard them as such, so far as they favor their own interests. These they embrace; they treat them with affection, confer on them their favors, and call them their brethren: nay more; because they are evil, they acknowledge them as neighbors in proportion as they love themselves, thus according to the quality and extent of their love. Men of this description deduce the origin of neighbor from self, and for this reason, that love constitutes and determines it. But those who do not love themselves above others, as is the character of all who belong to the kingdom of the Lord, derive the origin of neighbor from Him whom they ought to love supremely, thus from the Lord; and they esteem every one as neighbor according to the quality of his love to the Lord, thus according to his reception of the Lord's love in himself. Hence it is manifest what the members of the church ought to consider as the origin of the relationship of neighbor; and that every one is to be esteemed a neighbor according to the good which he possesses from the Lord; consequently, that good itself is the neighbor.

90. That this is the case, the Lord also teaches in Matthew, where, speaking of those who had lived in the practice of good works, He says, "that they had given Him to eat, that they had given Him to drink, that they had taken Him in, had clothed Him, had visited Him, and had come to Him when in prison;" and afterwards, where He says, "that inasmuch as they had done these things to the least of His brethren, they had done them to Himself," xxv. 34—40. In these six varieties of good, as understood in the spiritual sense, are comprehended all the particulars in the relationship of neighbor. Hence, also, it is evident, that when good is loved, the Lord

Himself is loved; for it is from the Lord that all good proceeds, —He is in it, and is good itself.

91. But not only is man the neighbor in his individual capacity, but also considered collectively, for a less or a greater society, the church, the kingdom of the Lord, and above all, the Lord himself is also the neighbor. These are our neighbor, and to these we are to do good from a principle of love. These also constitute the ascending degrees of this relationship: for a society consisting of many, is the neighbor in a higher degree than an individual; our country is so in a still higher degree; the church in a still higher degree than our country; and, in a degree higher still, the kingdom of the Lord: but in the supreme degree of all, the Lord himself is the neighbor. These degrees of ascent are like the steps of a ladder, at the top of which is the Lord.

92. The reason why a society is the neighbor more than an individual man, is, because it consists of many. Charity must be exercised towards a society in the same manner as towards an individual, namely, according to the quality of the good which it possesses; consequently, in a manner totally different towards a society of well-disposed persons, from what must be the case towards a society of an opposite character. A society is loved, when its good or welfare is consulted, under the influence of the love of good.

93. Our country is the neighbor more than a society, because it is like a parent; for therein a man is born, and by it he is nourished and protected from injuries. It is our duty to do good to our country from a principle of love according to its necessities, which principally regard the sustenance, and the civil and spiritual life of its inhabitants. The man who loves his country, and does good to it from a principle of benevolence, when he comes into the other life, loves the kingdom of the Lord; for, in that life, the kingdom of the Lord is his country: and he who loves the kingdom of the Lord, loves the Lord himself; for the Lord is all in all in his kingdom.

94. The church is the neighbor more than our country; for he who consults the welfare of the church, provides for the souls, and for the eternal life, of those who dwell in his country. He, therefore, who, from love, provides for the church, loves the neighbor in a superior degree; for he wishes, and earnestly desires, that heaven and the happiness of eternal life may be the portion of others.

95. The kingdom of the Lord is the neighbor in a still higher degree; for his kingdom consists of all who are influenced by good, both on earth and in heaven. Thus the kingdom of the Lord is good, with all its quality, in the aggregate; and when this is loved, the individuals who are in good are loved also.

96. These are the degrees of the relationship of neighbor and, according to these, love ascends in all who are influenced by the love of the neighbor. But these degrees are degrees of successive order, in which what is prior or superior is to be preferred to what is posterior and inferior. And since the Lord is the supreme degree, and is to be regarded in each degree as the end to which it tends, he, consequently, is to be loved above all persons, and above all things. Hence it may now be seen, in what manner love to the Lord conjoins itself with love towards the neighbor.

97. It is a common saying, that every man is his own neighbor, that is, that every one should first take care of himself; or, in other words, that charity begins at home: but the doctrine of charity teaches in what sense this is to be understood. Every one ought to provide for himself the necessaries of life, such as food, raiment, a place of habitation, and other things which his situation in civil life necessarily requires. And this he ought to do, not only for himself, but also for his family and his dependents; and not for the present time only, but also for the future. For unless a man provide for himself the necessaries of life, he cannot be in circumstances to exercise charity, being himself in want of all things.

98. In what sense every man ought to consider himself as his own neighbor, may appear from the following comparisons. Every man ought to provide food and raiment for his body; this must be the first object of his care; but then the end in view must be, to have a sound mind in a healthy body. Every man ought also to provide for the necessary requirements of his mind, that is, to store it with such things as will raise it in intelligence and wisdom, and thus qualify him for being of service to his fellow-citizens, to his country, to the church, and thus to the Lord. The man who thus acts, provides for his own spiritual welfare to eternity. Hence it is obvious that the end, whatever it be, is the primary object of attention; for all intermediate objects regard it. The case is similar to that of a man who builds a house: the first thing he does is to lay a solid foundation; and the foundation is laid for the sake of the house, and the house is built for the purpose of being inhabited. But the man who regards himself as his nearest neighbor, resembles him who considers the foundation of his house as the chief end, and not the house itself, as a place of abode: whereas the habitation is the first and ultimate end; and the house, with its foundation, is only a means to that end.

99. The end plainly shows the sense in which a man should consider himself as his own neighbor, and provide for himself in the first instance. If his end be to become richer than others, solely for the sake of riches, of pleasure, or of station, and the like, it is a bad end, and such a man does not love his

neighbor, but himself: but if, on the contrary, his end be to procure riches that he may thereby provide for the good of his fellow-citizens, of society in general, of his country, and of the church; as, also, if he procure for himself offices of usefulness for the same purposes, he loves his neighbor. And because every man's first and ultimate end is that which he loves supremely, the end for which he acts is what constitutes the man: for this end is his love.

What has hitherto been said has been confined to the relationship of neighbor; love towards him, OR CHARITY, shall now be considered.

100. It is the opinion of many, that charity consists in giving to the poor, in assisting the needy, and in doing good indiscriminately; charity, however, consists in acting with prudence, and with a view to good as the result. He who bestows his bounty on a poor or needy villain, does evil to his neighbor through such a person; for he thus confirms him in evil and supplies him with the means of doing evil to others. The case is otherwise with him who supplies the wants of the good.

101. But charity embraces operations much more extensive than those which relate to the relief of the poor and needy: it consists in doing what is right in every action of life, and in the faithful performance of our duty in every office. Thus, if a judge administers justice for its own sake, he exercises charity; if he punishes the guilty, and acquits the innocent, he exercises charity; for, in so doing, he promotes the welfare of his fellow-citizens, and of his country. The Christian minister, again, who teaches truth, and leads the people of his charge to good, for the sake of truth and of good, exercises charity: but he who does such things from selfish and worldly motives, does not exercise charity, for he does not love his neighbor, but only himself.

102. The case is similar in all other instances, whether in private or in public life; as with the behavior of children to their parents, and of parents to their children; of servants to their masters, and of masters to their servants; of subjects to their king, and of kings to their subjects. In all these cases, whoever performs his duty from a principle of duty, and does what is just from a principle of justice, exercises charity.

103. The reason why these things are included in the love of the neighbor, or charity, is, because, as was said above, every individual man is the neighbor, although in a different manner: a society, whether great or small, is the neighbor more than the individual; our country, more than a society; the kingdom of the Lord more than our country; and the Lord Himself above all; and, in the universal sense, good, which proceeds from the Lord; consequently, also, sincerity and justice. The man, therefore, who does good of any kind, for its

own sake, and who acts sincerely and justly for the sake of sincerity and justice, loves the neighbor, and exercises charity; for he acts from the love of good, sincerity, and justice; and, consequently, from love to those in whom good, sincerity, and justice dwell.

104. Charity, therefore, is an internal affection, from which man is desirous to do good, and to do so without the hope of remuneration; the delight of his life consisting in thus acting. Those who do good from this internal affection, are influenced by charity in all that they think and say, desire and practise. It may be said, that a man, or an angel, is, as to his interiors, charity itself, when he makes good to be the neighbor. So wide is the sphere of operation which charity embraces.

105. Those who propose to themselves the love of self and the world as the end of their actions, cannot, in any respect, be influenced by charity. They do not even know what charity is, and are utterly at a loss to comprehend how the desire of benefiting their neighbor, and performing acts of kindness to him, without a view to reward, should constitute heaven in man; and that there is inherent in such affection a degree of felicity equal to that experienced by the angels in heaven, which is ineffable. The reason is, that they imagine, that if they were to be deprived of the pleasure arising from honors and riches, they should experience joy no more: whereas it is only when such prospects are abandoned, that heavenly joy, which infinitely transcends all other, commences.

FROM THE ARCANA CŒLESTIA.

106. That heaven is distinguished into two kingdoms, one of which is called the celestial kingdom, and the other the spiritual; the love prevailing in the celestial kingdom is love to the Lord, and is called celestial love; and the love prevailing in the spiritual kingdom is love towards the neighbor, or charity, and is called spiritual love, n. 3325, 3653, 7257, 9002, 9833, 9961. That heaven is thus distinguished, see the work On Heaven and Hell, n. 20 to 28; and that the Divine [principle] of the Lord in the heavens is love to Him, and charity towards the neighbor, n. 13 to 19, in the same.

That it cannot be known what good is and what truth is, unless it be known what love to the Lord and love towards the neighbor are, because all good is of love, and all truth is of good, n. 7255, 7366. That to know truths, to will truths, and to be affected with them for truths' sake, that is, because they are truths, is charity, n. 3876, 3877. That charity consists in an internal affection of doing truth, and not in an external affection without an internal one, n. 2430, 2442, 3776, 4899, 4956, 8033. Thus that charity consists in performing uses for the sake of uses, n. 7038, 8253. That charity is the spiritual life of man, n. 7081. That the whole Word is the doctrine of love and charity, n. 6632, 7262. That it is unknown at this day what charity is, n. 2417, 3398, 4776, 6632. That nevertheless man may know from the light of his own reason, that love and charity constitute man n. 3957, 6273. Also that good and truth accord together, and that one is of the other, and so also love and faith, n. 7627.

That the Lord is the neighbor in the supreme sense, because He is to be loved above all things; and hence that all is the neighbor which is from Him, and in which He is,—thus that good and truth are, n. 2425, 3419, 6706, 6819, 6823, 8124. That the distinction of neighbor is according to the quality of good, thus according to the presence of the Lord, n. 6707, 6708, 6709, 6710. That every man and every society, also our country and the church, and, in a universal sense, the kingdom of the Lord, are the neighbor, and that to do good to them according to the quality of their state from a love of good, is tc love the neighbor; thus that the neighbor is their good, which is to be consulted, n. 6818 to 6824, 8123. That civil good, which is justice, and moral good, which is the good of life in society, and is called sincerity, are also the neighbor, n. 2915, 4730, 8120, 8121, 8122. That to love the neighbor does not consist in loving his person, but in loving that with him from which he is, consequently good and truth, n. 5025, 10,336. That they who love the person, and not that which is with him from which he is, love evil as well as good, n. 3820. And that they do good to the evil as well as to the good, when nevertheless doing good to the evil is doing evil to the good, which is not loving the neighbor, n. 3820, 6703, 8120. That the judge who punishes the evil that they may be amended, and that the good may not be contaminated by them, loves the neighbor, n. 3820, 8120, 8121.

That to love the neighbor is to do what is good, just, and right, in every work and in every office, n. 8120, 8121, 8122. Hence that charity towards the neighbor extends itself to every particular which man thinks, wills, and does, n. 8124. That to do what is good and true is to love the neighbor, n. 10,310, 10,336. That they who do this love the Lord, who in the supreme sense is the neighbor, n. 9212. That a life of charity is a life according to the commandments of the Lord; and that to live according to Divine Truths is to love the Lord, n. 10,143, 10,153, 10,310, 10,578, 10,648.

That genuine charity is not meritorious, n. 2340, 2373, 2400, 3887, 6388 to 6393. Inasmuch as it is from internal affection, consequently from the delight of the life of doing good, n. 2373, 2400, 3887, 6388, 6393. That they who separate faith from charity, in another life hold faith and the good works which they have done in an external form as meritorious, n. 2373. That they who are in evils from the love of self or the love of the world, know not what it is to do good without a view to reward; of consequence they know not what that charity is which is not meritorious, n. 8037.

That the doctrine of the Ancient Church was the doctrine of life, which is the doctrine of charity, n. 2487, 2385, 3419, 3420, 4844, 6628. That thence they had intelligence and wisdom, n. 2417, 6629, 7259 to 7262. That intelligence and wisdom increase immensely in the other life with those who have lived a life of charity in the world,

n. 1941, 5859. That the Lord flows in with Divine Truth into charity, because into the essential life of man, n. 2363. That the man with whom charity and faith are conjoined is like a garden; but like a desert when they are not conjoined, n. 7626. That man recedes from wisdom in proportion as he recedes from charity; and that they who are not in charity, are in ignorance concerning Divine Truths, however wise they think themselves, n. 2416, 2435. That the angelic life consists in performing the goods of charity, which are uses, n. 454. That the spiritual angels, who are they that are in the good of charity, are forms of charity, n. 553, 3804, 4735.

That all spiritual truths regard charity as their beginning and end, n. 4353. That the doctrinals of the church are of no avail, unless they regard charity as their end, n. 2049, 2116.

That the presence of the Lord with men and angels is according to their state of love and charity, n. 649, 904. That charity is the image of God, n. 1013. That love to the Lord, consequently the Lord, is within charity, although man does not know it, n. 2227, 5066, 5067. That they who live a life of charity are accepted as citizens both in the world and in heaven, n. 1121. That the good of charity is not to be violated, n. 2359.

That they who are not in charity cannot acknowledge and worship the Lord except from hypocrisy, n. 2132, 4424, 9833. That the forms of hatred and of charity cannot exist together, n. 1860.

107. To the above shall be added some particulars concerning the doctrine of love to the Lord, and the doctrine of charity, as it was held by the ancients who constituted the church of those times; in order that the former quality of that doctrine, which at this day exists no longer, may be known. The particulars are extracted from the Arcana Cœlestia, n. 7257 to 7263.

The good which belongs to love to the Lord, is called celestial; and the good which belongs to love towards the neighbor, or charity, is called spiritual good. The angels of the inmost or third heaven, are in the good of love to the Lord, being called celestial angels; but the angels of the middle or second heaven, are in the good of love towards the neighbor, being called spiritual angels.

The doctrine of celestial good, which is that of love to the Lord, is of most wide extent, and at the same time most full of arcana; being the doctrine of the angels of the inmost or third heaven, which is such, that if it were delivered from their mouths, scarcely a thousandth part of it would be understood: the things also which it contains are ineffable. This doctrine is contained in the inmost sense of the Word; but the doctrine of spiritual love, in the internal sense.

The doctrine of spiritual good, which is that of love towards the neighbor, is also of wide extent and full of arcana, but much less so than the doctrine of celestial good, which is that of love to the Lord. That the doctrine of love towards the neighbor, or charity, is of wide extent, may appear from the fact, that it reaches to all the things which man thinks and wills, consequently to all which he speaks and acts, even to the most minute particulars; and also from the fact, that the same charity does not exist with two different persons, and that no two persons are alike the neighbor.

As the doctrine of charity was so extensive, therefore the ancients, with whom it was the very doctrine of the church, distinguished charity towards the neighbor into several classes, which they again subdivided, and gave names to each class, and taught how charity was to be exercised towards those who are in one class, and towards those who are in another; and thus they reduced the doctrine and the exercises of charity into order, that they might distinctly fall under the view of the understanding.

The names which they gave to those towards whom they were to exercise charity were several; some they called the BLIND, some the LAME, some the MAIMED, some the POOR, some the MISERABLE and AFFLICTED, some the FATHERLESS, some WIDOWS; but in general they called them, the HUNGRY, to whom they should give to eat, the THIRSTY, to whom they should give to drink, STRANGERS, whom they should take in, the NAKED, whom they should clothe, the SICK, whom they should visit, and the BOUND IN PRISON, to whom they should come.

These names were given from heaven to the ancients who belonged to the church, and by those who were so named they understood those who were spiritually such. Their doctrine of charity not only taught who these were, but also the quality of the charity to be exercised towards each: hence it is, that the same names are in the Word, and signify those who are such in a spiritual sense. The Word in itself is nothing but the doctrine of love to the Lord, and of charity towards the neighbor, as the Lord teaches: *Thou shalt love the Lord thy God with all thy heart, and with all thy soul, and with all thy mind; this is the first and great commandment. The second is like unto it, Thou shalt love thy neighbor as thyself. On these two commandments hang all the law and the prophets.* Matt. xxii. 35, 36, 37, 38. The law and the prophets are the whole Word.

The reason why those same names are in the Word, is, in order that the Word, which is in itself spiritual, might, in its ultimate, be natural; and because they who are in external worship are to exercise charity towards such as are so named, and they who are in internal worship towards such spiritually understood; thus that the simple might understand and do the Word in simplicity, and the wise, in wisdom; also, that the simple, by the externals of charity, might be initiated into its internals.

OF FAITH.

108. It is impossible for any one to know the essence of faith, unless he know the essence of charity; because where there is no charity, there is no faith: for charity and faith form a one, like good and truth. What a man loves or holds dear, he esteems good; and what he believes, he esteems true: whence it is manifest that there is a similar oneness between charity and faith, as there is between good and truth. The

nature of their union may be clearly seen from what has been said above concerning GOOD and TRUTH.

109. The oneness existing between charity and faith is also similar to that between the will and understanding in man, for these two faculties are the respective receptacles of good and truth, the will receiving good, and the understanding, truth; thus, also, these two faculties receive charity and faith, for good belongs to charity, and truth to faith. Every one knows that charity and faith reside with man, and in man; and, since this is the case, they must reside in his will and understanding; for therein and thence is all the life of man. Man, it is true, is also endowed with memory; but this is only the outer court, where those things which are to enter into the understanding and the will are collected together. Hence, it is evident, there is a union, or oneness, of faith and charity, like that of the will and understanding; the nature of which union may be understood from what has been said above on the WILL and UNDERSTANDING.

110. Charity conjoins itself with faith in man, when he wills what he knows and perceives; to will has relation to charity;—to know and perceive to faith. Faith enters man, and becomes his own, when he wills and loves what he knows and perceives; but unless this be the case it remains without him.

111. Faith is not in reality faith in man, unless it become spiritual, and it does not become spiritual unless it belong to his love; and it may be said to belong to his love when man embodies truth and good in his life, that is, when he lives according to those things which are commanded in the Word.

112. Faith is the affection of truth arising from willing truth purely for its own sake; and to will truth for its own sake is the true spiritual principle of man: being entirely distinct from the natural principle, which consists in willing truth, not for the sake of truth, but for the sake of personal glory, reputation, or gain. To will truth abstractedly from such motives is spiritual, because it is from a Divine origin. Whatever proceeds from a Divine origin is spiritual; and this is conjoined to man by love; for love is spiritual conjunction.

113. Man may know, think, and understand much, but when he is left to solitary reflection, he rejects from himself everything that is not in accordance with his ruling love. Hence also he rejects such things after the life of the body, when he lives as a spirit: that alone remains in the spirit of man which has entered into his love; all other things, after death, are regarded by him as foreign, and are cast out, because they belong not to his love. It is said that this takes place with the spirit of man, because, after the dissolution of the body, man lives a spirit.

114. Some idea may be formed of the good of charity, and

the truth of faith, from the light and heat of the sun. When the light which proceeds from the sun is conjoined with the heat, as in the spring and summer, all the productions of the earth germinate and flourish; but when there is no heat in the light, as in the time of winter, all the productions of the earth become torpid and die. Just so it is with the truth of faith, which is spiritual light, and with love, which is spiritual heat. Hence, then, a correct idea may be formed of the state of every man who is a member of the church, and also of his quality when his faith is conjoined to charity, and when his faith is separated from charity: in the former case he resembles a garden and a paradise; in the latter, a desert, or a land covered with snow.

115. The confidence or trust, which is said to arise from faith, and which is called essential saving faith, is not spiritual confidence, or trust, but merely natural, when it is from faith alone. Spiritual confidence or trust has its essence and life from the good of love, but not from faith separate from that good. The confidence of faith separate from good is dead; on which account true confidence is impossible for those who live in the practice of evil; neither is that confidence which leads to the expectation of obtaining salvation on account of the Lord's merit with the Father, whatever may have been the nature of a man's life, a confidence founded on truth. All who possess spiritual faith, have a confidence that they shall be saved by the Lord; for they believe that the Lord came into the world to give eternal life to those who believe in Him, and who live according to the precepts which He taught;—that He regenerates them, and renders them meet for heaven;—and that He alone effects this, from pure mercy, and without the aid of man.

116. To believe those things which are taught in the Word, or which are enforced by the doctrine of the church, and not, at the same time, to live according to them, appears, indeed, as if it were faith, and by such faith some suppose they are saved; but by this alone no one can be saved; for it is merely persuasive faith, the real nature of which shall now be explained.

117. Faith is persuasive, when the Word and the doctrine of the church are believed and loved, not for the sake of truth and a life according to it, but for the sake of gain, of honor, and reputation for learning, as ends; wherefore, they who entertain this faith, do not look to the Lord and to heaven, but to themselves and the world. Those who aspire after great things in the world, and are covetous of extensive possessions, are under a stronger persuasion of the truth of what is taught by the church, than those whose aims are more humble, and whose desires are more moderate. The reason is, that the former

regard the doctrine of the church only as the means of attaining their own ends; and in proportion as the ends are coveted, the means are loved, and are also believed. But the real case stands thus. So far as men are inflamed by the love of self and the world, and from such excitement speak, preach, and act, they are under the influence of the above mentioned persuasion, and they know no otherwise than that all is reality; but when the ardor of those affections has abated, or is removed, they believe but little, and oftentimes, nothing at all. From this it is evident, that persuasive faith is the faith of the lips only, and not of the heart, and that in itself it is no faith.

118. Those who possess persuasive faith do not know from any internal enlightenment whether what they teach be true or false; neither, indeed, do they care, provided it be believed by the vulgar; for they have no affection of truth for its own sake; and hence they abandon their faith, whenever they are deprived of honor and gain, excepting when their reputation is in danger of being injured. Persuasive faith does not exist internally with man, but stands without, in the memory only, whence it is taken whenever it is required to be taught. On this account, both that faith and the truths belonging to it are dissipated after death; for then there remains only so much of faith as is within man, that is, as is rooted in good and has thus become a part of the life.

119. Those who have only this persuasive faith are described by the Lord in the gospel by Matthew, where He says: *Many will say to Me, in that day, Lord, Lord, have we not prophesied in Thy name, and in Thy name have cast out devils, and in Thy name done many wonderful works? And then will I profess unto them, I never knew you; depart from Me ye that work iniquity*, chap. vii. 22, 23. Also in Luke: *Then shall ye begin to say, We have eaten and drunk in Thy presence, and Thou hast taught in our streets. But He shall say, I tell you, I know you not whence ye are; depart from Me, all ye workers of iniquity*, chap. xiii. 26, 27. The same persons are understood also by the five foolish virgins who had no oil in their lamps, and who are thus described in Matthew: *Afterwards came also the other virgins, saying, Lord, Lord, open to us. But He answered and said, Verily, I say unto you, I know you not*, chap. xxv 11, 12. Oil in lamps, signifies the good of love in faith.

FROM THE ARCANA CŒLESTIA.

120. THAT they who do not know that all things in the universe have relation to TRUTH and GOOD, and to the conjunction of both, that anything may be produced, do not know that all things of the church have relation to FAITH and LOVE, and to the conjunction of both, that the church may be in man, n. 7752 to 7762, 9186, 9224. That all things in the universe which are according to Divine order have relation to good and truth, and to their conjunction, n. 2451, 3166, 4390, 4409, 5232, 7256, 10,122, 10,555. That truths are of faith and goods are of love, n. 4353, 4997, 7178, 10,367. This is the reason that good and truth have been treated of in this doctrine; wherefore from what has been adduced, conclusions may be drawn respecting faith and love; and it may be known what their quality is when they are conjoined, and what it is when they are not conjoined, by putting love in the place of good, and faith in the place of truth, and making applications accordingly.

That they who do not know that all and singular things in man have relation to the UNDERSTANDING and WILL, and to the conjunction of both, in order that man may be man, do not know clearly that all things of the church have relation to FAITH and LOVE, and to the conjunction of both, in order that the church may be with man, n. 2231, 7752, 7753, 7754, 9224, 9995, 10,122. That man has two faculties, the understanding and the will, n. 641, 803, 3623, 3939. That the understanding is designed for receiving truths, consequently the things of faith; and the will for receiving goods, consequently the things of love, n. 9300, 9930, 10,064. This is the reason why the will and understanding have been also treated of in this doctrine; for from what has been adduced, conclusions may be drawn respecting faith and love, and it may be known what their quality is when they are conjoined, and what it is when they are not conjoined, by considering love as in the will, and faith as in the understanding.

That they who do not know that man has an internal and an external, or an INTERNAL and EXTERNAL MAN, and that all things of heaven have relation to the internal man, and all things of the world to the external, and that their conjunction is like the conjunction of the spiritual world and the natural world, do not know what SPIRITUAL FAITH and SPIRITUAL LOVE are, n. 4392, 5132, 8610. That there is an internal and an external man, and that the internal is the spiritual man, and the external the natural, n. 978, 1015, 4459, 6309, 9701 to 9709. That faith is so far spiritual, consequently so far faith, as it is in the internal man; and love likewise, n. 1594, 3987, 8444. And that so far as the truths which are of faith are loved, so far they become spiritual, n. 1594, 3987. This is the reason why the internal and external man have been treated of, for from what has been adduced, conclusions may be drawn respecting faith and love, what their quality is when they are spiritual, and what when they are not spiritual; consequently how far they are of the church, and how far they are not of the church.

121. That faith separate from love or charity is like the light of

winter, in which all things on earth are torpid, and no harvests, fruits, or flowers, are produced; but that faith with love or charity is like the light of spring and summer, in which all things flourish and are produced, 2231, 3146, 3412, 3413. That the wintry light of faith separate from charity is changed into thick darkness when light from heaven flows in; and that they who are in that faith then come into blindness and stupidity, n. 3412, 3413. That they who separate faith from charity, in doctrine and life, are in darkness, consequently in ignorance of truth, and in falses, for these are darkness, n. 9186. That they cast themselves into falses, and into evils thence, n. 3325, 8094. The errors and falses into which they cast themselves, n. 4721, 4730, 4776, 4783, 4925, 7779, 8313, 8765, 9224. That the Word is shut to them, n. 3773, 4783, 8780. That they do not see or attend to all those things which the Lord so often spake concerning love and charity, and concerning their fruits, or goods in act, concerning which, n. 1017, 3416. That neither do they know what good is, nor consequently what celestial love is, nor what charity is, n. 2507, 3603, 4126, 9995.

That faith separate from charity is no faith, n. 654, 724, 1162, 1176, 2049, 2116, 2340, 2349, 2419, 3849, 3868, 6348, 7039, 7842, 9782. That such a faith perishes in the other life, n. 2228, 5820. That when faith alone is assumed as a principle, truths are contaminated by the falsehood of the principle, n. 2433. That such persons do not suffer themselves to be persuaded, because it is against their principle, n. 2385. That doctrinals concerning faith alone destroy charity, n. 6353, 8094. That they who separate faith from charity were represented by Cain, by Ham, by Reuben, by the first-born of the Egyptians, and by the Philistines, n. 3325, 7097, 7317, 8093. That they who make faith alone saving, excuse a life of evil, and that they who are in a life of evil have no faith, because they have no charity, n. 3865, 7766, 7778, 7790, 7950, 8094. That they are inwardly in the falses of their own evil, although they do not know it, n. 7790, 7950. That therefore good cannot be con joined to them, n. 8981, 8983. That in the other life they are against good, and against those who are in good, n. 7097, 7127, 7317, 7502 7945, 8096, 8313. That those who are simple in heart and yet wise, know what the good of life is, thus what charity is, but not what faith separate is, n. 4741, 4754.

That all things of the church have relation to good and truth, consequently to charity and faith, n. 7752, 7753, 7754. That the church is not with man before truths are implanted in his life, and thus become the good of charity, n. 3310. That charity constitutes the church, and not faith separate from charity, n. 809, 916, 1798, 1799, 1834, 1844. That the internal of the church is charity, n. 1899, 7755. Hence that there is no church where there is no charity, n. 4766, 5826. That the church would be one if all were regarded from charity, although men might differ as to the doctrinals of faith and the rituals of worship, n. 1286, 1316, 1798, 1799, 1834, 1844, 2385, 2982, 3267, 3451. How much of good would be in the church if charity were regarded in the first place, and faith in the second, n. 6269, 6272. That every church begins from charity, but in process of time turns aside to faith, and at length to faith alone, n. 1834

1835, 2231, 4683, 8094. That there is no faith at the last time of the church, because there is no charity, n. 1843. That the worship of the Lord consists in a life of charity, n. 8254, 8256. That the quality of the worship is according to the quality of the charity, n. 2190. That the men of the external church have an internal if they are in charity, n. 1100, 1102, 1151, 1153. That the doctrine of the ancient churches was the doctrine of life, which is the doctrine of charity, and not the doctrine of faith separate, n. 2417, 2385, 3419, 3420, 4844, 6628, 7259 to 7262.

That the Lord inseminates and implants truth in the good of charity when he regenerates man, n. 2663, 2189, 3310. That otherwise the seed, which is the truth of faith, cannot take root, n. 880. That then goods and truths increase, according to the quality and quantity of the charity received, n. 1016. That the light of a regenerate person is not from faith, but from charity by faith, n. 854. That the truths of faith, when man is regenerated, enter with the delight of affection, because he loves to do them, and that they are reproduced with the same affection, because the truths and the affection cohere, n. 2484, 2487, 3040, 3066, 3074, 3336, 4018, 5893.

That they who live in love to the Lord, and in charity towards the neighbor, lose nothing to eternity, because conjoined to the Lord; but that it is otherwise with those who are in separate faith, n. 7506, 7507. That man remains such as is his life of charity, not such as his separate faith, n. 8256. That all the states of delight of those who have lived in charity, return in the other life, and increase immensely, n. 823. That heavenly blessedness flows from the Lord into charity, because into the very life of man; but not into faith without charity, n. 2363. That in heaven all are regarded from charity, and none from separate faith, n. 1258, 1394. That all are associated in the heavens according to their loves, n. 7085. That no one is admitted into heaven by thinking, but by willing good, n. 2401, 3459. That unless doing good is conjoined with willing good and with thinking good, there is no salvation, neither any conjunction of the internal man with the external, n. 3987. That the Lord, and faith in him, are received by no others in the other life, than those who are in charity, n. 2340.

That good is in a perpetual desire and consequent endeavor of conjoining itself with truths, and charity with faith, n. 9206, 9207, 9495. That the good of charity acknowledges its own truth of faith, and the truth of faith its own good of charity, n. 2429, 3101, 3102, 3161, 3179, 3180, 4358, 5407, 5835, 9637. That hence there is a conjunction of the truth of faith and good of charity, concerning which, n. 3834, 4096, 4097, 4301, 4345, 4353, 4364, 4368, 5365, 7623 to 7627, 7752 to 7762, 8530, 9258, 10,555. That their conjunction is like a marriage, n. 1094, 2173, 2503. That the law of marriage is that two be one, according to the Word of the Lord, n. 10,130, 10,168, 10,169. So also faith and charity, n. 1094, 2173, 2503. That therefore faith which is faith, is, as to its essence, charity, n. 2228, 2839, 3180, 9783. That as good is the esse of a thing, and truth the existere thence, so also is charity the esse of a church, and faith the existere thence, n. 3409, 3180, 4574, 5002, 9144. That the truth of faith lives from the good of charity, consequently, that a life according to the truths of faith is charity, n. 1589, 1947, 2579, 4070, 4096, 4097, 4736, 4757, 4884, 5147, 5928, 9154, 9667, 9841, 10,729. That faith cannot exist but in charity, and if not in charity, that there is no good in faith, n. 2261, 4368. That faith is not alive with man when he only knows and thinks the things of faith, but when he wills them, and from will does them, n. 9224.

That there is no salvation by faith, but by a life according to the truths of faith, which life is charity, n. 379, 389, 2228, 4663, 4721. That they are saved who think from the doctrine of their church that faith alone saves, if they do what is just for the sake of justice, and good for the sake of good, for thus they are in charity notwithstanding, n. 2442, 3242, 3459, 3463, 7506, 7507. That if a mere cogitative faith could save, all would be saved, n. 2364, 10,659. That charity constitutes heaven with man, and not faith without it, n. 3815, 3513, 3584, 9832, 10,714, 10,715, 10,721, 10,724. That in heaven all are regarded from charity, and not from faith, n. 1258, 1394, 2364, 4802. That the conjunction of the Lord with man is not by faith, but by a life according to the truths of faith, n. 9380, 10,143, 10,153, 10,310, 10,578, 10,645, 10,648. That the Lord is the tree of life, the goods of charity the fruits, and faith the leaves, n. 3427, 9337. That faith is the lesser lnminary, and good the larger, n. 30 to 38.

That the angels of the Lord's celestial kingdom do not know what faith is, so that they do not even name it, but that the angels of the Lord's spiritual kingdom speak of faith, because they reason concerning truths, n. 202, 203, 337, 2215, 3246, 4448, 9166 10,786 That the angels of the Lord's celestial kingdom say only, yea, yea or nay, nay, but that the angels of the Lord's spiritual kingdom reason whether it be so or not so, when there is discourse concerning spiritual truths, which are of faith, n. 2715, 3246, 4448, 9166, 10,786, where the Lord's words are explained, *Let your discourse be yea, yea, nay, nay ; what is beyond these is from evil.* Matt. v. 37. The reason why the celestial angels are such, is, because they admit the truths of faith immediately into their lives, and do not deposit them first in the memory, as the spiritual angels do ; and hence the celestial angels are in the perception of all things of faith, n. 202, 585, 597, 607, 784, 1121, 1387, 1398, 1442, 1919, 5113, 5897, 6367, 7680, 7877, 1521, 8780, 9935, 9995, 10,124.

That trust or confidence, which in an eminent sense is called saving faith, exists with those only who are in good as to life, consequently, with those who are in charity, n. 2982, 4352, 4683, 4689, 7762, 8240, 9239 to 9245. That few know what that confidence is, n. 3868, 4352.

What difference there is between believing those things which are from God, and believing in God, n. 9239, 9243. That it is one thing to know, another to acknowledge, and another to have faith, n. 896, 4319, 5664. That there are scientifics of faith, rationals of faith and spirituals of faith, n. 2504, 8076. That the first thing is the acknowledgment of the Lord, n. 10,083. That all which flows in with man from the Lord is good, n. 1614, 2016, 2751, 2882, 2883 2891, 2892, 2904, 6193, 7643, 9128.

That there is a persuasive faith, which nevertheless is not faith, n. 2340, 2682, 2689, 3417, 3865, 8148.

That it appears from various reasonings as though faith were prior to charity, but that this is a fallacy, n. 3324. That it may be known from the light of reason, that good, consequently charity, is in the first place, and truth, consequently faith, in the second, n. 6273. That good, or charity, is actually in the first place, or is the first principle of the church, and truth, or faith, is in the second place, or is the second principle of the church, although it appears otherwise, n. 3324, 3325, 3330, 3336, 3494, 3589, 3548, 3556, 3570, 3576, 3603, 3701, 3995, 4337, 4610, 4925, 4926, 4928, 4930, 5351, 6256, 6269, 6272, 6273, 8042, 8080, 10,110. That the ancients disputed concerning the first principle or first-begotten of the church, whether it be faith or whether it be charity, n. 367, 2435, 3324.

122. That the twelve disciples of the Lord represented the church as to all things of faith and charity in the complex, as did also the twelve tribes of Israel, n. 2129, 3354, 3488, 3858, 6397. That Peter, James, and John represented faith, charity, and the goods of charity in their order, n. 3750. That Peter represented faith, n. 4738, 6000, 6073, 6344, 10,087, 10,580; and that John represented the goods of charity, see the preface to the 18th and 22nd chapters of Genesis. That there would be no faith in the Lord, because no charity, in the last time of the church, was represented by Peter's thrice denying the Lord before the cock crew the third time; for Peter there, in a representative sense, is faith, n. 6000, 6073. That cock-crowing, as well as twilight, signifies in the Word the last time of the church, n. 10,134. And that three or thrice, signifies what is complete to the end, n. 2788, 4495, 5159, 5198, 10,127. The like is signified by the Lord's saying to Peter, when Peter saw John follow the Lord, *What is it to thee, Peter? follow thou me, John;* for Peter said of John, *What [is] this [man]?* John xxi. 21, 22; n. 10,087. That John lay on the breast of the Lord, because he represented the good of charity, n. 3934, 10,081. That the good of charity constitutes the church, is also signified by the words of the Lord from the cross to John: *Jesus saw his mother, and the disciple whom he loved, who stood by, and he said to his mother, Woman, behold thy son: and he said to that disciple, behold thy mother; and from that hour that disciple took her to himself.* John xix. 26, 27. John signifies the good of charity, and woman and mother, the church; and the whole passage signifies that the church will be where the good of charity is; that woman in the Word means the church, see n. 252, 253, 749, 770, 3160, 6014, 7337, 8994. And likewise mother, n. 289, 2691, 2717, 3703, 4257, 5580, 8897, 10,490. That all the names of persons and places in the Word signify things abstractedly from them, n. 768 1888, 4310, 4442, 10 329.

OF PIETY.

123. MANY believe that spiritual life, or the life which leads to heaven, consists in *piety*, in *external sanctity*, and the *renunciation of the world:* yet piety without charity, external without internal sanctity, and a renunciation of the world without a life in the world, do not constitute spiritual life. Life truly spiritual consists in piety from charity; in external sanctity from internal sanctity; and in a renunciation of the world during a life in the world.

124. Piety consists in thinking and speaking piously; in devoting much time to prayer; in behaving with becoming humility during that time; in frequenting places of public worship, and attending devoutly to the discourses delivered there; in receiving the sacrament of the holy supper frequently every year; and in a due observance of the various other parts of Divine worship, according to the appointments of the church. But the life of charity consists in cultivating good will towards the neighbor, and endeavoring to promote his interest; in being guided in all our actions by justice and equity, good and truth, and in this manner discharging every duty; in one word, the life of charity consists in the performance of uses. Divine worship primarily consists in the life of charity, and secondarily in that of piety; he, therefore, who separates the one from the other, that is, who lives in the practice of piety, and not at the same time in the exercise of charity, does not worship God. He thinks, indeed, of God, yet not from God, but from himself: he thinks of himself continually, and not at all of the neighbor; and even if he does think of the neighbor, it is with disesteem, unless he be like himself. He likewise thinks of heaven as a reward, and he entertains in his mind the idea of merit, and also the love of self, together with a contempt or neglect of uses, and thus of the neighbor; while at the same time he trusts in himself that he is blameless. Hence it may be seen, that the life of piety, separate from the life of charity, is not the spiritual life which is essential to Divine worship. See Matt. vi. 7, 8.

125. External sanctity is like external piety, and is not holy with man, unless his internal be holy; for the quality of man's internal determines that of his external, since the latter proceeds from the former, as action from its cause: external sanctity, therefore, without internal, is natural and not spiritual. Hence it is that external sanctity is found with the evil as well as with the good; and they who place the whole of Divine worship in it, are, for the most part, extremely ignorant; that is, they are destitute of the knowledge of good and truth, which yet form the real sanctities that are to be known, believed, and loved, because they are from God, and God is in them. Inter

nal sanctity, therefore, consists in loving good and truth, justice and sincerity, for their own sakes. So far also as man thus loves these, so far he is spiritual, and his worship is spiritual, because so far he is desirous of knowing them and of doing them: but so far as he does not thus love them, he is natural, and his worship is natural; and so far he is unwilling either to know them or to do them. External worship, without internal, may be compared to the life of the respiration without the life of the heart; but external worship arising from internal may be compared to the life of the respiration conjoined to the life of the heart.

126. As regards a renunciation of the world: it is the opinion of many, that to renounce the world, and to live in the spirit and not in the flesh, means to reject all worldly concerns, especially riches and honors; to be continually engaged in pious meditation on God, on salvation, and on eternal life; to devote one's whole life to prayer, to the reading of the Word, and the perusal of pious books; and to suffer self-inflicted pain. This, however, is not what is meant by renouncing the world. To renounce the world is to love God and to love the neighbor; and a man loves God when he lives according to his commandments; and he loves the neighbor when he performs uses. In order therefore that man may receive the life of heaven, it is necessary that he should live in the world, and engage in the various offices and businesses of life. A life of abstraction from secular concerns is a life of thought and faith separate from a life of love and charity; and in such a life, the principle which prompts man to desire and to promote the good of the neighbor, must necessarily perish. When this is the case, the spiritual life becomes like a house without a foundation, which either gradually sinks to the ground, or becomes full of clefts and chinks, or totters till it falls.

127. That to do good is to worship the Lord, appears from the words of the Lord Himself: *Therefore whosoever heareth these sayings of Mine, and doeth them, I will liken him unto a wise man who built his house upon a rock.—And every one that heareth these sayings of Mine, and doeth them not, shall be likened unto a foolish man who built his house upon the sand.* Matt. vii. 24, 27; Luke vi. 47, 48, 49.

128. From these particulars it may be clearly seen, that a life of piety is valuable, and is acceptable to the Lord, so far as a life of charity is conjoined with it; for this is the primary, and such as the quality of this is, such is that of the former. Also, that external sanctity is of value, and is acceptable to the Lord, so far as it proceeds from internal sanctity; for such as the quality of this is, such is that of the former. And also, that the renunciation of the world is of value, and is acceptable to the Lord, so far as it is practised in the world;

for they renounce the world who remove the love of self and the world, and act justly and sincerely in every office, in every business, and in every work, from an interior, thus from a heavenly origin; which origin dwells in a man's life when he acts rightly, sincerely, and justly because it is according to the Divine laws.

FROM THE ARCANA CŒLESTIA.

129. That a life of piety without a life of charity, is of no avail [to salvation], but when united therewith conduces to it, n. 8252, *et seq.* That external sanctity without internal sanctity is not holy, n. 2190, 10,177. Of the quality of those in another life, who have lived in external sanctity, and not from internal sanctity, n. 951, 952.

That there is an internal and external of the church, n. 1098. That there is internal worship and external worship, and the quality of each, n. 1083, 1098, 1100, 1151, 1153. That internals are what constitute worship, n. 1175. That external worship without internal, is no worship, n. 1094, 7724. That there is an internal in worship, if man's life is a life of charity, n. 1100, 1151, 1153. That man is in true worship when he is in love and charity, that is, when he is in good of life, n. 1618, 7724, 10,242. That the quality of worship is according to good, n. 2190. That essential worship consists in a life according to the precepts of the church derived from the Word, n. 7884, 9921, 10,143, 10,153, 10,195, 10,645.

That true worship is from the Lord with man, not from man himself, n. 10,203, 10,299. That the Lord desires worship from man for the sake of man's salvation, and not for the sake of his own glory, n. 4593, 8263, 10,646. That man believes that the Lord desires worship for the sake of glory; but that they who thus believe know not what Divine glory is, nor that it consists in the salvation of the human race, which man partakes of, when he attributes nothing to himself, and when he removes his proprium by humiliation; because the Divine is then first able to flow in, n. 4347, 4593, 5957, 7550, 8263, 10,646. That humiliation of heart with man exists from an acknowledgment of himself, which is, that he is nothing but evil, and that he can do nothing from himself; and from a consequent acknowledgment of the Lord, which is, that nothing but good is from the Lord, and that he can do all things, n. 2327, 3994, 7478. That the Divine cannot flow in except into an humble heart, since so far as man is in humiliation, so far he is absent from his proprium, and of consequence from the love of self, n. 3994, 4347, 5957. Hence that the Lord does not desire humiliation for his own sake, but for man's sake, that man may be in a state for receiving the Divine, n. 4357, 5957. That worship is not worship without humiliation, n. 2327, 2423, 8873. The quality of external humiliation without internal, n. 5420, 9377. The quality of humiliation of heart, which is internal humiliation, n. 7478. That humiliation of heart does not exist with the evil, n. 7640.

That they who have not charity and faith are in external worship without internal worship, n. 1200. That if the love of self and of the world reigns interiorly with man, his worship is external without internal, however it may appear in its external form, n. 1182, 10,307, 10,308, 10,309. That external worship in which the love of self reigns inwardly, as is the case with those who are of Babylon, is profane, n. 1304, 1306, 1307, 1308, 1321, 1322, 1326. That to imitate heavenly affections in worship, when man is in evils from the love of self, is infernal, n. 10,309.

What the quality of external worship is when it proceeds from internal, and when it does not, may be seen and concluded from what has been said and adduced above concerning the INTERNAL and EXTERNAL MAN.

Further particulars concerning those who renounce the world and those who do not renounce it, their quality, and their lot in the other life, may be seen in the work ON HEAVEN AND HELL, under the following heads: *Of the Rich and Poor in Heaven*, n. 357 to 365; and *Of the Life that leads to Heaven* n. 528 to 535.

OF CONSCIENCE.

130. CONSCIENCE is formed in man from his religion, according to his inward reception of the same.

131. With the man who is a member of the church, conscience is formed by means of the truths of faith derived from the Word, or by teaching from the Word, according to the reception of those truths in the heart; for when man knows the truths of faith, and, after his own manner, assents to them, and carries them into practice, he acquires conscience; by reception in the heart is meant reception in the will, for man's will is what is called the heart. Hence it is, that they who have conscience speak from the heart in all that they say, and act from the heart in all that they do. The mind of such persons is simple or undivided, for they act in accordance with what they understand, and believe to be true and good.

132. A conscience approaching nearer to perfection may be enjoyed by those who are more enlightened in the truths of faith, and whose perception is clearer, than can be possessed by others who are less enlightened, and whose perception is obscure.

133. The real spiritual life of man resides in a true conscience, for that is the proper abode of his faith conjoined to charity. Hence, with those who possess it, to act from conscience is to act from their own spiritual life, and to act contrary to conscience is to act contrary to that life. Hence also it is, that such persons enjoy the tranquillity of peace and internal happiness when they act according to the dictates of

conscience, and that they experience perturbation and pain ot mind when these are disregarded. This mental pain is commonly called remorse of conscience.

134. Man is endowed with a conscience of what is good, and a conscience of what is just; the conscience of good is that of the internal man, and the conscience of what is just is that of the external man. The former of these consists in acting according to the precepts of faith from internal affection;—the latter, in acting according to civil and moral laws from external affection. They who have the conscience of what is good, have also the conscience of what is just; and they who have only the conscience of what is just, possess the means of obtaining the conscience of what is good, and also do obtain it when they are instructed.

135. Conscience, in those who are in charity towards the neighbor, is the conscience of truth, because it is formed by means of the faith of truth; but in those who are in love to the Lord, it is the conscience of good, because it is formed by means of the love of truth; the conscience of these is of a higher order, and is called the perception of truth from good. Those who possess the conscience of truth belong to the Lord's spiritual kingdom; but those who possess the conscience of good, which is superior, and is called perception, belong to the Lord's celestial kingdom.

136. The real nature of conscience shall now be illustrated by examples. If one man be in possession of another's property whilst the other is ignorant of it, and thus have it in his power to retain it without fear of the law, or the loss of honor and reputation, and yet restores it to the other because it is not his own, he has conscience; for in thus acting he does good for its own sake, and acts justly for the sake of justice. Again: if a person has it in his power to obtain an office of distinction, but knows that another person who is also a candidate for it possesses talents that might qualify him for being more serviceable to his country, and on that declines the competition, he has a good conscience. And so in all other cases.

137. From these instances it may be concluded of what quality they are who are devoid of conscience; they are known from their being of an opposite description. Thus they who for the sake of gain represent as just what is unjust, and as good what is evil, and the contrary, have no conscience; nor, indeed, do they know what conscience is; and if they are instructed respecting it, they do not believe, and some are even unwilling to know. Such, then, is the quality of those who, in all their transactions, have respect only to themselves and the world.

138. Those who have not received conscience during their abode in this world, cannot receive it in the other life, and thus

cannot be saved. The reason of this is, that they have no plane into which heaven, that is, the Lord through heaven, may flow, and by means of which he may operate upon them, and thus lead them to himself; for conscience is the plane and receptacle of the influx of heaven.

FROM THE ARCANA CŒLESTIA.

139. Of Conscience. That they who have no conscience, do not know what conscience is, n. 7490, 9121. That there are some who laugh at conscience, when they hear what it is, n. 7217. That some believe that conscience is nothing; some that it is a sad, painful, natural something, arising from bodily or worldly causes; and some, that it is an effect of religion on the minds of the vulgar, n. 950. That some know not that they have conscience, when yet they have it, n. 2380.

That the good have conscience, but not the evil, n. 831, 965, 7490. That they who are in love to God and in love towards their neighbor, have conscience, n. 2380. That conscience chiefly resides with those who are regenerated by the Lord, n. 977. That they who are in truths alone, and not in a life according to them, have no conscience, n. 1076, 1077, 1919. That they who do good from natural good, and not from religion, have no conscience, n. 6208.

That man's conscience is derived from the doctrine of his church, or from some religious principle, and is according thereto, n. 9112. That conscience is formed with man from those things which are of his religion, and which he believes to be truths, n. 1077, 2053, 9113. That conscience is an internal bond, by which man is obliged to think, speak, and do good; and by which he is withheld from thinking, speaking, and doing evil; and this not for the sake of self and the world, but for the sake of good, truth, justice, and uprightness, n. 1919, 9120. That conscience is an internal dictate, suggesting what ought to be done, and what ought not to be done, n. 1919, 1935. That conscience is in its essence a conscience of what is true and right, n. 986, 8081. That the new will with the spiritual regenerate man is conscience, n. 928, 1023, 1043, 1044, 4299, 4328, 4493, 9115, 9596. That the spiritual life of man is from conscience, n. 9117.

That there is a true conscience, a spurious conscience, and a false conscience, concerning which, see n. 1033. That conscience is more true, in proportion as it is formed from more genuine truths, n. 2053, 2063, 9114. That, in general, conscience is two-fold, interior and exterior, and that interior conscience is that of spiritual good, which in its essence is truth, and that exterior conscience is that of moral and civil good, which in its essence is sincerity and justice, and, in general, uprightness, n. 8042, 10,296.

That pain of conscience is anxiety of mind on account of injustice, insincerity, and any evil, which a man believes to be against God, and against the good of the neighbor, n. 7217. That if anxiety is felt when a man thinks evil, it is from conscience, n. 5470. That pain of conscience is an anguish felt on account of the evil which man does, and also on account of the privation of good and truth, n. 7217. Since temptation is a combat of truth and the false in the interiors of man, and since in temptations there is pain and anxiety, that therefore none are admitted into spiritual temptations, but those who have conscience, n. 847.

That they who have conscience speak and act from the heart, n. 7935, 9114. That they who have conscience do not swear in vain, 2842. That they who have conscience are in interior blessedness when they do what is good and just according to conscience, n. 9118. That they who have conscience in the world, have conscience in the other life, and are there amongst the happy, n. 965. That the influx of heaven flows into conscience with man, n. 6207, 6213, 9122. That the Lord governs the spiritual man by means of conscience, which is an internal restraint to him, n. 1835, 1862. That they who have conscience, have interior thought; but that they who have no conscience, have only exterior thought, n. 1919, 1935. That they who have conscience, think from the spiritual [principle], but that they who have no conscience, think only from the natural [principle], n 1820. That they who have no conscience, are only external men, n. 4459. That the Lord governs those who have no conscience by external restraints, which are all those things which are of the love of self and of the world, and which consequently relate to the fear of the loss of reputation, honor, office, gain, or wealth, and the fear of the law, and of the loss of life, n. 1077, 1080, 1835. That they who have no conscience, and yet suffer themselves to be governed by these external restraints, are capable of discharging the duties of high offices in the world, and of doing good, as well as those who have conscience; but the former do it in an external form, and from external obligations; whereas the latter do it in an internal form, and from internal obligations, n. 6707.

That they who have no conscience would destroy conscience with those who have it, n. 1820. That they who have no conscience in the world, have no conscience in the other life, n. 965, 9122. Hence that those who are in hell have no torment of conscience for their evils in the world, n. 965, 9122.

Who and of what quality, and how troublesome, the scrupulously conscientious are, and what they correspond to in the spiritual world, n. 5386, 5724.

That they who are in the Lord's spiritual kingdom, have conscience, and that it is formed in their intellectual part, n. 863, 865, 875, 895, 927, 1043, 1044, 1555, 2256, 4328, 4493, 5113, 6367, 8521, 9506, 9935, 9995, 10,124. That it is otherwise with those who are in the Lord's celestial kingdom, n. 927, 2256, 5113, 6367, 8521, 9935, 9995, 10,124.

140. Of Perception. That perception consists in seeing what is true and good by influx from the Lord, n. 202, 895, 7680, 9128. That perception exists only with those who are in the good of love from the Lord to the Lord, n. 202, 371, 1442, 5227. That perception exists with those in heaven, who whilst they lived in the world

brought the doctrinals of the church which are derived from the Word immediately into the life, and who did not first commit them to memory; that thus the interiors of their minds were formed to the reception of the Divine influx; and that thence their understanding is in heaven in continual enlightenment, n. 104, 495, 503, 521, 536, 1616, 1791, 5145. That they know innumerable things, and are immensely wise, n. 2718, 9543. That they who are in perception, do not reason concerning the truths of faith, and that if they reasoned their perception would perish, n. 585, 1398, 5897. That they who believe that they know and are wise from themselves, cannot have perception, n. 1386. That the learned do not comprehend what this perception is,—from experience, n. 1387.

That they who are in the Lord's celestial kingdom, have perception; but they who are in the spiritual kingdom, have no perception, but conscience in its place, n. 805, 2144, 2155, 8081. That they who are in the Lord's celestial kingdom do not think from faith, like those in the Lord's spiritual kingdom, because they who are in the celestial kingdom are in perception from the Lord of all things of faith, n. 202, 597, 607, 784, 1121, 1387, 1398, 1442, 1919, 7680, 7877, 8780. Wherefore the celestial angels say concerning the truths of faith only, Yea, yea, or Nay, nay, because they perceive them and see them; but the spiritual angels reason concerning the truths of faith, whether a thing be so or not, n. 2715, 3246, 4448, 9166, 10,786; where the words of the Lord are explained, *Let your discourse be Yea, yea, Nay, nay: what is beyond these is from evil*, Matt. v. 37. That the celestial angels, because they know the truths of faith from perception, are not even willing to name faith, n. 202, 337. The distinction between the celestial angels and the spiritual angels, n. 2088, 2669, 2708, 2715, 3235, 3240, 4788, 7068, 8521, 9277, 10,295. Of the perception of those who were of the most ancient church, which was a celestial church, n. 125, 597, 607, 784, 895, 1121, 5121.

That there is interior and exterior perception, n. 2145, 2171, 2831, 5920. That there exists in the world a perception of justice and equity, but seldom a perception of spiritual truth and good, n. 2831, 5937, 7977. That the light of perception is altogether different from that of confirmation; and that it is not like it, although it may appear so to some persons, n. 8521, 8780.

OF LIBERTY.

141. All liberty is the offspring of love; for what a man loves he performs freely; hence, all liberty originates in the will; for what a man loves he also wills: and because love and will constitute the life of man, so also does liberty. Hence it may readily be seen what liberty is, namely, that it is of the love and the will, and thence of the life of man; whence it is that what a man does from liberty, appears to him as if it proceeded from his very self.

142. When man does evil from liberty, it appears to him as if it were liberty, when yet it is slavery, because it arises from the love of self and of the world, and the love of these is from hell: and, after death, such liberty is actually turned into slavery, for then the man who has been led by it becomes a degraded slave in hell. But when man does good from liberty, he does in reality enjoy liberty, because it proceeds from love to the Lord and from love towards the neighbor, and the love of these is from heaven. This liberty also remains with man after death, and then becomes liberty in the highest sense of the word; for he who has lived in it on earth, becomes in heaven like a son in his father's house. This the Lord teaches where He says: "*Whosoever committeth sin is the servant of sin. And the servant abideth not in the house for ever; but the son abideth for ever. If the Son therefore shall make you free, ye shall be free indeed.*" John viii. 34, 35, 36. Now, because all good is from the Lord, and all evil from hell, it follows, that true liberty consists in being led by the Lord, and slavery in being led by hell.

143. Man has the liberty of thinking evil and falsity, and of doing the same, so far as he is not restrained by the laws, in order that he may be capable of being reformed; for goods and truths must be implanted in his love and in his will, that they may be incorporated with his life; and this cannot be effected unless he have the liberty of thinking evil and falsity, as well as good and truth. This liberty is granted to every man by the Lord; and so far as he rejects evil and falsity, when he is thinking of good and truth, the Lord implants these in his love and in his will, consequently in his life, and thus reforms him. Now, whatever is inseminated in the mind while in a state of liberty, remains; but what is inseminated by compulsion does not remain, because it is not from the will of the man himself, but from the will of him who compels. Hence, also, it is, that worship performed from liberty is pleasing to the Lord, and that worship from compulsion is not so; for the former worship is from love, but the latter is not so.

144. Although the liberty of doing good and the liberty of doing evil appear externally alike, they are as different and as distant from each other as heaven is from hell. The liberty of doing good also is from heaven, and is called heavenly liberty; but the liberty of doing evil is from hell, and is called infernal liberty. So far as man is in the one state of liberty, so far he is removed from the other; for no man can serve two masters. Matt. vi. 24. The same truth is also manifest from the fact, that they who are in a state of infernal liberty think it compulsion and slavery not to be allowed to will evil and to think falsity at their pleasure; while, on the contrary, they who are

in a state of heavenly liberty abhor willing evil and thinking falsity, and would feel tormented if compelled to do so.

145. And because acting from liberty appears to man like acting from his proprium, heavenly liberty may hence be called the heavenly proprium, and infernal liberty the infernal proprium. The infernal proprium is that into which man is born, and is evil; but the heavenly proprium is that into which man is brought by regeneration, and is good.

146. From this it may clearly appear that FREE WILL consists in doing good from choice or will, and that they who suffer themselves to be led by the Lord are in it; and they are led by the Lord, who love good and truth for their own sakes.

147. Man may readily discern of what quality his liberty is, from the nature of the delight which he experiences when he thinks, speaks, acts, hears, and sees; for all delight is of love.

FROM THE ARCANA CŒLESTIA.

148. THAT all liberty is of love or affection, for what a man loves, he does freely, n. 2870, 3158, 8907, 8990, 9585, 9591. As liberty is of love, that it is the life of every one, n. 2873. That there is heavenly liberty and infernal liberty, n. 2870, 2873, 2874, 9589, 9590. That heavenly liberty is of the love of good and truth, n. 1947, 2870, 2872. And because the love of good and truth is from the Lord, that being led by the Lord is true liberty, n. 892, 905, 2872, 2886, 2890, 2891, 2892, 9096, 9586, 9587 to 9591. That man by regeneration is introduced into heavenly liberty by the Lord, n. 2874, 2875, 2882, 2892. That man ought to possess liberty, that he may be capable of being regenerated, n. 1937, 1947, 2876, 2881, 3145, 3158, 4031, 8700. That otherwise the love of good and truth cannot be implanted in and appropriated to man, so as to appear his own, n. 2877, 2879, 8700, 2880, 2888. That nothing is conjoined to man which is done in compulsion, n. 2875, 8700. That if man could be reformed by compulsion, all would be saved, n. 2881. That compulsion is hurtful in reformation, n. 4031.

That worship from liberty is worship, but not worship from compulsion, n. 1947, 2880, 7349, 10,097. That repentance should take place in a free state, and that what is done in a forced state is of no avail, n. 8392. What forced states are, n. 8392.

That man is allowed to act from the liberty of reason, in order that good may be provided for him, and that therefore man is in the liberty of thinking and willing, and even of doing evil, so far as the laws do not forbid him, n. 10,777. That man is kept by the Lord between heaven and hell, in equilibrium, that he may be in liberty for the sake of reformation, n. 5982, 6477, 8209, 8907. That what is inseminated in liberty remains, but not what is inseminated in compulsion, n. 9588, 10,777. That therefore liberty is never taken away from any one, n. 2876, 2881. That no one is compelled by the Lord, n. 1937, 1947. How the Lord leads man by means of liberty into good; that by means of liberty he turns him from evil, and inclines him to good, so gently and tacitly that the man knows no other than that all proceeds from himself, n. 9587.

That for a man to compel himself is from liberty, but not for him to be compelled, n. 1937, 1947. That man ought to compel himself to resist evil, n. 1937, 1947, 7914. And also to do good as from himself, but still to acknowledge that it is from the Lord, n. 2883, 2891, 2892, 7914. That man has a stronger liberty in the combats of temptations, in which he conquers, since he then interiorly compels himself to resist evils, although it appears otherwise, n. 1937, 1947, 2881. That there is liberty in every temptation, but that that liberty is interiorly with man from the Lord; and that he therefore combats and wills to conquer, and not to be overcome, which he would not do without liberty, n. 1937, 1947, 2881. That the Lord does this by means of an affection of truth and good impressed on the internal man, the man himself being ignorant of it, n. 5044.

That infernal liberty consists in being led by the loves of self and of the world, and their concupiscences, n. 2870, 2873. That they who are in hell are unacquainted with any other liberty, n. 2871. That heavenly liberty is as far from infernal liberty as heaven is from hell, n. 2873, 2874. That infernal liberty in itself is slavery, n. 2884, 2890. Because it is slavery to be led by hell, n. 9586, 9589, 9590, 9591.

That all liberty is as the proprium, and according to it, n. 2880. That man receives a heavenly proprium from the Lord by regeneration, n. 1937, 1947, 2882, 2883, 2891. The nature of the heavenly proprium, n. 164, 5660, 8480. That this proprium appears to man as his own, but that it is not his, but the Lord's with him, n. 8497. That they who are in this proprium are in true liberty, because true liberty consists in being led by the Lord and his proprium, n. 892, 905, 2872, 2886, 2890, 2891, 2892, 4096, 9586, 9587, 9589, 9590, 9591.

149. That liberty originates from the equilibrium between heaven and hell, and that man, without liberty, cannot be reformed, is shown in the work ON HEAVEN AND HELL, in the articles concerning that equilibrium, n. 589—596, and concerning liberty, n. 597 to the end: but for the sake of instruction respecting what liberty is, and to show that man is reformed by means of it, I will here adduce the following extracts from that work. "It has been shown, that the equilibrium between heaven and hell is an equilibrium between the good which proceeds from heaven and the evil which proceeds from hell; and that, consequently, it is a spiritual equilibrium, which, in its essence, is freedom. The reason that spiritual equilibrium is, in its essence, freedom, is, because it is an equilibrium between good and evil, and between truth and falsity, which are spiritual things; wherefore, the power of willing either good or evil, and of thinking either truth or falsity, and of choosing the one in preference to the other, is the liberty of which we are here treating. This liberty is given to every man by the Lord, nor is it ever taken away from him. In its origin, indeed, it does not belong to man, but to the

Lord, it being from the Lord; but, nevertheless, it is given to man, together with life, as his own: and it is given him to this end,—that he may be capable of being reformed and saved; for without freedom there can be no reformation and salvation. Every one who takes any rational view of things may see, that man is at liberty to think either ill or well, sincerely or insincerely, justly or unjustly; and also, that he is at liberty to speak and to act well, sincerely, and justly, but is withheld from speaking and acting ill, insincerely, and unjustly, by spiritual, moral, and civil laws, by which his external is kept in bonds. From these facts it is evident, that the spirit of man, which is that which thinks and wills, is in the enjoyment of liberty; but that his external, which is what speaks and acts, is not, except in conformity with the above-mentioned laws. The reason that man would not be capable of being reformed, unless he were in the enjoyment of liberty, is, because he is born into evils of all kinds. These must be removed, in order that he may be saved: and they cannot be removed, unless he sees them in himself, and acknowledges them; and afterwards ceases to will them, and at length holds them in aversion. It is then that they are first removed. This could not be accomplished, unless man possessed in him good as well as evil; for he is capable, from good, of seeing evils, but not, from evil, of seeing goods. The spiritual goods which man is capable of making objects of his thoughts, he learns, from his infancy, by reading the Word and hearing sermons; and he learns moral and civil goods by living in the world. This is the first reason why man ought to be in the enjoyment of liberty. Another is, that nothing is appropriated to man, but what he does from an affection that is proper to his love: other things may indeed enter his mind, but no further than into his thought: nothing else enters into his will: and what does not enter into the will, also, does not become his own: for the thought draws its materials from the memory, but the will from the life itself. Nothing that man ever does or thinks is free, but what proceeds from his will, or, what is the same thing, from an affection belonging to his love. Whatever a man wills or loves, he does freely; in consequence of which, a man's liberty, and the affection which is that of his love or of his will, are one: on which account, therefore, man must be in the enjoyment of freedom, in order that he may be capable of being affected by truth and good, or of loving them, and that they may become, in consequence, as if they were his own. In one word, whatever does not gain admission to man in a state of freedom, does not remain in him, because it is not an object of his love or of his will; and whatever is not an object of a man's love or will does not belong to his spirit: for the *esse* of the spirit of man is his love or will. We use the terms 'his love or will,' because what a man loves, he also wills. These then are the reasons, that a man cannot be reformed, except he is in a state of liberty. In order that man may be in a state of liberty, as necessary to his being reformed, he is connected, as to his spirit, with heaven and with hell: for spirits from hell, and angels from heaven, are attendant on every man. By the spirits from hell, man is held in his evil; but by the angels from heaven, he is held in good by the Lord. Thus he is preserved in spiritual equilibrium, that is, in freedom. That angels from heaven, and spirits from hell, are adjoined to every man, may be seen in the Section on the Conjunction of Heaven with the Human Race n. 291—302."

OF MERIT.

150. They who do good with a view to merit are not influenced by the love of good, but by the love of reward; for they who are desirous of merit are also desirous of reward: and they who thus act, have respect to the reward, in which, and not in good, they place their delight. Such, therefore, are not spiritual men, but natural.

151. To do good which is really such, man must act from the love of good, and thus for the sake of good. They who are influenced by this love are unwilling so much as to hear of merit: for they love to do good, and have a lively perception of satisfaction in doing it; and, on the contrary, they are grieved when it is supposed by any one that what they do has respect to any selfish motive. They are like those who do good to their friends for the sake of friendship, to a brother for the sake of brotherhood, to a wife and children for their own sake, to their country for their country's sake, and thus from friendship and love. They who think rightly also say and insist, that the good which they do is not for their own sakes, but for the sake of those to whom it is done.

152. They who do good for the sake of reward, do not act from the Lord, but from themselves; they regard themselves in the first place, inasmuch as they regard their own good; the good of the neighbor, that is, of their fellow-citizens, of human society, of their country, and the church, they regard in no other light than as means to this end. Hence it is that the good of self-love and of the love of the world, is latent in the good of merit, which good is from man, and not from the Lord; and all good which is from man is not good; nay, so far as self and the world are latent in it, it is evil.

153. Genuine charity and faith entirely disclaim all merit; for the delight of charity is good itself, and the delight of faith is truth itself; they, therefore, who are in such charity and faith, know what the nature of non-meritorious good is, but not they who are not in charity and faith.

154. The Lord Himself plainly teaches that man is not to do good for the sake of reward, where He says: "*For if ye love them that love you, what thank have ye? for sinners also love those that love them. But love ye your enemies, and do good, and lend, hoping for nothing again; and your reward shall be great,*

and ye shall be the children of the Highest." Luke vi. 32, 35. That man cannot of himself do good that is really good, the Lord teaches in John: "*A man can receive nothing except it be given him from heaven,*" chap. iii. 27. And again, Jesus saith: "*As the branch cannot bear fruit of itself except it abide in the vine, no more can ye, except ye abide in Me. I am the vine, ye are the branches. He that abideth in Me, and I in him, the same bringeth forth much fruit; for without Me ye can do nothing,*" chap. xv. 4, 5.

155. Since all good and truth are from the Lord, and nothing from man; and since good that comes from man is not good in reality, it plainly follows, that no merit belongs to man, but that all merit is due to the Lord alone. The merit of the Lord consists in this, that by His own power He has effected the salvation of the human race; and also, that He saves those who do good from Him. Hence it is that, in the Word, he to whom the merit and righteousness of the Lord are ascribed is called righteous; and he to whom are ascribed his own righteousness and the merit of self, is called unrighteous.

156. The delight which is inherent in the love of doing good without any view to reward, is itself an eternal reward; for heaven and eternal happiness are inseminated into that good by the Lord.

157. They who think and believe that those who do good will enter heaven, and that man must do good in order to enter, do not view reward as an end, neither do they place merit in works; for even they who do good from the Lord both think and believe so; but they who, while they thus think, believe, and act, are not influenced by the love of good for its own sake, have respect to reward as an end, and consider their works as meritorious.

FROM THE ARCANA CŒLESTIA.

158. THAT merit and justice belong to the Lord alone, n. 9715, 9979. That the merit and justice of the Lord consist in his having saved the human race by his own proper power, n. 1813, 2025, 2026, 2027, 9715, 9809, 10,019. That the good of the Lord's justice and merit is the good which reigns in heaven, and is the good of his Divine Love from which he saved mankind, n. 9486, 9986. That no man can of himself become just, nor claim it by any right, n. 1813. The quality of those in the other life who claim justice to themselves, n. 942, 2027. That in the Word, the man to whom the justice and merit of the Lord are ascribed, is called just; and the man to whom self-justice and merit are ascribed, unjust, n. 5069, 9263. That whoever is once just from the Lord, will be continually just from him; for justice never becomes our own, but is continually from the Lord,

n. 3648. That they who believe in the justification taught in the church, know little of regeneration, n. 5398.

That man is so far wise as he ascribes all goods and truths to the Lord, and not to himself, n. 10,227. That as all real good and truth are from the Lord, and none from man, and as good from man is not good, it follows that merit belongs to no man, but to the Lord alone, n. 9975, 9981, 9988. That they who enter heaven put off all merit of their own, n. 4007. And that they do not think of reward for the good they have done, n. 6478, 9174. That they who think from merit so far do not acknowledge all things to be of mercy, n. 6478, 9174. That they who think from merit, think of reward and remuneration, and that therefore to will to merit is to will to be remunerated, n. 5660, 6392, 9975. That such persons cannot receive heaven, n. 1835, 9977, 8478. That heavenly happiness consists in the affection of doing good without regard to remuneration, n. 6388, 6478, 9174, 9984. That in the other life so far as any one does good without regard to remuneration, so far blessedness flows in, in an augmented degree from the Lord; and that the same is immediately dissipated when remuneration is thought of, n. 6478, 9174.

That good is to be done without regard to remuneration, n. 6392, 6478. Illustrated, n. 9981. That genuine charity is without any thing meritorious, n. 2340, 2373, 2400, 3887, 6388 to 6393. Because it is from love, thus from the delight of doing good, n. 3816, 3887, 6388, 6478, 9174, 9984. That reward in the Word, means delight and blessedness in doing good to others without reward, and that this delight and blessedness is felt and perceived by those who are in genuine charity, n. 3816, 3956, 6388.

That they who do good for the sake of reward, love themselves and not the neighbor, n. 8002, 9210. That mercenaries, in the spiritual sense of the Word, mean those who do good for the sake of reward, n. 8002. They who do good for the sake of remuneration, in the other life desire to be served, and are never contented, n. 6393. That they despise the neighbor, and are angry at the Lord himself, because they do not receive a reward, saying that they have merited it, n. 9976. That they who have separated faith from charity, in the other life make their faith, and also the good works which they have done in an external form, thus for the sake of themselves, meritorious, n. 2373. Further particulars respecting the quality of those in the other life who have placed their merit in works, n. 942, 1774, 1877, 2027. That they are there in the lower earth, and appear to themselves to cut wood, n. 1110, 4943, 8740. Because wood, especially Shittim wood, signifies the good of merit in particular, n. 2784, 2812, 9472, 9486, 9715, 10,178.

That they who have done good for the sake of remuneration, are servants in the Lord's kingdom, n. 6389, 6390. That they who place merit in works, fall in temptations, n. 2273, 9978. That they who are in the loves of self and of the world, do not know what it is to do good without a view to remuneration, n. 6392.

88

OF REPENTANCE, AND THE REMISSION OF SINS.

159. HE who would be saved must confess his sins, and do the work of repentance.

160. *To confess sins* is to know evils, to perceive them in oneself, to charge oneself with their guilt, and to condemn oneself on account of them. When this is done in the presence of God, it constitutes the confession of sins.

161. *To perform the work of repentance*, is to abstain from sins after they have been confessed, and supplication has been made for their remission, from humility of heart; and to live in newness of life, according to the precepts of charity and faith.

162. The man who makes only a general acknowledgment that he is a sinner, charging himself as guilty of all evils, and yet does not examine himself, that is, does not really see his own sins, may indeed make confession, but not the confession of repentance; for such a person, because he does not know his own evils, lives in the practice of them afterwards, just as he had done before.

163. He who lives in the practice of charity and faith, performs the work of repentance daily; he reflects on the evils that adhere to him, acknowledges them, guards against them, and supplicates the Lord for aid to resist them. For man, of himself, continually lapses into evil, but is continually raised by the Lord, and led to good. Such is the case with those who are in good; but they who are in evil lapse continually, and are also continually raised by the Lord; but they are only withheld from falling into the most dreadful evils, to which, of themselves, they tend with all their might.

164. The man who examines himself for the purpose of doing the work of repentance, must closely examine the thoughts and intentions of his will, and must thence infer what he would do, were he permitted, that is, if not restrained by the fear of the laws, and the loss of reputation, of honor, and of gain; for the evils of man reside in his thoughts and intentions, and from these proceed all the evil actions which he commits in the body. This is self-examination. But they who do not examine their evils of thought and will, cannot do the work of repentance; for they both think and desire afterwards as they did before; and to will or desire evil is virtually to do it.

165. Repentance which consists merely in words, and does not affect the life, is not repentance; neither are sins remitted by such repentance, but only by repentance of life. Sins are indeed continually remitted to man by the Lord, for the Lord is mercy itself; but still they adhere to man, however he may think they are remitted, nor are they removed from him but by

a life according to the precepts of true faith. So far as man lives according to those precepts, so far his sins are removed; and so far as they are removed, so far they are remitted.

166. It is commonly supposed that, when sins are remitted, they are wiped away, or washed off, as filth is by water; but sins are not wiped away, but removed, that is, man is withheld from them when he is kept in good by the Lord; and when this is the case, it appears to him as if he were without his sins, thus as if they were wiped away. And so far as man is reformed, so far he is capable of being kept in good. How this reformation is effected will be shown in the following chapter on regeneration. He who supposes that sins are remitted in any other way, is greatly deceived.

167. The evidences that accompany the remission, that is, the removal, of sins, are the following. They whose sins are remitted experience a delight in worshiping God for His own sake, and in serving the neighbor for the sake of the neighbor; —in doing good for the sake of good, and in speaking truth for the sake of truth. Such persons disclaim all merit in the exercise of their charity and faith; they are utterly averse to all evils, as enmity, hatred, revenge, adultery, and not only do they shun them, but they abhor the very thought of them connected with any intention. But the evidences that sins are not remitted, or removed, are these. They whose sins are not remitted do not worship God for His own sake, nor serve the neighbor for his own sake; thus they do not do good and speak truth for the sake of good and truth, but for the sake of themselves and the world. They claim merit on account of their deeds: they perceive nothing undelightful in evils, such as enmity, hatred, revenge, and adultery; and, inflamed with these lusts, they cherish the thought of them in all licentiousness.

168. The repentance which takes place in a state of freedom is effectual, but that which is produced in a state of compulsion is not so. A state of compulsion is that arising from sickness, or dejection of mind induced by misfortunes; from the expectation of imminent death; and, in short, from any state of fear which takes away the free use of reason. A wicked man, in a state of compulsion, may promise repentance, and perform good actions; but as soon as he regains a state of freedom, he returns to his former life of evil. With a good man the case is otherwise.

169. When a man has examined himself, acknowledged his sins, and done the work of repentance, he must continue steadfastly persevering in the practice of what is good, even to the end of his life. For should he afterwards relapse into his former evil life, and embrace it, he becomes guilty of profanation; since he then conjoins evil with good, and his latter state becomes worse than the former; according to the words of the Lord:

‘ *When the unclean spirit is gone out of a man, he walketh through dry places, seeking rest, and findeth none. Then he saith, I will return into my house from whence I came out; and when he is come, he findeth it empty, swept, and garnished. Then goeth he, and taketh with himself seven other spirits more wicked than himself, and they enter in and dwell there; and the last state of that man is worse than the first.*” Matt. xii. 43, 44, 45.

FROM THE ARCANA CŒLESTIA.

170. Of *Sin or Evil.* That there are innumerable kinds of evil and the false, n. 1188, 1212, 4818, 4822, 7574. That there is evil from the false, that there is the false from evil, and evil and the false again from thence, n. 1679, 2243, 4818. The nature and quality of the evil of the false, n. 2408, 4818, 7272, 8266, 8279. The nature and quality of the false of evil, n. 6359, 7272, 9304, 10,302. Of blameable evils, and of those which are not so blameable, n. 4171, 4172. Of evils from the understanding and of evils from the will, n. 9009. The difference between transgression, iniquity, and sin, n. 6563, 9156.

That all evils adhere to man, n. 2116. That evils cannot be taken away from man, but that man can only be withheld from them, and kept in good, n. 865, 868, 887, 894, 1581, 4564, 8206, 8393, 8988, 9014, 9333, 9446, 9447, 9448, 9451, 10,057, 10,059. That to be withheld from evil and kept in good, is effected by the Lord alone, n. 929, 2406, 8206, 10,059. That thus evils and sins are only removed, and that this is successively effected, n. 9334, 9335, 9336. That this is done by the Lord by means of regeneration, n. 9445, 9452, 9453, 9454, 9938. That evils shut out the Lord, n. 5696. That man ought to abstain from evils, that he may receive good from the Lord, n. 10,109. That good and truth inflow in proportion as man is withheld from evils, n. 2388, 2411, 10,675. That to be withheld from evil and kept in good, constitutes remission of sins, n. 8391, 8393, 9014, 9444 to 9450. The signs whether sins are remitted or not, n. 9449, 9450. That it is a consequence of the remission of sins to look at things from good and not from evil, n. 7697.

That evil and sin are a separation and turning away from the Lord; and that this is signified by evil and sin in the Word, n. 4997, 5229, 5474, 5746, 5842, 9346; that they are and signify a separation and aversion from good and truth, n. 7589. That they are and signify what is contrary to Divine order, n. 4839, 5076. That evil is damnation and hell, n. 3513, 6279, 7155. That it is not known what hell is, unless it be known what evil is, n. 7181. That evils are as it were heavy, and fall of themselves into hell; and so also falses that are from evil, n. 8279, 8298. That it is not known what evil is unless it be known what the love of self and the love of the world are, n. 4997, 7178, 8317. That all evils are from those loves, n.

1307, 1308, 1321, 1594, 1691, 3413, 7255, 7376, 7480, 7488, 8918, 9335, 9348, 10,038, 10,742.

That all men whatever are born into evils of every kind, their proprium being nothing but evil, n. 210, 215, 731, 874, 875, 876, 987, 1047, 2307, 2308, 3518, 3701, 3812, 8480, 8550, 10,283, 10,284, 10,731. That man must therefore be born again or regenerated, in order to receive a life of good, n. 3701.

That man casts himself into hell when he does evil from consent, afterwards from purpose, and at last from delight, n. 6203. That they who are in evil of life, are in the falses of their own evil, whether they know it or not, n. 7577, 8064. That evil would not be appropriated to man, if he believed, as is really the case, that all evil is from hell, and all good from the Lord, n. 6206, 4151, 6324, 6325. That in the other life evils are removed from the good and goods from the evil, n. 2256. That all in the other life are let into their interiors, thus, the evil into their evils, n. 8870.

That in the other life evil contains its own punishment, and good its own reward, n. 696, 967, 1057, 6559, 8214, 8223, 8226, 9049. That man is not punished in the other life for hereditary evils, as he is not to blame for these, but for his actual evils, n. 966, 2308. That the interiors of evil are foul and filthy, however they may appear otherwise in an external form, n. 7046.

That evil is attributed in the Word to the Lord, and yet nothing but good proceeds from Him, n. 2447, 6073, 6992, 6997, 7553, 7633, 7677, 7926, 8227, 8228, 8632, 9306. So also anger, n. 5798, 6997, 8284, 8483, 9306, 10,431. Why it is so said in the Word, n. 6073, 6992, 6997, 7643, 7632, 7679, 7710, 7920, 8282, 9009, 9128. What is signified by bearing iniquity, where it is predicated of the Lord, n. 9937, 9965. That the Lord turns evil into good with the good who are infested and tempted, n. 8631. That to leave man from his own liberty to do evil, is permission, n. 1778. That evils and falses are governed by the laws of permission by the Lord; and that they are permitted for the sake of order, n. 7877, 8700, 10,778. That the permission of evil by the Lord is not as of one who wills, but as of one who does not will, but who cannot bring aid on account of the end, n. 7877.

171. *Of the False.* That there are innumerable kinds of the false, namely, as many as there are evils, and that evils and falses are according to their origins, which are many, n. 1188, 1212, 4729, 4822, 7574. That there is a false from evil, or the false of evil; and that there is an evil from the false, or the evil of the false; and a false again from thence, n. 1679, 2243. That from one false that is assumed as a principle, falses flow in a long series, n. 1510, 1511, 4717, 4721. That there is a false from the desires of the love of self and of the world; and that there is a false from the fallacies of the senses, n. 1295, 4729. That there are falses of religion; and that there are falses of ignorance, n. 4729, 8318, 9258. That there is a false which contains good, and a false which contains no good, n. 2863, 9304, 10,109, 10,302. That there is what is falsified, n. 7318, 7319, 10,648.

The quality of the false of evil, n. 6359, 7272, 9304, 10,302. The quality of the evil of the false, n. 2408, 4818, 7272, 8266, 8279.

That the falses derived from evil appear like mists and impure waters over the hells, n. 8217, 8138, 8148. That such waters signify falses, n. 739, 790, 7307. That they who are in hell speak falses from evil, n. 1695, 7351, 7352, 7357, 7392, 7698. That they who are in evil cannot do otherwise than think what is false when they think from themselves, n. 7437.

That there are falses of religion which agree with good, and falses which disagree, n. 9258. That falses of religion, if they do not disagree with good, do not produce evil but with those who are in evil of life, n. 8318. That falses of religion are not imputed to those who are in good, but to those who are in evil, n. 8051, 8149. That every false may be confirmed, and then appear like truth, n. 5033, 6865, 8521, 8780. That care should be taken lest falses of religion be confirmed, since the persuasion of the false principally arises from thence, n. 845, 8780. How hurtful the persuasion of the false is, n. 794, 806, 5096, 7686. That a persuasion of the false is perpetually exciting such things as confirm falses, n. 1510, 1511, 2475. That they who are in the persuasion of the false are inwardly bound, n. 5096. That in the other life, they who are in a strong persuasion of the false, when they approach others, close up the rational [principle], and as it were suffocate them, n. 3895, 5128.

That truths which are not genuine, and also falses, may be consociated with genuine truths; but falses which contain good, and not falses in which is evil, n. 3470, 3471, 4551, 4552, 7344, 8149, 9298. That falses which contain good, are received by the Lord as truths, n. 4736, 8149. That the good which has its quality from the false is accepted by the Lord, if there is ignorance, and therein innocence, and a good end, n. 7887.

That evil falsifies truth, inasmuch as it draws aside and applies truth to evil, n. 8044, 8149. That truth is said to be falsified, when it is applied to evil by confirmations, n. 8602. That falsified truth is contrary to truth and good, n. 8602. For further particulars respecting the falsification of truth, see n. 7318, 7319, 10,648.

172. *Of profanity and profanation, spoken of above at* n. 169. That profanation is a commixion, in man, of good and evil, as also of truth and the false, n. 6348. That none can profane goods and truths, or the holy things of the church and the Word, except those who first acknowledge, believe, and still more live according to them, and afterwards recede from and deny their faith, and live to themselves and the world, n. 593, 1008, 1010, 1059, 3398, 3898, 4289, 4601, 10,284, 10,287. That he who believes truths in his childhood, and afterwards does not believe them, commits profanation slightly; but that he who confirms truths in himself after that period, and then denies them, commits profanation grievously, n. 6960, 6963, 6971. That they who believe truths, and live evilly, commit profanation; as also they who do not believe truths, and live holily, n. 8082. That if man, after repentance of heart, relapses to his former evils, he commits profanation, and that then his latter state is worse than his former, n. 8394. That those in the Christian world who defile the holy things of the Word by unclean thoughts and discourses, commit profanation, n. 4050, 5390. That there are various kinds of profanation, n. 10,287.

That they who do not acknowledge holy things cannot profane them, still less they who do not know them, n. 1008, 1010, 1059, 9188, 10,284. That they who are within the church, are capable of profaning holy things, but not they who are out of it, n. 2051. That the Gentiles, being out of the church, and not having the Word, cannot commit profanation, n. 1327, 1328, 2051, 2081. That neither can the Jews profane the holy interior things of the Word and the church, because they do not acknowledge them, n. 6963. That thus interior truths were not revealed to the Jews, for if they had been revealed and acknowledged, they would have profaned them, n. 3398, 3488, 6963. Profanation is meant by the words of the Lord above quoted at n. 169: *When the unclean spirit goes out of a man, he walks through dry places, seeking rest, but finding none; then he saith, I will return into my house from whence I went out; and when he comes and finds it empty, and swept, and garnished, then he goes away, and takes to himself seven other spirits worse than himself, and entering in they dwell there, and the latter things of the man become worse than the first.* Matt. xii. 43, 44, 45. The unclean spirit going out of a man, signifies the repentance of him who is in evil; his walking through dry places and not finding rest, signifies, that, to such a person, a life of good is of that quality; the house into which he returned, and which he found empty, swept, and garnished, signifies the man himself and his will, as being without good. The seven spirits which he took to himself and with whom he returned, signify evil conjoined to good; his state then being worse than his former, signifies profanation. This is the internal sense of these words, for the Lord spoke by correspondences. The same thing is meant by the words of the Lord to the man whom He cured at the Pool of Bethesda: *Behold, thou art made whole; sin no more, lest a worse thing come unto thee*, John v. 14. Also by these words of the Lord: *He hath blinded their eyes, and hardened their heart; that they should not see with their eyes, nor understand with their heart, and be converted, and I should heal them*, John xii. 40; where to be converted and healed, signifies to commit profanation, which takes place when truth and good are acknowledged, and afterwards rejected; which would have been the case if the Jews had been converted and healed.

That the lot of profaners in the other life is the worst of all, because the good and truth which they have acknowledged remain, and also the evil and the false; and because they cohere, a tearing asunder of the life takes place, n. 571, 582, 6348. That the greatest care is therefore taken by the Lord, to prevent the commission of profanation, n. 2426, 10,384. That therefore man is withheld from acknowledgment and faith, if he cannot remain therein to the end of life, n. 3398, 4402. That on this account also man is rather kept in ignorance, and in external worship, n. 301, 302, 303, 1327, 1328. That the Lord also stores up the goods and truths which man has received by acknowledgment, in his interiors, n. 6595.

That lest interior truths should be profaned, they are not revealed before the church is at its end, n. 3398, 3399. Wherefore the Lord came into the world, and opened interior truths, when the church was wholly vastated, n. 3398. See what is adduced on this subject in the work ON THE LAST JUDGMENT AND THE DESTRUCTION OF BABYLON, n. 73, 74.

That in the Word, Babel signifies the profanation of good, and Chaldea, the profanation of truth, n. 1182, 1283, 1295, 1304, 1306, 1307, 1308, 1321, 1322, 1326. That these profanations correspond to the prohibited degrees, or foul adulteries, spoken of in the Word, n. 6348. That profanation was represented in the Israelitish and Jewish church by eating blood, wherefore this was so severely prohibited, n. 1003.

OF REGENERATION.

173. THE man who does not receive spiritual life, that is, who is not born anew by the Lord, cannot enter heaven. This the Lord plainly teaches in John: *Verily, verily, I say unto thee, except a man be born again, he cannot see the kingdom of God.* iii. 3.

174. Man is not born of his parents into spiritual life, but only into natural life. The spiritual life of man consists in loving God above all things, and in loving the neighbor as himself, and this according to the precepts which the Lord has taught in the Word; but natural life consists in loving ourselves and the world more than the neighbor, yea, more than God himself.

175. Every man is born of his parents into the evils of self-love and of the love of the world; for every evil, which by habit has, as it were, contracted to itself a nature, is transmitted to the offspring. In this way evil descends successively from parents, from grandfathers, and from other ancestors, in a long series backwards; and the derivation of evil becomes at length so great, that the whole of man's proper life is nothing but evil. This continuous derivation of evil cannot be broken and altered, except by a life of faith and charity from the Lord.

176. Man is continually inclining to that which he derives from his hereditary nature, and lapsing into it; hence he confirms that evil in himself, and also superadds many more evils of himself. These evils are altogether contrary to spiritual life, and destroy it; so that unless man receives a new life, which is spiritual life, from the Lord,—unless he is conceived anew, born anew, and educated anew,—in a word, created anew, he must be damned: for his will and thoughts are wholly occupied with things of a selfish and worldly nature, as is the case with those who are in hell.

177. No one can be regenerated unless he be instructed in the knowledge of those things which belong to the new or spiritual life; and the things that belong to that life are the

truths which are to be believed, and the goods which are to be done; the former have respect to faith, and the latter to charity. Nor can any one know these things from himself; for man, in this respect, apprehends only those things which are obvious to the senses, and from these procures for himself what is called natural light; by means of which he discerns what has relation to the world and to himself, but not to heaven and to God. The truths relating to these must be learned from revelation; as, that the Lord, who is God from eternity, came into the world to save the human race;—that He has all power in heaven and on earth;—that faith and charity, with all that pertains to them, whether of truth or of good, are from Him; that there is a heaven, and a hell; and that man lives to eternity, in heaven if he has done good, but in hell if he has done evil.

178. These, with numerous other things, are objects of faith, and must be known by the man who undergoes the process of regeneration: for he who knows them may make them the objects of his thought, afterwards of his will, and finally reduce them to practice, and thus obtain new life. Thus he who does not know that the Lord is the Saviour of the human race, can neither believe in Him, love Him, nor do good for His sake. He who does not know that the Lord is the source of all good, cannot be persuaded that salvation is wholly from Him, still less can he desire that it should be so, and thus he cannot live from the Lord. He who is ignorant of the existence of heaven and hell, and of eternal life, cannot even think respecting the life of heaven, nor can he apply to receive it. The same holds true in other cases.

179. Every one has an internal man and an external; the internal is the spiritual man, and the external is the natural man; and each of these must be regenerated, in order that the entire man may be so. In the unregenerate the external or natural man rules, and the internal is in subjection; but in the regenerate, the internal or spiritual man has the ascendancy, and the external is in subjection. Hence it is evident that the true order of life is inverted in man from his birth; that is to say, the principle which serves ought to rule, and that which rules ought to serve. In order that man may be saved, this order of things must be inverted; and such inversion can only be effected by regeneration from the Lord.

180. What is meant by the internal man ruling and the external serving, and the reverse, may be thus explained. When a man places all his good in voluptuousness, in gain, and in pride, delights in hatred and revenge, and endeavors to find in his mind reasons to justify him, then his external man rules, and his internal serves; but when a man finds delight in thinking and willing well, sincerely, and justly, and outwardly

speaking and acting in the same manner, then the internal man rules, and the external obeys.

181. The internal man is first regenerated by the Lord, and the external afterwards, and the latter by means of the former; for the internal man is regenerated by embracing the things which belong to faith and charity, and the external, by a life in accordance with them. This is meant by the Lord's words, where He says: *Except a man be born of water and of the Spirit, he cannot enter into the kingdom of God.* John iii. 5. In the spiritual sense, water is the truth of faith, and the Spirit is a life according to it.

182. He who is regenerated, is, as to his internal man, in heaven, and is an angel there with the angels, into whose society he is admitted after the dissolution of the body; when he is capable of entering on a full enjoyment of the life of heaven, which consists in loving the Lord, in loving the neighbor, in understanding truth, loving good, and perceiving the felicity thence derived.

FROM THE ARCANA CŒLESTIA.

183. WHAT *Regeneration is, and why it is effected.* That at this day little is known concerning regeneration; the reason thereof, n. 3761, 4136, 5398. That man is born into evils of every kind, and that of consequence, his proprium by birth is nothing but evil, n. 210, 215, 731, 874, 875, 876, 987, 1047, 2307, 2308, 3518, 3701, 3712, 8480, 8549, 8550, 8552, 10,283, 10,284, 10,286. That man's HEREDITARY PRINCIPLE is nothing but evil, see the extracts above in this doctrine, n. 83. That man's PROPRIUM is nothing but evil, see the same, n. 82. That man of himself, so far as he is under the influence of his hereditary [principle] and proprium, is worse than the brutes, n. 694, 8480. That, therefore, if man should be led by his own proprium, he could not possibly be saved, n. 10,731.

That man's natural life is contrary to spiritual life, n. 3913, 3928. That the good which he does from himself, or from proprium, is not good, because he does it for the sake of self, and the world, n. 8478. That man's proprium must be removed that the Lord and heaven may be able to be present, n. 1023, 1044. That it is actually removed when he is regenerated by the Lord, n. 9334, 9335, 9336, 9452, 9455, 9938. That therefore he must be created anew, that is, regenerated, n. 8549, 9450, 9938. That creating man, in the Word, signifies to regenerate him, n. 16, 88, 10,634.

That man is conjoined to the Lord by regeneration, n. 2004, 9338. And consociated with angels in heaven, n. 2475. That he does not come into heaven, until he is in a state to be led by the Lord by means of good, which is the case when he is regenerated, n. 8516, 8539, 8722, 9139, 9832, 10,367.

That the external or natural man rules, and the internal man serves, in the man who is not regenerated, n. 3167, 8743. That thus the state of man's life is inverted from his birth, and must be entirely inverted again in order that he may be saved, n. 6507, 8552, 8553, 9258. That the end of regeneration is, that the internal or spiritual man may rule, and the external or natural man serve, n. 911, 913. That this is actually effected after man is regenerated, n. 5128, 5651, 8743. For after regeneration the love of self and the world no longer reigns, but love to the Lord and towards the neighbor, thus the Lord and not man, n. 8856, 8857. Hence it is plain that man cannot be saved unless he is regenerated, n. 5280, 8548, 8772, 10,156.

That regeneration is a plane whereon to perfect the life of man to eternity, n. 9334. That the regenerate man is perfected to eternity, n. 6648, 10,048. The quality of the regenerate and the unregenerate man described, n. 977, 986, 10,156.

184. *What persons are regenerated.* That man cannot be regenerated unless he be instructed in the truths of faith and the goods of charity, n. 677, 679, 711, 8635, 8638, 8639, 8640, 10,729. That they who are only in truths and not in good, cannot be regenerated, n. 6567, 8725. That no person is regenerated unless he be in charity, n. 989. That none can be regenerated but such as have conscience, n. 2689, 5470. That every one is regenerated according to his faculty of receiving the good of love to the Lord, and of charity towards the neighbor, by the truths of faith from the doctrine of the church, which is derived from the Word, n. 2967, 2975. Who can be regenerated, and who cannot, n. 2689. That they who lead a life of faith and charity, and are not regenerated in the world, are regenerated in the other life, n. 989, 2490.

185. *That regeneration is from the Lord alone.* That the Lord alone regenerates man, and that neither man nor angel contributes thereto, n. 10,067. That man's regeneration is an image of the Lord's glorification, that is, that as the Lord made His Human Divine, so He makes spiritual the man whom He regenerates, n. 3043, 3138, 3212, 3296, 3490, 4402, 5688, 10,057, 10,076. That the Lord wills to have the whole man whom He regenerates, and not part of him, n. 6138.

186. *Further particulars concerning regeneration.* That man is regenerated by the truths of faith, and by a life according to them, n. 1904, 2046, 9088, 9959, 10,028. That this is understood by the words of the Lord, *Unless a man be born of water and of the spirit, he cannot enter the kingdom of God.* John iii. 5. Water signifies the truth of faith, and spirit, a life according thereto, n. 10,240 That water in the Word signifies the truth of faith, n. 2702, 3058 5668, 8568, 10,238. That spiritual purification, which is from evils and falses, is effected by the truths of faith, n. 2799, 5954, 7044, 7918, 9089, 10,229, 10,237. That when man is regenerated, truths are inseminated and implanted in good, that they may become of the life, n. 880, 2189, 2475, 2697. What the quality of truths must be that they may be implanted in good, n. 8725. That in regeneration truth is initiated and conjoined to good, and good reciprocally to truth, n. 5365, 8516. How this reciprocal initiation and conjunction is effected, n. 3155, 10,067. That truth is implanted in good

when it becomes of the will, since it then becomes of the love, n 10,367.

That there are two states through which the regenerated man passes: a first, when he is led by truth to good; a second, when he acts from good, and from good sees truth, n. 7992, 7993, 8505, 8506, 8510, 8512, 8516, 8643, 8648, 8658, 8685, 8690, 8701, 8772, 9227, 9230, 9274, 9739, 10,048, 10,057, 10,058, 10,076. The quality of man's state when truth is in the first place, and good in the second, n. 3610. Hence it appears that when man is regenerating, he looks to good from truth; but when regenerated, he regards truth from good, n. 6247. Thus that a turning over as it were takes place, in that the state of man is inverted, n. 6507.

But it is to be noted, that when man is regenerating, truth is not actually in the first place and good in the second, but only apparently; but that when man is regenerated, good is in the first place and truth in the second, actually and perceptibly, n. 3324, 3325, 3330, 3336, 3494, 3539, 3548, 3556, 3563, 3570, 3576, 3603, 3701, 4243, 4244, 4247, 4337, 4925, 4926, 4928, 4930, 4977, 5351, 6256, 6269, 6273, 8516, 10,110. Consequently that good is the first and last of regeneration, n. 9337. Since truth appears to be in the first place and good in the second, when man is regenerating, or, which is the same thing, when man becomes a church, that on account of this appearance it was a matter of controversy among the ancients, whether the truth of faith or the good of charity is the first-born of the church, n. 367, 2435. That the good of charity is actually the first-born of the church, but the truth of faith only apparently so, n. 3325, 3494, 4925, 4926, 4928, 4930, 8042, 8080. That first-born in the Word signifies the first [principle] of the church, to which priority and superiority belongs, n. 3325. That the Lord is called the first-born, because in Him and from Him is all the good of love, of charity, and of faith, n. 3325.

That man ought not to return from the latter state wherein truth is regarded from good, to the former state, wherein good is regarded from truth, and why, n. 2454, 3650 to 3655, 5895, 5897, 7857, 7923, 8505, 8506, 8510, 8512, 8516, 9274, 10,184. Where these words of the Lord are explained: *Let not him who is in the field return back to take his clothes.* Matt. xxiv. 18; also, *Whosoever shall then be in the field, let him not return to those things which are behind him. Remember Lot's wife.* Luke xvii. 31, 32: for this is signified by those words.

The process of the regeneration of man described, and how it is effected, n. 1555, 2343, 2490, 2657, 2979, 3057, 3286, 3310, 3316, 3332, 3470, 3701, 4353, 5112, 5126, 5270, 5280, 5342, 6717, 8772, 8773, 9043, 9103, 10,021, 10,057, 10,367. That the arcana of regeneration are innumerable, since regeneration continues during the whole life of man, n. 2679, 3179, 3584, 3665, 3694, 3701, 4377, 4551, 4552, 5122, 5126, 5398, 5912, 6751, 9103, 9258, 9296, 9297, 9334. That scarce any of these arcana come to the knowledge and perception of man, n. 3179, 9336. That this is what is meant by the words of the Lord: *The wind bloweth where it listeth, and thou hearest the sound thereof, but knowest not whence it cometh and whither it goeth; so is every one that is born of the Spirit.* John iii. 8. Concerning the process of the regeneration of the man of the spiritual church, n. 2675, 2678, 2679, 2682. And concerning the process of the regeneration of the man of the celestial church, with the difference between the celestial and spiritual, n. 5113, 10,124.

That the case of the regenerate man is similar to that of an infant, who first learns to speak, then to think, afterwards to live well, until all those things flow from him spontaneously, as from himself, n. 3203, 9296, 9297. Thus that he who is regenerated is first led by the Lord as an infant, then as a youth, and afterwards as an adult, n. 3665, 3690, 4377, 4378, 4379, 6751. That when man is regenerated by the Lord, he is first in a state of external innocence, which is his state of infancy, and is afterwards successively led into a state of internal innocence, which is his state of wisdom, n. 9334, 9335, 10,021, 10,210. The nature and quality of the innocence of infancy, and of the innocence of wisdom, n. 1916, 2305, 2306, 3495, 4563, 4797, 5608, 9301, 10,021. A comparison between the regeneration of man, and the conception and formation of an embryo in the womb, n. 3570, 4931, 9258. That therefore generations and nativities in the Word signify spiritual generations and nativities, which belong to regeneration, n. 613, 1145, 1255, 2020, 2584, 3860, 3868, 4070, 4668, 6239, 10,197. The regeneration of man illustrated by the germinations in the vegetable kingdom, n. 5115, 5116. The regeneration of man represented in the rainbow, n. 1042, 1043, 1053.

That the internal or spiritual man, and the external or natural man, must each of them be regenerated, and the one by means of the other, n. 3868, 3870, 3872, 3876, 3877, 3882. That the internal man must be regenerated before the external, the internal man being in the light of heaven, and the external man in the light of the world, n. 3321, 3325, 3469, 3493, 4353, 8748, 9325. That the external or natural man is regenerated by means of the internal or spiritual, n. 3286, 3288, 3321. That man is not regenerate before the external or natural man is regenerate, n. 8742 to 8747, 9043, 9046, 9061, 9328, 9334. That the spiritual man is shut unless the natural man is regenerated, n. 6299. And that it is as it were blind with respect to the truth and goods of faith and love, n. 3493, 3969, 4353, 4587. That when the natural man is regenerate, the whole man is regenerate, n. 7442, 7443. That this is signified by the washing of the disciples' feet, and by these words of the Lord: *He that is washed hath no need to be washed except as to his feet, and the whole is clean.* John xiii. 9, 10; n. 10,243. That washing in the Word signifies spiritual washing, which is purification from evils and falses, n. 3147, 10,237, 10,241. And that feet signify those things that are of the natural man, n. 2162, 3761, 3986, 4280, 4938 to 4952. That therefore to wash the feet, is to purify the natural man, n. 3147, 10,241.

How the natural man is regenerated, n. 3502, 3508, 3509, 3510, 3573, 3576, 3579, 3616, 3762, 3786, 5373, 5647, 5650, 5651, 5660. The quality of the natural man when it is regenerate, and when it is not regenerate, n. 8744, 8745. That so far as the natural man does not combat with the spiritual man, so far the man is regenerate, n. 3286. That when a man is regenerate, the natural man perceives spiritual things by influx, n. 5651.

That the sensual [principle], which is the ultimate of the natural man, is not regenerated at this day, but that man is elevated above it, n. 7442. That all who are regenerated are actually elevated from sensual things into the light of heaven, n. 6183, 6454. The nature and quality of the sensual man may be seen in the extracts above, n. 50.

That man is regenerated by influx into his knowledges of good and truth, n. 4096, 4097, 4364. That when he is regenerated, he is introduced through mediate goods and truths into genuine goods and truths, and that afterwards the mediate goods and truths are relinquished, and the genuine succeed in their place, n. 3665, 3690, 3686, 3974, 4063, 4067, 4145, 6382. That then another order is induced amongst his truths and goods, n. 4250, 4251, 9931, 10,303. That they are disposed according to ends, n. 4104. Thus according to the uses of spiritual life, n. 9297. That they who are regenerated undergo several states, and are continually brought more interiorly into heaven, and nearer to the Lord, n. 6645. That the regenerate man is in the order of heaven, n. 8512. That his internal is open into heaven, n. 8512, 8513. That man by regeneration comes into angelic wisdom, which however lies concealed in his interiors so long as he remains in the world, but is opened in the other life, and that his wisdom is then like that of the angels, n. 2494, 8747. The enlightenment of those who are regenerated described, n. 2697, 2701, 2704. That by regeneration man receives a new understanding, n. 2657. How the case is with respect to the fructification of good, and the multiplication of truth, with those who are regenerated, n. 984. That with a regenerate person truths from good form as it were a constellation by successive derivations, and continually multiply themselves round about, n. 5912. That with a regenerate person, truths from good are disposed into such order, that the genuine truths of good, from which, as their parents, the rest proceed, are in the middle, whilst the rest succeed in order according to their relationship and affinities, down to the ultimates, where there is obscurity, n. 4128, 4551, 4552, 5134, 5270. That with a regenerate person truths from good are disposed in the form of heaven, n. 3316, 3470, 3584, 4302, 5704, 5709, 6028, 6690, 9931, 10,303; and in the work On Heaven and Hell, under the article *Concerning the Form of Heaven, which governs all heavenly consociation and communication*, n. 200 to 212; and in that *Concerning the Wisdom of the Angels of Heaven*, n. 265 to 275.

That with a regenerate person, there is a correspondence between spiritual things and natural things, n. 2850. That his order of life is altogether inverted, n. 3332, 5159, 8995. That he is altogether a new man as to his spirit, n. 3212. That he appears like the unregenerate man in externals, but not in internals, n. 5159. That spiritual good, which is to will and to do good from an affection of the love of good, can only be given to man by means of regeneration, n 4538. That truths, which enter with affection, are reproduced, n. 5893. That truths, so far as they are deprived of life from the proprium of man, are so far conjoined to good, and receive spiritual life, n. 3607, 3610. That so far as evils from the love of self and the love of the world are removed, so far there is life in truths, n. 3610.

That the first affection of truth with the man who is regenerated is not pure, but is purified successively, n. 3089, 8413. That evils and falses, with the man who is regenerated, are removed slowly, and not quickly, n. 9334, 9335. That the evils and falses of the proprium of man still remain, and are only removed by regeneration, n. 865, 868, 887, 929, 1581, 2406, 4564, 8206, 8393, 8988, 9014, 9333 to 9336, 9445, 9447, 9448, 9451 to 9454, 9938, 10,057, 10,059. That a man can never be so far regenerated as to be called perfect, n. 894, 5122, 6648. That evil spirits dare not assault a regenerate man, n. 1695. That they who believe the justification taught in the church, know little of regeneration, n. 5398.

That man must have liberty, to be capable of being regenerated, n. 1937, 1947, 2876, 2881, 3145, 3146, 3158, 4031, 8700. That man is introduced into heavenly liberty by regeneration, n. 2874, 2875, 2882, 2892. That there is no conjunction of good and truth by compulsion, thus no regeneration, n. 2875, 2881, 4031, 8700. Other particulars respecting liberty as it regards regeneration, may be seen in the doctrine above, where it treats of LIBERTY.

That he who is regenerated, must necessarily undergo temptations, n. 3696, 8403. Because temptations take place for the sake of the conjunction of good and truth, and also of the internal and external man, n. 4248, 4272, 5772.

OF TEMPTATION.

187. THOSE only who are regenerating, undergo spiritual temptations; such temptations being pains of mind induced by evil spirits, in those who are in good and truth. While those spirits excite the evils of such persons, there arises in the mind the anxiety of temptation. Man does not know whence this anxiety comes, because he is unacquainted with its spiritual origin.

188. There are both evil and good spirits attendant on every man; the evil spirits are in his evils, and the good spirits in his goods. When the evil spirits approach they draw forth his evils, while the good spirits, on the contrary, draw forth his goods; whence arise collision and combat, causing in the man an interior anxiety, which is temptation. Hence it is plain that temptations are not induced by heaven, but by hell; as is in accordance with the faith of the church, which teaches that God tempts no man.

189. Interior anxieties are also experienced by those who are not in goods and truths; but natural, not spiritual anxieties; the two are distinguished by this, that natural anxieties have worldly things for their objects, but spiritual anxieties, heavenly things.

190. The object contended for during temptations, is the dominion of good over evil, or of evil over good. The evil

which is desirous of obtaining the dominion, resides in the natural or external man, and the good, in the spiritual or internal man. If evil prevails, the natural man obtains the dominion; but if good prevails, the spiritual conquers.

191. These combats are carried on by the truths of faith derived from the Word. By these man must contend against evils and falses; for if he combats from any other principles, he cannot conquer, because in these alone the Lord is present. And as this warfare is carried on by the truths of faith, man is not permitted to enter on it until he has been instructed in the knowledge of good and truth, and has thence obtained some degree of spiritual life; such combats, therefore, do not take place till men arrive at years of maturity.

192. If man falls in temptation, his state after it becomes worse than before, because evil has acquired power over good, and falsity over truth.

193. Since at this day faith is rare, because there is no charity, the church being at its end, there are but few who are admitted into any spiritual temptations; hence it is scarcely known what they are, and to what salutary purpose they are conducive.

194. The ends to which temptations are conducive are these. They acquire for good dominion over evil, and for truth dominion over the false; they confirm truths in the mind, and conjoin them to good; and they disperse evils and the falsities thence derived. They serve also to open the internal spiritual man, and to bring the natural man into subjection to it; to destroy the loves of self and the world, and to subdue the concupiscences which proceed from them. When these things are effected, man acquires enlightenment and perception respecting the nature of good and its truth, and of falsity and its evil; whence he obtains intelligence and wisdom, which afterwards increase continually.

195. The Lord alone combats for man in temptation; and unless he believes that the Lord alone combats and conquers for him, he undergoes only an external temptation; which is in no respect conducive to his salvation

---

FROM THE ARCANA CŒLESTIA.

196. Before the particulars contained in the Arcana Cœlestia, respecting temptations, are summarily recited, something shall first be said concerning them, in order that it may be known still more clearly from whence they proceed. When the truths of faith which a man believes in his heart, and according to which he loves to live, are assaulted within him, it is called a spiritual temptation, especially when the good of love, in which he places his spiritual life, is

assaulted Those assaults take place in various ways; as by an influx of scandals against good and truth into the thoughts and the will; also by a continual drawing forth, and bringing to remembrance, of the evils which one has committed, and of the false persuasions by which one has been led, thus by an inundation of such things; and at the same time by an apparent shutting up of the interiors of the mind, and, consequently, of communication with heaven, by which the capacity of thinking from one's own faith, and of willing from one's own love, are intercepted. These things are effected by evil spirits who are present with man; and when they take place, they assume the appearance of interior anxieties and pains of conscience; for they affect and torment man's spiritual life, because he supposes that they proceed, not from evil spirits, but from his own interiors. Man does not know that such assaults proceed from evil spirits, because he is ignorant that spirits are present with him, evil spirits in his evils, and good spirits in his good; and that they reside in his affections. These temptations are most grievous, when they are accompanied with bodily pains; and still more so, when those pains are of long continuance, and no deliverance is granted, even although the Divine mercy is implored; hence results despair, which is the end.

Some particulars shall first be adduced from the ARCANA CŒLESTIA, concerning the spirits that are with man, because temptations proceed from them.

That spirits and angels are attendant on every man, n. 697, 5846 to 5866. That they are in his thoughts and affections, n. 2888, 5846, 5848. That if spirits and angels were taken away, man could not live, n. 2887, 5849, 5854, 5993, 6321. Because by spirits and angels man has communication and conjunction with the spiritual world, without which he would have no life, n. 697, 2796, 2886, 2887, 4047, 4048, 5846 to 5866, 5976 to 5993. That the spirits with man are changed according to the affections of his love, n. 5851. That spirits from hell are in the loves of man's proprium, n. 5852, 5979 to 5993. That spirits enter into all things of man's memory, n. 5853, 5897, 5859, 5860, 6192, 6193, 6198, 6199. That angels are in the ends from which and for the sake of which man thinks, wills, and acts in one particular manner and no other, n. 1317, 1645, 5844. That man is not visible to spirits, nor spirits to man, n. 5885. That spirits cannot see what is in our solar world by means of man, n. 1880. That though spirits and angels are with man, in his thoughts and affections, yet still he is in liberty as to thought, will, and action, n. 5982, 6477, 8209, 8307, 10,777; and in the work ON HEAVEN AND HELL, where the conjunction of heaven with the human race is treated of, n. 291 to 302.

197. *Whence and of what quality temptations are.* That temptations proceed from the evil spirits that are with man, who inject scandals against the goods and truths which a man loves and believes, and likewise excite the evils which he has done and the falses which he has thought, n. 741, 751, 761, 3927, 4307, 4572, 5036, 6657, 8960. That then evil spirits use all sorts of cunning and malice, n. 6666. That the man who is in temptations is near to hell, n. 8131.

That there are two forces which act in temptations, a force from within from the Lord, and a force from without from hell, n. 8168.

That the reigning love of man is assaulted in temptations, n. 847, 4274. That evil spirits attack those things only which are of man's faith and love, thus those things which relate to his spiritual life; wherefore at such times his eternal life is at stake, n. 1820. A state of temptations compared with that of a man among thieves, n. 5248. That in temptations angels from the Lord keep man in the truths and goods which are with him, but evil spirits keep him in the falses and evils which are with him, whence arises a conflict and combat, n. 4249.

That temptation is a combat between the internal or spiritual man, and the external or natural man, n. 2183, 4256. Thus between the delights of the internal and external man, which are then opposite to each other, n. 3928, 10,351. That it takes place on account of the disagreement between those delights, n. 3928. Thus that the dominion of one over the other is what is contended for in temptations, n. 3928, 8961.

That no person can be tempted unless he is in the acknowledgment, and likewise in the affection of truth and good, because there is otherwise no combat, for there is nothing spiritual to act against what is natural, thus there is no contest for dominion, n. 3928, 4299. That whoever has acquired any spiritual life, undergoes temptations, n. 8963. That temptations take place with those who have conscience, that is, with those who are in spiritual love; but that more grievous ones take place with those who have perception, that is, with those who are in celestial love, n. 1668, 8963. That dead men, that is they who are not in faith and love to God, and in love towards the neighbor, are not admitted into temptations, because they would fall, n. 270, 4274, 4299, 8964, 8968. That therefore very few at this day are admitted into spiritual temptations, n. 8965. But that they have anxieties on account of various causes in the world, past, present, or future, which are often attended with infirmity of mind and weakness of body, which anxieties are not the anxieties of temptations, n. 762, 8164. That spiritual temptations are sometimes attended with bodily pains, and sometimes not, n. 8164. That a state of temptation is an unclean and filthy state, inasmuch as evils and falses are injected, and also doubts concerning goods and truths, n. 5246. Also, because in temptations there are indignations, pains of the mind, and many affections that are not good, n. 1917, 6829. That there is also obscurity and doubt concerning the end, n. 1820, 6829. And likewise concerning the Divine Providence and hearing of prayer, because prayers are not heard in temptations as they are out of them, n. 8179. And because man when he is in temptation, seems to himself to be in a state of damnation, n. 6097. Because man perceives clearly what is doing in his external man, consequently the things which evil spirits inject and call forth, according to which he thinks of his state; but he does not perceive what is doing in his internal man, consequently the things which flow in by means of angels from the Lord, and therefore he cannot judge of his state therefrom, n. 10,236, 10,240.

That temptations are generally carried to desperation, which is their end, n. 1787, 2694, 5279, 5280, 6144, 7147, 7155, 7166, 8165, 8567. The reasons, n. 2694. That in the temptation itself there are also desperations, but that they terminate in a general one, n. 8567. That in a state of desperation a man speaks bitter things, but that the Lord does not attend to them, n. 8165. That when the temptation is finished, there is at first a fluctuation between truth and the false, n. 848, 857. But that afterwards truth shines, and becomes serene and cheerful, n. 3696, 4572, 6829, 8367, 8370.

That they who are regenerated undergo temptations not once only, but many times, because many evils and falses are to be removed, n. 8403. That if they who have acquired some spiritual life do not undergo temptations in the world, they undergo them in the other life, n. 7122. How temptations take place in the other life, and where, n. 537, 538, 539, 699, 1106 to 1113, 1122, 2694, 4728, 4940 to 4951, 6119, 6928, 7090, 7122, 7123, 7186, 7317, 7474, 7502, 7541, 7542, 7545, 7768, 7990, 9331, 9763. Concerning the state of enlightenment of those who come out of temptation, and are raised into heaven, and their reception there, n. 2699, 2701, 2704.

The nature of the temptation occasioned by failure of truth, attended with a desire thereof at the same time, n. 2682, 8352. The temptation of infants in another world, whereby they learn to resist evils, n. 2294. The difference between temptations, infestations, and vastations, n. 7474.

198. *How and when temptations take place.* That spiritual combats are chiefly fought by the truths of faith, n. 8962. That truth is the first [instrument] of combat, n. 1685. That the men of the spiritual church are tempted with regard to the truths of faith, and carry on the combat by truths; but that the men of the celestial church are tempted with regard to goods of love, and carry on the combat by goods, n. 1668, 8963. That the members of the spiritual church, for the most part, do not combat from genuine truths, but from such as they believe to be genuine from the doctrine of their own church; which doctrine however ought to be such, as to be capable of being conjoined with good, n. 6765.

That whoever is regenerated must undergo temptations, and that he cannot be regenerated without them, n. 5036, 5403; and that temptations therefore are necessary, n. 7090. That the man who is regenerating comes into temptations, when evil endeavors to gain dominion over good, and the natural man over the spiritual man, n. 6857, 8961; and when good ought to have the precedence, n. 4248, 4249, 4256, 8962, 8963. That they who are regenerated, are first let into a state of tranquillity, then into temptations, and afterwards return into a state of tranquillity of peace, which is the end, n. 3696.

199. *What good is effected by temptations.* The general effect of temptations, n. 1692, 1717, 1740, 6144, 8958 to 8969. That by temptations the spiritual or internal man acquires dominion over the natural or external man; consequently good acquires the dominion over evil, and truth over the false; because good resides in the spiritual man, which cannot exist without it, and evil resides in the natural man, n. 8961. Forasmuch as temptation is a combat between them, it follows that dominion is the object of contest, that is

whether the spiritual man shall have dominion over the natural man, thus whether good shall have dominion over evil, or *vice versa;* consequently, whether the Lord or hell shall have dominion over man, n. 1923, 3928. That the external or natural man, by means of temptations, receives truths corresponding to the affection thereof in the internal or spiritual man, n. 3321, 3928. That the internal spiritual man is opened and conjoined with the external by means of temptations, in order that man as to each may be capable of being elevated, and of looking to the Lord, n. 10,865. The internal spiritual man is opened and conjoined with the external by means of temptations, because the Lord acts from the interior, and flows in thence into the external, and removes and subjugates the evils therein, and at the same time subjects and renders it subordinate to the internal, n. 10,685.

That temptations take place for the sake of the conjunction of good and truth, and the dispersion of the falses which adhere to truths and goods, n. 4572. Consequently that good is conjoined to truths by means of temptations, n. 2272. That the vessels recipient of truth are softened by means of temptations, and put on a state receptive of good, n. 3318. That truths and goods, consequently the things which belong to faith and charity, are confirmed and implanted by means of temptations, 8351, 8924, 8966, 8967. And that evils and falses are removed, and room made for the reception of goods and truths, n. 7122. That by means of temptations the loves of self and the world, from whence proceed all evils and falses, are broken, n. 5356; and that thus man is humbled, n. 8966, 8967. That evils and falses are subdued, separated, and removed, but not abolished, by means of temptations, n. 868. That by means of temptations corporeal things with their concupiscences are subdued, n. 857, 858. That man by means of temptations learns what good and truth are, even from their relation to their opposites, which are evils and falses, n. 5356. That he also learns that of himself he is nothing but evil, and that all the good with him is from the Lord, and from his mercy, n. 2334.

That by means of the temptations in which man conquers, evil spirits are deprived of the power of rising up against him any more, n. 1695, 1717. That the hells dare not rise up against those who have suffered temptations and have conquered, n. 2183, 8273.

That after temptations in which man has conquered, there is joy arising from the conjunction of good and truth, although the man knows not that the joy he then feels proceeds therefrom, n. 4572, 6829. That there is then an illustration of the truth which is of faith, and a perception of the good which is of love, n. 8367, 8370. That thence he acquires intelligence and wisdom, n. 8966, 8967. That truths after temptations increase immensely, n. 6663; and that good has the precedence, or is in the first place, and truth in the second, n. 5773; and that man, as to his internal spiritual man, is admitted into the angelic societies, thus into heaven, n. 6611.

That before a man undergoes temptations, the truths and goods which are with him are arranged in order by the Lord, that he may be capable of resisting the evils and falses which are with him, and are excited from hell, n. 8131. That in temptations the Lord pro vides good where the evil spirits intend evil, n. 6574. That after temptations the Lord reduces truths with goods into a new order, and disposes them in a heavenly form, n. 10,685. That the interiors of the spiritual man are disposed into a heavenly form, see the work ON HEAVEN AND HELL, where it treats of the form of heaven, according to which are regulated the consociations and communications therein, n. 200 to 212.

That they who fall in temptations, come into damnation, because evils and falses conquer, and the natural man prevails over the spiritual man, and afterwards has the dominion; and that the latter state becomes worse than the former, n. 8165, 8169, 8961.

200. *That the Lord combats for man in temptations.* That the Lord alone combats for man in temptations, and that man does not combat at all from himself, n. 1692, 8172, 8175, 8176, 8273. That man cannot by any means combat against evils and falses from himself, because that would be to fight against all the hells, which the Lord alone can subdue and conquer, n. 1692. That the hells fight against man, and the Lord for him, n. 8159. That man combats from truths and goods, thus from the knowledges and affections thereof which are with him; but that it is not man who combats, but the Lord by means of these knowledges and affections, n. 1661. That man thinks that the Lord is absent in temptations, because his prayers are not heard as they are out of them, but that nevertheless the Lord is then more present with him, n. 840. That in temptations man ought to combat as from himself, and not to hang down his hands, nor to expect immediate help; but that nevertheless he ought to believe that all help is from the Lord, n. 1712, 8179, 8969. That man cannot otherwise receive a heavenly proprium, n. 1937, 1947, 2882, 2883, 2891. The quality of that proprium, that it is not man's, but the Lord's with him, n. 1937, 1917, 2882, 2883, 2891, 8497.

That temptation is of no avail, and productive of no good, unless a man believes, at least after the temptations, that the Lord has fought and conquered for him, n. 8969. That they who place merit in works, cannot combat against evils, because they combat from their own proprium, and do not permit the Lord to combat for them, n. 9978. That they who believe they have merited heaven by their temptations, are with much difficulty saved, n. 2273.

That the Lord does not tempt, but liberates, and leads to good, n. 2768. That temptations appear to be from the Divine, when yet they are not, n. 4299. In what sense the petition in the Lord's prayer—*Lead us not into temptation*—is to be understood, from experience, n. 1875. That the Lord does not concur in temptations by permitting them, according to the idea which man entertains of permission, n. 2768.

That in every temptation there is liberty, although it does not appear so, but that the liberty is interiorly with man from the Lord, and that he therefore combats and is willing to conquer, and not to be conquered, which he would not do without liberty, n. 1937, 1947, 2881. That the Lord effects this by means of the affection of truth and good impressed on the internal man, although the man is ignorant thereof, n. 5044. For all liberty is of affection or love, and according to its quality, n. 2870, 3158, 8907, 8990, 9585, 9591.

201. *Of the Lord's temptations.* That the Lord endured the most grievous and terrible of all temptations, of which there is but little said in the literal sense of the Word, but much in the internal sense, n. 1663, 1668, 1787, 2776, 2786, 2795, 2814, 9528. That the Lord combated from Divine Love towards the whole human race, n. 1690, 1691, 1812, 1813, 1820. That the love of the Lord was the salvation of the human race, n. 1820. That the Lord combated from His own proper power, n. 1692, 1813, 9937. That the Lord alone was made justice and merit, by means of temptations, and of the victories which He gained therein from His own proper power, n. 1813, 2025, 2026, 2027, 9715, 9809, 10,019. That by means of temptations the Lord united the Divine itself, which was in Him from conception, to His Human, and made this Divine, as He makes man spiritual by means of temptations, n. 1725, 1729, 1733, 1737, 3318, 3381, 3382, 4286. That the temptations of the Lord were attended with despair at the end, n. 1787. That the Lord, by means of the temptations with which He suffered Himself to be assaulted, subjugated the hells, and reduced to order all things in them, and in heaven, and at the same time glorified His Human, n. 1737, 4287, 9397, 9258, 9937. That the Lord alone fought against all the hells, n. 8273. That He permitted temptations from thence to assault Him, n. 2816, 4295.

That the Lord could not be tempted as to the Divine, because the hells cannot assault the Divine, wherefore He assumed a human from the mother, which could be tempted, n. 1414, 1444, 1573, 5041, 5157, 7193, 9315. That by means of temptations and victories He expelled all that was hereditary from the mother, and put off the human from her, until at length He was no longer her son, n. 2159, 2574, 2649, 3036, 10,829. That Jehovah, who was in Him from conception, appeared in His temptations to be absent, n. 1815. That this was His state of humiliation, n. 1785, 1999, 2159, 6866. That His last temptation and victory, by which He fully subjugated the hells, and made His Human Divine, was in Gethsemane and on the cross, n. 2776, 2803, 2813, 2814, 10,655, 10,659, 10,829.

That to eat no bread and drink no water for forty days, signifies an entire state of temptations, n. 10,686. That forty years, months, or days, signify a plenary state of temptations from beginning to end; and that such a state is understood by the deluge continuing forty days; by Moses abiding forty days upon Mount Sinai; by the sojourning of the children of Israel forty years in the desert; and by the Lord's temptation in the desert for forty days, n. 730, 862, 2272, 2273, 8098.

OF BAPTISM.

202. The ordinance of baptism is intended as a sign that the person baptized belongs to the church, and as a memorial that he must be regenerated; for the washing of baptism has no other signification than of spiritual washing, or regeneration.

203. All regeneration is effected by the Lord, through the instrumentality of the truths of faith, and of a life in accordance with them. Baptism, therefore, is a testification that the person baptized belongs to the church, and is capable of being regenerated: for it is in the church that the Lord, who alone regenerates man, is acknowledged, and there also is the Word, which contains the truths of faith, by which regeneration is effected.

204. These truths the Lord teaches in John: *Except a man be born of water and of the spirit, he cannot enter into the kingdom of God.* chap. iii. 5. Water, in the spiritual sense, here signifies the truth of faith derived from the Word; the spirit, a life according to that truth; and being born, being regenerated thereby.

205. Since every one who is regenerated also undergoes temptations, which are spiritual combats against evil and the false, the water used in baptism likewise signifies those temptations.

206. As baptism is appointed a sign and memorial of those things, man may be baptized as an infant, and if he has not been baptized in his infancy, he may be baptized as an adult.

207. Let those, therefore, who are baptized, remember, that baptism itself confers upon its subjects neither faith nor salvation, but merely testifies that they will receive faith, and that they will be saved, if they are regenerated.

208. Hence may be seen the import of the Lord's words in Mark: *He that believeth and is baptized, shall be saved; but he that believeth not shall be damned.* chap. xvi. 16. Here, to believe, signifies to acknowledge the Lord, and to receive Divine Truths from Him by means of the Word; and to be baptized, is to be regenerated by the Lord by means of those truths.

FROM THE ARCANA CŒLESTIA.

209. That baptism signifies regeneration by the Lord by the truths of faith derived from the Word, n. 4255, 5120, 9089, 10,239, 10,386, 10,387, 10,388, 10,392. That baptism is for a sign that man is of the church, which acknowledges the Lord, who is the source of regeneration, and which has the Word, from which the truths of faith, by means of which regeneration is effected, are derived, n. 10,386,

10,387, 10,388. That baptism gives neither faith nor salvation, but testifies that faith and salvation will be received by those who are regenerated, n. 10,391.

That washings in the ancient churches, and in the Israelitish church, represented and thence signified purifications from evils and falses, n. 3147, 9089, 10,237, 10,239. That washings of garments signified the purification of the understanding from falses, n. 5954. That washing of the feet signified the purification of the natural man, n. 3147, 10,241. What is signified by the washing of the disciples' feet by the Lord, is explained at n. 10,243.

That waters signify the truths of faith, n. 28, 2702, 3058, 5668, 8568, 10,238. That a fountain and a well of living waters signifies the truths of faith from the Lord, consequently the Word, n. 3424. That bread and water signify all the goods of love and truths of faith, n. 4976, 9323. That spirit signifies the life of truth, or the life of faith, n. 5222, 9281, 9818. What the spirit and the flesh signify,—that the spirit signifies life from the Lord, and flesh, life from man, n. 10,283. Hence it is evident what is signified by these words of the Lord: *Except a man be begotten of water and the spirit, he cannot enter into the kingdom of God;* namely, that unless man is regenerated by the truths of faith, and by a life according to them, he cannot be saved, n. 10,240. That all regeneration is effected by the truths of faith, and by a life according to them, n. 1904, 2046, 9088, 9959, 10,028.

That the total washing, which was effected by immersion in the waters of Jordan, signified regeneration, in the same manner as baptism, n. 9089, 10,239. What the waters of Jordan, and Jordan itself, signified, n. 1585, 4255.

That a deluge and inundation of waters signify temptations, n. 660, 705, 739, 756, 790, 5725, 6853. That baptism signifies the same, n. 5120, 10,389. In what manner baptism was represented from heaven, n. 2299.

OF THE HOLY SUPPER.

210. The Holy Supper was instituted by the Lord, to be a means whereby the church may have conjunction with heaven, and thus with the Lord; it is, therefore, the holiest solemnity of Divine worship.

211. The manner in which such conjunction is effected by the Holy Supper, is not understood by those who are unacquainted with the internal or spiritual sense of the Word, since they do not think beyond the external sense, which is that of the letter. It is only from the internal or spiritual sense of the Word, that it can be known what is signified by the Lord's body and blood, and by the bread and wine; and also what is signified by eating.

212. In the spiritual sense, the Lord's body or flesh, and the bread, signifies the good of love; the Lord's blood and the wine,

the good of faith; and eating, appropriation and conjunction. In no other sense do the angels, who are attendant on man, when he receives the sacrament of the Supper, understand those things, for they perceive all things spiritually. Hence it is, that, on such occasions, a holy principle of love and of faith flows into man from the angels, thus through heaven from the Lord, and hence conjunction is effected.

213. From these considerations it is evident, that when man partakes of the bread, which is the body, he is conjoined to the Lord by the good of love directed to Him and derived from Him; and that when he partakes of the wine, which is the blood, he is conjoined to the Lord by the good of faith, directed to Him and derived from Him. But it must be particularly observed, that conjunction with the Lord, by means of the sacrament of the Holy Supper, is effected with those alone who are influenced by the good of love to Him, and of faith in Him and from Him. With these there is conjunction by means of this most holy ordinance; with others, there is indeed the Lord's presence, but no conjunction with Him.

214. Besides, the Holy Supper includes and comprehends the whole of the Divine worship instituted in the Israelitish Church; for the burnt-offerings and sacrifices, in which the worship of that church principally consisted, were denominated by the single term BREAD; hence, also, the Holy Supper is the completion or fullness of that representative worship.

FROM THE ARCANA CŒLESTIA.

SINCE what is involved in the Holy Supper cannot be known, un less it be known what its particulars signify, for they correspond to spiritual things, therefore some passages shall be adduced respecting what is signified by body and flesh, by bread and wine, and by eating and drinking; as also concerning the sacrifices, wherein the worship of the Israelitish church principally consisted, showing that they were called bread.

215. OF SUPPER. That dinners and suppers signified consociation by love, n. 3596, 3832, 4745, 5161, 7996. That the Paschal supper signified consociation in heaven, n. 7836, 7997, 8001. That the feast of unleavened bread, or of the passover, signified deliverance from damnation, by the Lord, n. 7093, 7867, 9286 to 9292, 10,655; and in the inmost sense, the remembrance of the glorification of the Lord's Human, because deliverance comes therefrom, n. 10,655.

216. OF BODY AND FLESH. That the Lord's flesh signifies the Divine Good of His Divine Love, that is, of His Divine Human, n. 3813, 7850, 9127, 10,283. That His body has a like signification, n. 2343, 2359, 6135. That flesh in general signifies the will principle or proprium of man, which regarded in itself is evil; but which when vivified by the Lord, signifies good, n. 148, 149, 780, 999, 3813,

8409, 10,283. That hence flesh in the Word, signifies the whole man, and every man, n. 574, 1050, 12,803.

It is said here and in what follows, that these things signify, because they correspond; for whatever corresponds, signifies, see n. 2890, 2971, 2987, 2989, 3002, 3225. *That the Word is written by mere correspondences, and hence its internal or spiritual sense, the nature of which cannot be known, and scarcely its existence, without a knowledge of correspondences, n.* 3131, 3472 to 3485, 8615, 10,657. *That thus there is a conjunction of heaven with the man of the church by the Word, n.* 10,687. *For further particulars on this head see n.* 303 to 310, *in the work* ON HEAVEN AND HELL, *where it treats of the conjunction of heaven with the man of the church by means of the Word.*

217. OF BLOOD. That the Lord's blood signifies the Divine Truth proceeding from the Divine Good of His Divine Love, n. 4735, 4978, 7317, 7326, 7846, 7850, 7877, 9127, 9393, 10,026, 10,033, 10,152, 10,204. That the blood sprinkled upon the altar round about, and at its foundation, signified the unition of Divine Truth and Divine Good in the Lord, n. 10,047. That the blood of grapes signifies the truth of faith from the good of charity, n. 6378. That a grape and a bunch of grapes signify spiritual good, which is the good of charity, n. 5117. That to shed blood is to offer violence to Divine Truth, n. 374, 1005, 4735, 5476, 9127. What is signified by blood and water going out of the Lord's side, n. 9127. What by the Lord's redeeming men by His blood, n. 10,152.

218. OF BREAD. That bread, when mentioned in relation to the Lord, signifies the Divine Good of the Lord's Divine Love, and the reciprocal good of the man who eats it, n. 2165, 2177, 3478, 3735, 3813, 4211, 4217, 4735, 4976, 9323, 9545. That bread involves and signifies all food in general, n. 2165, 6118. That food signifies every thing that nourishes the spiritual life of man, n. 4976, 5147, 5915, 6277, 8418. Thus bread signifies all celestial and spiritual food, n. 276, 680, 2165, 2177, 3478, 6118, 8410. Consequently every thing which proceeds out of the mouth of God, according to the Lord's words, Matt. iv. 4, n. 681. That bread in general signifies the good of love, n. 2165, 2177, 10,686. The same is signified by wheat, of which bread is made, n. 3941, 7605. That bread and water when mentioned in the Word, signify the good of love, and the truth of faith, n. 9323. That breaking of bread was a representative of mutual love in the ancient churches, n. 5405. That spiritual food is knowledge, intelligence, and wisdom, and consequently good and truth, because the former are derived from the latter, n. 3114, 4459, 4792, 5147, 5293, 5340, 5342, 5410, 5426, 5576, 5582, 5588, 5656, 8562, 9003. And because they nourish the mind, n. 4459, 5293, 5576, 6277, 8418. That sustenance by food signifies spiritual nourishment, and the influx of good and truth from the Lord, n. 4976, 5915, 6277.

That the show-bread on the table in the tabernacle, signified the Divine Good of the Lord's Divine Love, n. 3478, 9545. That the meat-offerings of cakes and wafers in the sacrifices, signified worship from the good of love, n. 4581, 10,079, 10,137. What the various meat-offerings signified in particular, n. 7978, 9992, 9993, 9994 10,079.

That the ancients, when they mentioned bread, meant all food in general, see Gen. xliii. 16, 31; Exod. xviii. 12; Judges xiii. 15, 16; 1 Sam. xiv. 28, 29; chap. xx. 24, 27; 2 Sam. ix. 7, 10; 1 Kings iv. 22, 23; 2 Kings xxv. 29.

219. Of Wine. That wine, when mentioned with respect to the Lord, signifies the Divine Truth proceeding from His Divine Good, in the same manner as blood, n. 1071, 1798, 6377. That wine in general signifies the good of charity, n. 6377. That new wine signifies truth from good in the natural man, n. 3580. That wine is called the blood of grapes, n. 6378. That a vineyard signifies the church with respect to truth, n. 9139, 3220. That the drink-offering in the sacrifices, which was wine, signified spiritual good, which is holy truth, n. 1072. That the Lord alone is holy, and hence that all holiness is from Him, n. 9229, 9680, 10,359, 10,360. That the Divine Truth proceeding from the Lord is what is called holy in the Word, n. 6788, 8302, 9229, 9820, 10,361.

220. Of Eating and Drinking. That to eat signifies to be appropriated and conjoined by love and charity, n. 2187, 2343, 3168, 3513, 5643. That hence it signifies to be consociated, n. 8001 That to eat is predicated of the appropriation and conjunction of good, and to drink, of the appropriation and conjunction of truth, n. 3168, 3513, 3832, 9412. What eating and drinking in the Lord's kingdom signifies, n. 3832. Hence it is, that to be famished and hungry, in the Word, signifies to desire good and truth from affection, n. 4958, 10,227.

That the angels understand the things here spoken of according to their internal or spiritual sense alone, because the angels are in the spiritual world, n. 10,121. That hence holiness from heaven flows in with the men of the church, when they receive the sacrament of the supper with sanctity, n. 6789. And effects conjunction with the Lord, n. 1519, 3464, 3735, 5915, 10,521, 10,522.

221. Of Sacrifices. That burnt-offerings and sacrifices signified all things of worship from the good of love, and from the truths of faith, n. 923, 6905, 8680, 8936, 10,042. That burnt-offerings and sacrifices also signified Divine Celestial things, which are the internal things of the church, from which worship is derived, n. 2180, 2805, 2807, 2830, 3519. With a variation and difference according to the varieties of worship, n. 2805, 6905, 8936. That therefore there were many kinds of sacrifices, and various processes to be observed in them, and various beasts made use of, n. 2830, 9939, 9990. That the various things which they signified in general, may appear from unfolding the particulars by the internal sense, n. 10,042. What the beasts which were sacrificed signified in particular, n. 10,042. That arcana of heaven are contained in the rituals and processes of the sacrifices, n. 10,057. That in general they contained the arcana respecting the glorification of the Lord's Human; and in a respective sense, the arcana of the regeneration and purification of man from evils and falses; wherefore they were prescribed for various sins, crimes, and purifications, n. 9990, 10,022, 10,042, 10,053, 10 057. What is signified by the imposition of

hands on the beasts which were sacrificed, n. 10,023. What by the inferior parts of the slain beasts being put under their superior parts, in the burnt-offerings, n. 10,051. What by the meat-offerings that were offered at the same time, n. 10,079. What by the drink-offering, n. 4581, 10,137. What by the salt which was used, n. 10,300. What by the altar and all the particulars of it, n. 921, 2777, 2784, 2811, 2812, 4489, 4541, 8935, 8940, 9388, 9389, 9714, 9726, 9963, 9964, 10,028, 10,123, 10,151, 10,242, 10,245, 10,344. What by the fire of the altar, n. 934, 6314, 6832. What by eating together of the things sacrificed, n. 2187, 8682. That sacrifices were not commanded, but charity and faith, thus that they were only permitted, shown from the Word, n. 922, 2180. Why they were permitted, n. 2180, 2818.

That the burnt-offerings and sacrifices, which consisted of lambs, she-goats, sheep, kids, he-goats, and bullocks, were in one word called BREAD, is evident from the following passages: *And the priest shall burn it upon the altar;* IT IS THE BREAD OF THE OFFERING MADE BY FIRE UNTO THE LORD. Levit. iii. 11, 16. *The sons of Aaron shall be holy unto their God, neither shall they profane the name of their God; for the offerings of Jehovah made by fire, the* BREAD OF THEIR GOD, *they do offer. Thou shalt sanctify him, therefore, for he offereth* THE BREAD OF THY GOD. *A man of the seed of Aaron, in whom there shall be a blemish, let him not approach to offer the* BREAD OF HIS GOD. Levit. xxi. 6, 8, 17, 21. *Command the children of Israel, and say unto them, My offering,* MY BREAD, *for my sacrifices made by fire for an odor of rest, ye shall observe, to offer unto me in their due season.* Num. xxviii. 2. *He who shall have touched an unclean thing shall not eat of the holy things, unless he wash his flesh in water; and shall afterwards eat of the holy things, because it is his* BREAD. Levit. xxii. 6, 7. *Ye offer* POLLUTED BREAD *upon my altar,* Malachi i. 7.

From what has been observed, it may be seen what is meant by bread in John: *Jesus said, Verily, verily, I say unto you, Moses gave them not that* BREAD FROM HEAVEN, *but my Father giveth you the* TRUE BREAD FROM HEAVEN; *for* THE BREAD OF GOD *is He who came down from heaven, and giveth life unto the world. Then said they unto Him, Lord, evermore give us* THIS BREAD. *Jesus said unto them,* I AM THE BREAD OF LIFE; *he that cometh to me shall never hunger, and he that believeth on me shall never thirst. He that believeth on me hath eternal life.* I AM THE BREAD OF LIFE. THIS IS THE BREAD *which cometh down from heaven; that a man may eat thereof, and not die.* I AM THE LIVING BREAD *which came down from heaven; if any one shall eat* OF THIS BREAD, *he shall live for ever.* vi. 31 to 35, and 47 to 51. From these passages, and from what has been said above, it appears that bread is all the good which proceeds from the Lord, for the Lord Himself is in His own good; and thus that bread and wine in the holy supper are all worship of the Lord from the good of love and faith.

222. To the above shall be added some particulars from the A[r]CANA CŒLESTIA, n. 9127: "He who knows nothing of the intern[al] or spiritual sense of the Word, knows no other than that flesh a[nd] blood, when they are mentioned in the Word, mean natural fl[esh]

and blood. The internal sense, however, does not treat of the life of man's body, but of his soul, that is, of his spiritual life. which he is to live to eternity. This life is described in the literal sense of the Word, by things which belong to the life of the body, that is, by flesh and blood; and as the spiritual life of man subsists by the good of love and the truth of faith, therefore in the internal sense of the Word the good of love is meant by flesh, and the truth of faith by blood. These are understood by flesh and blood, and by bread and wine, in heaven; for bread means altogether the same there as flesh, and wine as blood. They who are not spiritual men, do not apprehend this; let such abide therefore in their own faith, only believing that in the holy supper, and in the Word, there is a sanctity, because they are from the Lord, although they may not know where that sanctity resides. On the other hand, let those who are endowed with interior perception, consider whether flesh means flesh, and blood, blood, in the following passages. In the Apocalypse: *I saw an angel standing in the sun, and he cried with a great voice, saying unto all the fowls that fly in the midst of heaven, Come and gather yourselves together to the supper of the great God; that ye may eat the flesh of kings, and the flesh of captains, and the flesh of mighty men, and the flesh of horses and of them that sit on them, and the flesh of all men, both free and bond, both small and great.* xix. 17, 18. Who can understand these words, unless he knows what flesh, kings, captains, mighty men, horses, them that sit on them, and freemen and bondmen, signify in the internal sense? And in Ezekiel: *Thus saith the Lord Jehovah: Say to every feathered fowl and to every beast of the field, Assemble yourselves and come; gather yourselves from every side to my sacrifice that I sacrifice for you, a great sacrifice upon the mountains of Israel, that ye may eat flesh and drink blood; ye shall eat the flesh of the mighty, and drink the blood of the princes of the earth; and ye shall eat fat till ye be full, and drink blood till ye be drunken, and of my sacrifice which I have sacrificed for you: thus shall ye be filled at my table, with horses and chariots, with mighty men, and with all men of war; and I will set my glory among the nations.* xxxix. 17, 18, 19, 20, 21. This passage treats of the calling together of all to the kingdom of the Lord, and in particular of the establishment of the church among the Gentiles; and eating flesh and drinking blood, signify to appropriate Divine Good and Divine Truth, thus the holy principle which proceeds from the Lord's Divine Humanity, to themselves. Who cannot see, that flesh does not here mean flesh, nor blood, blood; as when it is said, that they should eat the flesh of the mighty, and drink the blood of the princes of the earth, and that they should drink blood even to drunkenness; also that they should be filled with horses, with chariots, with mighty men, and with all men of war? What the feathered fowls and the beasts of the field signify in the spiritual sense, may be seen in the work ON HEAVEN AND HELL, n. 110 and the notes. Let us now consider what the Lord said concerning His flesh and His blood, in John: *The bread which I will give, is my flesh. Verily, verily, I say unto you, Except ye eat the flesh of the Son of Man, and drink His blood, ye have no life in you. Whoso eateth my flesh and drinketh my blood, hath eternal life, and I will raise him up at the last day; for my flesh is meat indeed, and my blood is drink indeed. He that eateth my flesh and drinketh my blood, dwelleth in me, and I in him. This is the bread which came down from heaven.* vi. 51 to 58. That the flesh of the Lord is Divine Good, and His blood, Divine Truth, each from Him, is evident, because these principles nourish the spiritual life of man: hence it is said, *My flesh is meat indeed, and my blood is drink indeed:* and as man is conjoined to the Lord by Divine Good and Truth, it is also said, *Whoso eateth my flesh and drinketh my blood, hath eternal life;* and, *He dwelleth in me and I in him;* and in the former part of the chapter, *Labor not for the meat which perisheth, but for that meat which endureth to eternal life.* verse 27. That to abide in the Lord is to be in love to Him, the Lord Himself teaches in John, chap. xv. 2—12."

OF THE RESURRECTION.

223. MAN is so created that, as to his internal, he cannot die; for he is capable of believing in and of loving God, and thus of being conjoined to God by faith and love; and to be thus conjoined to God is to live to eternity.

224. This internal exists in every man who is born: his external is that by which he brings into effect the things which belong to his faith and love. The internal of man is the spirit, and the external is the body. The external, or the body, is suited to the performance of uses in the natural world, and is rejected or put off at death; but the internal, which is called the spirit, and which is suited to the performance of uses in the spiritual world, never dies. After death, this internal exists as a good spirit and an angel, if the man had been good during his abode in his world, but if during that time he had lived in evil, he is, after death, an evil spirit.

225. The spirit of man, after the dissolution of the body, appears in the spiritual world in a human form, in every respect as in the natural world. He enjoys the faculty of sight, of hearing, of speaking, and of feeling, as he did in the world; and he is endowed with every faculty of thought, of will, and of action, as when he was in the world; in a word, he is a man in all respects, even to the most minute particular, except that he is not encompassed with the gross body which he had in the world. This he leaves when he dies, nor does he ever resume it.

226. This continuation of life is meant by the resurrection. The reason why men believe that they shall not rise again before the last judgment, when, as they suppose, the whole visible creation will be destroyed, is, that they do not understand the Word, and because sensual men place all their life in the

body, and imagine that unless the body be re-animated, the man can be no more.

227. The life of man after death is the life of his love and of his faith; hence the nature of his life to eternity is determined by the quality which had belonged to those during his life in the world. With those who loved themselves and the world supremely, this life is the life of hell; and with those who had loved God supremely, and the neighbor as themselves, it is the life of heaven. The latter are they who have faith; but the former are they who have no faith. The life of heaven is called eternal life, and the life of hell is called spiritual death.

228. That man continues to live after the death of the body, is plainly taught in the Word; as when it is said, that God is not the God of the dead, but of the living (Matt. xxii. 31); that Lazarus after death was carried into heaven, and that the rich man lifted up his eyes in hell (Luke xvi. 22, 23, and the following verses); that Abraham, Isaac, and Jacob, are in heaven (Matt. viii. 11; chap. xxii. 31, 32; Luke xxii. 37, 38); and when Jesus said to the thief on the cross, To-day shalt thou be with me in paradise (Luke xxiii. 43).

FROM THE WORK ON HEAVEN AND HELL.

229. It is unnecessary here to adduce from the Arcana Cœlestia any particulars concerning the resurrection and life of man after death, because these subjects have been fully treated in the work On Heaven and Hell, where they may be seen under the following articles. I. That every man is a spirit as to his interiors, n. 432 to 444. II. Of man's resuscitation from the dead, and his entrance into eternal life, n. 445 to 452. III. That after death man is in a perfect human form, n. 453 to 460. IV. That after death he retains every sense, and all the memory, thought, and affection, which he had in the world; and that he leaves nothing but his terrestrial body, n. 461 to 469. V. That man's nature after death is such as his life had been in the world, n. 470 to 484. VI. That the delights of every one's life are turned into corresponding things, n. 485 to 490. VII. Of man's first state after death, n. 491 to 498. VIII. Of his second state after death, n. 499 to 511. IX. Of his third state after death, which is a state of instruction for those that go to heaven, n. 512 to 520. X. That heaven and hell are from the human race, n. 311 to 317.

Concerning the last judgment, spoken of above at n. 226, see the work On the Last Judgment, and the Destruction of Babylon, throughout; where it is shown that the last judgment will not be attended with the destruction of the world.

OF HEAVEN AND HELL.

230. There are two things which constitute the life of man's spirit, namely, love and faith; love constituting the life of his will, and faith the life of his understanding. The love of good, and the faith of truth derived from good, constitute the life of heaven; and the love of evil, and the faith of the false thence derived, constitute the life of hell.

231. Love to the Lord and love towards the neighbor constitute heaven; and so does faith, so far as it derives life from those loves. And as each of these kinds of love, together with the faith thence derived, is from the Lord, it is evident that the Lord himself constitutes heaven.

232. Heaven is present with every man according to his reception of love and faith from the Lord; and they who receive heaven from the Lord during their abode in the world, are admitted into heaven after death.

233. They who receive heaven from the Lord are they who have heaven in them, for heaven is in man, as the Lord teaches: *Neither shall they say, Lo here! or, lo there! for the kingdom of God is within you.* Luke xvii. 21.

234. The abode of heaven in man is in his internal part, thus in his willing and thinking from love and faith, and thence in his external, which consists in acting and speaking from love and faith. But heaven is not in man's external without being in his internal; for all hypocrites are capable of acting and speaking well, but they are incapable of willing and thinking well.

235. On man's entering the other life, which takes place immediately after death, it is at once manifest whether heaven is in him or not; but this is not so manifest while he lives in the world. In the world the external appears, and the internal is concealed, but in the other life the internal is made manifest, because man then lives as to his spirit.

236. Eternal happiness, which is also called heavenly joy, is imparted to those who possess love to the Lord, and faith in Him derived from Him; for this love and faith have that happiness in them; and into the full enjoyment of it, the man who has heaven in him comes after death; in the meantime it lies stored up in his internal man. In the heavens there is a mutual participation of every good; the peace, the intelligence, the wisdom, and the happiness of all are communicated to each; yet to every one according to his reception of love and faith from the Lord. Hence it may be seen in how high a degree these enjoyments exist in heaven.

237. As love to the Lord and love towards the neighbor constitute the life of heaven in man, so the love of self and the

love of the world, when they reign, constitute the life of hell; for the two latter loves are in direct opposition to the two former. Those, therefore, in whom the loves of self and of the world reign, are incapable of receiving anything from heaven, so that what they receive comes from hell; for whatever a man loves, and whatever he believes, is either from heaven or from hell.

238. Those in whom the love of self and the love of the world predominate, can form no conception of heaven and heavenly happiness; and it even appears incredible to them that happiness should be found in anything but that in which they themselves delight. Nevertheless, the happiness of heaven enters the soul only in proportion as the loves of self and the world, regarded as ends, are removed; and the happiness which succeeds on their removal is so great as to exceed all human comprehension.

239. The life of man cannot be changed after death, but must forever remain such as it had been in this world; for the quality of man's spirit is in every respect the same as that of his love, and infernal love can never be transcribed into heavenly love, because they are in direct opposition to each other. This is what is meant by the words of Abraham addressed to the rich man in hell: *Between us and you there is a great gulf fixed; so that they which would pass from hence to you cannot; neither can they pass to us that would come from thence.* Luke xvi. 26. Hence it is evident, that all who go to hell remain there to eternity, and that all who go to heaven remain there to eternity.

---

240. Since the subject of heaven and hell has been treated of in a separate work, wherein is also adduced what is contained in the Arcana Cœlestia concerning it, it is therefore unnecessary here to add anything further.

OF THE CHURCH.

241. That which constitutes heaven with man, also constitutes the church with him; for as love and faith constitute heaven, so they also constitute the church; thus, from what has been already said concerning heaven, it may evidently be seen what the church is.

242. The church is said [to be] where the Lord is acknowledged and the Word exists, for the essentials of the church are love to the Lord, and faith in Him, both derived from Him; and the Word plainly teaches how man must live in order that he may receive love and faith from the Lord

243. In order to the existence of a church, there must be doctrine formed from the Word, since without doctrine the Word cannot be understood. Doctrine alone, however, does not constitute the church with man, but a life according to that doctrine; hence faith alone does not constitute the church with man, but the life of faith, which is charity. Genuine doctrine is the doctrine of charity and faith united, and not that of faith separate from charity; the doctrine of charity and faith united, is the doctrine of life, but the doctrine of faith without that of charity is not so.

244. They who are without the church, but at the same time acknowledge one God, and live according to the religious principles in which they have been instructed, and in a corresponding degree of charity towards the neighbor, are in communion with those who are within the church; for no man who believes in God and lives well, is damned. Hence it is evident, that the church of the Lord exists in every part of the world, although specifically, where the Lord is acknowledged, and where the Word is known.

245. Every man in whom the church exists, is saved; but every man in whom it does not exist, is condemned.

FROM THE ARCANA CŒLESTIA.

246. That the church exists specifically where the Word is, and where the Lord is thereby known, and thus where Divine Truths are revealed, n. 3857, 10,761. That still they who are born where the Word is, and where the Lord is thereby known, are not of the church, but they who are regenerated by the Lord by the truths of the Word, that is, they who live a life of charity, n. 6637, 10,143, 10,153, 10,578, 10,645, 10,829. That they who belong to the church, or in whom the church is, are in the affection of truth for the sake of truth, that is, they love truth because it is truth; and they examine from the Word whether the doctrinals of the church in which they were born are true, n. 5432, 6047. Otherwise the truth possessed by every one would be derived from another, and from his native soil, n. 6047.

That the church of the Lord is with all in the universal world who live in good according to their religious [principles], n. 3263, 6637, 10,765. That all who live in good, and acknowledge one God, are accepted by the Lord and enter heaven; since all who are in good acknowledge the Lord, because good is from the Lord, and the Lord is in good, n. 2589 to 2604, 2861, 2863, 3263, 4190, 4197, 6700, 9256. That the universal church on earth before the Lord is as one man, n. 7395, 9276. As heaven is, because the church is the heaven or kingdom of the Lord on earth, n. 2853, 2996, 2998, 3624 to 3649, 3636 to 3643, 3741 to 3745, 4625. But that the church, where the Lord is known and where the Word exists, is like the heart and lungs in man in respect to the other parts of the body, which live from the heart and lungs as the fountains of their life, n. 637, 931, 2054, 2853. Hence it is, that unless there were a church which possesses the Word, and where the Lord is thereby known, the human race could not be saved, n. 468, 637, 931, 4545, 10,452. That the church is the basis of heaven, n. 4060.

That the church is internal and external, n. 1242, 6587, 9375, 9680, 10,762. That the internal of the church is love to the Lord and charity towards the neighbor; consequently, that they who are in the affection of good and truth from love to the Lord and from charity towards the neighbor, constitute the internal church; and that they who are in external worship from obedience and faith, constitute the external church, n. 1083, 1098, 4288, 6380, 6587, 7840, 8762. That to know truth and good, and to act from thence, is the external of the church, but to will and love truth and good, and to act from thence, is the internal of the church, n. 4899, 6775. That the internal of the church is in the worship of those who are of the external church, although in obscurity, n. 6775. That the internal and external church constitute one church, n. 409, 10,762. That man has an internal and an external, an internal after the image of heaven, and an external after the image of the world; and that therefore, in order that the man may be a church, his external must act in unity with his internal, n. 3628, 4523, 4524, 6057, 6314, 9706, 10,472. That the church is in the internal of man and at the same time in the external, but not in the external without being in the internal, n. 1795, 6581, 10,691. That the internal of the church is according to truths and their quality, and according to their implantation in good by means of life, n. 1238.

That the church is in man as heaven is, and thus that the church in general consists of the men in whom the church is, n. 3884. In order that a church may exist, there must be a doctrine of life, that is, a doctrine of charity, n. 3445, 10,763, 10,764. That charity constitutes the church, and not faith separated from charity, n. 916. Consequently, not the doctrine of faith separated from charity, but the doctrine of faith conjoined therewith, and a life conformable to it, n. 809, 1798, 1799, 1834, 1844, 4468, 4672, 4676, 4766, 5828, 6637. That the church is not with man, unless the truths of doctrine are implanted in the good of charity with him, thus in the life, n. 3310, 3963, 5826. That there is no church with man, if he is only in truths, which are termed matters of faith, n. 5826. How much good would be in the church, if charity were in the first place and faith in the second, n. 6269. And how much evil, if faith is in the first place, n. 6272. That in the ancient churches charity was the principal and essential of the church, n. 4680. That the church would be like heaven, if all had charity, n. 2385, 2853. That if good were the characteristic of the church, and not truth without good, thus if charity were its characteristic, and not faith separate, the church would be one, and differences with respect to the doctrinals of faith, and external worship, would be accounted as nothing, n. 1285, 1316, 2982, 3267, 3445, 3451.

That every church begins from charity, but declines therefrom in process of time, n. 494, 501, 1327, 3773, 4649. Thus to falses from evil, and at length to evils, n. 1834, 1835, 2910, 4683, 4689. A comparison of a church at its beginning and decline with the infancy and old age of man, n. 10,134. And also with the rising and setting of the sun, n. 1837. Concerning the successive states of the Christian church, down to its last state; wherein are explained the particulars which the Lord foretold concerning the consummation of the age, and His coming, in Matthew, chap. xxiv. to the end, n. 3353 to 3356, 3486 to 3489, 3650 to 3655, 3571 to 3759, 3897 to 3901, 4057 to 4060, 4229 to 4231, 4332 to 4335, 4422 to 4424, 4635 to 4638, 4807 to 4810, 4954 to 4959, 5063 to 5071. That the Christian church is at this day in its last states, there being no faith therein because there is no charity, n. 3489, 4649. That the last judgment is the last time of the church, n. 2118, 3353, 4057, 4333, 4535. Of the vastation of the church, n. 407 to 411. That the consummation of the age and the coming of the Lord is the last time of the old church and the beginning of the new, n. 2243, 4535, 10,622. That when the old church is vastated, interior truths are revealed for the service of the new church which is then established, n. 3398, 3786. Concerning the establishment of the church with the Gentiles, n. 1366, 2986, 4747, 9256.

247. *Of the ancient churches.* That the first and most ancient church in this world was that which is described in the first chapters of Genesis, and that it was a celestial church, and the chief of all the rest, n. 607, 895, 920, 1121, 1122, 1123, 1124, 2896, 4493, 8891, 9942, 10,545. Of the states of those in heaven who belonged to it, n. 1114 to 1125. That they are in the highest degree of light, n. 1116, 1117. That there were various churches after the flood, called in one word, the ancient church, concerning which, see n. 1125, 1126, 1127, 1327, 10,355. Through how many kingdoms of Asia the ancient church was extended, n. 1238, 2385. The quality of the men of the ancient church, n. 609, 895. That the ancient church was a representative church, and that its representatives were collected into one by certain men of the most ancient church, n. 519, 521, 2896. That the ancient church was in possession of a Word, but that it was afterwards lost, n. 2897. The quality of the ancient church when it began to decline, n. 1128. The difference between the ancient and most ancient churches, n. 597, 607, 640, 641, 765, 684, 895, 4493. That both of them existed in Canaan, and that hence came the representative significations of the places therein, n. 3686, 4447, 4454. Of the church that began from Eber, which was called the Hebrew church, n. 1238, 1241, 1343, 4516, 4517. The difference between the ancient and Hebrew churches, n. 1342, 4874. That Eber instituted sacrifices which were wholly unknown in the ancient churches, n. 1343. That the ancient churches accorded with the Christian church as to internals, but not as to externals, n. 3478, 4489, 4772, 4904, 10,149. That in the most ancient church there was immediate revelation; in the ancient church, revelation by correspondences; in the Jewish church, by a living voice; and in the Christian church, by the Word, n. 10,355. That the Lord was the God of the most ancient church, and was called Jehovah, n. 1343, 6846. That the Lord is heaven, and that he is the church, n. 4766, 10,125 10,151, 10,157 That the Divine

of the Lord constitutes heaven, see the work ON HEAVEN AND HELL, n. 7 to 12, and 78 to 86; and thus also the church, since what constitutes heaven with man, constitutes also the church, as was shown in the doctrine above.

248. *Of the Jewish church and of the Jews.* That the statutes, judgments and laws, which were commanded in the Jewish church, were in part like those in the ancient church, n. 4449, 4834. In what respect the representative rites of the Jewish church differed from those of the ancient church, n. 4288, 10,149. That a representative church was instituted with that nation, but that there was no church in that nation itself, n. 4899, 4912, 6304. That therefore with respect to that nation itself, it was the representative of a church, but not a church, n. 4281, 4288, 4311, 4500, 6304, 7048, 9320, 10,396, 10,526, 10,531, 10,698. That the Israelitish and Jewish nation was not elected, but only received, in order that it might represent a church, on account of the obstinacy with which their fathers and Moses demanded it, n. 4290, 4293, 7051, 7439, 10,430, 10,535, 10,632. That their worship was merely external, without any internal worship, n. 1200, 3147, 3479, 8871. That they were entirely unacquainted with the internals of worship, and were not willing to know them, n. 301, 302, 303, 3479, 4429, 4433, 4680, 4844, 4897, 10,396, 10,401, 10,407, 10,694, 10,701, 10,707. In what manner they consider the internals of worship, of the church, and the Word, n. 4865. That their interiors were filthy, full of the loves of self and of the world, and of avarice, n. 3480, 9962, 10,454 to 10,457, 10,462 to 10,466, 10,575. That on this account the internals of the church were not discovered to them, because they would have profaned them, n. 2520, 3398, 3480, 4289. That the Word is wholly shut to them, n. 3769. That they see the Word from without and not from within, n. 10,549, 10,550, 10,551. That therefore their internal, when in worship, was shut, n. 8788, 8806, 9320, 9380, 9377, 9962, 10,390, 10,401, 10,407, 10,492, 10,498, 10,500, 10,575, 10,629, 10,692. That that nation was of such a quality, that they could be in a holy external, when the internal was shut, more than others, n. 4293, 4311, 4903, 9373, 9377, 9381. Their state at that time, n. 4311. That they are therefore preserved to this day, n. 3479. That their holy external was miraculously elevated by the Lord into heaven, and the interior things of worship, of the church, and the Word perceived thereby, n. 3480, 4309, 4311, 6304, 8588, 10,492, 10,500, 10.602. That for this purpose they were forced by external means strictly to observe their rites in their external form, n. 3147, 4281, 10,149. That because they were capable of being in a holy external without an internal, they were capable of representing the holy things of the church and heaven, n. 3479, 3881, 4208, 6306, 6588, 9377, 10,430, 10,500, 10,570. That still those holy things did not affect them, n. 3479. That the quality of the person who represents is of no importance, because the representation respects the thing represented, and not the person, n. 665, 1097, 1361, 3147, 3881, 4208, 4285, 4288, 4292, 4307, 4444, 4500, 6304, 7048, 7439, 8388, 8788, 8806.

That that nation was worse than other nations, with a description of their quality from the Word of both the Old and New Testa-

..ents, n. 4314, 4316, 4317, 4444, 4503, 4750, 4741, 4815, 4820, 4832, 5057, 5998, 7248, 8819, 9320, 10,454 to 10,547, 10,462 to 10,466. That the tribe of Judah was guilty of worse actions than the other tribes, n. 4815. How cruelly they treated the Gentiles, from delight, n. 5057, 7248, 9320. That that nation was idolatrous in heart, and more than other nations worshiped other gods, n. 3732, 4208, 4444, 4825, 5998, 6877, 7401, 8301, 8871, 8882. That even their worship was idolatrous when considered with respect to that nation itself, because it was external without internal, n. 4281, 4825, 8871, 8882. That they worshiped Jehovah only in name, n. 6877, 10,559, 10,560, 10,561, 10,566. And on account of miracles, n. 4299. That they who believe that the Jews will be converted at the end of the church, and brought again into the land of Canaan, think erroneously, n. 4847, 7051, 8301. Many passages adduced from the Word concerning this matter, but which are to be understood according to the internal sense, and differently from the sense of the letter, n. 7051. That the Word was changed on account of that nation, as to its external sense, but not as to its internal sense, n. 10,453, 10,461, 10,603, 10,604. That Jehovah appeared to them on Mount Sinai, according to their quality, in a consuming fire, a thick cloud, and smoke as of a furnace, n. 1861, 6832, 8814, 8819, 9434. That the Lord appears to every one according to his quality, as a vivifying and recreating fire to those who are in good, and as a consuming fire to those who are in evil, n. 934, 1861, 6832, 8814, 8819, 9434, 10,551. That one origin of that nation was from a Canaanite, and the two others from whoredom with a daughter-in-law, n. 1167, 4817, 4820, 4874, 4891, 4913. That these origins signify the nature of their conjunction with the church, as being like conjunction with the Canaanite, and whoredom with a daughter-in-law, n. 4868, 4874, 4899, 4911, 4913. Of the state of the Jews in the other life, n. 939, 940, 5057.

Since this nation, although of such a quality, represented the church; and since the Word was written among them and concerning them; therefore Divine Celestial things were signified by their names, as by Reuben, Simeon, Levi, Judah, Ephraim, Joseph, and the rest. That Judah, in the internal sense, signifies the Lord as to celestial love, and his celestial kingdom, n. 3654, 3881, 5583, 5603, 5782, 6363. The prophecy of Israel concerning Judah, in which the Lord is treated of, explained, Gen. xlix. 8 to 12; n. 6362 to 6382. That the tribe of Judah and Judea signify the celestial church, n. 3654, 6364. That the twelve tribes represented, and thence signified all things of love and faith in the complex, n. 3858, 3926, 4060, 6335; consequently also heaven and the church, n. 6337, 6637, 7836, 7891. That they signify according to the order in which they are named, n. 3862, 3926, 3939, 4603, *seq.* 6637, 6640. That the twelve tribes were divided into two kingdoms, in order that the Jews might represent the celestial kingdom, and the Israelites the spiritual kingdom, n. 8770, 9320. That the seed of Abraham, of Isaac, and of Jacob, signifies the goods and truths of the church, n. 3773, 10,445

OF THE SACRED SCRIPTURES, OR THE WORD.

249. WITHOUT a Divine revelation, man could know nothing of eternal life, or even of God; still less of love to God and of faith in Him; for man is born in utter ignorance, and must obtain all his knowledge, and form his understanding, from worldly objects. Moreover, man inherits by birth every evil proceeding from the love of self and the world; and the delights thence arising continually prevail, and insinuate into his mind things which are diametrically opposed to whatever is of God. Hence it is, that man is naturally destitute of the knowledge of eternal life; and hence the necessity of a Divine revelation, to communicate to him such knowledge.

250. That the evils of the love of self and of the world induce such ignorance concerning the things which relate to eternal life, manifestly appears from the case of many within the church, the learned as well as the unlearned, who, although they know from revelation that there is a God, that there is a heaven and a hell, that there is eternal life, and that that life is to be acquired by the good of love and faith, still lapse into unbelief concerning those subjects. Hence it is evident to what an awful extent ignorance would prevail, had no revelation been given.

251. Since, therefore, man lives after death, and even lives to eternity; and since the nature of his life to eternity is determined by that of his love and his faith; it follows that the Divine Being, in his love towards the human race, has revealed such things as may lead to that life, and conduce to man's salvation. What He has thus revealed, forms with us the Word.

252. As the Word is a revelation from God, it is Divine in all its parts, and in every particular; for what proceeds from God cannot be otherwise. That which proceeds from God descends through the heavens down to man; wherefore in the heavens it is accommodated to the wisdom of the angels who are there, and on earth it is accommodated to the apprehension of man. There is therefore in the Word an internal sense, which is spiritual, and suited to the capacity of the angels; and an external sense which is natural, and is intended for man. Hence it is that the conjunction of heaven with man is effected by the Word.

253. The genuine sense of the Word is understood only by those who are enlightened; and none are enlightened but those who have love to the Lord and faith in Him: the interior perceptions of such are elevated by the Lord into the light of heaven.

254. The Word cannot be understood in the letter, except by doctrine derived from it, by one who is enlightened; for the literal sense of the Word is accommodated to the apprehension

even of simple men ; wherefore doctrine drawn from the Word must be given them for a light.

FROM THE ARCANA CŒLESTIA.

255. Of *the Necessity and Excellency of the Word.* That from the light [*lumen*] of nature, nothing can be known concerning the Lord, concerning heaven and hell, concerning the life of man after death, and concerning the Divine Truths whereby man acquires spiritual and eternal life, n. 8944, 10,318, 10,319, 10,320. That this may be manifest from the fact, that many, and amongst them some who are learned, do not believe in such things, although they are born where the Word is, and are thereby instructed concerning them, n. 10,319. That it was therefore necessary that there should be some revelation from heaven, because man was born for heaven, n. 1775. That therefore in every age there has been a revelation, n. 2895. Concerning the various kinds of revelation which have been successively made on this earth, n. 10,355, 10,632. That the most ancient people who lived before the flood, and whose age was called the golden age, had immediate revelation, and hence Divine Truth was inscribed on their hearts, n. 2896. That in the ancient churches which were after the flood, there was a Word, both historical and prophetical, n. 2686, 2897; *concerning which churches, see above*, n. 247. That its historical parts were called the Wars of Jehovah, and its prophetical parts, Enunciations, n. 2897. That that Word was like our Word with respect to inspiration, n. 2897. That it is mentioned by Moses, n. 2686, 2897. But that that Word is lost, n. 2897. That there were also prophetic revelations with others, as appears from the prophecies of Balaam, n. 2898.

That the Word is Divine in the whole and in every particular part, n. 639, 680, 10,321, 10,637. That the Word is Divine and holy as to every iota and point, from experience, n. 1349. How it is explained at this day, that the Word is inspired as to every iota, n. 1886.

That the church exists specifically where the Word is, and where the Lord is thereby known and Divine Truths are revealed, n. 3857, 10,761. But that it does not follow from hence, that they are of the church who are born where the Word is, and where the Lord is thereby known, but they who by means of truths from the Word are regenerated by the Lord, that is, who live according to the truths therein, or lead a life of love and of faith, n. 6637, 10,143, 10,153, 10,578, 10,645, 10,829.

256. *That the Word is not understood except by those who are enlightened.* That the human rational [principle] cannot apprehend Divine things, nor even spiritual things, unless it is enlightened by the Lord, n. 2196, 2203, 2209, 2654. Thus that only they who are enlightened apprehend the Word, n. 10,323. That the Lord enables those who are enlightened, to understand truth, and to see how to reconcile those things in the Word which may appear to contradict

each other, n. 9382, 10,659. That the Word in the literal sense is not consistent with itself, and sometimes appears contradictory, n. 9025. And that therefore it may be explained and strained by those who are not enlightened, to confirm any opinion or heresy whatever, and to patronise any worldly and corporeal love, n. 4783, 10,399, 10,401. That they who read the Word from the love of truth and good, are enlightened from it, but not they who read it from the love of fame, gain, or honor, thus from the love of self, n. 9382, 10,548, 10,549, 10,550. That they who are in the good of life, and thereby in the affection of truth, are enlightened, n. 8694. That they whose internal is open, and who thus as to their internal man are capable of being elevated into the light of heaven, are enlightened, n. 10,401, 10,402, 10,691, 10,694. That enlightenment is an actual opening of the interiors of the mind, and elevation of them into the light of heaven, n. 10,330. That a holy [principle] from the internal, that is, through the internal from the Lord, inflows with those who esteem the Word to be holy, though they themselves are ignorant thereof, n. 6789. That they who are led by the Lord are enlightened, and see truths in the Word, but not they who are led by self, n. 10,638. That they who love truth because it is truth, that is, who love to live according to Divine Truths, are led by the Lord, n. 10,578, 10,645, 10,829. That the Word is vivified with man, according to his life of love and faith, n. 1776. That those things which are from self-intelligence have no life in them, since nothing good proceeds from man's proprium, n. 8491, 8944. That they who have much confirmed themselves in false doctrine, are incapable of enlightenment, n. 10,640.

That the understanding is enlightened, n. 6608, 9300. Because the understanding is recipient of truth, n. 6242, 6608, 10,659. That there are ideas concerning every doctrinal of the church, according to which is the understanding of the subject, n. 3310, 3825. That a man's ideas, so long as he lives in the world, are natural, because he then thinks in the natural [principle], but that nevertheless spiritual ideas lie concealed therein with those who are in the affection of truth for the sake of truth, n. 10,236, 10,240, 10,550. That there is no perception of any subject without ideas, n. 3825. That our ideas concerning the things of faith are opened in the other life, and their quality is then seen by the angels, n. 1869, 3310, 5510, 6201, 8885. That therefore the Word is not understood except by a rational man; for to believe anything without having an idea of the subject, and without a rational view of it, is only to retain words in the memory, destitute of all life of perception and affection, which is not believing, n. 2553. That the literal sense of the Word is what is enlightened, n. 3619, 9824, 9905, 10,548.

257. *That the Word cannot be understood but by means of doctrine from the Word.* That the doctrine of the church must be from the Word, n. 3464, 5402, 6832, 10,763, 10,765. That the Word without doctrine is not understood, n. 9025, 9409, 9424, 9430, 10,324, 10,431, 10,582. That true doctrine is a lamp to those who read the Word, n. 10,401. That genuine doctrine must be formed by those who are in enlightenment from the Lord, n. 2510, 2516, 2519, 2524, 10,105. That the Word is rendered intelligible by means of doc-

trine formed by one who is enlightened, n. 10,324. That they who are in enlightenment form doctrine for themselves from the Word, n. 9382, 10,659. The difference between those who teach and learn from the doctrine of the church, and those who teach and learn only from the literal sense of the Word, described, n. 9025. That they who abide in the literal sense of the Word, without doctrine, attain no understanding of Divine Truths, n. 9409, 9410, 10,582. That they fall into many errors, n. 10,431. That they who are in the affection of truth for the sake of truth, when they arrive at adult age, and are capable of using their own understanding, do not simply abide in the doctrinals of their own church, but examine from the Word whether they are truths, n. 5402, 5432, 6047. That otherwise every man's truth would be derived from others, and from his native soil, whether he were born a Jew or a Greek, n. 6047. That nevertheless such things as are become matters of faith from the literal sense of the Word, ought not to be rejected till after a full view, n. 9039.

That the true doctrine of the church is the doctrine of charity and faith, n. 2417, 4766, 10,763, 10,765. That the doctrine of faith does not constitute the church, but the life of faith, which is charity, n. 809, 1798, 1799, 1834, 4468, 4677, 4766, 5826, 6637. That doctrinals are of no value unless the life be directed by them, n. 1515, 2049, 2116. That in the churches at this day the doctrine of faith is taught, and not the doctrine of charity, the latter being degraded into a science which is called moral theology, n. 2417. That the church would be one, if men were acknowledged as members of the church according to their life, thus according to their charity, n. 1285, 1316, 2982, 3267, 3445, 3451, 3452. How much superior the doctrine of charity is to that of faith separate from charity, n. 4844. That they who do not know any thing concerning charity, are in ignorance concerning heavenly things, n. 2435. Into how many errors they fall who only hold the doctrine of faith, and not that of charity at the same time, n. 2417, 2383, 3146, 3325, 3412, 3413, 3416, 3773, 4672, 4730, 4783, 4925, 5351, 7623 to 7677, 7752 to 7762, 7790, 8094, 8313, 8530, 8765, 9186, 9224, 10,555. That they who are only in the doctrine of faith, and not in the life of faith, which is charity, were formerly called uncircumcised, or Philistines, n. 3412, 3413, 8093. That the ancients held the doctrine of love to the Lord, and of charity towards the neighbor, and made the doctrine of faith subservient thereto, n. 2417, 3419, 4844, 4955.

That doctrine deduced from the Word by an enlightened person, may be afterwards confirmed by means of rational [arguments], and that thus it is more fully understood, and is corroborated, n. 2553, 2719, 2720, 3052, 3310, 6047. *See more on this subject at* n. 51 *above.* That they who are in faith separate from charity would have the doctrinals of the church implicitly believed, without any rational intuition, n. 3394.

That it is not the part of a wise man to confirm a dogma, but to see whether it is true before he confirms it, as is the case with those who are in enlightenment, n. 1017, 4741, 7012, 7680, 7950. That the light of confirmation is natural light, and not spiritual, and may exist even with the evil, n. 8780. That all things, even falses, are capable of being confirmed so as to appear like truths, n. 2482, 2490, 5033, 6865, 8521.

258. *That in the Word there is a spiritual sense, which is called the internal sense.* That no one can know what the internal sense of the Word is, unless he know what correspondence is, 2895, 4322. That the whole and every part, even to the most minute, of the natural world, corresponds to spiritual things, and thence is significative of them, n. 2890 to 2893, 2897 to 3003, 3212 to 3227. That the spiritual things to which natural things correspond assume another appearance in the natural, so that they are not distinguished, n. 1887, 2396, 8920. That scarcely any one knows at this day, where, or in what part of the Word, its divinity is seated, when nevertheless it is in its internal or spiritual sense, which at this day is not known even to exist, n. 2890, 4989. That the mystery (*mysticum*) of the Word is nothing else than what its internal or spiritual sense contains, which treats of the Lord, of His kingdom, and of the church, and not of the natural things which are in the world, n. 4923. That the prophetic parts of the Word are in many places unintelligible, and therefore of no use without the internal sense; illustrated by examples, n. 2608, 8020, 8398. As with respect to what is signified by the White Horse, mentioned in the Apocalypse, n. 2760, *seq.* By the keys of the kingdom of the heavens that were given to Peter, see the preface to the 22nd chapter of Genesis, n. 9410. By the flesh, blood, bread, and wine, in the Holy Supper, and thus why it was instituted by the Lord, n. 8682. By the prophecies of Jacob concerning his sons in the 49th chapter of Genesis, n. 6306, 6333 to 6465. By many prophecies concerning Judah and Israel, which by no means tally with that people, nor in the literal sense have any coincidence with their history, n. 6331, 6361, 6415, 6438, 6444. Besides innumerable other instances, n. 2608.

Of the spiritual or internal sense of the Word in general, n. 1767 to 1777, 1869 to 1879. That there is an internal sense in the whole and in every particular part of the Word, n. 1143, 1984, 2135, 2333, 2395, 2495, 2619. That such things do not appear in the sense of the letter, but that nevertheless they are contained within it, n. 4442.

259. *That the internal sense of the Word is principally for the use of angels, and that it is also for the use of men.* In order that it may be known what the internal sense is, of what quality it is, and whence it is, it may here be observed in general, that speech and thought in heaven differ from speech and thought in the world; in heaven they are spiritual, but in the world they are natural; while, therefore, man is reading the Word, the angels who are with him perceive it spiritually, whilst he perceives it naturally; of consequence, the angels are in the internal sense, whilst men are in the external sense; nevertheless these two senses make one by correspondence.

That the Word is understood differently by the angels in the heavens and by men on earth, the angels perceiving the internal or spiritual sense, whilst men see only the external or natural sense n. 1887, 2396. That the angels perceive the W·rd in its internal sense, and not in its external sense, proved from the experience of those who spake with me from heaven, whilst I was reading the Word, n. 1769, 1770, 1771, 1772. That the ideas and speech of the angels are spiritual, but the ideas and speech of men are natural; that therefore there is an internal sense, which is spiritual, for the use of the angels, illustrated by experience, n. 2333. That nevertheless the literal sense of the Word serves the spiritual ideas of the angels as a medium of conveyance, just as the words of speech serve men to convey the sense of the subject whereon they converse, n. 2143. That the things relating to the internal sense of the Word, are such as belong to the light of heaven, and are therefore adapted to the perception of angels, n. 2618, 2619, 2629, 3086. That the things which the angels perceive from the Word are on this account precious to them, n. 2540, 2541, 2545, 2551. That the angels do not understand a single syllable of the letter of the Word, n. 64, 65, 1434, 1929. That they are unacquainted with the names of persons and places mentioned in the Word, n. 1434, 1888, 4442, 4480. That names cannot enter heaven, nor be pronounced there, n. 1876, 1888. That all names mentioned in the Word, signify things, and in heaven are changed into the ideas of the thing which they signify, n. 768, 1888, 4310, 4442, 5225, 5287, 10,329. That the angels think abstractedly from persons, n. 6613, 8343, 8985, 9007. How elegant the internal sense of the Word is, even where nothing but mere names occur, shown by examples from the Word, n. 1224, 1888, 2395. That many names in a series express one thing in the internal sense, n. 5905. That all numbers in the Word signify things, n. 482, 487, 647, 648, 755, 813, 1963, 1988, 2075, 2252, 3152, 4264, 6175, 9488, 9659, 10,217, 10,253. That spirits perceive the Word in its internal sense, so far as their interiors are open to heaven, n. 1771. That the literal sense of the Word, which is natural, is changed instantly with the angels into the spiritual sense, because there is a correspondence between the two senses, n. 5648. And that this is effected without their hearing or knowing what is contained in the literal or external sense, n. 10,215. Thus that the literal or external sense is confined to man, and proceeds no further, n. 2015.

That there is an internal sense of the Word, and likewise an inmost or supreme sense, concerning which see n. 9407, 10,604, 10,614, 10,627. That the spiritual angels, that is, those who belong to the spiritual kingdom of the Lord, perceive the Word in its internal sense, and that the celestial angels, that is, those who belong to the celestial kingdom of the Lord, perceive the Word in its inmost sense, n. 2157, 2275.

That the Word is for the use of men, and also for the use of angels, being accommodated to each, n. 7381, 8862, 10,322. That the Word is the medium of union between heaven and earth, n. 2310, 3495, 9212, 9216, 9357. That the conjunction of heaven with man is effected by means of the Word, n. 9396, 9400, 9401, 10,452. That therefore the Word is called a covenant, n. 9396. Because covenant signifies conjunction, n. 665, 666, 1023, 1038, 1864, 1996, 2003, 2021, 6804, 8767, 8778, 9396, 10,632. That there is an internal sense in the Word, in consequence of the Word having descended from the Lord through the three heavens to man, n. 2310, 6597. And that thereby it is accommodated to the angels of the three heavens, and also to men, n. 7381, 8862. Hence it is that the Word is Divine, n. 2980, 4989. And that it is holy, n. 10,276. And that it is spiritual, n. 4480. And that it is divinely inspired, n. 9094. That this is the meaning of inspiration, n. 9094.

That the regenerate man also, is actually in the internal sense of the Word, although he knows it not, since his internal man, which is endowed with spiritual perception, is open, n. 10,401. But that in this case the spiritual [principle] of the Word flows into natural ideas, and thus is presented naturally, because, while man lives in the world, he thinks in the natural [principle], n. 5614. That hence the light of truth, with the enlightened, is from their internal, that is, through their internal from the Lord, n. 10,691, 10,694. That by the same way a holy [principle] flows in with those who esteem the Word holy, n. 6789. As the regenerate man is actually in the internal sense of the Word, and in the sanctity of that sense, notwithstanding his ignorance of it, that therefore after death he comes into it, and is no longer in the sense of the letter, n. 3226, 3342, 3343.

260. *That the internal or spiritual sense of the Word contains innumerable arcana.* That the Word in its internal sense contains innumerable things, which exceed human comprehension, n. 3085, 3086. That it also contains inexplicable things, n. 1965. Which are represented only to angels, and understood by them, n. 167. That the internal sense of the Word contains arcana of heaven, which relate to the Lord and His kingdom in the heavens and on earth, n. 1, 2, 3, 4, 937. That those arcana do not appear in the sense of the letter, n. 937, 1502, 2161. That many things in the writings of the prophets, appear to be unconnected, when yet in their internal sense they cohere in a regular and beautiful connexion, n. 7153, 9022. That not a single word, nor even a single iota can be omitted in the literal sense of the Word, without an interruption in the internal sense, and that therefore, by the Divine Providence of the Lord, the Word has been preserved so entire as to every word and every point, n. 7933. That innumerable things are contained in every particular part of the Word, n. 6637, 6620, 8920. And in every expression, n. 1689. That there are innumerable things contained in the Lord's prayer, and in every part thereof, n. 6619. And in the precepts of the Decalogue; in the external sense of which, notwithstanding, some things are such as are known to every nation without revelation, n. 8867, 8900.

That in the Word, and particularly in the prophetical parts of it, two expressions are used that seem to signify the same thing, but that one expression has relation to good, and the other to truth; thus one relates to what is spiritual, the other to what is celestial, n. 683, 707, 2516, 8339. That good and truth are conjoined in a wonderful manner in the Word, and that that conjunction is apparent only to him who is acquainted with the internal sense, n. 10,554. And thus that there is a Divine marriage and a heavenly marriage in the Word, and in every part thereof, n. 683, 793, 801, 2173, 2516, 2712, 5138, 7022. That the Divine marriage is the marriage of Divine Good and Divine Truth, thus it is the Lord, in whom alone that marriage exists, n. 3004, 3005, 3009, 4158, 5194, 5502, 6343, 7945, 8339, 9263, 9314. That Jesus signifies Divine Good, and Christ Divine Truth; and both the Divine marriage in heaven, which is the marriage of Divine Good and Divine Truth, n. 3004, 3005, 3009. That this marriage is in every part of the Word, in its internal sense; thus the Lord, as to Divine Good and Divine Truth, is in every part of the Word, n. 5502. That the marriage of good and truth from the Lord in heaven and the church, is called the heavenly marriage, n. 2508, 2618, 2803, 3004, 3211, 3952, 6179. That therefore in this respect the Word is a kind of heaven, n. 2173, 10,126. That heaven is compared in the Word to a marriage, on account of the marriage of good and truth therein, n. 2758, 3132, 4434, 4834.

That the internal sense is the essential doctrine of the church, n. 9025, 9430, 10,401. That they who understand the Word according to the internal sense, understand the essential true doctrine of the church, inasmuch as the internal sense contains it, n. 9025, 9430, 10,401. That the internal of the Word is also the internal of the church, and likewise the internal of worship, n. 10,460. That the Word is the doctrine of love to the Lord, and of charity towards the neighbor, n. 3419, 3420.

That the Word in the letter is as a cloud, and that in the internal sense it is glory, see the Preface to the 18th chapter of Genesis, n. 5922, 6343, where the words, *The Lord shall come in the clouds of heaven with glory*, are explained. That a cloud in the Word signifies the Word in the literal sense, and that glory signifies the Word in the internal sense, see the Preface to the 18th chapter of Genesis, n. 4060, 4391, 5922, 6343, 6752, 8106, 8781, 9430, 10,551, 10,574. That those things which are in the literal sense, respectively to those which are in the internal sense, are like rude projections round a polished optical cylinder, by which nevertheless is exhibited in the cylinder a beautiful image of a man, n. 1871. That in the other life, they who only allow and acknowledge the literal sense of the Word, are represented by a deformed old woman; but they who allow and acknowledge the internal sense, together with the literal sense, are represented by a virgin beautifully clad, n. 1774. That the Word in its whole complex is an image of heaven, since the Word is Divine Truth, and Divine Truth constitutes heaven; and as heaven resembles one man, that therefore the Word is in that respect as an image of man, n. 1871. That heaven in one complex resembles one man, may be seen in the work ON HEAVEN AND HELL, n. 59 to 67. And that the Divine Truth proceeding from the Lord constitutes heaven, n. 126 to 140, 200 to 212. That the Word is beautifully and agreeably exhibited before the angels, n. 1767, 1768. That the literal sense is as the body, and the internal sense, as the soul of that body, n. 8943. That of consequence the life of the Word is from its internal sense, n. 1405, 4857. That the Word is pure in the internal sense, and does not appear so in the literal sense, n. 2362, 2396. That the things which are in the literal sense of the Word are holy on account of their internal contents, n. 10,126, 10,728.

That the historical parts of the Word also contain an internal sense, but remote from the letter, n. 4989. Thus that the historical as well as the prophetic parts of the Word contain arcana of heaven, n. 755, 1659, 1709, 2310, 2333. That the angels do not perceive those parts historically, but spiritually, n. 6884. The reason why the interior arcana which are in the historical parts, are less evident to man than those that are in the prophetical parts, n. 2176, 6597.

The quality of the internal sense of the Word further shown, n. 1756, 1984, 2004, 2663, 3035, 7089, 10,604, 10,614. And illustrated by comparisons, n. 1873.

261. *That the Word is written by correspondences, and thus by representatives.* That the Word, as to its literal sense, is written by mere correspondences, thus by such things as represent and signify spiritual things which relate to heaven and the church, n. 1404, 1408, 1409, 1540, 1619, 1659, 1709, 1783, 2179, 2763, 2899. That this was done for the sake of the internal sense, which is contained in every part, n. 2899. Thus for the sake of heaven, inasmuch as the inhabitants thereof do not understand the Word according to its literal sense, which is natural, but according to its internal sense, which is spiritual, n. 2899. That the Lord spake by correspondences, representatives, and significatives, because He spake from the Divine, n. 9049, 9063, 9086, 10,126, 10,728. That thus the Lord spake, at the same time, before the world and before heaven, n. 2533, 4807, 9049, 9063, 9086. That the things which the Lord spake filled the universal heaven, n. 4637. That the historical parts of the Word are representative, and the expressions significative, n. 1540, 1659, 1709, 1783, 2687. That the Word could not be written in any other style, consistently with its being the medium of communication and conjunction with the heavens, n. 2899, 6943, 9481. That they who despise the Word on account of the apparent simplicity and rudeness of its style, and who fancy that they should receive the Word, if it were written in a different style, are in a great error, n. 8783. That the mode and style of writing, which prevailed amongst the most ancient people, was by representatives and significatives, n. 605, 1756, 9942. That the ancient wise men were delighted with the Word, because of the representatives and significatives therein, from experience, n. 2592, 2593. That if a man of the most ancient church had read the Word, he would have seen the things which are in the internal sense clearly, and those which are in the external sense obscurely, n. 449. That the sons of Jacob were brought into the land of Canaan, because all the places in that land, from the most ancient times, were made representative, n. 1585, 3686, 4441, 5136, 6516. And thus that a Word might there be written, in which Word those places were to be mentioned for the sake of the internal sense, n. 3686, 4447, 5136, 6516. But that nevertheless the Word was changed, for the sake of that nation, as to the external sense, but not as to the internal sense, n. 10,453, 10,461, 10,603, 10,604. In order that it may be known what the correspondences and representatives in the Word are, and what is their quality, something shall also be said concerning them.

That all things which correspond are likewise representative, and thereby significative, thus that correspondences and representatives are one, n. 2890, 2897, 2971, 2987, 2989, 2990, 3002, 3225. What corespondences and representations are, from experience and examples, n. 2703, 2987 to 3002, 3213 to 3226, 3337 to 3352, 3472 to 3485, 4218 to 4228, 9280. That the science of correspondences and representations was the chief science amongst the ancients, n. 3021, 3419, 4280, 4749, 4844, 4964, 4965, 6004, 7729, 10,252. Especially among the people of the east, n. 5702, 6692, 7097, 7779, 9391, 10,252, 10,407; and in Egypt more than in other countries, n. 5702, 6692, 7097, 7779, 9391, 10,407. Also among the gentiles, as in Greece and other places, n. 2762, 7729. But that at this day it is among the sciences which are lost, particularly in Europe, n. 2894, 2895, 2994, 3630, 3632, 3747, 3748, 3749, 4581, 4966, 10,252. That nevertheless this science is more excellent than all other sciences, since without it the Word cannot be understoood, nor the signification of the rites of the Jewish church, which are recorded in the Word; neither can it be known what heaven is, nor what the spiritual [principle] is, nor in what manner spiritual influx takes place into what is natural, with many other matters, n. 4280, and in the places above cited. That all the things which appear before angels and spirits, are representatives, according to correspondences, of such things as relate to love and faith, n. 1971, 3213 to 3226, 3457, 3475, 3485, 9481, 9574, 9576, 9577. That the heavens are full of representatives, n. 1521, 1532, 1619. That representatives are more beautiful, and more perfect, in proportion as they are more interiorly in the heavens, n. 3475. That representatives there are real appearances, being derived from the light of heaven, which is Divine Truth, and which is the very essential of the existence of all things, n. 3485.

The reason why all and singular things in the spiritual world have representations in the natural world, is because what is internal assumes a suitable clothing in what is external, whereby it makes itself visible and apparent, n. 6275, 6284, 6299. Thus the end assumes a suitable clothing, that it may exist as the cause in a lower sphere, and afterwards that it may exist as the effect in a sphere lower still; and when the end, by means of the cause, becomes the effect, it then becomes visible, or appears before the eyes, n. 5711. That this may be illustrated by the influx of the soul into the body, whereby the soul assumes a clothing of such things in the body, as enable all the things which it thinks and wills, to appear and become visible; wherefore the thought, when it descends by influx into the body, is represented by gestures and actions which correspond thereto, n. 2988. That the affections, which are of the mind, are manifestly represented in the face, by the various configurations of the countenance, so that they may be seen therein, n. 4791 to 4805, 5695. Hence it is evident, that all and singular things in nature have in them a latent cause and end from the spiritual world, n. 3562, 5711. Since the things in nature are ultimate effects, which contain prior things, n. 4240, 4939, 5051, 6275, 6284, 6299, 9216. That internal things are represented, and external things represent n. 4292.

Since all things in nature are representative of spiritual and celestial things, therefore, in ancient times; there were churches, wherein all the externals, which are rituals, were representative; wherefore those churches were called representative churches, n. 519, 521, 2896. That the church founded among the children of Israel was a representative church, n. 1003, 2179, 10,149. That all its rituals were external things, which represented the internal things of heaven and the church, n. 4288, 4874. That representatives of the church and of worship ceased when the Lord came into the world, because the Lord opened the internal things of the church, and because all the externals of the church in a supreme sense regarded him, n. 4832.

262. *Of the literal or external sense of the Word.* That the literal sense of the Word is according to appearances in the world, n. 584, 926, 1719, 1720, 1832, 1874, 2242, 2520, 2533. And adapted to the capacity of the simple, n. 2533, 9049, 9063, 9086. That the Word in its literal sense is natural, n. 8783. Because what is natural is the ultimate wherein spiritual and celestial things terminate, and upon which they rest, like a house upon its foundation; and that otherwise the internal sense of the Word without the external, would be like a house without a foundation, n. 9369, 9430, 9824, 10,044, 10,436. That the Word is the continent of a spiritual and celestial sense, because it is of such a quality, n. 9407. And that it is holy and Divine in its literal sense as to all and singular the things therein, even to every iota, because it is of such a quality, n. 639, 680, 1319, 1870, 9198, 10,321, 10,637. That the laws ordained for the children of Israel, are yet the Holy Word, notwithstanding their abrogation, on account of the internal sense which they contain, n. 9210, 9259, 9349. That among the laws, judgments and statutes, ordained in the Israelitish and Jewish church, which was a representative church, there are some which are still in force, both in their external and internal sense; some which ought to be strictly observed in their external sense; some which may be of use, if people are disposed to observe them; and some which are altogether abrogated, n. 9349. That the Word is Divine, even as to those which are abrogated, n. 10,637.

What the quality of the Word is, as to the literal sense, if not understood at the same time as to the internal sense, or, which is the same thing, according to true doctrine from the Word, n. 10,402. That innumerable heresies arise from the literal sense without the internal sense, or without true doctrine from the Word, n. 10,401. That they who are in an external without an internal cannot endure the interior things of the Word, n. 10,694. That the Jews were of such a quality, and that they are also such at this day, n. 301, 302, 303, 3479, 4429, 4433, 4680, 4844, 4847, 10,396, 10,401, 10,407, 10,694, 10,701, 10,707.

263. *That the Lord is the Word.* That the Word in its inmost sense treats only of the Lord, and describes all the states of the glorification of His Human, that is, of its union with the Divine itself; and likewise all the states of the subjugation of the hells, and of the ordination of all things therein and in the heavens, n. 2249, 7014. Thus that the Lord's whole life in the world is described in that sense, and that thereby the Lord is continually present with the angels, n. 2523. Consequently that the Lord alone is in the inmost of the Word, and that the divinity and sanctity of the Word

is from thence, n. 1873, 9357. That the Lord's saying that all the Scripture concerning Him was fulfilled, signifies that all things which are contained in the inmost sense were fulfilled, n. 7933.

That the Word signifies Divine Truth, n. 4692, 5075, 9987. That the Lord is the Word because He is Divine Truth, n. 2533. That the Lord is the Word also because the Word is from Him, and treats of Him, n. 2859. And because it treats of the Lord alone in its inmost sense, thus because the Lord Himself is therein, n. 1873, 9357. And because in all and singular things of the Word there is a marriage of Divine Good and Divine Truth, n. 3004, 5502. That Jesus is Divine Good, and Christ Divine Truth, n. 3004, 3005, 3009. That Divine Truth is alone real, and that that in which Divine Truth is, which is from the Divine, is alone substantial, n. 5272, 6880, 7004, 8200. And as Divine Truth proceeding from the Lord is light in heaven, and Divine Good is heat in heaven; and as all things in heaven derive their existence from Divine Good and Divine Truth; and as the natural world has its existence through heaven, or the spiritual world; it is plain that all things which were created, were created from Divine Truth, or from the Word, according to these words in John: *In the beginning was the Word, and the Word was with God, and God was the Word, and by it were all things made which were made;* AND THE WORD WAS MADE FLESH; n. 2803, 2884, 5272, 7830. Further particulars concerning the creation of all things by Divine Truth, consequently by the Lord, may be seen in the work ON HEAVEN AND HELL, n. 137. And more fully in the two articles therein, n. 116 to 125, and n. 126 to 140.

That the conjunction of the Lord with man is effected through the Word, by means of the internal sense, n. 10,375. That conjunction is effected by all and singular the things of the Word, and that the Word is therefore to be admired above all other writings, n. 10,632, 10,633, 10,634. That since the Word has been written, the Lord thereby speaks with men, n. 10,290.

264. *Of those who are against the Word.* Of those who despise, mock at, blaspheme, and profane the Word, n. 1878. Their quality in the other life, n. 1761, 9222. That they may be compared to the viscous parts of the blood, n. 5719. The danger of profaning the Word, n. 571 to 582. How hurtful it is if principles of the false, particularly those which favor the loves of self and of the world, are confirmed by the Word, n. 589. That they who are in no affection of truth for the sake of truth, utterly reject the internal sense of the Word, and nauseate it, from experience, n. 5702. That some in the other life who have rejected the interior things of the Word, are deprived of rationality, n. 1879.

265. *Further particulars concerning the Word.* That the term WORD in the Hebrew tongue signifies various things, as speech, thought of the mind, every thing that has a real existence, and also anything, n. 9987. That Word signifies Divine Truth and the Lord, n. 4692, 5075, 9987. That words signify truths, n. 4692, 5075. That they signify doctrinals, n. 1288. That the ten words signify all Divine Truths, n. 10,688. That they signify things which really exist, n. 1785, 5075, 5272.

That in the Word, particularly in the prophetic parts, there are two expressions to signify one thing, and that the one has relation to good and the other to truth, which are thus conjoined, n. 683, 707, 5516, 8339. That it cannot be known what expression has relation to good, and what to truth, but from the internal sense of the Word; for there are proper words by which the things relating to good are expressed, and proper words by which the things relating to truth are expressed, n. 793, 801. And this so determinat·ly that it may be known merely from the words predicated, whether the subject treated of be good, or whether it be truth, n. 2722. That frequently one expression implies a universal, and the other expression implies a certain specific particular of that universal, n. 2212. That there is a species of reciprocation in the Word, concerning which see n. 2240. That many things in the Word have also an opposite sense, n. 4816. That the internal sense proceeds regularly according to the subject predicated, n. 4502.

That they who have been delighted with the Word in the other life receive the heat of heaven, wherein is celestial love, according to the quality and quantity of their delight from love, n. 1773.

266. The books of the Word are all those which have the internal sense; but those books which have not the internal sense, are not the Word. The books of the Word, in the Old Testament, are, the five Books of Moses, the Book of Joshua, the Book of Judges, the two Books of Samuel, the two Books of Kings, the Psalms of David, the Prophets Isaiah, Jeremiah, the Lamentations, Ezekiel, Daniel, Hosea, Joel, Amos, Obadiah, Jonah, Micah, Nahum, Habakkuk, Zephaniah, Haggai, Zechariah, Malachi: and in the New Testament, the four Evangelists, Matthew, Mark, Luke, John; and the Apocalypse. The rest have not the internal sense.

OF PROVIDENCE.

267. The Universal Government of the Lord is called Providence; and as the good of love and the truth of faith, by which salvation is effected, are wholly from Him, and in no respect from man, it is evident that the Divine Providence extends over all, and regulates the most minute particulars of those things which conduce to the salvation of the human race. This grand truth the Lord himself teaches in John, where He says, *I am the way, and the truth, and the life.* xiv. 6. And again: *As the branch cannot bear fruit of itself, except it abide in the vine: no more can ye, except ye abide in Me. For without Me ye can do nothing.* xv. 4, 5.

268. The Divine Providence extends to the most minute particulars of the life of man: for there is only One Fountain of Life; from whom we have our being, from whom we live, and from whom we act; and that fountain is the Lord.

269. They who think of the Divine Providence from worldly affairs, conclude that its operations are only of a general

nature, and that particulars depend on human agency. But such persons are unacquainted with the mysteries of heaven, because they form their conclusions under the influence of the love of self and the love of the world, and of their gross delights. Hence, when they see the wicked exalted to honors, and acquire riches, more than the good, and success attend the artifices of which they avail themselves, they say in their hearts, that these things would not be so if the Divine Providence were universally operative, and extended to every particular of the life of man; not considering that the Divine Providence does not regard that which is fleeting and transitory, and which terminates with the life of man in this world, but that it regards that which remains to eternity, thus which has no end. Of that which has no end it may be predicated that it IS; but of that which has an end, respectively, that it IS NOT. Let him who is able consider whether a hundred thousand years be anything when compared with eternity, and he will perceive that they are as nothing; what then are a few years of life in the world?

270. Whoever rightly considers the subject may know, that worldly rank and riches are not real divine blessings, although man from the pleasure which they yield him, calls them so; for they pass away, and also seduce many, and turn them away from heaven. But that eternal life, and the happiness thence resulting, are real blessings bestowed on man by the Lord, He himself plainly teaches in these words: *Provide yourselves bags which wax not old, a treasure in the heavens that faileth not, where no thief approacheth, neither moth corrupteth. For where your treasure is, there will your heart be also.* Luke xii 33, 34.

271. The devices of the wicked are attended with success, because it is according to Divine Order, that whatever man does, he should do in the free exercise of his reason, and from freedom of choice; unless therefore he were left to act according to his reason, consequently unless the artifices which he thence contrives were followed with success, he could in no wise be disposed to receive eternal life; for eternal life is insinuated into him when he is in a state of liberty and enlightened reason. No one can be compelled to do good, because nothing forced is permanent with man, it not being his own: that alone becomes his which he does from liberty, and in accordance with his reason. What he does from liberty, is done from his will or love; and the will or love is the man himself. If man were compelled to act contrary to his will, his thoughts would continually incline towards the dictates of his will. Besides, every one strives after what is forbidden, and this from a latent cause; for every one strives to act from liberty. Hence it is evident, that unless man were preserved in liberty, he could not be provided with good.

272. To leave man to think, to will, and, so far as the law does not restrain him, to do evil, from his own liberty, is called Permission.

273. When man is led, by the success of artful schemes, to the enjoyment of happiness in the world, it appears to him as the result of his own prudence; when at the same time the Divine Providence incessantly accompanies him,—permitting and continually withdrawing him from evil. But when man is led to the enjoyment of felicity in heaven, he knows and perceives that it is not effected by his own prudence, but by the Lord, and is the result of His Divine Providence, disposing and continually leading man to good.

274. That this is the case, man cannot comprehend from the light of nature; for from that light he cannot understand the laws of Divine Order.

275. Here it is to be particularly observed, that besides Providence, there is also Previdence (*foresight*). Good is provided by the Lord; but evil is previded. The one must needs accompany the other: for what proceeds from man is nothing but evil, but what proceeds from the Lord is wholly good.

FROM THE ARCANA CŒLESTIA.

Since all the good which is provided for man by the Lord flows in by influx, we shall therefore adduce from the Arcana Cœlestia the particulars concerning Influx: and since the Lord provides all things according to Divine Order, we shall also adduce from that work the particulars concerning Order.

276. *Of Providence.* That providence is the government of the Lord in the heavens and on the earth, n. 10,773. That the Lord, from providence, governs all things according to order, and thus that providence is government according to order, n. 1755, 2447. And that He governs all things either from will, or from leave, or from permission; and thus in various respects according to man's quality, n. 1755, 2447, 3704, 9940. That providence acts invisibly, n. 5580. That most things which are done from providence appear to man as contingencies, n. 5508. That providence acts invisibly, in order that man may not be compelled to believe from visible things, and thus that his free-will may not be hurt; for unless man is at liberty he cannot be reformed, thus he cannot be saved, n. 1937, 1947, 2876, 2881, 3854, 5508, 5982, 6477, 8209, 8907, 9588, 10,409 10,777. That the Divine Providence does not regard temporary things which soon pass away, but eternal things, n. 5264, 8717, 10,776; illustrated, n. 6491. That they who do not comprehend this, believe worldly rank and riches to be the only objects of providence, and call such things blessings from the Divine, when nevertheless they are not regarded as blessings by th Lord, but only as

means conducive to the life of man in the world; but that those things are regarded by the Lord which conduce to man's eternal happiness, n. 10,409, 10,776. That they who are in the Divine Providence of the Lord, are led in all general and particular matters to eternal happiness, n. 8478, 8480. That they who ascribe all things to nature and man's own prudence, and nothing to the Divine, do not think or comprehend this, n. 6481, 10,409, 10,775.

That the Divine Providence of the Lord is not, as believed in the world, universal only, and the particulars and singulars dependent on man's own proper prudence, n. 8717, 10,775. That no universal exists but from and with singulars, because singulars taken together are called a universal, as particulars taken together are called a general, n. 1919, 6159, 6338, 6482, 6483, 6484. That every universal is of the same quality as the singulars of which it is formed, and with which it co-exists, n. 918, 1040, 6483, 8858. That the providence of the Lord is universal, because existing in the most singular things, n. 1919, 2694, 4329, 5122, 5904, 6058, 6481 to 6486, 6490, 7004, 7007, 8717, 10,074; confirmed from heaven, n. 6486. That unless the Divine Providence of the Lord were universal, acting from and in the most singular things, nothing could subsist, n. 6338. That all things are disposed by it into order, and kept in order both in general and in particular, n. 6338. How the case herein is comparatively with that of a king on earth, n. 6482, 10,800. That man's own proper prudence is like a small speck of dirt in the universe, whilst the Divine Providence is respectively as the universe itself, n. 6485. That this can hardly be comprehended by men in the world, n. 8717, 10,775, 10,780. Because many fallacies assail them, and induce blindness, n. 6481. Of a certain person in the other life, who believed from confirmation in the world, that all things were dependent on man's own proper prudence, and nothing on the Divine Providence;—that the things belonging to him appeared infernal, n. 6484.

The quality of the Lord's providence with respect to evils, n. 6481, 6495, 6574, 10,777, 10,779. That evils are governed by the Lord by the laws of permission, and that they are permitted for the sake of order, n. 8700, 10,778. That the permission of evil by the Lord is not that of one who wills, but of one who does not will, but who cannot bring aid, on account of the urgency of the end, which is salvation, n. 7877. That to leave man from his own liberty to think and will evil, and, so far as the laws do not prevent him, to do evil, is to permit, n. 10,778. That without liberty, thus without this permission, man could not be reformed, thus could not be saved, may be seen in the doctrine of Liberty, n. 141 to 149 above.

That the Lord has providence and previdence, and that the one does not exist without the other, n. 5195, 6489. That good is provided by the Lord, and evil previded, n. 5155, 5195, 6489, 10,781.

That there is no such thing as predestination or fate, n. 6487. That all are predestined to heaven, and none to hell, n. 6488. That man is under no absolute necessity from providence, but at perfect liberty,—illustrated by comparison, n. 6487. That the elect in the Word are they who are in the life of good, and thence of truth, n.

3755, 3900, 5067, 5058. How it is to be understood that *God would deliver one man into another's hand*, Exod. xxi. 13; n. 9010.

That fortune, which appears in the world wonderful in many circumstances, is an operation of Divine Providence in the ultimate of order, according to the quality of man's state; and that this may afford proof, that the Divine Providence is in the most singular of all things, n. 5049, 5179, 6493, 6494. That this operation and its variations are from the spiritual world,—proved from experience, n. 5179, 6493, 6494.

277. *Of Influx.* Of the influx of heaven into the world, and of the influx of the soul into all things of the body,—from experience, n. 6053 to 6058, 6189 to 6215, 6307 to 6327, 6466 to 6495, 6598 to 6626. That nothing exists of or from itself, but from what is prior to itself, thus all things from the first, n. 4523, 4524, 6040, 6056. That as all things existed, they also subsist, because subsistence is perpetual existence, n. 2886, 2888, 3627, 3628, 3648, 4523, 4524, 6040, 6056. That influx takes place according to that order, n. 7270. Hence it is plain that all things subsist perpetually from the first esse, because they exist from it, n. 4523, 4524, 6040, 6056. That the all of life flows in from the first, because it is thence derived, thus from the Lord, n. 3001, 3318, 3337, 3338, 3344, 3484, 3619, 3741, 3742, 3743, 4318, 4319, 4320, 4417, 4524, 4882, 5847, 5986, 6325, 6468, 6469, 6470, 6479, 9279, 10,196. That every existere is from an esse, and that nothing can exist unless its esse be in it, n. 4523, 4524, 6040, 6056.

That all things which a man thinks and wills flow into him;—from experience, n. 904, 2886, 2887, 2888, 4151, 4319, 4320, 5846, 5848, 6189, 6191, 6194, 6197, 6198, 6199, 6213, 7147, 10,219. That man's ability of examining things, and of thinking and forming analytic conclusions, is from influx, n. 1288, 4319, 4320. That man could not live a moment if the influx from the spiritual world were taken away from him; but that still man is in liberty,—from experience, n. 2887, 5849, 5854, 6321. That the life which flows from the Lord, is varied according to man's state, and according to his reception of it, n. 2069, 5986, 6472, 7343. That with the evil, the good which flows from the Lord is turned into evil, and the truth into the false,—from experience, n. 3643, 4632. That the good and truth, which continually flow from the Lord, are so far received, as evil and the false do not oppose their reception, n. 2411, 3142, 3147, 5828.

That all good flows from the Lord, and all evil from hell, n. 904, 4151. That at this day man believes all things to be in himself and to be from himself, when nevertheless he receives them by influx, as he might know from the tenet of the church, that all good is from heaven, and all evil from hell, n. 4249, 6193, 6206. But that if he would believe the reality of this matter, he would not appropriate evil to himself, but cast it back from himself into hell, neither would he make good his own, and thus would not claim any merit from it, n. 6206, 6324, 6325. How happy the state of man would then be, as he would view both good and evil from within, from the Lord, n. 6325. That they who deny heaven, or know nothing about it, do not know that there is any influx thence, n. 4322, 5649, 6193

6479. What influx is, illustrated by comparisons, n. 6128, 6180, 9407.

That influx is spiritual, and not physical, thus that it is from the spiritual world into the natural, and not from the natural world into the spiritual, n. 3219, 5119, 5259, 5427, 5428, 5478, 6322, 9110, 9111. That spiritual influx passes through the internal man into the external, and not contrariwise, n. 1702, 1707, 1940, 1954, 5119, 5259, 5779, 6322, 9380. Because the internal man is in the spiritual world, and the external, in the natural world, n. 978, 1015, 3628, 4459, 4523, 4524, 6057, 6309, 9701 to 9709, 10,156, 10,472. That the appearance of influx passing from external into internal things, is a fallacy, n. 3721. That influx passes into man's rational [principles], and through these into things scientific, and not contrariwise, n. 1495, 1707, 1940. The order of influx, n. 775, 880, 1096, 1495, 7270.

That there is an immediate influx from the Lord, and also a mediate influx through the spiritual world or heaven, n. 6063, 6307, 6472, 9682, 9483. That the immediate influx from the Lord enters into the most singular of all things, n. 6058, 6474 to 6478, 8717, 8728. Of the mediate influx of the Lord through heaven, n. 4067, 6982, 6985, 6996. That it is effected by means of the spirits and angels who are adjoined to man, n. 697, 5846 to 5866. That the Lord, by means of angels, flows into the ends from which, and for the sake of which, a man thinks, wills, and acts after such or such a manner, n. 1317, 1645, 5844, 5854. And thus into those things which are of conscience with man, n. 6207, 6213. But by means of spirits into the thoughts, and thence into the things of the memory, n. 4186, 5858, 5864, 6192, 6193, 6198, 6199, 6319. That this can with difficulty be believed by man, n. 6214. That the Lord flows at once into first [principles] and last, or into inmost and outmost, and in what manner, n. 5147, 5150, 6473, 7004, 7007, 7270. That the influx of the Lord is into good with man, and through good into truth, and not contrariwise, n. 5482, 5649, 6027, 8685, 8701, 10,153. That good gives the faculty of receiving influx from the Lord, but not truth without good, n. 8321. That it is not what enters the thought, but what enters the will, that is hurtful, because this is appropriated to the man, n. 6308. That the Divine [principle] is tacit and pacific in the supreme [principles], but as it descends towards lower [principles] in man it becomes unpacific and tumultuous, on account of the things therein being inordinate, n. 8823. The quality of the Lord's influx with the prophets, n. 6212.

That there is a common influx, which is described, n. 5850. That it is a continual effort of acting according to order, n. 6211. That this influx takes place into the lives of animals, n. 5850. And also into the subjects of the vegetable kingdom, n. 3648. That thought is formed into speech, and will into gestures with man, according to this common influx, n. 5862, 5990, 6192, 6211.

278. *Of the influx of life with man in particular.* That there is one only fountain of life, from which all live both in heaven and in the world, n. 1954, 2021, 2536, 2658, 2886 to 2889, 3001, 3484, 3742, 5847, 6467. That this life is from the Lord alone, illustrated by various things, n. 2886 to 2889, 3344, 3484, 4319, 4320, 4524, 4882,

5986, 6325, 6468, 6469, 6470, 9276, 10,196. That the Lord is life itself, may be seen in John i. 1, 4; chap. v. 26; chap. xiv. 6. That life from the Lord flows in with angels, spirits, and men, in a wonderful manner, n. 2886 to 2889, 3337, 3338, 3484, 3742. That the Lord flows in from his Divine Love, which is of such a quality, that it wills that what is its own should be another's, n. 3742, 4320. That all love is of this quality, thus Divine Love infinitely more so, n. 1820, 1865, 2253, 6872. That hence life appears as if it were in man, and not as influent, n. 3742, 4320. Life appears as if it were in man, because the principal cause, which is life from the Lord, and the instrumental cause, which is the recipient form, act as one cause, which is felt in the instrumental, n. 6325. That the chief of the wisdom and intelligence of the angels consists in perceiving and knowing that the all of life is from the Lord, n. 4318. Concerning the joy of angels perceived and shown by their discourse to me, from the consideration, that they do not live from themselves, but from the Lord, n. 6469. That the evil are not willing to be convinced that life is received by influx, n. 3743. That doubts concerning the influx of life from the Lord cannot be removed, so long as fallacies, ignorance, and a negative principle prevail, n. 6479. That it is generally known in the church, that all good and truth is from heaven, that is, through heaven from the Lord, and that all evil and false is from hell; and yet the all of life has relation to good and truth, and to evil and the false, there being nothing of life without them, n. 2893, 4151. That the doctrinal tenets of the church derived from the Word teach the same thing, n. 4249. That nevertheless man does not believe that life is influent, n. 4249. That if communication and connection with spirits and angels were taken away, man would instantly die, n. 2887. That it is evident from hence, that the all of life flows in from the first esse of life, because nothing exists from itself, but from things prior to itself, thus all and singular things exist from that which is first; and because every thing must subsist from the same source from which it first existed, subsistence being perpetual existence, n. 4523, 4524. That angels, spirits, and men, were created to receive life, thus that they are only forms recipient of life, n. 2021, 3001, 3318, 3344, 3484, 3742, 4151, 5114, 5986. That their forms are such as the quality of their reception, n. 2888, 3001, 3484, 5847, 5986, 6467, 6472. That men, spirits, and angels, are therefore such as are their forms recipient of life from the Lord, n. 2888, 5847, 5986, 6467, 6472. That man is so created, that in his inmost [principles], and in those which follow in order, he is capable of receiving the Divine, and of being elevated to the Divine, and of being conjoined with the Divine by the good of love and the truths of faith, and on this account he lives to eternity, which is not the case with beasts, n. 5114.

That life from the Lord flows in also with the evil, thus also with those who are in hell, n. 2706, 3743, 4417, 10,196. But that they turn good into evil and truth into the false, and thus life into spiritual death, for such as the man is, such is his reception of life, n. 4319, 4320, 4417. That goods and truths from the Lord are continually influent with them, but that they either reject, suffocate, or pervert them, n. 3743. That they who are in evils, and thence in falses, have no real life,—and the quality of their life, n. 726, 4623, 4742, 10,284, 10,286.

279. *Of Order.* That Divine Truth proceeding from the Lord is the source of order, and Divine Good is the essential of order, n. 1728, 2258, 8700, 8988. That the Lord is order, since Divine Good and Divine Truth are from the Lord, yea, are the Lord, in the heavens and on earth, n. 1919, 2011, 5110, 5703, 10,336, 10,619. That Divine Truths are the laws of order, n. 2247, 7995. That where order is, the Lord is present, but that where order is not, the Lord is not present, n. 5703. As Divine Truth is order, and Divine Good the essential of order, therefore all and singular things in the universe have relation to good and truth, that they may be any thing, because they have relation to order, n. 2451, 3166, 4390, 4409, 5232, 7256, 10,122, 10,555. That good, being the essential of order, disposes truths into order, and not *vice versa*, n. 3316, 3470, 4302, 5704, 5709, 6028, 6690. That the universal heaven, as to all the angelic societies, is arranged by the Lord according to His Divine Order, because the Divine of the Lord with the angels constitutes heaven, n. 3038, 7211, 9128, 9338, 10,125, 10,151, 10,157. That hence the form of heaven is a form according to Divine Order, n. 4040 to 4043, 6607 to 9877.

That so far as man lives according to order, thus in good according to Divine Truths, which are the laws of order, so far is he a man, n. 4839. That so far as he thus lives, he appears in the other life as a perfect and beautiful man, but so far as he does not thus live, so far he appears as a monster, n. 4839, 6605, 6626. Hence it appears that all things of order are collected together in man, and that from creation he is Divine Order in form, n. 4219, 4220, 4223, 4523, 4524, 5114, 5368, 6013, 6057, 6605, 6626, 9706, 10,156, 10,472. That every angel is in a human form in consequence of being a recipient of Divine Order from the Lord, which form is perfect and beautiful according to his reception, n. 322, 1880, 1881, 3633, 3804, 4622, 4735, 4797, 4985, 5199, 5530, 6054, 9879, 10,177, 10,594. That the angelic heaven in its whole complex is also in a human form, because the universal heaven as to all its angelic societies, is disposed by the Lord according to Divine Order, n. 2996, 2998, 3624 to 3649, 3636 to 3643, 3741 to 3745, 4625. Hence it is evident, that the Divine Human is the source from which all these things are derived, n. 2996, 2998, 3624 to 3649, 3741 to 3745. Hence also it follows, that the Lord is the only Man, and that they are men who receive the Divine from Him, n. 1894. That so far as they receive it, so far they are images of the Lord, n. 8547.

That man is not born into good and truth, but into evil and the false, thus not into Divine Order, but into what is contrary to order, and on this account into mere ignorance, and that he ought therefore necessarily to be born anew, that is regenerated, which is done by Divine Truths from the Lord, and by a life according to them, to the intent that he may be inaugurated into order, and thus become a man, n. 1047, 2307, 2308, 3518, 3812, 8480, 8550, 10,283, 10,284, 10,286, 10,731. That when the Lord regenerates man, He disposes all things with him according to order, that is, according to the form of heaven, n. 5700, 6690, 9931, 10,303. That the man who is led by the Lord, is led according to Divine Order, n. 8512. That the interiors which are of the mind are open into heaven, even to the Lord, with the man who is in Divine Order, but shut with him who is not in Divine Order, n. 8513. That so far as man lives according to order, so far he has intelligence and wisdom, n. 2592.

That the Lord governs the first and last [principles] of order, and governs the first from the last, and the last from the first; and thus keeps all things in connection and order, n. 3702, 3739, 6040, 6056, 9828. Of successive order; and of the ultimate of order, in which things successive are together in their order, n. 634, 3691, 4145, 5114, 5897, 6239, 6326, 6465, 8603, 9216, 9217, 9828, 9836, 10,044, 10,099, 10,329, 10,335.

That evils and falses are contrary to order, and that still they are governed by the Lord, not according to order, but from order, n. 4839, 7877, 10,778. That evils and falses are governed by the laws of permission, and that this is for the sake of order, n. 7877, 8700, 10,778. That what is contrary to Divine Order is impossible, as that a man who lives in evil can be saved from mercy alone, as likewise that the evil can be consociated with the good in the other life, and many other things, n. 8700.

OF THE LORD.

280. There is One God, the Creator and Preserver of the universe; and consequently, the God of heaven and of earth.

281. There are two things which constitute the life of heaven in man, the good of love and the truth of faith. Man derives this life from God, and in no respect or degree from himself; therefore the primary principle of the church is, to acknowledge God, to believe in Him, and to love Him.

282. They who are born within the church ought to acknowledge the Lord, both as to His Essential Divinity and His Divine Humanity, to believe in Him and love Him; because salvation is wholly from Him. This the Lord plainly teaches in John: *He that believeth on the Son hath everlasting life; and he that believeth not the Son shall not see life; but the wrath of God abideth on him.* iii. 36. Again: *This is the will of Him that sent Me, that every one which seeth the Son, and believeth on Him, may have everlasting life; and I will raise him up at the last day.* vi. 40. And again: *Jesus said unto her, I am the resurrection and the life; he that believeth in Me, though he were dead, yet shall he live; and whosoever liveth and believeth in Me shall never die.* xi. 25, 26.

283. They, therefore, who are within the church, and yet do not acknowledge the Lord and His Divinity, cannot be conjoined to God, and thus cannot have any lot with the angels in heaven; for no one can be conjoined to God but from the Lord,

and in the Lord. That no one can be conjoined to God but from the Lord, the Lord teaches in John: *No man hath seen God at any time; the only begotten Son, who is in the bosom of the Father, He hath declared Him.* i. 18. Again: *Ye have neither heard His voice at any time, nor seen His shape.* v. 37. Again, it is said in Matthew: *No man knoweth the Son, but the Father; neither knoweth any man the Father, save the Son, and he to whomsoever the Son will reveal Him.* xi. 37. And again, in John: *I am the way, and the truth, and the life: no man cometh unto the Father but by Me.* xiv. 6. No one can be conjoined to God except in the Lord, because the Father is in Him, and they are one; as He teaches in John: *If ye had known Me, ye should have known my Father also. He that hath seen Me, hath seen the Father. Believest thou not that I am in the Father, and the Father in Me?* xiv. 7—11. And again: *I and my Father are one. That ye may know and believe that the Father is in Me, and I in Him.* x. 30, 38.

284. Since, therefore, the Father is in the Lord, and the Lord and the Father are ONE; and since the Lord must be believed in, and he who believes in HIM is declared to have eternal life; it plainly follows that the LORD IS GOD. And that the Lord is God, the Word also teaches; as in John: *In the beginning was the* WORD, *and the* WORD *was with God, and the* WORD WAS GOD. *All things were made by Him; and without Him was not anything made that was made. And the* WORD WAS MADE FLESH *and dwelt among us; and we beheld His glory, the glory as of the only begotten of the Father.* i. 1, 3. 14. And in Isaiah: *For unto us a child is born, unto us a Son is given; and the government shall be upon His shoulder; and His name shall be called Wonderful, Counsellor, the* MIGHTY GOD, *the everlasting* FATHER, *the* PRINCE OF PEACE. ix. 6. Again: *Behold, a virgin shall conceive and bear a Son, and shall call His name* IMMANUEL; *which being interpreted is,* GOD WITH US. vii. 14; Matt. i. 23. And in Jeremiah: *Behold, the days come, saith* JEHOVAH, *that I will raise unto David a righteous branch, and a* KING *shall reign and prosper; and this is His name whereby He shall be called,* JEHOVAH OUR RIGHTEOUSNESS. xxiii. 5, 6; xxxiii. 15, 16.

285. All who are really members of the church, and enlightened by the light of heaven, see the Divinity in the Lord; but they who are not thus enlightened can see in HIM nothing but the Humanity; while at the same time the Divinity and the Humanity are so united in Him, that they form a one. The Lord teaches this in John, where He says: *Father, all mine are thine, and thine are mine.* xvii. 10.

286. That the Lord was conceived by Jehovah the Father, and thus is God by virtue of such conception, is a truth well known in the church; also that He rose again with His whole body, for

He left nothing of it in the sepulchre. In the belief of this also He afterwards confirmed His disciples, when He said to them, *Behold my hands and my feet, that it is I myself; handle me, and see; for a spirit hath not flesh and bones, as ye see me have.* Luke xxiv. 39. And although He was a man as to flesh and bone, still He entered through the doors when they were shut; and after He had manifested Himself to the disciples, He became invisible. John xx. 19, 26; Luke xxiv. 31. With every mere man the case is otherwise; for he rises again as to his spirit alone, and not as to his body. When, therefore, the Lord said of Himself that He was not as a spirit, He plainly declared that He was not as another man. Hence it is evident that the Humanity of the Lord is Divine.

287. Every one derives the esse of his life, which is called his soul, from his father; the body is the existere of life thence proceeding: hence the body is the effigy, or form, of its soul; and the soul, through the medium of the body, exercises at pleasure the various activities of its life. Hence it is that men are born in the likeness of their parents, and that families are so readily distinguished from each other. From this circumstance it may be seen of what quality the Body or Humanity of the Lord was; namely, that it was as the Divinity Itself, which was the esse of His life, or the soul from the Father; on which account He said: *He that hath seen Me, hath seen the Father.* John xiv. 9.

288. That the Divinity and the Humanity of the Lord constitute One Person, is in agreement with the faith received throughout the whole Christian world; which, in effect, is this: that "Although Christ is God and Man, still He is not two, but one Christ;—one altogether, by unity of person. For as the reasonable soul and flesh are one man, so God and Man are one Christ." These are the words of the Athanasian Creed.

289. They who entertain respecting the Divinity an idea of three persons, cannot at the same time have an idea of one God; for if they even *say* that there is but one God, still they *think* of three. They, however, who entertain the idea of three essentials, or principles, existing in one person, can in reality both profess their belief in one God, and think in agreement with such profession.

290. The idea of three essentials existing in one person is attained, when the Father is thought of as being in the Lord, and the Holy Spirit as proceeding from Him. There is then perceived to be a TRINITY in the Lord: namely, the Divinity Itself, which is the Father; the Divine Humanity, which is the Son; and the Divine Proceeding, which is the Holy Spirit.

291. Since the whole Divinity is in the Lord, to Him belongs all power in heaven and earth. This He teaches in John: *The Father loveth the Son, and hath given all things into His*

hand. iii. 35. Again: *As thou hast given Him power over all flesh.* xvii. 2. And in Matthew: *All things are delivered unto me of my Father.* xi. 27. Again: *All power is given unto me in heaven and in earth.* xxviii. 18. This power is Divinity.

292. They who make the Humanity of the Lord like that of another man, do not think of His conception from the Divinity Itself: nor do they consider that the body of every one is the effigy of the soul. Neither do such persons reflect on the Lord's resurrection with His whole body; nor on His transfiguration, when His face shone as the sun. Nor do they think respecting those things which the Lord said of faith in Him, of His oneness with the Father, His glorification, and His power over heaven and earth; all which involve Divine attributes, and were mentioned in relation to His Humanity. Neither do they remember that the Lord is omnipresent even as to His Humanity (Matt. xxviii. 20); although the belief of His omnipresence in the holy supper is founded on this fact; and omnipresence is a Divine attribute. Yea, it is probably the case that they do not think that the Divine Principle, called the Holy Spirit, proceeds from the Lord's Humanity; when, nevertheless, it does proceed from His Glorified Humanity; for it is said, *The holy Spirit was not yet, because Jesus was not yet glorified.* John vii. 39.

293. The Lord came into the world that He might effect the salvation of the human race, which must otherwise have perished in eternal death. This salvation the Lord effected by the subjugation of the hells, which infested every man coming into the world, and going out of the world; and, at the same time, by the glorification of His Humanity: for thus He can keep the hells in subjection to eternity. The subjugation of the hells, and the glorification of the Lord's Humanity at the same time, were effected by means of temptations admitted into the Humanity which He derived from the mother, and by continual victories in those conflicts. His passion on the cross was the last of those temptations, and the completion of those victories.

294. That the Lord subjugated the hells, He Himself teaches in John, where, in the immediate prospect of the passion of the cross, He says: *Now is the judgment of this world; now shall the prince of this world be cast out.* xii. 31. Again: *Be of good cheer; I have overcome the world.* xvi. 33. And in Isaiah: *Who is this that cometh from Edom, travelling in the greatness of his strength? I that speak in righteousness, mighty to save. Mine own arm brought salvation to me. So He was their Saviour.* lxiii. 1—8. That the Lord glorified His Humanity, and that the passion of the cross was the last temptation, accompanied by complete victory, through which the glorification was effected, He teaches in John: *Therefore, when*

he (Judas) *was gone out, Jesus said, Now is the Son of Man glorified, and God is glorified in Him. If God be glorified in Him, God shall also glorify Him in Himself, and shall straightway glorify Him.* xiii. 31, 32. Again: *Father, the hour is come, glorify thy Son, that thy Son also may glorify thee.* xvii. 1, 5. And again: *Now is my soul troubled; Father, glorify thy name. Then came there a voice from heaven, saying, I have both glorified it, and will glorify it again.* xii. 27, 28. And in Luke: *Ought not Christ to have suffered these things, and to enter into His glory?* xiv. 26. These words were spoken in relation to the Lord's passion: to be glorified, is to be made Divine. Hence it is evident, that unless the Lord had come into the world, and been made man, and in this manner delivered from hell all who believe in Him and love Him, no mortal could have been saved; and this is what is meant when it is said, that without the Lord there is no salvation.

295. When the Lord had fully glorified His Humanity, He then put off the humanity derived from the mother, and put on a humanity derived from the Father, which is the Divine Humanity; wherefore, He was then no longer the son of Mary.

296. The grand and primary principle of the church is, to know and acknowledge its God; for without this knowledge and acknowledgment there can be no conjunction with Him; thus, there can be none in the church without the acknowledgment of the Lord. This the Lord teaches in John: *He that believeth on the Son hath everlasting life; and he that believeth not on the Son shall not see life, but the wrath of God abideth on him.* iii. 36. And in another place: *For if ye believe not that I am He, ye shall die in your sins.* viii. 24.

297. That there is in the Lord a threefold principle, namely, the Divinity Itself, the Divine Humanity, and the Divine Proceeding, is an arcanum from heaven, and is revealed for the benefit of those who shall have a place in the Holy Jerusalem.

FROM THE ARCANA CŒLESTIA.

298. THAT *the Divinity was in the Lord from His very conception.* That the Lord had a Divinity from the Father, n. 4641, 4963, 5041, 5157, 6716, 10,125. That the Lord alone had a Divine seed, n. 1438. That His soul was Jehovah, n. 1999, 2004, 2005, 2018, 2025. That thus the inmost of the Lord was the Divinity, the covering of which was from the mother, n. 5041. That the Divinity was the Lord's esse of life from which a human afterwards went forth, and became an existere from that esse, n. 3194, 3210, 10,270, 10,372.

299. *That the Divinity of the Lord is to be acknowledged.* That within the church where the Word is, and where the Lord is thereby known, the Divinity of the Lord ought not to be denied, nor the holy proceeding from Him, n. 2359. That they within the church who do not acknowledge the Lord, have no conjunction with the Divine, which is not the case with those who are out of the church, n. 10,205. That it is an essential of the church to acknowledge the Divinity of the Lord, and His unition with the Father, n. 10,083, 10,112, 10,370, 10,728, 10,730, 10,816, 10,817, 10,818, 10,820.

300. *That the Lord glorified His human in the world.* That the glorification of the Lord is largely treated of in the Word, n. 10,828; in the internal sense throughout, n. 2249, 2523, 3245. That the Lord glorified His human, but not His Divine, as this was glorified in itself, n. 10,057. That the Lord came into the world to glorify His human, n. 3637, 4286, 9315. That the Lord glorified His human by means of the Divine which was in Him from conception, n. 4727. That the idea of the regeneration of man may give an idea of the glorification of the Lord's human, since the Lord regenerates man in the same manner as He glorified His human, n. 3043, 3138, 3212, 3296, 3490, 4402, 5688. Some of the arcana respecting the glorification of the Lord's human, n. 10,057. That the Lord saved the human race by glorifying His human, n. 1676, 4180. Concerning the Lord's state of glorification and humiliation, n. 1785, 1999, 2159, 6866. That glorification, when predicated of the Lord, is the unition of His human with the Divine, and that to glorify is to make Divine, n. 1603, 10,053, 10,828.

301. *That the Lord from His human subjugated the hells when He was in the world.* That the Lord, when He was in the world, subjugated all the hells, and that He then reduced all things to order both in the heavens and in the hells, n. 4075, 4286, 9937. That the Lord then delivered the spiritual world from the antediluvians, n. 1266. What quality they were of, n. 310, 311, 560, 562, 563, 570, 581, 607, 660, 805, 808, 1034, 1120, 1265 to 1272. That by the subjugation of the hells, and the glorification of His human at the same time, the Lord saved mankind, n. 4180, 10,019, 10,152, 10,655, 10,659, 10,828.

302. *That the glorification of the Lord's human, and the subjugation of the hells, were effected by temptations.* That the Lord endured temptations infinitely more grievous than were ever endured by man, n. 1663, 1668, 1787, 2776, 2786, 2795, 2816, 4295, 9528. That the Lord fought therein from His Divine Love towards the human race, n. 1690, 1691, 1812, 1813, 1820. That the Lord's love was the salvation of the human race, n. 1820. That the hells fought against the love of the Lord, n. 1820. That the Lord alone, from His own proper power, fought against the hells, and overcame them, n. 1692, 1813, 2816, 4295, 8273, 9937. That hereby the Lord alone became justice and merit, n. 1813, 2025, 2026, 2027, 9715, 9809, 10,019. That the last temptation of the Lord was in the garden of Gethsemane and upon the cross, at which time He gained a complete victory, by which He subjugated the hells, and at the same time glorified His human, n. 2276, 2803, 2813, 2814, 10,655, 10,659, 10,829. That the Lord could not be tempted as to the Di-

vine itself, n. 2795, 2803, 2813, 2814. That therefore He assumed an infirm human from the mother, into which He admitted temptations, n. 1414, 1444, 1573, 5041, 5157, 7193, 9315. That by means of temptations and victories He expelled all that was hereditary from the mother, and put off the human which He had from her, till at length He was no longer her son, n. 2159, 2574, 2649, 3036, 10,829. That Jehovah, who was in Him, appeared in temptations as absent, and this so far as He was in the human from the mother, n. 1815. That this state was the Lord's state of humiliation, n. 1785, 1999, 2159, 6866. That the Lord by means of temptations and victories disposed all things in the heavens into order, n. 4287, 9397, 9528, 9937. That by the same means He united His human with His Divine, that is, He glorified His human, n. 1725, 1729, 1733, 1737, 3318, 3381, 3382, 4286, 4287, 9397, 9528, 9937.

303. *That the Lord's human, when He was in the world, was Divine Truth.* That the Lord, when He was in the world, made His human Divine Truth from the Divine Good which was in Him, n. 2803, 3194, 3195, 3210, 6716, 6864, 7014, 7499, 8127, 8724, 9199. That the Lord thus disposed all things in Himself into a heavenly form, which is according to Divine Truth, n. 1928, 3633. Consequently, that heaven was then in the Lord, and the Lord was as heaven, n. 911, 1900, 1982, 3624 to 3631, 3634, 3884, 4041, 4279, 4523, 4524, 4525, 6013, 6057, 6690, 9279, 9632, 9931, 10,303. That the Lord spake from Divine Truth itself, n. 8127. That therefore the Lord spake in the Word by correspondences, n. 3131, 3472 to 3485, 8615, 10,687. That hence the Lord is the Word, and is called the Word, which is Divine Truth, n. 2533, 2818, 2859, 2894, 3393, 3712. That in the Word the Son of Man signifies Divine Truth, and the Father Divine Good, n. 2803, 3704, 7409, 8724, 9194. That because the Lord was Divine Truth, He was Divine Wisdom, n. 2500, 2527. That the Lord alone had perception and thought from Himself, above all angelic perception and thought, n. 1904, 1914, 1915. That the Divine Truth could be tempted, but not the Divine Good, n. 2814.

304. *That the Lord united Divine Truth with Divine Good, thus His Human with the Divine itself.* That the Lord was instructed as another man, n. 1457, 1461, 2523, 3030. That the Lord successively advanced to union with the Father, n. 1864, 2033, 2632, 3141, 4585, 7014, 10,076. That so far as the Lord was united with the Father, so far He spake as with Himself; but that at other times He spake with the Father as with another [person], n. 1745, 1999, 7058. That the Lord united His human with the Divine from His own proper power, n. 1666, 1749, 1753, 1813, 1921, 2025, 2026, 2523, 3141, 5005, 5045, 6716. That the Lord united the Divine Truth, which was Himself, with the Divine Good which was in Himself, n. 10,047, 10,052, 10,076. That the unition was reciprocal, n. 2004, 10,067. That the Lord, when He went out of the world, made His human Divine Good, n. 3194, 3210, 6864, 7499, 8724, 9199, 10,076. That thus He came forth from the Father, and returned to the Father, n. 3194, 3210. That thus He became one with the Father, n. 2751, 3704, 4766. That the Lord, in His unition with the Divine itself which was in Him, regarded the conjunction

of Himself with the human race, n. 2034. That since the unition, Divine Truth proceeds from the Lord, n. 3704, 3712, 3969, 4577, 5704, 7499, 8127, 8241, 9199, 9398. In what manner Divine Truth proceeds from the Lord, illustrated, n. 7270, 9407.

That unless the Divine had been in the Lord's human from conception, the human could not have been united with the Divine itself, on account of the ardor of the infinite love in which the Divine itself is, n. 6849. That for this reason no angel can ever be united with the Divine itself except at a distance, and by means of a veil or covering; for otherwise he would be consumed, n. 6849. That the Divine Love is of such a quality, n. 8644. Hence it may appear that the human of the Lord was not like the human of another man, n. 10,125, 10,826. That His union with the Father, from whom He had His soul, was not like a union between two, but like that between soul and body, n. 3737, 10,824. That the union subsisting between the Lord's human and the Divine is properly union, but that subsisting between man and the Divine is more properly called conjunction, n. 2021.

305. *That thus the Lord made His human Divine.* That the human of the Lord is Divine, because it was derived from the esse of the Father, which was the Lord's soul,—illustrated by children partaking of their father's likeness, n. 10,270, 10,372, 10,823. And because it was derived from the Divine Love which was in Him, n. 6872. That every man is such as his love is, and that he is his own love, n. 6872, 10,177, 10,284. That the Lord was Divine Love, n. 2077, 2253. That the Lord made all His human, both internal and external, Divine, n. 1603, 1815, 1902, 1926, 2093, 2803. That therefore He rose again as to the whole body, differently from any man, n. 1729, 2083, 5078, 10,825. That the Lord's human is Divine, is acknowledged by the omnipresence of His human in the sacred supper, n. 2343, 2359. And that it is evident from His transformation before the three disciples, n. 3212. And likewise from the Word, n. 10,154. And that He is there called Jehovah, n. 1603, 1736, 1815, 1902, 2921, 3035, 5110, 6303, 6281, 8864, 9194, 9315. That in the literal sense of the Word there is a distinction made between the Father and the Son, or Jehovah and the Lord, but not in the internal sense, in which the angels are, n. 3035. That the Christian world does not acknowledge the human of the Lord to be Divine, in consequence of a decree passed by a council in favor of the Pope, that he might be acknowledged as the Lord's vicar;—proved from conversation with them in another life, n. 4738.

That the Divine human from eternity was the Divine Truth in heaven, thus the Divine existere, which was afterwards made in the Lord the Divine esse, from which the Divine existere in heaven [proceeded], n. 3061, 6280, 6880, 10,579. The previous state of heaven described, n. 6371, 6372, 6373. That the Divine was not perceptible, and therefore not capable of being received, until it passed through heaven, n. 6982, 6996, 7004. That the Lord from eternity, was the Divine Truth in heaven, n. 2803, 3195, 3704. That this is the Son of God born from eternity, n. 2628, 2798.

That in heaven no other Divine is perceived but the Divine Human, n. 6475, 9303, 9267, 10,067. That the most ancient people could not worship the infinite esse, but the infinite existere, which is the Divine Human, n. 4687, 5321. That the ancients acknowledged the Divinity, because it appeared in a human form, and that this was the Divine Human, n. 5110, 5663, 6846, 10,737. That the inhabitants of all the earths adore the Divinity under a human form, and that they rejoice when they hear that God actually became a man, n. 6700, 8541 to 8547, 9361, 10,736, 10,737, 10,738. *See also the little work* ON THE EARTHS IN OUR SOLAR SYSTEM, AND IN THE STARRY HEAVEN. That God cannot be thought of but in a human form, and that what is incomprehensible can be the object of no idea, n. 9359, 9972. That man can worship what he has some idea of, but not what he has no idea of, n. 4733, 5110, 5633, 7211, 9267, 10,667. That therefore the Divinity is worshiped under a human form by most nations in the globe, and that this is through an influx from heaven, n. 10,159. That all who are in good as to life, when they think of the Lord, think of a Divine Human, but not of the human separated from the Divine, n. 2326, 4724, 4731, 4766, 8878, 9193, 9198. That they in the church at this day who are in evil as to life, and they who are in faith separate from charity, think of the human of the Lord without the Divine, and do not comprehend what the Divine Human is, the causes thereof, n. 3212, 3241, 4689, 4692, 4724 4731, 5321, 6372, 8878, 9193, 9198.

306. *That there is a Trinity in the Lord.* That Christians were examined in the other life concerning the idea they entertained of one God, and it was found that they entertained an idea of three Gods, n. 2329, 5256, 10,736, 10,737, 10,738, 10,821. That a Divine Trinity may be conceived in one person, and thus one God, but not in three persons, n. 10,738, 10,821, 10,824. That the trinity in one person, that is, in the Lord, is the Divine itself, which is called the Father, the Divine Human, which is called the Son, and the Divine proceeding, which is called the Holy Spirit; and that thus the trinity is one, n. 2149, 2156, 2288, 2321, 2329, 2447, 3704, 6993, 7182, 10,738, 10,822, 10,823. That a Divine Trinity in the Lord is acknowledged in heaven, n. 14, 15, 1729, 2005, 5256, 9303. That the Lord is one with the Father, thus He is the Divine itself, and the Divine Human, n. 1729, 2004, 2005, 2018, 2025, 2751, 3704, 3736, 4706. That His Divine proceeding is also His Divine in heaven, which is called the Holy Spirit, n. 3969, 4673, 6788, 6993, 7499, 8127, 8302, 9199, 9228, 9229, 9270, 9407, 9818, 9820, 10,330. That therefore the Lord is the alone and only God, n. 1607, 2149, 2156, 2329, 2447, 2751, 3194, 3704, 3712, 3939, 4577, 4687, 5321, 6280, 6371, 6849, 6993, 7014, 7091, 7182, 7209, 8241, 8724, 8763, 8864, 8865, 9194, 9303.

307. *Of the Lord in heaven.* That the Lord appears in heaven both as a sun and a moon; as a sun, to those who are in the celestial kingdom, and as a moon, to those who are in the spiritual kingdom, n. 1053, 1521, 1529, 1530, 1531, 3636, 3643, 4321, 5097, 7078, 7083, 7173, 7270, 8812, 10,809. That the light which proceeds from the Lord as a sun is Divine Truth, from which the angels derive all their wisdom and intelligence, n. 1053, 1521 to 1533, 2776, 3138, 3195, 3222, 3223, 3225, 3399, 3341, 3636, 3643, 3993, 4180, 4302, 4415, 5400, 9399, 9407, 9548, 9571, 9684. And that the heat which

proceeds from the Lord as a sun, is Divine Good, from which the angels derive their love, n. 3338, 3636, 3643, 5215. That the Lord's Essential Divine is far above His Divine in heaven, n. 7270, 8760. That Divine Truth is not in the Lord, but proceeds from the Lord, as light is not in the sun, but proceeds from the sun, n. 3969. That esse is in the Lord, and existere from the Lord, n. 3938. That the Lord is the common centre to which all the angels in heaven turn, n. 3633, 9828, 10,130, 10,189. That nevertheless the angels do not turn to the Lord, but the Lord turns them to Him, n. 10,189: because the angels are not present with the Lord, but the Lord is present with the angels, n. 9415. That the Lord's presence with the angels is according to their reception of the good of love and charity from Him, n. 904, 4198, 4206, 4211, 4320, 6280, 6832, 7042, 8819, 9680, 9682, 9683, 10,106, 10,811. That the Lord is present with all in heaven, and all in hell, n. 2766. That the Lord from His Divine Love wishes to draw all men to Himself into heaven, n. 6645. That the Lord is in a continual endeavor at conjunction with man, but that His influx and conjunction are impeded by the loves of man's proprium, n. 2041, 2053, 2411, 5696.

That the Divine Human of the Lord flows into heaven, and constitutes heaven, and that there is no conjunction with the Divine in heaven, but with the Divine Human, n. 3038, 4211, 4724, 5633. And that the Divine Human flows in with men out of heaven and through heaven, n. 1925. That the Lord is the all of heaven, and the life of heaven, n. 7211, 9128. That the Lord dwells with the angels in what is His own, n. 9338, 10,125, 10,151, 10,157. Hence they who are in heaven are in the Lord, n. 3637, 3638. That heaven corresponds to the Divine Human of the Lord, and that man, as to all and singular things, corresponds to heaven, whence heaven collectively is as one man, and is therefore called the GRAND MAN, n. 2948, 2996, 3624 to 3629, 3636 to 3643, 3741 to 3745, 4625. That the Lord is the only man, and that they only are men who receive the Divine from Him, n. 1894. That so far as they receive the Divine, so far they become images of the Lord, n. 8547. That the angels are forms of love and charity in a human form, and that this is from the Lord, n. 3804, 4735, 4797, 4985, 5199, 5530, 9879, 10,177.

308. *That all good and truth are from the Lord.* That the Lord is good itself and truth itself, n. 2011, 5110, 10,336, 10,619. That all good and truth, consequently all peace, innocence, love, charity, and faith, are from the Lord, n. 1614, 2016, 2751, 2882, 2883, 2891, 2892, 2904. And that all wisdom and intelligence are from Him, n. 109, 112, 121, 124. That nothing but good comes from the Lord, but that the wicked turn the good which is from the Lord into evil, n. 7643, 7679, 7710, 8632. That the angels know that all good and truth are from the Lord, but that the wicked are not willing to know this, n. 6193, 9128. That angels at the presence of the Lord, are more in good, but infernals, at the presence of the Lord, are more in evil, n. 7989. That the wicked cast themselves into hell at the mere presence of the Lord, n. 8137, 8266. That the Lord judges all from good, n. 2335. That the Lord regards all from mercy, n. 223. That the Lord is never angry with any one, nor does evil to

any one, and does not send any one to hell, n. 245, 1683, 2335, 8632. In what sense those parts of the Word are to be understood, where it is said, that Jehovah or the Lord is angry, that He kills, that He casts into hell, and other things of the like nature, n. 592, 696, 1093, 1874, 1875, 2395, 2447, 3605, 3607, 3614, 6073, 6997.

309. *That the Lord has all power in the heavens and on earth.* That the universal heaven is the Lord's, n. 2751, 7086. And that He has all power in the heavens and on earth, n. 1607, 10,089, 10,827. That as the Lord governs the universal heaven, He also governs all things which depend thereon, thus all things in the world, n. 2026, 2027, 4523, 4524. That He also governs the hells, n. 3643. That the Lord governs all things from the Divine, by the Divine Human, n. 8864, 8865. That the Lord governs all things according to Divine Order, and that Divine Order has relation to those things which are of His will, to those things which are done from leave, and to those things which are done from permission, n. 1755, 2447, 3074, 9948; concerning order, see what is said above, at n. 238. That the Lord governs the last things from the first, and the first from the last, and that this is the reason why He is called the first and the last, n. 3702, 6040, 6056. That the Lord alone has the power of removing the hells, of withholding from evils, and of keeping in good, thus of saving, n. 10,019. That judgment belongs to the Lord, n. 2319, 2320, 2321, 10,810, 10,811. What the Lord's priesthood is, and what His royalty is, n. 1728, 2015.

310. *In what manner some expressions in the Word, which relate to the Lord, are to be understood.* What is meant by the seed of the woman, in the prophecy concerning the Lord, n. 256. What the Son of Man and the Son of God signify in the Word, n. 2159, 2813. What the two names, Jesus Christ, signify, n. 3004 to 3011. What is signified by the Lord's being said to be sent by the Father, n. 2397, 6831, 10,561. How it is to be understood, that the Lord bore the iniquities of all, n. 9937. How it is to be understood, that the Lord redeemed man by His blood, n. 10,152. How it is to be understood, that the Lord fulfilled the whole law, n. 10,239. How it is to be understood, that the Lord intercedes for mankind, n. 2250, 8573, 8705. How it is to be understood, that without the Lord there is no salvation, n. 10,828. That salvation is not effected by looking to the Father, or by praying Him to have mercy for the sake of His Son; for the Lord says, *I am the way, the truth, and the life; no one cometh to the Father but by Me*, John xiv. 6; n. 2854. The contradictions which are involved in the received faith, that the Lord reconciled the human race to the Father, by the passion of the cross, n. 10,659. That the coming of the Lord is His presence in the Word, n. 3900, 4060. That the Lord does not desire glory from man for the sake of Himself, but of man's salvation, n. 5957, 10,646. That wherever the name Lord occurs in the Word, it signifies Divine Good, n. 4973, 9167, 9194. That where the name Christ occurs, it signifies Divine Truth, n. 3003, 3004, 3005, 3009.

That the true acknowledgment and true worship of the Lord, is to do His precepts,—shown from the Word, n. 10,143, 10,153, 10,578, 10,645, 10,829.

OF ECCLESIASTICAL AND CIVIL GOVERNMENT.

311. There are two classes of affairs which ought to be [kept] in order amongst men; namely, those which relate to the things of heaven, and those which relate to the things of the world. The former are called ecclesiastical, and the latter civil affairs.

312. It is impossible for order to be maintained in the world without governors, to observe the proceedings of those who act according to order, and of those who act contrary to order, that they may reward the former, and punish the latter. Unless this were done, the human race would perish. The desire of ruling over others, and of possessing their property, being hereditary in every individual, and being the source whence all enmity, envying, hatred, revenge, deceit, cruelty, and numerous other evils proceed; unless men, in the exercise of their prevailing inclinations, were, on the one hand, restrained by fear of the laws and the dread of punishment, involving the loss of honor, of property, and of life, as the necessary consequences of a course of evil; and, on the other hand, encouraged by the hope of honor and of gain, as the reward of well-doing; there would be an end of the human race.

313. There should be governors, therefore, for the preservation of order in the various societies of mankind: and they ought to be persons well skilled in the laws, men of wisdom, having the fear of God. There must also be order among the governors themselves; lest any of them, from caprice, or ignorance, should sanction evils which are contrary to order, and thereby destroy it. This is guarded against by the appointment of superior and inferior governors, among whom there is subordination.

314. Governors appointed over those things amongst men which relate to heaven, or ecclesiastical affairs, are called priests, and their office is called the priesthood. But governors set over those things which relate to the world, or civil affairs, are called magistrates, and their chief, where such a form of government is established, is called the king.

315. With respect to priests, their duty is to teach men the way to heaven, and likewise to lead them therein. They are to teach them according to the doctrine of their church, which is derived from the Word; and to lead them to live according to that doctrine. Priests, who teach the doctrine of truth, and lead their flocks thereby to goodness of life, and so to the Lord, are the good shepherds spoken of in the Word; but they who only teach, and do not lead to goodness of life, and so to the Lord, are the bad shepherds.

316. Priests ought not to claim to themselves any power over the souls of men, inasmuch as they cannot discern the

real state of the interiors, or of the heart; much less ought they to claim the power of opening and shutting heaven, because that power belongs to the Lord alone.

317. Dignity and honor ought to be paid to priests on account of the sanctity of their calling; but they who are wise ascribe all such honor to the Lord, from whom all sanctity proceeds, and not to themselves; whereas, they who are not wise, attribute the honor to themselves, and take it from the Lord. They who claim honor to themselves on account of the sanctity of their calling, prefer honor and gain to the salvation of souls, which is the object for which they ought above all things to provide: but they who attribute honor to the Lord, and not to themselves, prefer the salvation of souls to honor and gain. The honor of any employment is not in the person of him who is employed, but is only annexed to him on account of the dignity of the duty in which he is engaged; and what is so annexed does not belong to the person, but to the employment, being separated from the person when he is separated from the employment. All personal honor is the honor of wisdom and the fear of the Lord.

318. Priests ought to instruct the people, and to lead them, by truths, to good of life, but they ought not to use compulsion, since no one can be compelled to believe contrary to what he thinks in his heart to be true. He who differs in opinion from the priest ought to be left in peace, provided he make no disturbance: but when such a person makes disturbances, he must be separated; for this also is agreeable to the order, for the sake of which the priesthood is established.

319. As priests are appointed to administer those things which belong to the Divine law and worship, so kings and magistrates are appointed to administer those things which belong to the civil law and judgment.

320. Since the king cannot, by himself, administer all things, subordinate governors are appointed, to each of whom a distinct province is assigned in the administration, where that of the king cannot extend immediately. These governors, in their collective capacity, constitute the royalty; the king himself being the chief.

321. The royalty itself is not in any person, but is annexed to the person. The king who believes that the royalty is in his own person, or the governor who supposes that the dignity of his office is in his own person, is not wise.

322. The royalty consists in administering and in judging from justice, according to the laws of the realm. The king who considers the laws as superior to himself, is wise; but the who considers himself as superior to the laws is not wise. The king who regards the laws as above himself, places the royalty in the law, and submits to its dominion; he knows that the

law is justice, and that all justice, which is really such, is Divine: but he who considers himself as above the laws, places the royalty in himself, and either believes himself to be the law, or the law, which is justice, to be derived from himself; hence he arrogates to himself that which is Divine, and to which, at the same time, he ought to be in subjection.

323. The law, which is justice, ought to be enacted in the realm, by persons well skilled in legislation, men of wisdom, who fear God; and both the king and his subjects ought afterwards to live according to it. The king who lives according to the laws enacted, and therein sets an example to his subjects, is truly a king.

324. The king who is vested with absolute power, and who believes that his subjects are such slaves that he has a right to their possessions and lives, and exercises such imaginary right, is not a king, but a tyrant.

325. The king ought to be obeyed according to the laws of the realm, and by no means to be injured either by word or deed; for on this depends the public security.

NOTE.—The word "governor," which occurs so frequently in the foregoing chapter, is, in the original, simply "præfectus," which in general signifies a "director," "officer," or "minister," rather than "governor," in the limited sense of that word, as it is popularly used at the present day. There are several other inaccuracies in the chapter as above given, but we have thought it best, on the whole, not to deviate much from the rendering of the English translator. Inasmuch, however, as this particular portion of the work has been the subject of considerable discussion, and its meaning variously interpreted, we append the following transcript of the original text from the edition published by Swedenborg himself, at London, in 1768.

DE REGIMINE ECCLESIASTICO & CIVILI.

311. Sunt duo, quæ apud homines in ordine erunt, nempe quæ Cœli sunt, & quæ Mundi: illa quæ Cœli sunt, vocantur Ecclesiastica, quæ Mundi sunt, vocantur Civilia.

312. Ordo non potest teneri in Mundo absque Præfectis, qui observaturi omnia quæ secundum ordinem, & quæ contra ordinem fiunt; & qui remuneraturi illos qui secundum ordinem vivunt, & punituri illos qui contra ordinem; si id non fit, peribit Genus humanum; nam cuivis ex hæreditario connatum est velle imperare aliis, ac possidere bona aliorum, unde inimicitiæ, invidiæ, odia, vindictæ, doli, sævitiæ, & plura alia mala; quapropter nisi in vinculis teneantur per leges, & per remunerationes convenientes amoribus illorum, quæ sunt honores & lucra, pro illis qui bona faciunt, ac per punitiones contrarias amoribus illis, quæ sunt jacturæ honorum, possessionum, & vitæ, pro illis qui mala faciunt, periturum esset Genus humanum.

313. Erunt itaque Præfecti, qui Cœtus hominum tenebunt in ordine qui, legisperiti, sapientes, & timentes Deum. Inter Præfectos etiam erit ordo, ne aliquis ex lubitu aut inscitia permittat mala contra ordinem, & sic destruat illum, quod cavetur cum Præfecti superiores & inferiores sunt, inter quos subordinatio.

314. Præfecti super illa apud homines quæ Cœli sunt, seu super Ecclesiastica, vocantur Sacerdotes, ac munus eorum Sacerdotium. Præfecti autem super illa apud homines quæ Mundi sunt, seu super Civilia, vocantur Magistratus, ac Summus eorum, ubi talia Imperia, Rex.

315. Quod concernit Sacerdotes, docebunt illi homines viam ad Cœlum, & quoque ducent illos; docebunt illos secundum Ecclesiæ suæ doctrinam ex Verbo, ac ducent

ut vivant secundum illam. Sacerdotes, qui docent vera, & per illa ducunt ad bonum vitæ, & sic ad Dominum, sunt Pastores ovium boni; qui autem docent, & non ducunt ad bonum vitæ, & sic ad Dominum, sunt Pastores mali.

316. Sacerdotes non sibi aliquam potestatem super animas hominum vindicabunt, quia non sciunt in quo statu sunt interiora hominis; minus sibi vindicabunt potestatem aperiendi & claudendi Cœlum, quoniam ea potestas est Solius Domini.

317. Sacerdotibus erit dignitas & honor propter Sancta quæ obeunt; sed qui sapiunt, dant honorem Domino a Quo Sancta, & non sibi; qui autem non sapiunt, tribuunt honorem sibi; hi illum adimunt Domino. Qui honorem tribuunt sibi propter Sancta quæ obeunt, illi præferunt honorem & lucrum saluti animarum, cui consulent; qui autem honorem dant Domino & non sibi, illi præferunt salutem animarum honori & lucro. Nullus honor alicujus functionis in persona est, sed ei adjungitur secundum dignitatem rei quam administrat; & quod adjungitur, hoc non ipsius personæ est, & quoque separatur cum functione: honor in persona est honor sapientiæ & timoris Domini.

318. Sacerdotes populum docebunt, ac ducent per vera ad bonum vitæ, sed usque nullum cogent, quoniam nullus cogi potest ad credendum contra id quod cogitavit ex corde esse verum; qui aliter credit quam Sacerdos, & non turbas facit, relinquetur in pace; at qui turbas facit, separabitur; nam hoc etiam est ordinis, propter quem Sacerdotium.

319. Sicut Sacerdotes præfecti sunt ad administrandum illa, quæ Legis Divinæ & Cultus sunt, ita Reges et Magistratus ad administrandum illa quæ Legis Civilis & Judicii sunt.

320. Quia Rex non solus potest administrare omnia, ideo sunt Præfecti sub illo, quorum unicuivis data est provincia administrandi quod Rex non potest & valet; hi Præfecti simul sumti constituunt Regium, sed ipso* Rex est Summus.

321. Ipsum Regium non est in persona, sed adjunctum est personæ: Rex qui credit quod Regium sit in sua persona, & Præfectus qui credit quod præfecturæ dignitas sit in sua persona, non sapit.

322. Regium consistit in administrando secundum leges Regni, & in judicando secundum illas ex justo: Rex qui spectat Leges supra se, is sapit, qui autem spectat se supra leges, is non sapit. Rex qui spectat Leges supra se, is Regium ponit in Lege, & Lex dominatur super illum, scit enim quod Lex sit Justitia & omnis Justitia quæ justitia est Divina: qui autem spectat se supra leges, is Regium ponit in se, & credit se vel esse Legem, vel Legem quæ Justitia esse a se; inde, quod Divinum est, sibi arrogat, sub quo tamen erit.

323. Lex quæ Justitia a Legisperitis sapientibus & timentibus Deum in Regno ferenda est, secundum quam dein & Rex & subditi vivent: Rex qui secundum Legem latam vivit, & in eo præcedit subditis exemplo, is vere Rex est.

324. Rex cui absoluta potestas, qui credit quod subditi ejus tales servi sint, ut jus habeat in eorum possessiones & vitas, & si id exercet, non Rex est sed Tyrannus.

325. Regi erit obedientia secundum leges Regni, nec factis & dictis ullo modo laedendus; inde enim pendet Securitas publica.

* Ipse?

FINIS.

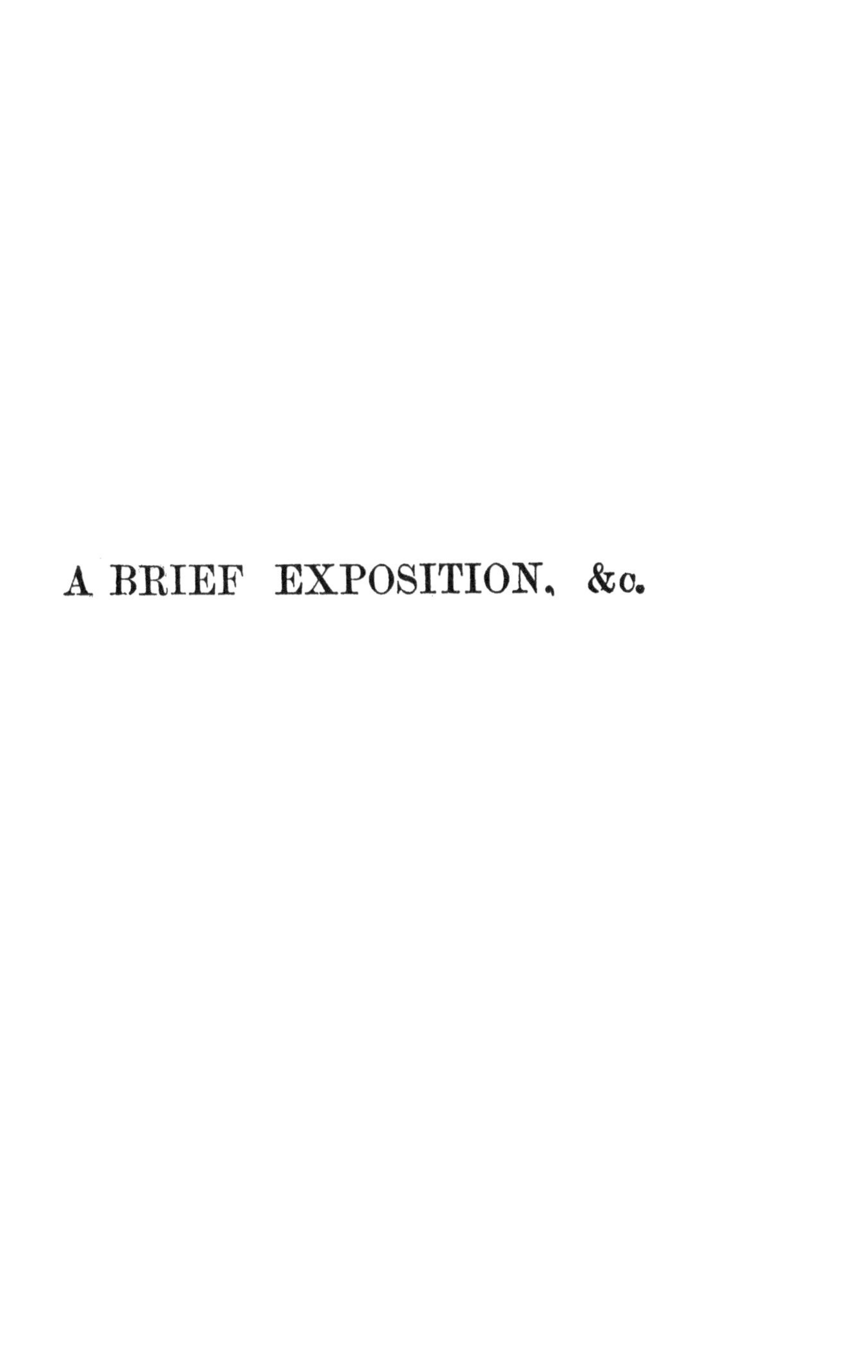

A BRIEF EXPOSITION, &c.

A

BRIEF EXPOSITION

OF THE

DOCTRINE

OF

THE NEW CHURCH,

SIGNIFIED BY THE

NEW JERUSALEM IN THE REVELATION.

From the Latin of

EMANUEL SWEDENBORG,

Servant of the Lord Jesus Christ.

BEING A TRANSLATION OF HIS WORK ENTITLED

"SUMMARIA EXPOSITIO DOCTRINÆ NOVÆ ECCLESIÆ, quæ per Novam Hierosolymam in Apocalypsi intelligitur: ab Emanuele Swedenborg, Sueco." Amstelodami, 1769.

NEW YORK.

AMERICAN SWEDENBORG PRINTING AND PUBLISHING SOCIETY,

REVELATION XXI. 2, 5.

I, John, saw the holy city, New Jerusalem, coming down from God out of heaven, prepared as a Bride adorned for her Husband. And He that sat upon the throne said, Behold, I make all things new: and He said unto me, Write, for these words are true and faithful.

CONTENTS.

APPENDIX.

A
BRIEF EXPOSITION
OF THE
DOCTRINE OF THE NEW CHURCH.

---

1. SEVERAL works and tracts having been published by me, during some years past, concerning the NEW JERUSALEM, whereby is meant a New Church about to be established by the Lord; and the Apocalypse having been revealed; I have come to a determination to lay before the world a complete view of the doctrine of that church in its full extent. But, as this is a work of some years, I have thought it advisable to draw up some sort of sketch thereof, in order that a general idea may first be formed of that church and its doctrine; because when general principles precede, then the several particulars will appear at full in a clear light, for these enter into general principles, as things homogeneous into their proper receptacles. This compendium, however, is not designed for critical examination, but is only offered to the world by way of information, as its contents will be proved at large in the work itself. But it is necessary first to state the doctrinals at present maintained concerning justification, that the following contrast between the doctrines of the present church, and those of the New Church, may be clearly understood.

THE DOCTRINALS OF THE ROMAN CATHOLICS CONCERNING JUSTIFICATION, FROM THE COUNCIL OF TRENT.

2. In the bull of Pope Pius IV., dated 13th November, 1564, are the following words: "I embrace and receive every thing, both generally and particularly, which the most holy Council of Trent hath determined and declared concerning *Original Sin and Justification*."

3. *From the Council of Trent, concerning Original Sin.* ([a]) That Adam, by his transgression, experienced an entire change and depravation of nature, both in body and soul; and

that the ill effects of Adam's transgression were not confined to himself, but also extended to his posterity ; and that it not only transmitted death and corporal sufferings upon all mankind, but likewise sin, which is the death of the soul, Sess. v. 1, 2. ([b]) That this sin of Adam, which originally was a single transgrēssion, and has been transmitted by propagation, and not by imitation, is so implanted in the nature of every man, as to be his own, and cannot be done away by any other means than by the merits of the only Saviour our Lord Jesus Christ, who has reconciled us to God by His blood, being made unto us righteousness, sanctification, and redemption, Sess. v. 3. ([c]) That by the transgression of Adam, all men lost their innocence, and became unclean, and by nature the children of wrath, Sess. vi. chap. 1.

4. *Concerning Justification.* ([a]) That our heavenly Father, the Father of Mercies, sent Christ Jesus His Son into the world, in the blessed fullness of time, as well to the Jews who were under the law, as to the Gentiles who followed not after righteousness, that they might all lay hold of righteousness, and receive the adoption of sons. Him God offered to be a propiti ation through faith in His blood, not only for our sins, but likewise for the sins of the whole world, Sess. vi. chap. 2. ([b]) Nevertheless all do not receive the benefit of His death, but only they to whom the merit of His passion is communicated ; so that unless they are born again in Christ, they can never be justified, Sess. vi. chap. 3. ([c]) That the beginning of justification is to be derived from the preventing grace of God through Christ Jesus, that is, from His call, Sess. vi. chap. 5. ([c]) That men are disposed to righteousness, when, being stirred up by Divine grace, and conceiving faith by hearing, they are freely moved towards God, believing those things to be true which are divinely revealed and promised ; and especially this, that the ungodly are justified by God through His grace, through redemption, which is by Christ Jesus ; and when, being convinced of sin from the fear of Divine justice, by which they are profitably disquieted, they are encouraged to hope, and to trust that God, for Christ's sake, will be propitious to them, Sess. vi. chap. 6. ([d]) That the consequence of this disposition and preparation is actual justification, which is not only a remission of sins, but likewise a sanctification and renovation of the interior man by the reception of Divine grace and gifts, whereby man from being unrighteous becomes righteous, and from being an enemy a friend, so as to be an heir according to the hope of eternal life, Sess. vi. chap. 7. ([e]) The *final cause* of justification is the glory of God and of Christ, and life eternal. The *efficient cause* is God, who freely cleanses and sanctifies. The *meritorious cause* is the dearly-beloved and only-begotten Son of God, our Lord Jesus Christ, who when we were enemies, through the

great love wherewith He loved us, by His most holy passion upon the cross merited for us justification, and made satisfaction for us to God the Father. The *instrumental cause* is the sacrament of baptism which is a sacrament of faith, without which none can ever be justified. The *formal cause* is the sole righteousness of God; not that whereby He is righteous Himself, but that whereby He makes us righteous, with which being gifted by Him, we are renewed in the spirit of our mind; and are not only reputed righteous, but are truly called righteous, and are so in reality, each according to that measure which the Holy Spirit imparts to every one as it pleases Him, Sess. vi. chap. 7, § 2. (f) That justification is a translation from that state, wherein man is born a child of the first Adam, into a state of grace and adoption among the sons of God by the second Adam, our Saviour Jesus Christ, Sess. vi. chap. 4.

5. *Concerning Faith, Charity, Good Works, and Merits.* (a) When the apostle declares, that man is justified by faith, and freely, these words are to be understood in the sense wherein the Catholic church has uniformly held and expressed them; to wit, that we are said to be justified by faith, because faith is the commencement of man's salvation, the foundation and root of all justification, without which it is impossible to please God, and attain to the fellowship of His children. But we are said to be justified freely, because none of those things which precede justification, whether faith or works, merit the actual grace of justification; for if it be grace, it is not of works, otherwise grace would not be grace, Sess. vi. chap. 8. (b) Although none can be righteous, but they to whom the merits of the passion of our Lord Jesus Christ are communicated, nevertheless that is effected in justification, when by the merit of the same most holy passion, the love of God is infused by the Holy Ghost into the hearts of those who are justified, and abides in them. Hence in the act of justification, man receives, together with the remission of his sins, all these things infused into him at once by Jesus Christ, in whom he is ingrafted by faith, hope, and charity. For faith, unless charity be added to it, neither unites perfectly to Christ, nor constitutes a living member of His body, Sess. vi. chap. 7, § 3. (c) That Christ is not only a Redeemer in whom they have faith, but also a Lawgiver, whom they obey, Sess. vi. chap. 16, can. 21. (d) That faith without works is dead and vain, because in Christ Jesus neither circumcision availeth any thing, nor uncircumcision, but faith which worketh by love: for faith without hope and charity cannot avail unto eternal life; wherefore also they hearken to the word of Christ, "If thou wilt enter into life, keep the commandments." Thus they who are born again, receiving true Christian righteousness, are commanded to keep it white and unspotted, as their first robe, given them by Jesus Christ,

instead of that which Adam lost both for himself and us by his disobedience, that they may present it before the tribunal of our Lord Jesus Christ, and obtain eternal life, Sess. vi. chap. 7, § 4. ([e]) That there is a continual influx of power from Jesus Christ Himself into those who are justified, as from a head into the members, and from a vine into the branches; which power always precedes, accompanies, and follows their good works, and without which they could not by any means be acceptable and meritorious in the sight of God; wherefore we are to believe, that nothing more is wanting to those who are justified, but they may be fully assured, that by those works which have been wrought in God, they have merited eternal life, which will be bestowed upon them in due time, Sess. vi. chap. 16. ([f]) When we speak of our own righteousness, we do not mean as though it were our own from ourselves; for that which is termed our righteousness, is the righteousness of God, being infused into us by God through the merit of Christ. Far be it therefore from any Christian man to trust or glory in himself, and not in the Lord, whose goodness towards us men is so great, that he vouchsafes to regard those things as our merits, which are His own gifts, Sess. vi. chap. 16. ([g]) For of ourselves, as of ourselves, we can do nothing; but by His co-operation, who strengthens us, we can do all things. Thus man has not whereof to glory, but all our glory is in Christ, in Whom we live, in Whom we merit, in Whom we make satisfaction, bringing forth fruits worthy of repentance, which have their efficacy from Him, are offered unto the Father by Him, and are accepted by the Father through Him, Sess. xiv. chap. 8. ([h]) Whosoever shall say that man may be justified in the sight of God, by his own works, which are done either through the powers of human nature, or through the teaching of the law, without Divine grace through Christ Jesus, let him be accursed, Sess. vi. can. 1. ([i]) Whosoever shall say that man may believe, hope, and love, (that is, have faith, hope, and charity,) as is necessary in order that the grace of justification may be conferred upon him, without the preventing inspiration of the Holy Spirit, and His assistance, let him be accursed, Sess. vi. can. 2. ([k]) Whosoever shall say that man is justified without the righteousness of Christ, whereby He has merited for us, let him be accursed, Sess. vi. can. 10. Not to mention many more passages, principally relating to the conjunction of faith with charity or good works, and condemning their separation.

6. *Concerning Free-will.* ([a]) That free-will is by no means destroyed by Adam's sin, although it is debilitated and warped thereby, Sess. vi. chap. 1. ([b]) Whosoever shall say that the free-will of man, when moved and stirred up by God, cannot at all co-operate by concurring with God, who stirs it up and calls it, whereby man may dispose and prepare himself to

receive the grace of justification; or that he cannot dissent if he would, but that, like a thing inanimate, he is merely passive, and has not the least power of action, let him be accursed, Sess. vi. can. 4.

7. *The Doctrinals of the Roman Catholics concerning Justification, as collected from the Decrees of the Council of Trent, may be summed up and arranged in a series thus.* That the sin of Adam is transfused into the whole human race, whereby his state, and likewise the state of all men, became perverted, and alienated from God, and thus they were made enemies and children of wrath; that therefore God the Father graciously sent His son to reconcile, expiate, atone, satisfy, and thus to redeem, by being made righteousness. That Christ accomplished and fulfilled all this, by offering up Himself a sacrifice to God the Father upon the cross, and thus by his passion and blood. That Christ alone has merited, and that this His merit is graciously imputed, attributed, applied, and transferred to the man who is recipient thereof, by God the Father through the Holy Spirit; and that thus the sin of Adam is removed from man; concupiscence however still remaining in him as an incentive to sin. That justification is the remission of sins, and that from thence a renovation of the interior man takes place, whereby man from an enemy becomes a friend, and from being a child of wrath, a child of grace; and that thus union with Christ is effected, and the regenerate person becomes a living member of His body.

8. That faith comes by hearing, when a man believes those things to be true which are revealed from heaven, and trusts in the promises of God. That faith is the beginning of man's salvation, the foundation and root of all justification, without which it is impossible to please God, and enter into the fellowship of His children. That justification is brought about by faith, hope, and charity; and that unless faith be accompanied by hope and charity, it is not living but dead, and incapable of effecting union with Christ. That it is man's duty to co-operate; that he has the power to approach and recede, otherwise nothing could be given unto him, for he would be like an inanimate corpse. That inasmuch as the reception of justification renews man, and as this is effected by the application of the merit of Christ, during man's co-operation, it follows that works are meritorious; but inasmuch as they are done from grace, and by the Holy Spirit, and as Christ alone has merited, therefore God considers His own gifts in man as meritorious; whence it follows, that no one ought to attribute any thing of merit to himself.

THE DOCTRINALS OF THE PROTESTANTS CONCERNING JUSTIFICATION, FROM THE FORMULA CONCORDIÆ.

9. The book from whence the following extracts are collected, is called *Formula Concordiæ*, or *Formula of Concord*, and was composed by persons attached to the Augsburg confession; and as the pages will be cited where the quotations are to be met with, it is proper to observe, that I have made use of the edition printed at Leipsic in the year 1756.

10. *From the Formula Concordiæ, concerning Original Sin.* ([a]) That since the fall of Adam, all men naturally descended from him are born in sin, which brings damnation and eternal death upon those who are not regenerated, and that the merit of Christ is the only means whereby they are regenerated, consequently the only remedy whereby they are restored, page 9, 10, 52, 53, 55, 317, 641, 644, and Appendix, p. 138, 139. ([b]) That original sin is such a total corruption of nature, that there is no spiritual soundness in the powers of man either as to his soul or body, p. 574. ([c]) That it is the source of all actual sins, p. 317, 577, 639, 640, 942, Appendix, p. 139. ([d]) That it is a total absence or privation of the image of God, p. 640. ([e]) That we ought to distinguish between our nature, such as God created it, and original sin which dwells in our nature, p. 645. ([f]) Moreover, original sin is there styled the work of the devil, spiritual poison, the root of all evils, an accident and a quality; whereas our nature is there styled the work and creature of God, the personality of man, a substance, and an essence; and that the difference between them is the same as the difference between a man infected with a disease and the disease itself.

11. *Concerning Justification by Faith.* The *general principles* are these. ([a]) That by the Word and sacraments the Holy Ghost is given, who effects faith when and where he pleases, in those who hear the gospel. ([b]) That contrition, justification by faith, renovation, and good works, follow in due order; that they are to be properly distinguished one from the other; and that contrition and good works do not avail any thing unto salvation, but faith alone. ([c]) That justification by faith alone, is remission of sins, deliverance from damnation, reconciliation with the Father, adoption as sons, and is effected by the imputation of the merit or righteousness of Christ. ([d]) That hence faith is that essential righteousness, whereby we are accounted righteous before God, and that it is a trust and confidence in grace. ([e]) That renovation, which follows, is vivification, regeneration, and sanctification. ([f]) That good works, which are the fruits of faith, being in themselves works of the Spirit, follow that renovation. ([g]) That this faith may be lost by grievous sins. *The general principles concerning the Law and the Gospel* are

these. (h) That we must carefully distinguish between the law and the gospel, and between the works of the law and the works of the Spirit, which are the fruits of faith. (i) That the law is a doctrine which teaches that man is in sin, and therefore under condemnation and the wrath of God, thus exciting terror; but that the gospel is a doctrine which teaches atonement for sin, and deliverance from damnation by Christ, and thus a doctrine of consolation. (k) That there are three uses of the law, namely, to keep the wicked within bounds, to bring men to an acknowledgment of their sins, and to hold up to the regenerate a rule of life. (l) That the regenerate are in the law, but not under the law, for they are under grace. (m) That it is the duty of the regenerate to exercise themselves in the law, because, during their life in the world, they are prompted to sin by the lusts of the flesh; but that they become pure and perfect after death. (n) That the regenerate are also chastised by the Holy Ghost, and endure various afflictions, but that nevertheless they keep the law willingly, and thus being the children of God, live in obedience to the law. (o) That with those who are not regenerated, the veil of Moses still remains before their eyes, and the old Adam bears rule; but that with the regenerate the veil of Moses is taken away, and the old Adam brought into subjection or crucified.

12. *Particulars from the Formula Concordiæ, concerning Justification by Faith without the works of the Law.* (a) That faith is imputed for righteousness without works, on account of the merit of Christ which is laid hold of by faith, p. 78, 79, 80, 584, 689. (b) That charity follows justifying faith, but that faith does not justify as being formed by charity, as the Papists say, p. 81, 89, 94, 117, 688, 691, Appendix, p. 169. (c) That neither the contrition which precedes faith, nor the renovation and sanctification which follow after it, nor the good works then performed, have anything to do with justification by faith, p. 688, 689. (d) That it is a folly to imagine that the works of the second table of the decalogue justify in the sight of God, for that table has relation to our transactions with men, and not properly with God; and the business of justification is between God and us, and to appease His wrath, p. 102. (e) If any one therefore, believes he can obtain the remission of his sins, because he is possessed of charity, he brings a reproach on Christ, by an impious and vain confidence in his own righteousness, p. 87, 89. (f) That good works are utterly to be excluded, in treating of justification and eternal life, p. 589. (g) That good works are not necessary as a meritorious cause of salvation, and that they do not enter into the act of justification, p. 589, 590, 702, 704, Appendix, p. 173. (h) That the position, that good works are necessary to salvation, is to be rejected, because it takes away the comfort of the gospel, gives

occasion to doubt of the grace of God, instils a conceit of self-righteousness, and because they are admitted by the Papists to support a bad cause, p. 704. ([i]) The expression that good works are necessary to salvation, is rejected and condemned, p. 591. ([k]) That expressions, implying that good works are necessary unto salvation, ought not to be taught and defended, but rather exploded and rejected by the churches as false, p. 705. ([l]) That works, which do not proceed from a true faith, are in fact sins in the sight of God, that is to say, they are defiled with sin, because a corrupt tree cannot bring forth good fruit, p. 700. ([m]) That faith and salvation are neither preserved nor retained by good works, because these are only evidences that the Holy Spirit is present, and dwells in us, p. 590, 705, Appendix, p. 174. ([n]) That the Decree of the Council of Trent is deservedly to be rejected, which affirms that good works preserve salvation, or that justification by faith, or even faith itself, is maintained and preserved, either in the whole, or in the least part, by our works. p. 707.

13. *Particulars from the Formula Concordiæ, concerning the Fruits of Faith.* ([a]) That a difference is to be observed between the works of the law, and the works of the Spirit; and that the works which a regenerate person performs with a free and willing mind are not works of the law, but works of the Spirit, which are the fruits of faith; because they who are born again are not under the law, but under grace, p. 589, 590, 721, 722. ([b]) That good works are the fruits of repentance, p. 12. ([c]) That the regenerate receive by faith a new life, new affections, and new works, and that these are from faith in repentance, p. 134. ([d]) That man after conversion and justification begins to be renewed in his mind, and at length in his understanding, and that then his will is not inac tive or backward in performing daily exercises of repentance, p. 582, 673, 700. ([e]) That we ought to repent as well on account of original sin, as on account of actual sins, p. 321, Appendix, p. 159. ([f]) That repentance with Christians continues until death, because they have to wrestle with the remains of sin in the flesh as long as they live, p. 327. ([g]) That we must enter upon, and advance more and more in the practice of the law of the decalogue, p. 85, 86. ([h]) That the regenerate, although delivered from the curse of the law, ought nevertheless still to exercise themselves in the Divine law, p. 718. ([i]) That the regenerate are not without the law, though not under the law, for they live according to the law of the Lord, p. 722. ([k]) That the law ought to be considered by the regenerate as a rule of religious life, p. 596, 717, Appendix, p. 156. ([l]) That the regenerate do good works, not by constraint, but of their own accord and freely, as though they had received no command, had heard of no threatenings, and expected no reward, p. 596,

701. (m) That with them faith is always occupied in some good work, and he who does not thus perform good works, is destitute of true faith, for where there is faith, there will be also good works, p. 701. (n) That charity and good fruits follow faith and regeneration, p. 121, 122, 171, 188, 692. (o) Faith and works agree well together, and are inseparably connected; but faith alone lays hold of the blessing without works, and yet it is not alone; hence it is that faith without works is dead, p. 692, 693. (p) That after man is justified by faith, his faith being then true and alive is operative by charity, for good works always follow justifying faith, and are most certainly discovered with it; thus faith is never alone, but always accompanied by hope and charity, p. 586. (q) We allow, that where good works do not follow faith, in such case it is a false and not a true faith, p. 336. (r) That it is as impossible to separate good works from faith, as heat and light from fire, p. 701. (s) That as the old Adam is always inherent in our very nature, the regenerate have continual need of admonition, doctrine, threatenings, and even the chastisements of the law, for they are reproved and corrected by the Holy Spirit through the law, p. 719, 720, 721. (t) That the regenerate must wrestle with the old Adam, and that the flesh must be kept under by exhortations, threatenings, and stripes, because renovation of life by faith is only begun in the present life, p. 595, 596, 724. (u) That there remains a perpetual wrestling between the flesh and the spirit, in the elect and truly regenerate, p. 675, 679. (x) That the reason why Christ promises remission of sins to good works, is, because they follow reconciliation, and also because good fruits must necessarily follow, and because they are the signs of the promise, p. 116, 117. (y) That saving faith is not in those who have not charity, for charity is the fruit which infallibly and necessarily follows true faith, p. 688. (z) That good works are necessary on many accounts, but not as a meritorious cause, p. 11, 17, 64, 95, 133, 589, 590, 702, Appendix, p. 172. (aa) That a regenerate person ought to co-operate with the Holy Spirit, by the new gifts and powers which he has received, but in a certain way, p. 582, 583, 674, 675, Appendix, p. 144. (bb) *In the Confession of the Churches in the Low Countries, which was received in the Synod of Dort, we read as follows:* "Holy faith cannot be inactive in man, for it is a faith working by charity; and works, which proceed from a good root of faith, are good and acceptable in the sight of God, as being fruits of a good tree; for we are debtors unto God to do good works, but God is no debtor unto us, inasmuch as it is God that doeth them in us."

14. *Concerning Merits, from the Formula Concordiæ.* (a) That it is false, that our works merit remission of sins; false, that men are accounted righteous by the righteousness of rea-

son; and false, that reason of its own strength is capable of loving God above all things, and of keeping His law, p. 64. ([b]) That faith does not justify because it is in itself so good a work, and so excellent a virtue, but because it lays hold of the merit of Christ in the promise of the gospel, p. 76, 684. ([c]) That the promise of remission of sins, and justification for Christ's sake, does not involve any condition of merit, because it is freely offered, p. 67. ([d]) That a sinner is justified in the sight of God, or absolved from his sins, and from the most just sentence of damnation, and adopted into the number of the children of God, without any merit of his own, and without any works of his own, whether past, present, or future, of mere grace, and only on account of the sole merit of Christ, which is imputed to him for righteousness, p. 684. ([e]) That good works follow faith, remission of sins, and regeneration; and whatever of pollution or imperfection is in them, is not accounted sinful or defective, and that for Christ's sake; and thus that the whole man, both as to his person and his works, is rendered and pronounced righteous and holy, out of mere grace and mercy in Christ, shed abroad, displayed, and magnified towards us; wherefore we cannot glory on account of merit, p. 74, 92, 93, 336. ([f]) He who trusts in works, thinking he can merit any thing thereby, despises the merit and grace of Christ, and seeks a way to heaven without Christ, by his own strength, p. 16, 17, 18, 19. ([g]) Whosoever desires to ascribe something to good works in the article of justification, and to merit the grace of God thereby, to such a man works are not only unprofitable, but even pernicious, p. 708. ([h]) The works of the decalogue are enumerated, and other necessary works, which God vouchsafes to reward, p. 176, 198. ([i]) We teach, that good works are meritorious, not indeed of remission of sins, grace, and justification, but of other temporal rewards, and even spiritual rewards in this life, and after this life, because Paul says, "Every one shall receive a reward according to his labor;" and Christ says, "Great will be your reward in heaven;" and it is frequently said, that "it shall be rendered unto every one according to his works;" wherefore we acknowledge eternal life to be a reward, because it is our due according to promise, and because God crowns His own gifts, but not on account of our merits, p. 96, 133, 134, 135, 136, 137, 138. ([k]) That the good works of believers, when they are performed upon right principles, and directed to right ends, such as God requires from the regenerate, are signs of eternal salvation; and that God the Father accounts them acceptable and pleasing for Christ's sake, and promises to them excellent rewards of the present life, and of that which is to come, p. 708. ([l]) That although good works merit rewards, yet neither from their worthiness nor fitness do they merit the remission of sins, or the glory of eternal life, p. 96, 135, 139, &c. Appendix, p. 174. ([m]) That Christ at the last judgment will pass sentence on good and evil works, as the genuine effects and evidences of men's faith, p. 134; Appendix, p. 187. ([n]) That God rewards good works, but that it is of grace that He crowns His own gifts, is asserted in the *Confession of the Churches in the Low Countries.*

15. *Concerning Free-will, from the Formula Concordiæ.* ([a]) That man has not the smallest degree of ability in spiritual things, p. 15, 18, 219, 318, 579, 656, &c., Appendix, p. 141. ([b]) That man by the fall of his first parents is become so totally corrupt, that he is by nature blind with respect to spiritual things which relate to conversion and salvation, and accounts the Word of God as a foolish thing; and that he is and continues to be an enemy to God, until by the power of the Holy Spirit, through preaching and hearing of the Word, he is of mere grace, without any the least co-operation on his part, converted, gifted with faith, regenerated, and renewed, p. 656, 657. ([c]) That man is altogether corrupt and dead to what is good, so that in the nature of man, since the fall, and before regeneration, there is not so much as a spark of spiritual strength subsisting or remaining, whereby he can prepare himself for the grace of God, or apprehend it when offered, or of and by himself be capable of receiving it, or understand, believe, embrace, think, will, begin, perfect, act, operate, co-operate in spiritual things, or apply or accommodate himself to grace, or contribute any thing towards his conversion, either in the whole, the half, or the least part, p. 656, 658. ([d]) That man in spiritual and Divine things, which regard salvation, is like the pillar of salt into which Lot's wife was turned, and like a stock or a stone without life, which have neither the use of eyes, mouth, nor any of the senses, p. 661, 662. ([e]) That still man has a locomotive power, by virtue whereof he can govern his outward members, attend public worship, and hear the Word and the gospel; but that in his private thoughts he despises it as a foolish thing; and in this respect is worse than a stock, unless the Holy Spirit is efficacious in him, p. 662, 671, 672, 673. ([f]) That still it is not with man in his conversion, as in the forming of a stone into a statue, or the stamping an impression upon wax, which have neither knowledge, sense, nor will, p. 662, 681. ([g]) That man in his conversion is a merely passive subject, and not an active one, p. 662, 681. ([h]) That man in his conversion does not at all co-operate with the Holy Spirit, p. 219, 579, 583, 672, 676, Appendix, p. 143, 144. ([h]) That man since the fall retains and possesses the faculty of knowing natural things, as also free-will in some measure to choose natural and civil good, p. 14, 218, 641, 664, Appendix, 142. ([i]) That the assertions of certain fathers, and modern doctors, that God draws man, but draws him in a manner consistent with his will, are not con-

sonant with Holy Scripture, p. 582, 583. (k) That man, when he is born again by the power of the Holy Spirit, co-operates, though in much weakness, from the new powers and gifts, which the Holy Spirit has begun to operate in him at his conversion, not indeed forcibly, but spontaneously, p. 582, &c., 673, 674, 675, Appendix, p. 144. (l) That in the regenerate, not only the gifts of God, but likewise Christ himself dwells by faith, as in His temples, p. 695, 697, 698, Appendix, p. 130. (m) There is a wide difference between baptized persons and persons not baptized; for it is the doctrine of Paul, that all who have been baptized, have put on Christ, and are truly regenerate, having thereby acquired a freedom of will, that is to say, being again made free, as Christ testifies, whence they not only hear the Word of God, but are likewise enabled, though in much weakness, to assent and embrace it by faith, p. 675.

It is proper to observe, that the foregoing extracts are taken from a book called *Formula Concordiæ*, which was composed by persons attached to the Augsburg confession; but that nevertheless the like doctrines concerning *justification by faith alone* are maintained and taught by the members of the Reformed Church in England and Holland; wherefore the following treatise is intended for all; see below, n. 17, 18.

A SKETCH

OF THE

DOCTRINALS OF THE NEW CHURCH.

---

16. WE now proceed to give a brief Exposition of the Doctrine of the New Church, which is signified by the New Jerusalem in the Apocalypse, chap. xxi. and xxii. This doctrine, which is not only a doctrine of faith, but also of life, will be divided in the larger work into three parts.

THE FIRST PART will treat: I. *Of the Lord God the Saviour, and of the Divine Trinity in Him.* II. *Of the Sacred Scripture, and its Two Senses, the Natural and the Spiritual, and of its Sanctity thence derived.* III. *Of Love to God and Love towards our Neighbor, and of the Agreement of those Loves with each other.* IV. *Of Faith, and its Conjunction with those Two Loves.* V. *The Doctrine of Life from the Commandments of the Decalogue.* VI. *Of Reformation and Regeneration.* VII. *Of Free-will, and Man's Co-operation with the Lord thereby.* VIII. *Of Baptism.* IX. *Of the Holy Supper.* X. *Of Heaven and Hell.* XI. *Of Man's Conjunction therewith, and of the State of Man's Life after Death according to that Conjunction.* XII. *Of Eternal Life.*

THE SECOND PART will treat: I. *Of the Consummation of the Age, or End of the present Church.* II. *Of the Coming of the Lord.* III. *Of the Last Judgment.* IV. *Of the New Church, which is the New Jerusalem.*

THE THIRD PART will point out the *Disagreements between the Tenets of the present Church, and those of the New Church.* But we will dwell a little upon these now, because it is believed both by the clergy and laity, that the present church is in the genuine light of the gospel and in the truths thereof, which cannot possibly be disproved, overturned, or controverted, not even by an angel from heaven: neither does the present church see any otherwise, because it has withdrawn the understanding from faith, and yet has confirmed its tenets by a kind of sight beneath the understanding, for falses may there be confirmed to such a degree, as to put on the appearance of truths; and when this is the case, they acquire a fallacious light, before which the light of truth appears as darkness. For this reason we shall here dwell a little upon this subject, mentioning the disagreements, and illustrating them by brief remarks, that such as have not their understandings closed by a blind faith, may see them at first as in a kind of twilight, and afterwards as in morning light, and at length, in the large work, as in the light of day. The disagreements in general are as follows.

I.

17. *That the Churches, which by the Reformation separated themselves from the Roman Catholic Church, dissent in various points of doctrine; but that they all agree in the articles concerning a Trinity of Persons in the Godhead, Original Sin from Adam, Imputation of the Merit of Christ, and Justification by Faith alone.*

BRIEF ANALYSIS OF THE ABOVE PROPOSITION.

18. The churches which by the Reformation separated themselves from the Romish church, are composed of such as call themselves Evangelical and Reformed, likewise Protestants, or, from the names of their leaders, Lutherans and Calvinists, among which the church of England holds the middle place: we shall say nothing here of the Greek church, which long ago separated from the church of Rome. That the Protestant churches dissent in various things, particularly concerning the holy supper, baptism, election, and the person of Christ, is well known to many; but that they all agree in the articles of a trinity of persons in the Godhead, original sin, imputation of the merit of Christ, and justification by faith alone, is not universally known. The reason of this is, because few persons apply themselves to inquire into the differences of sentiment

maintained by different churches, and consequently few understand wherein they agree: it is only the clergy that study the tenets of their church, while the laity rarely enter deeply into them, and consequently are unacquainted with differences in opinion. That nevertheless they agree in the four articles above-mentioned, both in their general principles, and in many of the particulars, will appear evident to any one who will be at the pains to consult their books, or attend to their sermons. This, however, it is necessary to make the reader acquainted with, on account of what follows.

II.

19. *That the Roman Catholics, before the Reformation, held and taught exactly the same things as the Reformed did after it, in respect to the four articles above-mentioned, namely, a Trinity of Persons in the Godhead, Original Sin, the Imputation of the Merit of Christ, and Justification by Faith therein, only with this difference, that they conjoined that Faith with Charity or Good Works.*

BRIEF ANALYSIS.

20. That there is such a conformity between the Roman Catholics and the Protestants in these four articles, as hardly to be any material difference, except that the former conjoin faith and charity, while the latter divide between them, is scarcely known to any one, and indeed is so generally unknown, that the learned themselves will be ready to wonder at the assertion. The reason of this ignorance is, because the Roman Catholics rarely approach God our Saviour, but instead of Him, the Pope as His vicar, and likewise the saints; hence they have deeply buried in oblivion their tenets concerning the imputation of the merit of Christ, and justification by faith. That nevertheless such tenets are received and acknowledged by them, evidently appears from the Decrees of the council of Trent, quoted above, n. 3, 4, 5, 6, 7, 8, and confirmed by Pope Pius IV., n. 2. If these be compared with the tenets extracted from the Augsburg Confession, and from the Formula Concordiæ thence derived, n. 9, 10, 11, 12, the difference between them will be found to consist more in words than in substance. The doctors of the church, by reading and comparing the above passages together, may indeed see some conformity between them, but still rather obscurely; that these therefore, as well as those who are less learned, and also the laity, may be fully satisfied in this matter, the subject shall be more clearly illustrated in what follows.

III.

21. *That the leading Reformers, Luther, Melancthon, and Calvin, retained all the tenets concerning a Trinity of Persons in*

the Godhead, Original Sin, Imputation of the Merits of Christ, and Justification by Faith, just as they were and had been among the Roman Catholics; but that they separated Charity or Good Works from that faith, and declared that they were not at the same time of a saving efficacy, with a view to be totally severed from the Roman Catholics as to the very Essentials of the Church, which are Faith and Charity.

BRIEF ANALYSIS.

22. That the four articles above mentioned, as at present taught in the reformed churches, were not new, and first broached by those three leaders, but were handed down from the time of the council of Nice, and taught by the writers after that period, and thus preserved in the Romish church, is very plain from ecclesiastial history. The reason why the Roman Catholics and the reformed agree in the article of a trinity of persons in the Godhead, is, because they both acknowledge the three creeds, the Apostles', the Nicene, and the Athanasian, in which a trinity is taught. That they agree in the article of the imputation of the merit of Christ, is plain from the extracts from the council of Trent, n. 3 to 8, compared with those from the Formula Concordiæ, n. 10 to 15. Their agreement in the article of justification, shall now be the subject of discussion.

23. The doctrine maintained by the council of Trent, concerning justifying faith, is as follows: "It has always been the uniform opinion of the Catholic church, that faith is the beginning of man's salvation, the foundation and root of all justification, without which it is impossible to please God, and attain to the fellowship of His children," see above, n. 5 ([a]). Also, "That faith comes by hearing the Word of God," n. 4 ([c]). Moreover that that Romish council conjoined faith and charity, or faith and good works, may clearly be seen from the quotations above, n. 4, 5, 7, 8. But that the reformed churches, from their leaders, have separated them, declaring salvation to consist in faith, and not at the same time in charity or works, to the intent that they might be totally severed from the Roman Catholics, as to the very essentials of the church, which are faith and charity, I have frequently heard from the above-mentioned leaders themselves. As also, that they established such separation by the following considerations, namely, that no one can do any good thing available to salvation of himself, nor can fulfil the law; and moreover, [that good works should be excluded] lest thereby any merit in man should enter into faith. That from these principles, and with this view, they excluded the good works of charity and faith, and thereby also from salvation, is plain from the quotations from the Formula Concordiæ above, n. 12; among which are these: "That faith

does not justify, as being formed by charity, as the Papists allege, n. 12 ([b]): that the position, that good works are necessary to salvation, ought to be rejected upon many accounts, and among others, because they are accepted by the Papists to support a bad cause, n. 12 ([h]): that the decree of the council of Trent that good works preserve and retain salvation and faith, is deservedly to be rejected," n. 12 ([n]): not to mention other passages to the same purport. That still, however, the Reformed conjoin faith and charity into one essential of salvation, and only differ from the Roman Catholics respecting the quality of works, will be shown in the following article.

IV.

24. *That nevertheless the leading Reformers adjoined good works, and even conjoined them, to their faith, but in man as a passive subject: whereas the Roman Catholics conjoin them in man as an active subject; and that notwithstanding there is actually a conformity between the one and the other as to faith, works, and merits.*

BRIEF ANALYSIS.

25. That the leading Reformers, although they separated faith and charity, did still adjoin and even conjoin them, but would not admit of their being united into one, so as to be both together necessary to salvation, is evident from their books, sermons, and declarations; for after they have separated them, they conjoin them, and even express this conjunction in clear terms, and not in such as admit of two senses; as for instance in the following. That faith after justification is never alone, but is always accompanied by charity or good works, and if not, that such faith is not a living but a dead faith, see above, n. 13 ([o]) ([p]) ([q]) ([r]) ([y]) ([bb]): nay, that good works necessarily follow faith, n. 13 ([x]) ([y]) ([z]): and that the regenerate person, by new powers and gifts, co-operates with the Holy Spirit, n. 13 ([aa]). That the Roman Catholics teach exactly the same doctrines, is plain from the passages collected from the council of Trent, n. 4, 5, 6, 7, 8.

26. That the Reformers profess nearly the same things with the Roman Catholics concerning the merits of works, is evident from the following quotations from the *Formula Concordiæ.* That good works are rewarded by virtue of the promise and by grace, and that from thence they merit rewards both temporal and spiritual, n. 14 ([i]) ([k]) ([l]) ([n]): and that God crowns His own gifts with a reward, n. 14 ([k]) ([n]). The like is asserted in the council of Trent, namely, That God of His grace makes His own gifts to be merits, n. 5 ([f]): and moreover, that salvation is not of works, but of promise and grace, because it

is God who operates them by His Holy Spirit, n. 5 ([e]) ([f]) ([g]) ([h]) ([i]) ([k]).

27. From comparing the one and the other, it appears at the first view, as though there was an entire conformity between them; but lest this should be the case, the reformers distinguished between the works of the law proceeding from man's purpose and will, and works of the Spirit proceeding from faith as from a free and spontaneous source, which latter they denominated the fruits of faith, as may be seen above, n. 11 ([h]) ([l]), and n. 13 ([a]) ([i]) ([l]), and n. 15 ([k]). Hence, on an accurate examination and comparison, there does not appear to be any difference in the works themselves, but only in the quality of them, namely, that the latter sort proceed from man as from a passive subject, but the former as from an active subject; consequently they are spontaneous when they proceed from man's understanding, and not at the same time from his will. This is said, because man, while he does good works, cannot but be conscious that he is doing them, and consciousness is from the understanding. Nevertheless, as the Reformed likewise preach up the exercise of repentance, and wrestlings with the flesh, n. 13 ([d]) ([e]) ([f]) ([g]) ([h]) ([k]), and these cannot be done by man but from his purpose and will, and thus by him as from himself, it follows, that there is still an actual conformity.

28. As regards free-will in conversion, or in the act of justification, it appears as if their sentiments were entirely opposite to each other; but that they still accord together, may be seen, if we duly consider and compare the passages transcribed from the council of Trent, n. 6 ([a]) ([b]), with those from the *Formula Concordiæ*, n. 15 ([m]); for in Christian countries all are baptized, and from thence are in a state of free-will, so as to be enabled not only to hear the Word of God, but likewise to assent to the same, and embrace it by faith; consequently no one in the Christian world is like a stock.

29. Hence then appears the truth of what is asserted in n. 19 and n. 21, namely, that the Reformers derived their opinions concerning a trinity of persons in the Godhead, original sin, the imputation of the merit of Christ, and justification by faith, from the Roman Catholics. These things have been advanced, in order to point out the origin of their tenets, especially the origin of the separation of faith from good works, or the doctrine of faith alone, and to show that it was with no other view than to be severed from the Roman Catholics, and that, after all, their disagreement is more in words than in reality. From the passages above adduced, it very evidently appears upon what foundation the faith of the Reformed churches has been erected and from what inspiration it took its rise.

V.

30. *That the whole system of Theology in the Christian world, at this day, is founded on an idea of Three Gods, arising from the Doctrine of a Trinity of Persons.*

BRIEF ANALYSIS.

31. We will first say something concerning the origin or source from whence the idea of a trinity of persons in the Godhead, and thereby of three Gods, proceeded. There are three Creeds, entitled the Apostles', the Nicene, and the Athanasian, which specifically assert a trinity: the Apostles' and the Nicene assert simply a trinity, but the Athanasian a trinity of persons. These three Creeds are to be met with in many of our Psalters, the Apostles' Creed next the Psalm which is sung, the Nicene after the Decalogue, and the Athanasian apart by itself.* The Apostles' Creed was written after the times of the Apostles; the Nicene Creed at the Council of Nice, a city of Bithynia, whereunto all the bishops in Asia, Africa, and Europe, were summoned by the Emperor Constantine, in the year 318; but the Athanasian Creed was composed since that council by one or more persons, with an intent utterly to overthrow the Arians, and was afterwards received by the churches as œcumenical. In the two former creeds the confession of a trinity was evident, but from the third or Athanasian Creed the profession of a trinity of persons was spread abroad: that hence arose the idea of three Gods, shall now be shown.

32. That there is a Divine Trinity, is manifest from the Lord's words in Matthew: "*Jesus said, go make disciples of all nations, baptizing them in the name of the Father, of the Son, and of the Holy Spirit,*" chap. xxviii. 19; and from these words in the same Evangelist: "*When Jesus was baptized, lo, the heavens were opened unto Him, and He saw the Holy Spirit descending like a dove, and coming upon Him, and lo, a voice from heaven, this is My beloved Son, in whom I am well pleased,*" chap. iii. 16, 17. The reason why the Lord sent His disciples to baptize in the name of the Father, Son and Holy Spirit, was, because in Him then glorified there was a Divine Trinity; for in the preceding verse 18, He says, *All power is given unto Me in heaven and in earth;*" and in the 20th verse following, *Lo, I am with you all the days, even unto the consummation of the age;*" thus He spoke of Himself alone, and not of three. And in John: "*The Holy Spirit was not yet, because Jesus was not yet glorified,*" chap vii. 39. The former words He uttered after His glorification, and His glorification was His complete unition with His Father, Who was the Essential Divine [Principle] in

* This relates to the Protestant churches on the continent.—*Editor.*

Him from conception; and the Holy Spirit was the Divine [Principle] proceeding from Him after His glorification; John xx. 22.

33. The reason why the idea of three Gods has principally arisen from the Athanasian Creed, where a trinity of persons is taught, is, because the word *person* begets such an idea, which is further implanted in the mind by the following words in the same Creed: *There is one person of the Father, another of the Son, and another of the Holy Ghost;*" and afterwards: "*The Father is God and Lord, the Son is God and Lord, and the Holy Ghost is God and Lord;*" but more especially by these: "*For like as we are compelled by the Christian verity to acknowledge every person by Himself to be God and Lord, so are we forbidden by the Catholic religion to say there be three Gods or three Lords;*" the result of which words is this, that by the Christian verity we are bound to confess and acknowledge three Gods and three Lords, but by the Catholic religion we are not allowed to say, or to make mention of three Gods and Lords; consequently we may have an idea of three Gods and Lords, but are not to make confession thereof with our mouth. Nevertheless, that the doctrine of the trinity in the Athanasian Creed is agreeable to truth, if only instead of a trinity of persons be there substituted a trinity of person, which trinity is in God the Saviour Jesus Christ, may be seen in the DOCTRINE OF THE NEW JERUSALEM CONCERNING THE LORD, published at Amsterdam, in the year 1763, n. 55 to 61.

34. It is to be observed, that in the Apostles' Creed it is said, "*I believe in God the Father, in Jesus Christ, and in the Holy Ghost;*" in the Nicene Creed, "*I believe in one God, the Father, in one Lord Jesus Christ, and in the Holy Ghost,*" thus only in one God; but in the Athanasian Creed it is, "*In God the Father, God the Son, and God the Holy Ghost,*" thus in three Gods. But whereas the authors and favorers of this creed clearly saw that an idea of three Gods would unavoidably result from the expressions therein used, therefore, in order to remedy this, they asserted that one substance or essence belongs to the three; but still there arises from thence no other idea, than that there are three Gods unanimous and agreeing together: for when it is said of the three that their substance or essence is one and indivisible, it does not remove the idea of three, but confounds it, because the expression is a metaphysical one, and the science of metaphysics, with all its ingenuity, cannot of three persons, each whereof is God, make one; it may indeed make of them one in the confession of the mouth, but never in the idea of the mind.

35. That the whole system of Christian theology at this day is founded on an idea of three Gods, is evident from the doctrine of justification, which is the head of the doctrinals of

the Christian church, both among Roman Catholics and Protestants. That doctrine sets forth that God the Father sent His Son to redeem and save mankind, and gives the Holy Spirit to operate the same: every man who hears, reads, or repeats this, cannot but in his thought, that is, in his idea, divide God into three, and suppose that one God sent another, and operates by a third. That the same thought of a Divine Trinity distinguished into three persons, each whereof is God, is continued throughout the rest of the doctrinals of the present church, as from a head into its body, will be demonstrated in its proper place. In the mean time consult what has been premised concerning justification, consult the system of theology in general and in particular, and at the same time consult yourself, while listening to sermons at church, or while praying at home, whether you have any other perception and thought thence resulting than of three Gods; and especially while you are praying or singing first to one, and then to the other two separately, as is the common practice. Hence is established the truth of the proposition, that the whole system of theology in the Christian world at this day, is founded on an idea of three Gods.

36. That a trinity of Gods is contrary to Holy Scripture, is well known, for it is written, "*Am not I Jehovah, and there is no God else beside me, a just God and a Saviour, there is none beside Me,*" Isa. xlv. 21, 22. "*I Jehovah am thy God, and thou shalt acknowledge no God beside Me, and there is no Saviour beside Me,*" Hos. xiii. 4. "*Thus said Jehovah the King of Israel and the Redeemer thereof, Jehovah Zebaoth, I am the First and the Last, and beside Me there is no God,*" Isa. xliv. 6. "*Jehovah Zebaoth is His name, and thy Redeemer the Holy One of Israel, the God of the whole earth shall He be called,*" Isa. liv. 5. "*In that day Jehovah shall be King over the whole earth; in that day there shall be one Jehovah, and His name One,*" Zech. xiv. 9 Beside many more passages elsewhere.

37. That a trinity of Gods is contrary to enlightened reason, may appear from many considerations. What man of sound reason can bear to hear that three Gods created the world; or that creation and preservation, redemption and salvation, together with reformation and regeneration, are the work of three Gods, and not of one God? And on the other hand, what man of sound reason is not willing to hear that the same God who is our Creator, is also our Redeemer, Regenerator and Saviour? As the latter sentiment, and not the former, accords with reason, there is therefore no nation upon the face of the whole earth, possessed of religion and sound reason, but what acknowledges one God. That the Mahometans, and certain nations in Asia and Africa, abhor Christianity, because they believe it inculcates the worship of three Gods, is well known; and the

only answer of the Christians to the charge, is, that the three possess one essence, and thus are one God. I can affirm, that from the reason which has been given me, I can clearly see, that neither the world, nor the angelic heaven, nor the church, nor anything therein, could have existed, or can still subsist, but from one God.

38. Here I will add a quotation from the *Confession of the Dutch Churches* received at the *Synod of Dort*, which is this: "I believe in one God, who is one essence, in which are three Persons, truly and really distinct, in communicable properties from eternity, namely, the Father, the Son, and the Holy Spirit; the Father is of all things, both visible and invisible, the cause, origin, and beginning; the Son is the Word, wisdom, and image of the Father; the Holy Spirit is the eternal virtue and power proceeding from the Father and the Son. However it must be allowed, that this doctrine far exceeds the comprehension of the human mind; we must therefore wait till we come to heaven for a perfect knowledge thereof."

VI.

39. *That the Tenets of the aforesaid Theology appear to be erroneous, after the idea of a Trinity of Persons, and the consequent idea of Three Gods has been rejected, and the idea of One God, in whom is a Divine Trinity, received in its stead.*

BRIEF ANALYSIS.

40. The reason why the tenets of the present church, which are founded upon the idea of three Gods, derived from the doctrine of a trinity of persons literally understood, appear erroneous, after the idea of one God, in whom is a Divine Trinity, has been received in its stead, is, because, till this truth is received, we cannot see what is erroneous. The case herein is like a person, who in the night time, by the light of some stars only, sees various objects, especially images, and believes them to be living men; or like one, who in the twilight before sunrise, as he lies in his bed, fancies he sees goblins in the air, and believes them to be angels; or like a person, who sees many things in the delusive light of fantasy, and believes them to be real; such things, it is well known, do not appear according to their true qualities, until the person comes to enjoy the light of the day, or, in other words, until his understanding is broad awake. The case is the same with the spiritual things of the church, which have been erroneously and falsely perceived, and even confirmed, when genuine truths present themselves in their own light, which is the light of heaven. Who is there that cannot understand, that all tenets founded on the idea of three Gods, must be interiorly erroneous and false? I say in-

teriorly, because the idea of God enters into every thing belonging to the church, religion, and worship; and theological matters have their residence above all others in the human mind, and among these the idea of God is the principal or supreme; wherefore if this be false, all beneath it, in consequence of the principle from whence they flow, must likewise be false or falsified: for that which is supreme, being also the inmost, constitutes the very essence of all that is derived from it; and the essence, like a soul, forms them into a body, after its own image; and when in its descent it lights upon truths, it even infects them with its own blemish and error. The idea of three Gods in theology may be compared to a disorder seated in the heart or lungs, in which the patient fancies himself to be in health, because his physician, not knowing his disease, persuades him that he is so; but if the physician knows it, and still persuades the patient that he is in health, he may justly be charged with deep malignity.

VII.

41. *That then true saving Faith, which is a Faith in One God, united with Good Works, is acknowledged and received.*

BRIEF ANALYSIS.

42. The reason why this faith, which is a faith in one God, is acknowledged and received as truly saving, when the former faith, which is a faith in three Gods, is rejected, is, because till this is the case it cannot be seen in its proper form: for the faith of the present day is set forth as the only saving faith, because it is a faith in one God, and a faith in a Saviour; but it must be observed, that this faith has two faces, the one internal, and the other external; its internal face is formed from the perception of three Gods (for who perceives or thinks any otherwise? Let every one examine himself); whereas its external face is formed from the confession of one God (for who confesses or speaks otherwise? Let every one examine himself). These two faces are altogether discordant with each other; so that the external is not acknowledged by the internal, nor is the internal known by the external. From this disagreement, and the vanishing of the one out of sight of the other, a confused idea of things pertaining to salvation has been conceived and brought forth in the church. It is otherwise, when the internal and external faces accord together, and mutually regard and acknowledge each other as one; that this is the case, when one God, in whom is a Divine Trinity, is not only perceived by the mind, but likewise acknowledged by the mouth, is self-evident. That the tenet of the Father's being alienated from mankind, is then abolished, together with that of His reconciliation, and that

quite another doctrine takes place concerning imputation, remission of sins, regeneration, and salvation thence derived, will clearly be seen in the work itself, in the light of reason illustrated by Divine Truths from the Sacred Scripture. This faith is called a faith united with good works, because without this union it is impossible to have faith in one God.

VIII.

43. *And that this Faith is in God the Saviour Jesus Christ, which in its simple Form is as follows:—I. That there is One God in Whom is a Divine Trinity, and that he is the Lord Jesus Christ. II. That saving Faith is to believe in Him. III. That Evils ought to be shunned, because they are of the Devil, and from the Devil. IV. That Good Works ought to be done, because they are of God, and from God. V. And that they ought to be done by man as of himself, but with a belief that they are from the Lord, operating in him and by him.*

BRIEF ANALYSIS.

44. This is the faith of the New Church in its simple form, which will appear more fully in the Appendix, and still more at large in the first part of the work itself, where I shall treat of the Lord God the Saviour, and of the trinity in Him; of love to God, and love towards our neighbor; of faith, and its conjunction with those two loves; also in the other parts, which will follow in their proper order. But it is necessary that this preliminary concerning the above-mentioned faith should here be briefly illustrated. The *first* position, namely, That there is one God, in whom there is a Divine Trinity, and that He is the Lord Jesus Christ, is summarily illustrated in the following manner. It is a certain and established truth, that God is one, that His essence is indivisible, and that there is a trinity; since therefore God is one, and His essence is indivisible, it follows, that God is one person, and that a trinity is in that person. That this is the Lord Jesus Christ, appears from hence, that He was conceived of God the Father, Luke i. 34, 35; and that thus as to His soul and essential life He is God; and therefore, as He Himself said, that the Father and He are one, John x. 30; that He is in the Father, and the Father in Him, John xiv. 10, 11; that he who seeth Him and knoweth Him, seeth and knoweth the Father, John xiv. 7, 9; that no one seeth and knoweth the Father, but He who is in the bosom of the Father, John i. 18; that all things belonging to the Father are His, John iii. 35; chap. xvi. 15; that He is the Way, the Truth, and the Life, and that no one cometh unto the Father but by Him, John xiv. 6; consequently from Him, because He is in

Him, and thus is He Himself; and according to Paul, that in Him dwells all the fulness of the Godhead bodily, Coloss. ii. 9; and according to Isaiah, "Unto us a Child is born, unto us a Son is given, whose name is God, *Father of Eternity*," ix. 5; and again, that He hath power over all flesh, John xvii. 2; and that He hath all power in heaven and earth, Matt. xxviii. 18: whence it follows, that He is the God of heaven and earth. The *second* position, namely, That saving faith is to believe in Him, is illustrated thus: "Jesus said, He that believeth in Me, shall not die eternally, but shall live," John xi. 25, 26; "This is the will of the Father, that every one who believeth in the Son may have eternal life," John vi. 40; "God so loved the world, that He gave His only begotten Son, that whosoever believeth in Him, should not perish, but have everlasting life," John iii. 15, 16; "He that believeth in the Son, hath everlasting life, but he that believeth not the Son, shall not see life, but the wrath of God abideth on him," John iii. 36. *The three remaining propositions*, namely, That evils ought to be shunned, because they are of the devil and from the devil; and that good works ought to be done, because they are of God and from God; but that man ought to believe that they are from the Lord, operating in him and by him, have no need of illustration and proof, for the whole Sacred Scripture, from beginning to end, proves them, and, in short, teaches nothing else but to shun evils, and do good, and to believe in the Lord. Besides, without these three there cannot be any religion, for all religion relates to life; and life consists in shunning evils and in doing good, which cannot be done by man except as of himself; wherefore if these three are removed from the church, the Sacred Scripture, together with religion, is likewise removed at the same time; in which case the church is no longer a church. For a further account of the faith of the New Church, in its universal and particular form, see below, n. 116, 117; all which will be demonstrated in the work itself.

IX.

45. *That the Faith of the present day has separated Religion from the Church, since Religion consists in the Acknowledgment of one God, and in the Worship of Him, from Faith grounded in Charity.*

BRIEF ANALYSIS.

46. What nation is there upon the face of the earth, possessed of religion and sound reason, that does not know and believe, that there is one God, and that to do evils is contrary to Him, and that to do good is well-pleasing to Him, and that man must do this from his soul, from his heart, and from his strength, although it is by influx from God; and that herein

consists religion? Who therefore does not see, that to confess three persons in the Godhead, and to assert that in good works there is nothing of salvation, is to separate religion from the church? Yet so it is asserted in these words: "That faith justifies without good works," n. 12 ([a]) ([b]); "that works are not necessary to salvation, nor to faith, because salvation and faith are neither preserved nor retained by good works," n. 12 ([g]) ([h]) ([m]) ([n]); consequently, that there is no bond of conjunction between faith and good works. It is indeed said afterwards, "that good works nevertheless follow faith, as fruit is produced from a tree," n. 13, ([l]) ([n]), but then, let us ask, who does them, nay, who thinks of them, or who is spontaneously led to perform them, while he knows or believes that they do not at all contribute to salvation, and also, that no one can do any good thing towards salvation of himself, and so on? If it be alleged that the leaders of the church have still conjoined faith with good works, it may be said in reply, that this conjunction, when closely inspected, is not conjunction, but mere adjunction, and this only like a superfluous appendage, that neither coheres nor adheres in any other manner than as a dark background to a portrait, which serves to set off the figure represented, and give it more the appearance of life. It may be said further, that inasmuch as religion has relation to life, and this consists in good works according to the truths of faith, it is evident that real religion is the portrait or figure represented itself, and not the mere shady appendage; yea, that when good works are regarded as such an appendage, they must be reputed by many as of no more account than the tail of a horse, which, as contributing nothing to the horse's strength, may be cut off at pleasure. Who can rationally conclude otherwise, while he understands such expressions as these according to their obvious meaning; "That it is a folly to imagine that the works of the second table of the decalogue justify in the sight of God," n. 12 ([d]); and these; "That if any one believes he shall therefore obtain salvation, because he hath charity, he brings a reproach upon Christ," n. 12 ([e]); as also these: "That good works are utterly to be excluded, in treating of justification and eternal life," n. 12 ([f]); with more to the same purpose? Who, therefore, when he reads afterwards, that good works necessarily follow faith, and that if they do not follow, the faith is a false and not a true faith, n. 13 ([p]) ([q]) ([y]), with more to the same purpose, attends to it? or if he attends to it, understands whether such good works are attended with any perception or consciousness? yet good which proceeds from man without his having a perception or consciousness of it, has no more life in it than if it came from a statue. But if we inquire more deeply into the rise of this doctrine, it will appear as though the leading Reformers first laid down faith alone as their rule, in order that they might be severed from the Roman Catholics, as mentioned above, n. 21, 22, 23; and that afterwards they adjoined thereto the works of charity, that their system might not appear to contradict the Sacred Scriptures, but have the semblance of religion, and thus be salved over.

X.

47. *That the Faith of the present Church cannot be conjoined with Charity, and produce any Fruits, which are Good Works.*

BRIEF ANALYSIS.

48. Before we proceed to the proof of this proposition, we shall first explain the origin and nature of charity, and the origin and nature of faith, and thus the origin and nature of good works, which are called fruits. Faith is truth, wherefore the doctrine of faith is the doctrine of truth; and the doctrine of truth has its seat in the understanding, and thence in the thought, and from the thought descends into the speech; wherefore it teaches what we are to will, and what we are to do, thus that evils, and what evils, are to be shunned, and that good works, and what good works, are to be done. When man from such a principle does good, then good conjoins itself with truth, because the will is conjoined with the understanding, for good appertains to the will, and truth to the understanding; from this conjunction arises the affection of good, which in its essence is charity, and the affection of truth, which in its essence is faith, and these two united together constitute a marriage; from which marriage good works are produced, as fruits from a tree; and hence they become the fruits of good, and the fruits of truth; the latter are signified in the Word by grapes, but the former by olives.

49. From this generation of good works, it is evident, that faith alone cannot possibly produce or beget any works, that deserve the name of fruits, any more than a woman can of herself produce any offspring without the concurrence of a man; wherefore the fruits of faith is a vain expression, and a word without meaning. Besides, throughout the whole world, nothing ever was or can be produced, but from a marriage of two, one whereof has relation to good, and the other to truth, or, in the opposite sense, one to evil, and the other to what is false; consequently no works can be conceived, much less brought into existence, but from such marriage, good works from the marriage of good and truth, and evil works from the marriage of evil and the false.

50. The reason why charity cannot be conjoined with the faith of the present church, and consequently why good works cannot spring from any marriage union between them is,

because imputation supplies every thing, remits guilt, justifies, regenerates, sanctifies, imparts the life of heaven and thus salvation, and all this freely, without any works of man: in this case, what is charity, which ought to be united with faith, but something vain and superfluous, and a mere addition and supplement to imputation and justification, to which nevertheless it adds no weight or value? Besides, a faith founded on the idea of three Gods is erroneous, as has been shown above, n. 39, 40; and with an erroneous faith, charity, that in itself is charity, cannot be conjoined. There are two reasons given for believing that there is no bond of union between that faith and charity; the one is, because they make their faith to be of a spiritual quality, but charity merely natural and moral, imagining that there can be no conjunction between what is spiritual and what is natural; the other reason is, lest any thing of man, and so any thing of merit, should gain admission into their faith, which they suppose to be alone of a saving nature. Furthermore, between charity and that faith there is no conjunction, but there is with the new faith, which may be seen below, n. 116, 117.

XI.

51. *That from the Faith of the present Church there results a Worship of the Mouth and not of the Life, whereas the Worship of the Mouth is accepted by the Lord, in proportion as it proceeds from the Worship of the Life.*

BRIEF ANALYSIS.

52. This is testified by experience. How few are there at this day, who form their lives after the precepts of the decalogue, and other precepts of the Lord, from a religious principle? And how few are there at this day, who desire to look their own evils in the face, and to perform actual repentance, and thus enter upon the worship of the life? or who, among those that make pretensions to piety, perform any other repentance than that of the mouth, which consists in words only, confessing themselves to be sinners, and praying, according to the doctrine of the church, that God the Father, for the sake of His Son, who suffered upon the cross for their sins, took away their damnation, and atoned for them with His blood, would mercifully forgive their transgressions, that so they might be presented without spot or blemish before His judgment-seat? Who does not see, that this worship is that of the lungs only, and not of the heart, consequently that it is external worship, and not internal? for it is a prayer for the remission of sins, when yet man is not conscious of a single sin that he has; and if he did know of any, he would cover it over with favor and indulgence, or with a faith that is to purify and absolve him,

without any works of his. But this conduct may be compared to that of a servant, who should go to his master with his face and clothes bedaubed with soot and filth, and say, Sir, wash me. Would not his master in such case naturally say to him, Thou foolish servant, what is it thou sayest? See! there is water, soap, and a towel, hast thou not hands of thine own, and strength to use them? wash thyself. Thus also the Lord God will say, The means of purification are provided by Me, and from Me also thou hast will and power, wherefore use these My gifts and talents, as thy own, and thou shalt be purified. Take another example by way of illustration. Suppose you should pray a thousand times at home and at church, that God the Father, for the sake of His Son, would preserve you from the devil, and should not at the same time, from that freedom of will in which you are perpetually kept by the Lord, keep yourself from evil, and so from the devil; you could not in this case be preserved even by legions of angels sent from the Lord; for the Lord cannot act contrary to His own Divine order, which is, that man should examine himself, discover his evils, resist them, and this as of himself, yet from the Lord. This does not indeed at this day appear to be the gospel, nevertheless it is the gospel, for the gospel is salvation by the Lord. The reason why the worship of the mouth is accepted by the Lord according to the worship of the life, is, because the speech of man before God, and before the angels, has its sound from the affection of his love and faith, and these two are in man according to his life; wherefore, reader, if the love of God and faith in Him are in your life, the sound of your voice will be like that of a dove; but if self-love and self-confidence are in your life, the sound of your voice will be like that of an owl, howsoever you may endeavor to imitate the dove. The spiritual principle, which is within the sound, is the cause of this.

XII.

53. *That the doctrine of the present Church is interwoven with many Paradoxes, which are to be embraced by Faith; and that therefore its tenets gain admission into the Memory only, and not into any part of the Understanding above the Memory, but merely into confirmatory augmentations below it.*

BRIEF ANALYSIS.

54. The rulers of the church insist, that the understanding is to be kept under obedience to faith, nay that faith, properly speaking, is a faith in what is unknown, which is blind, and only a faith of the night. This is their first paradox; for faith is of truth, and truth is of faith; and truth, before it can become an object of faith, must be seen in its own light and

understood; otherwise what is false may be believed as true. The paradoxes flowing from such a faith are many; as, that God the Father begat a Son from eternity, and that the Holy Spirit proceeds from both, and that each of these three is a person by Himself, and a God; that the Lord, both as to His soul and body, was from the mother; that the above three persons, consequently three Gods, created the universe; and that one of them descended, and assumed human nature, to reconcile the Father, and thus to save mankind; and that they who by grace obtain faith, and believe these paradoxes, are saved by the imputation, application, and translation of His righteousness to themselves; and that man, at his first reception of that faith, is like a statue, a stock, or a stone, and that faith comes by the mere hearing of the Word; that faith alone without the works of the law, or entirely independent of charity, is saving; and that it produces the remission of sins without any previous repentance; and that, merely by virtue of such remission of sins, the impenitent are justified, regenerated, and sanctified; and that afterwards charity, good works, and repentance, spontaneously follow. Besides many other paradoxes of a like nature, which, like offspring from an illegitimate bed, have all issued from the doctrine founded on the idea of three Gods.

55. What wise man does not see, that such paradoxes enter only into the memory, and not into the understanding above the memory, although they may be confirmed by reasonings from appearances and fallacies below it? for the human understanding is capable of seeing by two kinds of light, one of which is from heaven, and the other from the world; the light from heaven, which is spiritual, flows into the human mind above the memory, but the light from the world, which is natural, below it. That man, from this latter light, can establish whatever he pleases, and falses equally as well as truths, and that after confirmation he sees falses altogether as truths, has been shown in a memorable relation inserted in the work lately published concerning CONJUGIAL LOVE, n. 233.

56. To what has been said shall be added the following arcanum from heaven. All these paradoxes, according to their confirmations, abide in the minds of men, bound together as into one bundle, or wound up together as into one ball, and enter at the same time into every individual proposition that is stated from the doctrine of the church; so that when either faith, charity, or repentance, and still more when imputation or justification is mentioned, they all enter and are included in each particular. Man himself indeed does not perceive any such accumulation, or bundling together of the paradoxes in every individual proposition from the doctrine of the church, or on every mention of the above expressions; but the angels that

are with man perceive it, and they call it MALUA, that is, confusion and darkness.

57. I am well aware, that very many at this day, tinctured with the paradoxes of this faith, will be ready to say, how can theological truths be perceived by the understanding? are they not spiritual, and above its comprehension? Explain therefore, if thou canst, the mystery of redemption and justification, that reason may view it, and acquiesce therein. This mystery then shall be opened in the following manner. Who does not know that God is one, and that besides Him there is no other, and that God is essential love and essential wisdom, or that He is essential good and essential truth; and that the self-same God, as to Divine Truth, which is the Word, descended and assumed humanity to remove the hells, and consequently damnation, from man, which he effected by combats with, and victories over the devil, that is, over all the hells, which at that time infested and spiritually slew every man coming into the world; and that afterwards He glorified His humanity, by uniting in it Divine Truth with Divine Good, and thus returned to the Father from whom He came forth? When these things are perceived, then the following passage in John may be understood: "*The Word was with God, and God was the Word, and the Word became flesh,*" chap. i. 1, 14. And also the following in the same Evangelist: "*I went forth from the Father, and came into the world; again I leave the world and go to the Father,*" chap. xvi. 28. Hence also it is evident, that unless the Lord had come into the world, no person could have been saved, and that they are saved who believe in Him, and lead a good life. This view of faith presents itself as clear as the day to those who are enlightened by the Word, and is the frontispiece of the faith of the New Church. See the FAITH OF THE NEW HEAVEN AND OF THE NEW CHURCH IN ITS UNIVERSAL AND IN ITS PARTICULAR FORM, below, at n. 116, 117.

XIII.

58. *That the Tenets of the present Church cannot be learnt and retained without great difficulty, nor can they be preached or taught without using great care and caution to conceal their nakedness, because sound reason neither discerns nor receives them.*

BRIEF ANALYSIS.

59. That the understanding is to be kept under obedience to faith, is set as a motto before the tenets of the present church, to denote that their interiors are mysteries, or arcana, of too transcendent a nature to enter into the upper region of the understanding, and be there perceived, see above, n. 54. Those ministers of the church, who affect to excel in wisdom,

and wish to be looked upon as oracles in spiritual things, imbibe and swallow down in the schools, such things especially as surpass the comprehension of others, which they do with avidity, but nevertheless with difficulty. And because they are thence accounted wise, and they who have distinguished and enriched themselves from such hidden stores are honored with doctors' hats and episcopal robes, they revolve in their thoughts, and teach from their pulpits, scarce any thing else but mysteries concerning justification by faith alone, and good works as her humble attendants. And from their great erudition concerning both faith and good works, they in a wonderful manner sometimes separate and sometimes conjoin them; comparatively as if they held faith by itself in one hand, and the works of charity in the other, and at one time extend their arms and so separate them, and at another time bring their hands together and so conjoin them. But this shall be illustrated by examples. They teach, that good works are not necessary to salvation, because if done by man they are meritorious; at the same time they also teach, that good works necessarily follow faith, and that both together make one in the article of salvation. They teach that faith without good works, as being alive, justifies; and at the same time, that faith without good works, as being dead, does not justify. They teach, that faith is neither preserved nor retained by good works; and at the same time, that good works proceed from faith, as fruit from a tree, light from the sun, and heat from fire. They teach, that good works being adjoined to faith make it perfect; and at the same time, that being conjoined as in a marriage, or in one form, they deprive faith of its saving essence. They teach, that a Christian is not under the law; and at the same time, that he must be in the daily practice of the law. They teach, that if good works are intermixed in the business of salvation by faith, as in the remission of sins, justification, regeneration, vivification, and salvation, they are hurtful; but if not intermixed, that they are profitable. They teach, that God crowns His own gifts, which are good works, with rewards even of a spiritual nature, but not with salvation and eternal life, because faith without works, they say, is entitled to the crown of eternal life. They teach, that faith alone is like a queen, who walks in a stately manner with good works as her train of attendants behind her; but if these join themselves to her in front, and embrace her, she is cast from her throne and called an adulteress. But particularly, when they treat of faith and good works at the same time, they view merit on the one hand, and no merit on the other, making choice of expressions which they use in two different senses; one for the laity, and the other for the clergy; for the laity, that its nakedness may not appear, and for the clergy, that it may. Consider now, whether a person hearing such things can draw from them any doctrine leading to salvation, or whether he will not rather, from the apparent contradictions therein, become blind, and afterwards grope for the objects of salvation, like a person walking in the dark. Who in this case can tell from the evidence of works, whether he has any faith or not; and whether it is better to omit good works on account of the danger of merit, or to do them for fear of the loss of faith? But do you, my friend, separate and snatch yourself away from such contradictions, and shun evils as sins, and do good, and believe in the Lord, and saving justification will be given you.

XIV.

60. *That the doctrine of the Faith of the present Church ascribes to God human properties; as, that He viewed Man from anger, that He required to be reconciled, that He is reconciled through the love He bore the Son, and by His intercession; and that He required to be appeased by the sight of His Son's sufferings, and thus to be brought back to mercy; and that He imputes the Righteousness of His Son to an unrighteous Man who supplicates it from Faith alone; and that thus from an Enemy He makes him a Friend, and from a Child of Wrath a Child of Grace.*

BRIEF ANALYSIS.

61. Who does not know, that God is essential compassion and mercy, inasmuch as He is essential love and essential goodness, and that these properties are His being or essence? And who does not hereby see, that it is a contradiction to assert, that mercy itself, or goodness itself, can view man from anger, become his enemy, turn Himself away from him, and determine on his damnation, and still continue to be the same Divine Being or God? Such things can scarcely be attributed to a good man, but only to a wicked man, thus not to an angel of heaven, but only to an angel of hell; wherefore it is abominable to ascribe them to God. That they have been ascribed to Him, appears evident from the declarations of many fathers, councils, and churches, from the first ages to the present day; and also from the inferences which have necessarily followed from first principles into their derivatives, or from causes into their effects, as from a head into the members; such as, that He required to be reconciled; that He is reconciled through the love He bears towards the Son, and by His intercession and mediation; that He required to be appeased by the view of the extreme sufferings of His Son, and so to be brought back to mercy, and constrained as it were to show it, and thus from an enemy to be made a friend, and to adopt those who were the children of wrath as the children of grace. That the notion that God

can impute the righteousness and merits of His Son to an unrighteous man, who supplicates it from faith alone, is also a mere human invention, will be seen in the last analysis of this little work.

62. They who have perceived that mere human properties are unworthy of God, and yet are attributed to Him, have said, in order to defend the system of justification once conceived, and to varnish over its outside, that anger, revenge, damnation, and the like, are predicated of His justice, and are therefore mentioned in many parts of the Word, and as it were appropriated to God. But by the anger of God, in the Word, is signified evil in man, which, being contrary to God, is called the anger of God; not that God is ever angry with man, but that man from the evil that is in him, is angry with God; and because evil carries with it its own punishment, as good does its own reward, therefore while evil punishes the evil-doer, it appears to him as though he was punished by God. The case in this respect is the same as with a criminal who attributes his punishment to the law, or like a person who blames the fire for burning him when he puts his hand into it, or a drawn sword for wounding him when he rushes upon the point of it, while his adversary is standing upon his own defence: such is the nature of the justice of God. But of this more may be seen in the APOCALYPSE REVEALED, where it treats of justice and judgment in God and from God, n. 668. That anger is ascribed to Him, may be seen, n. 635; as likewise revenge, n. 658; but this is only in the literal sense, which is written by appearances and correspondences, and not in the spiritual sense, wherein truth is in its own light. This I can affirm, that whenever the angels hear any one say, that God determined in anger on the damnation of the human race, and as an enemy was reconciled by His Son, as by another God begotten from Himself, they are affected in a manner similar to those, who from an uneasiness in their bowels and stomach are excited to vomiting; on which occasions they say, what can be more insane than to affirm such things of God?

63. The reason why they have ascribed human properties to God, is, because all spiritual perception and illustration is from the Lord alone; for the Lord is the Word or Divine Truth, and "*is the true light which enlighteneth every man*," John i. 1, 9: He also says, "*I am come a light into the world, that whosoever believeth in Me, may not abide in darkness*," John xii. 46: and this light, and the perception thence derived, enter by influx into such only as acknowledge Him as the God of heaven and earth, and approach Him alone, and not into such as entertain an idea of three Gods, which has been the case from the time the Christian church began to be established. This idea of three Gods, being a merely natural idea, is receptive of no other light

than natural light, and cannot be opened to admit and receive spiritual light; hence it is, that they have seen no other properties in God, than such as are natural. Furthermore, had they seen how incongruous these human properties are to the Divine Essence, and had they removed them from the article of justification, they must then have entirely departed from their religion, which from the beginning was founded on the worship of three Gods, before the time appointed for the New Church, when the fulness and restoration [of the Christian religion] is to take place.

XV.

64. *That from the Faith of the present Church have been produced, and still may be produced, monstrous Births; such as, instantaneous Salvation by an immediate act of Mercy; Predestination; the notions that God has no respect unto the actions of Men, but unto Faith alone; that there is no connection between Charity and Faith; that Man in Conversion is like a Stock; with many more Heresies of the same kind; likewise concerning the Sacraments of Baptism and the Holy Supper, as to the advantages reasonably to be expected from them, when considered according to the Doctrine of Justification by Faith alone; as also with regard to the Person of Christ: and that the heresies from the first ages to the present day, have sprung up from no other source, than from the idea of Three Gods.*

BRIEF ANALYSIS.

65. That no other salvation is believed at this day, than such as is instantaneous, from an immediate act of mercy, is evident from hence, that a mere faith of the mouth, accompanied with a confidence proceeding from the lungs, and not with charity (whereby, nevertheless, the faith of the mouth becomes real, and the confidence of the lungs becomes that of the heart), is supposed to complete all the work of salvation; for if the co-operation is taken away which is effected through the exercises of charity by man as of himself, the spontaneous co-operation which is said to follow faith of itself, becomes passive action, which is nonsense and a contradiction in terms; for supposing this to be the case, what need would there be of any thing more than some such momentary and immediate prayer as this: "Save me, O God, for the sake of the sufferings of Thy Son, who hath washed me from my sins in His own blood, and presents me pure, righteous, and holy, before Thy throne?" and this ejaculation of the mouth might avail even at the hour of death, if not sooner, as a seed of justification. That nevertheless instantaneous salvation, by an immediate act of mercy, is at this day a fiery flying serpent in the church, and that

thereby religion is abolished, security introduced, and damnation imputed to the Lord, may be seen in n. 340 of the work concerning DIVINE PROVIDENCE, published at Amsterdam in the year 1764.

66. Predestination is also a birth conceived and brought forth from the faith of the present church, because it originates in a belief of instantaneous salvation by an immediate act of mercy, and in a belief that man has not the smallest degree of ability or free-will in spiritual things, concerning which, see below, n. 68. That this follows from the forementioned tenets, as one fiery serpent from another, or one spider from another, may be seen above. Predestination also follows from the supposition, that man is as it were inanimate in the act of conversion, that he is like a stock, and that afterwards he is unconscious whether he is a stock made alive by grace, or not; for it is said, that God, by the hearing of the Word, gives faith, when and where He wills, n. 10 ([a]), consequently of His good pleasure; and likewise that election is of the mere grace of God, independently of any action on man's part, whether such activity proceed from the powers of nature or of grace: *Formula Concordiæ*, p. 821, App. p. 182. The works which follow faith as evidences thereof, appear to the mind while it reflects on them like the works of the flesh, while the spirit which operates them does not make known from what origin they proceed, but supposes them, like faith, to be the effects of grace, and the good pleasure of God. Hence it is plain, that the tenet of predestination has sprung from the faith of the present church, as a sucker from its root; and I can venture to assert, that it has followed as the almost unavoidable consequence of such faith. This tenet was first broached by the Predestinarians, and afterwards adopted by Godoschalcus, then by Calvin and his followers, and lastly established and confirmed by the synod of Dort, whence it was conveyed into the church, by the Supra and Infra Lapsarians, as the palladium of religion, or rather as the head of Gorgon or Medusa engraved on the shield of Pallas. But what more detestable, or more cruel notion could have been devised and entertained of God, than that any part of the human race are predestinated to damnation? For it would be a horrible idea, that the Lord, who is essential love and essential mercy, designed that the bulk of mankind should be born for hell, or that myriads of myriads should be born devoted to destruction, or in other words, born to be devils and satans; and that, out of His Divine Wisdom, which is infinite, He should make no provision for those who lead good lives, and acknowledge God, whereby they might escape everlasting fire and punishment: whereas the Lord is the Creator and Saviour of all, and He alone leads all, and wills not the death of any. What then can be asserted or conceived more horrible, than that multitudes of

nations and people, should, under His auspices, and in His sight, from a predestinated decree, be delivered up to the devil as his prey, to glut his insatiate appetite? Yet this is a birth of the faith of the present Church; but the faith of the New Church abhors it as a monster.

67. That God has no respect unto the actions of men, but unto faith alone, is a new heresy, the offspring of the two former, concerning which we have already spoken above, n. 64, 65; and what is wonderful, it is derived from faith alone deeply examined and attentively considered, which has been done by the most sagacious divines of this age, and is a third offspring, begotten by that faith, and brought forth by predestination, that she-wolf, as a mother; but whereas it is insane, impious, and machiavelian, it has hitherto been kept included as it were in the uterine coats, or secundines, that came from the mother, lest its hideous form should appear: but the madness and impiety of it may be seen described and exploded in the APOCALYPSE REVEALED, n. 463.

68. That there is not any connection between charity and faith, follows from these passages in their doctrine of justification, namely: That faith is imputed for righteousness without works, n. 12 (a); that faith does not justify as being formed from charity, n. 12 (b); that good works are utterly to be excluded, in treating of justification and eternal life, n. 12 (f); that good works are not necessary unto salvation, and that the assertion of their necessity ought to be totally rejected by the church, n. 12 (g) (h) (i) (k); that salvation and faith are neither preserved nor retained by charity and the works thereof, n. 12 (m) (n); that good works, when blended in the matter of justification, are pernicious, n. 14 (g); that the works of the spirit, or of grace, which follow faith as its fruits, contribute nothing to man's salvation, n. 14 (d), and elsewhere; from all which it inevitably follows, that this faith of theirs has no connection with charity, and if it had, that the connection, according to their notion, would become injurious to salvation, because injurious to faith, which thus would no longer be the only means of salvation. That no connection between charity and that faith can actually exist, has been shown above, n. 47, 48, 49, 50; wherefore it may be said, that it was providentially ordered, that the Reformers should be so zealous to reject charity and good works from their faith; for had they conjoined them, it would have been like conjoining a leopard with a sheep, a wolf with a lamb, or a hawk with a dove. That this faith is also described in the Apocalypse by a leopard, may be seen in chap. xiii. 2; and also in the explanation thereof, in the APOCALYPSE REVEALED, n. 572. But what is a church without faith, and what is faith without charity, consequently what is a church without the marriage of faith and charity? see n. 48.

This marriage constitutes the real church, and is the New Church which is now establishing by the Lord.

69. That man in his conversion is like a stock, the faith of the present church acknowledges as its natural offspring in these express words. That man has not the smallest degree of ability in spiritual things, n. 15, (a) (b) (c); that in conversion he is like a stock, a stone, and a statue, and that he cannot so much as accommodate and apply himself to receive grace, but is like something that has not the use of any of the senses, n. 15, (c) (d); that man has only a locomotive power, whereby he is capable of going to church to hear the Word and the gospel, n. 15, (e); but that a person who is regenerate by virtue of the Holy Ghost, from the new powers and gifts which he has received, does in a certain manner co-operate, n. 15, (k); besides many other things to the same purpose. This description of man in his conversion, and during his repentance from evil works, is also an offspring produced from the said egg or womb, that is, from justification by faith alone, to the intent that man's works may be totally abolished, and not suffered to have the least conjunction with faith, not even to touch it. But seeing that such ideas are repugnant to the common perception of all men concerning man's conversion and repentance, they have added the following words. "*There is a wide difference between persons baptized, and persons unbaptized, for it is the doctrine of Paul, that all baptized persons have put on Christ, and are truly regenerated; they are then endowed with a freedom of will, whereby they not only can hear the Word of God, but can also assent to the same, and embrace it by faith*," n. 15, (m), and in the *Formula Concordiæ*, p. 675. I appeal to men of understanding, and beg them to weigh and consider, whether this latter quotation be any way consistent with the preceding ones, and whether it be not a contradiction to say that a Christian in a state of conversion is like a stock or a stone, so that he is not able so much as to accommodate himself to the receiving of grace, when yet every Christian is a baptized person, and by baptism became possessed, not only of a power to hear the Word of God, but also to assent to it, and embrace it by faith; wherefore the comparing a Christian to a stock or a stone is a simile that ought to be banished from all Christian churches, and to be done away, like a meteor that vanishes from before the eyes of a man waking out of sleep; for what can be more repugnant to reason? But in order to elucidate the doctrine of the New Church concerning man's conversion, I will transcribe the following passage from one of the *memorable relations* in the APOCALYPSE REVEALED. "How plain is it to see, that every man has liberty to think about God, or not to think about Him; consequently that every man has the same liberty in spiritual things, as he has in civil and moral things. The Lord gives

this liberty continually to all; wherefore man becomes guilty or not guilty accordingly. Man is man by virtue of this power, whereas a beast is a beast in consequence of its not possessing such a power; so that man is capable of reforming and regenerating himself as of himself, provided he only acknowledge in his heart that his ability is from the Lord. Every man who does the work of repentance, is reformed and regenerated. Both must be done by man as of himself, but this *as of himself* is also from the Lord, because the Lord gives both the power to will and perform, and never takes it away from any one. It is true that man cannot contribute any thing thereunto, nevertheless he is not created a statue, but a man, to do the work of repentance from the Lord as from himself. In this alone consists the reciprocality of love and faith, and of conjunction thereby, which the Lord earnestly wills to be done on the part of man. In a word, act of yourselves, and believe that you act from the Lord, for thus you will act as of yourselves. But the power so to act is not implanted in man by creation, because to act of himself is the prerogative of the Lord alone, but it is given continually; and in this case in proportion as man does good and acquires truth as of himself, he is an angel of heaven; but in proportion as he does evil, and in consequence thereof confirms himself in what is false, which also is done as of himself, in the same proportion he is a spirit of hell. That in this latter case also man acts as of himself, is evident from his prayers, as when he prays that he may be preserved from the devil, lest he should seduce him, and bring his own evils upon him. Every one however contracts guilt, who believes that he does of himself either good or evil; but not he who believes that he acts as of himself. For whatsoever a man believes he does of himself, that he appropriates to himself; if he believes that he does good of himself, he appropriates to himself that good, and makes it his own, when nevertheless it is of God and from God; and if he believes that he does evil of himself, he also appropriates that evil to himself, and makes it his own, when yet it is of the devil and from the devil.

That many other false tenets, even concerning the sacraments of baptism and the holy supper, as to the benefits reasonably to be expected from them, when considered according to the doctrine of justification by faith alone; as likewise concerning the person of Christ; together with all the heresies from the first ages down to the present day; have flowed from no other source, than from a doctrine founded on the idea of three Gods, we have not room to demonstrate within the limits of this epitome, but it shall be shown and proved at large in the work itself.

XVI.

70. *That the last state of the present Church, when it is at an end, is meant by the Consummation of the Age, and the Coming of the Lord at that period*, Matt. xxiv. 3.

BRIEF ANALYSIS.

71. We read in Matthew, "*The disciples came to Jesus, and showed Him the buildings of the temple; and Jesus said unto them, Verily, I say unto you, there shall not be left here one stone upon another, which shall not be thrown down. And the disciples said unto Him, tell us when these things shall be, and especially what shall be the sign of Thy coming, and of the consummation of the age*," chap. xxiv. 1, 2, 3. At this day the learned clergy and laity, understand, by the destruction of the temple, its destruction by Vespasian; and by the coming of the Lord, and the consummation of the age, they understand the end and destruction of the world: but by the destruction of the temple is not only meant the destruction thereof by the Romans, but likewise the destruction of the present church; and by the consummation of the age, and the coming of the Lord at that period, is meant the end of the present church and the establishment of a New Church by the Lord. That these things are there meant, is evident from the whole of that chapter from beginning to end, which treats solely of the successive declensions and corruptions of the Christian church, down to its destruction, when it is at an end. That by the temple, in a limited sense, is meant the temple at Jerusalem; in an extensive sense, the church of the Lord; in a more extensive sense, the angelic heaven; and, in the most extensive sense, the Lord as to His Humanity, may be seen in the APOCALYPSE REVEALED, n. 529. That by the consummation of the age is meant the end of the church, which comes to pass when there remains no truth of doctrine from the Word but what has been falsified, and thus consummated, is shown in n. 658, 676, 750, of the same work. That by the coming of the Lord is meant His coming in the Word, and at the same time the establishment of a New Church instead of the former, which is then brought to its consummation or end, evidently appears from His own words in the same chapter, from verse 30 to 34; as likewise from the two last chapters, xxi. and xxii., of the Apocalypse, where these words occur: "*I, Jesus, am the Root and the Offspring of David, the Bright and Morning Star. And the spirit and the bride say, Come; and let him that heareth say, Come; and him that is athirst, let him come. Yea, I come quickly: Amen, even so come, Lord Jesus*," chap. xxii. 17, 20.

72. That the church is at an end, when there are no longer any truths of faith, and hence no goods of charity

therein, is self-evident. That falses of faith extinguish the truths of doctrine, and evils of life consume the goods of charity, and that wherever falses of faith are, there likewise are evils of life, and that wherever evils of life are, there likewise are falses of faith, will be demonstrated in their proper places, when we come to treat of these matters. The reason why it has been hitherto unknown that by the consummation of the age is meant the end of the church, is, because when falses are taught, and when the doctrine resulting from them is believed and honored as orthodox, then it cannot possibly be known that the church is to be brought to a consummation, for falses are regarded as truths, and truths as falses, and then the false explodes the truth and blackens it, like ink poured into clear water, or soot thrown upon white paper. For it is the general opinion, and the most learned of the present age proclaim it, that they enjoy the purest light of the gospel, although they are enveloped in thick darkness; to such a degree of blindness are they reduced by the white speck that has covered over the pupils of their eyes.

73. That in the 24th chapter of Matthew, the 13th of Mark, and the 21st of Luke, where similar passages occur, is not described the destruction of the temple and Jerusalem, but that the successive changes of the state of the Christian church are foretold, in regular order, even to its last state, when it comes to an end, will be shown in the large work; and in the meantime, it may appear from these words in the above-mentioned evangelists: "*Then shall appear the sign of the Son of Man, and then shall all the tribes of the earth wail; and they shall see the Son of Man coming in the clouds of heaven with power and glory. And He shall send his angels with a great sound of a trumpet, and they shall gather together His elect from one end of the heavens to the other end thereof,*" Matt. xxiv. 30, 31; Mark xiii. 26, 27; Luke xxi. 27. It is well known that these things were neither seen nor heard at the destruction of Jerusalem, and that it is the prevailing opinion at this day, that they will come to pass at the day of the last judgment. We likewise read of similar things in the Apocalypse, which from beginning to end treats solely of the last state of the church, where are these words: "*Behold, Jesus Christ cometh in the clouds, and all the tribes of the earth shall wail because of Him,*" chap. i. 5, 7. The particular explication of these words may be seen in the APOCALYPSE REVEALED, n. 24 to 28; also what is signified by the tribes of the earth, and their wailing, n. 27, 348, 349.

XVII.

74. *That the Infestation from Falses, and thence the Consummation of every Truth, or the Desolation, which at this day*

prevails in the Christian Churches, is meant by the great affliction, such as was not from the beginning of the world, nor ever shall be, Matt. xxiv. 21.

BRIEF ANALYSIS.

75. That the successive declensions and corruptions of the Christian church are foretold and described by the Lord in the xxivth chapter of Matthew, may be seen above, n. 73. After having spoken of false prophets that should arise, and of the abomination of desolation wrought by them, verses 11, 15, He adds, "*Then shall be great affliction, such as was not from the beginning of the world until now, nor ever shall be,*" verse 21; whence it is evident, that by great affliction, in this as well as in other places throughout the Word, is meant the infestation of truth by falses, until there remains no genuine truth derived from the Word which is not falsified, and by that means consummated. This has come to pass, by reason that the churches have not acknowledged the unity of God in the trinity, and His trinity in unity, in one person, but in three, and hence have founded a church in the mind upon the idea of three Gods, and in the mouth upon the confession of one God; for by this means they have separated themselves from the Lord, and at length to such a degree, that they have no idea left of there being any Divinity in His Human Nature, (see the APOCALYPSE REVEALED, n. 294,) when nevertheless the Lord as to His Humanity is Divine Truth itself, and Divine Light Itself, as He abundantly teaches in His Word; hence comes the great affliction so prevalent at the present day. That this has been principally brought on by the doctrine of justification and imputation through the medium of faith alone, will be shown in the following pages.

76. This affliction, or infestation of truth by falses, is treated of in seven chapters of the Apocalypse; and is what is meant by the black horse and the pale horse going forth from the book, the seals whereof the Lamb had opened, chap. vi. 5 to 8; and by the beast ascending out of the abyss, which made war against the two witnesses, and slew them, chap. xi. 7, and following verses; as also by the dragon which stood before the woman who was ready to be delivered, in order to devour her child, and pursued her into the desert, and there cast out of his mouth water as a flood, that he might cause her to be carried away of the flood, chap. xii.; and likewise by the beast out of the sea, whose body was like that of a leopard, his feet like those of a bear, and his mouth like that of a lion, chap. xiii. 2; also by the three unclean spirits like frogs, which came out of the mouth of the dragon, out of the mouth of the beast, and out of the mouth of the false prophet, chap. xvi. 13; and moreover by these particulars, that after the seven angels had poured out the vials of the wrath of God, wherein were the

seven last plagues, upon the earth, upon the sea, upon the rivers and fountains, upon the sun, upon the throne of the beast, upon Euphrates, and last of all upon the air, there was a great earthquake, such as had never been seen since men were created upon the earth, chap. xvi. The earthquake here signifies an inversion of the church, which is occasioned by falses and falsifications of truth. The like things are understood by these words: "The angel put forth his sickle, and gathered the vine of the earth, and cast it into the great wine-press of the wrath of God; and the wine-press was trodden, and blood came out of the wine-press, even unto the horses' bridles, for the space of a thousand and six hundred furlongs," chap. xiv. 19, 20; where blood signifies truth falsified: besides many other passages to the same purpose, in those seven chapters. But if you desire further information in this matter, turn to the explication thereof, and the memorable relations at the end of the chapters.

XVIII.

77. *That there would be neither Love, nor Faith, nor the Knowledges of Good and Truth, in the last time of the Christian Church, when it draws to an end, is understood by these words: "After the affliction of those days, the sun shall be darkened, and the Moon shall not give her light, and the Stars shall fall from Heaven, and the Powers of the Heavens shall be shaken,"* Matt. xxiv. verse 29.

BRIEF ANALYSIS.

78. In the prophetic parts of the Word, the like things are said of the sun, moon, and stars, as here in Matthew, chap. xxiv. 29. Thus it is written in Isaiah: "*Behold the cruel day of Jehovah cometh; the stars of heaven and the constellations thereof shall not give their light, the sun shall be darkened at his rising, and the moon shall not cause her light to shine,*" Isaiah xiii. 9, 10. So in Ezekiel: "*When I shall put thee out, I will cover the heavens, and make the stars thereof dark; I will cover the sun with a cloud, and the moon shall not give her light, and I will set darkness upon thy land,*" xxxii. 7, 8. In Joel: "*The day of Jehovah cometh, a day of darkness, the sun and moon shall not give their light, and the stars shall withdraw their shining,*" ii. 10. Again, in the same prophet: "*The sun shall be turned into darkness, and the moon into blood, before the great day of Jehovah shall come,*" iii. 4. "*The day of Jehovah is near in the valley of decision; the sun and moon are darkened,*" iv. 15. In the Apocalypse: "*The fourth angel sounded, and the third part of the sun was smitten, and the third part of the stars, and the day shone not for a third part of it,*" vii. 12. And in another place, "*The sun became black as sackcloth of hair, and the moon*

became as blood," vi. 12. All the former passages treat of the last time of the Jewish church, which was when the Lord came into the world; the same thing is meant here in Matthew and in the Apocalypse, only in reference to the last time of the Christian church, when the Lord is to come again, but in the Word, which is Himself, and in which He is; wherefore immediately after those words in Matthew xxiv. 29, it follows, "*And then shall appear the sign of the Son of Man coming in the clouds of the heavens*," verse 30. By the sun, in the above passages, is meant love; by the moon, faith; and by the stars, the knowledges of good and truth; and by the powers of the heavens, those three as the supports and firmaments of the heavens where angels are, and of the churches where men are; by the above, therefore, collected into one sense, is meant, that there would be no love, nor faith, nor knowledges of good and truth, remaining in the Christian church, in the last time thereof, when it draws to its end. That the sun signifies love, has been shown in the APOCALYPSE REVEALED, n. 53, 54, 413, 796, 831, 961: that the moon signifies faith, n. 53, 332, 413, 423, 533: that the stars signify knowledges of good and truth, n. 51, 74, 333, 408, 419, 954.

79. That, according to the above prediction, there is at this day such great darkness throughout the Christian churches, that the sun gives no light by day, nor the moon and stars any light by night, is occasioned solely by the *doctrine of justification by faith alone;* for it inculcates faith as the only means of salvation; of the influx, progress, indwelling, operation, and efficacy of which no one has hitherto seen any sign; and into which neither the law of the decalogue, nor charity, nor good works, nor repentance, nor desires after newness of life, have any entrance, or are in the smallest degree connected with it; for it is asserted, that they spontaneously follow, without being of any use either to preserve faith or to procure salvation. The above doctrine likewise teaches, that faith alone imparts to the regenerate, or those who are possessed of it, full liberty, so as to be no longer under the law; moreover that Christ covers over their sins before God the Father, who forgives them as though they were not seen, and crowns them with renovation, holiness, and eternal life. These and many other things of a like nature are the interiors of that doctrine; the exteriors, which do not gain admission, are valuable sayings concerning charity, good works, acts of repentance, and exercises of the law; yet these are accounted by them merely as slaves and drudges, which follow their mistress, faith, without being permitted to join in her company. But forasmuch as they know that the laity account these things as equally necessary to salvation with faith, they carefully subjoin them in their sermons and discourses, and pretend to conjoin them with and insert them into justifica-

tion; this, however, they do merely to tickle the ears of the vulgar, and to defend their oracles, that they may not appear mere riddles, or like the vain responses of soothsayers.

80. In order to confirm the above assertions, I will adduce the following passages from the *Formula Concordiæ* (concerning which see n. 9), lest any one should think that these things have been unjustly laid to their charge. That the works of the second table of the decalogue are civil duties, and belong to external worship, which man is able to do of himself; and that it is a folly to dream that such works can justify, page 84, 85, 102. That good works are to be utterly excluded from the business of justification by faith, p. 589, 590, 591, 704 to 708. That good works do not in any wise enter into justification, p. 589, 702; Appendix, 62, 173. That good works do not preserve salvation nor faith, p. 590, 705; Appendix, p. 174. That neither does repentance enter into justification by faith, p. 165, 320; Appendix, p. 158. That repentance is nothing more than praying to God, acknowledging the truth of the gospel, giving of thanks, being obedient to the magistracy, and following one's calling, p. 12, 198, Appendix, 158, 159, 172, 266. That renovation of life has likewise nothing to do with justification, p. 585, 685, 688, 689; Appendix, p. 170. That attention to obedience for the time to come, in like manner, neither enters into faith, nor justifies, p. 90, 91, 690; Appendix, p. 167. That the regenerate are not under the law, but are delivered from the bondage thereof, and are only in the law, and under grace, p. 722, and elsewhere. That the sins of the regenerate are covered over by the merit of Christ, p. 641, 686, 687, 719, 720; besides many other passages to the same purport. It is to be observed, that all Protestants, as well those who call themselves Gospellers, as those who call themselves the Reformed, teach in like manner justification by faith alone, see above, n. 17, 18.

81. It is a wonderful circumstance, that the doctrine of justification by faith alone prevails at this day over every other doctrine throughout all reformed Christendom, and is esteemed almost as the only important point of theology in the sacred order. This is what all young students among the clergy greedily learn and imbibe at the universities, and what they afterwards teach in the churches, and publish in print, as if they were inspired with heavenly wisdom, and whereby they endeavor to acquire to themselves a name, and the reputation of superior learning, as well as diplomas, licences, and other honorary rewards. And these things are done, notwithstanding it is owing to this doctrine alone, that the sun is at this day darkened, the moon deprived of her light, and the stars have fallen from heaven, that is, have perished. It has been certified unto me, that the doctrine of faith in imputed righteous-

ness has blinded the minds of men at this day to such a degree, that they will not, and therefore as it were cannot, see any Divine Truth by the light of the sun, nor by the light of the moon, but only by the light of a fire by night; on which account I will venture to assert, that supposing Divine Truths concerning the conjunction of charity and faith, concerning heaven, the Lord, and eternal happiness, to be sent down from heaven engraven in silver characters, they would not be thought worthy to be read by the sticklers for justification; but the case would be quite otherwise supposing a paper concerning justification by faith alone to be brought them from hell. It is also said in the *Formula Concordiæ*, that the article of justification by faith alone, or the righteousness of faith, is the chief article in the whole Christian doctrine; and that the works of the law are utterly to be excluded from this article, p. 17, 61, 62, 72, 89, 683; Appendix p. 164.

XIX.

82. *That they who are in the present justifying Faith, are meant by the he-goats in Daniel and in Matthew.*

BRIEF ANALYSIS.

83. It is written in Daniel, "*I saw in a vision a ram, which had two horns that were high, but the higher came up last; and that the horn pushed westward, and northward, and southward, and made itself great. Then I saw a he-goat coming from the west, over the face of the whole earth, which had a horn between its eyes; and that he ran to the ram in the fury of his strength, and broke his two horns, and cast him down to the earth, and stamped upon him: but that the great horn of the he-goat was broken, and instead of it there came up four horns; and out of one of them came forth a little horn which waxed exceeding great towards the south, towards the east, and towards honorableness, and even to the host of heaven; and it cast down of the host and of the stars to the earth, and stamped upon them: yea, he magnified himself to the Prince of the host, and took from him the daily sacrifice, and cast away the place of his sanctuary, for he cast down truth to the earth. And I heard one saint saying, how long shall this vision be, the daily sacrifice, and the wasting transgression, that both the holy thing and the host should be given to be trodden under foot? And he said, even to the evening the morning, then shall the holy thing be justified,*" chap. viii. 2 to 14. That this vision is a prediction of the future states of the church is very evident, for it declares, that the daily sacrifice was taken away from the Prince of the host, the habitation of his sanctuary cast down, and that the he-goat cast down truth to the earth; moreover, that a saint said, How long shall

this vision be, that both the holy thing and the host should be given to be trodden under foot; and that this should be even to the evening the morning, when the holy thing shall be justified. By the evening the morning is meant the end of the old church, when a New Church commences.

84. In Matthew we read these words: "*Then shall the Son of Man say to the he-goats on His left hand, depart from Me, for I was hungry, and ye gave Me no meat; I was thirsty, and ye gave Me no drink; I was a stranger, and ye took Me not in; I was naked, and ye clothed Me not; I was sick and in prison, and ye visited Me not; and these shall go away into eternal punishment.*" That the same persons are here meant by he-goats and sheep, as by the he-goat and ram in Daniel, is very evident. That by he-goats are meant those who are in the present justifying faith, appears from this circumstance, that unto the sheep are enumerated works of charity, and it is said that they did them; and that unto the he-goats the same works of charity are enumerated, but it said that they did them not, and that they are therefore sentenced to condemnation; for they who are in the present justifying faith, neglect works, because they deny them to have any thing of salvation or of the church in them. When charity is thus removed, good works, which appertain to charity, become so totally forgotten and obliterated, that they are never more remembered, nor is the least effort made to recall them to mind when the law of the decalogue is read. It is a general rule in religion, that in proportion as any one does not will good, and hence does not do it, in the same proportion he wills evils, and hence does them; and on the contrary, that in proportion as any one does not will evils, and hence does not commit them, in the same proportion he wills good, and hence does good; these latter are the sheep, but the former are the he-goats. If all evil persons had been there meant by the he-goats, instead of the works of charity which they had not done, the evils which they had done would have been enumerated.

85. That no other than the persons above described are meant by the he-goats, has been manifested to me by experience in the spiritual world; in which world there appear all things that are in the natural world, such as houses and palaces, paradises and gardens, with trees of every kind; likewise fields and tillage lands, as also plains and green pastures, together with flocks and herds; and all resembling those upon our earth; nor is there any other difference, than that in the natural world they are from a natural origin, but in the spiritual world from a spiritual origin. There I have often seen sheep and he-goats, also combats between them, like that described in Daniel, chap. viii. I have seen he-goats with horns bent forwards and backwards, and rushing with fury upon the sheep; I have seen

some he-goats with two, and others with four horns, with which they vehemently struck at the sheep; and when I looked to discover what this meant, I saw some persons disputing together about faith conjoined with charity, and faith separated from charity; from whence it plainly appeared, that the present justifying faith, which considered in itself is a faith disjoined from charity, is the he-goat, and that faith conjoined with charity is the sheep.

86. The like persons are meant by he-goats in Zechariah, "*Mine anger was kindled against the shepherds, and I will visit the he-goats,*" x. 3. And in Ezekiel, "*Behold I judge between cattle and cattle, between the rams and the he-goats; seemeth it a small thing unto you, to have eaten up the good pasture, but ye must tread down with your feet also the residue of the pastures? Ye thrust all the infirm sheep with your horns, until ye have dispersed them; therefore will I save My flock, that it be no more a prey,*" xxxiv. 17, 18, 22, and following verses.

XX.

87. *That they who have confirmed themselves in the present justifying Faith, are meant in the Apocalypse by the Dragon, and his two Beasts, and by the Locusts; and that this same Faith, when confirmed, is there meant by the great City which is spiritually called Sodom and Egypt, where the two Witnesses were slain, as also by the Pit of the Abyss, frow which the Locusts came.*

BRIEF ANALYSIS.

88. That seven chapters of the Apocalypse treat of the perverted state of the church among the Reformed, and two chapters of the perverted state of the church among the Roman Catholics, and that the states of both churches, as existing at the present day, are sentenced to condemnation, has been shown in the explication thereof, in the work entitled, THE APOCALYPSE REVEALED, and that not by uncertain conjectures, but by full proofs. That by the dragon treated of in the 12th chapter, are meant those in the Reformed churches, who make God three, and the Lord two, and who separate charity from faith, by making their faith spiritual and saving, and not charity, see n. 532 to 565, and the *memorable relation* adjoined, n. 566. That they are further described by the two beasts, one rising out of the sea, and the other out of the earth, as related in chap. xiii. see n, 567 to 610, and the *memorable relation*, n. 611. That they are also described by the locusts, which came forth out of the pit of the abyss, as mentioned in chap. ix. see n. 419 to 442. That this same faith, when confirmed, is meant by the great city, which is spiritually called Sodom and Egypt, where the two faithful witnesses were slain, as related in chap.

xi. see n. 485 to 530, particularly n. 500 to 503, and the *memorable relation*, n. 531. That they are also meant by the pit of the abyss, out of which issued smoke as out of a great furnace, and the sun and the air were darkened, and then locusts came forth, as described in chap. ix., see n. 421 to 424.

89. That I might be assured and fully convinced, that by the pit of the abyss nothing else is meant than the faith of the dragon, which is a faith conceived from an idea of three Gods, and from having no idea of the Divinity of the Human Nature of Christ, and which is called faith alone justifying, regenerating, quickening, sanctifying, and saving; it was given me to look into that abyss, to converse with those who are therein, and likewise to see the locusts which came out thence; from which ocular demonstration, that pit together with the abyss is described by me in the APOCALYPSE REVEALED; and because a description from ocular demonstration may be relied on, it shall be transcribed from that work, where it is described as follows.

"That pit, which is like the mouth of a furnace, appears in the southern quarter; and the abyss beneath it is of great extent towards the east; they have light even there, but if light from heaven be let in, there is immediate darkness; wherefore the pit is closed up at the top. There appear in the abyss huts constructed of brick, which are divided into distinct cells, in each of which is a table, whereon lie papers, with some books. Every one there sits at his own table, who in this world had confirmed justification and salvation by faith alone, making charity a merely natural and moral act, and the works thereof only works of civil life, whereby men may reap advantage in the world, but if done for the sake of salvation, they condemn them, and some even rigorously, because human reason and will are in them. All who are in this abyss, have been scholars and learned men in the world; and among them are some metaphysicians and scholastic divines, who are there esteemed above the rest. But their lot is as follows: when first they come thither, they take their seats in the first cells, but as they confirm faith by excluding the works of charity, they leave the first seats, and enter into cells nearer the east, and thus successively till they come towards the end, where they are who confirm those tenets from the Word; and because they then cannot but falsify the Word, their huts vanish, and they find themselves in a desert. There is also an abyss beneath that abyss, where those are who in like manner have confirmed justification and salvation by faith alone, but who in their spirits have denied the existence of a God, and in their hearts have made a jest of the holy things of the church; there they do nothing but quarrel, tear their garments, get upon the tables, stamp with their feet, and assail each other with reproaches;

and because it is not permitted them to hurt any one, they use threatening words and shake their fists at each other."

90. That I might also be assured and convinced, that they who have confirmed themselves in the present justifying faith, are meant by the dragon, it was given me to see many thousands of them assembled together, and they then appeared at a distance like a dragon with a long tail, which seemed full of spikes like thorns, which signified falsities. Once also there appeared a still greater dragon, which raising up his back, lifted his tail towards heaven, and endeavored to draw down the stars from thence; stars there signify truths.

XXI.

91. *That unless a New Church be established by the Lord, no one can be saved; and that this is meant by these words, "Unless those days should be shortened, there should no flesh be saved."* Matt. xxiv. 22.

BRIEF ANALYSIS.

92. By shortening those days, is meant the putting an end to the present church, and establishing a new one; for, as has been already observed, the 24th chapter of Matthew treats of the successive declensions and perversions of the Christian church, even to the consummation and end thereof, and of the coming of the Lord at that period. The reason why no flesh could be saved, unless those days should be shortened, is, because the faith of the present church is founded on the idea of three Gods, and with this idea no one can enter heaven; consequently no one can enter heaven with the faith of the present church, because the idea of three Gods is in all and every part thereof; and besides, in that faith there exists no life from the works of charity. That the faith of the present church cannot be conjoined with charity, and produce any fruits which are good works, was shown above, n. 47 to 50. There are two things which form heaven in man, namely, the truths of faith and the goods of charity; the truths of faith occasion the presence of the Lord, and point out the way to heaven, and the goods of charity effect conjunction with the Lord, and introduce into heaven; and every one is there introduced into light according to his affection of truth, and into heat according to his affection of good. That the affection of truth is faith in its essence, and the affection of good charity in its essence, and that the marriage of them both constitutes the church, may be seen above, n. 48; the church and heaven make one. That these three are not in the churches of the present day, which are built upon faith alone, has been fully shown in the preceding pages.

93. I have sometimes in the spiritual world conversed with

the maintainers of justification by faith alone, and have told them that their doctrine is erroneous, and likewise absurd, that it brings on security, blindness, sleep, and night in spiritual things, and thereby death to the soul, thus exhorting them to desist from it. But I have received for answer, Why should we desist? Does not the pre-eminence of the clergy above the laity, in point of erudition, depend upon this doctrine? To which I replied, that it should seem from hence, that they regarded not so much the salvation of souls, as their own pre-eminence; and that because they had applied the truths of the Word to confirm their own false principles, and thereby had adulterated them, they were become angels of the abyss, called Abaddons and Apollyons, Apoc. ix. 11; by whom are signified the destroyers of the church by a total falsification of the Word. See the explication thereof, n. 440, and the *memorable relation*, n. 566, in the APOCALYPSE REVEALED. But they answered, How can this be? Are we not, by our knowledge of the mysteries of that doctrine, oracles? And do we not from that doctrine give answers as from our sanctuary? wherefore we are not Apollyons, but Apollos. On hearing this, I replied with indignation, If ye are Apollos, ye are also Leviathans, the first class of you are crooked Leviathans, and the second class of you are oblong Leviathans, whom God will visit with his sharp and great sword, Isaiah xxvii. 1. But they laughed at these words. What is meant by being visited and persishing by the sword, may be seen in the APOCALYPSE REVEALED, n. 52.

94. The great arcanum, why, unless a New Church be established by the Lord, no flesh can be saved, is this; that as long as the dragon with his crew remains in the world of spirits, into which he was cast from heaven, so long no Divine Truth, united with Divine Good, can pass from the Lord to men on earth, but it is either annihilated or perverted, so that salvation is thereby rendered impossible to be attained. This is what is meant in the Apocalypse by the following passage: "*And the dragon was cast out into the earth, and his angels were cast out with him; woe to the inhabitants of the earth and the sea, for the devil is come down unto them, having great wrath; and he persecuted the woman, who brought forth a Son*," chap. xii. 9, 12, 13. But after the dragon was cast into hell, xx. 10, then it was that John saw the new heaven and the new earth, and saw the New Holy Jerusalem coming down from God out of heaven, Apoc. xxi. 1, 2, &c. What is meant by the dragon, and who the dragons are, may be seen above, n. 47.

XXII.

95. *That the Opening and Rejection of the Tenets of the Faith of the present Church, and the Revelation and Reception of the*

Tenets of the Faith of the New Church, is meant by these words in the Apocalypse: "He that sat upon the throne said, Behold, I make all things New; and He said unto me, Write, for these Words are true and faithful," chap. xxi. 5.

BRIEF ANALYSIS.

96. He that sat upon the throne, that is, the Lord, said these things unto John, when he saw the New Jerusalem coming down from God out of heaven. That by the New Jerusalem is meant a New Church, will be shown in the following chapter. The reason why the falsities of the tenets of the faith of the present church must first be opened and rejected, before the truths of the tenets of the New Church can be revealed and received, is, because they do not agree together, no not in one single point or particular; for the tenets of the present church are founded upon a faith, in which it is unknown whether there be any essential of the church, or not. Now the essentials of the church, which conjoin themselves with a faith directed to one God, are charity, good works, repentance, and a life according to the Divine laws; and forasmuch as these together with faith affect and move the human will and thought, they conjoin man to the Lord, and the Lord to man. Since, therefore, none of these essentials enter into the faith of the present church at its first advent, which is called the act of justification, it cannot possibly be known whether this faith be in man, or not, consequently whether it be anything, or only an idea of something; for it is said, that man in the act of justification is like a stock or a stone, and that he can neither will, think, co-operate, no, nor even apply or accommodate himself to the reception thereof in the smallest degree, see above n. 15, (c) (d). Since, therefore, the case is such, that no one can guess, much less know, whether that faith be in him, and thus whether it be in him like a painted flower, or like a flower growing in a field; or whether it be like a bird flying by him, or like a bird that has built her nest in him; I ask by what tokens or signs is this to be known? If it be answered, that it is to be known by charity, good works, repentance, and exercises of the law, which follow after this faith, and yet have no connection with it; I leave it to men of sense to determine, whether things, that have no connection with faith, can possibly be proper signs and evidences thereof; for this faith of theirs, they say, is neither preserved nor retained by the above-mentioned works of charity, see above, n. 12, (m) (n). From what has been said we may draw the following conclusion, namely, that in the faith of the present day there exists nothing of the church, and consequently that it is not anything, but only an idea of something. Since then this faith is of such a

nature, it is deservedly to be rejected, yea, it rejects itself, as a thing that bears no relation to a church.

97. But widely different is the case with the tenets or doctrinals of the New Church; these are all essentials, in each of which there is heaven and the church; and they regard this as their end, namely, that man may be in the Lord, and the Lord in man, according to His own words in John, chap. xiv. 20; and chap. xv. 4, 5, 6. It is this conjunction alone which constitutes the Christian Church. From these few observations it may clearly appear what is meant by these words of the Lord: "*He that sat upon the throne said, behold I make all things new; and He said, write: for these words are true and faithful.*"

98. The sole reason why the Christian world has fallen into a faith, which has put away from itself all the truths and goods of heaven and the church, even to the separation thereof, is because they have divided God into three persons, and have not believed the Lord God the Saviour to be one with God the Father, and thus have not approached Him immediately; when nevertheless He alone as to His Humanity is essential Divine Truth, "*which is the Word, which was God with God, and is the true Light which enlighteneth every man; and became flesh,*" John. i. 1, 2, 9, 14. That He is essential truth, and thus essential light, is also testified in other places; for He says, "*I am the Light of the world,*" John viii. 22; chap. ix. 5. And in another place, "*While ye have the Light, believe in the Light, that ye may be the children of Light. I am come a Light into the world, that whosoever believeth in Me, may not abide in darkness,*" John xii. 36, 46. In the Apocalypse, "*I am Alpha and Omega, the Beginning and the End, the First, and the Last, the Bright and Morning Star,*" chap. xxii. 13, 16. And in Matthew, "*When Jesus was transformed, His face shone as the sun, and His raiment became as the light,*" chap. xvii. 12. Hence it appears why and whence this imaginary faith came into the world, namely, because they have not approached the Lord. And I can, from all my experience, as well as from positive assurance from heaven, with the utmost certainty declare, that it is impossible to derive a single genuine theological truth from any other source than from the Lord alone; nay, that to derive it from any other source is as impossible, as it is to sail from England or Holland to the Pleiades, or to ride on horseback from Germany to Orion in the skv.

XXIII.

99. *That the New Church about to be established by the Lord, is the New Jerusalem, treated of in the Apocalypse,* chap. xxi. and xxii. *which is there called the Bride and the Wife of the Lamb.*

BRIEF ANALYSIS.

100. The reason why the New Church is meant by the New Jerusalem coming down from God out of heaven, Apoc. xxi., is, because Jerusalem was the metropolis of the land of Canaan, and therein was the temple and the altar, and there also the sacrifices were offered, consequently Divine worship was there performed, which every male throughout the land was required to attend three times a-year. A further reason is, because the Lord was in Jerusalem, and taught in its temple, and afterwards glorified His Humanity there; hence it is, that by Jerusalem is signified the church. That by Jerusalem is meant the church, is very clear from the prophecies in the Old Testament concerning a New Church to be established by the Lord, wherein it is called Jerusalem. I shall only adduce the following passages, from which any one of interior reason may see, that by Jerusalem is meant the church: "*Behold I create a new heaven and a new earth, and the former shall not be remembered; behold I will create Jerusalem an exultation, and her people a gladness, that I may exult over Jerusalem, and be glad over My people. Then the wolf and the lamb shall feed together: they shall not do evil in all the mountain of My holiness,*" Isa. lxv. 17, 18, 19, 25. "*For Zion's sake I will not be silent, and for Jerusalem's sake I will not rest, until her righteousness goeth forth as splendor, and her salvation as a lamp that burneth. Then the Gentiles shall see thy righteousness, and all kings thy glory; and thou shalt be called by a new name, which the mouth of Jehovah shall utter; and thou shalt be a crown of beauty, and a diadem of a kingdom, in the hand of thy God. Jehovah shall be well pleased in thee, and thy land shall be married. Behold thy salvation shall come, behold His reward is with Him: and they shall call them the people of holiness, the redeemed of Jehovah; and thou shalt be called a city sought out, not deserted,*" Isaiah lxii. 1 to 4, 11, 12. "*Awake, awake, put on thy strength, O Zion; put on the garments of thy beauty, O Jerusalem, the city of holiness; for henceforth there shall no more come into thee the uncircumcised and the unclean. Shake thyself from the dust, arise, sit down, O Jerusalem. The people shall know my name in that day; for I am he that doth speak, behold it is I. Jehovah hath comforted His people, He hath redeemed Jerusalem,* Isaiah lii. 1, 2, 6, 9. "*Shout with joy, O daughter of Zion, be glad with all thy heart, O daughter of Jerusalem; the king of Israel is in the midst of thee; fear not evil any more; he will be glad over thee with joy, he will rest in thy love, he will rejoice over thee with shouting; I will make you a name and a praise among all the people of the earth,*" Zeph. iii. 14 to 17, 20. "*Thus saith Jehovah, thy Redeemer, saying to Jerusalem, thou shalt be inhabited,*" Isaiah xliv. 24, **26.** "*Thus saith Jehovah, I will return to Zion, and dwell in* *the midst of Jerusalem, whence Jerusalem shall be called the city of truth, and the mountain of Jehovah Zeboath the mountain of holiness,*" Zech. viii. 3, 20 to 23. "*Then shall ye know that I am Jehovah your God, dwelling in Zion, the mountain of holiness, and Jerusalem shall be holiness. And it shall come to pass in that day, that the mountains shall drop down with new wine, and the hills shall flow with milk, and Jerusalem shall sit fast from generation to generation,*" Joel iv. 17 to 21. "*In that day shall the branch of Jehovah be beauty and glory; and it shall come to pass that he that is left in Zion, and he that remaineth in Jerusalem, shall be called holy, every one that is written for life in Jerusalem,*" Isaiah iv. 2, 3. "*In the last days the mountain of the house of Jehovah shall be established as the head of the mountains, for out of Zion shall go forth doctrine, and the word of Jehovah from Jerusalem,*" Micah iv. 1, 2, 8. "*At that time they shall call Jerusalem the throne of Jehovah, and all nations shall be gathered to Jerusalem for the name of Jehovah, neither shall they go any more after the confirmation of their own evil heart,*" Jer. iii. 17. "*Look upon Zion, the city of our stated feasts, let thine eyes see Jerusalem, a quiet habitation, a tabernacle that shall not be taken down; the nails thereof shall never be removed, and the cords thereof shall not be broken,*" Isaiah xxxiii. 20; not to mention other passages, as Isaiah xxiv. 3; chap. xxxvii. 32; chap. lxvi. 10 to 14; Zech. xii. 3, 6 to 10; chap. xiv. 8, 11, 12, 21; Malachi iii. 2, 4; Psalm cxxii. 1 to 7; Psalm cxxx. 4, 5, 6. That by Jerusalem in the above passages is meant a church to be established by the Lord, and not the Jerusalem inhabited by the Jews, is plain from every particular of the description therein; as that Jehovah God was about to create a new heaven and a new earth, and also a Jerusalem at the same time; and that this Jerusalem would be a crown of beauty, and a diadem of a kingdom; that it is to be called holiness, and the city of truth, the throne of Jehovah, a quiet habitation, a tabernacle that shall not be taken down; that the wolf and the lamb shall feed together therein, and that the mountains shall drop down with new wine, and the hills flow with milk, and that it should remain from generation to generation; besides other circumstances, as respecting the people therein, that they should be holy, all written for life, and should be called the redeemed of Jehovah. Moreover, all those passages treat of the coming of the Lord, and particularly of His second coming, when Jerusalem shall be such as is there described; for heretofore she has not been married, that is, has not been the bride and the wife of the Lamb, as the New Jerusalem is said to be in the Apocalypse. The former or present church is meant by Jerusalem in Daniel, and its commencement is there described in these words: "*Know therefore and understand, that from the going forth of the Word, unto the restoring and building of Jerusalem, even unto Messiah the Prince, shall be seven weeks; afterwards in sixty and two weeks it shall be restored, and the street and the ditch shall be built, but in distress of times,"* chap. ix. 25. But its end is described by these words: "*At length upon the bird of abominations shall be desolation, and even to the consummation and decision it shall drop upon the devastation,"* verse 27. This last passage is alluded to in the following words of the Lord in Matthew: "*When ye shall see the abomination of desolation foretold by Daniel the prophet, standing in the holy place, let him that readeth note it well,"* chap. xxiv. 15. That Jerusalem in the places above adduced, does not mean the Jerusalem inhabited by the Jews, may appear from those places in the Word, where it is said of that city that it was entirely destroyed, and that it was to be destroyed, as in Jer. v. 1; chap. vi. 7; chap. vii. 17, 18, &c.; chap. viii. 6, 7, 8, &c.; chap. ix. 10, 11, 13, &c.; chap. xiii. 9, 10, 14; chap. xiv. 16; Lament. i. 8, 9, 17; Ezek. iv. 1 to the end; chap. v. 9 to the end; chap. xii. 18, 19; chap. xv. 6, 7, 8; chap. xvi. 1 to 63; chap. xxiii. 1 to 40; Matt. xxiii. 37, 38; Luke xix. 41 to 44; chap. xxi. 20, 21, 22; chap. xxiii. 28, 29, 30; besides many other passages; and also where it is called Sodom, as in Isa. iii. 9; Jer. xxiii. 14; Ezek. xvi. 46, 48; and in other places.

101. That the church is the Lord's, and that by virtue of a spiritual marriage, which is that of good and truth, the Lord is called the Bridegroom and the Husband, and the church the bride and the wife, is known among Christians from the Word, particularly from the following passages: John said of the Lord, "*He that hath the bride is the Bridegroom, but the friend of the Bridegroom is he who standeth and heareth Him, and rejoiceth because of the Bridegroom's voice,"* John iii. 29. "*Jesus said, while the Bridegroom is with them, the children of the marriage cannot fast,"* Matt. ix. 15. Mark ii. 19, 20. Luke v. 34, 35. "*I saw the holy city, New Jerusalem, coming down from God out of heaven, prepared as a bride adorned for her husband,"* Apoc. xxi. 2. "*The angel said unto John, come, and I will show thee the bride, the Lamb's wife; and from a mountain he showed him the holy city Jerusalem,"* Apoc. xxi. 9. "*The time of the marriage of the Lamb is come, and His wife hath made herself ready; blessed are they who are called unto the marriage supper of the Lamb,"* Apoc. xix. 7, 9. "*I am the Root and Offspring of David, the Bright and Morning Star. The spirit and the bride say, Come; and let him who heareth say, Come; and him that is athirst, let him come: and whosoever will, let him take the water of life freely,"* Apoc xxii. 16, 17.

XXIV

102. *That the Faith of the New Church cannot by any means be together with the Faith of the former Church, and that in*

case they be together, such a collision and conflict will ensue, as to destroy every thing relating to the Church in man.

BRIEF ANALYSIS.

103. The reason why the faith of the New Church cannot by any means be together with the faith of the former or present church, is, because they do not agree together in one third, no, nor even in one tenth part. The faith of the former church is described in the Apocalypse, chap. xii., by the dragon, but the faith of the New Church by the woman surrounded with the sun, having upon her head a crown of twelve stars, whom the dragon persecuted, and at whom he cast water as a flood, that he might swallow her up, see above, n. 87 to 90. These two cannot be together in one city, much less in one house, consequently they cannot be together in one mind; or should they be together, the unavoidable consequence must be, that the woman would be continually exposed to the rage and insanity of the dragon, and in fear lest he should devour her son; for it is said in the Apocalypse, chap. xii., that the dragon stood before the woman who was ready to be delivered, in order to devour her child, and that the woman, after she had brought forth the man-child, fled into the desert, verses 1, 4, 6, 14 to 17. The faith of the former church is a faith of the night, for human reason has no perception of it; wherefore it is also said, that the understanding must be kept in obedience thereunto; nay, it is not even known whether it be within man or without him, because nothing of man's will and reason enters into it, no, nor charity, good works, repentance, the law of the decalogue, with many other things which really exist in the mind of man. That this is the case, may be seen above, n. 79, 80, 96, 97, 98. But the faith of the New Church enters into a conjugial covenant with all these, and conjoins itself to them; and being thus in the heat of heaven, it is also in the light thereof, and is a faith of light. Now a faith of night and a faith of light can no more be together, than an owl and a dove in one nest; for in such case the owl would lay her eggs, and the dove hers, and after sitting, the young of both would be hatched, and then the owl would tear in pieces the young of the dove, and would give them to her own young for food; for an owl is a bird of prey. There is a further reason why the faith of the former church and the faith of the New Church cannot possibly be together, and that is, because they are heterogeneous; for the faith of the former church springs from an idea of three Gods, see n. 30 to 38, but the faith of the New Church from the idea of one God; and as there hence arises a heterogeneity or repugnance to each other, there must inevitably, supposing them to be together, be such a collision and conflict,

as would prove fatal to every thing relating to the church; or, in other words, man would either fall into a delirium, or into a state of insensibility as to spiritual things, until at length he would scarcely know what the church is, or whether there be any church at all. From what has been said, it follows, that they who have confirmed themselves in the faith of the old church, cannot, without endangering their spiritual life, embrace the faith of the New Church, until they first have narrowly examined, rejected, and thus extirpated the former faith, together with its young or eggs, that is to say, its tenets; the nature of which has been already shown in the foregoing pages, particularly at n. 64 to 69.

104. The like would happen if a person should embrace the faith of the New Church, and retain the faith of the old church concerning the imputation of the righteousness or merit of the Lord; for from this, as from their root, all the tenets of the former church, like so many young shoots, have sprung forth. Supposing this to be the case, it would comparatively be like a person extricating himself from three heads of the dragon, and becoming entangled in his four remaining ones; or like a person flying from a leopard, and meeting with a lion; or like a person escaping out of a pit where there is no water, and falling into a pit full of water, and being drowned. That this is the case, will be seen after the exposition of the following lemma, where something will be advanced concerning imputation.

XXV.

105. *That the Roman Catholics at this day know nothing of the Imputation of the Merit of Christ, and of Justification by Faith therein, into which their Church was formerly initiated, because it is entirely concealed under their external Forms of Worship, which are numerous; for which reason, therefore, if they recede but in part from their external forms of Worship, and immediately approach God the Saviour Jesus Christ, and administer the Holy Eucharist in both kinds, they may be brought into the New Jerusalem, or the New Church of the Lord, more easily than the Reformed.*

BRIEF ANALYSIS.

106. That the primates and rulers of the Romish church, at their consecration to the ministry, swear to observe the decrees of the council of Trent, appears from the bull of Pope Pius IV., where, in the form of the oath of their profession of faith, dated the 18th of November, 1564, we find these words: "*I firmly believe and profess all and every thing contained in the creed used by the holy church of Rome; and I receive, without any doubt, all such things as are maintained and declared in her holy canons,*

and general councils, and especially by the most holy council of Trent; so help me God." That they also bind themselves by an oath to believe and profess what the council of Trent has established, concerning the imputation of the merit of Christ, and justification by faith therein, is evident from these words in the same bull: "*I embrace and receive all and every thing, which has been determined and declared in the most holy council of Trent, concerning original sin and justification;*" what these are, may be seen from the extracts taken from that council, see above, n. 3, 4, 5, 6, 7, 8. From these principles established in that council, the following consequences have been drawn, namely, "That the Roman Catholics, previous to the Reformation, held precisely the same doctrines as the Reformed have done subsequent thereto, with respect to the imputation of the merit of Christ, and justification by faith therein, only with this difference, that they conjoined the same faith with charity and good works," see above, n. 19, 20. Also, "That the leading Reformers, Luther, Melancthon, and Calvin, retained all the tenets concerning the imputation of the merit of Christ, and justification by faith, just as they then were and had been held by the Roman Catholics; but that they separated charity and good works from that faith, and declared them to have no saving efficacy, to the intent that they might be severed from the Roman Catholics, as to the very essentials of the church, which are faith and charity," see above, n. 21, 22, 23. Moreover, "That nevertheless the aforesaid leading Reformers adjoined good works, and even conjoined them, to their faith, but at the same time considered man as a passive subject; whereas the Roman Catholics regarded him as an active subject; and that after all, there actually is a conformity of sentiment between both the one and the other, as to faith, works, and merits," see above, n. 24 to 29. From what has been shown, then, it is evident, that this faith is a faith which the Roman Catholics swear to observe, equally as well as the Reformed.

107. Nevertheless this faith is so far obliterated among the Roman Catholics at this day, that they scarcely know a syllable about it; not that it has been reprobated by any Papal decree, but because it has been concealed by the externals of worship, such as the adoration of Christ's vicar, the invocation of saints, the veneration of images, and moreover by such things as, from being accounted holy, affect the senses, as masses in an unknown tongue, garments, lights, incense, pompous processions; also mysteries respecting the eucharist; by these things, and others of a like nature, faith justifying by the imputation of the merit of Christ, although a primitive tenet of the Romish church, has been so removed out of sight, and withdrawn from the memory, that it is like something buried in the earth, and covered over with a stone, which the monks have set a watch over, to prevent

its being dug up and revived; for were it revived, the belief of their possessing a supernatural power of forgiving sins, and thus of justifying, sanctifying, and bestowing salvation, would cease, and therewith all their sanctity, pre-eminence, and prodigious gains.

108. The *first reason* why the Roman Catholics may be brought into the New Jerusalem, or New Church, more easily than the Reformed, is, because the faith of justification by the imputation of the merit of Christ, which is an erroneous faith, and cannot be together with the faith of the New Church (see n. 102 to 104), is with them obliterated, and is like to be still more fully so;' whereas it is as it were engraven upon the Reformed, inasmuch as it is the principal tenet of their church. A *second reason* is, because the Roman Catholics entertain an idea of Divine Majesty belonging to the Humanity of the Lord, more than the Reformed do, as is evident from their most devout veneration of the host. A *third reason* is, because they hold charity, good works, repentance, and attention to amendment of life, to be essentials of salvation, and these are also essentials of the New Church; but the case is otherwise with the Reformed, who are confirmed in faith alone; with these the above are neither regarded as essentials nor formalities belonging to faith, and consequently as not at all contributing to salvation. These are three reasons, why the Roman Catholics, if they approach God the Saviour Himself, not mediately but immediately, and likewise administer the holy eucharist in both kinds, may more easily than the Reformed receive a living faith in the room of a dead faith, and be conducted by angels from the Lord to the gates of the New Jerusalem or New Church, and be introduced therein with joy and shouting.

---

109. The imputation of the righteousness or merits of Christ, enters at this day like a soul into the whole system of theology throughout the Reformed Christian world. It is from imputation that faith, which is therein accounted the only medium of salvation, is affirmed to be righteousness before God, see above, n. 11 ([d]); and it is from imputation that man, by means of that faith, is said to be clothed with the gifts of righteousness, as a king when elected is invested with the insignia of royalty. But nevertheless imputation, from the mere assertion that a man is righteous, effects nothing, for it passes only into the ears, and does not operate in man, unless the imputation of righteousness be also the application of righteousness by its being communicated and so induced. This follows from its effects, which are said to be the remission of sins, regeneration, renovation, sanctification, and accordingly

salvation. It is asserted further, that by means of that faith Christ dwells in man, and the Holy Spirit operates in him, and that hence the regenerate are not only called righteous, but are in reality such. That not only the gifts of God, but likewise Christ Himself, yea, all the Holy Trinity, dwells by faith in the regenerate, as in their temples, see above, n. 15 ([l]); and that man, both in regard to person and works, is righteous, and pronounced to be so, see above, n. 14 ([e]); from which it clearly follows, that by the imputation of Christ's righteousness is meant its application, and thereby its being induced, by virtue of which man is made partaker thereof. Now, as imputation is the root, the beginning, and the foundation of faith, and all its operations towards salvation, and hence is as it were the sanctuary or sacred recess in the Christian temples at this day, it is necessary to subjoin here something relative to IMPUTATION by way of corollary; but this shall be distinctly arranged under proper articles in the following order: I. That to every one after death is imputed the evil in which he is, and in like manner the good. II. That the induction or translation of the good of one person into another, is a thing impossible. III. That a faith of the imputation or application of the righteousness or merits of Christ, is, inasmuch as such imputation or application is impossible, an imaginary faith.

110. I. THAT TO EVERY ONE, AFTER DEATH, IS IMPUTED THE EVIL IN WHICH HE IS, AND IN LIKE MANNER THE GOOD. In order to illustrate this with some degree of evidence, it shall be considered under the following distinctions. 1. That every one has a proper life of his own. 2. That the life of every one remains with him after death. 3. That to the evil person is then imputed the evil of his life, and that to the good person is imputed the good of his life. *First, that every one has a proper life of his own*, consequently a life distinct from that of another, is well known. For there is a perpetual variety, and no two things are alike; hence it is that every one has a property that is peculiarly his own. This manifestly appears from the faces of men, there not being one face exactly like another, nor ever can be to eternity, because there do not exist two minds alike, and the face is from the mind, for it is, as usually denominated, the type or index of the mind, and the mind derives it origin and form from the life. Unless a man had a proper life of his own, as he has a mind and face of his own, he could not enjoy any life after death distinct from that of another; nay, heaven could not exist, for this consists of a perpetual variety arising from the distinct life of each individual; its form solely proceeds from variety of souls and minds disposed into such an order, as to constitute one whole; and they constitute one from that One, whose life is in the whole and every particular there, as the soul is in man. Unless this were the case, heaven would be

dispersed, because its form would be dissolved. The One from whom the life of all and every one proceeds, and from whom that form coheres together, is the Lord. *Secondly, That the life of every one remains with him after death*, is known in the church from the Word, and particularly from the following passages: "The Son of Man shall come, and then He shall render unto every one according to his deeds," Matt. xvi. 27. "I saw the books opened, and all were judged according to their works," Apoc. xxi. 12, 13. "In the day of judgment God will render unto every one according to his works," Rom. ii. 6; 2 Cor. v. 10. The works, according to which it shall be rendered unto every one, are the life, for the life effects them, and they are according to the life. Forasmuch as it has been granted me for many years past to be in consort with angels, and to converse with those who have departed from the world, I can testify as a matter of certainty, that every one is there examined as to the quality of his past life, and that the life which he had contracted in the world, abides with him to eternity. I have spoken with those who lived many ages ago, whose life I was acquainted with from history, and I found them to be similar in quality to the description given of them. I have also heard from the angels, that no one's life can be changed after death, because it is organized according to his love and faith, and hence according to his works; and that if the life were changed, the organization would be destroyed, which never can be done. They further added, that a change of organization can only take place in the material body, and by no means in the spiritual body, after the former is rejected. *Thirdly, That to the evil person is then imputed the evil of his life, and that to the good person is imputed the good thereof.* The imputation of evil after death, does not consist in accusation, blame censure, or in passing judgment, as in the world; but the evil itself effects this. For the wicked of their own accord separate themselves from the good, because they cannot be together; the delights of the love of evil are in aversion to the delights of the love of good, and delights exhale from every one, as odors from every vegetable on earth; for they are no longer absorbed and concealed by the material body as before, but have a free efflux into the spiritual atmosphere from their loves; and inasmuch as evil is there perceived as it were in its odor, it is this which accuses, blames, finds guilty, and judges; not before any particular judge, but before every one who is in good; and this is what is meant by imputation. The imputation of good is effected in the same manner, and takes place with those who in the world had acknowledged that every good in them was and is from the Lord, and nothing thereof from themselves. These, after preparation, are let into the interior delights of their own good, and then a way is opened for them towards a society in heaven, whose delights are homogeneous. This is done by the Lord.

111. II. That the Induction or Translation of the Good of one Person to another, is a thing impossible. The proof hereof may also appear from the following observations in their order: 1. That every man is born in evil. 2. That man is led into good through regeneration by the Lord. 3. That this is effected by faith in the Lord, and by a life according to His commandments. 4. Wherefore the good of one person cannot by application be transferred to another, and so imputed. *First, That every man is born in evil*, is known in the church. This evil is said to be hereditary from Adam; but it is from parents, from whom every one derives his natural disposition or inclination; which is a fact proved by reason and experience; for likenesses of parents may be traced in the faces, characters, and manners of their children, and their children's children. Hence families are distinguished by many, and their propensities are also judged of: wherefore, the evils which parents have contracted, are transmitted by propagation to their posterity, and manifest themselves by a certain inclination towards them; hence are derived the evils into which men are born. *Secondly, That man is led into good through regeneration by the Lord.* That there is such a thing as regeneration, and that unless a person is regenerated, he cannot enter into heaven, is very evident from the Lord's words in John iii. 3, 5. That regeneration is purification from evils, and thus renovation of life, the Christian world cannot be ignorant of, for it is even discerned by reason, whilst it acknowledges that every one is born in evil, and that evil cannot be washed and wiped away, like filth by soap and water, but by repentance. *Thirdly, That this is effected by faith in the Lord, and by a life according to His commandments.* The precepts of regeneration are five, as may be seen above, n. 43, 44; among which are these. That evils ought to be shunned, because they are of the devil and from the devil; that good actions ought to be done, because they are of God and from God; and that the Lord is to be approached, that He may lead us so to do. Let every one consider and weigh with himself, whether good can be derived to man from any other source; and if he is not possessed of good he cannot be saved *Fourthly, Wherefore the good of one person cannot by application be transferred to another, and so imputed.* From what has been said above, it follows, that man by regeneration is renewed as to his spirit, and that this is effected by faith in the Lord, accompanied by a life according to His commandments. Who does not see, that this renewal can only be effected progressively; nearly in like manner as a tree takes root, and grows successively from a seed, and comes to perfection? They who

have a different notion of regeneration and renovation, know nothing of the state of man, nor anything about evil and good, as that they are diametrically opposite to each other, and that good cannot be implanted but in proportion as evil is removed; neither do they know, that so long as any one is in evil, he is averse to what is really good; wherefore if the good of one person were to be applied and so transferred to another who is in evil, it would be like casting a lamb to a wolf, or fastening a pearl to a hog's snout. From what has been said it is evident, that the induction or translation of the good of one person into another is a thing impossible.

112. III. That the Faith of Imputation, or Application of the Righteousness or Merits of Christ, is, inasmuch as such Imputation or application is impossible, an imaginary Faith. That to every one is imputed the evil in which he is, and in like manner the good, was demonstrated above, n. 110; hence it is evident, that if by imputation is meant the application, and thereby the translation, of the good of one person to another, it is a mere creature of the imagination. In the world, merits may be as it were transcribed by men, that is, benefits may be conferred on children for the sake of their parents, or on the friends of any favorite; yet the good of merit cannot be inscribed on their souls, but only externally adjoined. The like cannot take place with men in respect to their spiritual life. This, as was shown above, must be implanted, and if not implanted by a life according to the forementioned precepts of the Lord, man remains in the evil in which he was born; until this is brought to pass, no good can approach him, or if it does, it is instantly repelled, and rebounds like an elastic ball falling on a stone, or is absorbed like a diamond thrown into a bog. An unreformed man is, as to his spirit, like a panther or an owl, and may be compared to a thorn or a nettle; but a regenerate man is like a sheep or a dove, and may be compared to an olive-tree or a vine. Consider then, I pray, if thou art disposed, how can a man-panther be converted into a man-sheep, or an owl into a dove, or a thorn into an olive-tree, or a nettle into a vine, by any imputation, if thereby is meant transcription? In order that conversion may take place, must not the ferocious nature of the panther and the owl, and the noxious properties of the thorn and the nettle, be first removed, and thus the truly human and inoffensive properties be implanted? By what means this is effected, the Lord also teaches in John, chap. xv. 1 to 7.

113. To the above shall be added the following observations. It is said in the church, that none can fulfil the law, especially since whosoever offends against one commandment of the decalogue, offends against all. This form of speaking, however, is to be taken in a different sense from what it seems to convey; for it is to be understood in this manner, that whosoever from

purpose [of the will] or from confirmation [of the understanding], acts in opposition to one commandment, acts in opposition to the rest, inasmuch as to act thus from purpose or from confirmation is to deny that anything is a sin, and he who is guilty of such denial of sin, makes light of acting against all the rest of the commandments. Who does not know, that he who is a fornicator is not therefore a murderer, a thief, or a false witness, nor even willing to be such? But he who is an adulterer from purpose and confirmation, makes light of every thing relating to religion, and consequently pays no regard to murders, thefts, and false witness, not abstaining from them on account of their being sins, but for fear of the law or loss of character. The case is similar, if a person from set purpose or confirmation offends against any other commandment of the decalogue; he then also offends against the rest, because he does not account anything a sin. Just so it is, also, with those who are in good from the Lord. Such persons, if from their will and understanding, or from set purpose and confirmation, they abstain from one evil because it is a sin, abstain from all, and still more if they abstain from several; for whenever a person abstains, from purpose and confirmation, from any evil, because it is a sin, he is kept by the Lord in the purpose of abstaining from the rest; wherefore if through ignorance, or any predominant concupiscence of the body, he commits an evil, it nevertheless is not imputed to him, inasmuch as he did not purpose it to himself, neither does he afterwards confirm it in himself. A man comes into this kind of purpose, if he examines himself once or twice a year, and repents of the evil he discovers in himself. It is otherwise with him who never examines himself. It is permitted to confirm what has been advanced by the following experience. I have met with several in the spiritual world, who have lived like other people in the natural world, with respect to ornaments of dress, delicacies of food, making interest of money by trade and merchandise, frequenting play-houses, indulging in jocose conversation on love affairs, with other things of a similar nature, and yet the angels charged such things as evils of sin in some, and not as evils in others, declaring the latter innocent, and the former guilty. On being asked the reason of such distinction, when both had indulged in like practices, they replied, that they consider all according to their purpose, intention, and end, and distinguish them accordingly; and therefore that they excuse and condemn those whom the end excuses or condemns, inasmuch as good is the end that influences all who are in heaven, and evil is the end that influences all who are in hell. From what has been said it now plainly appears, to whom sin is imputed, and to whom it is not imputed.

114. To the above shall be added the two following MEMORABLE RELATIONS, taken from the APOCALYPSE REVEALED. FIRST. I was once seized suddenly with a disease that seemed to threaten my life; my whole head was oppressed with pain; a pestilential smoke was let in from the great city called Sodom and Egypt, Apoc. xi. 8; half dead with severe anguish, I expected every moment to be my last: thus I lay in bed for the space of three days and a half: my spirit was reduced to this state, and in consequence thereof my body. Then I heard about me the voices of persons saying, "Lo! he lieth dead in the street of our city, who preached repentance for the remission of sins, and Christ the man as the only God;" and they asked several of the clergy, whether he was worthy of burial? as was said concerning the two witnesses slain in that city, chap. xi. 8, 9, 10. And they answered, "No, let him lie to be made a spectacle of;" and they passed to and fro, and mocked. All this befel me of a truth, whilst I was writing the explication of the eleventh chapter of the Apocalypse. Then were heard shocking speeches from them, such as the following: "How can repentance be performed without faith? And how can Christ, a man, be adored as God? Whilst we are saved freely without any merit of our own, what need is there of anything besides the faith, that God the Father sent the Son to take away the curse of the law, to impute His merit to us, and so to justify us in His sight, and absolve us from our sins, and then to give the Holy Spirit to operate all good in us? Are not these doctrines agreeable to Scripture, and to reason also?" The crowd who stood by received these speeches with great applause. I heard all this without any power to reply, being almost dead: but after three days and a half my spirit recovered, and I went forth from the street into the city, (being in the spirit,) and again said, "Repent, and believe on Christ, and your sins shall be remitted, and ye shall be saved, but otherwise ye shall perish. Did not the Lord Himself preach repentance for the remission of sins, and that men should believe on Him? Did He not enjoin His disciples to preach the same? Is not a full and fatal security of life the sure consequence of your faith?" But they replied, "What idle talk! Has not the Son made satisfaction? And does not the Father impute it to us, and justify us who have believed in it? Thus we are led by the spirit of grace, and how then can sin have place in us, and what power has death to hurt us? Dost thou comprehend this gospel, thou preacher of sin and repentance?" At that instant a voice was heard from heaven, saying, "What is the faith of an impenitent man, but a dead faith? The end is come, the end is come, upon you that are secure, unblameable in your own eyes, justified in your own faith, yet devils;"—and suddenly a deep gulf was opened in the midst of the city,

which spread itself far and wide, and the houses fell one upon another, and were swallowed up; and presently water began to bubble up from a large whirlpool, and overflowed the waste.

When they were thus overwhelmed, and to appearance drowned, I was desirous to know their condition in the deep; and a voice from heaven said to me, "Thou shalt see and hear:" and immediately the waters wherein they seemed to be drowned disappeared, (for waters in the spiritual world are correspondences, and consequently appear to surround those who are under the influence of falses;) and then they appeared to me in a sandy bottom, where were large heaps of stones, among which they ran, and lamented that they were cast out of their great city: and they lifted up their voices and cried, "Why has all this befallen us? Are we not, through our faith, clean, pure, just, and holy?" Others exclaimed, "Are we not, through our faith, cleansed, purified, justified, and sanctified?" And others cried, "Are we not, through our faith, rendered worthy to be reputed and esteemed clean, pure, just, and holy, before God the Father, and before the whole trinity, and to be pronounced such before the angels? Are not we reconciled, atoned, expiated, and thereby absolved, washed, and cleansed from sins? And is not the curse of the law taken away by Christ? Why then are we cast down hither like condemned criminals? We have been told by a bold preacher of sin in our great city, *Believe on Christ, and do the work of repentance.* Have we not believed on Christ, whilst we believed on His merit? And have we not done the work of repentance, whilst we confessed ourselves sinners? Why then has all this befallen us?" But immediately a voice from one side said to them "Do ye know any one sin that ye are guilty of? Have ye ever examined yourselves? Have you in consequence thereof shunned any sin as evil against God? And whosoever does not shun sin, remains in it. Is not sin the devil? Wherefore ye are they, of whom the Lord saith, '*Then shall ye begin to say, we have eaten and drunk in Thy presence, and Thou hast taught in our streets; but He shall answer, I say unto you, I know you not, whence ye are; depart from Me all ye workers of iniquity,*' Luke xiii. 26, 27; Matt. vii. 22, 23. Depart therefore every one to his place; ye see the openings into those caverns, enter therein, and work shall be given each of you to do, and afterwards food in proportion to your work; but if ye refuse at present to enter, ye will presently be compelled by the calls of hunger."

Afterwards there came a voice from heaven to some on that land, who were without the great city, and who are also described in the Apocalypse, chap. xi. 13, crying aloud, "Take heed to yourselves, take heed how ye associate yourselves with such persons. Cannot ye understand, that evils, which are called sins and iniquities, render man unclean and impure? How can man be cleansed and purified from them, but by actual repentance, and faith in the Lord God the Saviour? Actual repentance consists in a man's examining himself, in knowing and acknowledging his sins, in making himself guilty, in confessing them before the Lord, in imploring help and power to resist them, and thus in desisting from them, and leading a new life, and doing all these things as of himself. Practise this once or twice in a year, when ye approach the holy communion; and afterwards when the sins, whereof ye made yourselves guilty, recur, then say to yourselves, we will not consent to them, because they are sins against God; this is actual repentance. Who cannot see, that where a man does not examine himself and see his sins, he remains in them? For all evil is pleasant to a man from his birth; it is pleasant to take revenge, to commit whoredom, to defraud, to blaspheme; does not the pleasure you find in them prevent their being seen? And, if you are told that they are sins, do you not on account of that pleasure, excuse them? Nay, do you not, by false reasonings, confirm them, and persuade yourselves that they are not sins! And so you continue in them, and practise them afterwards more than before; even till you do not know what sin is, or whether there be any such thing as sin or not. But the case is otherwise with every one who performs actual repentance; he calls his evils, which he has thus learnt to know and acknowledge, sins, and therefore begins to shun and detest them, and to feel their delights as undelightful; and in proportion as this is the case, he sees and loves what is good, and at length tastes the delights of goodness, which are the delights of heaven. In a word, so far as any one renounces the devil, so far he is adopted by the Lord, and by Him is taught, guided, withheld from evils, and preserved in what is good. This is the way, and there is no other, which leads from hell to heaven." It is something extraordinary, that there is in the Reformed a certain deep-rooted opposition and aversion to actual repentance, which is so violent, that they cannot force themselves to self-examination, and to see their sins, and to confess them before God; they are seized as it were with horror at the very intention of such a thing. I have inquired of many in the spiritual world concerning this circumstance, who have all told me, that it is above their power; and when they have been informed that the Roman Catholics practise such duties, namely, that they examine themselves, and confess their sins openly before a monk, they have been greatly astonished, and likewise wondered that the Reformed cannot do the same in private before God, although it is alike enjoined them previous to their approaching the holy supper. Some have examined into the cause of this, and found, that the doctrine of faith alone is what occasions such an impenitent state and such a heart; and then it was given them to see, that such of the Romish church as approach and adore Christ, and do not adore, but only honor, the leaders and heads of their church, are saved.

After the above admonition, was heard as it were a noise of thunder, and a voice speaking from heaven, saying, "We are amazed: say unto the body of the Reformed, believe on Christ, and do the work of repentance, and ye shall be saved." And I spake these words to them; and added further, "Is not BAPTISM A SACRAMENT OF REPENTANCE, and thereby an introduction into the church? What else do the sponsors promise for the person to be baptized, but that he will renounce the devil and his works? Is not the SACRED SUPPER A SACRAMENT OF REPENTANCE, and thereby an introduction into heaven? Is it not declared to the communicants, that they must do the work of repentance before they approach? Is not the DECALOGUE, WHICH INCULCATES REPENTANCE, THE DOCTRINE OF THE WHOLE CHRISTIAN CHURCH? Is it not there said, in the six commandments of the second table, thou shalt not do this and that evil, and not said, thou shalt do this and that good? Hence ye may understand, that in proportion as any one shuns evil, in the same proportion he loves good, and that before this, he does not know either what good is, or what evil is."

115. THE SECOND MEMORABLE RELATION is as follows. An angel once said to me, "If thou desirest to see clearly the nature of faith and charity, and thereby what faith is when separate from charity, and what it is when conjoined with charity, I will give thee ocular demonstration of it." I replied, "Show it me." And he said, "Instead of faith and charity, substitute light and heat, and thou wilt see clearly what I mean; for faith in its essence is the truth of wisdom, and charity in its essence is the affection of love, and the truth of wisdom in heaven is light, and the affection of love in heaven is heat; the light and heat which the angels feel and enjoy, are nothing else: hence thou mayest see clearly what faith is when separate from charity, and what it is when conjoined with charity. Faith separate from charity is like the light in winter, and faith conjoined with charity is like the light in spring; the light of winter, which is light separate from heat, and in consequence thereof conjoined with cold, strips the trees of all their leaves, kills every green herb, makes the ground hard, and freezes the water; but the light in spring, which is light conjoined with heat, causes the trees to vegetate, first into leaves, then into blossoms, and lastly into fruits; it opens and softens the ground, whereby it yields grass, herbs, flowers, and fruits; and it also dissolves the ice, so that the waters flow from their fountains. Exactly similar is the case with faith and charity; faith separate

from charity deadens all things, and faith conjoined with charity enlivens all things. The nature of such deadening and enlivening may be seen visibly in our spiritual world, because here faith is light, and charity, heat; for where faith is conjoined with charity, there are paradisal gardens, flowery walks, and verdant groves, gay and delightful in proportion to such conjunction; but where faith is separate from charity, there does not grow so much as a blade of grass, nor any green thing, except it be on thorns and briers." There were standing at a little distance from us some of the clergy, whom the angel called justifiers and sanctifiers of men by faith alone, and also arcanists, that is, dealers in mysteries; we related to them the same things concerning charity and faith, and likewise gave them ocular demonstration of the truth of our assertions; but when we asked them whether they believed it to be so, they turned their backs upon us, and said, "We did not hear you;" whereupon we raised our voices, and cried, "Hear us now then;" but immediately they stopped their ears with both hands, and exclaimed, "We will not to hear."

CONCLUSION.

Jeremiah, chap. vii. 2, 3, 4, 9, 10, 11.

Stand in the gate of the house of Jehovah, and proclaim there this word: Thus saith Jehovah of Hosts, the God of Israel: Amend your ways and your works; trust ye not in lying words, saying, the temple of Jehovah, the temple of Jehovah, the temple of Jehovah is here (*that is the Church*). *Will ye steal, murder, commit adultery, and swear falsely, and after that come and stand before Me in this house, whereon My name is called, and say, we are delivered, whilst ye do all these abominations? Is not this house become a den of robbers? Even I, behold, I have seen, saith Jehovah.*

APPENDIX.

116. THE FAITH OF THE NEW HEAVEN AND NEW CHURCH, IN ITS UNIVERSAL FORM, is this: That the Lord from eternity, who is *Jehovah*, came into the world that He might subdue the hells, and glorify His Humanity; that without this coming no

mortal could have been saved; and that all will be saved who believe in Him.

It is called faith in its universal form, because this is the universal of faith, and the universal of faith is what must enter into all and every particular part thereof. It is a universal of faith, that God is one in essence and person, in whom is a trinity, and that the Lord God the Saviour Jesus Christ is He. It is a universal of faith, that no mortal could have been saved, unless the Lord had come into the world. It is a universal of faith, that He came into the world to remove hell from man, which He effected by combats against it, and victories over it; whereby he subdued it, and reduced it to order, and under obedience to Himself. It is a universal of faith, that He came into the world to glorify the Humanity which He assumed in the world, that is, to unite it with the Divinity of which it was begotten; thus, having subdued hell, He keeps it eternally in order and under obedience to Himself. Inasmuch as both these works, [the subjugation of hell, and the glorification of His Humanity] could only be effected by means of temptations admitted into His Humanity, even to the last, which was the passion of the cross, therefore he endured that also. These are the universals of faith concerning the Lord.

The universal of Christian faith on man's part is, that he should believe on the Lord, for by believing on Him he has conjunction with Him, and by conjunction salvation. To believe on Him, is to have confidence that He will save; and because none can have such confidence but he who leads a good life, therefore this is also meant by believing on Him.

117. THE FAITH OF THE NEW HEAVEN AND NEW CHURCH, IN ITS PARTICULAR FORM, is this: That Jehovah God is essential love and essential wisdom, or that he is essential good and essential truth; and that as to His Divine Truth, which is the Word, and which was God with God, He came down and assumed Humanity, for the purpose of restoring to order all things which were in heaven, and which were in hell, and which were in the church; inasmuch as at that time, the power of the devil, that is, of hell, prevailed over the power of heaven, and on earth the power of evil prevailed over the power of good; in consequence whereof, a total destruction and damnation were at hand, and threatened every creature. This impending destruction and damnation Jehovah God removed by His Humanity, which was Divine Truth, and thus He redeemed both angels and men; and afterwards He united in His Humanity, Divine Truth and Divine Good, and thus returned into His Divinity, in which He was from eternity, together with His glorified Humanity. This is signified by these words in John: "*The Word was with God, and God was the Word; and the Word became flesh,*" chap. i. 1, 14: and in another place, "*I went forth from the*

Father, and am come into the world; again I leave the world, and go to the Father," chap. xvi. 28. Hence it appears, that unless the Lord had come into the world, no one could have been saved. The case is similar at this day; wherefore, unless the Lord come again into the world in Divine Truth, which is the Word, no person can be saved.

The particulars of faith on the part of man are these: I. That God is one, in whom is a Divine Trinity, and that the Lord God the Saviour Jesus Christ is that God. II. That a saving faith is to believe on Him. III. That evils ought to be shunned, because they are of the devil and from the devil. IV. That good actions ought to be done, because they are of God and from God. V. And that they should be done by man as of himself, nevertheless under this belief, that they are from the Lord operating in him and by him. The two first particulars have relation to faith; the two next to charity; and the last respects the conjunction of charity and faith, and thereby of the Lord and man: see also what has been said above, n. 44, on these subjects.

THREE MEMORABLE RELATIONS, FROM THE APOCALYPSE REVEALED.

118. The First Memorable Relation. When I was engaged in the explanation of the xxth chapter of the Apocalypse, and was meditating about the dragon, the beast, and the false prophet, an angelic spirit appeared before me, and asked, what was the subject of my meditation. I answered, "About the false prophet." Then he said, "I will lead you to the place where they are who are meant by the false prophet; and wh are the same that are understood in chap. xiii. by the beast that rose out of the earth, which had two horns like a lamb, and spake like a dragon." I followed him, and lo, I saw a multitude, in the midst of which there were prelates, who taught that nothing else saves man but faith, and that works are good, but not for salvation, and that still they are to be taught from the Word, in order that the laity, especially the simple, may be kept more strictly within the bounds of obedience to the magistracy, and forced, as if from religion, therefore interiorly, to exercise moral charity. Then one of them observing me, said, "Have you any desire to see our place of worship, wherein is an image representative of our faith?" I went and saw it; it was magnificent, and lo, in the midst of it there was the image of a woman clothed in a scarlet robe, and holding in her right hand a piece of gold coin, and in her left a string of pearls. But both

the place of worship and the image were the effect of fantasy, for infernal spirits can by fantasies represent magnificent objects, by closing the interiors of the mind, and opening only its exteriors. When I perceived, however, that it was a delusion of this kind, I prayed to the Lord, and suddenly the interiors of my mind were opened, and then, instead of a magnificent temple, I saw a house full of clefts and chinks from top to bottom, so that none of its parts cohered together, and instead of the woman I saw hanging up in that house an image, the head of which was like a dragon's, the body like a leopard's, and the feet like a bear's, thus like the beast which is described as rising out of the sea, Apoc. xiii.; and instead of a floor there was a bog containing a multitude of frogs; and I was informed, that beneath the bog was a large hewn stone, under which the Word lay entirely hidden. On seeing this, I said to the juggler, "Is this your place of worship?" and he said, "It is;" but then suddenly his interior sight was opened also, and he saw the same things that I did; whereupon he uttered a great cry, and said, "What and whence is all this?" And I said, "This is in consequence of light from heaven, which discovers the quality of every form, and thus the quality of your faith separate from spiritual charity." Then immediately an east wind blew, and carried away every thing that was there, and also dried up the bog, and thereby exposed the stone under which lay the Word; and afterwards there breathed a vernal warmth from heaven, and lo, then, in the very same place, there appeared a tabernacle, as to its outward form, plain and simple. And the angels who were with me said, "Behold, the tabernacle of Abraham, such as it was when the three angels came to him and announced the future birth of Isaac; it appears indeed simple to the eye, but nevertheless according to the influx of light from heaven it becomes more and more magnificent." And they were permitted to open the heaven which is the abode of angels who excel in wisdom, and then by virtue of the influx of light from thence the tabernacle appeared as a temple resembling that of Jerusalem; and on looking into it, I saw that the stone in the floor, under which the Word was deposited, was set with precious stones, from which there issued forth the bright rays as of lightning that shone upon the walls, and caused beautiful variegations of color on certain cherubic forms that were sculptured on them. As I was admiring these things, the angels said, "Thou shalt yet see something still more wonderful." And it was permitted them to open the third heaven, which is the abode of the celestial angels who excel in love, and then by virtue of the influx of flaming light from thence the whole temple disappeared, and in its stead was seen the Lord alone, standing on the foundation stone, which was the Word, in the same form that he appeared in before John, Apoc. i.

But inasmuch as the interiors of the minds of the angels were then filled with holiness, occasioning in them a strong propensity to fall prostrate upon their faces, suddenly the passage of light from the third heaven was closed by the Lord, and that from the second heaven opened again, in consequence of which the former appearance of the temple returned, and also of the tabernacle, but this was in the midst of the temple. Hereby was illustrated the meaning of these words in this chapter: "Behold, the *tabernacle of God* is with men, and He will dwell with them," verse 3, n. 882; and by these, "And I saw no *temple* (in the New Jerusalem), for the *Lord God Omnipotent and the Lamb are the temple of it*," verse 22, n. 918.

119. THE SECOND MEMORABLE RELATION. Awaking on a time out of sleep, I fell into a profound meditation about God; and when I looked upwards, I saw in the heaven above me a most clear shining light in an oval form; and as I fixed my eyes attentively upon the light, it removed gradually from the centre towards the circumference: and lo! then heaven was opened unto me, and I beheld magnificent scenes, and saw angels standing in the form of a circle, on the southern side of the opening, in conversation with each other; and because I earnestly desired to know what they were conversing about, it was permitted me first to hear the sound of their voices, which was full of celestial love, and afterwards to distinguish their speech, which was full of wisdom flowing from their love. They conversed together concerning the *One God*, of *conjunction with Him*, and *salvation* thereby. The matter of their discourse was for the most part ineffable, there being no words in any natural language adapted to convey its meaning; but as I had oftentimes been in consort with angels in their heaven, and, being at such times in a similar state with them, was also in the use and understanding of their language, therefore I was now able to comprehend what they said, and to collect some particulars from their conversation, which may be intelligibly expressed in the words of natural language. They said that the *Divine Esse is One, the Same, the Real* (*Ipsum*), *and Indivisible*; that so also is the Divine Essence, inasmuch as the Divine Esse is the Divine Essence; and that so, likewise, is God, for the Divine Essence, which is also the Divine Esse, is God. This they illustrated by spiritual ideas, saying, that the Divine Esse cannot possibly belong to several, so as to be a Divine Esse in each of them, and yet remain One, the Same, the Real, the Indivisible; for on such a supposition, each would think from his own esse of and by himself; or should the thoughts of each be influenced at the same time from and by the rest, to agreement and unanimity, they would then be several unanimous Gods, and not one God; for unanimity, being the consent of several, and at the same

time of each from and by himself, does not comport with the unity of God, but implies plurality. They did not say, of Gods, because they could not, inasmuch as the light of heaven, which gave birth to their thought, and which conveyed their words, was in opposition to that expression. They added further, that when they meant to pronounce the word Gods, and each as a distinct person by Himself, the power of pronunciation was diverted immediately to utter one God, yea, the only God. Again, they proved that the Divine Esse is the *Divine Esse in itself*, not from itself, because to be from itself supposes an Esse in itself from another: thus it supposes a God from a God, which is not possible. What is from God is not called God, but is called Divine; for what is God from God; consequently, what is God from God born from eternity; and what is God from God proceeding through a God born from eternity; but obscure words, that have no light in them from heaven? They said further, that the Divine Esse, which in itself is God, is *the Same;* not simply the Same, but infinitely the Same, that is, the Same from eternity to eternity; it is the Same in every place, and the Same with every one, and in every one; but that all variableness and changeableness is in the recipient, occasioned by the peculiar state and circumstances thereof. That the Divine Esse, which is God in Himself, is the *Real*, they thus explained: God is the *Real*, because He is Love itself, and Wisdom itself, or, what is the same, because He is Good itself, and Truth itself, and of consequence Life itself; which, unless they were real in God, could have no existence in heaven or in the world, inasmuch as there would be nothing in them that had relation to what is real; for all quality has its quality from this condition of its existence, that there be a something real, from whence it is derived, and to which it has relation as the cause of its peculiar quality. This Reality, which is the Divine Esse, is not in place, but with those and in those who are in place, according to its reception; inasmuch as neither place, nor progression from one place to another, is predicable of love and wisdom, or of goodness and truth, or of life derived thence, which are Reality in God, nay, Real God [or God Himself]; but such things exist in God without place, and this is the foundation of the Divine omnipresence; wherefore the Lord says, "*That He is in the midst of them, and that He is in them, and they in Him.*" But since He cannot be received by any creature such as He is in Himself, He appears such as He is in Himself as a sun above the angelic heavens; that which proceeds thence as light being Himself as to wisdom, and that which proceeds thence as heat being Himself as to love. Yet He Himself is not that sun, but Divine Love and Divine Wisdom in their proximate emanation from Him, and round about Him, appear as a sun before the angels: Himself in the sun is a Man,

OUR LORD JESUS CHRIST, both with respect to the All-begetting Divinity, and with respect to the Divine Humanity; inasmuch as the Real Esse, which is Love itself, and Wisdom itself, was His soul from the Father, and thus Divine Life, which is life in itself. The case is otherwise with man, for in him the soul is not life, but a recipient of life. This the Lord also teaches when He saith, "*I am the Way, the Truth, and the Life;*" and in another place, "*As the Father hath life in Himself, so hath He given to the Son to have life in Himself,*" John v. 26. Life in Himself is God. They further added, that whosoever is under the influence of any spiritual light, may see plainly from what has been said, that the Divine Esse, which is also the Divine Essence, being One, the Same, the Real, and of consequence Indivisible, cannot possibly exist in more than one; and that if it should be supposed to exist in more, manifest contradictions would follow upon such a supposition.

As I listened to this discourse, the angels perceived in my thought the common ideas respecting God entertained in the Christian church, of a trinity of persons in unity, and their unity in trinity; as also of the birth of the Son of God from eternity: whereupon they said to me, "What notions are these which thou entertainest? Are they not the offspring of natural light, wherewith our spiritual light has no agreement? Unless therefore thou removest these ideas from thy mind, we must shut heaven against thee and begone." But I replied, "Enter, I beseech you, more deeply into my thought, and possibly you will find it in agreement with your own." And they did so, and perceived, that by three persons I understood three proceeding Divine attributes, which are *creation, redemption,* and *regeneration*, and that those attributes belong to one God; and that by the birth of the Son of God from eternity, I understood His birth foreseen from eternity, and provided in time. I then acquainted them, that I had received this my natural idea of a trinity and unity of persons, and of the birth of the Son of God from eternity, from the doctrine of faith in the church, that has its name from Athanasius: and that that doctrine is right, if only instead of a trinity of persons is substituted therein a trinity of person, which solely exists in the *Lord Jesus Christ;* and if, instead of the birth of the Son of God from eternity, is understood His birth foreseen from eternity, and provided in time, because as to the Humanity which He assumed, He is expressly called the *Son of God.* Then the angels said, Well, well; and they desired me to declare upon their testimony, that whosoever does not approach the real God of heaven and earth, cannot have entrance into heaven, inasmuch as heaven is heaven from that God only; and that *that God is Jesus Christ,* who is Jehovah Lord, from eternity Creator, in time Redeemer, and to eternity Regenerator; of consequence, who is at once Father, Son, and Holy Spirit; and that this is the gospel, which is to be preached. After this, the heavenly light, which I had before seen over the aperture, returned, and by degrees descended thence, and filled the interiors of my mind, and illuminated my ideas concerning the unity and trinity of God; and then I perceived, that the ideas which I had originally entertained about them, and which were merely natural, were separated, as chaff is separated from the wheat by winnowing, and that they were carried away, as by a wind, to the northern part of heaven, and there disappeared.

120. The Third Memorable Relation. Inasmuch as the Lord has favored me with a sight of the wonderful things that are in the heavens and under the heavens, it is therefore my duty, in the discharge of my commission, to relate what I have seen. There was shown me a magnificent palace, with a temple in its inmost part, and in the midst of the temple was a table of gold, on which lay the Word, and two angels stood beside it. About the table were three rows of seats: the seats of the first row were covered with silk damask of a purple color; the seats of the second row with silk damask of a blue color; and the seats of the third row with white cloth. Below the roof, high above the table, there was seen a spreading curtain, which shone with precious stones, from whose lustre there issued forth a bright appearance as of a rainbow, when the firmament is clear and serene after a shower. Then suddenly there appeared a number of clergy sitting on the seats, all clothed in the garments of their sacerdotal office. On one side was a wardrobe, where stood an angel who had the care of it, and within lay splendid vestments in beautiful order. It was *a Council convened by the Lord;* and I heard a voice from heaven saying, *Deliberate;* but they said, on what? It was said, Concerning *the Lord the Saviour*, and concerning *the Holy Spirit.* But when they began to think on these subjects, they were without illustration; wherefore they made supplication, and immediately light issued down out of heaven, which first illuminated the hinder part of their heads, and afterwards their temples, and last of all their faces; and then they began their deliberation, and, as they were commanded, *First, concerning the Lord the Saviour.* The first proposition and matter of inquiry was, *who assumed the Humanity in the Virgin Mary?* And the angel standing at the table, on which the Word lay, read before them these words in Luke: "*The angel said unto Mary, Behold thou shalt conceive in thy womb, and bring forth a Son, and shall call His name Jesus He shall be great, and shall be called the Son of the Highest. And Mary said to the angel, How shall this be, seeing I know not a man? And the angel answering said, The Holy Spirit shall come*

upon thee, and the power of the Highest shall overshadow thee, wherefore also that Holy Thing which shall be born of thee shall be called the Son of God," chap. i. 31, 32, 34, 35. Then he also read from the 20th to the 25th verse of the first chapter of Matthew, and when he came to the 25th verse, he uttered it with a loud voice. Besides these passages he read many more out of the Evangelists, as Matt. iii. 17; chap. xvii. 5; John xx. 31; and several other places, where the Lord as to His Humanity is called the *Son of God*, and where He, from His Humanity, calls Jehovah *His Father;* and also out of the Prophets, where it is foretold that Jehovah Himself should come into the world; particularly these two passages in Isaiah. "*It shall be said in that day, lo! this is our God, whom we have expected, to deliver us; this is Jehovah, whom we have expected; let us exult and be glad in His salvation,*" chap. xxv. 9. "*The voice of him that crieth in the desert, prepare ye the way of Jehovah, make straight in the wilderness a highway for our God: for the glory of Jehovah shall be revealed, and all flesh shall see it together. Behold, the Lord Jehovah cometh in strength; He shall feed His flock like a shepherd,*" chap. xl. 3, 5, 10, 11. And the angel said, Inasmuch as Jehovah Himself came into the world, and assumed the Humanity, whereby He has redeemed and saved men, therefore He is called by the prophet *the Saviour and the Redeemer;* and then he read before them the following passages: "*Surely God is in Thee, and there is no God beside; verily Thou art a God that hidest Thyself, O God of Israel the Saviour,*" Isaiah xlv. 14, 15. "*Am not I Jehovah? and there is no God else beside Me? a just God, and there is no Saviour beside Me?*" chap. xlv. 21. "*I am Jehovah, and beside Me there is no Saviour,*" chap. xliii. 11. "*I am Jehovah thy God, and thou shalt acknowledge no God beside Me, and there is no Saviour beside Me,*" Hosea xiii. 4. "*That all flesh may know that I Jehovah am thy Saviour and thy Redeemer*, Isaiah xlix. 26; chap. xl. 16. "*As for our Redeemer, Jehovah of Hosts is His name,*" chap. xlvii. 4. "*Their Redeemer, the strong Jehovah of Hosts is His name,*" Jeremiah l. 34. *Jehovah is my Rock and my Redeemer,*" Psalm xix. 14. "*Thus saith Jehovah thy Redeemer, the Holy One of Israel, I Jehovah am thy God,*" Isaiah xlviii. 17; chap. xliii. 14; chap. xlix. 7; chap. liv. 8. "*Thou Jehovah art our Father; our Redeemer from the age is Thy name*, chap. lxiii. 16. "*Thus saith Jehovah thy Redeemer, I am Jehovah that maketh all things, and alone by Myself,*" Isaiah xliv. 24. "*Thus saith Jehovah the King of Israel, and His Redeemer Jehovah of Hosts, I am the First and the Last, and beside Me there is no God,*" chap. xliv. 6. "*Jehovah of Hosts is His name, and thy Redeemer the Holy One of Israel, the God of the whole earth shall He be called,*" chap. liv. 5. "*Behold the days shall come, when I will raise unto David a right-*

ous branch, who shall reign a King, and this is His name, Jehovah our Righteousness," Jer. xxiii. 5, 6; chap. xxxiii. 15, 16. "*In that day Jehovah shall be King over all the earth; in that day there shall be one Jehovah, and His name one,*" Zech. xiv. 9. From all these passages collected, they that sat on the seats were unanimously confirmed in this opinion, namely, that Jehovah Himself assumed the Humanity, for the purpose of redeeming and saving mankind. But instantly a voice was heard from some Roman Catholics, who had hid themselves behind the altar, saying, How can Jehovah the Father become a man? Is He not the Creator of the universe? And one of those who sat on the second row of seats turned himself towards the voice, and said, Who was it then? And he who had been behind the altar, standing now beside the altar, replied, *The Son from eternity.* But answer was returned, Is not the Son from eternity, according to your own confession, also the Creator of the universe? And what is a Son, or a God, born from eternity? And how is it possible for the Divine Essence, which is one and indivisible, to be separated, so that one part can descend without the whole? *The second matter of inquiry concerning the Lord was,* whether or no, according to this reasoning, the Father and He are one, as the soul and the body are one? And they said, that this must follow of consequence, inasmuch as the soul is from the Father. Then one of those, who sat on the third row of seats, read out of the Confession of Faith, called the Athanasian Creed, the following passage: "*Although our Lord Jesus Christ, the Son of God, is God and man, yet He is not two, but one Christ; yea, He is in every respect one, being one person; for as the soul and body make one man, so God and man are one Christ.*" He added, that this faith is received throughout the whole Christian world, even by the Roman Catholics. Then they said, what need have we of further proof? God the Father and He are one, as the soul and body are one; and since this is the case, we perceive that the Humanity of the Lord is Divine, because it is the Humanity of Jehovah; likewise that the Lord ought to be approached as to His Divine Humanity; and that thus and in no other possible way can access be had to the Divinity which is called the Father. This conclusion of theirs the angel confirmed by several passages out of the Word, amongst which were these, in Isaiah: "*Unto us a Child is born, unto us a Son is given, whose name shall be Wonderful, Counsellor, God, Hero, Father of Eternity, Prince of Peace,*" chap. ix. 5. Again, "*Abraham knoweth us not, and Israel doth not acknowledge us, Thou Jehovah art our Father, our Redeemer, from the age is Thy name,*" lxiii. 16. And in John, "*Jesus said, he that believeth on Me believeth on Him that sent Me, and he that seeth Me, seeth Him that sent Me,*" John xii. 44, 45. "*Philip said unto Jesus, show us the Father;*

Jesus said unto him, He that seeth Me, seeth the Father; how then sayest thou, show us the Father? believest thou not that I am in the Father, and the Father in Me? John xiv. 8, 9. "*Jesus said, I and the Father are one,*" chap. x. 30. And again, "*All things that the Father hath are Mine, and all Mine are the Father's,*" chap. xvi. 15; chap. xvii. 10. Lastly, "*Jesus said, I am the Way, the Truth, and the Life: no one cometh to the Father but by Me,*" chap. xvi. 6. When the angel had ended, they all declared with one mouth and one heart, that the Humanity of the Lord is Divine, and that this ought to be approached in order to come at the Father; inasmuch as Jehovah God, who is the Lord from eternity, by the Humanity sent Himself into the world, and made Himself visible to mankind, and thereby gave them access unto Him. In like manner He made Himself visible to men of old time, in a human form, and so gave them access unto Him; but then it was by means of an angel.

After this they proceeded to deliberate about *the Holy Spirit;* and previous thereto, they laid open the idea generally received concerning *God the Father, the Son, and the Holy Spirit,* which is, that God the Father is seated on high, with the Son at His right hand, and that by them is sent forth the Holy Spirit, to enlighten and instruct mankind. But instantly a voice was heard from heaven, saying, we cannot endure an idea formed on such a conception; who does not know, that Jehovah God is omnipresent? And whosoever knows and acknowledges this truth, must also acknowledge, that it is He who enlightens and instructs; and that there is not a mediating God distinct from Him; much less is there a third God distinct from two others, as one person is distinct from another person; wherefore let the former idea, which is vain and frivolous, be removed, and let this, which is just and right, be received, and then you will see clearly. But immediately a voice was heard again from the Roman Catholics, who had concealed themselves behind the altar of the temple, saying, what then is the *Holy Spirit,* mentioned in the writings of the Evangelists, and Paul, by whom so many learned men among the clergy, and particularly of our church, profess themselves to be guided? What person in Christendom at this day denies the Holy Spirit, and His operations? Upon this one who sat on the second row of seats, turned towards the altar, and said, ye insist that the Holy Spirit is a distinct person of Himself, and a distinct God of Himself; but what is a person coming forth and proceeding from a person, except the operation which comes forth and proceeds? One person cannot come forth and proceed from another, by another, but operation can; or what is a God coming forth and proceeding from a God, but the Divine Principle which comes forth and proceeds? One God cannot come forth and proceed from another, by another, but what is Divine may come forth and proceed from one God? Is not the Divine Essence one and indivisible, and inasmuch as the Divine Essence or the Divine Esse is God, is not God therefore one and indivisible? On hearing these words, they that sat on the seats unanimously agreed in this conclusion, that the Holy Spirit is not a distinct person of Himself, consequently not a distinct God of Himself; but that by the Holy Spirit is meant the Divine Sanctity coming forth and proceeding from the one only omnipresent God, who is the Lord. To this the angels, who stood at the golden table whereon the Word was placed, said, WELL: it is not written in any part of the Old Testament, that the prophets spake the Word from the Holy Spirit, but from Jehovah the Lord; and wherever the Holy Spirit is mentioned in the New Testament, it signifies the Divine Proceeding, which is the Divine Principle that enlightens, instructs, vivifies, reforms, and regenerates. After this came on another subject of inquiry, respecting the *Holy Spirit*, namely: From whom proceeds the Divine Principle which is called the Holy Spirit; whether from the Divine which is called the Father, or from the Divine Human which is called the Son? And whilst they were engaged in this inquiry, there shone a light from heaven, whereby they saw that the Divine Sanctity, which is signified by the Holy Spirit, proceeds from the Divine in the Lord by His glorified Humanity, which is the Divine Humanity, comparatively as all activity proceeds from the soul by the body with man. This the angel who stood at the table confirmed by the following passages: "*He, whom the Father hath sent, speaketh the words of God; He hath not given the Spirit by measure unto Him; the Father loveth the Son, aud hath given all things into His hand*," John iii. 34, 35. "*There shall come forth a rod out of the stem of Jesse, the Spirit of Jehovah shall rest upon Him, the Spirit of Wisdom and Understanding, the Spirit of Counsel and Might*," Isa. xi. 1, 2. "*That the Spirit of Jehovah was put upon Him, and was in Him*," chap. xlii. 1; chap. lix. 19, 21; chap. lxi. 1; Luke iv. 18. "*When the Holy Spirit shall come, whom I will send unto you from the Father*," John xv. 26. "*He shall glorify Me, for He shall receive of Mine, and shall show it unto you; all things that the Father hath are Mine, wherefore I said that He shall receive of Mine, and shall show it unto you*," John xvi. 14, 15. "*If I go away, I will send the Comforter unto you*," John xvi. 7. "*The Comforter is the Holy Spirit*," John xiv. 26. "*The Holy Spirit was not yet, because Jesus was not yet glorified*," John vii. 39. But after His glorification, "*Jesus breathed on His disciples, and said, Receive ye the Holy Spirit*," John xx. 22. And in the Apocalypse, "*Who shall not glorify Thy name, O Lord, because Thou Alone art Holy*," chap. xv. 4. Inasmuch as the Divine Operation of the Lord, by virtue of His

Divine Omnipresence, is signified by the Holy Spirit, therefore when the Lord spake to His disciples concerning the Holy Spirit, whom he would send from God the Father, He also said, "*I will not leave you comfortless, I go away and come again unto you; and in that day ye shall know that I am in My Father, and ye in Me, and I in you,*" John xiv. 18, 20, 28: and just before His departure out of the world He said, "*Lo! I am with you all the days, even to the consummation of the age,*" Matt. xxviii. 20. Having read these words in their presence, the angels said, From these, and many other passages in the Word, it is evident, that the Divine Principle which is called the Holy Spirit, proceeds from the Divine in the Lord by His Divine Human. Whereupon they that sat on the seats all exclaimed, *This is Divine Truth.*

Lastly, this decree was passed: That from what has been deliberated in this council, we clearly see, and of consequence acknowledge as holy truth, that in the Lord God the Saviour Jesus Christ there is a Divine Trinity, consisting of the All-begetting Divinity which is called Father, the Divine Humanity which is the Son, and the Divine Proceeding which is the Holy Spirit: then they lifted up their voices together, saying, "*In Jesus Christ dwelleth all the fulness of the Divinity bodily,*" Col. ii. 9. Thus there is One God in the church.

When these conclusions were determined in that magnificent council, they rose up to depart; and the angel, the keeper of the wardrobe, presented to each of them who sat on the seats, splendid garments, interwoven here and there with threads of gold, and said, Receive ye these *wedding garments.* And they were conducted in a glorious manner to the New Christian Heaven, with which the church of the Lord on earth, which is the New Jerusalem, will be in conjunction.

Zechariah, chap. xiv. ver. 7, 8, 9.

It shall be one day which is known to Jehovah, not day nor night, for about evening-time it shall be light. It shall come to pass in that day, living waters shall go out from Jerusalem: and Jehovah shall be King over all the earth: in that day there shall be One Jehovah, and His name One.

251

THE END.

THE NATURE OF

THE INTERCOURSE

BETWEEN

THE SOUL AND THE BODY.

THE NATURE

OF

THE INTERCOURSE

BETWEEN

THE SOUL AND THE BODY:

WHICH IS SUPPOSED TO BE EFFECTED

EITHER BY PHYSICAL INFLUX, OR BY SPIRITUAL INFLUX, OR BY PRE-ESTABLISHED HARMONY.

From the Latin of

EMANUEL SWEDENBORG,

Servant of the Lord Jesus Christ.

BEING A TRANSLATION OF HIS WORK ENTITLED

"DE COMMERCIO ANIMÆ ET CORPORIS QUOD CREDITUR FIERI, VEL PER INFLUXUM PHYSICUM, VEL PER INFLUXUM SPIRITUALEM, VEL PER HARMONIAM PRÆSTABILITAM." Londini, MDCCLXIX.

NEW YORK:

AMERICAN SWEDENBORG PRINTING AND PUBLISHING SOCIETY,

CONTENTS.

THE NATURE OF

THE INTERCOURSE

BETWEEN

THE SOUL AND THE BODY.

---

1. THERE are three opinions and tenets, or three hypotheses, respecting the intercourse between the soul and the body, or respecting the manner in which the one operates on the other, and in which they both operate in union; the first is called Physical Influx, the second Spiritual Influx, and the third Pre-established Harmony. The FIRST hypothesis, which is that of PHYSICAL INFLUX, draws its origin from the appearances of the senses, and the fallacies which spring from that source. For it appears as if the objects of sight, which affect the eyes, flowed into the thought, and produced it; in like manner speech, which affects the ears, appears to flow into the mind, and produce ideas there; and the case appears to be similar with respect to the smell, taste and touch. The organs of these senses first receive, by contact, impressions from surrounding objects; and the mind appears to think, and also to will, according to the affections of those organs; observing which, the ancient philosophers and schoolmen concluded there to be an influx from the organs of sense into the soul, and hence adopted the hypothesis of Physical or Natural Influx. The SECOND hypothesis, which is that of SPIRITUAL INFLUX, called by some Occasional Influx, draws its origin from order and its laws. For the soul is a spiritual substance, and is consequently purer, prior, and interior; but the body is material, and is consequently grosser, posterior, and exterior; and it is according to order for what is purer to flow into what is grosser, what is prior into what is posterior, and what is interior into what is exterior; thus what is spiritual into what is material; and not the contrary; consequently, it is according to order for the mind, as the seat of thought, to flow into the sight according to the state induced on the eyes by the objects before them,—which state, also, that mind disposes at its pleasure; and likewise for the mind as the seat of perception to flow into the hearing,

according to the state induced on the ears by speech. The THIRD hypothesis, which is that of PRE-ESTABLISHED HARMONY, originates from appearances and fallacies to which the rational faculty is subject. For in the operation itself, the mind acts together and simultaneously with the body; but, nevertheless, every operation is first successive and afterwards simultaneous. Now successive operation is influx, and simultaneous operation is harmony; which occur when the mind thinks and afterwards speaks, or when it wills and afterwards acts. It is therefore a fallacy of the rational faculty to establish that which is simultaneous and exclude that which is successive. No fourth opinion respecting the intercourse between the soul and the body can be framed; for either the soul must operate on the body, or the body on the soul, or both continually together.

2. Since the hypothesis of spiritual influx draws its origin, as just observed, from order and its laws, this opinion has been acknowledged and received by the wise in the learned world in preference to the other two; for every thing which draws its origin from order, is truth, and truth manifests itself by virtue of its inherent light, even in that shade which obscures the rational perception while the truth only exists in the form of an hypothesis. There are three things which involve this hypothesis in shade, viz., ignorance respecting what the soul is, ignorance respecting what anything spiritual is, and ignorance respecting the nature of influx: wherefore these three things must first be unfolded before the rational faculty can see the truth itself. For truth, while it only exists in the form of an hypothesis, is not truth itself, but a conjecture respecting it; it is like a picture seen at night on a wall by the light of the stars, to which the mind assigns a different form according to its fancy; whereas its proper form is seen when the sun illuminates it in the morning, and not only discovers and renders visible its general figure, but also its particular parts: just so, out of the shade in which the truth appears while this opinion exists in the form of an hypothesis, arises the open truth, when it is known what and of what nature that which is spiritual is respectively to that which is natural; what and of what nature the human soul is; and what is the nature of the influx that flows into the soul, and by the soul into the perceptive and thinking mind, and from this into the body. But these subjects can be explained by no man, unless he have received from the Lord the privilege of being in society with angels in the spiritual world and with men in the natural world at the same time; and since this privilege has been bestowed on me, I have been enabled to describe what and of what nature they are. This I have done in the work on CONJUGIAL LOVE, in the Memorable Relation respecting the nature of what is SPIRITUAL, n. 326—329; in that respecting the HUMAN SOUL, n. 315; in

that respecting INFLUX, n. 380; and more fully in that at n. 415—422.* Who does not know, or may not know, that the good of love and the truth of faith flow from God into man, and that they flow into his soul, and are felt in his mind; and that they flow again, from his thought into his speech, and from his will into his actions? That spiritual influx, and its origin and derivation, are from thence, shall be manifested in the following order. I. *That there are two worlds, a spiritual world, which is inhabited by spirits and angels, and a natural world, which is inhabited by men.* II. *That the spiritual world first existed and continually subsists from its own sun; and that the natural world first existed and continually subsists from its own sun.* III. *That the sun of the spiritual world is pure love from Jehovah God, who is in the midst of it.* IV. *That from that sun proceed heat and light; and that the heat proceeding from it is in its essence love, and the light thence is in its essence wisdom.* V. *That both that heat and that light flow into man, the heat into his will, where it produces the good of love; and the light into his understanding, where it produces the truth of wisdom.* VI. *That those two elements, viz., heat and light, or love and wisdom, flow conjointly from God into the soul of man, and by this into his mind, its affections and thoughts, and from these into the senses, speech and actions of the body.* VII. *That the sun of the natural world is pure fire; and that the world of nature first existed and continually subsists by this sun.* VIII. *That therefore every thing which proceeds from this sun, regarded in itself, is dead.* IX. *That that which is spiritual, clothes itself with that which is natural, as man clothes himself with a garment.* X. *That spiritual things thus clothed in man enable him to live as a rational and moral man, thus as a spiritually natural man.* XI. *That the reception of that influx is according to the state of love and wisdom with man.* XII. *That the understanding in man is capable of being elevated into the light, that is, into the wisdom, in which are the angels of heaven, according to the improvement of his rational faculty; and that his will is capable of being elevated, in like manner, into heat, that is, nto love, according to the deeds of his life; but that the love of the will is not elevated, except so far as man wills and does those things which the wisdom of the understanding teaches.* XIII. *That beasts are constituted quite otherwise.* XIV. *That there are three degrees in the spiritual world, and three degrees in the natural world, according to which all influx takes place.* XV. *That ends are in the first degree, causes in the second, and effects in the third.* XVI. *That hence may appear what is the nature of spiritual*

* Those who may not possess the work on CONJUGIAL LOVE, will find the same articles in the TRUE CHRISTIAN RELIGION, n. 280; n. 697; n. 35; n. 77, and n. 12

influx from its origin to its effects. Each of these propositions shall now be briefly illustrated.

I. *That there are two worlds, a spiritual world inhabited by spirits and angels, and a natural world inhabited by men.*

3. That there is a spiritual world inhabited by spirits and angels, distinct from the natural world inhabited by men, is a fact which, because no angel has descended and declared it, and no man has ascended and seen it, has been hitherto unknown, even in the Christian world; lest, therefore, from ignorance of the existence of such a world, and the doubts respecting the reality of heaven and hell which result from such ignorance, men should be infatuated to such a degreee as to become naturalists and atheists, it has pleased the Lord to open my spiritual sight, and, as to my spirit, to elevate me into heaven, and to let me down into hell, and to exhibit to my view the nature of both. It has thus been made evident to me that there are two worlds completely distinct from each other; one, all the objects of which are spiritual, whence it is called the spiritual world; and another, all the objects of which are natural, whence it is called the natural world: as also, that spirits and angels live in their own world, and men in theirs; and further, that every man passes by death from his world into the other, in which he lives to eternity. It is necessary, in order that the nature of influx, which is the subject of this little work, may be unfolded from its first origin, that some information respecting both these worlds should be first premised; for the spiritual world flows into the natural world, and actuates it in all its parts; it not only operates upon men, but on beasts too; and also constitutes the vegetative principle in trees and herbs.

II. *That the spiritual world first existed and continually subsists from its own sun; and that the natural world first existed and continually subsists from its own sun.*

4. There is one sun of the spiritual world, and another sun of the natural world, because those worlds are completely distinct from each other; and every world must derive its origin from a sun; for a world of which all the objects are spiritual, cannot originate from a sun, all the products of which are natural; for then there must be a physical influx, which, nevertheless, is contrary to order. That the world first existed from the sun, and not the sun from the world, is manifest by an effect from the former cause still observable; viz., that the world, in the whole and in every part, still subsists by the sun; and subsistence demonstrates existence; wherefore, it is

a common remark, that subsistence is perpetual existence; whence it is evident, that take away the sun, and its world would fall into a chaos, and this chaos into nothing. That, in the spiritual world, there is a sun different from that in the natural world, I am able to testify, for I have seen it; in appearance, it is a globe of fire, like our sun, is of much the same magnitude, and at the same distance from the angels as our sun is from men; but it does not rise or set, but stands immovable in a middle altitude between the zenith and the horizon; whence the angels enjoy perpetual light and perpetual spring. The man who reasons upon the subject without knowing any thing respecting the sun of the spiritual world, may easily fall into insane notions when he endeavors to form an idea of the creation of the universe; thus when he deeply considers it, he concludes that its origin must be from nature; and as the origin of nature is the sun, he conceives that the universe proceeded from the sun as its creator. Moreover, no one can form a right conception of spiritual influx, unless he knows the origin of it; for all influx proceeds from a sun, spiritual influx from its sun, and natural influx from its sun; thus the internal sight of man, which is that of his mind, receives influx from the spiritual sun, but his external sight, which is that of his body, receives influx from the natural sun; but, in operation, both act in conjunction, just as the soul acts in conjunction with the body. Hence it is evident into what blindness, darkness, and fatuity they may fall, who have no knowledge of the spiritual world and its sun; they may fall into *blindness*, because the mind which judges by the sight of the eye alone, becomes in its reasonings like a bat, which flies by night with a wandering course, and is attracted by a mere linen cloth that may any where be hanging up; they may fall into *darkness*, because the sight of the mind, when the sight of the eye flows into it from without, is deprived of all spiritual light, and becomes like the sight of an owl; and they may fall into *fatuity*, because the man still continues to think, but he thinks from natural things concerning spiritual things, and not contrariwise; thus he thinks like a madman, a fool, and an idiot.

III. *That the sun of the spiritual world is pure love, from Jehovah God, who is in the midst of it.*

5. Spiritual things cannot proceed from any other source than from love, nor love from any other source than Jehovah God, who is Love itself: hence the sun of the spiritual world, from which, as their fountain, all spiritual things issue, is pure love proceeding from Jehovah God, who is in the midst of it. That sun is not itself God, but it is an emanation from God, being the proximate sphere diffused around him and proceeding from him. By

means of this sun, the universe was created by Jehovah God by the universe, we mean, the whole expanse of worlds, which are as many as the stars in the expanse of our heaven). Creation was effected by means of that sun, which is pure love, thus by Jehovah God, because love is the very *esse* of life, and wisdom is the *existere* of life thence derived, and all things were created from love by wisdom; this is meant by these words in John: "The Word was with God, and God was the Word; all things were made by him, and without him nothing was made which was made; and the world was made by him" i. 3, 10: the Word here is the Divine Truth, thus likewise the Divine Wisdom; wherefore, also, the Word is called, ver. 9, the light which illuminates every man: in like manner the Divine Wisdom illuminates by means of the Divine Truth. They who deduce the origin of worlds from any other source than the Divine Love operating by the Divine Wisdom, fall into hallucinations like those of persons disordered in the brain, who see spectres as men, phantoms as luminous objects, and imaginary entities as real figures: for the created universe is a coherent work, originating from love operating by wisdom; as you will see, if you are able to examine the chain of things in their order, from those which are first to those which are last. As God is one, so also the spiritual sun is one; for the extension of space is not predicable of spiritual things, which are the derivations of that sun; and essence and existence that are independent of space are present everywhere in space without space: thus the Divine Love is present from the beginning of the universe to all its boundaries. That the Divine fills all things, and by such impletion preserves them in the state in which they were created, is a truth of which the rational faculty has a distant apprehension; which becomes a nearer one, in proportion as the mind has a knowledge of the nature of love, as it is in itself; of its conjunction with wisdom for the perception of ends; of its influx into wisdom for the exhibition of causes; and of its operation by means of wisdom for the production of effects.

IV. *That from that sun proceed heat and light; and that the heat proceeding from it in its essence is love, and the light thence in its essence is wisdom.*

6. It is known that in the Word, and thence in the common language of preachers, fire is mentioned to express Divine Love; thus it is usual to pray, that heavenly fire may fill the heart and kindle holy desires to worship God: the reason of which is, because fire corresponds to love, and thence signifies it. Hence it is that Jehovah God was seen by Moses, as a fire, in a bush; as also by the children of Israel at Mount Sinai; and that fire was

commanded to be perpetually kept upon the altar, and the lights of the candlestick in the tabernacle to be lighted every evening: these commands were given because fire signifies love. That such fire has heat proceeding from it, appears manifestly from the effects of love: thus, a man is set on fire, grows warm, and becomes inflamed, as his love is exalted into zeal, or into red-hot anger. The heat of the blood, or the vital heat of men and of animals in general, proceeds solely from love, which constitutes their life. Neither is infernal fire any thing else than love opposite to heavenly love. This then is the reason that the Divine Love appears to the angels as the sun in their world, with the aspect of a globe of fire, like our sun, as was said above; and that the angels enjoy heat according to their reception of love from Jehovah God by means of that sun. It follows from hence, that the light there is in its essence wisdom; for love and wisdom, like esse and existere, are incapable of being divided, since love exists by means of wisdom and according to it. This resembles a familiar phenomenon in our world: at the time of spring, heat unites itself with light, and causes the vegetable creation to bud, and at length to bear fruit. Moreover, every one knows experimentally, that spiritual heat is love and spiritual light is wisdom; for a man grows warm in proportion as he feels love, and has a perception of light in his understanding in proportion as he attains wisdom. I have often seen that spiritual light, which immensely exceeds natural light in clearness and in splendor, for it is as clearness and splendor themselves in their very essence; it appears like resplendent and dazzling snow, such as the garments of the Lord appeared when he was transfigured, Mark ix. 3; Luke ix. 28. As light is wisdom, therefore the Lord calls himself the Light which illuminates every man, John i. 9; and says in other places, that he is the Light, John iii. 19; viii. 12; xii. 35, 36, 47, that is, that he is Divine Truth itself, which is the Word, thus Wisdom itself. It is commonly imagined that natural light, which is the same as the light of reason, proceeds from the light of our world: but it proceeds from the light of the spiritual world; for the sight of the mind flows into the sight of the eye, thus also the light of the spiritual world into the light of the natural world, but not contrariwise: if the contrary took place, there would be physical influx and not spiritual influx.

V. *That both that heat and that light flow into man, the heat into his will, where it produces the good of love, and the light into his understanding, where it produces the truth of wisdom.*

7. It is known that all things universally have relation to good and truth, and that there is not a single object in exist-

ence which has not something relative to those two principles. On this account, there are in man two receptacles of life, one, which is the receptacle of good, called the will, and another, which is the receptacle of truth, called the understanding; and as good belongs to love, and truth to wisdom, the will is the receptacle of love, and the understanding is the receptacle of wisdom. That good belongs to love, is evident from this consideration; that what a man loves, this he wills, and when he brings it into act he calls it good; and that truth belongs to wisdom appears hence, that all wisdom is composed of truths; even the good which a wise man thinks, is truth, which becomes good when he wills it and does it. He who does not rightly distinguish between these two receptacles of life, which are the will and the understanding, and does not form to himself a clear notion respecting them, will in vain endeavor to comprehend the nature of spiritual influx: for there is influx into the will, and there is influx into the understanding; there is an influx of the good of love into the will of man, and there is an influx of the truth of wisdom into his understanding; each proceeding from Jehovah God immediately, by the sun in the midst of which he is, and mediately, by the angelic heaven. These two receptacles, the will and the understanding, are as distinct as heat and light are; for the will receives the heat of heaven, which in its essence is love, and the understanding receives the light of heaven, which in its essence is wisdom; as was said above. There is an influx from the human mind into the speech, and there is an influx into the actions; the influx into the speech takes place from the will by the understanding, and the influx into the actions takes place from the understanding by the will. They who are only acquainted with the influx into the understanding, and not at the same time with that into the will, are like persons having but one eye, who only see the objects on one side of them, and not those on the other; and they are like persons who are maimed, who do their work awkwardly with one hand only; and they are like persons that are lame, who walk by hopping on one foot, with the assistance of a crutch. From these few observations it is plain, that spiritual heat flows into the will of man, and produces the good of love, and that spiritual light flows into his understanding, and produces the truth of wisdom.

VI. *That those two elements, viz. heat and light, or love and wisdom, flow conjointly from God into the soul of man, and by this into the mind, its affections and thoughts, and from these into the senses, speech, and actions of the body.*

8. The spiritual influx hitherto treated of by men of learning, is, the influx from the soul into the body; but they have

not noticed the prior influx into the soul, and by that into the body. It nevertheless is well known, that all the good of love, and all the truth of faith, flow from God into man, and that no portion of them is from man himself; and whatever flows from God flows proximately into his soul, and by the soul into the rational mind, and by this into the organs which constitute the body. Any person, then, who investigates the nature of spiritual influx without taking this into the account, is like one who stops up the stream of a fountain and still looks there for unfailing waters; or one who deduces the origin of a tree from the branch and not from the seed; or one who examines principiates* without attending to the first principle. For the soul is not life in itself, but is a recipent of life from God, who is life in itself; and all influx belongs to life, thus is from God. This is meant by this passage: "Jehovah God breathed into the nostrils of the man the breath of life [lives], and the man became a living soul," Gen. ii. 7: to breathe into the nostrils the breath of life [lives], signifies, to implant the perception of good and truth. The Lord also says of himself, "As the Father hath life in himself, so hath he given to the Son to have life in himself," John v. 26; to have life in himself is to be God: and the life of the soul is life influent from God. Now forasmuch as all influx belongs to life, and life operates by means of its receptacles; and the inmost or first of the receptacles in man is his soul; therefore, in order that the nature of influx may be rightly apprehended, it is necessary to begin from God, and not from an intermediate station. Were we to begin from an intermediate station, our doctrine of influx would be like a chariot without wheels, or like a ship without sails. This being the case, therefore, in the preceding articles we have treated of the sun of the spiritual world, in the midst of which is Jehovah God, n. 5; and of the influx of love and wisdom, thus of life, n. 6, 7. The reason that life from God flows into man by the soul, and by this into the mind, that is, into the affections and thoughts of the mind, and from these into the senses, speech, and actions of the body, is, because these are the subjects of life in successive order. For the mind is subordinate to the soul, and the body is subordinate to the mind: and the mind has two lives, one belonging to the will and another to the understanding; the life of its will is the good of love, the derivations of which are called affections; and the life of its understanding is the truth of wisdom, the derivations of which are called thoughts: by means of these and the former, the mind lives: but the life of the body are the senses, speech, and actions: that these are derived from the soul by the mind, follows from the order in which they stand, and from which they manifest themselves to a wise man without scrutiny. The human soul, being a

* A logical term, denoting things derived from a first principle.

superior spiritual substance, receives influx immediately from God; but the human mind, being an inferior spiritual substance, receives influx from God mediately by the spiritual world; and the body, being composed of the substances of nature, which are called matter, receives influx from God mediately by the natural world. That the good of love and the truth of wisdom, flow from God into the soul of man conjointly, that is, united into one, but that they are divided by man in their progress, and are conjoined only with those who suffer themselves to be led by God, will be seen in the following articles.

VII. *That the sun of the natural world is pure fire; and that the world of nature first existed and continually subsists by means of this sun.*

9. That nature and its world, by which we mean the atmospheres and the earths which are called planets, among which is the terraqueous globe on which we dwell, together with all the productions which annually adorn its surface, subsist solely from the sun, which constitutes their centre, and which, by the rays of its light, and the modifications of its heat, is everywhere present, every one knows for certain, from his own experience, from the testimony of the senses, and from the writings of those who have treated of such subjects: and as these things owe their perpetual subsistence to the sun, reason may with certainty conclude, that they owe their existence also to the same; for perpetually to subsist is perpetually to exist as they first existed; hence it follows, that the natural world was created by Jehovah God by means of this sun as a secondary cause. That there are spiritual existences and natural existences, which are entirely distinct from each other; and that the origin and support of spiritual existences are derived from a sun which is pure love, in the midst of which is the Creator and Upholder of the universe, Jehovah God, has been demonstrated before; but that the origin and support of natural existences are derived from a sun which is pure fire, and that the latter is derived from the former, and both from God, follows of itself, as what is posterior follows from what is prior, and what is prior from the First Cause of all. That the sun of nature and its worlds is pure fire all its effects demonstrate; as the concentration of its rays into a focus by the art of optics, from which proceeds fire of a vehemently burning nature, and also flame; the nature of its heat, which is similar to heat from elementary fire; the graduation of that heat according to its angle of incidence, whence proceed the varieties of climate, and also the four seasons of the year; beside other facts; by which the rational faculty may be confirmed, even by the senses of its body, that the sun of the natural world is mere fire; and also,

that it is fire in its utmost purity. They who know nothing concerning the origin of spiritual existences from their sun, but are only acquainted with the origin of natural existences from theirs, can scarcely avoid confounding spiritual and natural existences together, and concluding, through the fallacies of the senses, and those to which the rational faculty is subject, that spiritual existences are nothing but a pure kind of natural existences, and that, from the activity of the latter excited by heat and light, arise wisdom and love. These persons, since they see nothing else with their eyes, and smell nothing else with their nostrils, and breathe nothing else in their breast, than nature, ascribe to it all the rational powers also; and thus they imbibe naturalism as a sponge sucks up water. Such persons may be compared to coachmen, who yoke the horses behind the carriage, and not before it. The case is otherwise with those who distinguish between spiritual and natural existences, and deduce the latter from the former; these, also, perceive that there is an influx of the soul into the body, thus that it is spiritual, and that natural things, which are those of the body, serve the soul for vehicles and mediums, by which to produce its effects in the natural world. He who concludes otherwise may be compared to a crab, which assists its progress in walking with its tail, and draws its eyes backwards at every step; and his rational sight may be compared to the sight of the eyes of Argus in the back of his head, when those in his forehead were asleep. Such persons, also, believe themselves to be Arguses in reasoning; for they say, "Who does not see that the origin of the universe is from nature? and what then is God but the inmost extension of nature?" and the like irrational observations; of which they boast more than wise men do of their rational sentiments.

VIII. *That, therefore, every thing which proceeds from this sun, regarded in itself, is dead.*

10. Who does not see from the rational faculty belonging to his understanding, if this be a little elevated above the sensual faculties of the body, that love, regarded in itself, is alive, and that the appearance of fire which it assumes is its life, and, on the contrary, that elementary fire, regarded in itself, is respectively dead—consequently, that the sun of the spiritual world, being pure love, is alive, and that the sun of the natural world, being pure fire, is dead? and that the case is the same with all the products which emanate and exist from them? There are two things which produce all the effects in the universe, LIFE and NATURE; and they produce them according to order, when life, from within, actuates nature; the case is otherwise, when nature, from without, draws

life to act; which takes place with those who place nature, which in itself is dead, above and within life, and thence wholly devote themselves to the pleasures of the senses, and the concupiscences of the flesh, esteeming the spiritual concerns belonging to the soul, and the truly rational objects belonging to the mind, as nothing. Such persons, on account of this inversion, are they who are called THE DEAD; such are all atheistic naturalists in the world, and all satans in hell. They are also called the dead in the Word; as in David: "They joined themselves to Baal-peor, and ate the sacrifices of *the dead*," Ps. cvi. 28. "The enemy hath persecuted my soul, he hath made me to sit in darkness, as those who have been long *dead*," Ps. cxliii. 3. "To hear the groaning of the bound, and to open to those that are appointed to *death*," Ps. cii. 20: and in the Revelation: "I know thy works, that thou hast a name, that thou livest, and art *dead;* be watchful, and strengthen the things which remain that are ready to *die*," iii. 1, 2. They are called the dead, because spiritual death is damnation, and damnation is the lot of those who believe life to be from nature, and thus believe the light of nature to be the light of life, and thereby bury, suffocate, and extinguish every idea of God, of heaven, and of eternal life. In consequence of so doing, such persons are like owls, which see light in darkness, and darkness in light: that is, they see false sentiments as true and evils as good: and as the delights of evil are the delights of their hearts, they are not unlike those birds and beasts which devour dead bodies as choice delicacies, and scent the stenches arising from graves as balsamic odors. Such persons can see no influx but such as is physical or natural; if, notwithstanding, they affirm influx to be spiritual, they do not possess any idea of it, but merely repeat the words of their preceptor.

IX. *That what is spiritual clothes itself with what is natural, as a man clothes himself with a garment.*

11. It is well known that both an active and a passive force are necessary to every operation, and that nothing can be produced by an active force alone, and nothing from a passive alone. The case is similar with what is spiritual and what is natural; what is spiritual, as a living force, being active, what is natural, as a dead force, being passive. Hence it follows that whatever existed in this solar world at its first creation, and whatever comes into existence from moment to moment since, exists from what is spiritual by what is natural: and this is true, not only in regard to the subjects of the animal kingdom, but also to those of the vegetable kingdom. Another fact is also known similar to the former, viz. that both

a principal and an instrumental cause are necessary to every production, and that these two causes, when anything is being produced, appear as one, though they are distinctly two; wherefore it is one of the canons of wisdom, that the cause principal and the cause instrumental make together one cause. So also do what is spiritual and what is natural. The reason that, in producing effects, these two forces and causes appear as one, is, because what is spiritual is within what is natural, as the fibre is within the muscle, and as the blood is within the arteries; or as the thought is inwardly in the speech, and the affection in the tones of the voice, causing themselves to be apprehended by these natural instruments. From these considerations, though, as yet, as through a glass darkly, it appears, that what is spiritual clothes itself with what is natural, as a man clothes himself with a garment. The organical body with which the soul clothes itself, is here compared to a garment, because a garment invests the body; and the soul also puts off the body, and casts it off as an old coat, when it emigrates by death from the natural into its own spiritual world: for the body grows old like a garment, but not the soul, because this is a spiritual substance, which has nothing in common with the changes of nature, which advance from a commencement to an end, and are periodically terminated. They who do not consider the body as the vesture or covering of the soul, and as being in itself dead, and only adapted to receive living forces flowing into it through the soul from God, cannot avoid concluding from fallacies, that the soul lives by itself, and the body by itself, and that there is, between their respective lives, a PRE-ESTABLISHED HARMONY; and likewise, that the life of the soul flows into the life of the body, or the life of the body into the life of the soul, indifferently, whence they conceive INFLUX to be both SPIRITUAL and NATURAL; when, nevertheless, it is a truth which is testified by every object in creation, that a posterior existence does not act from itself, but from the prior existence from which it proceeded; thus that neither does this act from itself, but from some existence still prior; and thus that nothing acts at all but by communication from the First Cause Itself, which does act of itself, and which is God. Besides there is but one only life, and this is not capable of being created, but is eminently capable of flowing into forms organically adapted to its reception: all the objects in the created universe, even to the most minute, are such forms. It is believed by many that the soul is itself a spark of life, and thus that man, since he lives from his soul, lives from his own life, thus of himself, consequently, not by an influx of life from God. But such persons cannot avoid twisting of fallacies a sort of Gordian knot in which they entangle all the judgments of their mind, till nothing but insanity, in regard to spiritual things, is the result: or they construct a labyrinth, from which the mind can never, by any clue which reason supplies, retrace its way, and extricate itself: they also actually let themselves down into caverns under ground, where they dwell in eternal darkness. For from such a belief proceed innumerable fallacies, each of which is horrible; as that God has transferred and transcribed himself into men, whence every man is a sort of deity that lives of himself; and thus that he does good, and enjoys wisdom from himself; likewise, that he possesses faith and charity in himself, and exercises them from himself, and not from God; beside other monstrous sentiments, such as prevail with those in hell, who, when they were in the world, believed nature to live, or to produce life by its own activity: when these look towards heaven its light appears to them as mere darkness. I formerly heard a voice saying from heaven, that if a spark of life in man were his own, and not of God in him, there would be no heaven nor anything belonging to it; whence also, there could be no church on earth, and, consequently, no life eternal. For further particulars relating to this subject, may be consulted the Memorable Relation in the work on CONJUGIAL LOVE, n. 132—136.*

X. *That spiritual existences so clothed in man, are what enable him to live as a rational and moral man, thus a spiritually natural man.*

12. From the principle established above, viz., that the soul clothes itself with a body as a man clothes himself with a garment, this follows as a conclusion: for the soul flows into the human mind, and by this into the body, and carries with it the life, which it continually receives from the Lord, and thus transfers it mediately into the body, where, owing to the closeness of its union, it makes the body appear to live; whence, and from a thousand testimonies of experience, it is evident, that what is spiritual united to what is material, as a living force with a dead force, causes man to speak rationally and to act morally. It appears as if the tongue and lips spoke from a certain life in themselves, and as if the arms and hands acted in a like manner; but it is the thought, which in itself is spiritual, which speaks, and the will, which likewise is spiritual, which acts, each by its own organs, which in themselves are material, being taken from the natural world. That this is the case, appears in the light of day, provided this consideration be attended to. Remove thought from speech, is not the tongue dumb in a moment? so, remove will from action, and do not the hands in a moment become still? Spiritual existences in

* And in the TRUE CHRISTIAN RELIGION, n. 48.

this state of union with natural, and the consequent appearance of life in material objects, may be compared to generous wine when absorbed by a clean sponge, to the saccharine juice in a grape, to the savory liquor in an apple, and to the aromatic odor in cinnamon; the fibres containing these things are portions of matter, which have neither taste nor smell of themselves, but derive them from the fluids in and between them; wherefore, if you squeeze out those juices, they become dead filaments; such are the organs proper to the body, if life be taken away. That man is a rational being by virtue of the union in him of spiritual existences with natural, is evident from the analytical nature of his thoughts; and that he is a moral being from the same cause, is evident from the propriety of his actions and the graces of his demeanor; these he possesses by virtue of his faculty of being able to receive influx from the Lord through the angelic heaven, which is the very abode of wisdom and love, thus of rationality and morality. Hence it may be perceived, that a spiritual and a natural constitution being united in man, is what enables him to live as a spiritually natural man. The reason that he lives in a similar and yet dissimilar manner after death, is, because his soul is then clothed with a substantial body, as in the world it was clothed with a material body. It is believed by many, that the perceptions and thoughts of the mind, being spiritual, flow in naked, and not by means of organized forms; but let them dream thus who have not seen the interiors of the head, where the perceptions and thoughts reside in their first principles, and who are ignorant that it contains the brains, interwoven and composed of the cineritious and medullary substances, together with glands, cavities, and septa, and with *meninges* and *matres* surrounding them all; and who, likewise, do not know that a man thinks and wills soundly or insanely according as all these organs are in a state of integrity or derangement, consequently, that he is rational and moral according to the organic structure of his mind. For the rational sight of man, which is the understanding without forms organized for the reception of spiritual light, would be an abstract nothing, just as his natural sight would be without the eyes; and so in regard to the other mental functions.

XI. *That the reception of that influx is according to the state of love and wisdom with man.*

13. That man is not life, but an organ recipient of life from God, and that love in union with wisdom is life; also, that God is Love itself and Wisdom itself, and thus Life itself, has been demonstrated above; hence it follows, that so far as a man loves wisdom, or so far as wisdom embosomed in love is

within him, so far he is an image of God, that is, a receptacle of life from God; and, on the contrary, that so far as he is possessed by opposite love and thence by insanity, so far he does not receive life from God, but from hell, which life is called death. Love and wisdom themselves are not life, but are the *esse* of life; but the delights of love and the amenities of wisdom, which are the affections of them, constitute life, for by these the *esse* of life comes into existence. The influx of life from God carries with it those delights and amenities, like the influx of light and heat at the time of spring into the human minds, and also into birds and beasts of every kind, yea, into vegetables, which then germinate and become prolific: for the delights of love and the amenities of wisdom expand men's minds and adapt them to the reception of the influx of life from God, as joy and gladness expand the face, and adapt it to the influx of the hilarities of the soul. The man who is affected with the love of wisdom, is like the garden in Eden, in which are two trees, the tree of life, and the tree of the knowledge of good and evil; the tree of life is the reception of love and wisdom from God, and the tree of the knowledge of good and evil is the reception of them from self: the man who eats of the latter tree is insane, but still believes himself to be wise like God; but the man who eats of the former tree is truly wise, and believes no one to be wise but God alone, and that man is wise so far as he believes this, and the more so as he feels that he wills it. But more on this subject may be seen in the Memorable Relation in the work on CONJUGIAL LOVE, n. 132—136.* I will here add an arcanum confirming these facts from heaven: All the angels of heaven turn the fore part of the head towards the Lord as a sun, and all the angels of hell turn the back of the head to Him, and the latter receive the influx into the affections of their will, which in themselves are concupiscences, and make the understanding favor them, but the former receive the influx into the affections of their understanding, and make the will favor them, whence these are in the enjoyment of wisdom, but the others are possessed by insanity. For the human understanding has its seat in the cerebrum, which is under the forehead, and the will in the cerebellum, which is in the back of the head. Who does not know that a man who is insane through cherishing false sentiments, favors the lusts of his own evil, and confirms them by reasons drawn from the understanding; whereas a wise man sees from truths the quality of the lusts of his own will, and restrains them? A wise man does this, because he turns his face to God, that is, he believes in God, and not in himself; but an insane man does the other, because he averts his face from God, that is, he

* Or TRUE CHRISTIAN RELIGION, n. 48.

believes in himself, and not in God. For a man to believe in himself, is to believe that he enjoys love and wisdom from himself, and not from God; and this is signified by eating of the tree of the knowledge of good and evil: but for a man to believe in God, is to believe that he enjoys love and wisdom from God, and not from himself; and this is signified by eating of the tree of life, Rev. ii. 7. From these considerations it may be perceived, but still only with a degree of clearness answering to the light of the moon by night, that the reception of the influx of life from God is according to the state of love and wisdom with man. This influx may further be illustrated by the influx of light and heat into vegetables, which blossom and bear fruit according to the structure of the fibres which form them, thus according to their reception of the light and heat; it may also be illustrated by the influx of the rays of light into precious stones, which modify them into colors according to the situation of the parts composing them, thus also according to their reception of the rays; and likewise by optical glasses and the drops of rain, which exhibit rainbows according to the incidence, the refraction, and thus the reception of the light. The case is similar with human minds in respect to spiritual light, which proceeds from the Lord as a sun, and perpetually flows in, but is variously received.

XII. *That the understanding in man is capable of being elevated into the light, that is, into the wisdom, in which are the angels of heaven, according to the improvement of his rational faculty; and that his will is capable of being elevated, in like manner, into the heat of heaven, that is, into the love of heaven, according to the deeds of his life; but that the love of the will is not elevated, except so far as man wills and does those things which the wisdom of the understanding teaches.*

14. By the human mind are to be understood its two faculties, which are called the understanding and the will. The understanding is the receptacle of the light of heaven, which in its essence is wisdom; and the will is the receptacle of the heat of heaven, which in its essence is love, as was shown above. These two principles, wisdom and love, proceed from the Lord as a sun, and flow into heaven universally and individually, whence the angels have wisdom and love; and they also flow into this world universally and individually, whence men have wisdom and love. But the two principles proceed in union from the Lord, and likewise flow in union into the souls of angels and men; but they are not received in union in their minds; light, which forms the understanding, being first received there, and love, which forms the will, being received gradually. This also is of Providence: for every man is to be

created anew, that is, reformed, and this is effected by means of the understanding; for he must imbibe from infancy the knowledges of truth and good, which are to teach him to live well, that is, to will and act rightly: thus the will is formed by means of the understanding. For the sake of this end, there is given to man the faculty of elevating his understanding al most into the light which is enjoyed by the angels of heaven, that he may see what he ought to will and thence to do, in order that he may be prosperous in the world for a time, and blessed after death to eternity. He becomes prosperous and blessed, if he procures to himself wisdom, and keeps his will under its obedience; but unprosperous and unhappy if he puts his understanding under obedience to his will: the reason is, because the will hereditarily tends to evils, even to those which are enormous; wherefore, unless it were restrained by means of the understanding, man would rush into acts of wickedness, yea, from his inherent savage nature, he would destroy and slaughter, for the sake of himself, all who did not favor and indulge him. Besides, unless the understanding could be separately perfected, and the will by means of it, man would not be a man but a beast. For without that separation, and without the ascent of the understanding above the will, he would not be able to think, and from thought to speak, but only to express his affection by sounds; neither would he be able to act from reason, but only from instinct; still less would he be able to know the things which are of God, and God by means of them, and thus to be conjoined to Him, and to live to eternity. For man thinks and wills *as from himself*, and this, *as from himself*, is what gives him the faculty of reciprocal conjunction: for there can be no conjunction without reciprocality, just as there can be no conjunction of an active with a passive force without re-action. God alone acts, and man suffers himself to be acted on, and re-acts in all appearance as from himself, though interiorly it is from God. From these considerations, rightly apprehended, may be seen what is the nature of the will of man if it is elevated by means of the understanding, and what is its nature if it is not elevated, consequently what is the nature of the man. But the latter subject, viz., what is the nature of man if the love of his will is not elevated by means of the understanding, shall be illustrated by comparisons. He is like an eagle flying on high, which, as soon as it sees the food below which is the object of its lust, as chickens, young swans, or even young lambs, casts itself down in a moment and devours them. He is also like an adulterer, who conceals a harlot in a cellar below, and who by turns goes up to the highest apartments of the house, and dis courses wisely with those who dwell there concerning chastity and alternately withdraws from the compan ythere, and indulges himself below with his harlot. He is also like a thief on a tower, who there pretends to act the part of a watchman, but who, as soon as he sees any object of plunder below, hastens down and seizes it. He may also be compared to gnats, which fly in a column over the head of a horse while he is running, but which fall down when the horse stops, and immerse themselves in the marsh. Such is the man whose will or love is not elevated by means of the understanding; for he then remains stationary below, immersed in the uncleanness of nature and the lusts of the senses. The case is altogether otherwise with those who subdue the allurements of the lusts of the will by the wisdom belonging to the understanding. With these, the understanding afterwards enters into a marriage covenant with the will; thus wisdom with love, and they dwell together in the upper apartment with the utmost delight.

XIII. *That it is altogether otherwise with Beasts.*

15. They who judge of things only as they appear before the senses of the body, conclude that beasts have will and understanding as well as men, and hence that the only distinction consists in man's being able to speak, and thus to describe the things which he thinks and desires, while beasts can only express them by sounds. Beasts, however, have not will and understanding, but only a resemblance of each, which the learned call an analogous endowment. A man is a man, because his understanding is capable of being elevated above the desires of his will, and it thus can know and see them, and also govern them; but a beast is a beast, because its desires drive it to do whatever it does. A man, then, is a man, in consequence of this, that his will is under obedience to his understanding; but a beast is a beast in consequence of this, that its understanding is under obedience to its will. From these considerations this conclusion follows, viz., That the understanding of man, forasmuch as it receives the light influent from heaven, and apprehends and perceives this as its own, and thinks from it analytically, with all variety, altogether as from itself, is alive, and is thence truly understanding; and that the will of man, forasmuch as it receives the influent love of heaven, and acts from it as from itself, is alive, and is thence truly will; but that the contrary is the case with beasts. Wherefore they who think under the influence of the lusts of the will, are compared to beasts, and in the spiritual world they likewise at a distance appear as beasts; they also act like beasts, with this only difference, that they are able to act otherwise if they will: but they who restrain the lusts of their will by means of the understanding, appear in the spiritual world as men, and are angels of heaven. In a word, the will

and the understanding in beasts always cohere, and forasmuch as the will is blind, being the receptacle of heat and not of light, it makes the understanding blind also: hence a beast does not know and understand its own actions, and yet it acts, for it acts by an influx from the spiritual world; and such action is instinct. It is imagined that a beast thinks from understanding what to act; but this is by no means the case: it is compelled to act solely by the natural love which is in it from creation, with the assistance of the senses of its body. The reason that man thinks and speaks is solely because his understanding is capable of being separated from his will, and of being elevated even into the light of heaven; for the understanding thinks, and thought speaks. The reason why beasts act according to the laws of order inscribed on their nature, and some beasts in a moral and rational manner, differently from many men, is, because their understanding is in blind obedience to the desires of their will, and thence they are not able to pervert those desires by depraved reasonings, as men do. It is to be observed, that when the terms "will" and "understanding" are here used in reference to beasts, a certain resemblance of, and an endowment analogous to, those faculties, are what are meant: analogous endowments are called by the names of the faculties themselves, on account of the appearance. The life of a beast may be compared with a sleep-walker, who walks and acts by virtue of the will while the understanding sleeps; and also with a blind man, who walks through the streets with a dog leading him; and also with an idiot, who, from custom, and the habit thence acquired, does his work in a regular manner. It may likewise be compared with a person void of memory, and thence deprived of understanding, who still knows or learns how to clothe himself, to eat the food which he prefers, to love the sex, to walk the streets from house to house, and to do such things as soothe the senses and indulge the flesh, by the allurements and pleasures of which he is drawn along, though he does not think, and thence cannot speak. From these considerations it is evident, how much they are mistaken who believe beasts to be endowed with rationality, and only to be distinguished from men by their external figure and by their not being able to express by speech the rational things which inwardly occupy their thoughts; from which fallacies many even conclude, that if man lives after death, beasts will do so too; and, on the contrary, that if beasts do not live after death, neither will man; beside other dreams, arising from ignorance in regard to the will and understanding, and also in regard to degrees; by the aid of which, as steps for its ascent, the mind of man mounts up to heaven.

XIV. *That there are three degrees in the spiritual world, and three degrees in the natural world, hitherto unknown, according to which all influx takes place.*

16. It is discovered by the investigation of causes from their effects, that degrees are of two kinds, one according to which things prior and posterior are constituted, and another according to which things greater and less are constituted. The degrees which distinguish things prior and posterior, are to be called DEGREES OF ALTITUDE, or DISCRETE DEGREES; but the degrees by which things greater and less are distinguished from each other, are to be called DEGREES OF LATITUDE, and also CONTINUOUS DEGREES. Degrees of altitude, or discrete degrees, are like the generations and compositions of one thing from another; as, for example, they are like the generation and composition of any nerve from its fibres, and of any fibre from its fibrils; or of any piece of wood, stone, or metal from its parts, and of any part from its particles: but degrees of latitude, or continuous degrees, are like the increments and decrements of the same degree of altitude with respect to breadth, length, height, and depth; as of greater and less bodies of water, or air, or ether; and as of large and small masses of wood, stone, or metal. All things, even to the most particular, in both worlds, both the spiritual world and the natural world, are, from creation, in degrees of both these kinds: the whole animal kingdom in this world is in those degrees both in general and in particular; so are the whole vegetable kingdom, and the whole mineral kingdom likewise; and so is the expanse of atmospheres from the sun even to the earth. There are therefore three atmospheres discretely distinct according to the degrees of altitude, both in the spiritual world and in the natural world, because each world has its sun: but the atmospheres of the spiritual world, by virtue of their origin, are substantial, and the atmospheres of the natural world, by virtue of their origin, are material; and since the atmospheres descend from their origins according to those degrees, and are the continents of light and heat, like vehicles to convey these principles to their destination, it follows that there are three degrees of light and heat: and since light in the spiritual world is in its essence wisdom, and heat there is in its essence love, as was demonstrated above in its proper article, it follows also, that there are three degrees of wisdom and three degrees of love, consequently three degrees of life; for they are graduated by the atmospheres through which they pass. Hence it is that there are three angelic heavens; a supreme, which is also called the third heaven, inhabited by angels of the supreme degree; a middle, which is also called the second heaven, inhabited by angels of the middle degree;

and an ultimate, which is also called the first heaven, inhabited by angels of the lowest degree. Those heavens are also distinguished according to the degrees of wisdom and love: the angels of the ultimate heaven are in the love of knowing truths and goods; the angels of the middle heaven are in the love of understanding them, and the angels of the supreme heaven are in the love of being wise, that is, of living according to those truths and goods which they know and understand. As the angelic heavens are distinguished into three degrees, so also is the human mind, because the human mind is an image of heaven, that is, it is a heaven in miniature. Hence it is that man is capable of becoming an angel of one of those three heavens: and he becomes such according to his reception of wisdom and love from the Lord; an angel of the ultimate heaven if he only receives the love of knowing truths and goods; an angel of the middle heaven if he receives the love of understanding them; and an angel of the supreme heaven if he receives the love of being wise, that is, of living according to them. That the human mind is distinguished into three regions, according to the three heavens, may be seen in the memorable relation inserted in the work on CONJUGIAL LOVE, n. 270. Hence it is evident, that all spiritual influx to man and into man descends from the Lord by these three degrees, and that it is received by man according to the degree of wisdom and love in which he is. A knowledge of these degrees is of the greatest utility at this day. For many, in consequence of not knowing them, tarry in the lowest degree, in which are the senses of their body, and on account of their ignorance, which is intellectual darkness, are incapable of being elevated into spiritual light, which is above them: hence naturalism takes possession of them, as it were spontaneously, as soon as they enter on any investigation and scrutiny concerning the human soul and mind, and its rationality, and more so if they extend their inquiries to heaven and the life after death: whence they become like persons standing in the market places with telescopes in their hands, looking at the sky and uttering vain predictions; and also like persons who chatter and reason about every object they see, and every thing they hear, without any rational ideas, resulting from an understanding of the subject, being contained in their remarks: these are like butchers, who believe themselves to be skilful anatomists, because they have examined the viscera of oxen and sheep outwardly, but not inwardly. But it is a truth that to think from the influx of natural light not cleared by the influx of spiritual light, is merely to dream, and to speak from such thought is to make vain assertions, like fortune-tellers. But further particulars concerning degrees may be seen in the work on the DIVINE LOVE AND THE DIVINE WISDOM, n. 173—281.

XV. *That ends are in the first degree, causes in the second, and effects in the third.*

17. Who does not see that the end is not the cause, but that it produces the cause? and that the cause is not the effect, but that it produces the effect? consequently, that they are three distinct things which follow each other in order? The end with man is the love of his will; for what a man loves, this he proposes to himself and intends: the cause with him is the reason of his understanding; for the end, by means of the reason, seeks for middle or instrumental causes: and the effect is the operation of the body, from, and according to, the end and cause. Thus there are three things in man, which follow each other in order, just as is done by the degrees of altitude. When these three things are exhibited to observation, the end is within the cause, and by the cause is in the effect: thus, in the effect, these three things co-exist. On this account it is said in the Word, that every one shall be judged according to his works: for the end, or the love of his will, and the cause, or the reason of his understanding, are contained together in the effects, which are the works of his body: thus in them is contained the quality of the whole man. They who are unacquainted with these truths, and do not thus distinguish the objects of rational contemplation, cannot avoid terminating the ideas of their thought either in the atoms of Epicurus, the monads of Leibnitz, or the simple substances of Wolff: they thus shut up their understandings as with a bolt, so that they cannot even exercise their reason upon the subject of spiritual influx, because they cannot think of any progression beyond those atoms, monads, or simple substances; for the author of the doctrine of simple substances says, that if they are divided they are annihilated. Thus the understanding remains stationary in its first light, which merely proceeds from the senses of the body, and does not advance a step further. Hence it is not known but that spiritual substance is merely a subtile natural substance; that beasts have rationality as well as men; and that the soul is a puff of wind, like that which is emitted from the breast when a person dies: beside other notions which do not partake of light but of darkness. As all things in the spiritual world, and all things in the natural world, proceed according to these degrees, as was shown in the preceding article, it is evident that intelligence properly consists in knowing and distinguishing them, and seeing them in their order. By these degrees, also, every man is known as to his quality, when his love is known; for, as observed above, the end, which is of the will, the causes, which are of the understanding, and the effects, which are of the body, follow from his love, as a tree from its seed, and as fruit from a tree. There are loves of three

kinds; the love of heaven, the love of the world, and the love of self: the love of heaven is spiritual, the love of the world is material, and the love of self is corporeal. When the love is spiritual, all things which follow from it, as forms from their essence, are spiritual likewise: so, also, when the principal love is the love of the world or of wealth, and thus is material, all things which follow from it, as principiates from their first principle, are material likewise; and so, again, when the principal love is the love of self, or of eminence above all others, and thus is corporeal, all things which follow from it are corporeal likewise; because the man who cherishes this love regards himself alone, and thus immerses the thoughts of his mind in his body. Wherefore, as just remarked, he who knows the reigning love of any one, and is at the same time acquainted with the progression of ends to causes and of causes to effects, which three things follow each other in order, according to the degrees of altitude, knows the quality of the whole man. Thus the angels of heaven know the quality of every one with whom they speak; they perceive his love from the sound of his voice, they see an image of it in his face, and the figure of it in the gestures of his body.

XVI. *That hence is evident what is the nature of spiritual influx from its origin to its effects.*

18. Spiritual influx has hitherto been deduced, by those who have treated of it, from the soul into the body, but not from God into the soul and thus into the body. The reason of their proceeding thus has been, because no one had any knowledge respecting the spiritual world, and respecting the sun there, from whence all spiritual things issue as from their fountain; and thus no one had any knowledge respecting the influx of spiritual things into natural things. Now since it has been granted me to be in the spiritual world and in the natural world at the same time, I am obliged by my conscience to communicate these facts. For of what use is the possession of knowledge without its communication? Without the latter, what is the former, but like collecting and storing up riches in a casket, and only looking at them occasionally and counting them over, without any intention of applying them to use? In fact, it is spiritual avarice. But in order that it may be fully known what spiritual influx is, and what is its nature, it is necessary to know what that which is SPIRITUAL is in its essence, and what that which is NATURAL; as also what the HUMAN SOUL is: lest, therefore, this short lucubration should be defective through ignorance of these subjects, it will be useful to consult some MEMORABLE RELATIONS inserted in the work on CONJUGIAL LOVE; viz. that respecting the SPIRITUAL PRINCIPLE,

n. 326—329; that respecting the HUMAN SOUL, n. 315; and that respecting THE INFLUX OF SPIRITUAL THINGS INTO NATURAL, n. 380; which latter subject is more fully treated of, n. 415—422.*

19. I will here subjoin this MEMORABLE RELATION. After these pages were written, I prayed to the Lord that I might be permitted to converse with some disciples of ARISTOTLE, and at the same time with some disciples of DES CARTES, and with some disciples of LEIBNITZ, in order that I might learn the opinions of their minds concerning the intercourse between the soul and the body. After my prayer was ended, there were present nine men, three Aristotelians, three Cartesians, and three Leibnitzians; and they arranged themselves round me, the admirers of Aristotle being on the left side, the followers of Des Cartes on the right side, and the favorers of Leibnitz behind. At a considerable distance, and also at a distance from each other, were seen three persons crowned with laurel, whom I knew, by an influent perception, to be those three great leaders or masters themselves. Behind Leibnitz stood a person holding the skirt of his garment, who, I was told, was Wolff. Those nine men, when they beheld one another, at first saluted each other, and conversed together in a mild tone of voice. But presently there arose from below a spirit with a torch in his right hand, which he shook before their faces, whereupon they became enemies, three against three, and looked at each other with a fierce countenance: for they were seized with the lust of altercation and dispute. Then the Aristotelians, who were also schoolmen, began to speak, saying, "Who does not see that objects flow through the senses into the soul, as a man enters through the doors into a chamber, and that the soul thinks according to such influx? When a lover sees a beautiful virgin, or his bride, does not his eye sparkle, and transmit the love of her into the soul? When a miser sees bags of money, do not all his senses burn toward them, and thence induce this ardor into the soul, and excite the desire of possessing them? When a proud man hears himself praised by another, does he not prick up his ears, and do not these transmit those praises to the soul? Are not the senses of the body like outer courts, through which alone entrance is obtained to the soul? From these considerations and innumerable others of a similar kind, who can conclude otherwise than that influx proceeds from nature, or is physical?" While they were speaking thus, the followers of Des Cartes held their fingers on their foreheads; and now withdrawing them they replied, saying, "Alas, ye speak from appearances; do ye not know that the eye does not

* The same articles are repeated in the TRUE CHRISTIAN RELIGION, and will be found at n. 280, 697, 35, 77, and 12.

love a virgin or bride from itself, but from the soul? and likewise that the senses of the body do not covet the bags of money from themselves, but from the soul; and also that the ears do not devour the praises of flatterers in any othermanner? Is it not perception that causes sensation? and perception is a faculty of the soul, and not of the organs of the body. Say, if you can, what causes the tongue and lips to speak, but the thought? and what causes the hands to work, but the will? and thought and will are faculties of the soul, and not of the body. Thus what causes the eye to see, and the ear to hear, and the other organs to feel, but the soul? From these considerations, and innumerable others of a similar kind, every one, whose wisdom is elevated above the sensual apprehensions of the body, must con clude, that influx does not flow from the body into the soul, but from the soul into the body; which influx we call occasional influx, and also spiritual influx." When these had finished, the three men who stood behind the former triads, and who were the favorers of Leibnitz, began to speak, saying, "We have heard the arguments on both sides, and have compared them; and we have perceived that in many particulars the latter are stronger than the former, and that in many others the former are stronger than the latter; wherefore, if you please, we will compromise the dispute." On being asked how, they replied, "There is not any influx from the soul into the body, nor from the body into the soul, but there is a unanimous and instantaneous operation of both together, to which a celebrated author has assigned an elegant name, when he calls it Pre-established Harmony." After this the spirit with a torch appeared again, but the torch was now in his left hand, and he shook it behind the back of their heads, whence the ideas of them all became confused, and they all cried out at once, "Neither our soul nor body knows what part to take; wherefore let us settle this dispute by lot, and we will abide by the lot which comes out first." So they took out three bits of paper, and wrote on one of them, PHYSICAL INFLUX, on another, SPIRITUAL INFLUX, and on the third, PRE-ESTABLISHED HARMONY; and they put them all into the crown of a hat. Then they chose one of their number to draw; who, on putting in his hand, took out that on which was written, SPIRITUAL INFLUX. Having seen and read it, they all said, yet some with a clear and flowing, some with a faint and indrawn voice, "Let us abide by this, because it came out first." But then an angel suddenly stood by, and said, "Do not imagine that the paper in favor of spiritual influx came out first by chance, for it was of providence: for you do not see the truth of that doctrine, on account of the confusion of your ideas, but the truth presented itself to the hand of him that drew the lots, that you might yield it your assent."

20. I was formerly asked, "How I, who was previously a philosopher, became a theologian;" I answered, "In the same manner that fishermen became the disciples and apostles of the Lord:" and I added that I also from early youth had been a spiritual fisherman. On this, my inquirer asked, "What is a spiritual fisherman?" To which I replied, "A fisherman, in the spiritual sense of the Word, signifies a man who investigates and teaches natural truths, and afterwards spiritual truths in a rational manner." On his inquiring, "How this is demonstrated?" I said, "From these passages of the Word: 'And the waters shall fail from the sea, and the rivers shall be wasted and dried up: therefore the *fishers* shall mourn, and all that cast a hook into the sea shall lament,' Is. xix. 5, 8. In another place it is said respecting the sea, whose waters were healed, 'the *fishers* shall stand from Engedi even unto Eneglaim, they shall be a place to spread forth nets; their *fish* shall be according to their kinds, as the *fish* of the great sea, exceedingly many,' Ezek. xlvii. 10. And in another place: 'Behold, I will send for many *fishers*, saith Jehovah, and they *shall fish them*,' Jerem. xvi. 16. Hence it is evident why the Lord chose fishermen for his disciples, and said, "Follow me, and I will make you *fishers* of men," Matt. iv. 18, 19; Mark i. 16, 17: and why he said to Peter, after he had caught a multitude of fishes, '*henceforth thou shalt catch men*,' Luke v. 9, 10." I afterwards demonstrated the origin of this signification of fishermen from the *Apocalypse Revealed;* viz. that since water signifies natural truths, n. 50, 932, as does also a river, n. 409, 932, therefore a fish signifies those who are in possession of natural truths, n. 405; whence fishermen signify those who investigate and teach truth. On hearing this, my interrogator raised his voice and said, "Now I can understand why the Lord called and chose fishermen to be his disciples; and therefore I do not wonder that he has also called and chosen you, since, as you have observed, you were from early youth a fisherman in a spiritual sense, that is an investigator of natural truths: the reason that you are now become an investigator of spiritual truths, is, because these are founded on the former." To this he added, being a man of reason, that "the Lord alone knows who is the proper person to apprehend and teach or communicate the truths which should be revealed for his New Church, and whether such a person is to be found among the dignitaries of the Church or among their domestic servants. Besides," he continued, "among Christians, what divine does not first study philosophy at college, before he is ordained? otherwise, whence could he obtain a sufficient degree of intelligence?" At last he said, "Since you are become a divine, explain what

is your system of divinity?" I answered, "These are the two principles of it, THAT GOD IS ONE, and THAT THERE IS A CONJUNCTION OF CHARITY AND FAITH." He replied, "Who denies these principles?" I rejoined, "The divinity of the present day, when interiorly examined."

THE END.

THE WHITE HORSE.

ON

THE WHITE HORSE,

MENTIONED IN

THE APOCALYPSE, CHAP. XIX.,

WITH PARTICULARS RESPECTING

THE WORD,

AND ITS SPIRITUAL SENSE,

EXTRACTED FROM THE ARCANA CŒLESTIA.

From the Latin of

EMANUEL SWEDENBORG,

Servant of the Lord Jesus Christ.

BEING A TRANSLATION OF HIS WORK ENTITLED

De Equo Albo de quo in Apocalypsi, Cap. xix., et dein de Verbo et ejus Sensu Spirituali seu Interno, ex Arcanis Cœlestibus." Londini, MDCCLVIII.

NEW YORK:
AMERICAN SWEDENBORG PRINTING AND PUBLISHING SOCIETY,

CONTENTS.

ON THE

WHITE HORSE,

MENTIONED IN THE APOCALYPSE,

CHAP. XIX.

---

1. In the Apocalypse of John the Word is thus described as to its spiritual or internal sense: "I saw heaven opened, and behold a *white horse*, and he that sat upon him was called Faithful and True, and in righteousness he doth judge and make war. His eyes were as a flame of fire; and on his head were many crowns; and he had a name written that no man knew but he himself. And he was clothed with a vesture dipped in blood; and his name is called the *Word of God*. And the armies which were in heaven followed him upon white horses, clothed in fine linen white and clean. And he hath on his vesture and on his thigh a name written, *King of kings* and *Lord of lords*," chap. xix. 11, 12, 13, 14, 16. It is impossible for any one to know what each of these expressions implies, except from the internal sense. It is manifest that every expression is in some respect representative and significative: as when it is said, that heaven was opened; that there was a white horse; that he that sat upon him was faithful and true; and that in righteousness he doth judge and make war; that his eyes were as a flame of fire; that on his head were many crowns; that he had a name that no man knew but he himself; that he was clothed with a vesture dipped in blood; that the armies which were in heaven followed him upon white horses; that they were clothed in fine linen white and clean; and that on his vesture and on his thigh he had a name written. It is expressly said, that it is the Word which is here described, and the Lord who is the Word; for it is said, "His name is called the *Word of God*;" and afterwards, "He hath on his vesture and on his thigh a name written, *King of kings* and *Lord of lords*." From the interpretation of each expression it evidently appears, that in the above passage the Word is described as to its spiritual or internal sense. By heaven being opened is represented and signified, that the internal sense of the Word is seen in heaven and consequently by those in the world to whom

heaven is open. The horse, which was white, represents and signifies the understanding of the Word as to its interiors; that this is the signification of a white horse, will be shown presently. That he that sat upon him is the Lord as to the Word, consequently the Word, is manifest, for it is said, "His name is called the Word of God;" who, by virtue of good, is called faithful, and is said to judge in righteousness; and by virtue of truth, is called true, and is said to make war in righteousness; for the Lord himself is righteousness. His eyes, which were as a flame of fire, signify Divine Truth derived from the Divine Good of his Divine Love. The many crowns on his head, signify all the goods and truths of faith. Having a name written that no man knew but he himself, signifies, that the quality of the Word in the internal sense is seen by no one but himself, and those to whom he reveals it. Clothed in a vesture dipped in blood, signifies the Word in the letter, to which violence has been offered. The armies in heaven which followed him upon white horses, signify those who are principled in the understanding of the Word as to its interiors. Clothed in fine linen, white and clean, signifies the same persons principled in truth originating in good. A name written on his vesture and on his thigh, signifies truth and good, and their quality. From these particulars, and from those which precede and follow in that chapter, it is evident, that therein is predicted, that about the last time of the church the spiritual or internal sense of the Word would be opened: what would come to pass at that time, is also described in the same chapter, verses 17—21. That this is the signification of the words above mentioned, it is unnecessary to prove in this place, as they are particularly explained in the ARCANA CŒLESTIA; where it is shown, That the Lord is the Word, because he is Divine Truth, n. 2533, 2803, 2884, 5272, 7835. That the Word is Divine Truth, n. 4692, 5075, 9987. That forasmuch as the Lord is righteousness, therefore it is said, that he who sat upon the horse doth in righteousness judge and make war; and that the Lord is called righteousness for this reason, because of his own proper power he has saved mankind, n. 1813, 2025, 2026, 2027, 9715, 9809, 10,019, 10,152. And that righteousness means the merit which belongs to the Lord alone, n. 9715, 9979. That his eyes, which were as a flame of fire, signify Divine Truth originating in the Divine Good of the Divine Love, is, because the eyes signify the understanding and the truth of faith, n. 2701, 4403—4421, 4523—4534, 6923, 9051, 10,569; and a flame of fire the good of love, n. 934, 4906, 5215, 6314, 6832. That the crowns which were on his head signify all the goods and truths of faith, n. 114, 3858, 6335, 6640, 9863, 9865, 9868, 9873, 9905. That his having a name written which no man knew but he himself, signifies, that the quality of the Word in the internal sense is known by no one but himself, and those to whom he reveals it, is, because a name signifies the quality of a thing, n. 144, 145, 1754, 1896, 2009, 2724, 3006, 3237, 3421, 6674, 9310. That clothed in a vesture dipped in blood, signifies the Word in the letter, to which violence has been offered, is, because a vesture signifies truth by reason that it invests good, n. 1073, 2576, 5248, 5319, 5954, 9212, 9216, 9952, 10,536 ; that it particularly signifies truth in the ultimates, consequently, the Word in the letter, n. 5248, 6918, 9158, 9212 ; and that blood signifies violence offered to truth by falsity, n. 374, 1005, 4735, 5476, 9127. That the armies in heaven which followed him upon white horses, signify those who are in the understanding of the Word as to its interiors, is, because armies signify those who are in the truths and goods of heaven and the church, n. 3448, 7236, 7988, 8019 ; and a horse signifies understanding, n. 3217, 5321, 6125, 6400, 6531, 6534, 7024, 8146, 8318 ; and white signifies such truth as is in the light of heaven, consequently interior truth, n. 3301, 3993, 4007, 5319. That clothed in fine linen white and clean, signifies the same persons principled in truth originating in good, is, because fine linen, or lawn, signifies truth from a celestial origin, which is truth derived from good, n. 5319, 9469. That a name written on the vesture and on the thigh, signifies truth and good, and their quality, is, because a vesture signifies truth, and a name quality, as observed above, and the thigh signifies the good of love, n. 3021, 4277, 4280, 9961, 10,485. King of kings, and Lord of lords, is the Lord with respect to Divine Truth and with respect to Divine Good ; that the Lord is called king from Divine Truth, n. 3009, 5068, 6148 ; and that he is called Lord from Divine Good, n. 4973, 9167, 9194. Hence it appears what is the quality of the Word in its spiritual or internal sense, and that there is no expression therein which does not signify something spiritual relative to heaven and the church.

2. In the prophetical parts of the Word mention is very often made of the horse, but heretofore no one has known that a horse signifies understanding, and his rider an intelligent person ; and this possibly, because it seems strange and wonderful, that by a horse such a thing should be signified in the spiritual sense, and hence in the Word. But nevertheless, that it is really so, may evidently appear from many passages therein; some of which only I will here adduce. In the prophecy of Israel, it is said of Dan, "Dan shall be a serpent by the way, an adder in the path, that biteth the horse's heels, so that his rider shall fall backward," Gen. xlix. 17, 18. No one can understand what this prophecy concerning one of the tribes of Israel signifies, unless he knows what is signified by a serpent, and what by a horse and his rider : every one, however, knows

that there is something spiritual involved therein; what therefore each particular expression signifies, may be seen in the ARCANA CŒLESTIA, n. 6398, 6399, 6400, 6401, where this prophecy is explained. So in Habakkuk: "Was the Lord displeased against the rivers? Was thine anger against the rivers; was thy wrath against the sea, that thou didst ride upon thy horses and thy chariots of salvation? Thou didst walk through the sea with thy horses," iii. 8, 15. That horses here have a spiritual signification, is evident, for the passage treats concerning God; in any other sense, what could be meant by saying, that the Lord rides upon his horses, and that he walked through the sea with his horses? So in Zechariah: "In that day there shall be upon the bells of the horses, holiness unto Jehovah," xiv. 20; where a like spiritual signification is implied. So in the same prophet: "In that day, saith Jehovah, I will smite every horse with astonishment, and his rider with madness; and I will open mine eyes upon the house of Judah, and will smite every horse of the people with blindness," xii. 4. The subject there treated of is the ruin of the church, which takes place when there no longer remains the understanding of any truth; and which is described thus by the horse and his rider; what else could be the meaning of smiting every horse with astonishment, and of smiting the horse of the people with blindness? What has this to do with the church? So in Job: "God hath deprived her of wisdom, neither hath he imparted to her understanding: what time she lifteth up herself on high, she scorneth the horse and his rider," xxxix. 17, 18, 19, &c. That the horse here signifies understanding, is manifestly evident. In like manner in David, where God is said "to ride prosperously because of truth," Psalm xlv. 4; and in many other places. Moreover, who can know the reason why Elijah and Elisha were called the chariot of Israel and the horsemen thereof; and why the lad of Elisha saw the mountain full of horses and chariots of fire; except it be known what is signified by chariots and horsemen, and what was represented by Elijah and Elisha? Elisha said to Elijah, "My father, my father, the chariot of Israel and the horsemen thereof," 2 Kings ii. 11, 12. And Joash the king said to Elisha, "My father, my father, the chariot of Israel and the horsemen thereof," 2 Kings xiii. 14; and, speaking of the lad of Elisha, it is said, "Jehovah opened the eyes of the young man, and he saw, and, behold, the mountain was full of horses and chariots of fire round about Elisha," 2 Kings vi. 17. The reason why Elijah and Elisha were called the chariot of Israel and the horsemen thereof, is, because they both represented the Lord as to the Word, and a chariot signifies doctrine drawn from the Word, and horsemen, intelligence. That Elijah and Elisha represented the

Lord as to the Word, may be seen in the ARCANA CŒLESTIA, n. 5247, 7643, 8029, 9327. And that chariots signify doctrine drawn from the Word, n. 5321, 8215.

3. This signification of the horse, as denoting understanding, is derived from no other source than from the representatives which exist in the spiritual world. In that world are frequently seen horses, and persons sitting upon horses, and also chariots; and there every one knows that they signify things intellectual and doctrinal. I myself have often observed, when any were thinking from their understanding, that at such times they appeared as if riding on horses; their meditation represented itself in this manner before others, although they themselves were ignorant of it. There is also a place in the spiritual world, where many assemble who think and speak from understanding concerning the truths of doctrine; and when others approach, they see the whole plain covered with chariots and horses; novitiate spirits, who are astonished at the sight, and wonder whence it proceeds, are instructed that it is an appearance resulting from their intellectual thought. That place is called the assembly of the intelligent and the wise. I have likewise seen bright horses and chariots of fire, when certain spirits were taken up into heaven, which was a sign that they were then instructed in the truths of heavenly doctrine, and became intelligent, and thus were taken up; on seeing which, it occurred to my mind, what is signified by the chariot of fire, which carried Elijah up into heaven; and what is signified by the horses and chariots of fire that were seen by the young man of Elisha, when his eyes were opened.

4. That such is the signification of chariots and horses was perfectly well known in the ancient churches; for those churches were representative churches, and the science of correspondences and representations was esteemed, among the members of those churches, the chief of all sciences. From those churches the signification of the horse, as expressive of understanding, was derived to the wise men round about, even into Greece. Hence it was, when they would describe the sun, in which they placed their God of wisdom and intelligence, that they attributed to it a chariot and four horses of fire; and when they would describe the God of the sea, since by the sea were signified sciences derived from understanding, that they also attributed horses to him; and when they would describe the rise of the sciences from understanding, that they also feigned a winged horse, which with its hoof broke open a fountain, at which sat nine virgins called the sciences. For from the ancient churches they received the knowledge that the horse signifies understanding; wings, spiritual truth; the hoof, what is scientific derived from understanding; and a fountain, doctrine from which sciences are derived. Nor is anything else

signified by the Trojan horse, than an artificial contrivance devised by their understanding for the purpose of destroying the walls. Even at this day, when understanding is described after the manner received from those ancients, it is usual to figure it by a flying horse or Pegasus; so, likewise, doctrine is described by a fountain, and the sciences by virgins; but scarcely any one knows, that the horse, in the mystic sense, signifies the understanding; still less that those significatives were derived to the Gentiles from the ancient representative churches.

5. Since the White Horse signifies the understanding of the Word as to its spiritual or internal sense, those particulars concerning the Word and that sense, which are shown in the ARCANA CŒLESTIA, are here subjoined: for in that work the whole contents of Genesis and Exodus are explained according to the spiritual or internal sense of the Word.

REFERENCES FROM THE ARCANA CŒLESTIA,

ON THE SUBJECT OF THE WORD, AND ITS SPIRITUAL OR INTERNAL SENSE.

6. OF *the necessity and excellency of the Word.* That from the light of nature nothing can be known concerning the Lord, concerning heaven and hell, concerning the life of man after death, nor concerning Divine Truths by which man acquires spiritual and eternal life, n. 8944, 10,318, 10,319, 10,320. That this may appear manifest from the consideration, that many, and amongst them men of learning, do not believe those things, although they are born in a country where the Word is received, and are thereby instructed concerning them, n. 10,319. That therefore it was necessary there should be some revelation from heaven, forasmuch as man was born to become an inhabitant of heaven, n. 1775. That therefore in every age of the world there has been a revelation, n. 2895. Of the various kinds of revelation which have successivelybeen made to the inhabitants of this earth, n. 10,355, 10,632. That to the most ancient men, who lived before the flood, whose time was called the golden age, there was an immediate revelation, and of consequence Divine Truth was inscribed on their hearts, n. 2896. That the ancient churches, which existed after the flood, had a historical and prophetical Word, n. 2686, 2897; concerning which churches see the NEW JERUSALEM AND ITS HEAVENLY DOCTRINE, n. 247. That its historical parts were called The

Wars of Jehovah, and its prophetical parts, Enunciations, n. 2897. That that Word, with respect to inspiration, was like our Word, but accommodated to those churches, n. 2897. That it is mentioned by Moses, n. 2686, 2897. But that that Word is lost, n. 2897. That prophetical revelations were also made to others, as appears from the prophecies of Balaam, n. 2898.

That the Word is divine in all and every particular part, n. 639, 680, 10,321, 10,637. That the Word is divine and holy as to every point and iota, from experience, n. 1349. How it is explained at this day, that the Word is inspired as to every iota, n. 1886.

That the church in an especial manner is where the Word is, and where the Lord is thereby known, and Divine Truths are revealed, n. 3857, 10,761. But that it does not follow from thence, that they are of the church, who are born where the Word is, and where the Lord is thereby known; but they who, by means of truths from the Word, are regenerated by the Lord, who are they who live according to the truths therein, consequently, who lead a life of love and faith, n. 6637, 10,143, 10,153, 10,578, 10,645, 10,829.

7. *That the Word cannot be understood, except by those who are enlightened.* That the human rational faculty cannot comprehend divine, nor even spiritual things, unless it be enlightened by the Lord, n. 2196, 2203, 2209, 2654. Consequently, that they only who are enlightened comprehend the Word, n. 10,323. That the Lord enables those who are enlightened to understand truths, and to see how to reconcile those things which appear contradictory to each other, n. 9382, 10,659. That the Word in its literal sense appears inconsistent, and in some places seems to contradict itself, n. 9025. And that therefore, by those who are unenlightened, it may be so explained and applied, as to confirm any opinion or heresy, and to defend any lust, however worldly and corporeal, n. 4738, 10,339, 10,401. That they are enlightened from the Word, who read it from the love of truth and goodness, but not they who read it from the love of fame, of gain, or of honor, that is, from the love of self, n. 9382, 10,548, 10,549, 10,550. That they are enlightened who are in the good of life, and thereby in the affection of truth, n. 8694. That they are enlightened whose internal is open, or who as to their internal man are capable of elevation into the light of heaven, n. 10,401, 10,402, 10,691, 10,694. That enlightenment is an actual opening of the interiors of the mind, and also an elevation into the light of heaven, n. 10,330. That there is an influx of sanctity from the internal, that is, from the Lord through the internal, to those who esteem the Word holy, though they themselves are ignorant of it, n. 6789. That they are enlightened, and see the truths of the Word, who are led by the Lord, but not they

who are led by themselves, n. 10,638. That they are led by the Lord, who love truth because it is truth, who also are they that love to live according to Divine Truths, n. 10,578, 10,645, 10,829. That the Word is made alive with man according to the life of his love and faith, n. 1776. That the things derived from self-intelligence have no life in themselves, because from man's proprium there proceeds nothing that is good, n. 8941, 8944. That they cannot be enlightened who have much confirmed themselves in false doctrine, n. 10,640.

That it is the understanding which is enlightened, n. 6608, 9300. That the understanding is the recipient of truth, n. 6242, 6608, 10,659. That in regard to every doctrine of the church, there are ideas of the understanding and of the thought thence proceeding, according to which the doctrine is perceived, n. 3310, 3825. That the ideas of man during his life in the world are natural, because he then thinks in the natural principle; but that still spiritual ideas are concealed therein, with those who are in the affection of truth for its own sake, and that man comes into these ideas after death, n. 3310, 5510, 6201, 10,236, 10,240, 10,550. That without ideas of the understanding, and of the thought thence derived, on any subject, there can be no perception, n. 3825. That ideas concerning the things of faith are laid open in the other life, and their quality clearly discerned by the angels, and that man is then conjoined with others according to those ideas, so far as they proceed from the affection which is of his love, n. 1869, 3320, 5510, 6201, 8885. That therefore the Word can be understood by none but a rational man; for to believe anything without an idea thereof, and without a rational view of the subject, is only to retain in the memory words destitute of all life of perception and affection, which in fact is not believing, n. 2533. That it is the literal sense of the Word which admits of illustration, n. 3619, 9824, 9905, 10,548.

8. *That the Word cannot be understood but by means of doctrine from the Word.* That the doctrine of the church must be derived from the Word, n. 3464, 5402, 6832, 10,763, 10,765. That the Word is unintelligible without doctrine, n. 9025, 9409, 9424, 9430, 10,324, 10,431, 10,582. That true doctrine is as a lamp to those who read the Word, n. 10,401. That genuine doctrine must be formed by those who are in illustration from the Lord, n. 2510, 2516, 2519, 2524, 10,105. That the Word is intelligible by means of doctrine formed by an enlightened person, n. 10,324. That they who are in illustration, form for themselves doctrine from the Word, n. 9382, 10,659. What is the difference between those who teach and learn from the doctrine of the church, and those who teach and learn from the literal sense of the Word alone, n. 9025. That they who are in the literal sense of the Word without doctrine, do not

attain to any understanding concerning Divine Truths, n. 9409, 9410, 10,582. That they may fall into many errors, n. 10,431. That they who are in the affection of truth for the sake of truth, when they come to years of maturity, and are capable of exercising their own understanding, do not implicitly abide in the doctrines of their respective churches, but examine from the Word whether they be true or not, n. 5402, 5432, 6047. That otherwise every man's views of truth would be derived from the authority of another, and from his native soil, whether he were born a Jew or a Greek, n. 6047. That nevertheless such things as are become matters of faith from the literal sense of the Word, are not to be extinguished till after a full view of their falsity, n. 9039.

That the true doctrine of the church is the doctrine of charity and faith, n. 2417, 4766, 10,763, 10,765. That the doctrine of faith does not constitute the church, but the life of faith, which is charity, n. 809, 1798, 1799, 1834, 4468, 4677, 4766, 5826, 6637. That doctrines are of no account, unless the life be directed thereby; and that every one may see they are for the sake of life, and not merely for the memory, and thought thence derived, n. 1515, 2049, 2116. That in the churches at this day the doctrine of faith is taught, and not the doctrine of charity, the latter being degraded to a science, which is called moral philosophy, n. 2417. That the church would be one, or undivided, if purity of life, and charity, were accounted the distinguished marks of church-membership, n. 1285, 1316, 2982, 3267, 3445, 3451, 3452. How much superior the doctrine of charity is to that of faith separate from charity, n. 4844. That they who know nothing concerning charity, are in ignorance with respect to heavenly things, n. 2435. That they who only hold the doctrine of faith, and not that of charity, fall into errors; which errors are also described, n. 2417, 2383, 3146, 3325, 3412, 3413, 3416, 3773, 4672, 4730, 4783, 4925, 5351, 7623—7677, 7752—7762, 7790, 8094, 8313, 8530, 8765, 9186, 9224, 10,555. That they who are only in the doctrine of faith, and not in the life of faith, which is charity, were formerly called the uncircumcised, or Philistines, n. 3412, 3413, 3463, 8093, 8313, 9340. That the ancients held the doctrine of love to the Lord and of charity towards the neighbor, and made the doctrine of faith subservient thereto, n. 2417, 3419, 4844, 4955.

That doctrine formed by an enlightened person, may afterwards be confirmed by things rational and scientific; and that thus it is more fully understood, and is corroborated, n. 2553, 2719, 2720, 3052, 3310, 6047. See more on this subject in the NEW JERUSALEM AND ITS HEAVENLY DOCTRINE, n. 51. That they who are in faith separate from charity, would have the doctrines of the church implicitly believed, without any rational intuition, n. 3394.

That it is not the mark of a wise man to confirm a received opinion, but to see whether it be true or not before he confirms it; and that this is the case with those who are in illustration, n. 1017, 4741, 7012, 7680, 7950. That the light of confirmation is a natural light, and not spiritual, and may exist even with the evil, n. 8780. That every thing, however false, may be so far confirmed, as to acquire the appearance of truth, n. 2482, 2490, 5033, 6865, 8521.

9. *That in the Word there is a spiritual sense, which is called the internal sense.* That no one can know what the spiritual or internal sense of the Word is, unless he know what correspondence is, n. 2895, 4322. That all and every thing, even the most minute particulars, which exist in the natural world, correspond to spiritual things, and thence are significative of them, n. 2890—2893, 2897—3003, 3213—3227. That the spiritual things to which natural things correspond, assume another appearance in the natural degree or principle, so that they are not distinguished, n. 1887, 2396, 8920. That scarcely any one knows wherein resides the divinity of the Word, when nevertheless it is in its internal and spiritual sense, which at this day is not known even to have any existence, n. 2980, 4989. That the mystical contents of the Word are no other than those of its internal or spiritual sense, which treats of the Lord, of the glorification of His Humanity, of His kingdom, and of the church, and not of the natural things of this world, n. 4923. That the prophetic writings are in many places unintelligible, and therefore of no use, without the internal sense,—illustrated by examples, n. 2608, 8020, 8398. As, for instance, with respect to what is signified by the white horse spoken of in the Apocalypse, n. 2760, &c. What by the keys of the kingdom of heaven, that were given to Peter, see the preface to the 22nd chapter of Genesis, and n. 9410. What by flesh, blood, bread, and wine, in the holy supper, n. 8682. What by the prophecies of Jacob concerning his sons, recorded in the 49th chapter of Genesis, n. 6306, 6333—6465. What by many prophecies concerning Judah and Israel, which by no means tally with that nation, nor in the literal sense have any coincidence with their history, n. 6331, 6361, 6415, 6438, 6444. Besides many other instances, n. 2608. More may be seen of the nature of correspondence, in the work on HEAVEN AND HELL, n. 87—102, 104—115, and 303—310.

Of the internal or spiritual sense of the Word in general, n. 1767—1777, 1869—1879. That in all and every particular of the Word there is an internal sense, n. 1143, 1984, 2135, 2333, 2395, 2495, 2619. That such things do not appear in the literal sense, but that nevertheless they are really contained within it, n. 4442.

10. *That the internal sense of the Word is principally intended for the use of angels, and that it is also intended for the use of men.* In order that it may be known what the internal sense is, the quality thereof, and whence it is, it may here be observed in general, that thought and speech in heaven are different from thought and speech in the world; for in heaven they are spiritual, but in the world natural; when, therefore, man reads the Word, the angels that are with him have a spiritual perception thereof, whilst men understand it naturally; hence it follows, that angels are in the internal sense, whilst men are in the external sense; but that nevertheless these two senses make a one by correspondence. That angels not only think spiritually, but also speak spiritually; that they are likewise present with man; and that they have conjunction with man by means of the Word, may be seen in the work on HEAVEN AND HELL, where it treats of the wisdom of the angels of heaven, n. 265—275; of their speech, n. 234—245; of their conjunction with man, n. 291—302; and of their conjunction with man by means of the Word, n. 303—310.

That the Word is understood differently by angels in heaven, and by men on earth; the former perceiving the internal or spiritual sense, whilst the latter see only the external or natural sense, n. 1887, 2396. That the angels perceive the Word in its internal sense, and not in its external sense, proved from the experience of those who have conversed with me from heaven, when I was reading the Word, n. 1769, 1770, 1771, 1772. That the ideas of the thought and also the speech of angels are spiritual, but the ideas and speech of men natural; that therefore there is an internal sense, which is spiritual, for the use of angels, illustrated from experience, 2333. That nevertheless the literal sense of the Word serves the spiritual ideas of angels as a medium of conveyance, comparatively as the words of speech do with men to convey the sense of a subject whereon they discourse, n. 2143. That the things relating to the internal sense of the Word are manifested in the light of heaven, and consequently to the perception of angels, n. 2618, 2619, 2629, 3086. That therefore those things which the angels perceive from the Word, are of high estimation with them, n. 2540, 2541, 2545, 2551. That angels do not understand a single syllable of the Word in its literal sense, n. 64, 65, 1434, 1929. That they are unacquainted with the names of persons and places recorded in the Word, n. 1434, 1888, 4442, 4480. That names cannot enter into heaven, nor be pronounced there, n. 1876, 1888. That all names in the Word signify things, and that in heaven they are changed into ideas of the things signified, n. 768, 1888, 4310, 4442, 5225, 5287, 10,323. That angels also think abstractedly from persons, n. 6613, 8343, 8985, 9007. How elegant the internal sense of the Word is, even where nothing but mere names occur, shown by examples from the Word, n. 1224, 1888, 2395. That many names also in series express one thing in the internal sense, n. 5905. That likewise all numbers in the Word signify things, n. 482, 487, 647, 648, 755, 813, 1963, 1988, 2075, 2252, 3152, 4264, 6175, 9488, 9659, 10,217, 10,253. That spirits also have a perception of the Word in its internal sense in proportion as their interiors are open to heaven, n. 1771. That the literal sense of the Word, which is the natural sense, is instantly changed into the spiritual sense with the angels, from the correspondence there is between the two senses, n. 5648. And this without their hearing or knowing what is in the literal or external sense, n. 10,215. Thus that the literal or external sense is confined to man, and proceeds no further, n. 2015.

That there is an internal sense in the Word, and likewise an inmost or supreme sense, concerning which, see n. 9407, 10,604, 10,614, 10,627. That the spiritual angels, or those who belong to the spiritual kingdom of the Lord, perceive the Word in its internal sense; and that the celestial angels, or those who belong to the celestial kingdom of the Lord, perceive the Word in its inmost sense, n. 2157, 2275.

That the Word is for the use of men, and also for the use of angels, being accommodated to each, n. 7381, 8862, 10,322. That the Word is the medium of union between heaven and earth, n. 2310, 2493, 9212, 9216, 9357. That the conjunction of heaven with man is by means of the Word, n. 9396, 9400, 9401, 10,452. That therefore the Word is called a covenant, n. 9396. Because a covenant signifies conjunction, 665, 666, 1023, 1038, 1864, 1996, 2003, 2021, 6804, 8767, 8778, 9396, 10,632. That there is an internal sense in the Word, in consequence of the Word's having descended from the Lord, through the three heavens down to man, n. 2310, 6397. And that thereby it is accommodated to the angels of the three heavens and also to men, n. 7381, 8862. That hence it is that the Word is divine, n. 2980, 4989. And that it is holy, n. 10,276. And that it is spiritual, n. 4480. And that it is divinely inspired, n. 9094. That this is the meaning of inspiration, n. 9094.

That the regenerate man is actually in the internal sense of the Word, although he knows it not, inasmuch as his internal man, which is endowed with spiritual perception, is open, n. 10,401. But that in such case the spiritual principle of the Word flows into natural ideas, and thus is represented naturally, because while he lives in the world this spiritual principle thinks in the natural man, so far as it comes to the perception thereof, n. 5614. That hence the light of truth, with such as are enlightened, is derived from their internal, that is, through the internal, from the Lord, n. 10,691, 10,694. That also by the same way there is an influx of sanctity communicated to those who esteem the Word holy, n. 6789. Inasmuch as the regenerate man is actually in the internal sense of the Word, and in the sanctity thereof, although he knows it not, that therefore after death he comes into it of himself, and is no longer in the sense of the letter, n. 3226, 3342, 3343. That the ideas of the internal man are spiritual; but that man during his life in the world does not attend thereto, inasmuch as they are within his natural thought, and give it its rational faculty, n. 10,236, 10,240, 10,550. But that man after death comes into those his spiritual ideas, because they are proper to his spirit, and then not only thinks, but also speaks therefrom, n. 2470, 2478, 2479, 10,568, 10,604. Hence it is that it was said, that the regenerate man knows not that he is in the spiritual sense of the Word, and that he receives illustration thence.

11. *That in the internal or spiritual sense of the Word there are innumerable arcana.* That the Word in the internal sense contains innumerable things which exceed human comprehension, n. 3085, 3086. That it also contains things ineffable and inexplicable, n. 1965. Which are manifested only to angels, and understood by them, n. 167. That the internal sense of the Word contains arcana of heaven, which relate to the Lord and His kingdom in heaven and on earth, n. 1—4, 937. That those areana do not appear in the sense of the letter, n. 937, 1502, 2161. That many things in the writings of the prophets appear to be unconnected, which yet in the internal sense cohere in a beautiful series, n. 7153, 9022. That not a single expression, nor even a single iota, in its original language, can be taken from the literal sense of the Word, without an interruption in the internal sense; and that therefore, by the Divine Providence of the Lord, the Word is preserved so entire as to every point, n. 7933. That innumerable things are contained in every particular part of the Word, n. 6637, 8920. And in every expression, n. 1689. That there are innumerable things contained in the Lord's prayer and in every particular part thereof, n. 6619. And in the precepts of the decalogue; in the external sense whereof, notwithstanding, some things are such as are known to every nation without revelation, n. 8867, 8900. That in every tittle of the letter of the Word, in the original language, there is a sanctity, shown from heaven; see the work on HEAVEN AND HELL, n. 260, where these words of the Lord are explained, "That not one jot or one tittle shall pass away from the law," Matt. v. 18.

That in the Word, particularly in the prophetical parts, there are two expressions which seem to signify the same thing: but that one has relation to good, and the other to truth, n. 683,

707, 2516, 8339. That in the Word goods and truths are conjoined in a wonderful manner, and that such conjunction is only apparent to him who is acquainted with the internal sense, n. 10,554. And thus that in the Word, and in every part thereof, there is a Divine marriage and a heavenly marriage, n. 683, 793, 801, 2173, 2516, 2712, 5138, 7022. That the Divine marriage is the marriage of Divine Good and Divine Truth, consequently it is the Lord in heaven, in whom alone that marriage exists there, n. 3004, 3005, 3009, 4158, 5194, 5502, 6343, 7945, 8339, 9263, 9314. That Jesus also signifies Divine Good, and Christ Divine Truth, and thus both signify the Divine marriage in heaven, n. 3004, 3005, 3009. That this marriage is in every particular part of the Word in its internal sense, and thus the Lord is therein as to Divine Good and Divine Truth, n. 5502. That the marriage of good and truth from the Lord in heaven and in the church is called the heavenly marriage, n. 2508, 2618, 2803, 3004, 3211, 3952, 6179. That, therefore in this respect the Word is a kind of heaven, n. 2173, 10,126. That heaven is compared in the Word to a marriage, on account of the marriage of good and truth therein, n. 2758, 3132, 4434, 4834.

That the internal sense is the real genuine doctrine of the church, n. 9025, 9430, 10,401. That they who understand the Word according to the internal sense, know the real and true doctrine of the church, inasmuch as it is contained in the internal sense, n. 9025, 9430, 10,401. That the internal of the Word is also the internal of the church, as it is likewise the internal of worship, n. 10,460. That the Word is the doctrine of love to the Lord, and of charity towards the neighbor, n. 3419, 3420.

That the Word in the literal sense is as a cloud, and that in the internal sense it is glory, see the preface to the 18th chapter of Genesis, and n. 5922, 6343, where these words are explained, "That the Lord shall come in the clouds of heaven with glory." That clouds also in the Word signify the Word in its literal sense, and glory the Word in its internal sense, see the preface to the 18th chapter of Genesis, and n. 4060, 4391, 5922, 6343, 6752, 8106, 8781, 9430, 10,551, 10,574. That the things contained in the literal sense, respectively to those which are in the internal sense, are like rude projections round a polished optical cylinder, from which nevertheless is exhibited in the cylinder a beautiful image of a man, n. 1871. In the spiritual world they who allow and acknowledge only the literal sense of the Word, are represented by a deformed old woman; but they who allow and acknowledge the internal sense together with the literal sense, are represented by a virgin in beautiful clothing, n. 1774. That the Word in its whole complex is an image of heaven; for the Word is Divine Truth, and Divine Truth constitutes heaven, and heaven resembles one man, and therefore in this respect the Word is as it were an image of man, n. 187. That heaven in one complex resembles one man, may be seen in the work on HEAVEN AND HELL, n. 59—67. And that the Divine Truth proceeding from the Lord constitutes heaven, n. 126—140, 200—212. That the Word is represented before the angels under the most beautiful and agreeable forms, n. 1767, 1768. That the literal sense is as the body, and the internal sense as the soul of that body, n. 8943. That hence the life of the Word is from the internal sense, n. 1405, 4857. That the Word is pure in the internal sense, but that it does not appear so in the literal sense, n. 2362, 2396. That the things which are in the literal sense derive their sanctity from the internal contents, n. 10,126, 10,728.

That the historical parts of the Word also have an internal sense, but more remote from the letter, n. 4989. Consequently that the historical as well as the prophetical parts of the Word contain arcana of heaven, n. 755, 1659, 1709, 2310, 2333. That the angels do not perceive those parts historically, but according to their spiritual signification, n. 6884. That the interior arcana contained in the historical parts are less evident to man than those contained in the prophetical parts, by reason that the mind is engaged in viewing and considering the historical transactions, n. 2176, 6597.

The nature of the internal sense of the Word is further shown, n. 1756, 1984, 2004, 2663, 3033, 7089, 10,604, 10,614. And illustrated by comparisons, n. 1873.

12. *That the Word is written by correspondences, and thus by representatives.* That the Word as to its literal sense is written by mere correspondences, that is, by such things as represent and signify the spiritual things of heaven and the church, n. 1404, 1408, 1409, 1540, 1619, 1659, 1709, 1783, 2179, 2763, 2899. That this was done for the sake of the internal sense, which there is in every part, n. 2899. Consequently for the sake of heaven, inasmuch as the inhabitants thereof do not understand the Word according to the literal sense, which is natural, but according to the internal sense, which is spiritual, n. 2899. That the Lord spake by correspondences, representatives, and significatives, because he spake from the Divine, n. 9049, 9063, 9086, 10,126, 10,728. That the Lord thus spoke to the world, and at the same time to heaven, n. 2533, 4807, 9049, 9063. 9086. That the things spoken by the Lord went through the whole heaven, n. 4637. That the historical parts of the Word are representative, and the expressions significative, n. 1540, 1659, 1709, 1783, 2687. That the Word could not be written in any other style, consistently with its being the medium of communication and conjunction with the heavens, n. 2899 6943, 9481. That they are in a great error, who despise the

Word on account of the apparent simplicity and rudeness of its style, and who fancy that they should receive the Word, if it were written in a different style, n. 8783. That the method and style of writing, which prevailed amongst the most ancient inhabitants of the earth, was by correspondences and representatives, n. 605, 1756, 9942. That the ancient wise men were delighted with the Word, because of the representatives and significatives therein, from experience, n. 2592, 2593. That if a man of the most ancient church had read the Word, he would have seen clearly the things contained in the internal sense, and but obscurely the things contained in the external sense, n. 449. That the sons of Jacob were brought into the land of Canaan, because all the places in that land, from the most ancient times, were made representative, n. 1585, 3686, 4441, 5136, 6516. And that thus the Word might be there written, wherein those places should be mentioned for the sake of the internal sense, n. 3686, 4447, 5136, 6416. But that nevertheless the Word as to the external sense was changed for the sake of that nation, but not as to the internal sense, n. 10,453, 10,461, 10,603, 10,604. Many passages adduced from the Word concerning that nation, which must be understood according to the internal sense, and not according to the sense of the letter, n. 7051. Inasmuch as that nation represented the church, and the Word was written with them and concerning them, that therefore Divine Celestial things were signified by their names, as by Reuben, Simeon, Levi, Judah, Ephraim, Joseph, and the rest: and that by Judah in the internal sense is signified the Lord as to celestial love, and his celestial kingdom, n. 3654, 3881, 3882, 5782, 6362—6382.

For the better understanding of the nature and meaning of correspondences and representatives in the Word, something shall be here said concerning them. That all things which correspond are likewise representative, and thereby significative, so that correspondences and representations are one, n. 2890, 2897, 2971, 2987, 2989, 2990, 3002, 3225. The nature of correspondences and representations shown from experience and examples, n. 2703, 2987—3002, 3213—3226, 3337—3352, 3472—3485, 4218—4228, 9280. That the science of correspondences and representations was the chief science amongst the ancients, n. 3021, 3419, 4280, 4749, 4844, 4964, 4965, 6004, 7729, 10,252. Especially among the people of the east, n. 5702, 6692, 7097, 7779, 9391, 10,252, 10,407. And in Egypt more than in other countries, n. 5702, 6692, 7097, 7779, 9391, 10,407. Also among the Gentiles, as in Greece, and in other places, n. 2762, 7729. But that at this day the science of correspondences and representations is lost, particularly in Europe, n. 2894, 2895, 2994, 3630, 3632, 3747, 3748, 3749, 4581, 4966, 10,252. That nevertheless this science is more excellent than all other sciences, inasmuch as without it the Word cannot be understood, nor the signification of the rites of the Jewish church which are recorded in the Word, nor can it be known what the nature of heaven is, nor what the spiritual principle is, nor in what manner a spiritual influx takes place into what is natural, nor how the case is with respect to the influx of the soul into the body, with many other matters, n. 4180, and in the places above cited. That all things which appear before spirits and angels, are representative according to correspondences, n. 1971, 3213—3226, 3457, 3475, 3485, 9481, 9574, 9576, 9577. That the heavens are full of representatives, n. 1521, 1532, 1619. That representatives are more beautiful, and more perfect, in proportion as they are more interior in the heavens, n. 3475. That representatives there are real appearances, inasmuch as they are derived from the light of heaven which is Divine Truth, and which is the very essence of the existence of all things, n. 3485.

The reason why all and every particular existence in the spiritual world has its representation in the natural world, is, because what is internal assumes to itself a suitable clothing in what is external, whereby it makes itself visible and apparent, n. 6275, 6284, 6299. Thus the end assumes a suitable clothing, that it may exist as the cause in a lower sphere, and afterwards that it may exist as the effect in a sphere still lower; and when the end, by means of the cause, becomes the effect, it then becomes visible, or appears before the eyes, n. 5711. This may be illustrated by the influx of the soul into the body, whereby the soul assumes a clothing of such things in the body as enable it to express all its thoughts and affections in a visible form; wherefore thought, when it descends by influx into the body, is there represented by such gestures and actions as correspond to it, n. 2988. The affections of the mind are manifestly represented in the face, by the various configurations of the countenance, so as to be there rendered visible, n. 4791—4805, 5695. Hence it is evident, that all and every particular existence in nature has in it a latent cause and end from the spiritual world, n. 3562, 5711. Inasmuch as the things which are in nature are the ultimate effects, within which are prior or superior things, n. 4240, 4939, 5051, 6275, 6284, 6299, 9216. That internal things are the objects represented, and external things the objects representing, n. 4292. What is further meant by correspondences and representations may be seen in the work on Heaven and Hell, where it treats of the correspondence between all things of heaven, and all things of man, n. 87—102. Of the correspondence of heaven with all things on earth, n. 103—115. And of representatives and appearances in heaven, n. 170—176.

Forasmuch as all things in nature are representative of spiritual and celestial things, therefore in the churches which existed in ancient times, all the externals, which were rituals, were representative, and therefore these churches were called representative churches, 519, 521, 2896. That the church founded among the children of Israel was a representative church, n. 1003, 2179, 10,149. That all the rituals therein were externals, which represented internals, such as belong to heaven and the church, n. 4288, 4874. That the representatives of the church and of worship ceased when the Lord came into the world and manifested Himself, because the Lord opened the internals of the church, and because all things of that church in a supreme sense regarded Him, n. 4832.

13. *Of the literal or external sense of the Word.* That the literal sense of the Word is according to appearances in the world, n. 584, 926, 1719, 1720, 1832, 1874, 2242, 2520, 2533. And adapted to the conceptions of the simple, 2533, 9049, 9063, 9086. That the Word, in the literal sense, is natural, n. 8783; because what is natural is the ultimate, wherein spiritual and celestial things find their limits, and upon which they rest like a house upon its foundation; and that otherwise the internal sense of the Word, without the external, would be like a house without a foundation, n. 9360, 9430, 9824, 9433, 10,044, 10,436. That the Word being of such a nature contains both a spiritual and celestial sense, n. 9407. And of consequence, that it is holy and divine in the literal sense, as to all and every part thereof, even to every single iota, n. 639, 680, 1319, 1870, 9198, 10,321, 10,637. That the laws ordained for the sons of Israel, notwithstanding their being repealed, are yet the holy Word, on account of the internal sense which they contain, n. 9210, 9259, 9349. That among the laws, judgments and statutes, ordained in the Israelitish or Jewish church, which was a representative church, there are some which are still in force both in their external and internal sense; which ought strictly to be observed in their external sense; some which may be of use, if people are disposed to observe them; and some which are absolutely repealed, n. 9349. That the Word is divine even in those statutes which are repealed, on account of the heavenly things which lie concealed in their internal sense, n. 10,637.

What the quality of the Word is in the literal sense, if not understood at the same time as to the internal sense, or, what is the same thing, according to true doctrine from the Word, n. 10,402. That innumerable heresies spring up from the literal sense of the Word without the internal sense, or without genuine doctrine drawn from the Word, n. 10,401. That they who are in externals without internals, cannot bear the interior things of the Word, n. 10,694. That the Jews were of this description, and that they are such also at the present day, n. 301,

302, 303, 3479, 4429, 4433, 4680, 4844, 4847, 10,396, 10,401, 10,407, 10,695, 10,701, 10,707.

14. *That the Lord is the Word.* That the Word in its inmost sense treats solely of the Lord, describing all the states of the glorification of His Humanity, that is, of its union with the Essential Divinity, and likewise all the states of the subjugation of the hells, and the reducing to order of all things therein, as well as in the heavens, n. 2249, 7014. Thus that the inmost sense describes the Lord's whole life on earth, and that thereby the Lord is continually present with the angels, n. 2523. That therefore the Lord alone is in the inmost part of the Word, and that the divinity and sanctity of the Word is from thence, n. 1873, 9357. That the Lord's saying, that the Scripture was fulfilled concerning Him, signifies, that all things were fulfilled which are contained in the inmost sense, n. 7933.

That the Word signifies Divine Truth, n. 4692, 5075, 9987. That the Lord is the Word, because He is Divine Truth, n. 2533. That the Lord is the Word also for this reason, because the Word is from Him, and treats of Him, n. 2859. And because it treats of the Lord alone in its inmost sense; thus the Lord Himself is therein, n. 1873, 9357. And because in all and in every part of the Word there is a marriage of Divine Good and Divine Truth, which marriage is in the Lord alone, n. 3004, 3005, 3009, 4158, 5194, 5502, 6343, 7945, 8339, 9263, 9314. That Divine Truth is the only real existence in the universe; and that the substance in which it is, and which is the Divine, is the only substantial existence, n. 5272, 6880, 7004, 8200. And inasmuch as Divine Truth proceeding from the Lord as the sun in heaven is light there, and Divine Good is heat there; and inasmuch as all things in heaven derive their existence therefrom, as all things in the world derive their existence from light and heat, which are also in their own substances, and act by means thereof; and inasmuch as the natural world exists by means of heaven or the spiritual world; it is plain that all things were created from Divine Truth, and consequently from the Word, according to this passage in John, "In the beginning was the Word, and the Word was with God, and the Word was God, and by it all things were made that were made; and THE WORD WAS MADE FLESH," chap. i. 1, 2, 3, 14; n. 2803, 2884, 5272, 7830. Further particulars concerning the creation of all things from Divine Truth, consequently by the Lord, may be seen in the work on HEAVEN AND HELL, n. 137; and more fully in the article concerning the sun in heaven, where it is shown that the Lord is that sun, and that it is His Divine Love, n. 116—125. And that Divine Truth is light, and Divine Good is heat, proceeding from that sun in heaven, n. 126—140.

That the conjunction of the Lord with man is effected by

the Word, through the medium of the internal sense, n. 10,375. That this conjunction is effected by all and every part of the Word, and that herein the Word is to be admired beyond all other writings, n. 10,632, 10,633, 10,634. That since the time of writing the Word, the Lord thereby speaks with men, n. 10,290. For further particulars respecting the conjunction of heaven with man by means of the Word, see the work on Heaven and Hell, n. 303—310.

15. *Of those who are against the Word.* Of those who despise, blaspheme, and profane the Word, n. 1878. Their quality in the other life, n. 1761, 9222. That they represent the viscous parts of the blood, n. 5719. How great the danger is which arises from profaning the Word, n. 571—582. How hurtful it is, if principles of falsity, particularly those which favor self-love and the love of the world, are confirmed by the Word, n. 589. That they who are in no affection of truth for its own sake, utterly reject the things appertaining to the internal sense of the Word, and nauseate them, from experience of such in the world of spirits, n. 5702. Of some in the other life, who endeavored altogether to reject the interior things of the Word, and that such are deprived of rationality, n. 1879.

16. *Which are the books of the Word.* That the books of the Word are all those which have the internal sense; but that those books which have not the internal sense are not the Word. That the books of the Word in the Old Testament are, The five books of Moses; the book of Joshua; the book of Judges; the two books of Samuel; the two books of Kings; the Psalms of David; The Prophets Isaiah, Jeremiah, the Lamentations, Ezekiel, Daniel, Hosea, Joel, Amos, Obadiah, Jonah, Micah, Nahum, Habakkuk, Zephaniah, Haggai, Zechariah, Malachi. In the New Testament, the four Evangelists, Matthew, Mark, Luke, John; and the Apocalypse. The rest have not the internal sense, n. 10,325.

That the book of Job is an ancient book, which indeed contains an internal sense, but not in series, n. 3570, 9942.

17. *Further particulars respecting the Word.* That the term Word, in Hebrew, signifies various things; as speech, or discourse, thought of the mind, every thing that has a real existence, and also something, n. 9987. That the Word signifies Divine Truth and the Lord, n. 2533, 4692, 5075, 9987. That words signify truths, n. 4692, 5075. That they signify doctrinals, n. 1288. That the ten words signify all Divine Truths, n. 10,688.

That in the Word, particularly in the prophetic parts, there are two expressions that signify one thing, and that the one has relation to good and the other to truth, which are thus conjoined, n. 683, 707, 5516, 8339. That it can be known only from the internal sense of the Word, what expression refers to good and what to truth ; for there are proper words by which things appertaining to good are expressed, and proper words by which things appertaining to truth are expressed, n. 793, 801. And this so determinately, that it may be known merely from the words made use of, whether the subject treated of be good, or whether it be truth, n. 2722. That frequently one expression implies a universal, and the other expression implies a certain specific particular of that universal, n. 2212. That there is a species of reciprocation in the Word, concerning which see n. 2240. That most expressions in the Word have also an opposite sense, n. 4816. That the internal sense proceeds regularly according to the subject predicated, n. 4502.

That they who have been delighted with the Word, in the other life receive the heat of heaven, wherein is celestial love, according to the quality and degree of their delight arising from love, n. 1773.

END OF THE WHITE HORSE.

AN APPENDIX

TO

THE TREATISE

ON

THE WHITE HORSE,

From the Latin of

EMANUEL SWEDENBORG,

Servant of the Lord Jesus Christ.

NEW YORK:

AMERICAN SWEDENBORG PRINTING AND PUBLISHING SOCIETY,

APPENDIX

TO THE

TREATISE ON THE WHITE HORSE.

---

1. That a horse should signify the understanding of truth, and, in the opposite sense, reasonings, which appear as if they were the result of understanding, in confirmation of the false, must needs appear strange at this day; I shall therefore bring together some other passages from the Word, where the expression, Horse, occurs. Thus in the following: "Is thy wrath against the sea, O Jehovah, that *thou ridest on thine horses?* Thy chariots are salvation. Thou hast trodden the sea *with thine horses*, even the mire of the waters," Habakkuk, chap. iii. 8, 15. "*The hoofs of the horses* [of Jehovah] are counted as rocks," Isaiah v. 28. "At thy rebuke both the chariot and *the horse* have fallen asleep," Psalm lxxvi. 6. "I will overthrow the throne of kingdoms, and I will overthrow the chariot, and those that ride in it, and *the horses* and their riders shall come down," Haggai ii. 22. "I will cut off *the horse* from Jerusalem; but to the Gentiles he will speak peace," Zechariah ix. 10.

2. In these passages, *horse* signifies the understanding of truth in the church; and chariot, doctrine thence derived; and they who ride in the chariots, and on the horses, signify those who understand, and are in the doctrine of truth derived from the Word. But this may appear yet more evident from the following passages: "Gather yourselves on every side, on account of the sacrifice; ye shall be filled at my table *with horse and with chariot;* thus will I set my glory among the Gentiles," Ezekiel xxxix. 17, 20, 21. "Gather yourselves together unto the supper of the great God, that ye may eat the flesh of *horses*, and of *them that sit on them*," Apocalypse xix. 17, 18. In addition to these, the following may be taken as a still further evidence of the signification of horse and chariot: "Gird thy sword upon the thigh, O Mighty One, *ride* upon the Word of Truth," Psalm xlv. 3, 4. "Sing ye, extol him that *rideth* on the clouds," Psalm lxviii. 4. "Jehovah is *riding* upon a cloud," Isaiah xix. 1. "Sing ye praises unto the Lord, who *rideth* on the heaven of heavens, which was of old," Psalm lxviii. 32, 33. "God *rode* upon a cherub," Psalm xviii. 10. "Then shalt thou

delight thyself in Jehovah, and *I will cause thee to ride* upon the high places of the land," Isaiah lviii. 14. "I will make Ephraim to ride," Hosea x. 11. In these places, *to ride* signifies to instruct and be instructed in the truths of doctrine, and so to become wise. The high places of the land signify the sublimer truths of the church, and Ephraim also the understanding of the Word. The like significations are to be applied to the horses and chariots mentioned in Zechariah ; and to the four chariots which came out from between two mountains, to each of which were attached four horses that were red, black, white, and grisled ; these are called spirits, and are said to have gone forth from standing before the Lord of the whole land, chap. vi. 1 to 15. And also to these in the Apocalypse : "When the Lamb opened the seals of the Book, there went forth in order horses, the first *a white horse*, the second *a red horse*, the third *a black horse*, and the fourth *a pale horse*," vi. 1 to 8. The Book whose seals the Lamb opened is the Word, and from this Word it is evident that nothing but the understanding of it could go forth ; for what else could be meant by four horses going forth from an open book?

3. But take the same expressions when applied in an opposite sense, and it will be clear that *horse* signifies the understanding of truth, and chariot doctrine ; in that opposite sense, however, a horse signifies the understanding of truth when falsified by reasonings ; and a chariot, the doctrine or heresy thence derived ; as, "Woe to them that go down to Egypt for help, and stay on *horses*, and look not unto the Holy One of Israel ; for Egypt is man and not God, and his *horses* flesh and not spirit," Isaiah xxxi. 1, 3. "Then shalt thou set him as king over Israel whom Jehovah thy God shall choose. But he shall not multiply *horses* to himself, nor bring back the people unto Egypt, to the end that he may multiply *horses*," Deuteronomy xvii. 15, 16. These expressions are used, because Egypt represents the natural man, who, by reasonings drawn from the bodily senses, perverts the truths of the Word. For what else could be meant by the horses of Egypt being flesh and not spirit, and what that the king should not multiply horses, but false doctrines of religion? "Ashur shall not save us, *we will not ride upon a horse*," Hosea xiv. 4. "Some trust in *a chariot*, and some in *horses*, but we will make our boast in the name of Jehovah our God," Psalm xx. 7. "*Horses* are a lying thing for safety," Psalm xxxiii. 17. "Thus saith the Holy One of Israel, in confidence shall be your strength ; but ye said, no ; we will flee upon *a horse*, we will ride upon the swift," Isaiah xxx. 15, 16. "Jehovah shall make the house of Judah as *a horse of glory* ; and *the riders on horses* shall be confounded," Zechariah x. 3, 5. "I will bring upon Tyre, Nebuchadnezzar king of Babylon, with *horse*, and with *chariot*, and with *horsemen* ; by reason of

the abundance of *horses*, their dust shall cover thee, thy walls shall shake at the voice of the *horsemen* and of the *chariot*; with the hoofs of his *horses* shall he tread down all thy streets," Ezekiel xxvi. 7—11. In the Word, Tyre signifies the church as to the knowledges of truth; and the king of Babylon, their falsification and profanation; and it is on this account said that he would come with horse, with chariot, and with horsemen, and that by reason of the abundance of horses their dust should cover it. "Woe to the city of blood, the whole is full of a lie; there are the neighing *horse* and the bounding *chariot*," Nahum iii. 1—4. A city of blood signifies doctrine drawn from the truths of the Word when those truths are falsified. To understand the truth of the Word when it is falsified and as truth destroyed, is also meant by *the red*, *the black*, and *the pale horses*, in the Apocalypse, vi. 4, 5, 8. Since, then, the understanding of truth is signified by a horse, and in an opposite sense the understanding of the false, it may appear from this what the Word is in its spiritual sense.

4. It is commonly known, that in Egypt there were hieroglyphics, and that they were inscribed on the columns and walls of the temples and other buildings; it is acknowledged, however, that, at this day, no one is able to determine their signification. Those hieroglyphics were no other than the correspondences between *the spiritual* and *the natural*, to which science the Egyptians more than any people in Asia applied themselves, and according to which the very early nations of Greece formed their fables; for this, and this only, was the most ancient style of composition; to which I can add the new information, that every object seen by spirits and angels in the spiritual world is a mere correspondence; and the Holy Scripture is on this account written by correspondences, that so it might be the medium of conjunction between the men of the church and the angels of heaven. But as the Egyptians, and along with them the people of the kingdoms of Asia, began to convert these correspondences into idolatry, to which the children of Israel were prone, these latter were forbidden to make any use of them. This is evident from the first commandment of the decalogue, which says, "Thou shalt not make unto thee any graven image, nor any likeness [*of any thing*] that is in the heavens above, or that is in the earth beneath, or that is in the waters under the earth. Thou shalt not bow down thyself to them, nor serve them, for I Jehovah thy God am a jealous God," Deuteronomy v. 8, 9. Besides this, there are in other parts many passages to the same purport. From that time, the science of correspondences became extinct, and successively to such an extent, that at this day it is scarcely known that the science ever existed, and that it is an object of importance. But the Lord being now about to establish a New

Church, which will have its foundation in the Word, and which church is meant by the New Jerusalem in the Apocalypse; it has pleased Him to reveal this science, and thus to disclose what the Word is in its bosom or spiritual sense. This I have done in the works entitled, Arcana Cœlestia, published at London, and Apocalypse Revealed, published at Amsterdam. As the science of correspondences was esteemed by the ancients, the science of sciences, and constituted their wisdom, it would surely be of importance for some one of your Society to devote his attention to it; and for this purpose he may begin, if it be agreeable, with the correspondences disclosed in the Apocalypse Revealed. Should it be desired, I am willing to unfold the meaning of the Egyptian hieroglyphics, which are nothing else but correspondences, these being discovered and proved from the Word, in the Apocalypse Revealed, and to publish their explication—a work which no other person could accomplish. E. S.

END OF THE APPENDIX.

NOTE.

The following paragraph is from the Advertisement prefixed to the translation of the "Appendix," published at London, 1824, *by T. Goyder.*

"The history of this little work may be given in a few words: it was originally written in Latin, and sent by the author under the title of 'An Appendix to the Treatise on the White Horse,' to the Rev. Thomas Hartley. By this gentleman a copy was sent to Dr. Messiter, a name well known to the readers of the New Doctrines. After his decease, it came into the possession of his eldest daughter, along with his other papers; and I am indebted to her kindness for the copy, from which this translation has been made."

To this it may be added, that the original edition contains the particulars of the receipt of the "Appendix" by the Rev. T. Hartley, which have likewise been printed in the New Jerusalem Magazine, August, 1840*: Boston, U. S. The Latin has never been printed. The paragraphs are numbered in the present edition for convenience of reference, but there are no numbers in the original.*

THE

EARTHS IN THE UNIVERSE.

THE

EARTHS IN THE UNIVERSE,

AND THEIR INHABITANTS;

ALSO,

THEIR SPIRITS AND ANGELS:

FROM WHAT HAS BEEN HEARD AND SEEN.

From the Latin of

EMANUEL SWEDENBORG,

Servant of the Lord Jesus Christ.

BEING A TRANSLATION OF HIS WORK ENTITLED

"DE TELLURIBUS IN MUNDO NOSTRO SOLARI, QUÆ VOCANTUR PLANETÆ: ET DE TELLURIBUS IN CŒLO ASTRIFERO: DEQUE ILLARUM INCOLIS; TUM DE SPIRITIBUS ET ANGELIS IBI: EX AUDITIS ET VISIS." LONDINI: MDCCLVIII.

NEW YORK:

AMERICAN SWEDENBORG PRINTING AND PUBLISHING SOCIETY,

CONTENTS.

ON THE

EARTHS IN THE UNIVERSE.

1. INASMUCH as, by the Divine mercy of the Lord, things interior are open to me, which appertain to my spirit, and thereby it has been granted me to discourse not only with spirits and angels who are near our earth, but also with those who are near other earths; and whereas I had a desire to know whether other earths exist, and of what sort they are, and what is the nature and quality of their inhabitants, therefore it has been granted me of the Lord to discourse and converse with spirits and angels who are from other earths, with some for a day, with some for a week, and with some for months; and to be instructed by them concerning the earths, from which and near which they were; and concerning the lives, customs, and worship of the inhabitants thereof, with various other things worthy to be noted: and whereas in this manner it has been granted me to become acquainted with such things, it is permitted to describe them according to what has been heard and seen. It is to be observed, that all spirits and angels are from the human race;[a] and that they are near their respective earths;[b] and that they are acquainted with things on those earths; and that by them man may be instructed, if his interiors be so open as to be enabled to speak and converse with them; for man in his essence is a spirit,[c] and together with spirits as to his interiors;[d] wherefore he whose interiors are opened by the Lord, may discourse with them, as man with man;[e] which privilege has been granted me now for twelve years daily.

EXTRACTS FROM THE ARCANA CŒLESTIA.

[a] That there are no spirits and angels, but what were of the human race, n. 1880.

[b] That the spirits of every earth are near to their own particular earth, because they are from the inhabitants of that earth, and of a similar genius and temper; and that they are serviceable to those inhabitants, n. 9968.

[c] That the soul, which lives after death, is the spirit of man, which is the real man in him, and also appears in another life in a perfect human form, n. 322, 1880, 1881, 3633, 4622, 4735, 6054, 6605, 6626, 7021, 10,594.

[d] That man, even during his abode in the world, as to his interiors, consequently as to his spirit or soul, is in the midst of spirits and angels, of a nature and quality agreeing to his own, n. 2378, 3645, 4067, 4073, 4077.

[e] That man is capable of discoursing with spirits and angels, and that the ancients on our earth did frequently discourse with them, n. 67, 68, 69, 784, 1634, 1636, 7802. But that at this day it is dangerous to discourse with them, unless man be in a true faith, and be led of the Lord, n. 784, 9438, 10,751.

2. That there are several earths, and men upon them, and thence spirits and angels, is a thing most perfectly well known in another life, for it is there granted to every one who desires it from a love of truth, and consequent use, to discourse with the spirits of other earths, and thereby to be confirmed concerning a plurality of worlds, and to be informed, that the human race is not confined to one earth only, but extends to earths innumerable; and moreover to know, what is the particular genius, manner of life, and also Divine worship, prevailing amongst the inhabitants of each particular earth.

3. I have occasionally discoursed on this subject with the spirits of our earth, and the result of our conversation was, that any man of an enlarged understanding may conclude, from various considerations, that there are several earths, and that they are inhabited by men; for it is a suggestion of reason, that so great material masses as the planets are, some of which far exceed this earth in magnitude, are not empty masses, and created only to be conveyed in their revolutions round the sun, and to shine with their scanty light for the benefit of one earth, but that their use must needs be more enlarged and distinguished. He who believes, as every one ought to believe, that the Deity created the universe for no other end than that mankind, and thereby heaven, might have existence, (for mankind is the seminary of heaven,) must needs believe also, that wheresoever there is any earth, there are likewise men-inhabitants. That the planets which are visible to our eyes, as being within the boundaries of this solar system, are earths, may appear manifest from this consideration, that they are bodies of earthly matter, because they reflect the light of the sun, and when seen through optical glasses, they appear, not as stars glittering by reason of their flame, but as earths variegated by reason of their opaque spots. The same may further appear from this consideration, that they, in like manner as our earth, are conveyed by a progressive motion round the sun, in the way of the zodiac, whence they have their years, and seasons of the year, as spring, summer, autumn, and winter; and in like manner, revolve about their own axis, whence they have their days, and times of the day, as morning, mid-day, evening and night. Moreover some of them have moons, which are called satellites, and which perform their revolutions round their central globes, as the moon does round our earth. The planet Saturn has besides a large luminous belt, as being furthest distant from the sun, which belt supplies that earth with much light, although reflected. How is it possible for any reasonable person, acquainted with these circumstances, to assert that such bodies are void, and without inhabitants?

4. Moreover, in my discourse with spirits, I have at such times suggested, that it is very credible that in the universe

there are more earths than one, from this consideration, that the starry heaven is so immense, and the stars therein are so innumerable, each of which in its place, or in its world, is a sun, and like our sun, in various magnitude. Every considerate person is led to conclude, that so immense a whole must needs be a means to some end, the ultimate of creation, which end is the kingdom of heaven, wherein the Divine [being or principle] may dwell with angels and men: for the visible universe, or the heaven resplendent with stars so innumerable, which are so many suns, is only a means, or medium, for the existence of earths, and of men upon them, of whom may be formed a celestial kingdom. From these considerations every reasonable person must needs be led to conceive, that so immense a means, adapted to so great an end, was not constituted for a race of men from one earth only, and for a heaven thence derived: for what would this be to the Divine [being or principle] which is infinite, and to which thousands, yea, ten thousands of earths, all full of inhabitants, are comparatively small, and scarce of any amount.

5. Moreover, the angelic heaven is so immense, that it corresponds with all and singular the things appertaining to man, myriads corresponding to every member and organ, and to all the viscera, and the respective affections of each; and it has been given to know, that that heaven, as to all its correspondences, can by no means exist, except by the inhabitants of very many earths.[f]

6. There are spirits whose sole duty is to acquire to themselves knowledges, because they are delighted only with knowledges. These spirits are permitted to wander at large, and even to pass out of this solar system into others, and to procure for themselves knowledges. They have declared, that there are not only earths inhabited by men, in this solar system, but also out of it in the starry heaven, to an immense number. These spirits are from the planet Mercury.

7. As to what in general concerns the Divine worship of the inhabitants of other earths, such amongst them as are not idolaters, all acknowledge the Lord to be the only God; for they adore the Divine [being or principle] not as invisible, but as visible, for this reason amongst others, because when the Divine [being or principle] appears to them, he appears in a

f That heaven corresponds to the Lord, and that man, as to all and singular the things appertaining to him, corresponds to heaven, and that hence heaven, before the Lord, is a man in a large effigy, and may be called the Grand Man, n. 2996, 2998, 3624—3649, 3636—3643, 3741—3745, 4625. Concerning the correspondence of man, and of all things appertaining to him, with the Grand Man, which is heaven, in general, from experience, n. 3021, 3624—3649, 3741—3751, 3883—3896, 4039—4051, 4218—4228. 4318—4331, 4403—4421, 4527—4533, 4622—4633, 4652—4660, 4791—4805, 4931—4953, 5050—5061, 5171—5189, 5377—5396, 5552—5573 57 1—5727, 10,030.

human form, as he also formerly appeared to Abraham and others on this earth;[g] and they who adore the Divine [being or principle] under a Human Form are all accepted of the Lord.[h] They say also, that no one can rightly worship God, much less be joined to Him, unless he comprehends Him by some idea, and that God cannot be comprehended except in a Human Form; and if He be not so comprehended, the interior sight, which is of the thought, concerning God, is dissipated, as the sight of the eye is, when looking upon the boundless universe; and that in this case the thought must needs sink into nature, and worship nature instead of God.

8. When they were told that the Lord on our earth assumed the human [nature,] they mused awhile, and presently said, that it was done for the salvation of the human race.

OF THE EARTH OR PLANET MERCURY, ITS SPIRITS AND INHABITANTS.

9. THAT the universal heaven resembles one man, who is therefore called the GRAND MAN, and that all and singular the things appertaining to man, both his exteriors and interiors, correspond to that man or heaven, is an arcanum not as yet known in the world; but that it is so, has been abundantly proved.[f] To constitute that Grand Man, there is need of spirits from several earths, those who come from our earth into heaven not being sufficient for this purpose, being respectively few; and it is provided of the Lord, that whensoever there is a deficiency in any place as to the quality or quantity of correspondence, a supply be instantly made from another earth, to fill up the deficiency, that so the proportion may be preserved, and thus heaven be kept in due consistence.

10. It was also discovered to me from heaven, in what relation to the Grand Man the spirits from the planet Mercury stand, viz., that they have relation to the memory, but to the memory of things abstracted from terrestrial and merely material objects. Since however it has been granted to discourse with them, and this during several weeks, and to learn their nature and quality, and to observe how the inhabitants of that earth are particularly circumstanced, I shall adduce what has been thus experimentally made known to me.

11. On a time some spirits came to me, and it was declared

[g] That the inhabitants of all the earths adore the Divine [being or principle] under a Human Form, consequently the Lord, n. 8541—8547, 10,159, 10,736, 10,737, 10,738. And that they rejoice when they hear that God was actually made Man, n. 9361. That it is impossible to think of God except in a Human Form, n. 8705, 9359, 9972. That man may worship and love what he has some idea of, but not what he has no idea of, n. 4733, 5110, 5633, 7211, 9267, 10,067.

[h] That the Lord receives all who are principled in good, and who adore the Divine [being or principle] under a Human Form, n. 9359, 7173.

from heaven, that they were from the earth which is nearest to the sun, and which in our earth is known by the name of the planet Mercury. Immediately on their coming, they explored my memory in search of all that I knew: (spirits can do this most dexterously, for when they come to man, they see in his memory all things contained therein).[i] During their search after various things, and amongst others, after the cities and places where I had been, I observed that they had no inclination to know any thing of temples, palaces, houses, or streets, but only of those things which I knew were transacted in those places, also of whatever related to the rule and government therein prevailing, and to the tempers and manners of the inhabitants, with other things of a similar nature: for such things cohere with places in man's memory; wherefore when the places are excited in remembrance, those things also are brought to view at the same time. I was much surprised to find them of such a nature and quality; wherefore I asked them, why they disregarded the magnificence of the places, and only attended to the things and circumstances connected therewith. They answered, because they had no delight in looking at things material, corporeal, and terrestrial, but only at things real: hence it was confirmed, that the spirits of that earth, in the Grand Man, have relation to the memory of things abstracted from what is material and terrestrial.

12. It was told me, that such is the life of the inhabitants of that earth, viz. that they have no concern about things terrestrial and material, but only about the statutes, laws, and forms of government, which prevail among the nations therein; also about the things of heaven, which are innumerable: and I was further informed, that several of the men of that earth converse with spirits, and that thence they have the knowledges of spiritual things, and of the states of life after death; and thence also their contempt of things corporeal and terrestrial; for they who know of a certainty, and believe, that they shall live after death, are concerned about heavenly things, as being eternal and happy, but not about worldly things, only so far as the necessities of life require. Inasmuch as the inhabitants of the planet Mercury are of such a nature and quality, therefore also the spirits who are from thence are of a like nature and quality.[i]

13. With what eagerness they inquire into and imbibe the knowledges of things, such as appertain to the memory elevated above the sensualities of the body, was made manifest to me from this circumstance, that when they looked into those things

[i] That spirits enter into all the things of man's memory, n. 2488, 5863, 6192, 6193, 6198, 6199, 6214. That angels enter into the affections and ends, from which and for the sake of which man thinks, wills, and acts in such and such a manner, in preference to every other, n 1317, 1645, 5844.

which I knew respecting heavenly subjects, they passed hastily through them all, declaring every instant the nature and quality of each: for when spirits come to man, they enter into all his memory, and excite thence whatever suits themselves: yea, what I have often observed, they read the things contained therein, as out of a book.[k] These spirits did this with greater dexterity and expedition, because they did not stop at such things as are heavy and sluggish, and which confine and consequently retard the internal sight, as all terrestrial and corporeal things do, when regarded as ends, that is, when alone loved: but they looked into things essential: for such things, which are not clogged with things terrestrial, elevate the mind upwards, whereas mere material things sink the mind downwards, and at the same time contract and shut it up. Their eagerness to acquire knowledges, and to enrich the memory, was manifest also from the following circumstance: on a time whilst I was writing somewhat concerning things to come, and they were at a distance, so that they could not look into those things from my memory, because I was not willing to read them in their presence, they were very indignant, and contrary to their usual behaviour, they were desirous to abuse me, saying that I was one of the worst of men, with such like indignities; and that they might give proof of their resentment, they caused a kind of contraction attended with pain on the right side of my head even to the ear; but these things did not hurt me: nevertheless, in consequence of having done evil, they removed themselves to a yet greater distance, but presently they stood still again, desirous to know what I had written: such is their eager thirst after knowledges.

14. The spirits of Mercury, above all other spirits, possess the knowledges of things, as well respecting this solar system, as respecting the earths which are in the starry heaven; and what they have once acquired to themselves, that they retain, and also recollect it as often as anything similar occurs. Hence also it may appear manifest, that spirits have memory, and that it is much more perfect than the memory of men; and further, that what they hear, see, and perceive, they retain, and especially such things as delight them, as these spirits are delighted with knowledges; for whatever things cause delight, and affect the love, these flow in as it were spontaneously, and remain; other things do not enter, but only touch the surface and pass by.

15. When the spirits of Mercury come to other societies, they explore and collect from them what they know, and then they depart; for such communication is granted amongst spirits and especially amongst angels, that when they are in a society,

[k] That the spirits who are attendant on man, are in possession of all things appertaining to his memory, n. 5853, 5857, 5859, 5860.

if they are accepted and loved, all things which they know are communicated.[1]

16. In consequence of their knowledges, the spirits of Mercury have an extraordinary degree of haughtiness; wherefore they are given to understand, that although they know innumerable things, yet there are infinite things which they do not know; and that if their knowledges should increase to eternity, the notice even of all general or common things would still be unattainable. They are told likewise of their haughtiness and high-mindedness, and how unbecoming such a temper is; but on such occasions they reply, that it is not haughtiness, but only a glorying by reason of the faculty of their memory; thus they have the art of exculpating themselves, and excusing their foibles.

17. They are averse to discourse consisting of vocal expressions, because it is material; wherefore when I conversed with them without intermediate spirits, I could only do it by a species of active thought. Their memory, as consisting of things not of images purely material, affords a nearer supply of its objects to the thinking principle; for the thinking principle, which is above the imagination, requires for its objects things abstracted from material. But notwithstanding this, the spirits of Mercury are little distinguished for their judgment, having no delight in the exercise of that faculty, and the deducing of conclusions from knowledges; for bare knowledges alone are the things which give them pleasure.

18. They were questioned, whether they proposed to themselves any use from their knowledges; and at the same time it was represented to them, that it is not enough to be delighted with knowledges, because knowledges have respect to uses, and uses ought to be the ends of knowledges; from knowledges alone no use results to them, but to others with whom they are disposed to communicate their knowledges; and that it is very inexpedient for any one, who wishes to become wise, to rest satisfied with mere knowledges, these being only administering causes, intended to be subservient to the investigation of things appertaining to life: but they replied, that they were delighted with knowledges, and that knowledges to them are uses.

19. Some of them are also unwilling to appear as men, like the spirits of other earths, and would rather appear as crystalline globes; the reason why they are desirous to appear so, although they do not appear so, is, because the knowledges of things immaterial are represented in another life by crystals.

20. The spirits of Mercury differ totally from the spirits of

[1] That in the heavens there is given a communication of all good things, inasmuch as it is the property of heavenly love to communicate all its possessions with others; and that hence the angels derive wisdom and happiness, n. 549, 550, 1390, 1391, 1399, 10,130, 10,723.

our earth, for the spirits of our earth have not so much concern about immaterial things, but about worldly, corporeal, and terrestrial things, which are material; wherefore the spirits of Mercury cannot abide together with the spirits of our earth, and of consequence, wheresoever they meet them, they fly away: for the spiritual spheres, which are exhaled from each, are altogether contrary the one to the other. The spirits of Mercury have a common saying, that they have no inclination to look at a sheath, but at things stripped of their sheath, that is, at interior things.

21. On a time there appeared a whitish colored flame, which burnt briskly, and this for nearly an hour. That flame signified the approach of spirits of Mercury, who for penetration, thought, and speech, were more prompt than the former spirits. When they were come, they instantly ran through the things contained in my memory, but I could not perceive what observations they made, by reason of their promptitude. I heard them afterwards express the nature and quality of some particulars; in respect to what I had seen in the heavens and in the world of spirits, they said that they knew those things before. I perceived that a multitude of spirits consociated with them was behind, a little to the left in the plane of the *occiput*.

22. At another time I saw a multitude of such spirits, but at some distance from me, in front a little to the right, and thence they discoursed with me, but by means of intermediate spirits; for their speech was as quick as thought, which does not fall into human speech, but by means of other spirits; and what surprised me, they spake not singly, but in a volume together [*volumatim*], and yet readily and rapidly. Their speech appeared undulatory, in consequence of the numbers who spake at the same time, and what is remarkable, it was conveyed towards my left eye, although they were to the right. The reason was, because the left eye corresponds to the knowledges of things abstracted from what is material, consequently to such things as appertain to intelligence: whereas the right eye corresponds to such things as appertain to wisdom.[m] They likewise perceived and judged of what they heard with the same promptitude with which they discoursed, saying of such a thing that it was so, and of such a thing that it was not so; their judgment was as it were instantaneous.

23. There was a spirit from another earth, who was well qualified to discourse with them, being a quick and ready speaker, but

[m] That the eye corresponds to the understanding, because the understanding is internal sight, and the sight of things immaterial, n. 2701, 4410, 4526, 9051, 10,569. That the sight of the left eye corresponds to truths, consequently to intelligence; and the sight of the right eye corresponds to the goods of truth, consequently to wisdom, n. 4410.

who affected elegance in his discourse. They instantly decided on whatever he spake, saying of this, that it was too elegant; of that, that it was too polished: so that the sole thing they attended to was, whether they could hear anything from him which they had never known before, rejecting thus the things which were as shades to the substance of the discourse, as all affectations of elegance and erudition especially are; for these hide real things, and instead thereof present expressions, which are only material forms of things; for the speaker keeps the attention fixed herein, and is desirous that his expressions should be regarded more than the meaning of them, whereby the ears are more affected than the minds of the audience.

24. The spirits of the earth Mercury do not abide long in one place, or within companies of the spirits of one world, but wander through the universe. The reason is, because they have relation to the memory of things, which memory must be continually stored with fresh supplies; hence it is granted them to wander about, and to acquire to themselves knowledges in every place. During their sojourning in this manner, if they meet with spirits who love material things, that is, things corporeal and terrestrial, they avoid their company, and betake themselves where such things are no subjects of discourse. Hence it may appear, that their mind is elevated above things of sense, and thus that they are in an interior luminous principle. This was also given me actually to perceive, whilst they were near me, and discoursed with me: I observed at such times, that I was withdrawn from things of sense, insomuch that the luminous principle of external vision began to grow dull and obscure.

25. The spirits of that earth go in companies and phalanxes, and when assembled together, they form as it were a globe; thus they are joined together by the Lord, that they may act in unity, and that the knowledges of each may be communicated with all, and the knowledges of all with each, as is the case in heaven.[1] That they wander through the universe to acquire the knowledges of things, appeared to me also from this circumstance, that once, when they appeared very remote from me, they discoursed with me thence, and said, that they were then gathered together, and journeying out of the sphere of this world into the starry heaven, where they knew such spirits existed as had no concern about terrestrial and corporeal things, but only about things elevated above them, and that they were desirous to associate with those spirits. It was given to understand, that they themselves do not know whither they are journeying, but that they are led by the Divine guidance to those places where they may be instructed concerning such things as they are yet unacquainted with, and which agree with the knowledges that they have already. It was given to understand further, that they do not know how to find the companies

with whom they are joined together, and that this also is of Divine direction.

26. In consequence of their thus journeying through the universe, and thereby being enabled to know more than others respecting the worlds and earths out of the sphere of our solar system, I have also discoursed with them on this subject. They said that in the universe there are very many earths inhabited by men; and that they wonder how any should suppose (whom they called men of little judgment), that the heaven of the Omnipotent God consisted only of spirits and angels who come from one earth, when these comparatively are so few, that in respect of the Omnipotence of God they are scarce anything, nor would it alter the case even supposing there were myriads of worlds, and myriads of earths. They declared moreover, that they knew there were earths existing in the universe to the number of some hundred thousands and upwards; and yet what is this to the Divine [being or principle] who is Infinite?

27. The spirits of Mercury, who were attendant upon me whilst I was writing and explaining the Word as to its internal sense, and who perceived what I wrote, said that the things which I wrote were very gross [*admodum crassa*] and that almost all the expressions appeared as material; but it was given to reply, that to the men of our earth what was written seemed subtle and elevated, and many things incomprehensible. I added, that several on this earth do not know that it is the internal man which acts on the external, and causes the external to live; and that they persuade themselves from the fallacies of the senses that the body has life, and that in consequence thereof, such as are wicked and unbelieving entertain doubts respecting a life after death; also, that the [part or principle] of man which is to live after death is not by them called spirit, but soul; and that they dispute what soul is, and where is its abode, and believe that the material body, although dispersed throughout the atmosphere, is to be joined again to it, in order that man may live as man; with many other things of a like nature. The spirits of Mercury, on hearing these things, asked, whether such men could become angels; and it was given to answer, that those become angels who have lived in the good of faith and charity, and that then they are no longer in external and material things, but in internal and spiritual; and when they come into that state, that they are in a light superior to that in which the spirits from Mercury are. To convince them that it was so, an angel was allowed to discourse with them, who had come into heaven from our earth, having lived in the good of faith and charity, concerning whom more will be said presently.

28. On another occasion, there was sent me by the spirits of Mercury a long piece of paper, of an irregular shape, con-

sisting of several pieces pasted together, which appeared as if covered with print, like our printed books. I asked whether they had the art of printing amongst them; but they said they had not, nevertheless they knew that on our earth we had such printed papers. They had no inclination to say more; but I perceived that they thought that knowledges with us were upon our paper, and not so much in our understandings, thus in a sneering way insinuating, that our papers knew more than we ourselves did; they were instructed, however, how the real case was in this respect. After some time they returned, and sent me another paper, which appeared also printed like the former, but not so pasted together and irregular, but neat and handsome. They said, that they were further informed, that in our earth there are such papers, and books made of them.

29. From the above account it appears manifest, that spirits retain in the memory what they see and hear in another life, and that they are capable of being instructed alike as when they were men in the world, consequently of being instructed in things appertaining to faith, and thereby of being perfected. In proportion as spirits and angels are of a more interior character and quality, in the same proportion they receive instruction more readily, and in a greater fulness, and retain it more perfectly: and inasmuch as this faculty abides forever, it is evident that they are continually advancing in wisdom. With the spirits of Mercury there is a constant growth in the science of things, but not in wisdom thence derived, because they love knowledges, which are means, but not uses which are ends.

30. The particular genius and character of the spirits who are from the planet Mercury, may still further appear from the following account. It is to be observed, that all spirits and angels whatsoever were once men; for the human race is the seminary of heaven; also that the spirits are altogether such, as to affections and inclinations, as they were during their life in the world whilst men; for every one's life follows him into another world.[n] This being the case, the genius and character of the men of every earth may be known from the genius and character of the spirits who come from thence.

31. Inasmuch as the spirits of Mercury in the Grand Man have relation to the memory of things abstracted from what is material, therefore when any one discourses with them concerning things terrestrial, corporeal, and merely worldly, they are altogether unwilling to hear him; and if they are forced to hear, they transmute the things spoken of into other things, and

[n] That every one's life remains with him and follows him after death, n. 4227, 7440. That the externals of life are kept closed after death, and the internals opened, n. 4314, 5128, 6495. That then all and singular the things of thought are made manifest, n. 4633, 5128.

for the most part into things contrary, that they may avoid attending to them.

32. That I might be fully convinced of this their particular genius and character, it was allowed to represent to them meadows, fallow lands, gardens, woods, and rivers (to represent such things is imaginatively to exhibit them before another, in which case, in another world, they appear to the life); but they instantly transmuted them, obscuring the meadows and fallow fields, and by representations filling them with snakes. The rivers they made black, so that the water no longer appeared limpid. When I asked them why they did so, they said that they had no inclination to think of such things, but of things real, which are the knowledges of things abstracted from what is terrestrial, especially of such things as exist in the heavens.

33. Afterwards I represented to them birds of different sizes, both large and small, such as exist on our earth; for in another life such things may be represented to the life. When they saw the birds represented, they were disposed at first to change them, but afterwards they were delighted with them and seemed satisfied; the reason was, because birds signify the knowledges of things, and the perception of this signification flowed in also at that instant;[o] thus they desisted from transmuting them, and thereby from averting the ideas of their memory. Afterwards it was allowed to represent before them a most pleasant garden full of lamps and lights; instantly they paused, and their attention was fixed, by reason that lamps with lights signify truths which are lucid by virtue of good.[p] Hence it was made manifest that their attention might be fixed in viewing things material, if the signification of those things in a spiritual sense was but insinuated at the same time; for the things appertaining to such spiritual sense are not so abstracted from things material, being representative thereof.

34. Morever I discoursed with them concerning sheep and lambs, but they were not disposed to hear of such things, because they were perceived by them as things terrestrial. The reason was, because they did not understand what innocence is, which lambs signify, as was perceivable from this circumstance, that when I told them that lambs, represented in heaven, signify innocence,[q] they immediately said that they did not know what innocence was, but only knew it as to the name; and this was, because they are affected only with knowledges,

o That birds signify things rational, things intellectual, thoughts, ideas, and knowledges, n. 40, 745, 776, 778, 866, 988, 993, 5149, 7441. And this with a variety according to the genera and species of birds, n. 3219.

p That lamps with lights signify truths which are lucid by virtue of good, n. 4638, 9548, 9783.

q That lambs in heaven, and in the Word, signify innocence, n. 3994, 7840, 10,132.

and not with uses, which are the ends of knowledges, consequently they cannot know, from internal perception, what innocence is.

35. Some of the spirits of the earth Mercury on a time came to me, being sent by others, with intent to learn what I was employed about, to whom one of the spirits of our earth said, that they might tell those who sent them not to speak any thing but what was true, and not, according to their usual practice, suggest things opposite to what they are questioned about; for if any of the spirits of our earth were to do so, they would be chastised for it. But immediately the company which was at a distance, from which those spirits were sent, made answer, that if they must be chastised on that account, they must all be chastised, inasmuch as by reason of acquired habit they could not do otherwise. They added, that when they discourse with the men of their own earth, they also do so, but this not with any intention of deceiving, but to inspire a desire of knowledge; for when they suggest things opposite, and conceal things in a certain manner, then a desire of knowledge is excited, and thereby from an earnestness to search out and discover those things, the memory is perfected. I also discoursed with them at another time on the same subject, and because I knew that they conversed with the men of their earth, I asked them in what manner they instruct their inhabitants. They said that they do not instruct them as to all particulars in relation to the subject matter of instruction, but still insinuate some perception thereof, that thus a desire of examining and acquiring the knowledge of it may be excited and cherished; which desire would die away, in case they fully explained all particulars. They added, that they suggest objections of things opposite also, for this reason, that the truth afterwards may appear more striking; for all truth is made manifest by relation to its opposites.

36. It is their constant custom not to declare to another what they know, but still they desire to learn from all others what is known to them: nevertheless, with their own society they communicate all things, insomuch that what one knows all know, and what all know each one knows in that society.[1]

37. Inasmuch as the spirits of Mercury abound with knowledges, they are principled in a species of haughtiness; hence they imagine that they know so much, that it is almost impossible to know more. But it has been told them by the spirits of our earth, that their knowledge is not so extensive as they imagine, but comparatively scanty, and that the things which they do not know are infinite in respect to what they do know, and as the waters of the largest ocean compared with the waters of a very small fountain; and further, that the first step in the ladder of wisdom is to know, acknowledge, and perceive that

what is known is little and scarce anything in comparison with what is unknown. To convince them that this is the case, it was granted, that a certain angelic spirit should discourse with them, and should tell them in general what they knew, and what they did not know, and that there were infinite things which they did not know, also that eternity would not suffice for their acquiring even a general knowledge of things: he discoursed by angelic ideas much more readily than they did, and because he discovered to them what they knew, and what they did not know, they were struck with amazement. Afterwards I saw another angel discoursing with them; he appeared in some altitude to the right; he was from our earth, and enumerated very many things which they did not know; afterwards he discoursed with them by changes of state, which they said they did not understand; then he told them that every change of state contains infinite things, as did also every smallest part of such change. When they heard these things, inasmuch as they had been puffed up with self-conceit by reason of their knowledges, they began to humble themselves: their humiliation was represented by the sinking downwards of their volume [*voluminis*]; (for that company then appeared as a volume, in front at a distance towards the left, in the plane of the region below the navel,) but the volume appeared as it were hollowed in the middle, and elevated on the sides; a reciprocal moving was also observed therein. They were likewise given to understand what that signified, viz. what they thought in their humiliation, and that they who appeared elevated on the sides were not as yet in any humilation. Then I saw that the volume was separated, and that they who were not in humiliation were remanded back towards their orb, the rest remaining where they were.

38. On a time the spirits of Mercury came to a certain spirit from our earth who, during his abode in the world, had been most distinguished for his great learning, (it was Christian Wolf,) desiring to receive information from him on various subjects; but when they perceived that what he said was not elevated above the sensual things of the natural man, inasmuch as in his discourse his thoughts were intent on fame and honorary distinction, and he was desirous, as in the world, (for in another life every one is like his former self,) to connect various things into series, and from those series again and continually to form other conclusions, and thus to construct a chain of several consequences and deductions grounded therein, which they did not see or acknowledge to be true, and which therefore they declared to be chains which neither cohered in themselves, nor with the conclusions, calling them obscurity grounded in authority [*obscurum auctoritatis*]; they then desisted from asking him further questions, inquiring only, *how this is called, and how that;* and whereas he answered these inquiries also

by material ideas, and by no spiritual ones, they retired from him; for every one, in another life, discourses spiritually, or by spiritual ideas, only so far as he had believed on God during his abode in the world, and materially, so far as he had not believed on God. An occasion here offering itself, it may be expedient to mention how it fares in another life with the learned who imbibe intelligence from their own meditation, kindled with the love of knowing truths, for the sake of truths, thus for the sake of uses abstracted from worldly considerations, and how with those who imbibe intelligence from others, without any meditation of their own, as is the common case with such as desire to know truths solely for reputation's sake, that they may be accounted learned, and thereby attain worldly honor or gain, thus who desire to know truth, not for the sake of uses abstracted from worldly considerations: concerning such, it is allowed to relate the following experience. There was perceived on a time somewhat noisy, or sonorous [*sonorum quoddam,*] penetrating from beneath, near the left side even to the left ear. I observed that they were spirits, who there attempted to force a way; but of what sort they were I could not know. However, when they had forced a way, they spake with me, saying that they were logicians and metaphysicians, and that they had immersed their thoughts in the sciences of logic and metaphysics, with no other end than to acquire the character of being learned, and thus to be advanced to honor and emolument, lamenting that they now led a miserable life in consequence of applying to those sciences with no other end, and thus not having cultivated thereby their rational principle; their speech was slow, and of a mute tone [*mute sonans.*]. In the mean time there were two discoursing with each other above my head, and on inquiring who they were, it was said that one of them was a most distinguished character in the learned world, and it was given me to believe that it was Aristotle. Who the other was, remained untold. The former was then let into the state in which he was during his life in the world; for every one may easily be let into the state of his life which he had in the world, inasmuch as he has with him every state of his former life: but, what surprised me, he applied himself to the right ear, and there spake, but in a hoarse tone of voice, yet with sound sense. From the purport of his discourse I perceived, that he was altogether of a different genius and temper from those schoolmen who first ascended, in that he wrote from a ground of thought and discernment in himself, and thence produced his philosophical discoveries: so that the terms which he invented, and which he imposed on speculative subjects, were forms of expression by which he described interior things; also that he was excited to such pursuits by a delight of the affection, and by a desire of knowing the things appertaining to the thinking and intellectual faculties, and that he followed obedientlywhatever his spirit had dictated; wherefore he applied himself to the right ear, contrary to the custom of his followers, who are called schoolmen, and who do not go from thought to terms, but from-terms to thoughts, thus in a contrary way; and several of them do not even proceed to thoughts, but stick solely in terms, which if they apply, it is to confirm whatever they desire, and to impose on false principles an appearance of truth according to their eagerness to persuade others. Hence philosophical investigations lead them rather to folly than to wisdom; and hence they have darkness instead of light. Afterwards I discoursed with him concerning the analytic science, observing, that a child, in half an hour's conversation, speaks more philosophically, analytically, and logically, than would be in his power to describe by a volume, inasmuch as all things appertaining to thought, and to human speech thence derived, are analytical, the laws whereof are from the spiritual world; and he who desires to think artificially from terms, is not unlike a dancer, who would learn to dance by the science of the moving fibres and muscles, in which science, if he should fix his mind whilst he is dancing, it would be almost impossible for him to move a foot; and yet without that science, he moves all the moving fibres throughout the whole body, and in subordination thereto he moves the lungs, the diaphragm, the sides, the arms, the neck, and other organs of the body, to describe all which would require many volumes; and the case is exactly similar with those who are desirous to think from terms. He approved of these observations, and said, that to learn to think in that way is proceeding in an inverted order: adding if any one will be so silly, let him so proceed; but let the thoughts be grounded in use, and flow from an interior principle. He next showed me, what idea he had conceived of the Supreme Deity, viz. that he had represented Him to his mind as having a human face, and encompassed about the head with a radiant circle; and that now he knew that the Lord is Himself that Man, and, that the radiant circle is the Divine principle proceeding from Him, which not only flows into heaven, but also into the universe, disposing and ruling all things therein. He added, Whosoever disposes and rules heaven, he also disposes and rules the universe, because the one cannot be separated from the other: he also said that he believed only in one God, whose attributes and qualities were distinguished by a variety of names, and that these names were by others worshiped as so many gods. There appeared to me a woman, who stretched out her hand, desiring to stroke my cheek, at which, when I expressed my surprise, he said that whilst he was in the world such a woman had often appeared to him, as it were stroking his cheek, and that her hand was beautiful. The angelic spirits said that such women sometimes appeared to the ancients, and were by them called Pallases, and that she appeared to him from the spirits, who, during their abode on earth, in ancient times, were delighted with ideas, and indulged in thoughts, but without philosophy: and whereas such spirits were attendant upon him, and were delighted with him, because he thought from an interior principle, therefore they representatively exhibited such a woman to his view. Lastly, he informed me what idea he had conceived of the soul or spirit of man, which he called Pneuma, viz. that it was an invisible vital principle, like somewhat of ether; and he said that he knew that his spirit would live after death, inasmuch as it was his interior essence, which cannot die, because it is capable of thinking; and that moreover he was not able to think clearly concerning it, but only obscurely, because he had not formed any thought about it from any other source but that of his own mind, and a little also from the ancients. It is to be noted that Aristotle is amongst sound and sober spirits in another life, and that several of his followers are amongst the infatuated.

39. On a time I saw that spirits of our earth were with spirits of the earth Mercury, and I heard them discoursing together, and the spirits of our earth, amongst other things, asked them on whom they believed. They replied that they believed on God; but when they inquired further concerning the God on whom they believed, they would give no answer, it being customary with them not to answer questions directly. Then the spirits from the earth Mercury, in their turn, asked the spirits from our earth on whom they believed. They said that they believed on the Lord God. The spirits of Mercury then said that they perceived that they believed on no God, and that they had contracted a habit of professing with the mouth that they believe, when yet they do not believe. (The spirits of Mercury have exquisite perception, in consequence of their continually exploring, by means of perception, what others know.) The spirits of our earth were of the number of those who in the world had made profession of faith agreeable to the doctrine of the church, but still had not lived the life of faith; and they who do not live the life of faith, in another life have not faith, because it is not in the man.[r] On hearing this they were silent, inasmuch as, by a perception then given them, they acknowledged that it was so.

40. There were certain spirits who knew from heaven, that on a time a promise was made to the spirits of the earth Mercury, that they should see the Lord; wherefore they were asked

[r] That they who make profession of faith agreeable to doctrine, and do not live the life of faith, have no faith, n. 3865, 7766, 7778, 7790, 7950, 8094. And that their interiors are contrary to the truths of faith, although in the world they do not know this, n. 7790, 7950.

by the spirits about me whether they recollected that promise. They said that they did recollect it; but that they did not know whether the promise was of such a nature as that they might depend with certainty on its accomplishment. Whilst they were thus discoursing together, instantly the Sun of heaven appeared to them. (The Sun of heaven, which is the Lord, is seen only by those who are in the inmost or third heaven; others see the light thence derived.) On seeing the Sun, they said that this was not the Lord God, because they did not see a face. In the mean while the spirits discoursed with each other, but I did not hear what they said. But on a sudden, at that instant, the Sun again appeared, and in the midst thereof the Lord, encompassed with a solar circle: on seeing this, the spirits of Mercury humbled themselves profoundly, and subsided. Then also the Lord, from that sun, appeared to the spirits of this earth, who, when they were men, saw Him in the world; and they all, one after another, and thus several in order, confessed that it was the Lord Himself. This confession they made before all the company. At the same instant also the Lord, out of the Sun, appeared to the spirits of the planet Jupiter, who declared with open voice that it was He Himself whom they had seen on their earth when the God of the universe appeared to them.[s]

41. Certain of them, after that the Lord appeared, were led off frontwards to the right, and as they advanced, they said that they saw a light much clearer and purer than they had ever seen before, and that it was impossible any light could exceed it; and it was then even-tide here. There were several who made this declaration.[t]

42. It is to be observed that the sun of this world does not appear at all to any spirit, nor anything of light thence derived. The light of that sun is as thick darkness to spirits and angels. That sun remains only in the perception appertaining to spirits from having seen it during their abode in the world, and is presented to them in idea as somewhat darkish, and this behind at

[s] That the Lord is the Sun of heaven, from whom all light therein is derived, n. 1053, 3636. 4060. And that the Lord thus appears to those who are in His celestial kingdom, where love to Him is prevalent, n. 1521, 1529, 1530, 1531, 1837, 4696. That He appears at a middle distance above the plane of the right eye, n. 4321, 7078. That therefore by sun in the Word is signified the Lord as to Divine Love, n. 2495, 4060, 7083. That the sun of this world does not appear to spirits and angels, but in the place thereof there appears somewhat as it were darkish, not in front, but behind, in a direction opposite to the Sun of heaven, or to the Lord, n. 9755.

[t] That there is in the heavens great light, which exceeds, by many degrees, the mid-day light of this world, n. 1117, 1521, 1533, 1619—1632, 4527, 5400, 8644. That all light in the heavens is from the Lord as a Sun there, n. 1053, 1521, 3195, 3341, 3636, 3643, 4415, 9548, 9684, 10,809. That the Divine Truth proceeding from the Divine Good of the Divine Love of the Lord appears in the heavens as light, and presents all the light that is therein, n. 3195, 3222, 5400, 8644, 9399, 9548, 9684. That the light of heaven illuminates both the sight and the understanding of the angels, n. 2776, 3138. That when heaven is said to be in light and heat, it signifies being in wisdom and in love, n. 3643, 9399, 9401.

a considerable distance, in an altitude a little above the plane of the head. The planets which are within the system of that sun appear according to a determinate situation in respect to the sun; Mercury behind, a little towards the right; Venus to the left, a little backwards; Mars to the left in front; Jupiter in like manner to the left in front, but at a greater distance; Saturn directly in front, at a considerable distance; the Moon to the left, at a considerable height: the satellites also to the left in respect to their particular planet. Such is the situation of the above planets in the ideas of spirits and angels: spirits also appear near their respective planets, but out of them. As to what particularly concerns the spirits of Mercury, they do not appear in any certain determinate quarter, or at any certain determinate distance, but sometimes in front, sometimes to the left, sometimes a little to the back; the reason is, because they are allowed to wander through the universe to procure for themselves knowledges.

43. On a time the spirits of Mercury appeared to the left in a globe, and afterwards in a volume extending itself lengthways. I wondered whither they were desirous of going, whether to this earth or elsewhere; and presently I observed that they inclined to the right, and as they rolled along, approached to the earth or planet Venus towards the quarter in front. But when they came thither they said that they would not abide there, because the inhabitants were wicked; wherefore they turned about to the back part of that earth, and then said that they would willingly stay there, because the inhabitants were good. Immediately on this, I was made sensible of a remarkable change in the brain, and of a powerful operation thence proceeding. Hence I was led to conclude that the spirits of Venus, who were on that part of the planet, were in concord with the spirits of Mercury, and that they had relation to the memory of things material which was in concord with the memory of things immaterial, to which latter memory the spirits of Mercury have relation: hence a more powerful operation was felt from them when they were there.

44. I was desirous to know what kind of face and body the men in the earth Mercury had, whether they were like the men on our earth. Instantly there was presented before my eyes a woman exactly resembling the women in that earth. She had a beautiful face, but it was smaller than that of a woman of our earth; her body also was more slender, but her height was equal; she wore on her head a linen cap, which was put on without art, but yet in a manner becoming. A man also was presented to view, who was more slender in body than the men of our earth are. He was clad in a garment of dark blue color, closely fitted to his body, without any foldings or protuberances. It was given me to understand that such was the form of

body and such the dress of the men of that earth. Afterwards there was presented to view a species of their oxen and cows, which indeed did not differ much from those on our earth, only that they were less, and in some degree approached to a species of deer.

45. They were questioned also concerning the sun of the system, how it appears from their earth. They said that it appears large, and larger there than when seen from other earths, and that they knew this from the ideas of other spirits concerning the sun. They said further that they enjoy a middle temperature, neither too hot nor too cold. It was on this occasion granted me to tell them, that it was so provided of the Lord in regard to them that they should not be exposed to too much heat by reason of their greater nearness to the sun, inasmuch as heat does not arise from the sun's nearness, but from the altitude and density of the atmosphere, as appears from the cold on high mountains even in hot climates; also, that heat is varied according to the direct or oblique incidence of the sun's rays, as is plain from the seasons of winter and summer in every region. These are the things which it was given me to know concerning the spirits and inhabitants of the earth Mercury.

OF THE EARTH OR PLANET JUPITER, ITS SPIRITS AND INHABITANTS.

46. It was granted me to enjoy longer intercourse with the spirits and angels of the planet Jupiter, than with the spirits and angels from the rest of the planets; wherefore I am at liberty to be more particular in regard to the state of life of them, and of the inhabitants of that planet. That those spirits were from that planet was evident from many circumstances, and was also confirmed by a declaration from heaven.

47. The real earth or planet Jupiter does not indeed appear to spirits and angels: for to the inhabitants of the spiritual world no material earth is visible, but only the spirits and angels who come thence. They who are from the planet Jupiter appear in front to the left, at a considerable distance, and this constantly (see above, n. 42); there also is the planet. The spirits of every earth are near their respective earth in consequence of having been inhabitants thereof (for every man after death becomes a spirit), and in consequence of being thus of a similar genius and temper with the inhabitants, and of being in a capacity thereby of associating with and serving them.

48. The spirits from the earth Jupiter related that the multitude of men therein was as great as the earth could sup-

port; that the earth was fruitful and plentiful in all productions; that the inhabitants had no desires beyond the necessaries of life; that they accounted nothing useful but so far as it was necessary; and that hence the number of inhabitants was so great. They said that the education of their children was their greatest concern, and that they loved them most tenderly.

49. They further related that the inhabitants are distinguished into nations, families, and houses, and that they all live apart with their own kindred, and that hence their connections are confined to relatives; likewise, that no one covets another's property, and that it never enters into their minds to desire the possessions of another, still less to obtain them fraudulently, and least of all to extort them by violence. Such violence they consider as a criminal act contrary to human nature, and regard it as horrible. When I would have told them that on this earth there are wars, depredations, and murders, they instantly turned away from me, and expressed an aversion to hear. It was declared to me by the angels that the most ancient people on this earth lived in like manner as the inhabitants of the planet Jupiter, viz. that they were distinguished into nations, families, and houses; that all at that time were content with their own possessions; that it was a thing altogether unknown for one person to enrich himself at the expense of another, or to aspire at dominion from a principle of self-love; and that on this account the ancient times, and especially the most ancient, were more acceptable to the Lord than succeeding times: and such being the state of the world, innocence also then reigned, attended with wisdom; every one did what was good from a principle of good, and what was just from a principle of justice. To do what is good and just with a view to self-advancement, or for the sake of gain, was a thing unknown. At the same time they spake nothing but what was true, and this not so much from a principle of truth as from a principle of good, that is, not from an intellectual principle separate from the will principle, but from a will principle joined with the intellectual. Such were the ancient times; wherefore angels could then converse with men, and convey their minds, almost separate from things corporeal, into heaven, yea, would conduct them through the heavenly societies, and show them the magnificent and blessed things abounding therein, and likewise communicate to them their happinesses and delights. These times were known also to the ancient writers, and were by them called the golden and also Saturnian ages. The superior excellence of those times, as was observed, was owing to this, that men were then distinguished into nations, nations into families, and families into houses, and every house lived apart by itself; and it then never entered into any one's mind to invade another's

inheritance, and thence acquire to himself opulence and dominion. Self-love and the love of the world were then far from men's affections; every one rejoiced in his own, and not less in his neighbor's good. But in succeeding times this scene was changed, and totally reversed, when the lust of dominion and of large possessions invaded the mind. Then mankind, for the sake of self-defence, collected themselves into kingdoms and empires; and inasmuch as the laws of charity and of conscience, which were inscribed on the hearts, ceased to operate, it became necessary to enact external laws in order to restrain violence, and to secure obedience thereto by temporal rewards and punishments. When the state of the world was thus changed, heaven removed itself from man, and this more and more even to the present time, when the very existence of heaven and hell is unknown, and by some denied. This account of the primitive state of the inhabitants of this earth is given, in order to show more clearly by the parallel what is the state of the inhabitants of the earth Jupiter, and whence they have their probity, and also their wisdom, concerning which more will be said hereafter.

50. By long and frequent conversation with the spirits of the earth Jupiter, it was made very manifest to me that they were better disposed than the spirits of several other earths. The manner of their approach to me, their abode with me, and their influx at that time, was inexpressibly gentle and sweet. In another life the quality of every spirit manifests itself by an influx, which is the communication of its affection. Goodness of disposition manifests itself by gentleness and sweetness; by gentleness, in that it is afraid to do hurt, and by sweetness, in that it loves to do good. I could clearly distinguish a difference between the gentleness and the sweetness of the influx proceeding from the spirits of Jupiter and of that which proceeds from the good spirits of our earth. When any slight disagreement exists among them, they said that there appears a sort of slender bright irradiation, like that of lightning, or like the little swath encompassing glittering and wandering stars; but all disagreements among them are soon adjusted. Glittering stars, which are at the same time wandering, signify what is false; but glittering and fixed stars signify what is true; thus the former signify disagreement.[u]

51. I could distinguish the presence of the spirits of Jupiter, not only by the gentleness and sweetness of their approach and influx, but also by this circumstance, that for the most part their influx was into the face, to which they communicated a smiling cheerfulness, and this continually during their presence. They said that they communicate a like cheerfulness of countenance to the inhabitants of their earth, when they come to

[u] That stars in the Word signify the knowledges of good and truth, consequently truths, n. 2495, 2849, 4697. And that in another life truths are represented by fixed stars, but falses by wandering stars, n. 1128.

them, being desirous thus to inspire them with heartfelt tranquillity and delight. That tranquillity and delight with which they inspired me filled my breast and heart very sensibly; at the same time there was a removal of all evil lusts and anxiety concerning things to come, which cause unquiet and disturbance, and excite various commotions in the mind. Hence was discoverable the nature and quality of the life of the inhabitants of the earth Jupiter; for the disposition of the inhabitants of any earth may be known by the spirits who come thence, inasmuch as every one retains his own proper life after death, and continues to live it when he becomes a spirit. It was very observable that they had a state of blessedness or happiness still more interior, which was manifest from this circumstance, that their interiors were perceived not to be closed, but open to heaven; for in proportion as the interiors are more open to heaven, in the same proportion they are the more susceptible of receiving Divine Good, and therewith blessedness and interior happiness. The case is altogether otherwise with those who do not live in the order of heaven: the interiors with such are closed, and the exteriors open to the world.

52. It was further shown me what sort of faces the inhabitants of the earth Jupiter had: not that the inhabitants themselves appeared to me, but that the spirits appeared with faces similar to what they had during their abode on their earth. But previous to this manifestation, one of their angels appeared behind a bright cloud, who gave permission; and instantly two faces were presented to view. They were like the faces of the men of our earth, fair and beautiful; sincerity and modesty seemed to beam forth from them. During the presence of the spirits of Jupiter, the faces of the men of our earth appeared less than usual, which circumstance was owing to this, that there was an influx from those spirits of the idea which they had concerning their own faces as being larger; for they believe, during their abode in their earth, that after their decease their faces will be larger and of a round shape; and whereas this idea is impressed on them, it consequently remains with them, and when they become spirits they appear to themselves as having larger faces. The reason why they believe that their faces will be larger is, because they say that the face is not body, inasmuch as through it they see, hear, speak and manifest their thoughts; and whereas the mind is thus transparent through the face, they hence form an idea of the face as of mind in a form; and inasmuch as they know that they shall become wiser when they cease to live in the body, therefore they believe that the form of the mind or the face will become larger. They believe also that after their decease they will perceive a fire which will communicate warmth to their faces. This belief takes its rise from hence, that the wiser amongst them know that fire in a spiritual sense signifies

love, and that love is the fire of life, and that the angels have life from this fire.[x] Such of them also as have lived in celestial love have their wishes herein gratified, and perceive a warmth in the face, and at the same time the interiors of the mind are kindled with love. It is on this account that the inhabitants of that earth frequently wash and make clean their faces, and also carefully secure them from the sun's heat. They use a covering for the head, made of the bark of a tree of a bluish color, which serves as a shade for the face. Concerning the faces of the men of our earth, which they saw through my eyes,[y] they said that they were not handsome, and that the beauty which they had consisted in the external skin, but not in the fibres derived from what is internal. They were surprised to see the faces of some full of warts and pimples, and in other respects deformed, and said that they have no such faces amongst them. Some of their faces retained a smiling cast, viz. such as were of a cheerful and smiling habit, and such as were a little prominent about the lips.

53. The reason why the faces which were prominent about the lips retained a smiling cast, was, because the chief part of their discourse is effected by the face, and especially by the region about the lips, and also because they never use deceit, that is, never speak otherwise than they think, the consequence of which is, that they use no restraint in regard to the face, but let all the features and fibres have free play. The case is other-with those who from their childhood have been practised in deceit. The face is thereby contracted from within, to prevent the inward thoughts from being manifested; neither has it free play from without, but is kept in readiness either to put itself forth or to contract itself, according to the suggestions of craft and cunning. The truth of this may appear from an examination of the fibres of the lips, and of the parts thereabouts; for the series of fibres in those parts are manifold, complex, and interwoven together, being created not only for the purposes of receiving and chewing the food, and of forming expressions of speech, but also of manifesting the ideas of the mind by their various configurations.

54. It was also shown me how the thoughts are expressed by the face: the affections, which appertain to the love-principle are manifested by the features and their changes, and the thoughts in those affections by variations as to the forms of

x That fire in the Word signifies love in both senses, n. 934, 4906, 5215. That sacred and celestial fire is Divine Love, and every affection which is of that love, n. 934, 6314, 6832. That infernal fire is self-love and the love of the world, and every concupiscence appertaining to those loves, n. 965, 1861, 5071, 6314, 6832, 7575, 10,747. That love is the fire of life, and that life itself is actually derived from that fire, n. 4906, 5071, 6032.

y That spirits and angels do not see the things of this solar world, but that they saw through my eyes, n. 1881.

interior things therein; it is impossible to describe them further. The inhabitants of the earth Jupiter use also vocal discourse, but it is not so loud as with us. One kind of discourse is an aid to the other, and life is insinuated into vocal discourse by that of the countenance. I am informed by the angels that the first discourse of all in every earth was effected by the face, and this from two origins, the lips and the eyes. The reason why this kind of discourse was first in use is because the face was formed to express by its features all a man's thoughts and inclinations; hence the face is called an effigy and index of the mind: a further reason is, because in the most ancient or primitive times man was influenced by a principle of sincerity, and cherished no thought, nor wished to cherish any, but what he was willing should beam forth visibly in his face: thus also the affections of the mind, and the thoughts therein originating, might be exhibited to the life, and in their fulness. Hereby likewise they were made visible, as several things united together in a form. This kind of discourse therefore excelled vocal discourse as much as the sense of seeing excels that of hearing, or as the sight of a fine country excels a verbal description of it. Add to this, that such discourse was in agreement with the discourse of angels, with whom men in those times had communication; and also that when the face speaks, or the mind by the face, the angelic discourse is exhibited with man in its ultimate natural form, but not so in verbal discourse. Every one also may conceive that the most ancient people could not at first practise verbal discourse, inasmuch as the expressions of vocal language are not infused immediately, but must have been invented, and applied to the things they were intended to express; and this would require a course of time to effect.[z] So long as man continued to be influenced by a principle of sincerity and rectitude, so long also such discourse remained; but as soon as the mind began to think one thing and speak another, which was the case when man began to love himself and not his neighbor, then verbal discourse began to increase, the face being either silent or deceitful. Hence the internal form of the face was changed, contracted itself, acquired stiffness, and began to be nearly void of life; whilst the external form, inflamed by the fire of self-love, appeared in the eyes of men as if it were alive; for a want of life in the internal forms, which are hid underneath the external, does not appear before men, but is manifest to the angels, inasmuch as the latter see interior things. Such are the faces of those who think one thing and speak another; for simulation, hypocrisy, cunning, and deceit, which at this day are called prudence, have a tendency

[z] That the most ancient people on this earth used to discourse by the face and lips, by means of internal aspiration, n. 607, 1118, 7361. That the inhabitants of some other earths used to discourse in like manner, n. 4799, 7359, 8248, 10,587. Concerning the perfection and excellence of that discourse, n. 7360, 10,587, 10,708

to produce such effects. But the case is otherwise in another life, where it is not allowable for the speech and thoughts to be at variance. Their variance also is there clearly perceived in every single expression, and when it is perceived, the spirit who is found guilty, is separated from his associates, and fined. Afterwards he is reduced by various methods to speak as he thinks, and to think as he wills, until his mind be one, and not divided. If he be a good spirit, he is reduced to a state of willing what is good, and of thinking and speaking what is true, from a principle of good; and if he be an evil spirit, he is reduced to a state of willing what is evil, and of thinking and speaking what is false, from a principle of evil. Until this is effected, the good spirit is not elevated into heaven, nor is the evil one cast into hell; and this to the end that in hell there may be nothing but evil and the false grounded in evil, and in heaven nothing but good and truth grounded in good.

55. I was further informed by the spirits from that earth, concerning various particulars relating to its inhabitants, as concerning their manner of walking, their food, and their habitations. With respect to their manner of walking, they do not walk erect like the inhabitants of this and of several other earths, nor do they creep on all four, like four-footed beasts; but as they go along, they assist themselves with their hands, and alternately half elevate themselves on their feet, and also at every third step turn the face sideways and behind them, and likewise at the same time bend the body a little, which is done suddenly; for it is thought indecent among them to be seen in any other point of view than with the face in front. In walking thus they always keep the face elevated as with us, that so they may look at the heavens as well as the earth. Holding the face downwards so as to see the earth alone, they call an accursed thing: the most vile and abject amongst them give into this habit, but if they continue in it, they are banished the society. When they sit, they appear like men of our earth, erect as to the upper part of the body, but they usually sit cross-legged. They are particularly cautious, not only when they walk, but also when they sit, to be seen with the face in front, and not as to the back parts. They are also very willing to have their faces seen, because thence their mind appears; for with them the face is never at variance with the mind, nor indeed have they power to make it so; hence it evidently appears, on an interview with them, what dispositions they entertain towards all who are present, especially whether their apparent friendship be sincere or forced, for this they never conceal. These particulars were declared to me by their spirits, and confirmed by their angels. Hence also their spirits are seen to walk, not erect like others, but almost like persons swimming, appearing to help themselves forward with their hands, and by turns to look around them.

56. They who live in their warm climates go naked, except about the loins; nor are they ashamed of their nakedness, inasmuch as their minds are chaste, loving none but such as they are in conjugial connection with, and abhorring adultery. They were very much surprised at the spirits of our earth, who on hearing of their method of walking, and also that they were naked, made a joke of it, and gave way to lascivious thoughts, without attending at all to their heavenly life. They said that this was a proof that things corporeal and terrestrial were of more concern to them than heavenly things, and that things of an indecent nature had place in their minds. Those spirits of our earth were told that nakedness gives no occasion either of shame or of scandal to such as live in chastity and a state of innocence, but only to such as live in lasciviousness and immodesty.

57. When the inhabitants of that earth lie in bed, they turn their faces forward, or towards the chamber, but not backward, or towards the wall. This was told me by their spirits, who assigned also the reason for their so doing, viz. that they believe that in turning the face forward they turn it to the Lord, but if they turn it backward they avert it from the Lord. I have sometimes observed, in regard to myself, whilst I was in bed, such a direction of the face; but never knew before whence it was.

58. They take delight in making long meals, not so much for the pleasure of eating as for the pleasure of discoursing at such times. Whilst they sit at table, they do not sit on chairs or stools, nor upon an elevated turf, nor yet upon the bare ground; but on the leaves of a certain tree. They were not willing to tell of what tree the leaves were; but when I guessed at several, and at last named the leaves of the fig-tree, they affirmed that to be the tree. They said moreover that they did not dress their food with any view to gratify the palate, but chiefly with a view to wholesomeness, and that the food which was wholesome was also savory. In a conversation which took place amongst the spirits on this subject, it was urged that it would be well for man to prepare his food according to this rule, for by so doing he would show his attention to the health of his mind and body at the same time; whereas, when the gratification of the palate is the chief thing attended to, the bodily health is frequently lost thereby, at least loses much of its inward vigor; and consequently the mind also is affected, inasmuch as the exertions of the mind depend on the interior state of the recipient bodily parts, as seeing and hearing depend on the state of the eye and ear. Hence the madness of supposing that all the delight of life consists in luxury and pleasurable indulgences: hence also comes dulness and stupidity in things which require thought and judgment, whilst the mind is disposed only for the exertions of cunning and contrivance respecting bodily and worldly things. Hereby man acquires a brutal image and like-

ness, and therefore such persons are not improperly compared with brutes.

59. Their habitations were also shown me. They are low, and constructed of wood, but within they are coated over with bark of a palish blue color, the walls and ceiling being spotted as with small stars, to represent the heavens; for they are fond of thus picturing the visible heavens and stars in the insides of their houses, because they believe the stars to be the abodes of angels. They have also tents, which are round above, and stretched out to a considerable length, spotted likewise within with little stars in a blue plane; in these they betake themselve in the middle of the day, to prevent their faces suffering from the heat of the sun. They are very attentive to the construction, neatness, and cleanliness of these their tents: they have also their meals in them.

60. When the spirits of Jupiter saw the horses of this earth, the horses appeared to me of a less size than usual, although they were tolerably robust and large. This was in consequence of the idea of those spirits concerning the horses they saw. They said that they also had horses amongst them, but of a much larger size, and that they were wild, running at large in the woods, and that when they came in sight, the inhabitants are terrified, although they never suffer any hurt from them. They added, that the fear of horses is innate or natural to them: this led me to a consideration of the cause of that fear, and it seemed to be grounded in the spiritual signification of horses; for a horse in a spiritual sense signifies the intellectual principle formed of scientifics,[aa] and inasmuch as the inhabitants of Jupiter are afraid of cultivating the intellectual principle by worldly sciences, hence comes an influx of the fear of horses. That they pay no attention to scientifics, which appertain to human erudition, will be seen presently.

61. The spirits of the earth Jupiter are not willing to associate with the spirits of our earth, because they differ both in minds and manners. They say that the spirits of our earth are cunning, and that they are prompt and ingenious in the contrivance of evil; and that they know and think little about what is good. Moreover, the spirits of the earth Jupiter are much wiser than the spirits of our earth. They say also of our spirits, that they talk much and think little, and thus that they are not capable of an interior perception of many things, not even of what is good; hence they conclude, that the men of our earth are external men. On a time also it was permitted the spirits of our earth, by their wicked arts, to act upon and infest the spirits of Jupiter who were with me. The latter endured such action

[aa] That horse signifies the intellectual principle, n. 2760—2762, 3217, 5321, 6125, 6400, 6534, 7024, 8146, 8148. And that the white horse in the Revelation signifies the understanding of the Word, n. 2760.

for a considerable time, but at length confessed that they could endure no longer, and that they believed it impossible for worse spirits to exist, inasmuch as they perverted their imagination and also their thoughts in such a manner that they seemed to themselves as it were bound, and that they could not be extricated and set at liberty without Divine aid. Whilst I was reading in the Word some passages concerning our Saviour's passion, certain European spirits infused dreadful scandals, with intent to seduce the spirits of Jupiter. Inquiry was made who they were, and what had been their profession in the world, and it was discovered that some of them had been preachers; and that the greater part were of those who call themselves of the Lord's society, or Jesuits. I said that they, during their abode in the world, by their preaching concerning the Lord's passion, were able to move the vulgar to tears. I further added what was the cause of the difference between what they appeared to be in the world, and what they were at present, viz. that in the world their thoughts and their words were at variance, consequently they entertained one opinion in their hearts, and professed another with their lips, but that now they are not allowed to speak under such disguise, for in becoming spirits they are compelled to speak in all respects as they think. The spirits of Jupiter expressed the utmost astonishment at hearing of such variance between men's interiors and exteriors, and that they were able to think one thing and say another, which to themselves (viz. the spirits of Jupiter) was impossible. They were surprised also, when they were informed that great numbers who are from our earth become angels, and that such are in heart altogether different from the above spirits; for they imagined at that instant that in our earth all were like the spirits then present; but they were informed that there are not many of such a character, and that there are also some whose thoughts are under the influence of goodness, and not of evil like the above, and that all whose thoughts are under the influence of goodness become angels. To convince them that this was the case, there came choirs out of heaven, consisting of angels from our earth, one choir after another, who together with one voice and in harmonious concert glorified the Lord. Those choirs affected the spirits of Jupiter who were present with such delight, that they seemed to themselves to be caught up as it were into heaven: the glorification by the choirs[bb] lasted about an hour. It was given me to perceive sensibly a communication of the delights occasioned

[bb] That it is called a chorus or choir when several spirits speak together and unanimously, concerning which see n. 2595, 2596, 3350. That in their speech there is an harmonious agreement, concerning which see n. 1648, 1649. That by choirs in another life there is a preparation for an introduction to unanimity, n. 5182.

thereby. The spirits of Jupiter said that they would relate what had happened to the other spirits from their earth who were in other parts of the spiritual world.

62. The inhabitants of the earth Jupiter make wisdom to consist in thinking well and justly on all occurrences in life. They imbibe this wisdom from their parents at an early age, and it is successively transmitted to posterity, receiving an increase in each generation from the love thereof, in consideration of its having been the wisdom of their forefathers. They are altogether unacquainted with the sciences, such as are cultivated in our earth, nor have they any desire to be acquainted with them. They call them shades, and compare them to clouds which intercept the light of the sun. This idea concerning the sciences they have conceived, in consequence of some spirits from our earth boasting that they were wise by reason of their skill in the sciences. The spirits from our earth who thus boasted were such as made wisdom to consist in things appertaining merely to the memory, as in languages, especially the Hebrew, Greek, and Latin, in a knowledge of all important particulars respecting the learned world, in criticism, in bare experimental discoveries, and in terms, particularly such as are philosophical, with other things of a like nature, not using such things as means leading to wisdom, but making wisdom to consist in the things themselves. Such persons, inasmuch as they have not cultivated their rational faculty by the sciences, as by means leading to wisdom, have little perception in another life; for they see only in terms, and from terms, in which case those things are as clots and clouds obstructing the intellectual sight (see above, n. 38); and they who have been vain and conceited by reason of their erudition thus grounded, have still less perception; but they who have used the sciences as means of invalidating and annihilating the things appertaining to the church and to faith, are found to have totally destroyed their intellectual principle, in consequence whereof they see in the dark like owls, mistaking what is false for what is true, and what is evil for what is good. The spirits of Jupiter, from the conversation they had with such, concluded that the sciences occasion a shade in the intellect and tend to make it blind. But they were informed that on our earth the sciences are means of opening the intellectual sight, which sight is in the light of heaven; but inasmuch as there is a prevalence of such things as appertain to the mere natural and sensual life, therefore the sciences to the men of our earth are means of becoming unwise, or of confirming them in favor of nature against Divine agency, and in favor of the world against heaven. They were further informed that the sciences in themselves are spiritual riches, and that they who possess them are like those who possess worldly riches, which in like manner are

means whereby man may do service to himself, his neighbor, and his country, and whereby also he may do mischief; moreover, that they are like dress, which serves for use and ornament, and also for the nourishing of pride and vanity, as in the case of those who would be honored for their fine clothes. This was perfectly intelligible to the spirits of Jupiter; but they were surprised at the inhabitants of our earth, that, being men, they should rest in means, and prefer things leading to wisdom before wisdom itself; and that they should not see, that to immerse the mind in such things, and not to elevate it above them, was to becloud and blind it.

63. A certain spirit at that instant, rising from the lower earth, came to me, and said that he had heard what I had been discoursing upon with other spirits, but that he did not understand at all what was said concerning spiritual life and the light thereof. He was asked whether he was willing to be instructed on that head. He said that he did not come with any such intention: hence it was given me to conclude that he would not comprehend what might be said on the subject. He was exceedingly stupid; yet it was declared by the angels, that during his abode in the world, he was much celebrated for his learning. He was cold, as was manifestly perceived from his breathing, which was a sign of an illumination merely natural, and of none spiritual, consequently, that by the sciences he had not opened but closed his way to the light of heaven.

64. Inasmuch as the inhabitants of the earth Jupiter procure intelligence for themselves by a way different from that of the inhabitants of our earth, and are moreover of a different genius and temper as grounded in the life, therefore they cannot abide long together, but either shun or remove each other. There are spheres, which may be called spiritual spheres, which continually flow forth, yea, overflow from every spirit; they flow from the active principle of the affections and consequent thoughts, thus from the life itself.[cc] All consociations in another life are regulated according to these spheres; those which agree being joined together according to their agreement, and those which disagree being separated according to their disagreement. The spirits and angels, who are from the earth Jupiter, in the GRAND MAN have relation to the IMAGINATIVE PRINCIPLE OF THOUGHT, and consequently to an active state of the interior parts; but the spirits of our earth have relation to the various functions of the exterior parts of the body, and when these are desirous to have dominion, the active or imaginative principle

cc That a spiritual sphere, which is the sphere of the life, flows forth and overflows from every man, spirit, and angel, and encompasses them about, n. 4464, 5179, 7454. That it flows forth from the life of their affections and consequent thoughts, n. 2489, 4464, 6206. That in another life consociations and also dissociations are regulated according to spheres, n. 6206, 9606, 9607, 10,312.

of thought from the interior cannot flow in: hence come the oppositions between the spheres of the life ot each.

65. As to what concerns their Divine worship, it is a principal characteristic thereof, that they acknowledge our Lord as the Supreme, who governs heaven and earth, calling Him the ONLY Lord; and inasmuch as they acknowledge and worship Him during their life in the body, they hence seek Him after death and find Him; He is the same with our Lord. They were asked, whether they know that the ONLY Lord is a Man. They replied that they all know that He is a man, because in their world He has been seen by many as a Man; and that He instructs them concerning the truth, preserves them, and also gives eternal life to those who worship Him from a principle of good. They said further, that it is revealed to them from Him how they should live, and how believe; and that what is revealed is handed down from parents to children, and hence there flows forth doctrine to all the families, and thereby to the whole nation which is descended from one father. They added, that it seems to them as if they had the doctrine written on their minds, and they conclude so from this circumstance, because they perceive instantly, and acknowledge as of themselves, whether it be true or not what is said by others concerning the life of heaven in man. They do not know that their only Lord was born a man on our earth; they said that it is of no concern to them to know it, only that He is a Man, and governs the universe. When I informed them that on our earth He is named Christ Jesus, and that Christ signifies Anointed or King, and Jesus, Saviour, they said that they do not worship Him as a king, because king suggests the idea of what is worldly, but that they worship Him as a Saviour. On this occasion a doubt was injected from the spirits of our earth, whether their only Lord was the same with our Lord; but they removed it by the recollection that they had seen Him in the sun, and had acknowledged that it was He Himself whom they saw on their earth (see above, n. 40). On a time also, the spirits of Jupiter who were with me were seized with a momentary doubt whether their only Lord was the same with our Lord; but this doubt, which was instantaneously injected, was also instantaneously dispersed. It was suggested by an influx from some spirits of our earth; and what surprised me much on this occasion, the spirits of Jupiter were so ashamed of themselves for having doubted herein, though but for a moment, that they requested me not to publish it, lest they should be charged with any incredulity, when yet they were now convinced of the truth more than others. They were most exceedingly affected and rejoiced when they heard it declared that the only Lord is alone Man, and that all have from Him what entitles them to be called men; but that they are only so far men as they are images of

Him, that is, as they love Him, and love their neighbor, consequently, as they are principled in good; for the good of love and faith is an image of the Lord.

66. There were with me some spirits of the earth Jupiter, while I was reading the seventeenth chapter in John, concerning the Lord's Love, and concerning His Glorification; and when they heard the contents, a holy influence seized them, and they confessed that all things therein were Divine. But at that instant, some spirits of our earth, who were infidels, suggested various scandals, saying that He was born an infant, lived as a man, appeared as another man, was crucified, with other circumstances of a like nature. The spirits of the earth Jupiter, however, paid no attention to these suggestions. They said that such are their devils, whom they abhor; adding, that nothing of a celestial principle has any place in their minds, but only an earthly principle, which they called dross; and which they said they had discovered from this circumstance, that when mention was made of going naked on their earth, obscene ideas immediately occupied their thoughts, and they paid no attention to their celestial life, which was also spoken of at the same time.

67. The clear perception which the spirits of Jupiter have concerning spiritual things, was made manifest to me from their manner of representing how the Lord converts depraved affections into good affections. They represented the intellectual mind as a beautiful form, and impressed upon it an activity suitable to the form answering to the life of affection. This they executed in a manner which no words can describe, and with such dexterity that they were commended by the angels. There were present on this occasion some of the learned from our earth, who had immersed the intellectual principle in scientific terms, and had thought and written much about form, about substance, about materiality and immateriality, and the like, without applying such things to any use: these could not even comprehend that representation.

68. They are exceedingly cautious on their earth, lest any one should fall into wrong opinions concerning the only Lord; and if they observe that any begin to think not rightly concerning Him, they first admonish, then use threats, and lastly deter by punishment. They said that they had observed, if any such wrong opinions insinuate themselves into any family, that family is taken from amongst them, not by the punishment of death inflicted by their fellows, but by being deprived of respiration, and consequently of life, by spirits, when they have first threatened them with death: for in that earth spirits speak with the inhabitants, and chastise them if they have done evil, and even if they have intended to do evil, of which we shall say more presently. Hence if they think evil concerning the only Lord, and do not repent, they are threatened with death.

In this manner the worship of the Lord, who to the inhabitants of that earth is the Supreme Divinity, is preserved pure.

69. They said that they have no particular days set apart for Divine worship, but that every morning at sun-rise, and every evening at sun-setting, they perform holy worship to their only Lord in their tents; and that they also sing psalms after their manner.

70. I was further informed, that in that earth there are also some who call themselves saints, and who command their servants, of whom they wish to have great numbers, to give them the title of lords, threatening them with punishment if they omit it. They likewise forbid their servants to adore the Lord of the universe, saying that themselves are lords-mediators, and that they will present the supplications of others to the Lord of the universe. They call the Lord of the universe, who is our Lord, not only the Lord, as the rest do, but the Supreme Lord, by reason that they call themselves also lords. The sun of the world they call the Face of the Supreme Lord, and believe that His abode is there, wherefore they also adore the sun. The rest of the inhabitants hold them in aversion, and are unwilling to converse with them, as well because they adore the sun as because they call themselves lords, and are worshiped by their servants as mediatory gods. There was shown me by spirits the covering of their head, which was a tufted cap of darkish color. In the other life such appear to the left in a certain altitude, and there sit as idols; and for some time are also worshiped by the servants who have attended upon them, but are afterwards held in derision by the same servants. What surprised me was, that their faces shine there as by the light of a fire, which is in consequence of their having believed that they were saints; but notwithstanding this fiery appearance of their faces, they are nevertheless cold, and have an intense desire to be made warm. Hence it is evident that the fire, whereby they seem to shine, is the fire of self-love, and a false fire. In order to make themselves warm, they seem to themselves to cut wood, and whilst they are thus employed, there appears underneath the wood something of a man, whom at the same time they attempt to strike. This appearance is in consequence of their attributing to themselves merit and sanctity; for all who do so in this life seem to themselves in another life to cut wood, as was the case likewise with some spirits from our earth, who have been spoken of elsewhere. For the further illustration of this subject, I shall here adduce what has been experimentally made known to me: "In the lower earth beneath the soles of the feet, are those who have placed merit in their good deeds and works. Several of them appear to themselves to cut wood. The place where they are collected is very cold, and they seem to themselves to acquire warmth by their labor. I have

also discoursed with them, and it was given me to ask them whether they had any inclination to leave that place. They replied that as yet they had not merited it by their labor. When that state however is finished and past, they are taken away thence. All such spirits are in a mere natural state, inasmuch as in the desire of meriting salvation there is nothing of a spiritual principle, such desire originating in self, and not in the Lord. Moreover such prefer themselves above others, and in some cases despise others; and if in another life they do not receive more bliss than others, they have indignation against the Lord, wherefore whilst they are cutting wood, it appears as if somewhat of the Lord was underneath the wood. This is in consequence of their indignation."[dd]

71. It is common in the earth Jupiter for spirits to discourse with the inhabitants, to instruct them, and also to chastise them if they have done evil; on which subject I wish to be more particular, as several things were related to me by their angels concerning it. The reason why spirits in that earth discourse with men is, because they think much about heaven and a life after death; and because respectively they are little solicitous about the present life; for they know that they shall live after their decease, and in a happy state according to the state of their internal man, formed in the world. To discourse with spirits and angels was also common on this earth in ancient times, and for the same reason, viz. because they then thought much of heaven and little of the world. But that living communication with heaven in process of time was closed, as man from internal became external, or what is the same thing, as he began to think much about the world and little about heaven; and especially when he ceased to believe in the existence of heaven or hell, and that in himself there was a spiritual man which would live after death; for at this day it is believed that the body lives by a virtue of its own, and not by virtue of its spirit; wherefore unless man now entertained a belief that he should rise again with his natural body, he would have no belief at all about the resurrection.

72. As to what particularly concerns the presence of spirits with the inhabitants of Jupiter, there are some spirits who chastise, some who instruct, and some who rule over them. The spirits who chastise apply themselves to the left side, and incline themselves towards the back, and when they are there, they press forth from man's memory all that he has done or

[dd] That the Lord alone has merit and righteousness, n. 9715, 9975, 9979, 9981, 9982. That such as place merit in their works, or wish to merit heaven by their good deeds, in another life wish to be served. and are in no wise contented, n. 6393. That they despise their neighbor, and are angry at the Lord Himself, if they do not receive a reward, n. 9976. What their lot is in another life, n. 942, 1774, 1877, 2027. That they are of those who in the lower earth appear to cut wood, n. 1110 4943.

thought, for this is an easy thing to spirits, inasmuch as when they come to man, they enter into all his memory.[i] If they find that he has done evil, or has thought evil, they reprove him, and also chastise him by pain in the joints of his feet or hands, or about the region of the belly; this also spirits can effect with much dexterity when they are permitted. On the approach of such spirits to man, he is struck with horror attended with fear, and hence he is aware of their coming. Fear may be excited in any person by evil spirits, on their approach, especially by those who during their abode in the world have been thieves and robbers. In order that I might know how those spirits act when they come to a man of their own earth, it was permitted that such a spirit should also come to me. When he was near, horror attended with fear manifestly affected me, yet it was not an interior but exterior horror, because I was aware of the spirit from whom it proceeded. He was also seen by me, and appeared as a darkish cloud with moveable stars in it: (moveable stars signify falsities, but fixed stars truths[u]). He applied himself to my left side towards the back, and likewise began to reprove me on account of things done and thought, which he produced from my memory, and also interpreted unfavorably; but he was checked by the angels. When he perceived that he was with a man who did not belong to his own earth, he began to discourse with me, saying that when he came to any man he knew all and singular the things which the man was doing and thinking; also that he severely reproved him, and likewise chastised him by various pains. At another time again such a chastising spirit came to me, and applied himself to my left side below the middle of the body, like the former, and also desired to punish me; but he likewise was restrained by the angels. He showed me however the kinds of punishment which they are permitted to inflict on the men of their earth, if they do evil, or intend to do evil. Besides pains of the joints, they cause also a painful compression about the middle of the belly, which seems as if it proceeded from a tight sharp belt; likewise a cessation of respiration at times even to apparent suffocation. Another kind of punishment is that of prohibition, whereby the person punished is forbid eating anything but bread for a time. Lastly, death is denounced in case the offender does not cease from his evil acts and intentions, and at the same time he is deprived of all satisfaction arising from the company of his wife, his children, and associates. Grief is also insinuated on such occasions by reason of such deprivation.

73. The spirits who instruct, apply themselves also to the left side of the persons instructed, but more to the front. They reprove likewise, but mildly, and presently teach them how they ought to live. They appear also of a darkish hue, yet not like clouds as the former, but as if they were clad in sackcloth.

These are called instructors, but the former chastisers. When the instructing spirits are present, angelic spirits are present also, sitting close to the head, and filling it in a peculiar manner. Their presence likewise is perceived there like a mild and gentle aspiration; for they are afraid of man's perceiving the least pain or anxiety from their approach and influx. They govern the chastising and instructing spirits, preventing the former from putting man to more pain than is permitted by the Lord, and prompting the latter to teach what is true. During the time that a chastising spirit was with me, there were present also angelic spirits, who kept my countenance in a constant smile and cheerfulness, and the region about the lips prominent, and my mouth a little open. This the angels easily effect by influx, when it is permitted of the Lord. They said that with the inhabitants of their earth, they induce such a countenance when they are present.

74. If man, after chastisement and instruction, again does evil, or thinks to do evil, and does not check himself by the precepts of truth, when the chastising spirit returns, he is punished more severely; but the angelic spirits moderate the punishment according to the intention in what was done, and according to the will principle in what was thought. Hence it may appear, that their angels who sit at the head, exercise a species of judicatory power over man, inasmuch as they permit, moderate, restrain, and operate by influx; but it was declared, that they do not judge, but that the Lord alone is Judge, and that from Him into them flow all things which they enjoin to the chastising and instructing spirits, and that it appears as if it was from them.

75. In the earth Jupiter, spirits speak with man, but man in his turn does not speak with spirits, only these words when he is instructed,—*I will do so no more:* nor is it allowed him to tell any one that a spirit has spoken with him, for if he does this, he is afterwards punished. Those spirits of Jupiter, when they were with me, supposed at first that they were with a man of their own earth; but when I spake with them again, and when they perceived that I had thoughts of publishing what passed between us, and thus of telling it to others, and that it was not allowed them either to chastise or instruct me for so doing, they then discovered that they were with a stranger.

76. There are two signs which appear to those spirits during their abode with man: they see an elderly man [*virum*] of a fair countenance, which is a sign to them to speak nothing but what is true, and to do nothing but what is just; they see also a face in a window, which is a sign to them to depart thence. Such an elderly man also appeared to me, and likewise a face was seen in a window, and on seeing the face those spirits immediately departed from me.

77. Besides the spirits above mentioned, there are also spirits who suggest contrary persuasions. These are they who, during their abode in the world, were banished from the society of the rest on account of their wickedness. When they approach, there appears as it were a flying fire, which passes downwards near the face. They place themselves beneath near man's back parts, and speak thence towards the upper parts. What they say is directly contrary to the instructions which the instructor spirit gave from the angels, and is to this purport, that they need not live according to instruction, but according to their own will and pleasure, without any check or restraint. They generally make their approach as soon as the former spirits are departed; but the men on that earth are aware who and what those spirits are, and therefore are unconcerned about them. Nevertheless they are taught hereby what is evil, and consequently what is good; for by evil is learnt what good is, the quality of good being discerned by its opposite, because all perception in every case is according to reflection, in relation to differences and distinctions suggested by opposites, in various manners and various degrees.

78. The chastising and instructing spirits do not approach those who call themselves saints and lords-mediators (concerning whom see above, n. 70), because these do not suffer themselves to be instructed, nor are amended by discipline, being inflexible in consequence of being under the influence of self-love. The chastising and instructing spirits say, that they discern such by their coldness, and that when they perceive cold they depart from them.

79. There are also spirits amongst those from the earth Jupiter whom they call sweepers of chimneys, because they appear in like garments, and likewise with sooty faces. Who they are, and what is their nature and quality, I shall also describe. One of these spirits came to me, and anxiously requested that I would intercede for him to be admitted into heaven. He said that he was not conscious of having done any evil, only that he had reprimanded the inhabitants of his earth, and that after reprimanding, he instructed them. He applied himself to my left side, a little lower than the elbow, and spake as it were with a divided faith. He had also the power of exciting pity. But all I could say in reply was, that it was not in my power to help him, for that all help was from the Lord alone; nor could I intercede for him, because I did not know whether it was useful or not; but that if he was deserving, he might have hope. At that instant he was remanded back amongst some upright spirits from his own earth; but they said that he could not be in consort with them, because he differed in quality. Still however he requested with an intense desire to be let into heaven, and in consequence thereof he was introduced to a society of

upright spirits of this earth; but these also declared that he could not abide with them. He was likewise of a black color in the light of heaven; but he himself said that he was not a black color, but of a darkish brown. I was informed that those are such at first who are afterwards received amongst those who constitute the province of the SEMINAL VESSELS in the GRAND MAN, or heaven; for in those vessels the semen is collected and is encompassed with a covering of suitable matter fit to preserve the prolific principle of the semen from being dissipated, but which may be put off in the neck of the uterus, that thus what is reserved within may serve for conception or the impregnation of the ovulum; hence also that seminal matter has a strong tendency and as it were a burning desire to put itself off, and leave the semen to accomplish its end: somewhat similar to this appeared likewise in this spirit. He came again to me, in vile raiment, and again said that he had a burning desire to be admitted into heaven, and that now he perceived himself to be qualified for that purpose. It was granted me to tell him that possibly this was a token that he would shortly be admitted. At that instant the angels called to him to cast off his raiment, which he did immediately with inconceivable quickness, from the vehemence of his desire; whereby was represented what is the nature of their desires who are in the province to which the seminal vessels correspond. I was informed that such, when they are prepared for heaven, are stripped of their own garments, and are clothed with new shining raiment, and become angels. They are likened unto caterpillars, which having passed through that vile state of their existence are changed into nymphs, and thus into butterflies; in which last state they are gifted with new clothing, and also with wings of various colors, as blue, yellow, silver, or golden. At the same time they have liberty to fly in the open air as in their heaven, and to celebrate their marriage, and to lay their eggs, and thus to provide for the propagation of their kind; and then also sweet and pleasant food is allotted them from the juices and odors of various flowers.

80. Hitherto nothing has been said concerning the nature and quality of the angels who are from the earth Jupiter; for they who come to the men of their earth, and sit at the head (concerning whom, see n. 73), are not angels in their interior heaven, but are angelic spirits, or angels in their exterior heaven; and inasmuch as the nature and quality of the former angels have been made known to me, I shall here relate what has been discovered on that subject. A certain spirit belonging to those of the earth Jupiter, who inspire terror, approached to my left side beneath the elbow, and thence spake to me; but his speech was harsh, nor were his expressions very distinct, so that

I was obliged to wait some time before I could collect his meaning. And whilst he was speaking, he injected somewhat of terror, admonishing me hereby to give a kind reception to the angels when they came: but it was given me to reply, that this did not depend upon myself, for that all were received by me according to what they were in themselves. Presently the angels of that earth approached, and I was permitted to perceive from their discourse that they differed altogether from the angels of our earth; for they did not discourse by verbal expressions, but by ideas which diffused themselves through every part of my interiors: and hence also they had an influx into the face, so that the face concurred in every particular, beginning from the lips, and proceeding towards the circumference in every direction. The ideas which were instead of verbal expressions, were discrete, but in a small degree. Afterwards they discoursed with me by ideas still less discrete, so that scarce anything of interstice was perceivable. It appeared in my perception like the meaning of verbal expressions with those who attend only to the meaning abstracted from the expressions. This discourse was more intelligible to me than the former, and was also more full. It flowed, in like manner as the former, into the face; but the influx was more continuous according to the quality of the discourse; it did not, however, begin as the former, from the lips, but from the eyes. Afterwards they discoursed in a manner still more continuous and full; and then the face could not concur by a suitable motion, but the influx was made sensible on the brain, which was acted upon in like manner. Lastly, they discoursed so, that the discourse fell only on the interior intellect; its volubility was like that of an attenuated atmosphere. I was made sensible of the influx, but not distinctly of the particulars discoursed on. These several kinds of discourse may be compared with different fluids,—the first kind with fluent water, the second with water more attenuated, the third with the atmospherical air, and the fourth with attenuated air. The spirit above mentioned, who was on the left side, sometimes interrupted the discourse, admonishing me particularly to behave modestly with his angels; for there were attendant spirits from our earth who suggested things which gave displeasure. He said that he did not understand at first what the angels discoursed about, but that he did afterwards when he removed to my left ear. Then also his speech was not harsh as before, but like that of other spirits.

81. I afterwards discoursed with the angels concerning some extraordinary particulars on our earth, especially concerning the art of printing, concerning the Holy Word, and concerning the doctrinals of the church derived from the Word; and I informed them that the Word and the doctrinals of the church

were printed and published, and were thus learnt. They wondered exceedingly that things of such a nature could be made public by writing and printing.

82. I was allowed to see how the spirits of that earth, when they are prepared, are taken up into heaven, and become angels. On such occasions there appear chariots and bright horses as of fire, by which they are carried away in like manner as Elias. The reason of this appearance of chariots and bright horses as of fire is, because thus it is represented that they are instructed and prepared to enter heaven, inasmuch as chariots signify the doctrinals of the church, and bright horses signify an enlightened understanding.[ee]

83. The heaven into which they are carried away, appears on the right to their earth, consequently separate from the heaven of the angels of our earth. The angels who are in that heaven appear clothed in shining blue raiment spotted with little stars of gold, and this by reason of their having loved that color in the world, and having believed also that it was the very essential celestial color, and especially because they are principled in such good of love as that color corresponds to.[ff]

84. There appeared to me a bald head, but only the upper part thereof, which was bony; and I was told that such an appearance is seen by those who are to die within a year, and that they instantly prepare themselves. The inhabitants of that earth do not fear death, except on this account, that they leave their conjugial partner, their children, or parents, for they know that they shall live after death, and that in dying they do not quit life, because they go to heaven; wherefore they do not call it dying, but being heaven-made. Such amongst them as have lived in true conjugial love, and have taken such care of their children as becomes parents, do not die of diseases, but in tranquillity as in sleep; and thus they emigrate from the world to heaven. The age to which the inhabitants live is, on an average, about thirty years, estimated according to years on our earth. It is by the providence of the Lord that they die at so early an age, lest their numbers should increase beyond what that earth is capable of supporting; and whereas, when they have fulfilled those years, they do not suffer themselves to

[ee] That chariots signify the doctrinals of the church, n. 2760, 5321, 8215. That horses signify the intellectual principle, n. 2760, 2761, 2762, 3217, 5321, 6125, 6400, 6534, 7024, 8136, 8148, 8381. That the white horse in the Apocalypse signifies the understanding of the Word, n. 2760. That by Elias in a representative sense is meant the Word, n. 2762, 5247. And whereas all doctrine of the church and the understanding thereof are from the Word, Elias is called the chariots of Israel and the horsemen thereof, n. 2762. That on this account he was taken up by a fiery chariot and fiery horses.

[ff] That blue originating in red or flame-color, corresponds to the good of celestial love; and that blue grounded in white or lightish color, corresponds to the good of spiritual love, n. 9868.

be guided by spirits and angels like those who are not so far advanced in age, therefore spirits and angels seldom attend them when arrived at their thirtieth year. They come to maturity sooner than on our earth. Even in the first flower of youth they connect themselves in marriage, and then it is their chief delight to love the partner of such connection, and to take care of their children. Other delights they indeed call delights, but respectively external.

OF THE EARTH OR PLANET MARS, ITS SPIRITS AND INHABITANTS.

85. The spirits of Mars are amongst the best of all spirits who come from the earths of this solar system, being for the most part celestial men, not unlike those who were of the most ancient church on this earth.[gg] When they are represented according to their true nature and quality, they are represented with the face in heaven and the body in the world of spirits; and such of them as are angels are represented with the face towards the Lord and with the body in heaven.

86. The planet Mars appears in the idea of spirits and angels, (like all the other planets,) in its place constantly, which place is to the left in front, at some distance in the plane of the breast, and thereby out of the sphere where the spirits of our earth are. Spirits of one earth are separate from the spirits of another earth, by reason that the spirits of each particular earth have relation to some particular province in the GRAND MAN[f] and consequently they are each in other and different states; and it is owing to this diversity of state that they appear separate from each other, either to the right or to the left, at a greater or lesser distance.[hh]

87. Spirits came thence to me, and applied themselves to my left temple, where they breathed upon me with their discourse; but I did not understand it. As to its flow, it was soft beyond what I had ever before perceived, being like the softest breeze. It breathed first upon the left temple and upon the upper part of the left ear; and the breathing proceeded thence to the left eye, and by degrees to the right, and flowed down after-

gg That the first and most ancient church on this earth was a celestial church, which is the chief of all, concerning which see n. 607, 895, 920, 1121, 1122, 1123, 1124, 2896, 4493, 8891, 9942, 10,545. That a church is called celestial wherein love to the Lord is the ruling principle, but spiritual wherein the ruling principle is charity and faith, n. 3691, 6435, 9468, 9680, 9683, 9780.

hh That distances in another life are real appearances, which are presented visibly by the Lord, according to the states of the interiors of angels and spirits, n 5604, 9104, 9440. 10,146.

wards, especially from the left eye, to the lips; and when it was at the lips, it entered through the mouth, and by a way within the mouth, and thus through the eustachian tube into the brain. When the breathing arrived thither, then I understood their speech, and was permitted to discourse with them. I observed, whilst they were speaking with me, that my lips were put in motion, and also my tongue in a slight degree, and this by reason of the correspondence of interior speech with the exterior. Exterior speech is that of articulate sound conveyed to the external membrane of the ear, and thence to the brain by means of the small organs, membranes and fibres, which are within the ear. Hence it was granted me to know that the speech of the inhabitants of Mars was different from that of the inhabitants of our earth, in that it was not sonorous, but almost tacit, insinuating itself into the interior hearing and sight by a shorter way; and consequently that it was more perfect, fuller of ideas, and thereby approaching nearer to the speech of spirits and angels. The essential affection also of the speech is represented amongst them in the face, and the thought thereof in the eyes; for the thought and the speech, and likewise the affection and the face, with them act in unity. They account it wicked to think one thing and speak another, and to will or desire one thing whilst the features of the face express the contrary. They are altogether unacquainted with hypocrisy, and likewise with fraudulent pretence and deceit. That the same kind of speech prevailed amongst the most ancient people on our earth, I was permitted to know by conversation with some of them in another life; and for the further elucidation of this subject I shall here relate the following particulars, communicated to me on the occasion: "It was shown me by an influx which I cannot describe what was the nature and quality of the speech which prevailed amongst the men of the most ancient church; that it was not articulate, like the verbal speech of our time, but tacit, being effected not by external respiration, but by internal: thus it was speech cogitative. It was also permitted me to perceive the nature of their internal respiration, how it proceeded from the navel towards the heart, and thus through the lips without any thing of sound whilst they were speaking; and that it did not enter into the ear of another by an external way, and beat on what is called the drum of the ear, but by a certain internal way, and by what is called at this day the *tuba eustachiana*. It was further shown me that by such speech they were enabled to express more fully the purposes of the mind, and the ideas of the thought, than can possibly be done by articulate sounds or expressions of the outward voice, which speech is in like manner directed by respiration, but such as is external; for there is not a single expression, nor any constituent of expression which is not directed by applications of the respiration. This however was effected with the antediluvians more perfectly, as being directed by internal respiration, which being of a more interior nature, is also more perfect, and more applicable and conformable to the ideas of thought. Moreover they were enabled to express their meaning by slight motions of the lips, and by corresponding changes of the countenance; for being celestial men, whatsoever was the object of their thoughts shone forth from their faces and their eyes, which underwent a conformable variation, the face as to its form according to the life of the affection and the eyes as to light. It was not possible for them on any account to express with the countenance what they did not think in their hearts; and whereas their speech was effected by internal respiration, which is that of the spirit of man, therefore they were enabled to hold consort and discourse with angels." The respiration of the spirits of Mars was also communicated to me,[ii] and it was perceivable that their respiration proceeded from the region of the thorax towards the navel, and thence flowed upwards through the breast with an imperceptible breathing towards the mouth; from which circumstances it was manifest to me, as also other experimental proofs, that they were of a celestial genius, consequently not unlike those who were of the most ancient church on this earth.

88. I was instructed that the spirits of Mars, in the GRAND MAN, have relation to the middle principle between the intellectual and the will principle, consequently that they have relation to THOUGHT GROUNDED IN AFFECTION, and the best of them to the AFFECTION OF THOUGHT: hence it is that their faces act in unity with their thoughts, nor can they in any case play the hypocrite. And inasmuch as this is their relation in the GRAND MAN, therefore the middle province, which is between the cerebrum and the cerebellum, corresponds to them: for where the cerebrum and the cerebellum are joined together as to spiritual operations, with such persons the face acts in unity with the thoughts, so that the very affection of thought beams forth from the face, and the general principle of the thought beams forth from the affection, which is discoverable also by certain signs from the eyes: wherefore whilst the spirits of Mars were with me, I had a sensible perception of a drawing back of the fore-part of the head towards the hind-part, consequently of the cerebrum towards the cerebellum.[kk]

89. On a time whilst the spirits of Mars were with me, and occupied the sphere of my mind, there came some spirits from

ii That spirits and angels have respiration, n. 3884, 3885, 3891, 3893.

kk That human faces on our earth in ancient times received influx from the cerebellum, and that then faces acted in unity with men's interior affections; but that afterwards they received influx from the cerebrum, when man began to pretend to affections which were not his own, and to fashion his countenance falsely according to such pretence: concerning the changes hereby occasioned in faces in process of time, see n. 4325—4328.

our earth, and desired also to infuse themselves into that sphere; but instantly the spirits of our earth became as it were insane, by reason of the utter disagreement between them and the spirits of Mars. For the spirits of our earth, in the GRAND MAN, have relation to external sense; hence they were in idea turned to the world and to self, whereas the spirits of Mars were in idea turned from self to heaven and their neighbor; hence came the contrariety. But at that instant there approached some angelic spirits of Mars, and at their approach the communication was closed, and thus the spirits of our earth retired.

90. The angelic spirits discoursed with me concerning the life of the inhabitants on their earth, informing me that they are not under any forms of government, but that they live arranged into greater and lesser societies, and that they are associated with each other according to their agreement in mind, which agreement they discover instantly by the face and speech, being seldom deceived in their judgment herein, and that then they are instantly united in friendship. They informed me further that their consociations are delightful, and that they discourse with each other about what passes in their societies, and especially about what passes in heaven, for several of them have manifest communication with the angels of heaven. Such amongst them as begin to think perversely in their societies, and thereby to incline to evil, are dissociated, and left to themselves alone, in consequence whereof they lead a most wretched life out of all society, in dens or other places, being no longer regarded by the rest. Certain societies endeavor to compel such persons to repentance by various methods; but if they cannot succeed herein, they separate themselves from all connection with them. Thus they are careful to provide against the contagion of the lust of dominion and the lust of gain, that is, against any persons under the influence of the lust of dominion, subjecting to themselves any society, and by degrees several societies; and against any, under the influence of the lust of gain, depriving others of their possessions. Every one on that earth lives content with his own property, and every one with his own share of honor, accounting it enough to be reputed upright and a lover of his neighbor. This delightful and tranquil principle of mind would perish unless such as incline to evil thoughts and dispositions were banished from the rest, and unless a prudent but severe check was given to the first incroachments of self-love and the love of the world; for it was owing to these loves that empires and kingdoms were first established, under which establishments there are few but what desire to have dominion, and to possess the property of others, there being few who do what is just and right out of a real love thereto, and still fewer who do good from a real principle of charity, being rather influenced by other motives, such

as the fear of the law, and a regard to gain, honor, reputation and the like.

91. In regard to Divine worship as practised by the inhabitants of that earth, they informed me that they acknowledge and adore our Lord, saying that He is the only God, and that He governs both heaven and the universe; and that every good thing is from Him, and that He leads and directs them; also that He often appears amongst them on their earth. It was then granted me to tell them, that Christians also on our earth know that the Lord governs heaven and earth, agreeably to His own words in Matthew, "*All power is given to Me in heaven and in earth,*" xxviii. 18; but that they do not believe it like the inhabitants of the earth Mars. They acquainted me further that on their earth the inhabitants believe that with themselves there is nothing but what is filthy and infernal, and that all good is of the Lord; yea, they added further, that of themselves they are devils, and that the Lord draws them out of hell, and continually keeps them from falling into it again. On a certain occasion, when the name of the Lord was mentioned, I observed that those spirits humbled themselves in such inward and profound abasement as no words can describe; for in their humiliation it was suggested to them that of themselves they were in hell, and thus that they were altogether unworthy to look to the Lord, who is essential Holiness; and so deeply was this suggestion implanted in them, being grounded in a true faith, that they were in a measure out of themselves, and remained in that state on their knees, until the Lord elevated them, and at the same time, as it were, drew them out of hell. When they emerge thus from humiliation, they are full of goodness and love, and thereby replenished with joy of heart. During their abasement they do not turn their faces to the Lord, for this they dare not do, but turn them in a contrary direction. The spirits who were about me said that they never before were witnesses to such humiliation.

92. It was a matter of surprise to some spirits who were from that earth, that there were about me so many spirits from hell, and that they also discoursed with me; but I was allowed to reply, that this was permitted them to the intent that I might know their natures and qualities, and why they were in hell, and that their infernal state was in consequence of and according to their evil lives. I was further allowed to declare, that there were several amongst them whom I had been acquainted with during their abode in the world, and that some of them had lived in high stations of dignity and pre-eminence, at which time the world alone had possession of their hearts; but it was not in the power of any evil spirit, even the most infernal, to hurt me, being continually under the Lord's protection.

93. There was presented before me an inhabitant of that

earth. He was not indeed an inhabitant, but like one. His face resembled the faces of the inhabitants of our earth, but the lower region of the face was black, not owing to his beard, for he had none, but to blackness instead of a beard: this blackness extended itself underneath the ears on both sides; the upper part of the face was yellowish, like the faces of the inhabitants of our earth who are not perfectly fair. They said moreover that on that earth they feed on the fruits of trees, especially on a kind of round fruit which buds forth from the ground; and likewise on pulse; and that they are clothed with garments wrought from the fibrous bark of certain trees, which has such a consistence that it may be woven, and also stiffened by a kind of gum which they have amongst them. They related further that they are acquainted with the art of making fluid fires, whereby they have light during evening and night.

94. I observed on a time a sort of flaming principle most beautiful. It was of various colors, as purple, and also a palish red, and the colors likewise sparkled beautifully by reason of the flame. I saw also a kind of hand to which that flaming principle adhered, at first on the back part, afterwards on the palm, and thence it played round the hand on all sides. This continued for some time. Presently the hand with the flaming principle was removed at a distance, and where it rested there was a bright lucid appearance. In that bright lucid appearance the hand retired from view, and instantly the flaming principle was changed into a bird, which at first was of like colors with the flaming principle, the colors sparkling in like manner, but they successively changed, and as the colors changed, the vigor of life in the bird changed also. It flew all around, and at first about my head, afterwards in a direction in front into a kind of narrow chamber, which appeared like some consecrated place; and as it flew more in a front direction its life in proportion departed, till at length it was changed into a stone, at first of the color of a pearl, but afterwards of an obscure color; but notwithstanding its being without life, it still continued flying. During the flight of this bird around my head, and whilst it was still in the vigor of life, there appeared a spirit from beneath rising through the region of the loins to the region of the breast, who thence desired to take away the bird; but inasmuch as it was so beautiful, he was prevented by the spirits around me, who all kept their eyes fixed attentively upon it. But the spirit who rose from below powerfully persuaded them that the Lord was with him, and consequently that what he did was from the Lord. Although most of them did not believe this, still they no longer hindered him from taking away the bird: he was not able, however, to retain it, by reason of an influx from heaven at that instant, and therefore presently let it fly out of his hand at perfect liberty. When this had

passed, the spirits around me, who had been exceedingly attentive to the bird and its successive changes, began to discourse with each other concerning it, and continued their discourse for a considerable time. They had a perception that such appearance must needs signify somewhat celestial; they knew that a flaming principle signifies celestial love and its affections; that hand to which the flaming principle adhered signifies life and its power; that changes of color signify the varieties of life as to wisdom and intelligence; that bird has also a similar signification, but with this difference, that a flaming principle signifies celestial love and the things appertaining to that love, whereas bird signifies spiritual love and the things appertaining to that love; (celestial love is love to the Lord, and spiritual love is charity towards our neighbor;[gg]) and that the changes of colors and at the same time of life in the bird, till at length it became a bird of stone, signify the successive changes of spiritual life as to intelligence. They knew further that the spirits, who ascend from beneath, through the region of the loins to the region of the breast, are in a principle of strong persuasion that they are in the Lord, and hence believe that whatever they do, howsoever evil it may be, is done by them agreeably to the Lord's will. But though they knew all this, yet they could not hence know who were meant by this appearance. At length they were instructed from heaven, that the inhabitants of Mars were meant; that their celestial love, wherein as yet several are principled, was signified by the flaming principle which adhered to the hand; and that the bird in the beginning, whilst it was in the beauty of its colors and in the vigor of its life, signified their spiritual love; but that by the bird's becoming as it were a bird of stone and void of life, and at length of an obscure color, were signified such of the inhabitants as had removed themselves from the good of love, and were in evil, and still believe that they are in the Lord. The like was signified by the spirit, who rose up and was desirous to take away the bird.

95. By a bird of stone were also represented the inhabitants of that earth, who after a strange manner transmute the life of their thoughts and affections into almost no life, concerning which circumstance I received the following information. There was a certain spirit above my head who discoursed with me, and from the sound of his voice it seemed as if he was in a state of sleep. In this state he spake many things, and all with a prudence equal to that of a person awake. It was given me to perceive that he was a subject by which the angels spake, and he in that state perceived and produced what was said by them;[ll] for he

[ll] That communications are effected by means of spirits sent forth from societies of spirits and angels to other societies, and that those emissary spirits are called subjects, n. 4403, 5856, 5983, 5985—5989.

spake nothing but what was true. If anything flowed in from another source, he admitted it indeed, but did not bring it forth. I questioned him concerning his state. He said that that state was to him a peaceable state; that it was free from all solicitude respecting the future; and that at the same time he was fruitful in producing uses, whereby he had communication with heaven. I was told that such, in the GRAND MAN, have relation to the longitudinal sinus, which lies in the brain between the two hemispheres thereof, and is there in a quiet state, howsoever the brain be disturbed on each side. During my conversation with this spirit, some spirits introduced themselves towards the fore-part of the head where he was, and pressed upon him; wherefore he retired to one side, and gave them place. The stranger spirits discoursed with each other; but their discourse was unintelligible both to myself and to the spirits about me. I was instructed by the angels that they were spirits from the earth Mars, who had the art of discoursing with each other in such a manner that the spirits present could neither understand or perceive what they said. I wondered how such discourse could possibly be contrived, because all spirits have one speech, which flows from the thinking principle, and consists of ideas which are heard as expressions in the spiritual world; but I was informed that those spirits by a certain method form ideas expressed by the lips and the countenance unintelligible to others, and that in the same instant they artfully withdraw the thoughts, being particularly cautious lest anything of affection should manifest itself, because in such case the thought would appear, inasmuch as thought flows from affection, and is as it were in it. I was further instructed that the inhabitants of the earth Mars, who make heavenly life to consist in knowledges alone, and not in a life of love, contrived such speech, but not all; and that the contrivers thereof, when they become spirits, retain the same kind of speech. These are they who were particularly signified by the bird of stone; for to form a speech by modifications of the countenance and foldings of the lips, with a removal of the affections, and a withdrawing of the thoughts from others, is to deprive speech of its life and soul, and to make it like a dead image, and by degrees to do the like also to themselves. But although they suppose that their discourse is not understood by others, yet angelic spirits have a perception of all and singular the things which they discourse about. The reason is, because it is not possible for any thought to be withdrawn from angelic spirits. This was also proved to them by living evidence. I was thinking concerning this circumstance, that the wicked spirits of our earth are not affected with shame when they infest others. This thought entered into me by influx from some angelic spirits who had a perception of their discourse. Those spirits of Mars instantly acknowledged that that was the subject of their discourse, and they were much surprised. Moreover several things, which they both spake and thought, were discovered by an angelic spirit, notwithstanding all their endeavors to withdraw their thoughts from him. Afterwards those spirits entered by influx from above into my face. The influx felt like small striated rain, which was a sign that they were not in the affection of truth and of good, for this is represented by what is striated [*striatum*]. They then spake plainly with me, saying that the inhabitants of their earth discourse in like manner with each other. They were then told that this is evil, because hereby they obstruct the influence of things internal, and recede from them to things external, which external things also they deprive of their proper life; and particularly, because to speak in such a manner is not sincere. For they who are sincere are never disposed to speak or even to think anything but what others may know, not caring if the whole world, yea if the whole heaven, was acquainted with their words and thoughts; but they who are otherwise disposed judge and think evil of others, and well of themselves, and at length are betrayed through habit to think and speak evil of the church, of heaven, yea, and of the Lord Himself. I have been informed that they who love knowledges, and not so much a life according to knowledges, in the GRAND MAN, have relation to the interior membrane of the skull; but that they who accustom themselves to speak without affection, and to draw the thought to themselves and withdraw it from others, have relation to that membrane when become bony, because from having some spiritual life, they come at length to have none.

96. Inasmuch as by a bird of stone are also represented those who are principled in knowledges alone, and in no life of love, and inasmuch as hence they have no spiritual life, therefore, by way of appendix, we shall take this opportunity of showing that they alone have spiritual life who are principled in celestial love, and thence in knowledges; and that each kind of love contains in itself every principle of knowledges appertaining thereto. This may be exemplified by the case of all living creatures, whether they be the inhabitants of earth or of air. Each is in possession of the science of all things appertaining to its particular love, which love has respect to nourishment, a safe habitation, the propagation of their kind, the care of their young, and with some to providing for themselves during winter; wherefore each is in possession of all science that is requisite, such science being implanted in its love, and flowing into each animal as into its proper receptacle; and in some cases being of such an extraordinary nature, that man cannot but be amazed at it. With the animals, however, science is connate, and is called instinct; nevertheless it appertains to the natural love in which they are principled: and if man was principled in

his proper love, which is love to God and towards his neighbor (this is man's proper love, as distinguishing him from the beasts, being heavenly love), then man would not only be principled in all requisite science, but likewise in all intelligence and wisdom; for intelligence and wisdom would flow from heaven into those two kinds of love, that is, through heaven from the Divine [principle or being]. But inasmuch as man is not born to those two kinds of love, but to their contraries, viz. to self-love and the love of the world, therefore he must needs be born in all ignorance and want of knowledge. Nevertheless by Divine means he is brought to somewhat of intelligence and wisdom, but still not actually so, unless the love of self and of the world be removed, and thus a way be opened for love to God and towards his neighbor. That love to God and neighborly love contain in them all intelligence and wisdom, may appear from the case of those in another life who, during their abode in this world, have been principled in such love. When these after death are admitted into heaven, they there come into such knowledge and wisdom as they before had no conception of; yea, they think and speak there like the rest of the angels, such things as ear has not heard, neither has it entered into the heart of man to conceive, which are ineffable. The reason is, because those two kinds of love have the faculty of receiving in themselves such things.

OF THE EARTH OR PLANET SATURN, ITS SPIRITS AND INHABITANTS.

97. The spirits from the earth Saturn appear in front at a considerable distance, beneath in the plane of the knees, where the earth itself is; and when the eye is opened to see thither, a multitude of spirits come into view who are all from that earth. They are seen on this part of that earth, and to the right of it. I was permitted also to discourse with them, and thereby to discover their natures and qualities in respect to others. They are upright, and they are modest; and inasmuch as they esteem themselves little, therefore they also appear little in another life.

98. In acts of Divine worship they are exceedingly humble, for on such occasions they account themselves as nothing. They worship our Lord, and acknowledge Him as the only God. The Lord also appears to them at times under an angelic form, and thereby as a Man, and at such times the Divine [nature or principle] beams forth from the face and affects the mind. The inhabitants also, when they arrive at a certain age, discourse with spirits, by whom they are instructed concerning the Lord, how He ought to be worshiped, and likewise how they ought to

live. When any attempt is made to seduce the spirits who come from the earth Saturn, and to withdraw them from faith in the Lord, or from humiliation towards Him, and from uprightness of life, they say that they would rather die ; on such occasions there appear in their hands little knives, with which they seem desirous to strike their bosoms ; on being questioned why they do so, they say, that they would rather die than be drawn aside from the Lord. The spirits of our earth sometimes deride them on this account, and infest them with reproaches ; but their reply is, that they are well aware they do not kill themselves, and that this is only an appearance flowing from their will principle, inclining them rather to die than to be withdrawn from the worship of the Lord.

99. They said that sometimes spirits from our earth come to them, and ask them what God they worship ; and that the answer they give them is, that they are out of their senses, and that there cannot be a greater proof of insanity than to ask what God any one worships, when there is but one only God for all in the universe to worship ; and that they are still more beside themselves in this, that they do not acknowledge the Lord to be that one only God, and that He rules the universal heaven, and thereby the universal world ; for whosoever rules heaven rules also the world, inasmuch as the world is ruled by and through heaven.

100. They said that on their earth there are also some who call the nocturnal light, which is great, the Lord ; but that they are separated from the rest, and are not tolerated by them. That nocturnal light comes from the great belt, which at a distance encompasses that earth, and from the moons which are called Saturn's satellites.

101. They related further that another kind of spirits, who go in companies, frequently come to them, desiring to know all particulars relative to their circumstances, and that by various methods they extract from them whatever they know. They observed concerning these spirits, that they were not beside themselves, only in this, that they desire to know so much for no other intent than to possess knowledge. They were afterwards instructed that these spirits were from the planet Mercury, or the earth nearest the sun, and that they are delighted with knowledges alone, and not so much with the uses thence derived.

102. The inhabitants and spirits of the planet Saturn have relation, in the Grand Man, to the middle sense between the spiritual and the natural man, but to that which recedes from the natural and accedes to the spiritual. Hence it is that those spirits appear to be carried or snatched away into heaven, and presently to be let back again ; for whatever appertains to spiritual sense is in heaven, but whatever appertains to natural sense is beneath heaven. Inasmuch as the spirits of

our earth, in the GRAND MAN, have relation to natural and corporeal sense, it was permitted me to know by manifest experience how the spiritual man and the natural fight and strive with each other, when the latter is not principled in faith and charity. The spirits of the earth Saturn came from afar into view, and instantly there was opened a living communication between them and such spirits of our earth as were not principled in faith and charity. The latter, on thus perceiving the former, became like persons insane, and began to infest them, by infusing unworthy suggestions concerning faith, and also concerning the Lord; and whilst they were busied in these invectives and abuses, they also cast themselves into the midst of them, and in the spirit of insanity by which they were possessed endeavored to do them mischief. But the spirits of Saturn were not at all afraid, because they were secure and in tranquillity; whereas the spirits of our earth, when they were in the midst of them, began to be tortured, and to respire with difficulty, and in consequence thereof made their escape with all precipitation, one in this way and another that, till they all disappeared. The spirits who were present perceived from this circumstance what is the nature and quality of the natural man when separate from the spiritual, and when he comes into a spiritual sphere, viz. that he is insane; for the natural man separate from the spiritual is wise only with a wisdom that originates in the world, and not with the wisdom that is from heaven; and he who is wise only with the wisdom that originates in the world, believes nothing but what he can apprehend with his senses, and the things which he believes are grounded in the fallacies of the senses, which, unless they are removed by an influx from the spiritual world, produce false principles and persuasions. Hence it is that spiritual things are things of nought to such persons, insomuch that they can scarce bear to hear mention made of anything spiritual; wherefore they become insane when they are kept in a spiritual sphere. It is otherwise during their abode in the world, where they either think naturally concerning spiritual things, or avert their ears that they may not hear them; that is, they hear and do not attend. It was also manifest from this experimental evidence, that the natural man cannot introduce himself into the spiritual, that is, ascend; but when man is principled in faith, and thereby in spiritual life, in this case the spiritual man flows into the natural, and thinks therein; for there is given a spiritual influx, that is, an influx from the spiritual world into the natural, but not the reverse, or from the natural into the spiritual.[mm]

[mm] That influx is spiritual, and not physical or natural, consequently that influx is from the spiritual world into the natural, and not from the natural into the spiritual, n. 3214, 5119, 5259, 5427, 5428, 5477, 6322. That it appears as if influx is from externals into man's internals, but this is a fallacy, n. 3721.

103. I was further informed by the spirits of that earth respecting the consociations of the inhabitants, with several other particulars. They said that they live divided into families, every family apart by itself; each family consisting of a man and his wife with their children; and that the children, when they enter the married state, are separated from the house, and have no further care about it; wherefore the spirits from that earth appear two and two: that they are little solicitous about food and raiment; that they feed on the fruits and pulse which their earth produces; and that they are clothed slightly, being encompassed with a coarse skin or coat, which repels the cold: moreover, that all on that earth know that they shall live after death; and that on this account also they make light of their bodies, only so far as regards that life, which they say is to remain and serve the Lord. It is for this reason likewise that they do not bury the bodies of the dead, but cast them forth, and cover them with branches of forest trees.

104. Being questioned concerning that great belt, which appears from our earth to rise above the horizon of that planet, and to vary its situations, they said, that it does not appear to them as a belt, but only as somewhat whitish like snow in the heaven in various directions.

OF THE EARTH OR PLANET VENUS. ITS SPIRITS AND INHABITANTS.

105. The planet Venus, in the idea of spirits and angels, appears to the left a little backwards, at some distance from our earth. It is said, "in the idea of spirits," because neither the sun of this world, nor any planet, appears to any spirit; but spirits have only an idea that they exist. It is in consequence of such idea that the sun of this world is presented behind as somewhat darkish, and the planets not moveable as in the world, but remaining constantly in their several places: see above, n. 42.

106. In the planet Venus there are two kinds of men, of tempers and dispositions opposite to each other; the first mild and humane, the second savage and almost brutal. They who are mild and humane appear on the further side of the earth, they who are savage and almost brutal appear on the side looking this way. But it is to be observed that they appear thus according to the states of their life, for in the spiritual world the state of life determines every appearance of space and of distance.

107. Some of those who appear on the further side of the planet, and who are mild and humane, came to me, and were

presented visibly above my head, and discoursed with me on various subjects. Amongst other particulars, they said that during their abode in the world, and more so since they were become spirits, they acknowledged our Lord as their only God. They added that on their earth they had seen Him, and they represented also how they had seen Him. These spirits in the GRAND MAN have relation to THE MEMORY OR THINGS MATERIAL, AGREEING WITH THE MEMORY OF THINGS IMMATERIAL, to which the spirits of Mercury have relation: wherefore the spirits of Mercury have the fullest agreement with these spirits of Venus, and on this account, when they were together, a remarkable change, and a powerful operation in my brain, was perceivable from their influx: see above, n. 43.

108. I did not however discourse with those spirits who are on the side that looks this way, and who are savage and almost brutal; but I was informed by the angels concerning their nature and quality, and whence it comes that they are so brutal. The cause is this, that they are exceedingly delighted with rapine, and more especially with eating their booty; the delight thence arising, when they think about eating their booty, was communicated to me, and was perceived to be most extraordinary. That on this earth there have been inhabitants of a like brutal nature, appears from the histories of various nations; also from the inhabitants of the land of Canaan, 1 Sam. xxx. 16; and likewise from the Jewish and Israelitish nation, even in the time of David, in that they made yearly excursions, and plundered the Gentiles, and rejoiced in feasting on the spoils. I was informed further, that those inhabitants are for the most part giants, and that the men of our earth reach only to their navels; also that they are stupid, making no inquiries concerning heaven or eternal life, but immersed solely in earthly cares and the care of their cattle.

109. In consequence of this their nature and quality, when they come into another life they are exceedingly infested there by evils and false persuasions. The hells, which appertain to them, appear near their earth, and have no communication with the hells of the wicked of our earth, by reason of their different tempers and dispositions: hence also their evils and false persuasions are totally of a different sort.

110. Such, however, amongst them, as are in the capacity of being saved, are in places of vastation, and are there reduced to the last state of desperation; for there is no other method whereby evils and false persuasions of that kind can be subdued and removed. When they are in a state of desperation, they cry out that they are beasts, that they are abominations, that they are hatreds, and that thereby they are damned. Some of them, when they are in this state, exclaim even against heaven; but as this proceeds from desperation, it is forgiven them. The

Lord moderates on these occasions, and restrains within proper limits their harsh and bitter expressions. These, when they have passed through extreme suffering, are finally saved, inasmuch as the corporeal principles are hereby brought to a kind of death. It was further declared concerning these spirits, that during their life on their earth they believed in some great Creator without a Mediator; but when they are saved, they are also instructed that the Lord alone is God, the Saviour and Mediator. I have seen some of them, after they have passed through extreme suffering, taken up into heaven; and when they were received there, I have been made sensible of such a tenderness of joy from them as drew tears from my eyes.

OF THE SPIRITS AND INHABITANTS OF THE MOON.

111. Certain spirits appeared over my head, and thence were heard voices like thunder; for the thunder of their voices exactly resembled the sound of thunder from the clouds after lightning. I at first conjectured that it was owing to a great multitude of spirits, who had the art of uttering voices attended with so loud a noise. The more simple spirits who were with me smiled on the occasion, at which I was much surprised; but the cause of their smiling was presently discovered to be this, that the spirits who thundered were not many, but few, and were also as little as children; and that on former occasions they had terrified them by such noises, and yet were unable to do them any hurt. In order that I might know their nature and quality, some of them descended from on high where they were thundering; and what surprised me, one carried another on his back, and thus two of them approached me. Their faces appeared not unhandsome, but longer than the faces of other spirits. In regard to stature, they appeared like children of seven years old, but more robust; thus they were dwarfs [*homunciones*]. It was told me by the angels, that they were from the Moon. He who was carried on the other's back, on coming to me, applied himself to my left side under the elbow, and thence discoursed with me, saying that whenever they utter their voices they thus thunder; and that thereby they terrify the spirits who are inclined to do them mischief, and put some to flight, and that thus they go with security whithersoever they are disposed. To convince me that the noise they make was of such a sort, he retired from me to some other spirits, but not entirely out of sight, and thundered in like manner. They showed moreover, that the voice being uttered from the abdomen, like an eructation, made this thundering sound. It was perceived that this was owing to this particular circumstance, that

the inhabitants of the Moon do not speak from the lungs like the inhabitants of other earths, but from the abdomen, and thus from a certain quantity of air there collected, by reason that the Moon is not encompassed with an atmosphere like that of other earths. I was instructed that the spirits of the Moon, in the GRAND MAN, have relation to the ensiform cartilage or *xiphoides*, to which the ribs in front are joined, and from which descends the *fascia alba*, which is the *fulcrum* of the abdominal muscles.

112. That there are inhabitants in the moon, is well known to spirits and angels, and in like manner that there are inhabitants in the moons or satellites which revolve about Jupiter and Saturn. They who have not seen and discoursed with spirits coming from those moons, still entertain no doubt but there are men inhabiting them, because they are earths, alike with the planets, and wherever an earth is, there are men inhabitants; for man is the end for which every earth was created, and nothing was made by the Great Creator without an end. That the human race, as constituent of heaven, is the end of creation, may appear to every one who thinks from a rational principle at all enlightened.

THE REASONS WHY THE LORD WAS WILLING TO BE BORN ON OUR EARTH, AND NOT ON ANOTHER.

113. THERE are several reasons, concerning which I had information from heaven, why it pleased the Lord to be born and to assume a humanity on our earth, and not on another. The PRINCIPAL REASON *was because of the Word, in that it might be written on our earth; and when written be afterwards published throughout the whole earth; and when once published be preserved to all posterity; and that thus it might be made manifest, even to all in another life, that God was made man.*

114. *That the principal reason was because of the Word*, is in consequence of the Word being essential Divine Truth, which teaches man that there is a God, that there is a heaven and a hell, and that there is a life after death; and teaches moreover how man ought to live and believe, in order to his admission into heaven, and thereby to eternal happiness. All these things would have been altogether unknown without a revelation, consequently on this earth without the Word; and yet man is so created that as to his interiors he cannot die.[nn]

[nn] That by mere natural light nothing can be known concerning the Lord, concerning heaven and hell, concerning the life of man after death, and concerning Divine Truths, by which man has spiritual and eternal life, n. 8944, 10,318, 10,319 10,320. That this may appear from this consideration, that se-eral, and amongst

115. *That the Word might be written on our earth*, is in consequence of the art of writing having existed here from the most ancient time, first on the rind or bark of trees, next on skins or parchment, afterwards on paper, and lastly by types as in printing. This was provided of the Lord for the sake of the Word.

116. *That the Word might afterwards be published throughout the whole earth*, is in consequence of the communication opened here amongst all nations, both by land and water, to all [illegible] [illegible]he globe ; hence that the Word once written might be [illegible]ed from one nation to another, and be taught in all p[illegible]

[illegible]17. *That the Word once written might be preserved* [illegible] *[illegible]terity*, consequently for thousands and thousands of [illegible] [illegible] that it has been so preserved, is well known.

118. *That thus it might be made manifest that God was made man ;* for it was with a view to this chief and most essential object that the Word was revealed, inasmuch as no one can believe in a God, and love a God, whom he cannot comprehend under some appearance; wherefore they who acknowledge an invisible and thus incomprehensible principle, in thought sink into nature, and consequently believe in no God : hence it pleased the Lord to be born on this earth, and to make this manifest by the Word, that it might not only be known on this globe, but also *might be made manifest thereby to spirits and angels even from other earths, and likewise to the Gentiles from our own earth.*[oo]

119. It is to be observed that the Word on our earth, given through heaven from the Lord, is the union of heaven and the world; for which end there is a correspondence of all things contained in the letter of the Word with Divine things in heaven; and the Word in its supreme and inmost sense treats of the Lord, of His kingdom in the heavens and the earths, and of love and faith from Him and in Him, consequently of life from Him and in Him. Such things are presented to the angels in heaven, when the Word of our earth is read and preached.[pp]

120. In every other earth Divine Truth is manifested by

them the learned, do not believe those things, although they are born where the Word is, and where there is instruction by the Word concerning those things, n. 10,319. That therefore it was necessary there should be a revelation from heaven, because man was born for heaven, n. 1775.

[oo] That the Gentiles in another life are instructed by angels, and that they who have lived good lives according to their religious principles, receive the truths of faith, and acknowledge the Lord, n. 2049, 2595, 2598, 2600, 2601, 2603, 2661, 2863, 3263.

[pp] That the Word is understood by the angels in the heavens after a different manner from what it is understood by men on the earths, and that the internal or spiritual sense is for the angels, but the external or natural sense for men, n. 1769—1772, 1887, 2143, 2333, 2396, 2540, 2541, 2545, 2551. That the Word is conjunctive of heaven and earth, n. 2310, 2495, 9212, 9216, 9357, 10,357. That the Word therefore was written by mere correspondences, n. 1404, 1408, 1409, 1540, 1619, 1659, 1709, 1783, 8615, 10,687. That in the inmost sense of the Word the Lord alone and His kingdom are treated of, n. 1873, 2249, 2523, 7014, 9357.

word of mouth by spirits and angels, as was said above in speaking of the inhabitants of the earths in this solar system. But this manifestation is confined to families; for mankind in most earths live distinct according to families; wherefore Divine Truth thus revealed by spirits and angels is not conveyed far beyond the limits of families, and unless a new revelation constantly succeeds, truth is either perverted or perishes. It is otherwise on our earth, where Divine Truth, which is the Word, remains for ever in its integrity.

121. It is to be observed that the Lord acknowledges and receives all, of whatsoever earth they be, who acknowledge and worship God under a human form, inasmuch as God under a human form is the Lord: and whereas the Lord appears to the inhabitants in the earths in an angelic form, which is a human form, therefore when the spirits and angels from those earths are informed by the spirits and angels of our earth that God is actually Man, they receive that Word, acknowledge it, and rejoice that it is so.

122. To the reasons above adduced, may be added, that the inhabitants and spirits of our earth, in the GRAND MAN, have relation to natural and external sense, which sense is the ultimate wherein the interiors of life close, and rest as in their common basis. The case is similar in regard to Divine Truth in the letter, which is called the Word, and which for this reason also was given on this earth, and not on any other:[qq] and whereas the Lord is the Word, and is the First and the Last thereof, therefore, that all things might exist according to order, He was willing to be born on this earth, and be made the Word, according to what is written in John, "In the beginning was the Word, and the Word was with God, and God was the Word. This was in the beginning with God. All things were made by Him, and without Him was not anything made which was made. *And the Word was made flesh, and dwelt among us, and we beheld His glory, the glory as of the Only-begotten of the Father.* No one hath seen God at any time; the Only-begotten Son, who is in the bosom of the Father, He hath exposed Him to view," i. 1, 2, 3, 4, 14, 18. The Word is the Lord as to Divine Truth, consequently Divine Truth from the Lord.[rr] But this is an arcanum which will be intelligible only to very few.

[qq] That the Word in the sense of the letter is natural, n. 8783. By reason that what is natural is the ultimate, wherein spiritual and celestial things close, and on which they subsist as on their foundation, and that otherwise the internal or spiritual sense of the Word would be as a house without a foundation, n. 9430, 9433, 9824, 10,044, 10,436.

[rr] That the Word is the Lord as to Divine Truth, consequently Divine Truth from the Lord, n. 2859, 4692, 5075, 9987. That by Divine Truth all things were created and made, n. 2803, 2884, 5272, 7835.

OF THE EARTHS IN THE STARRY HEAVEN.

123. They who are in heaven can discourse and converse with angels and spirits who are not only from the earths in this solar system, but also from other earths in the universe out of this system; and not only with the spirits and angels there, but also with the inhabitants themselves, only however with those whose interiors are open, so that they can hear such as speak from heaven. The same is the case with man during his abode in the world, to whom it has been granted by the Lord to discourse with spirits and angels; for man is a spirit as to his interiors, the body which he carries about in the world only serving him for performing functions in this natural or terrestrial sphere, which is the ultimate of all spheres. But it is allowed to no one to discourse as a spirit with angels and spirits, unless he be such that he can consociate with angels as to faith and love; nor can he so consociate, unless he have faith and love to the Lord; for man is joined to the Lord by faith and love to Him, that is, by truths of doctrine and good principles of life derived from Him; and when he is joined to the Lord, he is secure from the assaults of evil spirits from hell. With others the interiors cannot be so far opened, since they are not in the Lord. This is the reason why there are few at this day who are permitted to speak and converse with angels; a manifest proof whereof is, that the existence of spirits and angels is scarcely believed at this day, much less that they are attendant on every man, and that by them man has connection with heaven, and by heaven with the Lord. Still less is it believed that man, when he dies as to the body, lives a spirit, even in a human form as before.

124. Inasmuch as there are many at this day in the church who have no faith concerning a life after death, and scarce any concerning heaven, or concerning the Lord as being the God of heaven and earth, therefore the interiors appertaining to my spirit are open by the Lord, so that I am enabled, during my abode in the body, to have intercourse with the angels in heaven; and not only to discourse with them, but also to see the astonishing things of their kingdom, and to describe the same, in order to check from henceforth the cavils of those who urge, "Did ever any one come from heaven and assure us that such a place exists, and acquaint us with what is doing there?" Nevertheless, I am aware that they who in heart have heretofore denied a heaven and a hell and a life after death, will even still continue in the obstinacy of unbelief and denial; for it is easier to make a raven white than to make those believe who have once in heart rejected faith; the reason of which is, that such persons always think about matters of faith from a negative principle, and not from an affirmative. May the things, however,

which have been hitherto declared, and which we have further to declare, concerning angels and spirits, be for the use of those few who are principled in faith! whilst it is permitted me, in order to bring others to somewhat of acknowledgment, to relate such particulars as delight and engage the attention of persons desirous of knowledge; for which purpose we shall now proceed to give an account of the earths in the starry heaven.

125. He who is unacquainted with the arcana of heaven cannot believe that man is capable of seeing earths so remote, and of giving any account of them from sensible experience; but let such a one know that the spaces and distances, and consequent progressions, which exist in the natural world, are, in their origin and first cause, changes of the state of interior things; that with angels and spirits they appear according to such changes;[ss] and that therefore angels and spirits may by such changes be apparently translated from one place to another, and from one earth to another, even to earths at the extreme boundaries of the universe. The case is the same also with man as to his spirit, and therefore he also may be so translated, whilst his body still continues in its own place. This has been the case with myself, since by the Divine mercy of the Lord I have been permitted to converse with spirits as a spirit, and at the same time with men as a man. The sensual man is not capable of conceiving that man as to his spirit can be thus translated, inasmuch as the sensual man is immersed in space and in time, and measures his progressions accordingly.

126. That there are several worlds or systems may appear to every one from this consideration, that so many stars appear in the universe; and it is well known to the learned, that every star is like a sun in its own place, remaining fixed as the sun of our earth in its place: and that it is owing solely to distance that it appears in a small form like a star; consequently, that each star has planets revolving around it, which are so many earths, in like manner as the sun of our system has; and that the reason why those planets, or earths, do not appear, is because of their immense distance, and of their having no light but what they receive from their own star, which light cannot be reflected so far as to reach us. For what other end or purpose shall we say, was so large a firmament created with so many stars? The end of the creation of the universe is man, in order that an angelic heaven might be formed of men: but what would mankind and an angelic heaven from one single earth avail to answer the purposes of an Infinite Creator, for which a thousand, yea ten thousands earths, would not suffice? By calculation it appears that supposing there were in the universe

[ss] That motions, progressions, and changes of place, in another life, are changes of the states of the interiors of life, and that nevertheless it really appears to spirits and angels as if they actually existed, n. 1273—1277, 1377. 3356, 5606, 10,734.

a million earths, and on every earth three hundred millions of men, and two hundred generations within six thousand years, and that to every man or spirit was allotted a space of three cubic ells, in this case the sum of men or spirits collectively would not occupy a space equal to a thousandth part of this earth, consequently not more than the space possessed by one of the satellites of Jupiter or Saturn, which would be a space so diminutive in respect to the universe, that it would be scarcely discernible; for a satellite of Jupiter or Saturn is scarcely visible to the naked eye: and what would this be in regard to the purposes of the Creator of the universe, to answer which, the whole universe, though filled with earths, would be inadequate, for He is Infinite! In discoursing on this subject with the angels, they have told me that they have a like idea concerning the fewness of the human race in respect to the infinity of the Creator; but that their thoughts on the subject originate not from spaces, but from states, and that according to their idea, supposing the number of earths to be as many myriads as could be conceived in thought, they would still be as nothing to the Lord. The information, which I am about to give concerning the earths in the starry heaven, is from experimental testimony, whereby it will likewise appear, how I was translated thither as to my spirit, whilst my body continued in its own place.

OF THE FIRST EARTH IN THE STARRY HEAVEN, ITS SPIRITS AND INHABITANTS.

127. I WAS led by angels from the Lord to a certain earth in the starry heaven, where I was permitted to take a view of the earth itself, yet not to speak with the inhabitants, but with spirits who came from thence (for all the inhabitants or men of every earth, after finishing their course of life in the world, become spirits, and remain near their own earth). From these however I received information concerning the earth, and concerning the state of the inhabitants thereof; for men, when they leave the body, carry with them all their former life, and all their memory.[tt] To be led to earths in the universe, is not to be led and translated thither as to the body, but as to the spirit; and the spirit is led by variations of the state of interior life, which appear to it as progressions through spaces. Approaches, or near advancements, are also effected according to agreements or resemblances of states of life; for agreement or resemblance produces conjunction, whereas disagreement and dissimilitude

[tt] That man after death retains the memory of all his concerns in the world, n 2476—2486.

produces disjunction. Hence it may appear how translation is effected as to the spirit, and its approach or near advancement to things remote, whilst the man still remains in his own place. But to lead a spirit, by variations of the state of his interiors, out of his own orb, and to cause the variations successively to advance even to a state agreeing with or like to those to whom he is led, is in the power of the Lord alone; for there must be a continual direction and foresight from first to last, both in advancing and in returning back again; especially when the translation is to be effected with a man who is still as to the body in the natural world, and thereby in space. That such a translation has been effected, will appear incredible to those who are immersed in the sensual-corporeal life, and whose thoughts originate in sensual-corporeal things, nor can they be induced to believe it. The reason is, because the sensual-corporeal-life cannot conceive of progression without space; but they who think from the sensual principle of their spirit, somewhat removed or withdrawn from the sensual principle of the body, consequently who think from an interior principle in themselves, may be induced to believe and to conceive it, since in the idea of interior thought there is neither space nor time, but instead thereof the original principles whence spaces and times had birth. For the use of these latter the following account is written respecting the earths in the starry heaven, and not for the former (viz. such as are immersed in the sensual-corporeal life), unless they be in a state to suffer themselves to be instructed.

128. At a time when I was broad awake, I was led as to the spirit by angels from the Lord to a certain earth in the universe, accompanied by some spirits from this world. Our progression was in a direction to the right, and continued for two hours. Near the boundary of our solar system there appeared first a whitish cloud, but thick; and behind it a fiery smoke ascending from a great chasm. It was a vast gulf, separating on that side, our solar system from some other systems of the starry heaven. The fiery smoke appeared at a considerable distance. I was conveyed through the midst of it, and instantly there appeared beneath in the chasm or gulf several men who were spirits (for spirits appear all in a human form, and are actually men). I also heard them discoursing with each other, but whence they were, or of what sort, it was not given me to know. One of them, however, told me that they were guards, to prevent spirits passing from this world to any other in the universe without having obtained leave. That such was the case, was also confirmed by this circumstance, that some spirits who were in company, to whom it was not permitted to pass, when they came to that great gulf or interstice, began to cry out vehemently that they were lost and undone; for they were as persons struggling in the agonies of death; wherefore they halted on

that side of the gulf, nor could they be conveyed further; for the fiery smoke exhaling from the gulf affected them powerfully with its influence, and thus put them to torture.

129. After I was conveyed through that great chasm, I at length arrived at a place where I stopped; and immediately there appeared to me spirits from above, with whom I was permitted to discourse. From their discourse and their particular manner of apprehending and explaining things, I clearly perceived that they were from another earth; for they differed altogether from the spirits of our solar system. They also perceived from my discourse that I came from afar.

130. After discoursing for some time on various subjects, I asked what God they worshiped. They said that they worshiped some angel, who appeared to them as a Divine Man, being bright and shining with light; and that he instructed them, and gave them to perceive what they ought to do. They said further, that they knew that the Most High God is in the sun of the angelic heaven, and that He appears to His angel, and not to them; and that He is too great for them to dare to adore Him. The angel whom they worshiped was an angelic society, to which it was granted by the Lord to preside over them, and to teach them the way of what is just and right; therefore they have light from a kind of flame, which appears like a torch, fiery and yellow to a considerable degree. The reason is, because they do not adore the Lord, consequently they have not light from the sun of the angelic heaven, but from an angelic society; for an angelic society, when it is granted by the Lord, can exhibit such a light to spirits who are in an inferior region. That angelic society was also seen by me, and was on high above them; there was also seen the flaming principle whence the light proceeded.

131. As to the rest of their character, they were modest, somewhat simple, but still under tolerable good influence as to their thoughts. From the light which was amongst them might be concluded what was the nature and quality of their intellectual principle; for the intellect is according to the reception of the light which is in the heavens, inasmuch as Divine Truth, proceeding from the Lord as a sun, is what shines there, and enables the angels not only to see but also to understand.[uu]

132. I was instructed that the inhabitants and spirits of that earth, in the GRAND MAN, have relation to somewhat in the

[uu] That there is great light in the heavens, n. 1117, 1521, 1522, 1533, 1619–1632, 4527, 5400, 8644. That all light in the heavens is from the Lord as a Sun there, n. 1053, 1521, 3195, 3341, 3636, 4415, 9548, 9684, 10.809. That Divine Truth proceeding from the Lord appears in the heavens as light, n. 3195, 3222, 5400, 8644, 9399, 9548, 9684. That that light illuminates both the sight and the understandings of angels and spirits, n. 2776, 3138. That the light of heaven also illuminates the understanding of man, n. 1520, 3138, 3167, 4408, 6608, 8707, 9126 9399, 10,569.

SPLEEN, in which I was confirmed by an influx into the spleen whilst they were discoursing with me.

133. Being questioned concerning the sun of their system, which enlightens their earth, they said that the sun there has a flaming appearance, and when I represented the size of the sun of our earth, they said that theirs was less; for their sun to our eyes is a star, and I was told by the angels that it was one of the lesser stars. They said also, that from their earth is likewise seen the starry heaven, and that a star larger than the rest appears to them westward, which was declared from heaven to be our sun.

134. After this my sight was opened, so that I could look in some degree upon their earth; and there appeared several green fields and forests with trees in full foliage, and also fleecy sheep. Afterwards I saw some of the inhabitants, who were of the meaner class, clothed nearly like the country-people in Europe. There was seen also a man and his wife. She appeared of handsome stature and a graceful mien; so likewise did the man; but what surprised me, he had a stately carriage, and a deportment which had a semblance of haughtiness, but the woman's deportment was humble. I was informed by the angels that such is the fashion on that earth, and that the men, who are such, are beloved, because they are nevertheless well disposed. I was informed likewise, that it is not allowed them to have more wives than one, because it is contrary to the laws. The woman whom I saw had before her bosom a cloak or covering, broad enough to conceal herself behind it, which was so contrived, that she could put her arms in it, and use it as a garment to cover her, and so walk about her business. It might be tucked up as to the lower part, and when tucked up, and applied to the body, it appeared like a stomacher, such as are worn by the women of our earth; but the same also served the man for a covering, and he was seen to take it from the woman, and apply it to his back, and loosen the lower part, which thus flowed down to his feet like a gown, and clothed in this manner he walked off. The things seen on that earth were not seen with the eyes of my body, but with the eyes of my spirit; for a spirit may see the things which are on any earth, when it is granted by the Lord.

135. Being well aware that many will doubt the possibility of man's being able to see, with the eyes of his spirit, anything on so distant an earth, it may be expedient to declare how the matter is. Distances in another life are not like distances here on earth. In another life they are altogether according to the states of the interiors of every particular person. They who are in a similar state are together in one society and in one place; everything is present by virtue of a similitude of state, and everything is distant by virtue of a dissimilitude of state;

hence it was that I was near to the above earth, when I was brought by the Lord into a state similar to the state of the spirits and inhabitants thereof, and that in this case being present I discoursed with them. Hence it is evident, that earths in the spiritual world are not distant as in the natural world, but only apparently according to the states of life of the inhabitants and spirits of each. The state of life is the state of the affections as to love and faith. In regard to a spirit, or what is the same thing, a man as to his spirit, seeing things on any earth, we shall also explain how this is. Neither spirits nor angels by their own proper sight can see anything that is in the natural world; for the light of the natural world, or the solar light, is to them as gross darkness. In like manner man by his bodily sight cannot see anything that is in the other life; for the light of heaven is to him as gross darkness. Nevertheless, both spirits and angels, when it pleases the Lord, may see things in the natural world through the eyes of man; but this is not granted by the Lord except with those whom He permits to discourse with spirits and angels, and to be in consort with them. It has been allowed them to see through my eyes the things of this world, and as plainly as I myself did; and also to hear men discoursing with me. Sometimes it has happened that through me they saw their friends, with whom they had been intimate when in the body, altogether present as before, at which they were amazed. Wives have in this manner seen their husbands and children, and have wished me to tell them that they were present and looking on them, and that I would mention the particulars of their state in the other life; but this, I said, was not allowed, by reason that they would have called me mad, or would have pronounced my information to be all a delirium of the imagination, inasmuch as I was well aware that, although they gave assent with their lips to the doctrine of the existence of spirits and of the resurrection of the dead, and of their being amongst spirits, and that spirits can see and hear by means of man, yet they did not believe these things in their hearts. When my interior sight was first opened, and they who are in another life saw through my eyes the world and the things contained therein, they were so amazed that they called it the miracle of miracles, and were affected with a new joy, to think that a communication was thus opened of earth with heaven, and of heaven with earth. This joy continued for some months, but afterwards the circumstance which occasioned it became so familiar that now the wonder has ceased. I am informed that spirits and angels attendant on other men see not the least of the things of this world, but only perceive the thoughts and affections of those on whom they attend. Hence it may appear, that man was so created, that during his life here amongst men in the world, he might at the same time live in heaven amongst angels, and *vice versâ*, so that heaven and the world might be united together and act in unity in man, and men might know what passes in heaven, and angels what passes in the world; and that when men depart this life, they might pass thus from the Lord's kingdom on the earths into the Lord's kingdom in the heavens, not as into another, but as into the same, in which also they were during their life in the body; but in consequence of becoming so corporeal, man closed heaven against himself.

136. Lastly, I discoursed with the spirits who were from the above earth concerning various particulars on our earth, especially concerning this circumstance, that there are sciences cultivated on our earth which are not cultivated on other earths, as astronomy, geometry, mechanics, physics, chemistry, medicine, optics, and natural philosophy; and likewise arts, which are not known elsewhere, as the art of ship-building, of smelting metals, of writing, and of printing, and thus of communicating with others in distant parts of the earth, and also of preserving what is communicated for thousands of years, and that this art has been practised in regard to the Word which was revealed by the Lord, and that consequently revelation is for ever permanent on our earth.

137. At length there was presented to my view the hell of those who are from that earth, and very terrible was the appearance of the infernals seen therein, insomuch that I dare not describe their monstrous faces. There were seen also female magicians, who practise direful arts. They appeared clad in green, and struck me with horror.

OF A SECOND EARTH IN THE STARRY HEAVEN, ITS SPIRITS AND INHABITANTS.

138. I WAS afterwards led of the Lord to an earth in the universe which was further distant from our earth than the foregoing of which we have been just speaking. That it was further distant was plain from this circumstance, that I was two days in being led thither as to my spirit. This earth was to the left, whereas the former was to the right. Inasmuch as remoteness in the spiritual world does not arise from distance of place, but from difference of state, as was said above, therefore from the tediousness of my progression thither, which lasted two days, I might conclude that the state of the interiors with the inhabitants of that earth, which is the state of affections and of consequent thoughts, differed proportionably from the state of the interiors with spirits from our earth. Being conveyed thither as to the spirit by changes of the state of the interiors, I was enabled to observe the successive changes themselves before I arrived thither. This was done whilst I was awake.

139. When I arrived thither, the earth was not seen by me, but only the spirits who were from that earth; for, as was said above, the spirits of every earth appear about their own particular earth, by reason that they are of a genius and temper similar to that of the inhabitants, and in order that they may serve them. Those spirits were seen at a considerable height above my head, whence they beheld me as I approached. It is to be observed that they who stand on high in another life can behold those who are beneath them, and the higher they stand the greater is the extent of their vision; and they can not only behold those who are beneath them, but likewise discourse with them. From their state of elevation they observed that I was not from their earth, but from some other at a greater distance; wherefore they accosted me in questions concerning various particulars, to which it was given me to reply; and amongst other things I related to them to what earth I belonged, and what kind of earth it was. Afterwards I spake to them concerning the other earths in our solar system; and at the same time also concerning the spirits of the earth or planet Mercury, in that they wander about to several earths for the purpose of procuring for themselves knowledges of various matters. On hearing this, they said that they had likewise seen those spirits amongst them.

140. It was told me by the angels from our earth that the inhabitants and spirits of that earth, in the GRAND MAN, have relation to KEENNESS OF VISION, and therefore they appear on high; and that they are also remarkably clear-sighted. In consequence of their having such relation, and of their seeing clearly and distinctly what was beneath them, in discoursing with them I compared them to eagles, which fly aloft, and enjoy a clear and extensive view of objects beneath. At this they expressed indignation, supposing that I compared them to eagles as to their rapaciousness, and consequently that I thought them wicked; but I replied, that I did not liken them to eagles as to rapaciousness, but as to sharp-sightedness.

141. Being questioned concerning the God whom they worshiped, they replied that they worshiped a God visible and invisible, a God visible under a human form, and a God invisible not under any form; and it was discoverable from their discourse, and also from the ideas of their thought as communicated to me, that the visible God was our Lord himself, and they also called Him Lord. To this I was permitted to reply, that on our earth also there is worshiped a God invisible and visible; that the invisible God is called Father, and the visible is called Lord; and that both are One, as He himself taught, saying that no one had ever seen the appearance of the Father, but that the Father and He are One, and that whoso seeth Him seeth the Father, and that the Father is in Him and He in the

Father; consequently that both Divine principles are in One Person. That these are the Lord's own words, may be seen, John v. 37; chap. x. 30; chap. xiv. 7, 9, 10, 11.

142. Presently I saw other spirits from the same earth, who appeared in a place beneath the former, with whom also I discoursed; but they were idolaters, for they worshiped an idol of stone, like to a man, but not handsome. It is to be observed, that all who come into another life have at first a worship like what they practised in the world, but that they are successively separated from it. The reason is, because all worship remains implanted in a man's interior life, from which it cannot be removed and eradicated but by degrees. On seeing this, I was permitted to tell them that they ought not to worship what was dead, but what was living; to which they replied that they knew that God lives and not a stone, but that they thought of the living God when they looked on a stone like a man, and that otherwise the ideas of their thought could not be fixed upon and determined to the invisible God. It was then granted me to tell them, that the ideas of thought may be fixed upon and determined to the invisible God, when they are fixed upon and determined to the Lord, who is God visible in thought under a human form; and thus that man may be joined with the invisible God in thought and affection, consequently in faith and love, when he is joined with the Lord, but not otherwise.

143. The spirits who were seen on high were questioned, whether on their earth they live under the rule of princes or kings; to which they replied, that they know not what such rule is, and that they live under themselves, being distinguished into nations, families, and houses. They were questioned further, whether they are thus in a state of security. They replied in the affirmative, inasmuch as one family never envies another in any respect, or desires to deprive another of its just rights. They expressed a degree of indignation at being asked these questions, as implying a suspicion of their hostility, or of their want of protection against robbers. What, said they, have we need of but food and raiment, and thus to live content and quiet one under another?

144. Being further questioned concerning their earth and its produce, they said that they had green fields, flower-gardens, forests full of fruit trees, and also lakes abounding with fish; and that they had birds of a blue color, with golden feathers, and also greater and lesser animals. Among the lesser, they mentioned one sort which had the back elevated like camels on our earth; nevertheless, that they did not feed on their flesh, but only on the flesh of fishes, and besides on fruits of trees and pulse of the earth. They said, moreover, that they did not live in houses regularly built, but in groves, in which amongst the

leaves they made to themselves shelter against rain and the heat of the sun.

145. Being questioned concerning their sun, which appears as a star from our earth, they said that it has a fiery appearance, and not larger to look at than a man's head. I was told by the angels, that the star which was their sun was among the lesser stars, not far distant from the equator.

146. There were seen some spirits who were like what they had been during their abode on their earth as men. They had faces not unlike those of the men of our earth, except that their eyes and noses were less. This appearing to me somewhat of deformity, they said that little eyes and a little nose were accounted marks of beauty with them. A female was seen clad in a gown ornamented with roses of various colors. I asked whence they were supplied with materials for clothing on their earth. They answered that they gathered from certain plants a substance which they spun into thread; and that immediately afterwards they laid the threads in double and triple rows, moistening them with a glutinous liquor, and thus giving them consistence. Afterwards they color the cloth thus prepared with a substance procured from the juices of herbs. It was also shown me how they prepare the thread. The women sit down on the ground, and wind it by means of their toes; and when wound they draw it towards them, and with the hand spin it out to any fineness they please.

147. They said also, that on that earth every husband has no more than one wife; and that the number of children in a family is from ten to fifteen. They added, that there are found likewise harlots amongst them; but that all such, after the life of the body, when they become spirits, are magicians, and are cast into hell.

OF A THIRD EARTH IN THE STARRY HEAVEN, ITS SPIRITS AND INHABITANTS.

148. There appeared some spirits from afar who were not willing to approach. The reason was, because they could not be together with the spirits of our earth who were then about me. Hence I perceived that they were from another earth; and I was afterwards informed that they were from a certain earth in the universe; but where that earth is, was not made known to me. Those spirits were unwilling to think at all about the body, or even about anything corporeal and material, contrary to the spirits of our earth; hence it was that they were

not willing to approach ; nevertheless after the removal of some of the spirits of our earth, they came nearer and discoursed with me. But instantly there was felt an anxiety arising from the collision of spheres ; for spiritual spheres encompass all spirits and societies of spirits ;[cc] and inasmuch as they issue from the life of the affections and consequent thoughts, therefore where the affections are contrary, collision takes place, and hence comes anxiety. The spirits of our earth related, that they even durst not approach those other spirits ; since on their approach, they were not only seized with anxiety, but also appeared to themselves as if they were bound hand and foot with serpents, from which they could not be loosed but by retiring. This appearance had its ground in correspondence ; for the spirits of our earth, in the GRAND MAN, have relation to the external sense, consequently to the sensual corporeal principle, and this sensual principle is represented in another life, by serpents.[xx]

149. Such being the nature and quality of the spirits of that earth, they appear in the eyes of other spirits, not as others, in a distinct human form, but as a cloud, in many cases like a dusky cloud, with whitish tints, resembling somewhat human ; but they said, that within they are white, and that when they become angels, that duskiness is changed into a beautiful blue, which was also shown me. I asked whether they entertained such an idea concerning their bodies during their abode in the world as men. They replied, that the men of their earth make no account of their bodies, but only of the spirit in the body, as knowing that the spirit will live for ever, but that the body must perish. They said also, that several on their earth believe that the spirit of the body has existed from eternity, and was infused into the body when they were conceived in the womb ; but they added, that now they know that it is not so, and that they repent for having even entertained so false an opinion.

150. When I asked them whether they were willing to see any objects on our earth, informing them that it was possible to do so through my eyes (see above, n. 135), they answered first that they could not, and afterwards that they would not, inasmuch as they were merely terrestrial and material objects, from which they remove their thoughts as far as possible. Nevertheless, there were represented to their view magnificent palaces, resembling those in which kings and princes dwell on our earth; for such things may be represented before spirits, and when they are represented they appear exactly as if they existed. But the spirits from that earth made light of them, calling them marble images ; and then related that they have more magnificent

xx That the sensual external principle of man in the spiritual world is represented by serpents, as being in the lowest principles, and in respect to interior things in man, lying on the ground, and as it were creeping ; and that hence they were called serpents who reasoned from that sensual principle, n. 195—197, 6398, 6949.

objects with them, which are their sacred temples, not built of stone, but of wood. When it was objected that these were still terrestrial objects, they replied that they were not terrestrial, but celestial, because in beholding them they conceived not a terrestrial but a celestial idea; believing that they should see like objects in heaven after death.

151. They then represented their sacred temples before the spirits of our earth, who declared that they never saw anything more magnificent; and as they were seen also by myself, therefore I can describe them. They are constructed of trees not cut down, but growing in the place where they were first planted. On that earth, it seems there are trees of an extraordinary size and height; these they set in rows when young, and arrange them in such order that they may serve as they grow up to form porticos and galleries. In the mean while, by cutting and pruning the tender shoots, they fit and prepare them to entwine one with another, and join together so as to form the ground-work and floor of the temple to be constructed, and by a side elevation to serve as walls, and, being bended into an arch above, to make the roof. In this manner they construct the temple with admirable art, elevating it high above the ground. They prepare also an ascent into it, by continuous branches of the trees extended from the trunk, and firmly connected together. Moreover, they adorn the temple without and within in various ways, by disposing the leaves into particular forms; thus they build entire groves. But it was not permitted me to see the nature of the construction of these temples within, only I was informed that the light of their sun is let in by apertures among the branches, and is everywhere transmitted through crystals; whereby the light falling on the walls is refracted in divers colors like those of the rainbow, particularly the colors of blue and orange, which they are most fond of. Such is the nature of their architecture, the works whereof they prefer to the most magnificent palaces of our earth.

152. They said further, that the inhabitants do not dwell in high places, but on the earth in low cottages, by reason that high places are for the Lord who is in heaven, and low places for men who are on earth. Their cottages were also shown me; they were oblong, having within along the walls a continued couch or bed, on which they lie one next to another. On the side opposite to the door was a kind of alcove, before which was a table, and behind it a fire-place, by which the whole chamber is enlightened. In the fire-place there is not a burning fire, but a luminous wood, from which issues as much light as from the flame of a common fire. They said that in an evening this wood appeared as if it contained in it lighted charcoal.

153. They informed me further, that they do not live in societies, but in houses apart by themselves: that they are

joined in societies when they meet at Divine worship; and that on these occasions they who are teachers walk beneath in the temple, and the rest in piazzas at the sides; and that at their meetings they experience interior joys, arising from the sight of the temple, and from the worship therein celebrated.

154. In respect to Divine worship, they said that they acknowledge God under a Human form, consequently our Lord; for all who acknowledge the God of the universe under a Human form are accepted and led by our Lord. The rest cannot be so led, because they think without a determination of the thought to some specific appearance. They added, that the inhabitants of their earth are instructed concerning the things of heaven by some immediate commerce with angels and spirits, which may be more easily opened to them than to others, by reason of their rejecting corporeal things from their thoughts and affections. I asked what became of those amongst them who are wicked. They replied that on their earth it was not allowed that a wicked person should exist; but if any one gave in to evil thoughts or evil actions, he was reprimanded by a certain spirit, and threatened with death if he persisted therein; and in case he still persisted, he was taken off by a swoon; and that by this means the men of that earth are preserved from the contagion of evils. A certain spirit of this kind was sent to me. He spake with me as with them; moreover, he occasioned somewhat of pain in the region of my abdomen, informing me that this was the method he uses with those who give in to evil thoughts and evil actions, and to whom he threatens death if they persist. I was given to understand that they who profane holy things are grievously punished; and that before the punishing spirit comes, there appear to them in vision the jaws of a lion, wide open, of a livid color, who seems as if he would swallow their head, and tear it asunder from the body, and hence they are seized with horror. They call the punishing spirit the devil.

155. Inasmuch as they were desirous to know how we are circumstanced on our earth in regard to revelation, I informed them that it is effected by writing and preaching from the Word, and not by immediate commerce with spirits and angels, and that what is written may be printed and published, and thus be read and comprehended by whole societies, whereby the life may be corrected and amended. They were exceedingly surprised that such an art as writing and printing, utterly unknown in other places, could exist on our earth; but they comprehended that on this earth, where corporeal and terrestrial things are so much loved, Divine things from heaven could not otherwise flow in and be received; and that it would be dangerous for persons in such circumstances to discourse with angels.

156. The spirits of that earth appear upwards in the plane of

the head towards the right. All spirits are distinguished by their situation in respect to the human body, which is in consequence of the universal heaven corresponding with all things appertaining to man. These spirits keep themselves in that plane, and at that distance, because their correspondence is not with the externals but with the interiors of man. Their action is upon the left knee, a little above and beneath, with a kind of vibration very sensibly felt. This is a sign that they correspond ˙˙˙ CONJUNCTION OF THINGS NATURAL AND THINGS CELESTIAL.

A FOURTH EARTH IN THE STARRY HEAVEN, ITS SPIR... AND INHABITANTS.

157. I WAS further conducted to another earth which is in the universe, out of our solar system, which was effected by changes of the state of my mind, consequently as to the spirit; for, as has been frequently observed above, a spirit is conducted from place to place no otherwise than by changes of the state of his interiors, which changes appear to him in all respects like advancements from place to place, or like journeyings. These changes continued without intermission for about ten hours, before I came from the state of my own life to the state of life peculiar to the spirits of that earth, consequently, before I arrived there as to my spirit. I was carried towards the east, to the left, and seemed to be gradually elevated from an horizontal plane. I was also enabled to observe clearly a progression and promotion from a former place, till at length the spirits from whom I departed no longer appeared; and in the mean time I discoursed on various subjects with the spirits who were with me. A certain spirit was also with us who, during his abode in the world, had been a prelate, and a preacher, and likewise a very pathetic writer. From the idea concerning him in me, the attendant spirits supposed that he was a Christian in heart superior to the rest; for in the world an idea is conceived, and judgment formed from preaching and writing, and not from the life, if it is not attended with some extraordinary circumstances; and in case anything in the life appears which does not agree with the preaching and writing, it is nevertheless excused; for the idea or thought and perception concerning any particular person, gives a bias to the judgment in all things, inclining it in favor of such idea, thought, and perception.

158. After this I observed that I was in the starry heaven as to my spirit, far out of our solar system; for this may be observed from the changes of state, and consequent apparent continued progression, which lasted nearly ten hours. At length I heard spirits discoursing near some earth, which was afterwards also seen by me. When I was come near them, after some dis-

course together, they said that strangers sometimes come to them from a distance who discourse with them concerning God, and confuse the ideas of their thought. They pointed also at the way by which such strangers came, whereby it was perceivable that they were from the spirits of our earth. On questioning them as to the confusion caused in their ideas, they said that it arose from those strangers asserting that they ought to believe on a Divine Principle distinguished into three persons, which they nevertheless call one God; and on examining the idea of their thoughts, it is presented as a threefold principle [*trinum*], not continuous, but discrete, with some as three persons discoursing with each other, and with some as two seated together, one near the other, and a third hearkening to them, and going from them; and although they call each person God, and form a different idea concerning each, still they declare them but one God. They complained exceedingly, that hereby their ideas were confused, in that these strangers conceived three in thought, and in speech profess one, when nevertheless thought and speech ought ever to be in agreement with each other. The spirit who in the world had been a prelate and a preacher, and who also was with me, was then examined as to the idea he entertained respecting one God and three persons, when it was discovered that he represented to himself three gods, but making one by continuity. He conceived, however, this threefold unity as invisible because it was Divine, and from this conception it was perceivable that he thought only of the Father, and not of the Lord, and that his idea concerning the invisible God was no other than as of nature in her first principles, the result of which idea was, that the inmost principle of nature was his Divine Principle, and thus that he might easily be hence led to acknowledge nature as God. It is well to be observed, that the idea which any person entertains concerning anything is in another world presented to the life, and thereby every one is examined as to the nature of his thought and perception respecting the things of faith; and that the idea of the thought concerning God is the chief of all others, inasmuch as by that idea, if it be genuine, conjunction is effected with the Divine Being, and consequently with heaven. They were afterwards questioned concerning the nature of their idea respecting God. They replied that they did not conceive God as invisible, but as visible under a Human form; and that they knew Him to be thus visible, not only from an interior perception, but also from this circumstance, that He has appeared to them as a man. They added that if, according to the idea of some strangers, they should conceive God as invisible, consequently without form and quality, they should not be able in anywise to think about God, inasmuch as such an invisible principle falls not upon any idea of thought. On hearing this, it was granted me to tell them that they do well to think of God under a Human form, and that many on our earth think in like manner, especially when they think of the Lord; and that the ancients also thought according to this idea. I then told them concerning Abraham, Lot, Gideon, Manoah, and his wife, and what is related of them in our Word, viz. that they saw God under a Human form, and acknowledged Him thus seen to be the Creator of the universe, and called Him Jehovah, and this also from an interior perception; but that at this day that interior perception was lost in the Christian world, and only remains with the simple who are principled in faith.

159. Previous to this discourse, they believed that our company also consisted of those who are desirous to confuse them in their thoughts of God by an idea of three; wherefore on hearing what was said they were affected with joy, and replied that there were also sent from God (whom they then called the Lord) those who teach them concerning Him; and that they are not willing to admit strangers, who perplex them, especially by the idea of three persons in the Divinity, inasmuch as they know that God is One, consequently that the Divine Principle is One, and not consisting of three in unanimity, unless such threefold unanimity be conceived to exist in God as in an angel, in whom there is an inmost principle of life, which is invisible, and which is the ground of his thought and wisdom, and an external principle of life, which is visible under a human form, whereby he sees and acts, and a proceeding principle of life, which is the sphere of love and of faith issuing from him (for from every spirit and angel there proceeds a sphere of life whereby he is known at a distance);[cc] which proceeding principle of life, when considered as issuing from the Lord, is the essential Divine principle which fills and constitutes the heavens, because it proceeds from the very Esse of the life of love and of faith. They said that in this, and in no other manner, they can perceive and apprehend a threefold unity. When they had thus expressed themselves, I was permitted to inform them that such an idea concerning a threefold unity agrees with the idea of the angels concerning the Lord, and that it is grounded in the Lord's own doctrine respecting Himself; for He teaches that the Father and Himself are One; that the Father is in Him and He in the Father; that whoso seeth Him seeth the Father; and whoso believeth on Him believeth on the Father and knoweth the Father, also that the Comforter, whom He calls the Spirit of Truth, and likewise the Holy Ghost, proceeds from Him, and does not speak from Himself, but from Him, by which Comforter is meant the Divine Proceeding principle. I was further permitted to tell them that their idea concerning a threefold unity agrees with the Esse and Existere of the life of the Lord when in the world: the Esse of His life was the Essential Divine principle, for he was conceived of Jehovah, and the Esse of

every one's life is that whereof he is conceived; the Existere of life derived from that Esse is the Human principle in form; the Esse of the life of every man, which he has from his father, is called soul, and the Existere of life thence derived is called body. Soul and body constitute one man. The likeness between them resembles that which subsists between a principle which is in effort [*conatus*], and a principle which is in act derived from effort, for act is an effort acting, and thus two are one. Effort in man is called will, and effort acting is called action; the body is the instrumental part, whereby the will, which is the principal, acts, and the instrumental and principal in acting are one. Such is the case in regard to soul and body, and such is the idea which the angels in heaven have respecting soul and body: hence they know that the Lord made His Human principle Divine by virtue of the Divine principle in Himself, which was to Him a Soul from the Father. This is agreeable also to the creed received throughout the Christian world, which teaches, that "*Although Christ is God and Man, yet He is not two but one Christ; yea, He is altogether One and a single Person; for as body and soul are one man, so also God and man are one Christ.*"[yy] Inasmuch as there was such a union or such a oneness in the Lord, therefore He rose again, not only as to Soul, but also as to Body, which is not the case with any man; concerning which circumstance He also instructed His disciples in these words, "*HandleMe and see, for a spirit hath not flesh and bones, as ye see Me have.*"[zz] Those spirits understood clearly this discourse, such things being suited to the understanding of angelic spirits. They instantly added, that the Lord alone has power in the heavens, and that the heavens are His; to which it was granted me to reply, that this is known also to the church on our earth from the Lord's declaration before He ascended into heaven; for He then said, "*All power is given to Me in heaven and in earth.*"

160. Afterwards I discoursed with those spirits concerning their earth; for all spirits have knowledge of the things relating to the earth they came from, when their natural or external memory is opened by the Lord; inasmuch as this memory remains with them after death, but is not opened except at the Lord's good pleasure. Then they related concerning their earth from which they came, that when it is allowed them, they appear to the inhabitants, and discourse with them as men; and that this is effected by their being let into their natural or external me-

yy From the Athanasian Creed.

zz That immediately after death man rises again as to his spirit; and that he is in a human form, and that he is a man in all and every respect, n. 4527, 5006, 5078, 8939, 8991, 10,594, 10,597, 10,758. That a man rises again only as to spirit, and not as to body, n. 10,593, 10,594. That the Lord alone rose again as to body also, n. 1729, 2083, 5078. 10.825.

mory, and consequently into the thoughts which they had during their abode in the world; and that on such occasions the inhabitants have their interior sight, or sight of their spirits, opened, whereby they are seen. They added, that the inhabitants at such times know no other than that they are men of their earth, and that they then first perceive them not to be men when they are suddenly taken away from their sight. I told them that this was the case also on our earth in ancient times, as when angels appeared to Abraham, Sarah, Lot, the inhabitants of Sodom, Manoah and his wife, Joshua, Mary, Elizabeth, and the prophets in general; and that the Lord appeared in like manner, and they who saw Him knew no other than that He was a man of the earth before He revealed Himself: but that at this day such appearances are seldom exhibited; the reason whereof is, lest men by such things should be compelled to believe; for faith wrought by compulsion, such as is the faith which enters by miracles, is not inherent, and would also be hurtful to those in whom faith may be implanted by the Word in a state without compulsion.

161. The spirit, who had been a prelate and a preacher in the world, was altogether indisposed to believe that any other earths existed besides our own, in consequence of having thought in the world that the Lord was born on this earth alone, and that none could be saved without the Lord; wherefore he was reduced into a state similar to that which spirits are reduced into when they appear on their own earth as men, concerning which state see above: and thus he was let into that earth, so that he not only saw it, but also discoursed with its inhabitants. Hereupon a communication was also thereby granted me, so that I in like manner saw the inhabitants, and likewise some particular things on that earth. (See above, n. 135.) There appeared then four kinds of men, but one kind after the other in succession: at first there were seen men clothed; next to them, in order of succession, men naked, of a human flesh color; afterwards men naked, but with inflamed bodies; and lastly, black men.

162. Whilst the spirit who had been a prelate and preacher was with those who were clothed, there appeared a woman of a very beautiful countenance, in a plain simple dress; her gown flowing gracefully behind her, with sleeves also for the arms; her head-dress was beautiful, in the form of a chaplet of flowers. That spirit was exceedingly delighted at the sight of this virgin; he discoursed with her, and also took her by the hand; but inasmuch as she perceived that he was a spirit, and not of that earth, she rushed hastily away from him. Afterwards there appeared to him on the right several other women, who had the care of sheep and lambs, which at that time they were leading to a watering-trough, which was supplied with water by a small

drain from a certain lake. These women were clothed in like manner with the former: they had in their hands shepherds' crooks, by which they led the sheep and lambs to drink. They said that which way soever they pointed with their crooks, thither the sheep went: the sheep which we saw were large, with broad woolly tails. The faces of the women, when viewed more closely, were full and handsome. There were seen also men: their complexion was like that of the men of our earth, but with this difference, that the lower part of the face was black instead of a beard, and the nose was more of a snowy white than a flesh color. Afterwards the spirit who, as was said, had been a preacher in the world, was led on further, but reluctantly, because his thoughts were still engaged about the woman with whom he was delighted, as was evident from this circumstance, that there still appeared somewhat of his shadow in the former place. Then he came to those who were naked; they were seen walking together two and two, husband and wife, having a covering about the loins, and also around the head. That spirit, when he was with these inhabitants, was led into the state in which he was in the world when he was disposed to preach, and instantly said that he would preach before them the Lord crucified; but they said that they were not willing to hear any such thing, because they knew not what was meant by the Lord crucified, but knew that the Lord is living. He then said that he would preach the living Lord; but this also they refused to hear, saying that they perceived in his discourse somewhat not celestial, because it had much respect to himself, his own fame and reputation; that they could distinguish from the tone of voice, whether the discourse came from the heart or not! and that hence they pronounced him incapable of teaching them; wherefore he was silent. During his life in the world he had been a very pathetic preacher, so that he could excite in his hearers very holy influences: but this pathetic manner had been acquired by art, consequently it was derived from self and the world, and not from heaven.

163. They said, moreover, that they had a perception whether there be any conjugial principle with those of their nation who are naked; and it was shown that they perceive this by virtue of a spiritual idea concerning marriage, which idea being communicated to me was to this effect, that a likeness of interiors was formed by the conjunction of goodness and truth, consequently of love and faith, and that conjugial love existed from that conjunction descending by influx into the body; for all things appertaining to the mind are presented in some natural appearance in the body, consequently in the appearance of conjugial love, when the interiors of two persons mutually love each other, and also by virtue of that love are desirous to

will and to think the one as the other, and thus to abide and be joined together as to the interiors of the mind. Hence spiritual affection, which appertains to the mind, becomes natural affection in the body, and clothes itself with the sense of conjugial love. Spiritual affection appertaining to the mind is the affection of goodness and truth, and of their conjunction; for all things appertaining to the mind, or to the thinking principle and the will principle have relation to truth and good. They said further that it is altogether impossible for any conjugial principle to exist between one man and several wives, inasmuch as the marriage of goodness and truth, which appertains to the mind, can exist only between two.

164. After this the above spirit came to those who were naked, but whose bodies were inflamed; and lastly, to those who were black, some of whom were naked, and some clothed; but both the latter and the former dwelt in a distant part of the same earth; for a spirit may be led in an instant to places far asunder, inasmuch as he does not proceed and advance like man by spaces, but by changes of state. See above, n. 125, 127.[ss]

165. I lastly discoursed with the spirits of that earth concerning the belief of the inhabitants of our earth in regard to a resurrection, in that they cannot conceive that men come into another life immediately after death, and then appear like men as to the face, the body, the arms, the feet, and all the external and internal senses; still less can they conceive that they are then clothed in raiment and that they have places of abode and habitations; and this solely by reason that the thoughts of the generality of persons on this earth are grounded in the things of sense, which appertain to the body, and therefore they believe in the existence of nothing but what they see and touch; and few can be withdrawn from external and sensible things to things of an interior nature, and thus be elevated into the light of heaven, in which such interior things are perceived. Hence it is, that in regard to the soul or spirit, they cannot form any idea of it as of a man, but as of wind, of air, or of a phantom without form, in which notwithstanding there is some vital principle. This is the reason why they do not believe that they shall rise again till the end of the world, which they call the last judgment, at which time they suppose that the body, although mouldered into dust, and dissipated by every wind, will be brought back again and joined to its soul or spirit. I added, that it is permitted they should thus believe, inasmuch as it cannot otherwise be conceived by those whose thoughts, as was said, are grounded in things of sense, that the soul or spirit can live as a man in a human form, unless it receives again that body with which it was clothed in the world; wherefore unless it was asserted that that body is to rise again, they would reject in heart the doctrine concerning a resurrection and

eternal life as incomprehensible. But stil. this thought concerning a resurrection has this advantage attending it, that it leads them to believe in a life after death, the consequence of which belief is, that when they come to lie on a sick bed, and their thoughts are not influenced as before by worldly and corporeal things, that is, by things of sense, they then believe that they shall live immediately after their decease; they then also speak about heaven, and about the hope of living there immediately after death, with ideas very different from those suggested by their doctrine concerning the last judgment. I related further, that it had sometimes been matter of surprise to me, that when they who are principled in faith speak of a life after death, and of their friends and relatives who are deceased, and at such times do not think about the last judgment, they then believe that their friends and relatives live as men immediately on their decease; but this idea, as soon as ever a thought concerning the last judgment flows in, is changed into a material idea concerning their terrestrial body, that it is again to be joined to their soul; for they do not know that every man is a spirit as to his interiors, and that it is this spirit which lives in the body and in all its parts, and not the body which lives of itself; and that it is from the spirit of every one that the body has its human form, consequently it is the spirit of every one which is principally man, and in like form as man, but invisible to the eyes of the body, yet visible to the eyes of spirits. Hence also, when the sight of man's spirit is opened, which is effected by the removal of the bodily sight, angels appear as men: thus angels appeared to the ancients, according to what is written in the Word. In my discourse also with spirits, whom I had been acquainted with during their abode in the world, I have occasionally asked them whether they had any inclination to be clothed again with their terrestrial bodies, as they had once thought would be the case. But they started at the very idea of such a conjunction, being full of confusion and amazement to think, that whilst they were in the world they should be under the influence of so blind a belief, void of all understanding.

166. Moreover on that earth were seen the habitations of the inhabitants, which were low houses of a considerable length, with windows on the sides according to the number of the rooms or chambers into which they were divided. The roof was round, and there was a door on both sides at each end. We were told that they were built of common soil, and covered with turf; and that the windows were constructed of threads of grass so entwined together as to render them transparent. Little children were also seen; and we were told that their neighbors visit them especially for the sake of their children, that they may be in company with other children in the presence and under the control of their parents. There appeared also fields

full of growing corn, which was at that time nearly ripe for harvest. The seeds or grains of their corn were shown us, and they were like those of Chinese wheat. We saw likewise some bread made thereof, which was in small square loaves. There appeared also plains of grass adorned with flowers, and trees laden with fruit like pomegranates, besides shrubs, which were not vines, but still produced berries of which they made wine.

167. The sun of that earth, which is to us a star, appears there flaming, in size about a fourth part of our sun. Their year is nearly two hundred days, and each day fifteen hours, computed according to the length of days on our earth. The earth itself is one of the least in the starry heaven, being scarcely five hundred German miles in circumference. This information we had from the angels, who made a comparison in all these particulars with things of a like nature on our earth, according to what they saw in me, or in my memory. Their conclusions were formed by angelic ideas, whereby are instantly known the measures of spaces and times, in a just proportion with respect to spaces and times elsewhere. Angelic ideas, which are spiritual, in such calculations infinitely excel human ideas.

OF A FIFTH EARTH IN THE STARRY HEAVEN, ITS SPIRITS AND INHABITANTS.

168. I WAS led at another time to another earth which is in the universe out of our solar system, and on this occasion also by changes of state, continued nearly for twelve hours. There were in company with me several spirits and angels from our earth, with whom I discoursed in the way of progress thither. I was carried at times obliquely upwards and obliquely downwards, continually towards the right, which in another life is towards the south. In two places only I saw spirits, and in one I discoursed with them. In this journey or progress I was enabled to observe how immense is the Lord's heaven, which is designed for angels and spirits; for from the parts uninhabited I was led to conclude that it was so immense, that in case there were several myriads of earths, and on each earth a multitude of men equal in number to the inhabitants of our earth, there would still be a place of abode for them to eternity, and it would never be filled. This I was enabled to conclude from a comparison made with the extent of the heaven which is about our earth and designed for it, which extent was respectively so small, that it did not equal one ten thousandth thousandth part of the extent uninhabited.

169. When the angelic spirits who were from that earth

came into view, they accosted us, asking who we were, and what we wanted. We said that we came for the sake of journeying, that we were directed thither, and that they had nothing to fear from us; for they were afraid we were of those who disturb them in regard to God, to faith, and things of a like nature, on account of whom they had betaken themselves to that quarter of their earth, shunning them as much as possible. We asked them in what particulars they were disturbed. They replied, by an idea of three, and by an idea of a Divine principle without a human, in God, when yet they knew and perceived that God is one, and that He is a man. It was then perceived by us that they who disturb them, and whom they shunned, were from our earth. This was manifest also from this consideration, that there are spirits from our earth who thus wander about in another life in consequence of their fondness for and delight in travelling, which they have contracted in the world; for on other earths there is no such custom of travelling as on ours. It was afterwards discovered that they were monks, who had travelled on our globe from a desire of converting the gentiles; wherefore we told them that they did well to shun such spirits, because their intention was not to teach, but to secure gain and dominion; and that they study by various arts first to captivate men's minds, but afterwards to subject them to themselves as slaves: moreover, that they did well in not suffering their ideas concerning God to be disturbed by such. They informed us further, that the above spirits confuse them by asserting that they ought to have faith and to believe the things they declare; but their reply to this was, that they knew not what faith or believing meant, since they perceive in themselves whether a thing be true or not. They were of the Lord's celestial kingdom, where all know by an interior perception the truths which with us are called the truths of faith, for they are in illumination from the Lord; but it is otherwise with those who are in the spiritual kingdom. That the angelic spirits of that earth were of the Lord's celestial kingdom, it was granted me to see, from the flaming principle whence their ideas flowed; for the light in the celestial kingdom is flaming, and in the spiritual kingdom it is white. They who are of the celestial kingdom, when the discourse is about truths, say no more than yea, yea, or nay, nay, and never reason about truths whether they be so or not. These are they of whom the Lord speaks in these words, "*Let your discourse be yea, yea, and nay, nay, for whatsoever is more than this cometh of evil.*" Hence it was that those spirits said that they did not know what is meant by having faith or believing. They consider an exhortation to believe, like a person's saying to his companion who sees houses or trees with his own eyes, that he ought to have faith or to believe that they are houses and trees, when he sees clearly that they are so. Such are they who are of the Lord's celestial kingdom, and such were these angelic spirits.[aaa] We told them that there are few on our earth who have interior perception, by reason that they learn truths in their youth, and do not practise them: for man has two faculties, which are called understanding and will; they who admit truths no further than into the memory, and thence in some small degree into the understanding, and not into the life, that is, into the will, these, inasmuch as they are not capable of any illumination or interior sight from the Lord, say that those truths are to be believed, or that they are objects of faith, and also reason concerning them whether they be truths or not; yea, they are not willing that they should be perceived by any interior sight, or by a kind of illumination in the understanding. They say this, because truths with them are without light from heaven, and to those who see without light from heaven, what is false may appear like what is true, and what is true like what is false; hence so great blindness has seized several on our earth, that although they do not practise truths or live according to them, still they say that they may be saved by faith alone, as if it were the mere knowledge of things appertaining to faith which constitute man, and not a life according to that knowledge. We afterwards discoursed with them concerning the Lord, concerning love to Him, concerning neighborly love, and concerning regeneration. In regard to the Lord, we said that to love Him is to love the commandments which are from Him, which is from a principle of love to do those commandments;[bbb] in regard to neighborly love, that it consists in willing good and thence doing good to a fellow-citizen, to a man's country, to the church, or to the Lord's kingdom, not with a view to vain applause, or to establish self-merit, but from an affection of good.[ccc] Concerning regeneration, we observed that they who are regenerated by the Lord, and commit truths immediately to life, come into an interior perception concerning them; but that they who receive truths first in the memory, and afterwards will them and do

[aaa] That heaven is distinguished into two kingdoms, one of which is called the celestial kingdom, the other the spiritual kingdom, n. 3887, 4138. That the angels in the celestial kingdom have vastly more knowledge and wisdom than the angels in the spiritual kingdom, n. 2718. That the celestial angels do not think and speak from a ground of faith, like the spiritual angels, but from an internal perception that a thing is so, n. 202, 597, 607, 784, 1121, 1387, 1398, 1442, 1919, 7680, 7877, 8780. That the celestial angels say only concerning the truths of faith, yea, yea, or nay, nay, but that the spiritual angels reason whether it be so or not so, n. 202. 337, 2715, 3246, 4448, 9196.

[bbb] That to love the Lord is to live according to His commandments, n. 10,143, 10,153, 10,310, 10,578, 10,648.

[ccc] That neighborly love consists in doing what is good, just, and right, in every work and in every function, from an affection of what is good, just, and right, n. 8120—8122, 10,310, 10,336. That a life of neighborly love is a life according to the Lord's commandments, n. 3249.

them, are they who are principled in faith; for they act from a principle of faith, which is then called conscience. They said that they perceived these things to be so, and thus perceived also what faith is. I discoursed with them by spiritual ideas, whereby such things may be exhibited and comprehended in ight.

170. The spirits with whom I now discoursed were from the northern part of their earth. I was afterwards led to those who were on the western part. These also, being desirous to discover who and what I was, immediately said that there was nothing in me but evil, thinking thus to deter me from approaching nearer. I was enabled to perceive that this was their manner of accosting all who come to them; and it was granted me to reply that I well knew it to be so, and that in them also there was nothing but evil, by reason that every one is born to evil, and therefore whatever comes from man, spirit, or angel, as from what is his own, or from his selfhood, is nothing but evil, inasmuch as all good in every one is from the Lord. Hence they perceived that I was in the truth, and I was admitted to discourse with them. They then showed me their idea concerning evil in man, and concerning good from the Lord, how they are separated from each other. They placed one near the other, almost contiguous, but still distinct, yet as it were bound in a manner inexpressible, so that the good led the evil, and restrained it, insomuch that it was not allowed it to act at pleasure; and thus the good bended the evil in whatever direction it desired, without the evil knowing anything of it. In this manner they exhibited the dominion of good over evil, and at the same time a state of freedom. They then asked how the Lord appeared amongst the angels from our earth. I said that he appeared in the sun as a man, encompassed therein with a fiery solar principle, whence the angels in the heavens derive all light; and that the heat which proceeds thence is Divine Good, and that the light which proceeds thence is Divine Truth, each originating in the Divine Love, which is the fiery principle appearing around the Lord in that sun; but that that sun only appears to the angels in heaven, and not to the spirits who are beneath, since they are more removed from the reception of the good of love and of the truth of faith, than the angels who are in the heavens. See above, n. 40. It was granted them thus to inquire concerning the Lord, and concerning His appearance before the angels from our earth, inasmuch as it pleased the Lord at that instant to present himself before them, and to reduce into order the things which had been disturbed by the evil spirits of whom they complained. This also was the reason why I was led thither, that I might be an eye-witness of these things.

171 There was then seen an obscure cloud towards the east

descending from on high, which in its descent appeared by degrees bright and in a human form. At length the human form appeared in beams of flaming lustre, encompassed with small stars of the same radiance; thus the Lord presented Himself before the spirits with whom I was discoursing. At His presence all the spirits thereabouts were instantly gathered together from all sides; and when they were come they were separated, the good from the evil, the good to the right and the evil to the left, and this in an instant as of their own accord. Those on the right were arranged in order according to the nature and quality of their good, and those on the left according to the nature and quality of their evil; and they who were good were left to form amongst themselves a celestial society, but the evil were cast into the hells. Afterwards I saw that those beams of flaming lustre descended to the lower parts of the earth thereabouts to a considerable depth, and then they appeared at one time in a flaming lustre verging to lucidity, at another time in a lucidity verging to obscurity, and lastly in obscurity; and I was told by the angels that that appearance is according to the reception of truth from good, and of the false principle from evil, with those who inhabit the lower parts of that earth, and that the beams of flaming lustre themselves were subject to no such variableness. I was told also, that the lower parts of that earth were inhabited both by the good and by the evil; but that they were carefully separated, to the intent that the evil might be ruled by the good from the Lord. The angels added, that the good were by turns elevated thence into heaven by the Lord, and that others succeed in their place, and so on perpetually. In that descent, the good were separated from the evil in like manner as above, and all things were reduced to order; for the evil, by various arts and cunning contrivances, had insinuated themselves into the dwellings of the good there, and had infested them; and this was the cause of the present visitation. That cloud, which in descending appeared by degrees bright and in a Human form, and afterwards as beams of flaming lustre, was an angelic society with the Lord in the midst. Hence was shown the meaning of the Lord's words in the Gospels, where, speaking of the last judgment, He says, "*That He should come with the angels in the clouds of heaven, with glory and power.*"

172. Afterwards there were seen some monkish spirits, viz., such as had been travelling monks or missionaries in the world, of whom mention was made above; and there was also seen a crowd of spirits who were from that earth, several of them evil, whom the monkish spirits had seduced and drawn over to favor their opinions: these were seen on the eastern side of that earth, from whence they drove away the good, who betook themselves to the northern side of the earth, of whom we have spoken above. That crowd with their seducers was collected into one body,

amounting to some thousands, and was separated when the evil were cast into the hells. I was permitted to discourse with one spirit who was a monk, and to ask him what he did there. He replied that he taught them concerning the Lord. I asked, what besides. He said, concerning heaven and hell. I asked, what further. He said, concerning a belief in all that he should say. I asked again, if he taught anything else. He said, concerning the power of remitting sins, and of opening and shutting heaven. He was then examined as to what he knew concerning the Lord, concerning the truths of faith, concerning the remission of sins, concerning man's salvation, and concerning heaven and hell; and it was discovered that he knew scarce anything, that he was in an obscure and false principle concerning all and singular the truths appertaining to the above subjects, and that he was possessed solely by the lust of gain and dominion which he had contracted in the world and brought with him thence; wherefore he was told that, inasmuch as he had travelled so far as that earth under the instigation of that lust, and was so very ignorant in points of doctrine, he must needs deprive the spirits of that earth of celestial light, and cause in them the darkness of hell, and thus bring them under the dominion of hell, and not of the Lord. Moreover he was cunning and crafty to seduce others, but dull and stupid in heavenly things; wherefore he was cast thence into hell. Thus the spirits of that earth were freed from those monkish spirits.

173. The spirits of that earth mentioned also, among other particulars, that those strangers, who, as has been said, were monkish spirits, used all their endeavors to persuade them to live in society, and not separate and solitary; for spirits and angels dwell and associate in like manner as in the world; they who have dwelt in a collected state in the world, dwell also in a collected state in another life; and they who have dwelt in a separate state, divided into houses and families, dwell also in a separate state in another life. These spirits on their earth, while they lived there as men, had dwelt in a separate state, house and house, families and families, and thus nation and nation apart, and hence they knew not what it was to dwell together in society; wherefore when it was told them that those strangers wished to persuade them to dwell in society, to the intent that they might reign and rule over them, and that they could not otherwise subject them to themselves and make them slaves, they replied that they were totally ignorant what was meant by reigning and ruling. That they fly away at the very idea of rule and dominion, was made manifest to me from this circumstance, that one of them, who accompanied us back again, when I showed him the city in which I dwelt, at the first sight of it fled away, and was no more seen.

174. I then discoursed with the attendant angels concerning

dominion, observing that there were two kinds of dominion, one of neighborly love, and the other of self-love; and that the dominion of neighborly love has place among those who dwell separated into houses, families, and nations; whereas the dominion of self-love has place among those who dwell together in society. Among those who live separated into houses, families, and nations, he has dominion who is the father of the nation, and under him the father of families, and under these the father of each particular house: he is called the father of the nation in whom the families originate, from which families the houses are derived; but all these exercise a dominion of love, like that of a father towards his children, who teaches them how they ought to live, provides for their good to the utmost of his power, and distributes among them all that he possesses; while it never enters into his mind to subject them to himself, as subjects or as servants, but he loves that they should obey him as children obey their father: and inasmuch as this love increases in descending, as is generally known, therefore the father of the nation acts from a principle of more inward love than the father himself from whom the children are next descended. Such also is the dominion which has place in the heavens, inasmuch as such is the Lord's dominion; for His dominion is grounded on a principle of Divine Love towards the whole human race. But the dominion of self-love, which is opposite to the dominion of neighborly love, began when man alienated himself from the Lord; for in proportion as man does not love and worship the Lord, in the same proportion he loves and worships himself, and in the same proportion also he loves the world. Then it was, that, compelled by motives of self-preservation and security from injustice, nations, consisting of families and houses, cemented themselves into one body, and established governments under various forms; for in proportion as self-love increased, in the same proportion all kinds of evil, as enmity, envy, hatred, revenge, cruelty and deceit, increased with it, being exercised towards all who opposed that love; because from man's selfhood, which has rule in those who are principled in self-love, nothing but evil springs, inasmuch as man's selfhood is nothing else but mere evil, and of consequence is not receptive of any good from heaven. Hence self-love, while it has dominion, is the father of all such evils;[ddd] and it is

[ddd] That man's selfhood, which he derives from his parents, is nothing but dense evil, n. 210, 215, 731, 874, 876, 987, 1047, 2307, 2318, 3518, 3701, 3812, 8480, 8550, 10,283, 10,284, 10,286, 10,731. That man's selfhood consists in loving himself more than God, and the world more than heaven, and in making light of his neighbor in respect to himself, except it be for the sake of himself, and thus from motives of self-love and the love of the world, n. 694, 731, 4317, 5660. That all evils flow from self-love and the love of the world, when they have dominion, n. 1307, 1308, 1321, 1594, 1691, 3413, 7255, 7376, 7480, 7488, 8318, 9335, 9348, 10,038, 10,742 These evils are contempt of others, enmity, hatred, revenge, cruelty, and deceit

also a love of such a nature, that where it is left without restraint, it grasps at a universal dominion over the whole earth, and wishes to possess the property of all; nay, it is not even content with this, but would have dominion over heaven also, as may appear from the example of modern Babylon. Such then is the dominion of self-love, from which the dominion of neighborly love differs as much as heaven does from hell. But notwithstanding the dominion of self-love is such in societies, or in kingdoms and empires, there is still existing a dominion of neighborly love, even in those collective bodies of men, with those who are wise from a principle of faith and love towards God, for such love their neighbor. That such also in the heavens dwell distinct as to nations, families, and houses, although in societies together, but according to spiritual affinities, which have relation to the good of love and the truth of faith, by the divine mercy of the Lord will be shown elsewhere.

175. I afterwards questioned those spirits concerning various particulars in regard to the earth from whence they came, and first, concerning their Divine worship and concerning revelation. In regard to Divine worship, they said that nations with their families, every thirtieth day, meet together in one place, and hear preaching; and that the preacher on those occasions, from a pulpit a little raised from the ground, teaches them Divine truths which lead to the good of life. In regard to revelation, they said that it is communicated early in the morning in a state between sleeping and waking, when they are in an interior light not as yet disturbed by the bodily senses and worldly things; that on such occasions they hear the angels of heaven discoursing concerning Divine truths, and concerning a life in conformity thereto; and that when they are awake, an angel appears to them in a white garment by the bed-side, and then suddenly vanishes out of sight; and that hereby they know that what they heard was from heaven. Thus Divine vision is distinguished from vision not Divine; for in vision not Divine no angel appears. They added, that in this manner revelations are made to their preachers, and sometimes also to others.

176. On questioning them concerning their houses, they said that they were low, being built of wood, with a flat roof, having a cornice sloping downwards; and that in front dwelt the husband and wife, in the next chamber the children, and the men-servants and maid-servants to the back. In regard to food, they said that they drink milk with water, and have it from cows, which are woolly like sheep. Of their manner of life, they said that they go naked, and are not ashamed of it; also that their connections are with those of their own families.

n. 6667, 7372—7374, 9348, 10,038, 10,742. And that from these evils every false principle flows, n. 1047, 10,283, 10,284, 10,286.

177. In regard to the sun of that earth they related that it appears to the inhabitants of a flaming color; that the length of their years is two hundred days, and that a day equals nine hours of our time, which they could conclude from the length of the days of our earth perceivable in me; and further, that they have a perpetual spring and summer, and consequently that the fields are ever green, and the trees ever bearing fruit: the reason of this is, because their year is so short, being equal only to seventy-five days of our time; and when this is the case, the cold does not continue long in winter nor the heat in summer, and of consequence the ground is in a continual state of vegetation.

178. Concerning the ceremonies preparatory to and attending marriage, they related that a daughter, when she arrives at a marriageable age, is kept at home, nor is she allowed to leave the house till the day she is to be married; that then she is conducted to a certain connubial house, where there are also several other young women arrived at the same age brought together, and there they are placed behind a screen, which reaches to the middle of the body, so that they appear naked as to the breast and face: and that on such occasions the young men come thither to choose for themselves a wife; and when a young man sees a young woman that seems to suit him, and to whom his mind inclines him, he takes her by the hand; and if she then follows him, he leads her to a house prepared for the purpose, and she becomes his wife; for they discover from the face whether they agree in mind, inasmuch as every one's face on that earth is an index of the mind, being free from deceit and dissimulation. For the preservation of decency, aud to suppress lasciviousness, an old man is seated behind the young women, and an old woman at the side of them, to make their observations. There are several such places to which the young women are conducted: and also stated times for the young men to make their choice: for if they do not find a young woman to suit them in one place, they go to another; and if not at one time, they return again at a future time. They said further, that a husband has only one wife, and in no case more than one, because to have more than one is contrary to Divine order.

THE END.

THE LAST JUDGMENT.

AN ACCOUNT

OF

THE LAST JUDGMENT,

AND THE

BABYLON DESTROYED:

SHEWING THAT

ALL THE PREDICTIONS IN THE APOCALYPSE ARE AT THIS DAY FULFILLED.

FROM

THINGS HEARD AND SEEN

From the Latin of

EMANUEL SWEDENBORG,

Servant of the Lord Jesus Christ.

BEING A TRANSLATION OF HIS WORK ENTITLED

"DE ULTIMO JUDICIO, ET DE BABYLONIA DESTRUCTA: ITA QUOD OMNIA QUÆ IN APOCALYPSI PRÆDICTA SUNT, HODIE IMPLETA SINT. EX AUDITIS ET VISIS." LONDINI: MDCCLVIII.

NEW YORK:

AMERICAN SWEDENBORG PRINTING AND PUBLISHING SOCIETY,

CONTENTS.

OF

THE LAST JUDGMENT,

AND

THE BABYLON WHICH HAS BEEN DESTROYED.

THAT THE DAY OF THE LAST JUDGMENT DOES NOT MEAN THE DESTRUCTION OF THE WORLD.

1. THOSE who have been unacquainted with the spiritual sense of the Word, have always understood that everything in the visible world will be destroyed in the day of the last judgment; for it is said, that heaven and earth are then to perish, and that God will create a new heaven and a new earth: in which opinion they have also confirmed themselves because it is said, that all men are then to rise from their graves, and that the good are then to be separated from the evil, with more to the same purport: but it is thus expressed in the literal sense of the Word, because this sense of the Word is natural, and in the ultimate of Divine order, of which the whole and every part contains a spiritual sense within it: for which reason, he who comprehends the Word only according to the sense of the letter, may be led into various opinions, as actually is the case in the Christian world, where so many heresies exist from this ground, and every one of them is confirmed from the Word. But since no one has hitherto known, that in the whole, and in every part of the Word there is a spiritual sense, nor even what a spiritual sense is, therefore they who have embraced this opinion concerning the last judgment are pardonable. But still they may now know, that neither the visible heaven nor the habitable earth will perish, but that both will remain for ever; and that by a new heaven and a new earth is to be understood a new church, both in the heavens and on the earth: it is said a new church in the heavens, for there is a church in the heavens, as well as on the earth; for there also is the Word, and likewise preachings, and Divine worship like that on the earth; yet with a difference, that all these things are in a more perfect state, because they are not in the natural world, but in the spiritual; hence all who dwell there are spiritual men, and not natural as they were in the world. That it is so, may be seen in the work on HEAVEN, in a special article, on the conjunction of heaven

with man by the Word, n. 303 to 310; and on Divine worship in heaven, n. 221 to 227.

2. The passages in the Word, in which mention is made of the destruction of heaven and earth, are the following: "*Lift up your eyes to heaven, and look upon the land beneath; the heavens are about to perish like smoke, and the land shall wax old like a garment*," Isaiah li. 6. "*Behold, I am about to create new heavens, and a new earth; neither shall former things be remembered*," Isa. lxv. 17. "*I will make new heavens and a new earth*," Isa. lxvi. 22. "*The stars of heaven have fallen to the earth, and heaven has departed like a scroll rolled together*." Rev. vi. 13, 14. "*I saw a great throne, and one sitting thereon, from whose face the earth and the heaven fled away, and their place was not found*," Rev. xx. 11. "*I saw a new heaven and a new earth, for the first heaven and the first earth had passed away*," Rev. xxi. 1. In these passages, by a new heaven is not meant a visible heaven, but the very heaven where the human race is assembled; for a heaven was formed from all the human race, who had lived since the commencement of the Christian church; but they who were in it were not angels, but spirits of various religions; this heaven is understood by the first heaven which was to perish: but how this was, shall be specially declared in what follows; here is related only so much as serves to show what is meant by the first heaven which was to perish. Every one even, who thinks from a somewhat enlightened reason, may perceive, that it is not the starry heaven, the so immense firmament of creation, which is here meant, but that it is heaven in a spiritual sense, where angels and spirits are.

3. That a new earth (*or land*) means a new church on earth, has hitherto been unknown, for every one by land in the Word has understood the land, when yet by land is meant the church; in a natural sense, land is the land, but in a spiritual sense it is the church, because they who are in the spiritual sense, that is, who are spiritual, as the angels are, when land is named in the Word, do not understand the land itself, but the nation which is there, and its Divine worship; hence it is that by land is signified the church; that it is so, may be seen in the ARCANA CŒLESTIA, as quoted below.[a]

[a] From the ARCANA CŒLESTIA. That by land in the Word is signified the kingdom of the Lord and the church, n. 662, 1066, 1067, 1262, 1413, 1607, 2928, 3355, 4447, 4535, 5577, 8011, 9325, 9643. Chiefly for this reason, because by land is understood the land of Canaan, and the church was there from the most ancient times; hence also it is, that heaven is called the heavenly Canaan, n. 567, 3686, 4447, 4454, 4516, 4517, 5136, 6516, 9325, 9327. And because in a spiritual sense by land is understood the nation which is there, and its worship, n. 1262. That hence the land signifies various things pertaining to the church, n. 620, 636, 1067, 2571, 3368, 3379, 3404, 8732. That the people of the land are they who belong to the spiritual church, n. 2928. That an earthquake is a change of the state of the church, n. 3355. That a new heaven and a new earth signify a church, n. 1733, 1850, 2117, 2118, 3355. 4535, 10,373.

I will here adduce one or two passages from the Word, by which in some measure it may be comprehended, that the land signifies the church. "*The cataracts from on high were opened, and the foundations of the land were shaken; in breaking, the land is broken; in agitating, the land is agitated; in reeling, the land reels like a drunkard; it moves to and fro like a cottage; and heavy upon it is the transgression thereof,*" Isa. xxiv. 18, 19, 20. "*I will cause a man to be more rare than pure gold; therefore I will remove the heaven, and the land shall be removed out of her place, in the day of the fierce anger of Jehovah,*" Isa. xiii. 12, 13. "*The land was agitated before Him, the heavens have trembled, the sun and the moon are become black, and the stars have withdrawn their splendor,*" Joel ii. 10. "*The land was shaken and agitated, and the foundations of the mountains trembled and were shaken,*" Psalm xviii. 7, 8: and in many other places.

4. Creating, moreover, in the spiritual sense of the Word, signifies to form, to establish, and to regenerate; so that creating a new heaven and a new earth signifies to establish a New Church in heaven and on earth; as may appear from the following passages: "*The people who shall be created shall praise Jah,*" Psalm cii. 18. "*Thou sendest forth the spirit, they are created; and thou renewest the faces of the land,*" Psalm civ. 30. "*Thus said Jehovah, thy Creator O Jacob, thy Former O Israel, for I have redeemed thee, and I have called thee by thy name, thou art Mine; every one called by My name, and for My glory I have created, I have formed him, yea I have made him,*" Isaiah xliii. 1, 7; and in other places: hence it is, that the new creation of man is his reformation, since he is made anew, that is, from natural he is made spiritual; and hence it is that a new creature is a reformed man.[b]

5. Concerning the spiritual sense of the Word, the small work on the WHITE HORSE, mentioned in the Apocalypse, may be consulted.

That the most ancient church, which was before the flood, and the ancient church, which was after the flood, were in the land of Canaan, n. 567, 3686, 4447, 4454, 4516, 4517, 5136, 6516, 9327. That thence all the places there became representative of such things as are in the Lord's kingdom and in the church, n. 1505, 3686, 4447, 5136. That therefore Abraham was commanded to go thither, since among his posterity from Jacob, a representative church was to be instituted, and a Word written, whose ultimate sense should consist of the representatives and significatives which were there, n. 3686, 4447, 5136, 6516. Hence it is that by land and by the land of Canaan is signified the church, n. 3038, 3481, 3705, 4447, 4517, 5757, 10,658.

[b] That to create is to create anew, or to reform and regenerate, n. 16, 88, 10,373, 10,634. That to create a new heaven and a new earth, is to institute a new church, n. 10,373. That by the creation of heaven and earth in the beginning of Genesis, in the internal sense, is described the institution of the celestial, which was the most ancient church, n. 8891, 9942, 10,545.

THAT THE PROCREATIONS OF THE HUMAN RACE ON THE EARTH WILL NEVER CEASE.

6. THEY who have adopted as their belief concerning the last judgment, that all things in the heavens and on the earth are then to perish, and that a new heaven and a new earth will become extant in their place, believe, because it follows of consequence, that the generations and procreations of the human race are therefore to cease; for they think that all things will be then accomplished, and that man's future state will be quite different from his former one: but since the day of the last judgment does not mean the destruction of the world, as was shown in the preceding article, it also follows that the human race will continue, and that procreations will never cease.

7. That the procreations of the human race will continue to eternity, is plain from many considerations, of which some are adduced in the work on HEAVEN, and of which the following are the principal:—

I. That the human race is the basis on which heaven is founded.

II. That the human race is the seminary of heaven.

III. That the extension of heaven, which is for angels, is so immense, that it cannot be filled to eternity.

IV. That they are but few respectively, of whom heaven at present is formed.

V. That the perfection of heaven increases according to plurality.

VI. And that every Divine work has respect to Infinity and Eternity.

9. *That the human race is the basis on which heaven is founded*, is because man was last created, and that which is last created is the basis of all that precedes. Creation commenced from the supreme or inmost, because from the Divine; and proceeded to ultimates or extremes, and then first subsisted. The ultimate of creation is the natural world, including the terraqueous globe, with all things on it. When these were finished, then man was created, and into him were collated all things of Divine order from first to last; into his inmost were collated those things of that order which are primary; and into his ultimates those which are ultimate; so that man was made Divine order in form: hence it is that all things in man and with man, are both from heaven and from the world, those of his mind from heaven, and those of his body from the world; for the things of heaven in-flow into his thoughts and affections, and dispose them according to reception by his spirit, and the things of the world in-flow into his sensations and pleasures, and dispose them according to reception in his body, but still in accommodation to their agreement with the thoughts

and affections of his spirit. That it is so, may be seen in several articles in the work on HEAVEN and HELL, especially in the following: That the universal heaven, in one complex, has reference to one man, n. 59 to 67. That every society in heaven has the like, n. 68 to 72. That hence every angel is in a perfect human form, n. 73 to 77. And that this is from the Divine Human of the Lord, n. 78 to 86. And moreover under the article of the correspondence of all things of heaven with all of man, n. 87 to 112. Of the correspondence of heaven with all things on earth, n. 103 to 115. And of the form of heaven, n. 200 to 212. From the above order of creation it may appear, that such is the binding chain of connection from first to last, that all things together make one, in which the prior cannot be separated from the posterior (just as a cause cannot be separated from its effect): and that thus the spiritual world cannot be separated from the natural, nor the natural world from the spiritual: nor the angelic heaven from the human race, nor the human race from the angelic heaven; wherefore it is provided by the Lord, that each shall afford a mutual assistance to the other, that is the angelic heaven to the human race, and the human race to the angelic heaven. Hence it is, that the angelic mansions are indeed in heaven, and to appearance separate from the mansions of men, and yet are with man in his affections of good and truth; their presentation to sight, as separate, is but an appearance; as may be seen in an article in the work on HEAVEN and HELL, where space in heaven is treated of, n. 191 to 199. That the mansions of angels are with men in their affections of good and truth, is understood by these words of the Lord, "*He who loveth me, keepeth my words, and my Father will love him, and we will come unto him, and make our mansion with him*," John xiv. 23; by the Father and the Lord in the above passage is also signified heaven, for where the Lord is, there is heaven, since the Divine Proceeding from the Lord makes heaven, as may be seen in the work on HEAVEN and HELL, n. 7 to 12; and n. 116 to 125. And likewise by these words of the Lord, "*The Comforter the Spirit of Truth abideth with you, and is in you*." John xiv. 17; the Comforter is Divine Truth proceeding from the Lord, for which reason he is also called the Spirit of Truth, and Divine Truth makes heaven, and also angels, because they are recipient of it; that the Divine Proceeding from the Lord is Divine Truth, and that the angelic heaven is from It, may be seen in the work on HEAVEN and HELL, n. 126 to 140. The like is also understood by these words of the Lord, "*The kingdom of God is within you*," Luke xvii. 21; the kingdom of God is Divine Good and Truth, in which the angels are. That angels and spirits are with man, and in his affections, has been given me to see a thousand times, from their presence and abode with me; but angels and spirits do not know the men with whom they are, neither do men know the angels and spirits they cohabit with, for the Lord alone knows and disposes this. In a word, there is an extension into heaven of all the affections of good and truth, and communication and conjunction with those who are in the like affections there; and there is an extension into hell of all the affections of evil and the false, and a communication and conjunction with those who are in the like affections there. The extension of the affections into the spiritual world, is almost like that of sight into the natural world; communications in both are nearly similar; yet with this difference, that in the natural world there are objects, but in the spiritual world angelic societies. Hence it appears, that the connection of the angelic heaven with the human race is such that the one subsists from the other, and that the angelic heaven without mankind would be like a house without a foundation, for heaven closes into mankind and rests upon them. The case in this is the same as with each particular man; his spiritual things, which pertain to his thought and will, inflow into his natural things, which pertain to his sensations and actions, and in these they terminate and subsist; if man were not in possession of them, that is, if he were without these boundings and ultimates, his spiritual things, which pertain to the thoughts and affections of his spirit, would dissolve away, like things unbounded, or like those which have no foundation: and it happens, moreover, when a man passes from the natural into the spiitual world, which takes place when he dies, that then, since he is a spirit, he no longer subsists on his own basis, but upon the common basis, which is mankind. He who knows not the mysteries of heaven, may believe that angels subsist without men, and men without angels; but I can asseverate from all my experience of heaven, and from all my discourse with the angels, that no angel or spirit subsists apart from man, and no man apart from spirits and angels, but that there is a mutual and reciprocal conjunction. From this, it may now be seen that mankind and the angelic heaven make one, and subsist mutually from, and interchangeably with each other, and thus that the one cannot be removed from the other.

10. *That mankind is the Seminary of heaven*, will appear from a subsequent article, in which it will be shown, that heaven and hell are from mankind, and that therefore mankind is the seminary of heaven. It must, however, first be mentioned, that as heaven has been formed of the human race, from the first creation until now, so it will be formed and enlarged from the same source hereafter. It is indeed possible that the human race on one earth may perish, which comes to pass when they separate themselves entirely from the Divine, for then man no longer has spiritual life, but only natural, like that of beasts; and when man is such no society can be formed, and held bound by laws,

since without the influx of heaven, and thus without the Divine government, men would become insane, and rush unchecked into every wickedness, the one against the other. But although mankind, by separation from the Divine, were to perish on one earth, which however is provided against by the Lord, yet still they would continue on other earths; for that there are earths in the universe to some hundreds of thousands, may be seen in the little work, "OF THE EARTHS IN OUR SOLAR SYSTEM CALLED PLANETS, AND OF THE EARTHS IN THE STARRY HEAVEN." It was declared to me from heaven, that the human race on this earth would have perished, so that not one man would have existed on it at this day, if the Lord had not come into the world, and on this earth assumed the Human, and made it Divine; and also, unless the Lord had given to this earth such a Word as might serve for a basis to the angelic heaven, and for its conjunction *with mankind*; that the conjunction of heaven with man is by the Word, may be seen in the work on HEAVEN AND HELL, n. 303 to 310. But that such is the case can be comprehended only by those who think spiritually, that is, by those who through the acknowledgment of the Lord's Divinity are conjoined with heaven, for they alone are able to think spiritually.

11. *That the extension of heaven, which is for angels, is so immense, that it cannot be filled to eternity*, appears from what has been said in the work on HEAVEN AND HELL, On the immensity of heaven, n. 415 to 420: and *That they are but few respectively of whom heaven is at present formed*, in the little work on the EARTHS IN THE UNIVERSE, n. 126.

12. *That the perfection of heaven increases according to plurality*, results from its form, according to which its associations are disposed in order, and its communications flow, for it is of all *forms* the most perfect; and in proportion to the increase of numbers in that most perfect form, there is given a direction and consent of more and more to unity, and therefore a closer and a more unanimous conjunction; the consent and the conjunction derived from it increase by plurality, for every thing is there inserted as a mediate relation between two or more, and what is inserted confirms and conjoins. The form of heaven is like the form of the human mind, the perfection of which increases according to the increase of truth and good, from whence are its intelligence and wisdom. The form of the human mind, which is in heavenly wisdom and intelligence, is like the form of heaven, because the mind is the least image of that form; hence it is, that on all sides there is a communication of the thoughts and affections of good and truth in such men, and in angels, with surrounding societies of heaven; and an extension according to the increase of wisdom, and thus according to the plurality of the knowledges of truth implanted

in the intellect and according to the abundance of the affections of good implanted in the will; and therefore in the mind, for the mind consists of the intellect and the will. The human and angelic mind is such that it may be enlarged to eternity, and as it is enlarged, so it is perfected; and this is especially the case, when man is led by the Lord, for he is then introduced into genuine truths, which are implanted in his intellect, and into genuine goods, which are implanted in his will; for the Lord then disposes all things of such a mind into the form of heaven, until at length it is a heaven in the least form. From this comparison, which is a true parallel, it is evident, that the plurality of the angels perfects heaven. Moreover, every form consists of various parts; a form which does not consist of the various parts, is not a form, for it has no quality, and no changes of state; the quality of every form results from the arrangement of various things within it, from their mutual respectiveness, and from their consent to unity, by virtue of which every form is considered as one thing; such a form, in proportion to the multitude of the various things arranged within it, is the more perfect, for every one of them, as before observed, confirms, corroborates, conjoins, and so produces perfection. But this is still more plain from what has been shown in the work on HEAVEN AND HELL, especially where it treats on the following subject: That every society of heaven is a heaven in a lesser form, and every angel a heaven in the least form, n. 51 to 58; and also in the article, Of the form of heaven, according to which associations and communications have place there, n. 200 to 212; and On the wisdom of the angels of heaven, n. 265 to 275.

13. *That every Divine work has respect to Infinity and Eternity*, is evident from many things which exist both in heaven and in the world: in neither of them is there ever given any one thing exactly similar to, or the same as, any other: no two faces are either alike or identical, nor will be to eternity: in like manner the disposition of one is never altogether like that of another; wherefore there are as many faces and as many dispositions, as there are men and angels; there never exists in any one man [in whom yet there are innumerable parts which constitute his body, and innumerable affections which constitute his disposition], any one thing quite alike to, or identical with any one thing in another man; hence it is that every one leads a life distinct from the life of another. The same order exists in the whole and in every part of nature; that such infinite variety is in each and in all, is because they all originate from the Divine, who is Infinite; hence there is a certain image of Infinity every where, to the end, that the Divine may regard all things as His own work, and at the same time, that all things, as His work, may have respect to the Divine. A familiar instance may serve

to illustrate the manner in which everything in nature has respect to Infinity and Eternity; any seed, be it the produce of a tree, or of corn, or of a flower, is so created, that it may be multiplied to Infinity, and endure to Eternity; for from one seed are produced many, five, ten, twenty, to a hundred, and from each of these again as many more; such fructification from one seed continuing but for a century, would cover the surface not only of one, but of myriads of earths; the same seeds are so created, that their durations may be eternal; hence it is evident, that the idea of Infinity and Eternity is contained in them; and the like is true in all other cases. The angelic heaven is the end for which all things in the universe were created, for it is the end on account of which mankind exists, and mankind is the end regarded in the creation of the visible heaven, and the earths included in it; wherefore that Divine work, namely, the angelic heaven, primarily has respect to Infinity and Eternity, and therefore to its multiplication without end, for the Divine Himself dwells within it. Hence also it is clear, that the human race will never cease, for were it to cease, the Divine work would be limited to a certain number, and thus its respectiveness to Infinity would perish.

THAT HEAVEN AND HELL ARE FROM MANKIND.

14. It is altogether unknown in the Christian world, that heaven and hell are from mankind; for it is believed that angels were created at the beginning, and that heaven was formed of them; and, that the devil or satan was an angel of light, who, becoming rebellious, was cast down with his crew, and that this was the origin of hell. The angels are greatly astonished at such a faith in the Christian world, and still more, that nothing at all is there known of heaven, when yet it is a primary subject of doctrine in the church; and since such ignorance prevails, they are rejoiced in heart that it has now pleased the Lord to reveal to men many things concerning heaven, and also concerning hell, and by this means, as far as possible, to dissipate the darkness which daily increases, because the church has come to its end: wherefore they wish me to declare from them, that there is no one in the universal heaven, who was created an angel from the first, nor any devil in hell who was created an angel of light, and *then* cast down, but that all both in heaven and in hell are from the human race: in heaven those who had lived in the world in heavenly love and faith, and in hell those who had lived in hellish love and faith; and that it is hell in the whole complex, which is called the devil and satan; that the hell behind, which is the

abode of evil genii, is the Devil, and the hell in front, which is the abode of evil spirits, is Satan.[c] What the one hell is, and what the other, may be seen in the work on HEAVEN AND HELL, towards the end. The angels said, that the Christian world have conceived such a belief about those in heaven and hell, from certain passages in the Word no otherwise understood than according to the sense of the letter, and not illustrated and explained by genuine doctrine from the Word; when yet the sense of the letter, if the genuine doctrine of the church does not shine before it, divides the mind into various opinions; whence come ignorance, heresies, and errors.[d]

15. Another cause of such a belief in the man of the church is, that he believes that no one can go to heaven or hell before the time of the last judgment, of which he has conceived this opinion that the visible world is then to perish, and to become extant anew, and that then the soul will return into its body, and that their conjunction will again enable man to live as man. This belief involves another about the angels, that they were created from the beginning; for it is impossible to believe that heaven and hell are from mankind, when it is believed that no man goes to either till the end of the world. But in order that man may be convinced that it is not so, it has been granted me to have fellowship with angels, and also to speak with those who are in hell, and this now for many years, sometimes continuously from morning till evening, and thus to be instructed concerning heaven and hell; to the end that the man of the church may no longer remain in his erroneous belief, about a resurrection at the day of judgment, about a state of the soul in the interval, as well as about angels, and about a devil; which belief, since it is a belief of the false, induces darkness; and with those who think of such things from self-intelligence, brings on doubt, and at length denial; for they say in heart, how can so vast a heaven, and so many stars, with sun and moon, be destroyed and dissipated? and how can the stars fall from heaven upon the earth, which yet are larger than the earth? or how can bodies, eaten up by worms, consumed by putrefaction, and scattered to all the winds, be re-collected for

[c] That the hells, or the infernals, taken collectively, are called the devil and satan, n. 694. That they who have been devils in the world, become devils after death, n. 968.

[d] That the doctrine of the church must be from the Word, n. 3464, 5402, 6832, 10,763, 10,765. That the Word cannot be understood without doctrine, n. 9021, 9409, 9424, 9430, 10,324, 10,431, 10,582. That true doctrine is a lamp to those who read the Word, n. 10,401. That genuine doctrine must come from those who are in illustration from the Lord, n. 2510, 2516, 2519, 9424, 10,105. That they who dwell in the literal sense of the Word without doctrine, can arrive at no understanding of Divine Truths, n. 9409, 9410, 10,582. And that they are led into many errors, n. 40,431. The difference between those who teach and learn from the doctrine of the church derived from the Word, and those (who teach and learn) only from the literal sense of the Word, n. 9025.

their souls? in the mean time, where is the soul, and what is it without the senses which it had in the body? with such like sayings on matters, which being incomprehensible, fall not within belief, and destroy in many the faith in man's eternal life, in a heaven and a hell, and with them, in all the remaining tenets of the faith of the church. That they have wrought this destruction is evident from those who say, Who ever came from heaven to tell us that it does exist? What is hell? Is it anything at all? What is the meaning of man's being tormented with eternal fire? What is this day of judgment? Has it not been expected for ages in vain? Questions such as these imply complete denial. Lest therefore, they who think thus (as do many who, from their knowledge in worldly matters are reputed skilful and learned), should any longer disturb and seduce the simple in faith and heart, and induce infernal darkness concerning God, heaven, eternal life, and other subjects dependent upon these, the interiors of my spirit have been opened by the Lord, and thus it has been granted me to speak with all those of the dead whom I ever knew in the life of the body, with some for days, with some for months, and with some for a year, and also with so many others, that I should come short if I reckoned them at an hundred thousand, of whom many were in the heavens, and many in the hells. I have also spoken with some two days after their decease, and told them that solemn preparations were then making for their funerals; to which they said, that it was well to reject that which had served them for a body and its functions in the world: and they desired me to declare that they are not dead, but alive and equally men as before, and that they had only passed out of one world into another, and did not know that they had lost anything, since they are in a body and possessed of senses as before, and in intellect and will as before, and have like thoughts and like affections, like sensations, pleasures, and desires, as when they were living in the world. Most of those who were newly deceased, when they saw that they were living men as before, and in a similar state (for after death the state of every one's life is at first similar to what it was in the world, but is successively changed with each either into heaven or into hell), were affected with new joy at being alive, and said that they had believed nothing of this; but greatly wondered that they could have been so ignorant and so blind, concerning the state of their own lives after death; and more especially, that the men of the church should be so, when yet they of all men in the world, have the greatest opportunities of light afforded them.[e] Then for the

[e] That at this day few in christendom believe that man rises again immediately after death, Pref. to chap. xvi. of Gen. n. 4622, 10,758. But at the time of the last judgment, when the visible world is to perish, n. 10,594. The cause of such delief, n. 10,594, 10.758. That nevertheless man does rise again immediately after

first time they saw the cause of this blindness and ignorance, which is, that external things, such as relate to the world and the body, had occupied and filled their minds to such an extent, that they could not be elevated into the light of heaven and behold the things of the church, which are beyond its doctrinals; for mere darkness inflows from corporeal and worldly things (if they are so much loved as they are at the present day), whenever man wishes to think of the things of heaven, beyond the dictate of the doctrine of faith which belongs to his church.

16. Very many of the learned from the Christian world, are bewildered when they find themselves after death in a body, in garments, and in houses as they were in the world; and when they recall to memory, what they had thought of the life after death, of the soul, of spirits, of heaven and of hell, they are affected with shame, declare that they have thought like fools, and that the simple in faith are much wiser than they are. The learned were explored, who had confirmed themselves in such errors, and who had attributed all things to nature, and it was found, that the interiors of their minds were closed, and the exteriors opened, so that they had not looked to heaven, but to the world, and hence also to hell; for in so far as the interiors of the mind are opened, so far man looks to heaven, but in so far as the interiors are closed, and the exteriors opened, in so far he looks to hell; for the interiors of man are formed for the reception of the all of heaven, and his exteriors for the reception of the all of the world, and they who receive the world, and not at the same time heaven, receive hell.[f]

17. That the spirit of man, after its release from the body, is a man, and in a human form, has been attested to me by the daily experience of many years; for I have seen, heard, and conversed with spirits a thousand times; and even on this very subject; that men in the world do not believe them to be men, and that they who do believe it, are accounted simpletons by the learned. The spirits were grieved in heart, that such ignorance should still prevail in the world, and most of all in the church; but this, they said, proceeded principally from the

death, and that then he is a man in the general and in every particular, n. 4527, 5006, 7078, 8939, 8991, 10,594, 10,758. That the soul, which lives after death, is man's spirit, which is the real man in the man, and which also in the other life is in a perfect human form, n. 322, 1880, 1881, 3633, 4622, 4735, 5883, 6054, 6605, 6626, 7021, 10,594. The same from experience, n. 4527, 5006, 8939. And from the Word, n. 10,597. What is understood by the dead being seen in the holy city, Matt. xxvii. 53, is explained, n. 9229. How man is raised from the dead; by experience, n. 168 to 189. Of his state after resuscitation, n. 317, 318, 319. 2119, 5070, 10,596. False opinions about the soul and the resurrection, n. 444, 445, 4527, 4622, 4658.

f That in man the spiritual and the natural worlds are conjoined, n. 6057. That man's internal is formed in the image of heaven, but his external in the image of the world, n. 3628, 4523, 4524, 6057, 6314, 9706, 10,156, 10,472.

learned, whose thoughts of the soul have been sensual-corporeal; wherefore they have conceived no other idea of it, than such as they have of mere thought; which, when it is regarded without any subject in which *it may be*, and from which *it may proceed*, [in quo et ex quo] is like some volatile form of pure ether, which is necessarily dispersed when the body dies; but since the church derives a belief in the immortality of the soul from the Word, they were obliged to ascribe to it some vitality, such as they assign to thought, though not the sensitivity which man enjoys, till it is again united to its body. On this opinion is founded the doctrine of a resurrection at the time of the last judgment, and a belief in a conjunction (of the soul and the body then); for when this hypothesis about the soul, is coupled with the church-belief in man's eternal life, no other conclusion can be come to: hence it is, that when any one thinks of the soul, from the doctrine and hypothesis together, he quite fails to perceive that it is a spirit, and that this spirit is in a human form. Add to this, that scarcely any one at this day knows what the spiritual is, and still less that they who are spiritual, as all spirits and angels are, have anything of the human form. Hence it is, that almost all who come from the world are in the greatest amazement that they are alive, and equally men as before, with no difference whatever: but when they cease to be amazed at themselves, they then wonder that the church should know nothing of this state of men after death, when yet all who have ever lived in the world, are in the other life, and live as men; and because they have also wondered why this was not disclosed to man by visions, it was told them from heaven, that this could be done, for nothing is easier, when the Lord pleases, but that still they who had confirmed themselves in falses against it, would not believe, even though themselves were to see it; and moreover, that it is perilous to manifest anything from heaven to those who are in worldly and corporeal *loves*, for in this case they would first believe and afterwards deny, and thus profane an essential truth; for to believe and afterwards to deny, is to profane; and they who profane, are thrust down into the lowest and most grievous of all the hells. It is this peril which is understood by these words of the Lord, "*He hath blinded their eyes, and hardened their hearts, lest they should see with the eyes and understand with the heart, and convert themselves, and I should heal them*," John xii. 40; and that they who are in worldly and corporeal loves, still would not believe, *is understood* by these words, "*Abraham said to the rich man in hell, They have Moses and the prophets, let them hear them; but he said, Nay, father Abraham, but if one from the dead come to them, they will be converted; but Abraham said to him, if they hear not Moses and the prophets, neither will they believe even if one rose from the dead,*" Luke xvi. 29, 30, 31.

18. That heaven is from mankind, is evident from this, that angelic and human minds are similar; both enjoying the faculty of understanding, of perceiving, and of willing; both being formed for receiving heaven; for the human mind possesses wisdom as well as the angelic; but it is not so wise in the world, because it is in a terrestrial body, in which its spiritual mind thinks naturally, for its spiritual thought, which it has in common with an angel, then flows down into natural ideas correspondent with spiritual, and is thus perceived in them; but it is otherwise when the mind of man is freed from its connection with the body; then it no longer thinks naturally but spiritually; and when spiritually, it has thoughts incomprehensible and ineffable to the natural man, as an angel has. Hence it is evident, that man's internal, which is called his spirit, in its own essence is an angel.[g] That an angel is in a perfect human form, may be seen in the work on Heaven and Hell, n. 73 to 77: but when man's internal is not opened above, but only below, then still, after its removal from the body, it is in a human form, but a direful and diabolical one, for it cannot look upwards to heaven, but only downwards to hell.

19. That heaven and hell are from mankind, the church moreover might have known from the Word, and made *part* of its own doctrine, had it been admissive of illustration from heaven, and attended to the Lord's words to the thief, that "*to-day he should be with Him in paradise*," Luke xxiii. 43; or to those which the Lord spake concerning Dives and Lazarus, that, "*the one went to hell, and thence spoke with Abraham, and that the other went to heaven*," Luke xvi. 19 to 31; or to what the Lord told the Sadducees respecting the resurrection, that "*God is not the God of the dead, but of the living*," Matt. xxii. 32: and furthermore *the church might have known it* from the common faith of all who live well, especially from their faith in the hour of death, when they are no longer in worldly and corporeal *states*, in that they believe they shall go to heaven, as soon as the life of their body ceases; this faith prevails with all, so long as they do not think, from the doctrine of the church, of a resurrection at the time of the last judgment. Inquire into the subject and you will be confirmed that it is so.

20. He who has been instructed on Divine order, may moreover understand, that man was created to become an an-

[g] That there are as many degrees of life in man, as there are heavens, and that they are opened after death according to his life, n. 3747, 9594. That heaven is in man, n. 3884. That the men who are living a life of love and charity, have angelic wisdom in them, but that it is then latent, and that they come into it after death, n. 2494. That in the Word, the man who receives the good of love and of faith from the Lord, is called an angel, n. 10,528.

gel, because in him is the ultimate of order, [see n. 9] in which *ultimate*, whatever belongs to celestial and angelic wisdom may be formed, renewed and multiplied: Divine order never subsists in the mediate, so as to form anything there without an ultimate, for it is not in its own fulness and perfection *there*, but it proceeds to an ultimate: and when it is in its own ultimate, it then forms, and also by mediates there collated, renews and produces itself farther, which is brought about by procreations: wherefore the seminary of heaven is in the *ultimate*. This also is the meaning of the things related of man, and of his creation in the first chapter of Genesis, v. 26, 27, 28. "*God said, We will make man into our image, according to our likeness; and God created man into the image of Himself, into the image of God He created him; male and female He created them; and God blessed them, and God said unto them, be ye fruitful and multiply:*" to create into the image of God, and into the likeness of God, is to confer upon man all things of Divine order from first to last, and thus to make him an angel, as regards the interiors of his mind.

21. That the Lord rose again not only as to the Spirit, but also as to the Body, is because the Lord, when He was in the world, glorified His whole Human, that is, made it Divine: for the Soul, which He had from the Father, of Itself was the Essential Divine, and the body was made a similitude of the Soul, that is of the Father, and therefore also Divine: hence it is that He Himself, [unlike any other man], rose again as regarded both;[h] which He also disclosed to His disciples, who believed they saw a spirit when *they beheld* Him; for He said, *behold my hands and my feet, that it is I Myself: handle Me and see, for a spirit has not flesh and bones, as ye see Me have,*" Luke xxiv. 36, 37, 38; by which *words* He pointed out that He was not only a Man as to the Spirit, but also as to the Body.

22. Moreover that heaven and hell are from mankind, has been shown in many articles in the work on HEAVEN and HELL; as for instance in these following, Of the nations and people in heaven who are not within the church, n. 318 to 328. Of infants in heaven, n. 329 to 345. Of the wise and the simple in heaven, n. 346 to 356. Of the rich and the poor in heaven, n. 357 to 365. That every man is a spirit, as regards his own interiors, n. 432 to 444. That man after death is in a perfect human form, n. 453 to 460. That man after death is in *possession of* all the sense, memory, thought, and affection, which he had in the world, and leaves nothing but his terrestrial body, n. 461 to 469. Of the first state of man after death, n. 491 to

h That man rises again as to the spirit only, n. 10,593, 10,594. That the Lord alone rose as to the body also, n. 1729, 2083, 5078, 10,825.

498. Of the second state of man after death, n. 499 to 511. Of his third state, n. 512 to 517. See moreover what is said of the hells, n. 536 to 588. From all these articles it may be seen to result, that heaven does not consist of any angels created in the beginning, nor hell of any devil and his crew, but solely of those who have been born men.

THAT ALL WHO HAVE EVER BEEN BORN MEN FROM THE BEGINNING OF CREATION, AND ARE DECEASED, ARE EITHER IN HEAVEN OR IN HELL.

23. I. This is a consequence of what was declared and shown in the preceding article, namely, that heaven and hell are from mankind.

II. And of this, that every man after the life in the world, lives to eternity.

III. That thus all who have ever been born men from the creation of the world, and are deceased, are either in heaven or in hell.

IV. That since all who are to be born hereafter, must also go into the spiritual world, that world is so vast, and such a world, that the natural world, the abode of men on earth, cannot be compared with it.

But in order that all these things may be the more distinctly perceived, and the more evident, I wish to expound and describe them one by one.

24. *That it is a consequence of what was declared and shown in the preceding article,* [*namely, that heaven and hell are from mankind*], that all who have ever been born men from the beginning of creation, and are deceased, are either in heaven or in hell, is clear without explication. It has been the common belief hitherto, that men are not to go to heaven or to hell before the day of the last judgment, when souls are to return into their own bodies, and thus to realize such *conditions*, as are believed to be the properties of the body: the simple have been led into this belief by men professing wisdom, who have made the interior state of man the subject of their inquiry. These men, having never entertained any thought of the spiritual world, but only of the natural world, nor therefore of the spiritual man, knew not that the spiritual man which is in every natural man, is in the human form, as well as the natural man; and hence it never entered their minds that the natural man draws his own human form from his spiritual man; although they might have seen that the spiritual man acts at will upon the whole, and upon every part of the natural man, and that the natural man of himself does absolutely nothing. It is the

spiritual man who thinks and wills, for this the natural man of himself cannot do, and thought and will are the all in all of the natural man, for he is put in action as the spiritual man wills, and speaks as *the spiritual* thinks, and that so entirely, that action is nothing without will, and speech is nothing without thought, for on the removal of thought and will, speech and action cease in a moment. From this it is evident that the spiritual man is indeed a man, and that he is in the whole, and in every part of the natural man, and that therefore their effigies are alike, for the part or particle of the natural man, in which the spiritual does not act, has no life in it. But the spiritual man cannot appear to the eyes of the natural man, for, although it is according to order, that the spiritual should see the natural, it is contrary to order, that the natural should see the spiritual; since there is given an influx, and therefore also a sight, of the spiritual into the natural, (for sight too is influx), but not the reverse. It is the spiritual man who is called the spirit of man, and who appears in the spiritual world in a perfect human form, and lives after death. Because they who are intelligent have *hitherto* known nothing of the spiritual world, and therefore nothing of the spirit of man, [as was said above], they have conceived a notion, that man cannot live as man after death, before his soul returns into the body, and again puts on the senses: hence have arisen their so trifling ideas about man's resurrection, to wit, that corpses, though eaten up by worms and fish, or quite gone to dust, are to be re-collected by Divine Omnipotence, and re-united to souls; and that this is not to happen till the end of the world, when the visible universe is to perish; with many more such notions, which are every one of them inconceivable, and at the first glance of the mind, strike it as impossibilities, and contrary to Divine Order, tending thus to weaken the faith of many; for those who think wisely, cannot believe what they do not in some measure comprehend; no belief in impossibilities can exist, that is, no belief in such things as man thinks to be impossible: hence also those who disbelieve the life after death, derive an argument in support of their denial. But that man rises again immediately after death, and that then he is in a perfect human form, may be seen in the work on HEAVEN AND HELL, in many of its articles. These things have been said, that it may be still more confirmed that heaven and hell are from mankind, from which it follows, that all who were ever born men from the beginning of creation, and are deceased, are either in heaven or in hell.

25. *That every man after the life in the world lives to eternity*, results from this, that man is then spiritual, and no longer natural, and that the spiritual man, separated from the natural, maintains his quality to eternity, for man's state cannot be changed after death. Moreover, the spiritual of every man is

in conjunction with the Divine, since it has the power of thinking of the Divine, and also of loving the Divine, and of being affected with all things which are from the Divine, [such as those which the church teaches], and therefore of being conjoined to the Divine by thought and will, which are the two faculties of the spiritual man, and constitute his life; and that which can thus be conjoined to the Divine, can never die, for the Divine is with it, and conjoins it to Himself. Furthermore, as regards his spirit, man is created to the form of heaven, and the form of heaven is from the Divine Himself, as may be seen in the work on HEAVEN AND HELL, where it has been shown, That the Divine of the Lord makes and forms heaven, n. 7 to 12, and n. 78 to 86. That man is created to be a heaven in the least effigy, n. 57. That heaven in the whole complex, has reference to one man, n. 59 to 66. That hence an angel is in a perfect human form, n. 73 to 77; an angel is a man regarded as to his spiritual. On this subject moreover, I have often conversed with the angels, who wondered vastly, that of those who are called intelligent in the Christian world, and who even have credit given them for intelligence by others, there are very many who utterly reject the belief of their own immortality, believing that the soul of a man is dissipated at death, just as the soul of a beast is; not perceiving the distinction between the life of a man and the life of a beast; that man has the power of thinking above himself, of God, of heaven, of love, of faith, of good, spiritual and moral, of truths, and the like, and that thus he may be elevated to the Divine Himself, and be conjoined by all those things to Him; but that beasts cannot be elevated above their own natural, to think of such things, and of consequence that their spiritual, at death, cannot be separated from their natural,[i] so as to live by itself, as man's spiritual can: whence also it is, that the life of a beast ceases, on the dissipation of its natural life. The reason why many of the so-called intelligent in the Christian world, have no faith in the immortality of their own lives, the angels declared to be this, that in heart they deny the Divine, and acknowledge nature instead of the Divine, and they who think from such principles, are not able to think of any eternity by conjunction with the Divine, nor consequently, of the state of man as dissimilar to that of beasts, for in rejecting the Divine from thought, they also reject eternity. *The angels* declared moreover, that with every man there is an inmost or supreme

That there is also an influx from the spiritual world into the lives of beasts, but that it is common, and not special as with man, n. 1633, 3646. That the distinction between men and beasts is this, that men may be elevated above themselves to the Lord, may think of the Divine, may love Him, and may thus be conjoined to the Lord, whence they have eternal life; but it is otherwise with beasts, which cannot be elevated to such things, n. 4525, 5323, 9231.

degree of life, or an inmost or supreme somewhat (quoddam) into which the Divine of the Lord primarily or proximately inflows, and from which He disposes all the remaining interiors belonging to the spiritual and natural man, which are successive in both according to gradations of order: this inmost or supreme they called the Lord's entrance into man, and His veriest dwelling place with him; and *they said*, that by this inmost or supreme, man is man, and is distinguished from brute animals which have it not; and that hence it is, that men, as regards the interiors which belong to their minds, rational and natural, unlike animals, may be elevated by the Lord to himself, may have faith in Him, may be affected by love to Him, may receive intelligence and wisdom, and speak from reason. When I asked them concerning those who deny the Divine, and the Divine Truths, by which the conjunction of the life of man with the Divine Himself is *effected*, and who live to eternity, notwithstanding their denial, they replied, that these also have the faculty of thinking and of willing, and therefore of believing and loving the things which are from the Divine, as well as those who acknowledge the Divine, and that by virtue of this faculty, they too live to eternity; and they added, that this faculty is from that inmost or supreme which is in every man, [of which mention was made above]: (that it is possessed even by those who are in hell, and that they derive from it a power of reasoning and speaking against Divine Truths, has been shown in many places): hence it is, that every man lives to eternity, be he what he may. Because every man after death lives to eternity, no angel or spirit ever thinks of death; nay they are utterly ignorant of what it is to die; wherefore, when death is mentioned in the Word, the angels understand by it either damnation, which is death in the spiritual sense, or continuation of life and resurrection.[k] These things have been said in confirmation that all the men who have ever been born, and have died, from the beginning of creation, are alive, some in heaven, and some in hell.

26. In order that I might know *that all who have ever been born men from the beginning of creation, and are deceased, are either in heaven or in hell*, it has been granted me to speak with some who lived before the deluge; and also with some who lived after the deluge; and with certain of the Jewish nation, who are made known to us by the Word of the Old Testament; with some who lived in the Lord's time; with many who lived in the ages succeeding, even down to the present day; and moreover

[k] That when death is mentioned in the Word, and spoken of the wicked, in heaven are understood damnation, (which is spiritual death), and also hell, n. 5407, 6119, 9008. That they who are in goods and truths are called living, but they who are in evils and falses dead, n. 81, 290, 7494. That by death, when spoken of the good who die, resurrection and continuation of life are understood in heaven, for at death man rises again, continues his own life, and advances in it to eternity, n. 3498, 3506, 4618, 4621, 6036, 6222.

with all those of the dead, whom I had been acquainted with during their lives in the body; and likewise with infants, and with many of the Gentiles. From this experience I have been fully convinced, that there is not one, who was ever born a man, from the first creation of this earth, who is not in heaven or in hell.

27. *That since all, who are to be born hereafter, must also go into the spiritual world, that world is so vast and such a world, that the natural world, the abode of men on earth, cannot be compared with it*, is evident, from the immense multitude of men who have passed into the spiritual world since the first creation, and who are together there; as well as from the continual increase which the spiritual world *will receive* from mankind hereafter, for from mankind it will receive accessions, and that without end, in conformity with what has been shown above, in an article for the purpose, [n. 6 to 13] namely, that the procreations of the human race on the earth will never cease. When my eyes have been opened for me, it has sometimes been granted me to see how immense, even now, is the multitude of men who are there; it is so great that it can scarcely be numbered,—such myriads are there—and that only in one place, towards one quarter; what then must the numbers be in the other quarters? For all are there collected into societies, and the societies exist in vast numbers, and each society, in its own place, forms three heavens, and three hells under them; wherefore there are some *spirits* who are on high, some who are in the middle, and some who are below them; and underneath, there are those who are in the lowest places, or in the hells; and those who are above, dwell among themselves as men dwell, in cities, in which hundreds of thousands are together: whence it is evident, that the natural world, the abode of men on earth, cannot be compared with that world, as regards the multitude of the human race; so that when man passes from the natural world into the spiritual, it is like going from a village into a mighty city. That neither can the natural world be compared with the spiritual world in kind, may appear from this, that not only have all the things which are in the natural world an existence there, but innumerable others besides, which never were seen in this world, nor can be presented to the sight, for spiritual things are there effigied by natural-seeming appearances which fully represent them, each several thing with an infinite variety; for the spiritual so far exceeds the natural in excellence, that the things are few which can be produced to the natural sense; the natural sense not receiving one, for thousands which the spiritual mind receives; and all things which belong to the spiritual mind, are presented, even in forms to the sight *of spirits*, and this is the reason why it is impossible to describe what the spiritual world is, as regards its own mag-

nificent and stupendous things. These moreover increase in proportion to the multiplication of the human race in the heavens, for all things are there presented in forms which correspond to the state of each *spirit* as to love and faith, and thence as to wisdom and intelligence; and thus with a variety which increases continually, as the multitude increases; whence it has been said by those who were elevated into heaven, that they saw and heard things there, which no eye has ever seen, and no ear has ever heard. From these observations it may appear, that the spiritual world is such, that the natural world cannot be compared with it. Moreover, what it is, may be seen in the work on HEAVEN AND HELL, where it treats of the two kingdoms of heaven, n. 20 to 28. Of the societies of heaven, n. 41 to 50. Of representatives and appearances in heaven, n. 170 to 176. Of the wisdom of the angels of heaven, n. 265 to 275. The things there described however are very few.

THAT THE LAST JUDGMENT MUST BE WHERE ALL ARE TOGETHER, AND THEREFORE IN THE SPIRITUAL WORLD, AND NOT UPON EARTH.

28. CONCERNING the last judgment, it is believed that the Lord will then appear in the clouds of heaven with the angels in glory, and awaken from the sepulchres all who have ever lived since the beginning of creation, clothing their souls with bodies; and when they are thus summoned together, that He will judge them, those who have done well, to eternal life or heaven, those who have done ill, to eternal death or hell. The churches derive this belief from the sense of the letter of the Word, nor could it be removed, so long as men did not know that there is a spiritual sense within every thing which is related in the literal sense of the Word, and that that sense is the Essential Word, to which the sense of the letter serves for a foundation and a basis, and that without such a letter *as it has*, the Word could not have been Divine, or have served in heaven, as in the world, for the doctrine of life and faith, and for conjunction. He therefore who is acquainted with the spiritual things, to which the natural expressions of the Word correspond, has the power of knowing that by the Lord's advent in the clouds of heaven, is not to be understood that He will thus appear, but that He will appear in the Word; for the Lord is the Word, because He is the Divine Truth, the clouds of heaven in which He is to come, are the sense of the letter of the Word, and the Glory is its spiritual sense; the angels are the heaven, from which He will appear, and

moreover they are the Lord as to Divine Truths.[1] Hence the meaning of these words is now evident, namely, that when the end of the church is, the Lord will reveal the spiritual sense of the Word, and thus the Divine Truth, such as It is in Itself; therefore that this is the sign that the last judgment is at hand. That there is a spiritual sense within each thing and expression in the Word, and what it is, may be seen in the ARCANA CŒLESTIA, in which all the contents of Genesis and Exodus are explained according to that sense; and a collection of passages extracted from it, on the Word and its spiritual sense, may be seen in the little work, ON THE WHITE HORSE, MENTIONED IN THE APOCALYPSE.

29. That the last judgment must be in the spiritual world, and not in the natural world, or on the earth, is evident from the two preceding articles, and will be seen further in what is to follow. In the previous articles it has been shown, that heaven and hell are from mankind, and that all who were ever born men since the beginning of creation, and are deceased, are either in heaven or in hell, and that therefore they are all assembled *in the spiritual world* [ibi]: but in the articles which follow it comes tc be shown that the last judgment has already been accomplished.

30. And moreover, no one is judged from the natural man, or therefore during the life in the natural world, for man is then in a natural body: but every one is judged in the spiritual man, and therefore when he comes into the spiritual world, for man is then in a spiritual body. It is the spiritual in man which is judged, but not the natural, for no blame or criminality can be imputed to it, since it does not live of itself, but is only the servant, and passive instrument of the spiritual man. [See n. 24.] Hence also it is, that judgment is effected upon men when they have put off their natural, and put on their spiritual bodies. In the spiritual body moreover, man appears such as he is with respect to love and faith, for every one in the spiritual world is the effigy of his own love, not only as regards the face and the body, but even as regards the speech and the actions. [See the work on HEAVEN AND HELL, n. 481.] Hence

[1] From the ARCANA CŒLESTIA. That the Lord is the Word, because He is the Divine Truth in heaven, n. 2533, 2818, 2859, 2894, 3393, 3712. That the Lord is the Word, also because it is from Him, and treats of Him, n. 2859; and because it treats of the Lord alone, and primarily of the Glorification of His Human in its inmost sense, so that the Lord Himself is in it, n. 1873, 9357. That the coming of the Lord is His Presence in the Word, and revelation, n. 3900, 4060. That clouds in the Word signify the Word in the letter, or in its literal sense, n. 4060, 4391, 5922, 6343, 6752, 8106, 8781, 9430, 10,551, 10,574. That Glory in the Word signifies Divine Truth, such as it is in heaven, and such as it is in the spiritual sense, n. 4809, 5292, 8267, 8427, 9429, 10,574. That angels in the Word signify Divine Truths from the Lord, since angels are receptions of them, and do not speak them from themselves, but from the Lord, n. 1925, 2821, 3039, 4085, 4295, 4402, 6280 8192, 8301. That trumpets or cornets, which the angels then have, signify Divine Truths in heaven and revealed from heaven, n. 8815, 8823, 8915.

it is, that the true qualities of all are known, and their instantaneous separation effected, whenever the Lord pleases. From what has been said it is plain, that judgment is effected in the spiritual world, but not in the natural world, or on the earth.

31. That the natural life in man has no efficiency, but his spiritual life in the natural, since what is natural, of itself is void of life; and that the life which appears in it, is from the life of the spiritual man, and that therefore it is the spiritual man who is judged; and moreover that being judged according to deeds, means that man's spiritual is judged, may be seen in the work on HEAVEN AND HELL, in the article headed, That man after death is such as his life in the world has been, n. 470 to 484.

32. I am here desirous of adducing a certain heavenly arcanum, which is indeed mentioned in the work on HEAVEN AND HELL, but has never yet been described. Every one after death is bound to some society, even when first he comes into the spiritual world, [see that work, n. 427 to 497], but a spirit in his first state is ignorant of it, for he is then in externals and not yet in internals. When he is in this state, he goes hither and thither, wherever the desires of his animus impel him, but still actually, he is where his love is, that is, in a society composed of those who are in a love like his own. When a spirit is in such a state he then appears in many other places, in all of them also present as it were with the body, but this is only an appearance; wherefore as soon as he is led (perducitur) by the Lord into his own ruling love, he vanishes instantly from the eyes of others, and is among his own, in the society to which he was bound. This peculiarity exists in the spiritual world, and is a wonder to those who are ignorant of its cause. Hence it is then, that as soon as ever spirits are congregated together, and separated, they are also judged, and every one is presently in his own place, the good in heaven, and in a society there among their own, and the wicked in hell, and in a society there among their own. From these things it is moreover evident, that the last judgment can exist nowhere but in the spiritual world, both because every one there is in the likeness of his own life, and because he is with those who are in similar life, and is thus in society with his own. But in the natural world it is not so; the good and the evil may dwell together there, the one ignorant of what the other is, and the life's love of each producing no separation between them. Indeed it is impossible for any one in the natural body, to be either in heaven or in hell; wherefore in order that man may go to one of them, it is necessary that he put off the natural, and be judged in the spiritual body. Hence it is, as was said above, that the spiritual man is judged, and not the natural.

THAT THE LAST JUDGMENT EXISTS, WHEN THE END OF THE CHURCH IS: AND THAT THE END OF THE CHURCH IS, WHEN FAITH IS NOT, BECAUSE CHARITY IS NOT.

33. THERE are many reasons why the last judgment exists, when the end of the church is; the principal is, that then, the equilibrium between heaven and hell, and man's essential liberty along with it, begin to perish; and when man's liberty perishes, he can no longer be saved, for he cannot then be led to heaven in freedom, but is hurried into hell apart from freedom; for no man can be reformed without free-will, and all man's free-will is the result of the equilibrium between heaven and hell. That it is so, may appear from two articles in the work on HEAVEN AND HELL, where it treats, Of the equilibrium between heaven and hell, n. 589 to 596: and shows, That man is in freedom by means of that equilibrium; n. 597 to 603; and further, That no man can be reformed except in freedom.

34. That the equilibrium between heaven and hell begins to perish at the end of the church, may appear from this, that heaven and hell are from mankind, [as shown above in its proper article], and that when many go to hell, and few to heaven, evil on the one part, increases over good on the other; for evil increases in proportion as hell increases, and all evil is derived to man from hell, and all good from heaven. Now since evil increases over good at the end of the church, all are then judged by the Lord, the evil are separated from the good, all things are reduced into order, and a new heaven is established, with a new church upon earth, and thus the equilibrium is restored. It is this then which is called the last judgment, of which more will be said in the following articles.

35. It is known from the Word, that the end of the church is, when faith no longer exists within it, but it is not yet known, that faith is not, if charity is not; therefore something shall now be said upon this subject. It is foreshown by the Lord that there is no faith at the end of the church, "*When the Son of Man comes shall He find faith upon the earth*," Luke xviii. 8; and, moreover, that there is no charity then, "*In the consummation of the age iniquity will be multiplied, the charity of many will grow cold, and this gospel will be preached in all the world, and then shall the end come*," Matthew xxiv. 12, 14. The consummation of the age is the last time of the church: the state of the church successively decreasing in regard to love and faith, is described by the Lord in this chapter, but it is described by mere correspondences, and therefore the things therein predicted by the Lord cannot be understood, without a knowledge of the correspondent spiritual sense in each expression; on which account it has been granted me by the Lord to explain in the Arcana Cœlestia the whole of that chapter and a

part of the next, *both of them treating* of the consummation of the age, of His advent, of the successive vastation of the church, and of the last judgment. See the ARCANA CŒLESTIA, n. 3353 to 3356, 3486 to 3489, 3650 to 3655, 3751 to 3759, 3897 to 3901, 4056 to 4060, 4229 to 4231, 4332 to 4335, 4422 to 4424, 4635 to 4638, 4661 to 4664, 4807 to 4810, 4954 to 4959, 5063 to 5071.

36. Something shall now be said on this point, that there is no faith, if there is no charity. It is supposed that faith exists, so long as the doctrinals of the church are believed; or that they who believe, have faith; and yet mere believing is not faith, but willing and doing what is believed, is faith. When the doctrinals of the church are merely believed, they are not in man's life, but only in his memory, and thence in the thought of his outer man; nor do they enter into his life, before they enter into his will, and thence into his actions: then for the first time does faith exist in man's spirit; for man's spirit, the life of which is his essential life, is formed from his will, and from so much of his thought as proceeds from his will; the memory of man, and the thought derived from it, being only the court-yard, by which introduction is effected. Whether you say the will, or the love, it is the same, since every one wills what he loves, and loves what he wills, and the will is the receptacle of love, and the intellect, whose province it is to think, is the receptacle of faith. A man may know, think, and understand many things, but those which do not accord with his will or love, he rejects from him when he is left to himself, to meditate from his own will or love, and therefore he also rejects them after the life of the body, when he lives in the spirit; for that alone remains in man's spirit which has entered into his will or love, [as was said above]; other things after death being viewed as foreign, which he turns out of doors, and regards with aversion, because they are not properties of his love. But it is another thing when man not merely believes those doctrinals of the church which are derived from the Word, but wills them, and does them too; then faith is effected (fit); for faith is the affection of truth from the act of willing truth, because it is truth; the act of willing truth for its own sake being the spiritual essence of a man, and divested of the natural, which consists in willing truth, not for truth's sake, but for the sake of self-glory, fame and gain. Truth regarded apart from such things is spiritual, because in its own essence, it is Divine; wherefore, to will truth because it is truth, is also to acknowledge, and to love the Divine. These two are perfectly conjoined, and moreover are regarded as one in heaven, for that the Divine which proceeds from the Lord in heaven is Divine Truth, may be seen in the work on HEAVEN AND HELL; n. 128 to 132: and they are angels in the heavens, who receive it, and make it

constituent of their lives. These things are said, in order that it may be known, that faith does not consist in bare believing, but in willing and in doing, and that therefore there is no faith if there is no charity. Charity or love is to will and to do.

37. That within the church at this day, faith is so rare, that it can scarcely be said to exist at all, was made evident, from many of the learned and many of the simple, whose spirits were explored after death, as to what their faith had been in the world, and it was found, that every one of them supposed faith to be bare believing, and persuaded themselves that it was so; and that the more learned of them placed it entirely in believing, with trust or confidence, that they are saved by the Lord's passion, and His intercession, and that hardly one among them knew that there is no faith, if there is no charity, or love; nay, that they did not know what charity to the neighbor is, nor the difference between thinking and willing. For the most part they turned their backs ubon charity, saying that charity does nothing, but that faith *is* alone *effective.* When it was replied to them, that charity and faith are one, as the will and the intellect *are one*, and that charity has its seat in the will, and faith in the intellect, and that to separate the one from the other, is, as it were, to separate the will from the intellect, this they did not understand: whence it was made evident to me that scarcely any faith exists at the present day. This also was shown them to the life: they who were in the persuasion that they had faith, were led to an angelic society, where genuine faith existed, and when they were made to communicate with it, they clearly perceived that they had no faith, which afterwards moreover, they confessed in the presence of many. The same thing was also made apparent by other means to those who had made a profession of faith, and had thought they believed, without having lived the life of faith, which is charity; and they all confessed that they had no faith, because they had nothing of it in the life of their spirits, but only in some thought extrinsic to it, whilst they lived in the natural world.

38. Such is the state of the church at this day, namely, that in it there is no faith because there is no charity; and where there is no charity, there is no spiritual good, for that good exists from charity alone. It was declared from heaven that there is still good with some, but that it cannot be called spiritual, but natural good, because Essential Divine Truths are in obscurity, and Divine Truths introduce to charity, for they teach it, and regard it as their end and aim; whence no other charity can exist than such as accords with the truths which form it. The Divine Truths from which the doctrines of the chnrches are derived, respect faith alone, on which account they are called the doctrines of faith, and have no respect to

life; but truths which regard faith alone and not life, cannot make man spiritual, for so long as they are external to the life they are only natural, being merely known and thought of like common things: hence it is that spiritual good is not given at the present day, but only natural good with some. Moreover every church at the commencement is spiritual, for it begins from charity, but in the course of time it turns aside from charity to faith, and then from being an internal church it becomes an external one, and when it becomes external its end is, since it then places every thing in knowledge, and little or nothing in life. Thus also in proportion as man from being internal becomes external, spiritual light is darkened within him, until he no longer sees Divine Truth from Truth Itself, that is from the light of heaven, for Divine Truth is the light of heaven, but only from natural light, which is of such a nature, that when it is alone, and not illustrated by spiritual light, it sees Divine Truth as it were in night, and recognizes it as truth for no other reason, than that it is so called by the heads, and received as such by the commonality of the church. Hence it is, that the intellectual *faculty* of persons *in this state* cannot be illustrated by the Lord, for in as far as natural light shines in the intellectual *faculty*, in so far is spiritual light obscured; (natural light shines in the intellectual *faculty*, when the mundane, the corporeal, and the earthly, are loved in preference to the spiritual, the celestial, and the Divine); in so far also is man external.

39. But since it is not known in the Christian world that there is no faith if there is no charity, nor what charity to the neighbor is, nor even that the will constitutes the real [ipsum] man, and the thought only in as far as it proceeds from the will, therefore, in order that these subjects may come into the light of the intellect, I am desirous of adjoining a collection of passages concerning them from the Arcana Cœlestia, which may serve for illustration.

EXTRACTS FROM THE ARCANA CŒLESTIA.

OF FAITH. That they who know not that all things in the universe refer themselves to TRUTH and GOOD, and to the conjunction of both, in order to the production of anything, know not that all things of the church refer themselves to FAITH and LOVE, and to the conjunction of both, n. 7752 to 7762, 9186, 9224. That all things in the universe refer themselves to truth and good, and to their conjunction, n. 2451, 3166, 4390, 4409, 5232, 7256, 10,122, 10,555. That truths belong to faith, and goods to love, n. 4353, 4997, 7178, 10,367.

That they who know not that the whole, and all the parts in man, have relation to the INTELLECT and the WILL, and to the conjunction of both, in order that man may be man, also know not that all things of the church have relation to FAITH and LOVE, and to their conjunction, in order that the church may be in man, n. 2231, 7752, 7753, 7754, 9224, 9995, 10,122. That man has two faculties, one of which is called the intellect, and the other the will, n. 641, 803, 3623, 3939. That the intellect is dedicated to the reception of truths, or of those things which belong to faith; and the will to the reception of goods, or of those things which belong to love, n. 9300, 9930, 10,064. That hence it follows, that love or charity makes the church, and not faith alone, or faith separated from love of charity, n. 890, 916, 1798, 1799, 1834, 1844, 4766, 5826.

That faith separated from charity is no faith, n. 654, 724, 1162, 1176, 2049, 2116, 2340, 2349, 2419, 3849, 3868, 6348, 7039, 7842, 9782. That such faith perishes in another life, n. 2228, 5820. That doctrinals concerning faith alone, destroy charity, n. 6353, 8094. That they who separate faith from charity are represented in the Word by Cain, by Ham, by Reuben, by the first-born of the Egyptians, and by the Philistines, n. 3325, 7097, 7317, 8093. That in as far as charity departs, in so far prevails a religion respecting faith alone, n. 2231. That the church in process of time turns aside from charity to faith, and at length to faith alone, n. 4683, 8094. That in the last time of the church there is no faith, because there is no charity, n. 1843, 3489, 4649. That they who make faith alone salvific, excuse a life of evil; and that they who are in a life of evil, have no faith, because they have no charity, n. 3865, 7766, 7778, 7790, 7950, 8094. That they are inwardly in the falses of their own evil, although they are not aware of it, n. 7790, 7950. That therefore good cannot be conjoined to them, n. 8981, 8983. That also in another life they are opposed to good, and to those who are in good, n. 7097, 7127, 7317, 7502, 7945, 8096, 8313. That the simple in heart know better than the learned what the good of life is, and thus what charity is, but not what separated faith is, n. 4741, 4754.

That good is the esse, and truth the existere derived from it, and that thus the truth of faith has its own esse of life from the good of charity, n. 3049, 3180, 4574, 5002, 9144. Hence, that the truth of faith lives from the good of charity, or that charity is the life of faith, n. 1589, 1947, 1997, 2579, 4070, 4096, 4097, 4736, 4757, 4884, 5147, 5928, 9154, 9667, 9841, 10,729. That faith is not alive in man, when he only knows and thinks over the things of faith, but when he wills them, and from the act of willing, does them, n. 9224. That the conjunction of the Lord with man is not by faith, but by the life of faith, which is charity, n. 9380, 10,143, 10,153.

10,578, 10,645, 10,648. That worship from the good of charity is true worship, but worship from the truth of faith, without the good of charity, is merely an external act, n. 7724.

That faith alone, or faith separated from charity, is as the light of winter, in which all terrestrial growths are topid, and nothing is produced; but that faith in union with charity is as the light of spring and of summer, in which they all bloom and are made productive, n. 2231, 3146, 3412, 3413. That the wintry light, which is that of separated faith, in another life is turned into dense darkness, when the light of heaven inflows; and that they who are in that faith, are then overtaken by blindness and stupidity, n. 3412, 3413. That they who separate faith from charity, are in darkness, and thus in ignorance of truth, and thence in falses, for falses are darkness, n. 9186. That they cast themselves into falses, and thence into evils, n. 3325, 8094. The errors and falses into which they cast themselves, n. 4721, 4730, 4776, 4783, 4925, 7779, 8313, 8765, 9224. That the Word is closed against them, n. 3773, 4783, 8780. That they do not see and attend to all the things which the Lord so often spake concerning love and charity, which see, n. 1017, 3416. That they neither know what good is, what heavenly love is, nor what charity is, n. 2507, 3603, 4136, 9995.

That charity makes the church, and not faith separated from charity, n. 809, 916, 1798, 1799, 1834, 1844. How much of good would exist in the church, if charity were regarded as primary, n. 6269, 6272. That the church would be one, and not divided into many, if charity were its essential; and that then it would be unimportant if men did differ on the doctrines of faith and the rites of external worship, n. 1285, 1316, 2385, 2853, 2982, 3267, 3445, 3451, 3452. That all in heaven are regarded from charity, and none from faith without it, n. 1258, 1394, 2364, 4802.

That the twelve disciples of the Lord represented the church, as to the all of faith and charity, in one complex, as in like manner did the twelve tribes of Israel, n. 2129, 3354, 3488, 3858, 6397. That Peter, James and John, represented faith, charity, and the goods of charity, in their order, n. 3750. That Peter represented faith, n. 4738, 6000, 6073, 6344, 10,087, 10,580. And John the goods of charity; Pref. to c. xviii. and xxii. of Genesis. That in the last times, there would be no faith in the Lord, because no charity, was represented by Peter's denying the Lord three times, before the cock crew thrice; for Peter there in a representative sense is faith, n. 6000, 6073. The cock-crowing, as well as twilight, signifies in the Word the last time of the church, n. 10,134. And that three, or thrice, signify completion to the end, n. 2788, 4495, 5159, 5198, 10,127. The like is signified by what the Lord said to Peter, when Peter saw John following the Lord; "*What is it to thee, Peter? Do thou follow Me, John;*" for Peter said of John, "*What is he?*" John xxi. 21, 22, n. 10,087. That John rested on the breast of the Lord, because he represented the goods of charity, n. 3934, 10,081. That all the names of persons and places in the Word signify things abstracted from them, n. 768, 1888, 4310, 4442, 10,329.

Of Charity. That heaven is distinguished into two kingdoms, one of which is called the celestial kingdom, and the other the spiritual; love in the celestial kingdom is love to the Lord, and is called celestial love; and love in the spiritual kingdom is charity towards the neighbor, and is called spiritual love, n. 3325, 3653, 7257, 9002, 9833, 9961. That heaven is distinguished into those two kingdoms, may be seen in the work on Heaven and Hell, n. 20 to 28. And that the Divine of the Lord in the heavens is love to Him, and charity towards the neighbor, n. 13 to 19, in the same work.

That it is not known what good and truth are, unless it be known what love to the Lord and charity to the neighbor are, because all good is of love and charity, and all truth is of good, n. 7255, 7366. That to know truths, to will truths, and to be affected by truths for truth's sake, that is, because they are truths, is charity, n. 3876, 3877. That charity consists in an internal affection of doing truth, and not in an external affection without it, n. 2430, 2442, 3776, 4899, 4956, 8033. That therefore charity consists in performing uses for the sake of uses, and that its kind is according to the uses, n. 7038, 8253. That charity is man's spiritual life, n. 7081. That the whole Word is the doctrine of love and charity, n. 6632, 7262. That men at this day do not know what charity is, n. 2417, 3398, 4776, 6632. That still it may be known from the light of reason, that love and charity constitute man, n. 3957, 6273. Also that good and truth accord, that the one belongs to the other; therefore that charity and faith do the like, n. 7627.

That in the supreme sense the Lord is the Neighbor, because He is to be loved above all things; hence that every thing proceeding from Him, which contains Him (quod ab Ipso est in quo Ipse) is the neighbor; therefore that good and truth are, n. 2425, 3419, 6706, 6819, 6823, 8124. That the distinction of neighbor is according to the kind of good; thus according to the Presence of the Lord, n. 6707, 6708, 6709, 6710. That every man, and every society, also our country, and the church, and in a universal sense the kingdom of the Lord, are the neighbor; and that to do well by them, from the good of love, according to their several states, is to love the neighbor; thus that the neighbor is that good of theirs, which we ought to consult, n. 6818 to 6824, 8123. That civil good, which is justice, and moral good, which is the good of life in society, are also the neighbor, n. 2915, 4730, 8120, 8121, 8122. That to love the neighbor is not to love the person, but that in him which makes him the neighbor, that is, good and truth, n. 5025, 10,336. That they who love the person, and not that which makes the neighbor in him, love evil as well as good, n. 3820. And that they do service to the wicked as well as to the good, when yet to serve the wicked is to injure the good, and this is not to love the neighbor, n. 3820, 6703, 8120. That the judge who punishes the wicked to amend them, and lest they should corrupt the good, loves the neighbor, n. 3820, 8120, 8121.

That to love the neighbor is to do what is good, just, and upright in every work, and in every function, n. 8120, 8121, 8122. Hence, that charity towards the neighbor extends itself, both in general and in particular, to all that a man thinks, wills, and does, n. 8124. That to do good and truth for the sake of good and truth, is to love the neighbor, n. 10,310, 10,336. That they who do this, love the Lord, who in the supreme sense, is the Neighbor, n. 9212. That a life of charity is a life according to the Lord's precepts; so that to live according to Divine Truths, is to love the Lord, n. 10,143, 10,153, 10,310, 10,578, 10,648.

That genuine charity does not appropriate merit, n. 2340, 2373, 2400, 3887, 6388 to 6393. Because it is from an internal affection, thus from joy in doing good, n. 2373, 2400, 3887, 6388, 6393. That they who separate faith from charity, in the other life make a merit of faith, and of the good works they did, as matters of external form, n. 2373.

That the doctrine of the ancient church was the doctrine of life, which is the doctrine of charity, n. 2385, 2487, 3419, 3420, 4844, 6628. That the ancients, who belonged to the church, arranged the goods of charity in order, and distinguished them into classes, giving names to each, and that this was the source of their wisdom, n. 2417, 6629, 7259 to 7262. That wisdom and intelligence increase immensely in the other life, with those who have lived a life of charity in the world, n. 1941, 5859. That the Lord inflows with Divine Truth into charity, because into the very life of man, n. 2363. That man is as a garden, when charity and faith are conjoined in him, but as a desert when they are not conjoined, n. 7626. That man recedes from wisdom in proportion as he recedes from charity, n. 6630. That they who are not in charity, are in ignorance of Divine Truths, howsoever wise they may think themselves, n. 2416, 2435. That the angelic life consists in performing the goods of charity, which are uses, n. 454. That the spiritual angels are forms of charity, n. 553, 3804, 4735.

Of the Will and the Intellect. That man has two faculties, one of which is called the intellect, and the other the will,

n. 35, 641, 3939, 10,122. That those two faculties make the man himself, n. 10,076, 10,109, 10,110, 10,264, 10,284. That the man is such, as those two faculties are in him, n. 7342, 8885, 9282, 10,264, 10,284. That by them also man is distinguished from the beasts, because the intellect of man may be elevated by the Lord, and see Divine Truths, and his will may be elevated equally, and perceive Divine Goods; and thus man may be conjoined to the Lord by those two faculties, which make him man; but that it is not so with beasts, n. 4525, 5302, 5114, 6323, 9232. And since man, in that power, is above the beasts, that he cannot die as to his own interiors, which belong to his spirit, but that he lives for ever, n. 5302.

That all things in the universe refer themselves to good and truth; thus in man to the will and the intellect, n. 803, 10,122. For the intellect is the recipient of truth, and the will the recipient of good, 3332, 3623, 5332, 6065, 6125, 7503, 9300, 9930. It amounts to the same whether you say truth, or faith, for faith is of truth, and truth is of faith; and also whether you say good, or love, for love is of good, and good is of love; for what a man believes, he calls truth; and what he loves, he calls good, n. 4353, 4997, 7178, 10,122, 10,367. Hence it follows, that the intellect is the recipient of faith, and that the will is the recipient of love, n. 7178, 10,122, 10,367. And since man's intellect may be receptive of faith towards God, and his will of love towards God, that he may be conjoined to God by faith and love, and whoso can be conjoined to God by faith and love, can never die, n. 4525, 6323, 9231.

That the will of man is the very esse of his life, since it is the receptacle of love or good, and that the intellect is the existere of his life derived from it, since it is the receptacle of faith or truth, n. 3619, 5002, 9282. Thus that the life of the will is the principal life of man, and that the life of the intellect proceeds from it, n. 585, 590, 3619, 7342, 8885, 9282, 10,076, 10,109, 10,110. Just as light proceeds from fire or flame, n. 6032, 6314. That the things which enter the intellect and the will at the same time, are appropriated to man, but not those which enter the intellect alone, n 9009, 9069, 9071, 9129, 9182, 9386, 9393, 10,076, 10,109, 10,110. That those things become properties of man's life, which are received by the will, n. 3161, 9386, 9393. Hence it follows, that man is man from the will, and from its derivative intellect, n. 8911, 9069, 9071, 10,076, 10,109, 10,110. Every man moreover is loved and esteemed by others, according to the good of his will and its derivative intellect; for he who wills well, and understands well, is loved and esteemed, but he who understands well, and does not will well, is rejected and despised, n. 8911, 10,076. That man also after death remains as his will, and its derivative intellect are, n. 9069, 9071, 9386, 10,153. And that those things which belong to the intellect, and not at the same time to the will, then vanish away, because they are not in man, n. 9282. Or, what amounts to the same, that man remains after death as his love, and its derivative faith are, or as his good and its derivative truth are; and that the things which belong to faith, and not at the same time to love, or the things which belong to truth, and not at the same time to good, then vanish away, because they are not in man, and thus not of man, n. 553, 2364, 10,153. That man may receive in the intellect what he does not do from the will, or that he may understand what he cannot will, because it is against his love, n. 3539. The reason why man scarcely knows the distinction between thinking and willing, n. 9991.

How perverted is the state of those, whose intellect and will do not act in unity, n. 9075. That such is the state of hypocrites, of deceivers, of flatterers, and of dissemblers, n. 4326, 3573, 4799, 8250.

That all the will of good, and all the derivative understanding of truth are from the Lord; not so the understanding of truth, separated from the will of good, n. 1831, 3514, 5483, 5649, 6027, 8685, 8701, 10,153. That it is the intellect which is enlightened by the Lord, n. 6222, 6608, 10,659. That the intellect is enlightened in as far as man receives truth in the will, that is, in as far as he wills to do according to it, n. 3619. That the intellect has light from heaven, as the sight has light from the world, n. 1524, 5114, 6608, 9128. That the intellect is such, as are the truths from good of which it is formed, n. 10,064. That that is the intellect, which is from truths derived from good, but not that which is from falses derived from evil, n. 10,675. That the intellect is the seeing, from matters of experience and science, truths, the causes of things, connections, and consequences, in series, n. 6125. That the intellect is the seeing and perceiving whether a thing be truth, before it is confirmed, but not the being able to confirm every thing, n. 4741, 7012, 7680, 7950, 8521, 8780. That the seeing and perceiving whether a thing be truth before confirmation, is only given to those who are affected with truth for the sake of truth, and are thus in spiritual light, n. 8521. That the light of confirmation is natural light, communicable even to the wicked, n. 8780. That all dogmas, even false ones, may be confirmed, until they appear like truths, n. 2482, 2490, 5033, 6865, 7950.

THAT ALL THE THINGS, WHICH ARE PREDICTED IN THE APOCALYPSE, ARE AT THIS DAY FULFILLED.

40. No one can know what all the things which are contained in the Apocalypse signify and involve, unless he knows the internal or spiritual sense of the Word; for every thing there is written in a style similar to that of the prophecies of the Old Testament, in which each word signifies some spiritual thing, which is not apparent in the sense of the letter. Besides, the contents of the Apocalypse cannot be explained as to their spiritual sense, except by one who also knows how it went with the church, even down to its end, which can only be known in heaven, and is the thing contained in the Apocalypse: for the spiritual sense of the Word treats every where of the spiritual world, that is, of the state of the church in the heavens, as well as in the countries of the earth; hence the Word is Spiritual and Divine. It is this state which is there expounded in its own order. Hence it may appear, that the things contained in the Apocalypse can never be explained by any one but him to whom a revelation has been made concerning the successive states of the church in the heavens; for there is a church in the heavens as well as on the earth, of which something shall be said in the following articles.

41. The quality of the Lord's church in the countries of the earth, cannot be seen by any man, so long as he lives in the world,—still less how the church in process of time has turned aside from good to evil. The reason is, that man whilst he is living in the world, is in externals, and only sees those things which are palpable to his natural man; but the quality of the church as to spiritual things, which are its internals, does not appear in the world; yet it does appear in heaven as in clear day, for the angels are in spiritual thought, and also in spiritual sight, and hence see none other than spiritual things. Furthermore, all the men who have been born in this world from the beginning of creation are together in the spiritual world (as shown above) and are all there distinguished into societies according to the goods of love and faith, (as may be seen in the work on HEAVEN AND HELL, n. 41 to 50) whence it is that the state of the church, and its progressions, are manifest in heaven before the angels. Now since the state of the church as to love and faith is described in the spiritual sense of the Apocalypse, therefore no one can know what all the things in its series involve, but he to whom it has been revealed from heaven, and to whom at the same time has been imparted a knowledge of the internal or spiritual sense of the Word. This I can asseverate, that each thing there, nay, that every word, contains within it a spiritual sense, and that the all of the church, as to its spiritual state, from the beginning to the end, is fully described in that

sense; and because every word there signifies some spiritual thing, therefore not a word can be wanting without the series of things in the internal sense thereby suffering a change; on which account, at the end of that Book, it is said, "*If any one shall take away from the words of the book of this prophecy, God will take away his part from the Book of Life, and from that holy city, and from those things which are written in that Book.*" Rev. xxii. 19. It is the same with the books of the Old Testament; in them also every thing, and every word, contains an internal or spiritual sense, wherefore not one word can be taken away from them either. Hence it is that, of the Lord's Divine Providence, those books have been preserved entire to an iota since the time in which they were written, and that by the care of many who have enumerated their minutest particulars; this was provided by the Lord on account of the sanctity which is within each iota, letter, word, and thing they contain.

42. Since in like manner there is an internal or spiritual sense in every word in the Apocalypse, and since that sense contains the arcana of the state of the church in the heavens, and on the earth; and since those arcana can be revealed to no one, but to him who knows that sense, and to whom at the same time it has been granted to have consort with the angels, and to speak spiritually with them, therefore, lest the things which are therein written should be hidden to men, and should hereafter be disregarded, because they are not understood, its contents have been disclosed to me; but they are too numerous to be described in this little work; on which account I am desirous of explaining the whole book from beginning to end, and of unveiling the arcana which are within it: and the explication shall be published in less than two years, together with certain things in Daniel, which have hitherto lain hidden, because their spiritual sense was unknown.

43. He who knows not the internal or spiritual sense, never can divine what is meant in the Apocalypse by the dragon, and by the battle of Michael and his angels with it; what by the tail with which the dragon drew down the third part of the stars from heaven; what by the woman who brought forth the man-child which was caught up to God, and whom the dragon persecuted; what by the beast ascending from the sea, and the beast ascending from the earth, which had so many horns; what by the whore, with whom the kings of the earth committed whoredom; what by the first and second resurrection, and by the thousand years; what by the lake of sulphur and of fire, into which the dragon, the beast, and the false prophet were cast; what by the white horse; also what by the former heaven, and the former earth which passed away; and what by the new heaven and the new earth, in the place of the former; and

by the sea, which was no more; or what by the city New Jerusalem descending from heaven, and by its measures, wall, gates, and foundation of precious stones; what by the various numbers; besides other things, which are the veriest mysteries (arcanissima) to those who know nothing of the spiritual sense of the Word. But the meaning of all these things shall be unfolded in the promised explication on that book.

44. It has been remarked before, that all the things which are contained in that book, in the heavenly sense, are now fulfilled: in this little work I will deliver some general account of the last judgment, the Babylon destroyed, the first heaven and the first earth which passed away, the new heaven, the new earth, and the New Jerusalem; in order that it may be known, that all *its predictions* are now accomplished. But the details can only be delivered, where all these things are explained according to the description of them in the Book of Revelation.

THAT THE LAST JUDGMENT HAS BEEN ACCOMPLISHED.

45. It was shown above, in an article for the purpose, that the last judgment does not exist on the earth, but in the spiritual world, where all *who have lived* from the beginning of creation are together; and since it is so, it is impossible for any man to know when the last judgment is accomplished, for every one expects it to exist on earth, accompanied by a change of all things in the visible heaven, and in the countries of the earth and in mankind who dwell there. Lest therefore the man of the church from ignorance should live in such a belief, and lest they who think of a last judgment should expect it for ever, whence at length the belief of those things which are said of it in the literal sense of the Word must perish, and lest haply therefore many should recede from *their* faith in the Word, it has been granted me to see with my own eyes that the last judgment is now accomplished; that the evil are cast into the hells, and the good elevated into heaven, and thus that all things are reduced into order, the spiritual equilibrium between good and evil, or between heaven and hell, being thence restored. It was granted me to see from beginning to end how the last judgment was accomplished, and also how the Babylon was destroyed, how those who are understood by the dragon were cast into the abyss, and how the new heaven was formed, and a new church instituted in the heavens, which is understood by the New Jerusalem. It was granted me to see all these things with my own eyes, in order that I might be able to testify of them. This last judgment was commenced in the

beginning of the year 1757, and was fully accomplished at the end of that year.

46. But it ought to be known that the last judgment was effected upon those who had lived from the Lord's time to this day, but not upon those who had lived before: for a last judgment had twice before existed on this earth. Of these two judgments, the one is described in the Word by the flood, the other *was effected* by the Lord Himself when He was in the world, which moreover is understood by the Lord's words, "*Now is the judgment of this world, now is the prince of this world cast out*," John xii. 31; and by His words, "*These things I have spoken unto you that in Me ye may have peace; be of good cheer, I have overcome the world*," John xvi. 33; and also by these words in Isaiah, "*Who is this that cometh from Edom, walking in the multitude of his strength, great to save? I have trodden the wine press alone, therefore I have trodden them in My anger; whence their victory is sprinkled upon My garments, for the day of vengeance is in My heart, and the year of My redeemed has come; therefore He became a Saviour*," Isaiah lxiii. 1 to 8: and in many other places. A last judgment has twice before existed on this earth, because every judgment exists at the end of a church, [as shown above in an article for the purpose,] and there have been two churches on this earth, one before the flood, and one after it. The church before the flood is described in the beginning of Genesis by the new creation of the heaven and the land, and by paradise; its end, by the eating of the tree of science, and the subsequent particulars; and its last judgment by the flood; the whole by mere correspondences, according to the style of the Word; in the internal or spiritual sense of which, by the creation of the heaven and the land, the institution of a new church is understood, [see the first article]; by the paradise in Eden, its celestial wisdom; by the tree of science, and by the serpent, the scientific which destroyed it; and by the flood, the last judgment upon the men of whom it consisted. But the other church, which was after the flood, is also described in certain passages in the Word, as in Deut. xxxii. 7 to 14, and elsewhere. This church was extended through much of the Asiatic world, and was continued among the posterity of Jacob. Its end was, when the Lord came into the world. A last judgment was then effected by Him upon all who belonged to that church from its first institution; and, at the same time, upon the residue of the first church. The Lord came into the world for that end, to reduce all things in the heavens into order, and all things in the countries of the earth, by means of the heavens, and at the same time to make His Human Divine; for if this had not been done, no man could have been saved. That there were two churches on this earth before the Lord's advent, is

shown in various passages in the ARCANA CŒLESTIA, a collection of which may be seen below;[m] and that the Lord came into the world to reduce all things in the heavens into order, and all things in the countries of the earth by means of the heavens, and to make His Human Divine, *is also shown there.*[n] The third church on this earth is the Christian. Upon this church, and, at the same time, upon all those who had been in the first heaven since the Lord's time, the last judgment of which I now treat, was effected.

47. The manner in which this last judgment was effected cannot be described in all its details in this little work, for they are many, but shall be described in the explication on the Apocalypse. For the judgment was accomplished not only

m That the first and most ancient church on this earth was that which is described in the first chapters of Genesis, and that it was a celestial church, the chie of all the churches, n. 607, 895, 920, 1121, 1122, 1123, 1124, 2896, 4493, 8891, 9942, 10,545. What they who were of that church are in heaven, n. 1114 to 1125. That they are in the greatest light there, n. 1117. That there were various churches after the flood, which are called, in one word, the ancient church, n. 1125, 1126, 1127, 1327, 10,355. Through what kingdoms of Asia the ancient church was extended, n. 1238, 2385. What manner of men they of the ancient church were, n. 609, 895. That the ancient church was a representative church, n. 519, 521, 2896. What the ancient church was, when it began to decline, n. 1128. The distinction between the most ancient and ancient churches, n. 597, 607, 640, 641, 765, 784, 895, 4493. Of the church that commenced from Eber, which was called the Hebrew church, n. 1238, 1241, 1343, 4516, 4517. The distinction between the ancient and the Hebrew churches, n. 1343, 4874. Of the church instituted among the posterity of Jacob, or children of Israel, n. 4281, 4288, 4310, 4500, 4899, 4912, 6304, 7048, 9320, 10,396, 10,526, 10,531, 10,698. That the statutes, judgments and laws, which were commanded among the children of Israel, were in part like those which existed in the ancient church, n. 4449. In what manner the representative rites of the church which was instituted among the children of Israel, differed from the representative rites of the ancient church, n. 4288, 10,149. That in the most ancient church there was immediate revelation from heaven; in the ancient church revelation by correspondences; in the church among the children of Israel by an audible voice; and in the Christian church by the Word, n. 10,355. That the Lord was the God of the most ancient church, and also of the ancient church, and was called Jehovah, n. 1343, 6848.

n That the Lord, when He was in the world, reduced all things in the heavens and in the hells into order, n. 4075, 4286, 9937. That the Lord then freed the spiritual world from the antediluvians, n. 1266. What manner of men they were, n. 310, 311, 560, 562, 563, 570, 581, 586, 607, 660, 805, 808, 1034, 1120, 1265 to 1272. That the Lord by temptations and victories subjugated the hells, and reduced all things into order, and at the same time glorified His Human, n. 4287, 9397. That the Lord effected this by Himself, or by His own Power, n. 1692, 9937. That the Lord alone fought, n. 8273. That hence the Lord alone became Righteousness and Merit, n. 1813. 2025, 2026, 2027, 9715, 9809, 10,019. That thus the Lord united His Human with the Divine, n. 1725, 1729, 1733, 1737, 3318, 3381, 3382, 4286. That the passion of the cross was the last temptation, and plenary victory, by which He glorified Himself, that is, made His Human Divine, and subjugated the hells, n. 2776. 10,655, 10,659, 10,829. That the Lord could not be tempted as to the Essential Divine, n. 2795, 2803, 2813, 2814. That therefore He assumed a human from the mother, into which He admitted temptations, n. 1414, 1444, 1573, 5041, 5157, 7193, 9315. That He expelled whatever was hereditary from the mother, and put off the human He received from her, even until He was her son no longer, and that He put on the Human Divine, n. 2159. 2574, 2649, 3036, 10,829. That the Lord saved mankind by the subjugation of the hells, and the glorification of His Human, n. 4180, 10,019, 10,152, 10,655, 10,659, 10,828.

upon all the men of the Christian church, but also upon all who are called Mahometans, and, moreover, upon all the Gentiles in the whole circle of the earth; and it was effected in this order:—first upon those of the Papal religion; then upon the Mahometans; afterwards upon the Gentiles; and lastly upon the Reformed. The judgment upon the Papists shall be shown in the following article, ON THE BABYLON WHICH HAS BEEN DESTROYED; the judgment upon the Reformed in the article, ON THE FIRST HEAVEN WHICH PASSED AWAY; but something shall be said in this article, on the judgment upon the Mahometans and Gentiles.

48. The following was seen to be the arrangement in the spiritual world of all the nations and people to be judged. Collected in the middle, appeared those who are called the Reformed, where they were also distinct according to their countries; the Germans there towards the north; the Swedes there towards the west; the Danes in the west; the Dutch towards the east and the north; the English in the centre. Surrounding this whole mid-region of the Reformed, appeared collected those of the Papal religion, the greater part of them in the western, some part in the southern quarter. Beyond them were the Mahometans, also distinct according to their countries, who all appeared in the south-west. Beyond these, the Gentiles were congregated in vast numbers, constituting the very circumference; and on their outer side an appearance, as of a sea, was the boundary. This arrangement of the nations in the various quarters, was an arrangement according to each nation's common faculty of receiving Divine Truths; for in the spiritual world every one is known from the quarter, and the part of it, in which he dwells; and, moreover, in a society with many, he is known from his tarryings being made with a reference to the quarters; concerning which, see the work on HEAVEN AND HELL, n. 148, 149. It is the same when he goes from place to place; all advance to the quarters is then effected according to the successive states of the thoughts derived from the affections which belong to his proper life [propriæ]; in accordance with which all those who are spoken of in what follows were led to their own places. In a word, the ways in which every one walks in the spiritual world are actual determinations of the thoughts of the mind; whence it is, that ways, walkings, and the like, in the spiritual sense of the Word, signify the determinations and progressions of spiritual life.

49. In the Word, the four quarters are called the four winds, and a gathering is called a gathering from the four winds; as in Matthew, where the last judgment is the subject treated of, "*He shall send his angels, and they shall gather together the elect from the four winds, from one end of the heavens to the other:*" xxiv. 31; and elsewhere, "*All nations shall be*

gathered together before the Son of Man, and He shall separate them one from another, as a shepherd separates the sheep from the goats, and He shall set the sheep on the right and the goats on the left," Matthew xxv. 31, 32; which signifies that the Lord will then separate those who are in truths and at the same time in good, from those who are in truths and not in good; for in the spiritual sense of the Word, the right signifies good, and the left truth, and sheep and goats the same. The last judgment was effected upon these alone; the evil who were in no truths being in the hells already; for all the wicked who have denied the Divine in their hearts, and have rejected the truths of the church as incredible, are cast thither when they die, and therefore before the judgment. The first heaven which passed away, consisted of those who were in truths, and not in good, and the new heaven was formed of those who were in truths, and at the same time in good.

50. As regards the judgment upon the Mahometans and Gentiles, which is treated of in this article, it was thus effected. The Mahometans were led forth from their places, where they were gathered together in the south-west, by a way round the Christians, from the west, through the north, to the east, as far as its southern confine; and the good were separated from the evil in the way: the evil being cast into marshes and lakes, many too being scattered about in a certain far desert. But the good were led through the east to a land of great extent near the south, and habitations were there given them. They who were led thither had in the world acknowledged the Lord as the greatest Prophet, and as the Son of God, and had believed that He was sent by the Father to instruct mankind, and at the same time had lived a life moral-spiritual, in accordance with their religion [religiosum]. Most of these, when instructed, receive faith in the Lord, and acknowledge Him to be One with the Father. Communication is also granted them with the Christian heaven, by influx from the Lord; but they are not commingled with it, because religion separates them. All of that religion, as soon as they come into the other life, among their own, first seek Mahomet, yet he appears not, but in his place two others, who call themselves Mahomets, and who have obtained seats in the middle, under the Christian heaven, towards the left part of it. These two are in the place of Mahomet, because all after death, whatever be their religion, are first led to those they had worshiped in the world, (for every one's religion adheres to him), but secede on perceiving that these can render them no assistance. They are thus yielded up into their own religion at first, as the only possible means of effecting their withdrawal from it. Where Mahomet himself is, and what he is, and whence come those two who fill

his place, shall be told in the book in which the Apocalypse is explained.

51. The judgment was effected upon the Gentiles in nearly the same manner as upon the Mahometans; but they were not led like them in a circuit, but only a short way in the west, where the evil were separated from the good, the evil being there cast into two great gulfs, which stretched obliquely into the deep. But the good were conducted above the middle, where the Christians were, towards the land of the Mahometans in the eastern quarter, and dwellings were given them behind and beyond the Mahometans, to a great extent in the southern quarter. But those of the Gentiles who in the world had worshiped God under a human form, and had led lives of charity according to their religious principles, were conjoined with Christians in heaven, for they acknowledge and adore the Lord more than others; the most intelligent of them are from Africa. The multitude of the Gentiles and Mahometans who appeared was so great, that it could be numbered only by myriads. The judgment on this vast multitude was effected in a few days, for every one after being yielded up into his own love and into his own faith, is immediately destined and carried to his like.

52. From all these particulars appears the truth of the Lord's prediction concerning the last judgment, that "*they shall come from the east, and from the west, and from the north, and from the south, and shall sit down in the kingdom of God,*" Luke xiii. 29.

OF THE BABYLON AND ITS DESTRUCTION.

53. THAT all the things which are predicted in the Apocalypse are at this day fulfilled, may be seen above, n. 40 to 44; and that the last judgment has already been accomplished, may be seen in the preceding article; where it is also shown how the judgment was effected upon the Mahometans and Gentiles. Now follows an account of the manner in which it was effected upon the Papists, who are understood by the Babylon which is treated of in many parts of the Apocalypse, and whose destruction is the special subject of the 18th chapter, where it is thus described, "*An angel cried vehemently with a great voice, Babylon hath fallen, hath fallen, and is become the habitation of devils, and the hold of every foul spirit, and the cage of every unclean and hateful bird,*" v. 2. But before it is told how that destruction was effected, I shall premise,—

I. What is understood by the Babylon, and the manner of thing it is, (et quale ejus.)

II. What manner of men they of the Babylon are in the other life.

III. Where their habitations have hitherto been.

IV. Why they were there tolerated until the day of the last judgment.

V. The mode in which they were destroyed, and their habitations made a desert.

VI. That all those among them who were in the affection of truth from good were preserved.

VII. Of the state of those hereafter who come thence from the countries of the earth.

54. *What is understood by the Babylon, and the manner of thing it is.* By the Babylon are understood all who will to rule by religion [per religiosum]. To rule by religion, is to rule over men's souls, thus over their very spiritual lives, and to use the Divine things, which are in *their* religion, as the means *to rule.* All those who have dominion for an end, and religion for the means, in the general, are Babylon. They are called Babylon, because such dominion began in ancient times; but it was destroyed in its beginning. Its commencement is described by the city and the tower, whose head was to be in heaven; and its destruction, by the confusion of lips, whence its name Babel was derived; GENESIS xi. 1 to 9. What the particulars there related mean in the internal or spiritual sense of the Word, may be seen explained in the ARCANA CŒLESTIA, n. 1283 to 1328. Moreover that this dominion began and was instituted in Babel, appears in Daniel, where it is said of Nebuchadnezzar, that he set up an image which all were to adore, chap. iii.; and is understood by Belshazzar and his peers drinking out of the golden and silver vessels, which Nebuchadnezzar had carried away from the temple of Jerusalem, at the same time that they worshiped gods of gold, silver, copper, and iron; wherefore it was written on the wall, "*He hath numbered, he hath weighed, he hath divided;*" and on the same night the king himself was slain, chap. v. The vessels of gold and silver of the temple of Jerusalem, signify the goods and truths of the church; drinking out of them, and at the same time worshiping gods of gold, silver, copper, and iron, signify profanation; and the writing upon the wall, and the death of the king signify visitation, and destruction denounced against those who make use of Divine Goods and Truths as means. What manner of men those who are called Babylon are, is also described continually in the prophets; as in Isaiah, "*Thou mayest take up this parable concerning the king of Babylon: Jehovah hath broken the staff of the wicked, the sceptre of the rulers: thou, Lucifer, hast fallen from heaven; thou art cut down even to the earth; thou hast said in thy mind, I will ascend into heaven; I will exalt my throne over the stars of*

God, and I will sit on the mountain of the convention, in the sides of the north, I will become like the Most High. Nevertheless thou shalt be cast down into hell, to the sides of the pit; I will cut off the name and residue of Babylon, and will cause her to become an hereditary possession of the bittern," xiv. 4, 12, 13, 14, 15, 23: and again it is said in the same book, "*The lion said, Babylon is fallen, is fallen, and all the graven images of her god are cast down,*" xxi. 9; see moreover the whole of chap. xlvii. and chap. xlviii. 14 to 20; and Jeremiah, chap. l. 1, 2, 3. From these passages it is now evident what the Babylon is. It ought to be known that the church becomes a Babylon when charity and faith cease, and the love of self begins to rule in their stead; for this love, in proportion as it is unchecked, rushes on, aiming to dominate not merely over all whom it can subject to itself on earth, but even over heaven; nor does it rest there, but it climbs the very throne of God, and transfers to itself His Divine Power. That it did this, even before the Lord's coming, appears from the passages of the Word adduced above. But the Babylon here treated of, was destroyed by the Lord, when He was in the world, as well by those who composed it being reduced to mere idolaters, as by a last judgment upon them in the spiritual world, which is understood by the prophetic sayings, that "Lucifer," who there is Babylon, "was cast into hell," and that "Babylon has fallen;" and moreover by the writing on the wall, and the death of Belshazzar; and also by the stone, hewn from the rock, which destroyed the statue, of which Nebuchadnezzar dreamed.

55. But the Babylon treated of in the Apocalypse, is the Babylon of this day, which arose after the Lord's coming, and is known to be among the Papists. This Babylon is more pernicious and more abominable than that which existed before the Lord's coming, because it profanes the interior goods and truths of the church, which the Lord revealed to the world, when He *revealed* Himself. How pernicious, how inwardly abominable it is, may appear from the following summary. They who belong to it, acknowledge and adore the Lord apart from all power of saving: they entirely separate His Divine from His Human, and transfer to themselves His Divine Power, which belonged to His Human;[o] for they remit sins; they send to heaven; they cast into hell; they save whom they will; they sell salvation; thus arrogating things to themselves which are properties of Divine Power alone: and since they exercise this Power, it follows that they make gods of themselves, each

[o] That the attribution by the church, of two natures to the Lord, and the consequent separation of His Divine from His Human, was effected in a council, on the Pope's account, that the Pope might be acknowledged as the Lord's vicar, discovered from heaven in the ARCANA CŒLESTIA, n. 4738.

one according to his station, by transference from their highest, whom they call Christ's vicar, down to the lowest of them; thus they regard themselves as the Lord, and adore Him, not for His, but for their sakes. They not only adulterate and falsify the Word, but even take it away from the people, lest they should enter into the smallest light of truth; and not satisfied with this, they moreover annihilate it, acknowledging a divinity in the decrees of Rome, superior to the Divine in the Word; so that they exclude all from the way to heaven; for the acknowledgment of the Lord, faith in Him, and love to Him, are the way to heaven; and the Word is what teaches the way: whence it is, that without the Lord, by the medium of the Word, there is no salvation. They strive with all diligence to extinguish the light of heaven, which is from Divine Truth, in order that ignorance may exist in the place of it, and the denser the ignorance, the more acceptable it is to them. They extinguish the light of heaven by prohibiting the reading of the Word, and of books which contain its doctrines; instituting worship by masses destitute of Divine Truth, in a language unintelligible to the common people; and besides, they fill their world (orbem suum) with falses, those essential [ipsa] darknesses, which remove and dissipate the light. They teach, the vulgar moreover, that they have life (*eternal*) in the faith of their priests, consequently not in their own, but in that of other men. [ita in alienâ et non in suâ.] They also place all worship in a devout external, apart from the internal, making the internal into vacuum, for they deprive it of the knowledges of good and truth; and yet Divine worship is external, only in as far as it is internal, since the external proceeds from the internal. Besides this, they introduce idolatries of various kinds. They make and multiply saints; they see and tolerate the adoration of these saints, and even the prayers put up to them, almost as to gods; they expose their idols in all sorts of places; boast of their multitudinous miracles; set them over cities, temples, and monasteries: make sacred their bones—their veriest cast-away bones, which have been taken out of sepulchres; thus turning the minds of all from the worship of God, to the worship of men. Moreover, they use much artful precaution lest any one should come out of their darkness into light, from idolatrous to Divine worship; for they multiply monasteries, from which they send out spies and guards in all directions; they extort the confessions of the heart, which are also confessions of the thoughts and intentions, and if any one will not confess, they threaten him with infernal fire and torments in purgatory; and those who dare to speak against the Papal throne, and their dominion, they shut up in a horrible gaol, which is called the Inquisition. All this they do for one sole end;—that they may possess the world and its treasures, and live in congenial delights, (vivant genio) and be the mightiest of men, while the rest are their slaves. But domination such as this, is not that of heaven over hell, but of hell over heaven, for in as far as the love of ruling prevails in man, especially in the man of the church, in so far hell reigns. That this love reigns in hell, and makes hell, may be seen in the work on HEAVEN AND HELL, n. 551 to 565. From this summary it may appear that they have no church, but a Babylon among them. The church is, where the Lord Himself is worshiped, and where the Word is read.

56. *What manner of men they of the Babylon are in the other life*, can be apparent only to one who has been allowed by the Lord to be together with those who are in the spiritual world: since this has been granted to me, I am able to speak from experience, for I have seen them, I have heard tnem, and I have spoken with them. Every man after death is in a life similar to his life in the world; this cannot be changed, save only as regards the delights of the love, which are turned into correspondent things, as may appear from two articles in the work on HEAVEN AND HELL, n. 470 to 484; and n. 485 to 490. The same holds of the life of those now treated of, which is altogether such as it was in the world, with this difference, that the hidden things of their hearts are there uncovered, for they are in the spirit, in which reside the interior things of the thoughts and intentions, which they had concealed in the world, and had covered over with a devout external. And, since these hidden things were now laid open, it was perceived that more than half of those who had usurped the power of opening and shutting heaven, were downright atheists; but since dominion is rooted in their minds as in the world, and is based on this, that all power was given by the Father to the Lord Himself, and that it was transferred to Peter, and by order of succession to the heads of the church, therefore an oral confession about the Lord remains adjoined to their atheism; but even this remains only so long as they enjoy some dominion by means of it. But the rest of them, who are not atheists, are so empty (tam vacui), as to be entirely ignorant of man's spiritual life, of the means of salvation, of the Divine Truths which lead to heaven; and they know nothing at all of heavenly love and faith, believing that heaven may be granted of the Pope's grace to any one, whatever he be. Now since every one is in a life in the spiritual world, similar to his life in the natural world, without any difference, so long as he is neither in heaven nor in hell, (as is shown, and may be seen in the work on HEAVEN AND HELL, n. 453 to 480), and since the spiritual world, as regards its external appearance, is altogether like the natural world, (n. 170 to 176), therefore they also live a similar moral and civil life, and above all have similar worship, for this is inradicated in,

and inheres to man in his inmost, nor can any after death be withdrawn from it, except he be in good from truths, and in truths from good. But it is more difficult to withdraw the nation now treated of from its own worship, than other nations, because it is not in good from truths, and still less in truths from good; for its truths are not derived from the Word, with the exception of some few, which it has falsified by applying them to dominion; and hence it has none other than spurious good, for such as the truths are, such does the good become. These things are said, in order that it may be known, that the worship of this nation, in the spiritual world, is altogether similar to its worship in the natural world. Premising this, I will now relate some particulars of the worship and life of the Papists in the spiritual world. They have a certain session, in place of the session or consistory at Rome, in which their leaders meet, and consult on various matters touching their religion, especially on the means of holding the vulgar in blind obedience, and of enlarging their own dominion. This session is situated in the southern quarter, near the east, but none who have been Popes or Cardinals in the world dare to enter it, because the semblance of Divine authority possesses their minds, from their having in the world arrogated the Lord's power to themselves; wherefore, as soon as ever they present themselves there, they are carried out, and cast to their like in a desert. But those among them, who have been of sincere mind, and have not, from belief confirmed, usurped such power, are in a certain obscure chamber, situate behind this session. There is another convention in the western quarter, near the north; the business there, is the intromission of the credulous vulgar into heaven. They there dispose around them a number of societies which live in various external jollities; in some of the societies they play, in some they dance, in some they compose the face into the various expressions of hilarity and mirthfulness; in some they converse, friend-like; in some they discuss civil, in others religious matters; in other societies again, they talk obscenities; and so on. They admit their dependents into such one of these societies as each may desire, and call it heaven; but all of them, after being there a few hours, are wearied and depart, because those joys are external, and not internal: in this way, moreover, many are withdrawn from a belief in their doctrinal concerning intromission into heaven. As regards their worship in particular, it is almost like their worship in the world; as in the world, it consists in masses, not performed in the common language of spirits, but in one composed of lofty-sounding words, which induce an external devoutness and awe, and are utterly unintelligible. In like manner they adore saints, and expose idols to view; but their saints are no where to be seen, for all those who have sought to be worshiped as gods, are in hell; the rest who did not seek it, are among common spirits. This their prelates know, for they seek and find them, and when found they despise them; yet conceal it from the people, that the saints may still be worshiped as tutelar gods, but that the primates themselves, who rule over the people, may be worshiped as the lords of heaven. In like manner, moreover, they multiply churches and monasteries as they did in the world, they scrape together riches, and accumulate costly things, which they hide in cellars; for costly things exist in the spiritual, as well as in the natural world, and far more abundantly. In like manner they send forth monks, to allure the Gentiles to their religion, in order that they may subject them to their rule. They commonly have towers of espial erected in the middle of their assemblies, from which they are enabled to enjoy an extended vision into all the surrounding region: and moreover, by various means and arts they establish for themselves communications with persons far and near, joining in league with them, and drawing them over to their own party. Such is their state in general; but as to particulars, many prelates of that religion take away all power from the Lord, and claim it for themselves, and doing this, they acknowledge no Divine. They still counterfeit a devoutness in externals; yet this devoutness in itself is profane, because in their internals there is no acknowledgment of the Divine. Hence it is that they communicate with certain societies of the ultimate heaven by a devout external, and with the hells by a profane internal, so that they are at once in either (utrobivis): on which account, moreover, they allure simple good spirits, and appoint them habitations near themselves, and also congregate evil spirits, and dispose them around the society in all directions, by the simple good conjoining themselves with heaven, and by the evil with hell. Hence they are enabled to accomplish abominations, which they perpetrate from hell. For the simple good who are in the ultimate heavens, look only to their devotional external, and their very devout adoration of the Lord in outward things, but they see not their wickedness, and therefore they favor them, and this *favor from the good* is their greatest protection; yet in process of time they all recede from their devout external, and then, being separated from heaven, they are cast into hell. It may now be known in some degree, what manner of men they of the Babylon are in the other life. But I am aware that they who are in this world, and have no idea of man's state after death, of heaven, or of hell, but an inane and an empty one, will wonder at the existence of such things in the spiritual world. But, that man is equally a man after death, that he lives in fellowships as he did in the world, that he inhabits houses, hears preaching in churches, discharges duties, and sees things in that world, similar to those in the former world he has left, may appear from all that has been said and shown of the things I have heard and seen, in the work on HEAVEN AND HELL.

57. I have spoken with certain of that nation, concerning the keys given to Peter; whether they believed that the power of the Lord over heaven and earth was transferred to him? and because this was a fundamental of their religion, they vehemently insisted on it, saying, that there was no doubt about it, because it was manifestly said so. But when I asked them whether they knew that in each expression of the Word there is a spiritual sense, which is the sense of the Word in heaven, they said at first, that they did not know it, but afterwards they said they would inquire; and on inquiring, they were instructed that there is a spiritual sense within each expression of the Word, which differs from the sense of the letter, as spiritual differs from natural; and they were also instructed that no person named in the Word is named in heaven, but that some spiritual thing is there understood in place of him: finally, they were informed, that instead of Peter in the Word is understood the truth of the faith of the church, derived from the good of charity, and that the same is understood by a rock, which is there named with Peter, for it is said, "*Thou art Peter, and upon this rock will I build My Church*," Matt xvi. 18; by which is not understood that any power was given to Peter, but that power is the property of truth derived from good, for in the heavens, all power is in truth from good, or from good by means of truth; and since all good, and all truth, are from the Lord, and nothing from man, that all power is from the Lord. When they heard this they replied indignantly, that they wished to be certain whether or no that spiritual sense is contained in the words, whereupon the Word which is in heaven was given them, in which Word there is not the natural sense, but the spiritual, because it is for the angels, who are spiritual; (that there is such a Word in heaven, may be seen in the work on HEAVEN AND HELL, n. 259 to 261;) and when they read it, they saw manifestly that Peter is not named there, but truth from good, which proceeds from the Lord, instead of him.[p]

[p] FROM THE ARCANA CŒLESTIA. That the twelve disciples of the Lord represented the church as to the all of truth and good, or of faith and love, as in like manner did the twelve tribes of Israel, n. 2179, 3354, 3488, 3858, 6397. That Peter, James, and John, represented faith, charity, and the goods of charity, n. 3750. That Peter represented faith, n. 4738, 6000, 6073, 6344, 10,087, 10,580. That the keys of the kingdom of heaven being given to Peter, signifies that all power is given to truth from good, or to faith from charity, proceeding from the Lord; thus that all power belongs to the Lord, n. 6344. That a key signifies the power of opening and shutting, n. 9410. That all power is in good by truths, or in truths from good, proceeding from the Lord, n. 3091, 3563, 6344, 6413, 6948, 8200, 8304, 9327, 9410, 9639, 9643, 10,019, 10.182. That a rock in the Word signifies the Lord as to Divine Truth, n. 8581, 10,580. That all names of persons and places in the Word signify things and states, n. 768, 1888, 4310, 4442, 10,329. That their names

Seeing this, they rejected it with anger, and would have torn it in pieces with their teeth, had it not instantly been taken away from them. Hence they were convinced, although unwilling to be convinced, that that power is the property of the Lord alone, and cannot belong to any man, because it is a Divine Power.

58. *Where their habitations in the spiritual world have hitherto been.* It was said above, n. 48, that all the nations and people in the spiritual world were seen to be thus arranged;—collected in the middle those who are called the Reformed; around this middle, those of the Papal religion; the Mahometans beyond them; and the various Gentiles in the outmost circuit. Hence it may appear that the Papists formed the nearest circumference around the Reformed in the centre. The reason of this was, that they who are in the light of truth from the Word are in the centre, and they who are in the light of truth from the Word are also in the light of heaven, for the light of heaven is from Divine Truth, of which the Word is the continent. That the light of heaven is from Divine Truth, may be seen in the work on HEAVEN AND HELL, n. 126 to 140, and That it is Divine Truth, n. 303 to 310. Light, moreover, proceeds from the centre towards the circumferences, and illuminates. Hence it is that the Papists proximately surround the centre, for they have the Word, and it is also read by the rulers of their church, though not by the people. This is the reason why the Papal nation in the spiritual world have habitations around those who are in the light of truth from the Word. Their manner of dwelling, before their habitations were utterly destroyed, and made into a desert, shall now be told. The greatest part of them dwelt in the south and in the west; only a small part in the north and in the east. In the SOUTH dwelt those who had been possessed of more powerful abilities than their fellows in the world, (polluerunt ingenio), and had more confirmed themselves in their own religion. Great numbers of the rich and the noble also dwelt there, in habitations which were not above the earth's surface, but which, from dread of robbers, were subterranean, and were guarded at the entrances. In that quarter, moreover, there was a great city, extending nearly from east to west, and somewhat into the west, situated very near the centre where the Reformed were. Myriads of men or spirits tarried in that city. It was full of churches and monasteries. The ecclesiastics also carried into it all the treasures which they were enabled by their various artifices to scrape together, and they hid them in its cells and subterranean crypts, which were so curiously formed, that no one

do not enter heaven, but are turned into the things they signify, and that they cannot be pronounced in heaven, n. 1878, 5225, 6516, 10,216, 10,282. The delicate fitness of the internal sense of the Word, where mere names occur *in the letter*, illustrated by examples, n. 1224, 1264. 1888.

besides themselves could enter them, for they were disposed around in the form of a labyrinth. On the treasures there amassed, in the full confidence that they could never be destroyed, they had set their hearts. When I saw those crypts I was amazed at the art displayed in constructing them, and increasing them without end. The most of those who call themselves members of the society of Jesus were there, and cultivated amicable relations with the rich who dwelt in their neighborhood. Towards the east in that quarter was the session where they consulted on the enlargement of their dominion, and on the means of keeping the people in blind obedience, (see above, n. 56.) Thus much of their habitations in the southern quarter. In the NORTH, dwelt those who had been possessed of less powerful abilities, and had less confirmed themselves in their own religion, because they were in an obscure faculty of discerning, and thence in blind faith. The multitude was not so great there as in the south. The chief part of them dwelt in a great city, extending lengthwise from the angle of the east to the west, and also some little into the south. It also was full of churches and monasteries. On its outmost side which was near the east dwelt many of various religions, and also some of the Reformed. A few places, moreover, beyond the city in that quarter, were occupied by the Papists. In the EAST dwelt those who had been in the greatest delight of ruling in the world, and at the same time in somewhat of natural lumen; they appeared there on mountains, but only in the quarter which faces the north; there were none in the other part which faces the south. In the angle towards the north, there was a mountain, on whose summit they had placed a certain person of unsound mind, whom, by communications of the thoughts, which are known in the spiritual, but unknown in the natural world, they were enabled to inspire to command anything they chose; and they gave out that he was the very god of heaven, appearing under a human form, and thus paid him Divine worship. They did this, because the people were desirous of seceding from their idolatrous worship, wherefore, they devised it as a means of keeping them in obedience. That mountain is understood in Isaiah xiv. 13, by "*the mountain of convention in the sides of the north*," and those on the mountains are there understood by Lucifer, verse 12; for such of the Babylonish crew as dwelt in the east, were in greater lumen than others, which lumen also, they had prepared for themselves by artifice. They once appeared to be building a tower, whose head should reach to the very heaven where the angels are, but the appearance was a mere representative of their machinations; for machinations are presented in the spiritual world, before the eyes of those who stand at a distance, by many *representatives*, which yet do not exist actually to those who are busied in the machinations: in that world, this is a common thing. By this appearance it was given me to know what *the tower whose head should be in heaven, whence the place was called Babel*, Gen. xi. 1 to 10, signifies. Thus much for their habitations in the east. In the WEST, in front, dwelt those of that religion who had lived in the dark ages, for the most part under-ground, one progeny beneath another. The whole anterior tract, which looked to the north, was, as it were, excavated, and filled with monasteries; the entrances to them lay through caverns, closed at top, through which they went out and in. They rarely spoke with those who lived in the following ages, being of a different disposition, and not so craftily wicked; for as, in their times, there was no contention with the Reformed, there was therefore less of the craft and malice of hatred and revenge. In the western quarter beyond that tract, were many mountains, on which dwelt the wickedest of that nation, who denied the Divine in their hearts, and yet orally professed their belief in Him, and gesticulated their adoration of Him more devoutly than others. They who were there, devised nefarious artifices to keep the vulgar under the yoke of their sway, and also to force others to submit to that yoke: these artifices I may not describe, they are so unspeakably wicked. In general they are such as are mentioned in the work on HEAVEN AND HELL, n. 580. The mountains on which they dwelt, are understood in the Apocalypse by the seven mountains, and the dwellers themselves are described by the woman sitting upon the scarlet beast: "*I saw a woman sstting upon a scarlet beast, full of names of blasphemy, having seven heads, and ten horns: she had on the forehead a name written, mystery, Babylon the great, mother of the whoredoms and abominations of the land: the seven heads are seven mountains, on which the woman sitteth*," Apoc. xvii. 3, 5, 9. By a woman in the internal sense, is understood the church; here in the opposite sense, a profane religion; by the purple beast, the profanation of celestial love; by the seven mountains, the profane love of ruling. Thus much of their habitations in the west. The reason why they dwell distinct according to quarters is, because all in the spiritual world are carried into that quarter, and into that part of it, which corresponds to their affections and loves, and no one to any other place; concerning which see the work on HEAVEN AND HELL, where it treats Of the four quarters of heaven, n. 141 to 153. In general, all the consultations of the Babylonish race tend to this, that they may dominate, not only over heaven, but over the whole earth, and thus that they may possess heaven and earth, obtaining each by means of the other. To effect this, they continually devise and hatch new laws and new doctrinals. They make the same endeavor also in the other life as they made in the world, for every one after death is such as he was in the world, most especially as regards his religion. It was granted me to hear certain of the primates consulting about a doctrine, which was to be a law to the people: it consisted of many articles, but they all tended to one thing; fraudulent dominion over the heavens, and the earth, and the ascription of all power to themselves, and of none to the Lord. These doctrinals were afterwards read before the bystanders, and thereupon a voice was heard from heaven, declaring, that they were dictated from the deepest hell, though the hearers knew it not; which was further confirmed by this; a crowd of devils from that hell, of the blackest and direst appearance, ascended, and tore those doctrinals from them, not with their hands, but with their teeth, and carried them down to their own hell; to the amazement of those who saw it.

59. *Why they were there tolerated, until the day of the last judgment.* The reason was, because it is of Divine order that all who can possibly be preserved, shall be preserved, even until they can no longer remain among the good. All those, therefore, who can imitate spiritual life in externals, and present it, to appearance, in a moral life, as if it were really within, whatever they may be as to love and faith in internals, are preserved; as are those also, who have outward, though they have not inward, sanctity. Such were many of that nation, for they could discourse piously with the vulgar, and adore the Lord devotionally with them, could implant religion in their minds, and lead them to think of heaven and hell, and could uphold them in doing good (bona), by preaching works. Thus they were enabled to lead numbers to a life of good, and therefore into the way to heaven; on which account also, many of that religion were saved, although few of their leaders; the leaders being such as the Lord means by "*false prophets, who come in sheep's clothing, but inwardly are ravening wolves,*" Matt. vii 15. By prophets, in the internal sense of the Word, are understood those who teach truth, and lead to good by means of it; and by false prophets, those who teach the false, and seduce by means of it. They are also like the scribes and pharisees, who are described by the Lord in these words, "*They sit in Moses' seat; all things that they bid you observe, observe and do, but do not according to their works, for they say and do not; all their works they do to be seen of men; they shut up the kingdom of heaven against men, but go not in themselves: they eat widows' houses, for a pretence pouring forth long prayers. Woe unto you, hypocrites, ye make clean the outside of the cup and platter, but within they are full of rapine and iniquity; cleanse first the inside of the cup and platter, that the outside may be clean also: ye are like whited sepulchres, which appear outwardly beautiful, but within are full of the bones of*

the dead: thus ye outwardly appear just before men, but within ye are full of hypocrisy and iniquity," Matt. xxiii. 1 to 34. Another reason moreover why they were there tolerated was, because every man after death retains the religion he has made his own (imbuit) in the world; into which therefore, when first he comes into the other life, he is yielded up. Now with this nation, the religious principle was implanted by those who gave an oral preference to sanctity, and feigned holy gestures, and moreover, impressed the people with a belief in their power of saving; on which ground also they were not removed, but were preserved among their own. But the principal reason was, that all are preserved from one judgment to another, who live the semblance of a spiritual life in externals, and imitate, as it were, internal piety and sanctity; all, indeed, from whom the simple may receive instruction and guidance: for the simple in faith and heart look no farther than to see what is external, and apparent before the eyes. Hence all such were tolerated from the commencement of the Christian church, until the day of the last judgment. (That a last judgment has existed twice before, and now exists for the third time, was shown above). Of the whole of these the former heaven consisted, and they are understood in the Apocalypse, xx. 5, 6, by "*those who are not of the first resurrection;*" but since they were such as they are above described, that heaven was destroyed, and they of the second resurrection were cast out. But it ought to be known that they only were preserved who suffered themselves to be held bound by laws both civil and spiritual, they being capable of living together in society; howbeit, they who could not be restrained by those laws were not preserved, but were cast into hell long before the day of the last judgment: for societies are continually purified from, and defended against such. Hence, they who led a wicked life, who enticed the vulgar into the commission of evils, and entered on abominable arts, such as exist among spirits in the hells, (see the work on HEAVEN AND HELL, n. 580), were cast out of societies, and this in *their* turns. In like manner also the inwardly good are removed from societies, lest they should be contaminated by the inwardly evil; for the good perceive the interiors, and therefore pay no regard to the exteriors, except just so far as they agree with the interiors; they are sent in *their* turns, to places of instruction (concerning which see the work on HEAVEN AND HELL, n. 512 to 520), and are carried thence into heaven; for the new heaven is formed of them, and they are understood by "*those who are of the first resurrection.*" Thus much is here declared, in order that it may be known why so many of the Papal religion were tolerated and preserved until the day of the last judgment; but more will be said on the same subject in the following article, where the first heaven which passed away is to be treated of.

60. *The mode in which they were destroyed, and their habitations made a desert.* This I will here describe in few words; more fully in the explication on the Apocalypse. That the Babylon there treated of has been destroyed, no one but he who saw it can know, and to me it was given to see how the last judgment was brought about and thoroughly accomplished upon all, especially upon those of the Babylon. I, therefore, will describe it. This was granted me, principally, in order to reveal to the world, that all things predicted in the Apocalypse are divinely inspired, and that the Apocalypse is a prophetic book of the Word; for if this, and at the same time the internal sense which there is in each expression of that book, as in each expression of the Prophets of the Old Testament, were not revealed to the world, that book might possibly be rejected, on account of being not understood; which would further make men totally incredulous of its contents, nay, of any such thing as a last judgment to come: in which disbelief those of the Babylon would confirm themselves more strongly than others. Lest this should be, it pleased the Lord to make me an eye-witness. But the whole of what I saw of the last judgment upon those of the Babylon, in other words, of the destruction of the Babylon, being in itself sufficient to fill a volume, cannot be here adduced: in this place I shall merely relate certain general aspects of it, reserving the particulars for the explication on the Apocalypse. Inasmuch as the Babylonish nation was settled in, and extended over, many tracts in the spiritual world, and had formed to itself societies in all the quarters, I will describe in regular succession the mode in which it was destroyed in each several quarter.

61. Destruction was effected after visitation, for visitation always precedes. The act of exploring what the men are, and moreover the separation of the good from the evil, is visitation; and the good are then removed, and the evil are left behind. This having been done, there were great earthquakes, from which they perceived that the last judgment was at hand, and trembling seized them all. Then those in the SOUTHERN QUARTER, and especially in the great city there, (see n. 58), were seen running to and fro, some with the intention of betaking themselves to flight, some of hiding themselves in the crypts, others of hiding in the cellars and caves beside their treasures, out of which others again carried anything they could lay their hands on. But after the earthquakes there burst up an ebullition from below, (ab inferiori) which overturned everything in the city and in the region round it. After this ebullition came a vehement wind from the east, which laid bare, shook, and overthrew everything to its foundations, upon which

all who were there were led forth, from every part, and from all their hiding-places, and cast into a sea of black waters: those who were cast into it, amounted to many myriads. Afterwards, from that whole region, a smoke ascended, as after a conflagration, and finally a thick dust, which was borne by the east wind to the sea, and strewn over it; for their treasures were turned into dust, with all those things they had called holy because they possessed them. This dust was strewn over the sea, because such dust signifies damnation. In the last place, there were seen, as it were a blackness flying over that whole region, which, when it was viewed narrowly, appeared like a dragon; a sign that the whole of that vast city and region was become a desert. This was seen, because dragons signify the falses of such a religion, and the abode of dragons signifies the desert *state* which remains after their overthrow; as in Jeremiah ix. 11; x. 22; xlix. 33; Malachi i. 3. Certain persons were also seen to have, as it were, a mill-stone around their left arms, which was a representative of their having confirmed their abominable dogmas from the Word; a mill-stone signifying such *things:* hence it was plain what these words in the Apocalypse signify, "*The angel took up a stone, like a great mill-stone, and hurled it into the sea, saying, thus with violence shall that great city Babylon be thrown down, and shall no more be found,*" Apoc. xviii. 21. But they who were in the session, which also was in that region, but nearer to the east, and in which they were consulting on the modes of enlarging their dominion, and of keeping the people in ignorance, and thence in blind obedience, (see above, n. 58) were not cast into that black sea, but into a gulf which yawned into length and depth beneath and around them. Such was the accomplishment of the last judgment upon the Babylonians in the southern quarter. But the last judgment upon those in front in the Western Quarter, and upon those in the Northern Quarter, where the other great city stood, was thus effected. After great earthquakes, which rent everything in those quarters to the very foundations, (these are the earthquakes which are understood in the Word, in Matthew xxiv. 7; Luke xxi. 11; likewise Apoc. vi. 12; viii. 5; xi. 13; xvi. 18; and in the prophecies of the Old Testament, and not any earthquakes in this world) an east wind went forth by the way of the south, through the west, into the north, despoiling the whole region, first that part of it in front of the western quarter, where the people of the dark ages dwelt underground, and afterwards the great city, which extended from that quarter, quite through the north, to the east, and laid it bare so utterly, that all things were exposed to view. But because there were not such riches there, no ebullition, and sulphurous treasure-consuming fire, were seen, but mere overturn and destruction, and at length exhalation of the whole into smoke; for the east wind went forth continually, blowing to and fro; it overthrew, it destroyed all things, and blew them clean away. The monks and common people were led forth to the amount of many myriads; some were cast into the black sea, on that side of it which faces the west; some into the great southern gulf, mentioned above; some into a western gulf, and some into the hells of the Gentiles, for a part of those who lived in the dark ages were idolaters, like the Gentiles. A smoke also was seen to ascend from that region, and to proceed as far as the sea; over which it hovered, depositing a black crust there; for that part of the sea into which they were cast, was encrusted over with the dust and smoke, into which their dwellings and their riches had been reduced; wherefore that sea has no longer a visible existence, but in its place is seen, as it were a black soil, and their hell is under it. The last judgment upon those who dwelt upon the mountains in the EASTERN QUARTER (see n. 58), was thus accomplished. Their mountains were seen to subside into the deep, and all those who were upon them to be swallowed up; and he whom they had placed upon one of the mountains, and whom they proclaimed to be god, was seen to become first black, then fiery, and with his *worshipers* to be cast headlong into hell. For the monks of the various orders who dwelt upon those mountains, declared that he was god and that they were Christ, and wherever they went, they took with them the abominable persuasion that themselves were Christ. Finally, judgment was accomplished upon those who dwelt more remotely in the WESTERN QUARTER, upon the mountains there, and who are understood by the woman sitting upon the scarlet beast, who had seven heads which are seven mountains, of whom also something is related at n. 58. Their mountains too were seen, of which some yawned open in the middle, and the apertures widened into huge spiral gulfs, into which those on the mountains were cast. Other mountains were torn up by their foundations, and turned upside down, so that summit and basis were inverted; those who were thence in the plains were inundated as with a deluge, and covered over, and those who were among them from other quarters were cast into gulfs. But the things now related are only a small part of all I saw; more will be given in the explication on the Apocalypse. They were brought about and thoroughly accomplished in the beginning of the year seventeen hundred and fifty-seven. As regards the gulfs into which the whole *of the Babylonians* were cast, excepting those who were cast into the black sea, they are many in number. Four of them were discovered to me; one great gulf in the southern quarter, to the east there; another in the western quarter, to the south; a third in the western quarter, to the north there; a fourth still further in the angle between the west and the north: the gulfs and the sea are their hells. These were seen, but in addition to these there are many more, which were not seen; for the hells of the Babylonish nation are distinct according to the various profanations of spiritual things, which belong to the good and the truth of the church.

62. Thus now was the spiritual world freed from such spirits, and the angels rejoiced on account of its liberation from them, because they of the Babylon infested and seduced whomsoever they could, and in that world more than in this, their cunning being more mischievous there, because they are spirits; for it is the spirit of each in which all his wickedness is hidden, since the spirit of the man is what thinks, wills, intends, and devises. Many of them were explored, and it was found that they had no belief in anything at all, and that the abominable lust of seducing, the rich for the sake of their riches, and the poor for the sake of dominion, was rooted in their minds, and that they kept all men in the densest ignorance in order to obtain that end; thus blocking up the way to light, and therefore the way to heaven: for the way to light and to heaven is obstructed, when the knowledges of spiritual things are overwhelmed by idolatries, and when the Word is adulterated, invalidated, and taken away.

63. *That such among them as were in the affection of truth from good were preserved.* Those of the Papal religion who lived piously, and were in good, although not in truths, and still from affection desired to know truths, were taken and carried into a certain region, in front in the western quarter, near the north, habitations being given them, and societies of them instituted there, and then priests from the Reformed were sent thither, who instructed them from the Word, and as they are instructed, they are accepted into heaven.

64. *Of the state of those hereafter who come thence from the countries from the earth.* Since the last judgment is now accomplished, and all things are reduced by the Lord into order through means of it, and since all who are inwardly good are taken into heaven, and all who are inwardly evil are cast into hell, it is no longer permitted them, as heretofore it was, to form societies below heaven and above hell, or to have anything in common with other spirits, but as soon as ever they come thither, that is, at the death of each of them, they are altogether separated, and after passing a certain time in the world of spirits, they are carried into their own places. They therefore who profane holy things, that is who claim for themselves the power of opening and shutting heaven, and of remitting sins, (which are powers belonging to the Lord alone), and who place Papal bulls on an equality with the Word, and have dominion for an end, are henceforth carried away into that black sea, or into those gulfs, which are the hells of pro-

faners. But it was declared to me from heaven, that those of that religion who are of such a nature, do not look at all to the life after death, because they deny it in their hearts, but that they look solely to the life in the world; and that hence they care not a straw (floccipendant) for this lot of theirs after death, which yet is to endure to eternity, but laugh at it, as a thing of nought.

OF THE FORMER HEAVEN AND ITS ABOLISHMENT.

65. It is said in the Apocalypse, "*I saw a great throne, and One sitting upon it, from whose face the heaven and the land fled away, and their place was not found,*" xx. 11. And afterwards, "*I saw a new heaven and a new land; the first heaven and the first land had passed away,*" xxi. 1. That a new heaven and a new land, after the passing away of the former heaven and the former land, do not mean the visible heaven or the land we inhabit, but an angelic heaven and a church, was shown above in the first article, and also in those which follow it. For the Word in itself is spiritual, and therefore treats of spiritual things; spiritual things being those which are proper to heaven and the church; these are expounded by natural things in the sense of the letter, because natural things serve as a basis to spiritual things, without which basis the Word would not be a Divine work, because it would not be complete; for the natural, which is the ultimate in Divine Order, completes, and makes the interiors, which are spiritual and celestial, to subsist upon it, as a house upon its foundation. Now whereas men have thought of the contents of the Word from a natural and not from a spiritual ground, therefore, by the heaven and the land which are mentioned here and elsewhere, they have understood none other than the sky and land which exist in the world of nature; hence it is that they all expect the passing away and destruction of these, followed too by a creation of new ones. But lest they should expect this everlastingly, from age to age in vain, the spiritual sense of the Word is opened, that thus it may be known what is understood by much in the Word, which, when thought of naturally, does not enter the understanding, and, at the same time, what is understood by the heaven and the land which will pass away.

66. But before showing what is understood by the first heaven and the first land, it ought to be known, that by the first heaven is not understood the heaven formed of those who have become angels from the first creation of the world to the present time, for that heaven is abiding, and endures to eternity; for all who enter heaven are under the Lord's protection,

and he who has once been received by the Lord, can never be plucked away from Him. But by the first heaven is understood a heaven which was composed (conflatum) of others than those who have become angels, and for the most part of those who could not become angels. Who they were, and what, shall be told in the following pages. This heaven it is, of which it is said, that it "passed away." It was called heaven, because they who were in it dwelt on high, forming societies upon rocks and mountains, and living in similar to natural delights, but never in any that were spiritual; for very many who depart from the earth into the spiritual world, believe themselves in heaven, when they are on high, and in heavenly joy, when they are in world-like delights. Hence it was called heaven, but "the first heaven which passed away."

67. It is moreover to be noted, that this heaven which is called the first, did not consist of any who had lived before the Lord's coming into the world, but that all who composed it lived after His coming, for (as was shown above, n. 33 to 38) a last judgment is effected at the end of every church, a former heaven being then abolished, and a new heaven created or formed; for all who led an outwardly moral life, and lived in piety and sanctity that was external, although not internal, were tolerated from the beginning to the end of the church, and this so long as the internals which belong to the thoughts and intentions could be held in bonds by the laws of society, civil and moral; but at the end of the church their internals are unveiled, and the judgment is then effected upon them. Hence it is, that a last judgment has been effected upon the inhabitants of this planet twice before, and now is, for the third time (see n. 46); thus also a heaven and a land have twice passed away, and a new heaven and a new land have been created; for the heaven and the land are the church in either world, as shown above, n. 1 to 5. Hence it is plain, that the new heaven and the new land, mentioned in the prophets of the Old Testament, are now that new heaven and new land mentioned in the Apocalypse, but that the former existed from the Lord when He was in the world, and that the latter exist from Him now. Concerning the heaven and the land in the prophets of the Old Testament, it is thus written, "*Behold I am about to create a new heaven and a new land, neither shall the former be remembered,*" Isaiah lxv. 17. And in another place, "*I am about to make a new heaven and a new land.*" Isaiah lxvi. 22; besides what is said in Daniel.

68. Since the first heaven which passed away is the subject now treated of, and since no one knows anything concerning it, I will describe it in order.

I. Of whom the first heaven consisted.

II. What kind of heaven it was.

III. How it passed away.

69. *Of whom the first heaven consisted.* The first heaven was composed of all upon whom the last judgment was effected, for it was not effected upon those in hell, nor upon those in heaven, nor upon those in the world of spirits, (concerning which world see the work on HEAVEN AND HELL, n. 421 to 520), nor upon any who were yet living *in this world*, but solely upon those who had made to themselves the likeness of a heaven, of whom the greater part were on mountains and rocks; these also were they whom the Lord meant by the goats, which he placed on the left, Matthew xxv. 32, 33, and following verses. Hence it may appear, that the first heaven existed, not merely from Christians, but also from Mahometans and Gentiles, who had all formed to themselves such heavens in their own places. What manner of men they were shall be told in few words. They were those who lived in the world in external, and never in internal, sanctity; who were just and sincere for the sake of civil and moral laws, but not for the sake of Divine laws, therefore, who were external or natural, and not internal or spiritual men; who also were in the doctrinals of the church, and were able to teach them, but whose lives were not accordant with them; and who filled various offices, and did uses, but not foi the sake of uses. These, and all throughout the whole world who were like them, and lived after the Lord's coming, constituted the first heaven. This heaven therefore was such as the world and church upon earth is, among those who do good, not because it is good, but because they fear the laws, and the loss of fame, honor, and lucre; they who do good from no other origin, do not fear God, but men, and are destitute of conscience. In the first heaven of the Reformed, there was a large proportion of spirits, who believed that man is saved by faith alone, and did not live the life of faith, which is charity; and who loved much to be seen of men. In all these spirits, so long as they were associated together, the interiors were closed, that they might not appear, but when the last judgment was at hand they were opened; and it was then found that inwardly they were obsessed by falses and evils of every kind, and that they were against the Divine, and were actually in hell: for every one after death is immediately bound to his like, the good to their like in heaven, but the evil to their like in hell, yet they do not go to them before the interiors are unveiled; in the mean time they may live together in society with those who resemble them in externals. But it is to be noted, that all who were inwardly good or spiritual, were separated from those *spirits*, and elevated into heaven, and that all who were outwardly, as well as inwardly, evil, were also separated from them, and cast into hell; and this from the time immediately succeeding the Lord's advent, down to the last time,

when the judgment was; and that those only were left, to form societies among themselves, who constituted the first heaven, and who were of the kind above described.

70. There were many reasons why such societies, or such heavens were tolerated; the principal reason was, that by external sanctity, by external sincerity and justice, they were conjoined with the simple-good, who were either in the ultimate heaven, or were still in the world of spirits and not yet introduced into heaven. For in the spiritual world, there is a communication, and thence a conjunction, of all with their like; and the simple-good, in the ultimate heaven, and in the world of spirits, look principally to externals, yet are not inwardly evil; wherefore if these spirits had been forcibly removed from them before the appointed time, heaven would have suffered in its ultimates; and yet it is the ultimate, upon which the superior heaven subsists, as upon its own basis. That these spirits were tolerated until the last time on this account, the Lord teaches in the following words: "*The servants of the householder came and said unto him, Didst thou not sow good seed in thy field, whence then are the tares? and they said, Wilt thou then that we go and gather them up? but he said, Nay, lest, whilst ye gather up the tares, ye root up also the wheat with them; let both therefore grow together until the harvest, and at the time of harvest I will say to the reapers, gather ye together first the tares, and bind them in bundles to burn; but gather the wheat into barns. He that hath sowed the good seed, is the Son of Man; the field is the world; the good seed are the sons of the kingdom, the tares are the sons of evil; the harvest is the consummation of the age: as therefore the tares are gathered together, and burnt with fire, so shall it be in the consummation of the age,*" Matt. xiii. 27 to 30, 37 to 40. The consummation of this age, is the last time of the church; the tares are those who are inwardly evil; the wheat are those who are inwardly good; the gathering the tares together, and binding them in bundles to burn, is the last judgment.[q] The like is understood in the same chapter by the Lord's parable of the fishes of all kinds, which were ga-

[q] That bundles in the Word signify the arrangement of the truths and falses a man has, into series, thus also the arrangement of men in whom truths and falses are, n. 4686, 4687, 5339, 5530, 7408, 10,303. That the Son of Man is the Lord as to Divine Truth, n. 1729, 1733. 2159, 2628, 2803, 2813, 3255, 3704, 7499, 8897, 9087. That sons are the affections of truth from good, n. 489, 491, 533, 2623, 3373, 4257, 8649, 9807; therefore, that the sons of the kingdom are those who are in the affections of truth from good; and the sons of evil, those who are in the affections of the false from evil; whence the latter are called tares, and the former good seed; for tares signify the false from evil, and good seed, truth from good; that the seed of the field is truth from good, in man, from the Lord, n. 1940, 3038, 3310, 3373, 10,248, 10,249. That seed in the opposite sense is the false from evil, n. 10.248. That the seed of the field is also the nutrition of the mind by Divine Truth from the Word, and that sowing is instruction, n. 6158, 9272. That the consummation of the age is the last time of the church, n. 4535, 10,622.

thered together, and the good placed in vessels, but the bad cast away; concerning which it is also said, "*so shall it be in the consummation of the age; the angels shall go forth, and separate the evil from the midst of the just,*" verses 47, 48, 49. They are compared to fishes, because fishes in the spiritual sense of the Word, signify natural and external men, both good and evil; what the just signify may be seen below.[r]

71. *What kind of heaven it was*, may be concluded from the things already said of it; as also from this, that they who are not spiritual by an acknowledgment of the Lord, by a life of good, and by an affection of truth, and still appear as spiritual by external sanctity, by talk [sermocinatio] on Divine things, and by sincerities for the sake of themselves and the world, rush into the abominations which accord with their lusts, when they are left to their own internals; for nothing detains them, neither fear of God, nor faith, nor conscience. Hence it was, that as soon as ever they who were in the first heaven were yielded up into their own interiors, they were in open conjunction with the hells.

72. *The manner in which the first heaven passed away*, was described before, in describing the last judgment upon the Mahometans and Gentiles, n. 50 to 51; and upon the Papists, n. 61, 62, 63, since they also in their own places were constituents of the first heaven. It remains that something be said of the last judgment upon the Reformed, who are also called Protestants and Gospellers, or of the manner in which the first heaven composed of them passed away; for (as was said above) judgment was effected upon those only of whom the first heaven consisted. After being visited, and yielded up into their own interiors, they were separated from each other, and divided into classes according to evils and their derivative falses, and according to falses and their derivative evils, and were cast into hells correspondent with their loves. Their hells surrounded the middle region on all sides, for the Reformed were in the middle, the Papists around them, the Mahometans around the Papists, and the Gentiles in the outmost circuit. (See n. 48.) Those who were not cast into hells, were ejected into deserts; yet there were some sent down to the plains in the southern and northern quarters, there to form societies, and be instructed and prepared for heaven; these are they who were preserved. But how all these things were accomplished, cannot be minutely described in this place, for the judgment upon the Reformed

r That fishes, in the spiritual sense of the Word, signify scientifics, which belong to the natural or external man, and hence also natural or external men, both evil and good, n. 40, 991. That animals of all kinds correspond with such things as are in man, n. 45, 46, 246, 714, 716, 719, 2179, 2180, 3519. 9280, 10,609. That, in the Word, they to whom the Lord's justice and merit are attributed, are called just; they to whom self-justice and self-merit are attributed, are called unjust, n. 3648 5069, 9263.

was of longer continuance than upon others, and was effected by successive changes. Now since much that is worthy of mention was then heard and seen, I will present the particulars in their own order in the explication on the Apocalypse.

OF THE STATE OF THE WORLD, AND OF THE CHURCH HEREAFTER.

73. THE state of the world hereafter will be quite similar to what it has been heretofore, for the great change which has been effected in the spiritual world, does not induce any change in the natural world as regards the outward form; so that the affairs of states, peace, treaties, and wars, with all other things which belong to societies of men, in general and in particular, will exist in the future, just as they existed in the past. The Lord's saying, that "*in the last times there will be wars, and that nation will then rise against nation, and kingdom against kingdom, and that there will be famines, pestilences, and earthquakes in divers places,*" Matthew xxiv. 6, 7, does not signify that such things will exist in the natural world, but that the things correspondent with them will exist in the spiritual world, for the Word in its prophecies does not treat of the kingdoms, or of the nations upon earth, or consequently of their wars, or of famines, pestilences, and earthquakes in nature, but of such things as correspond to them in the spiritual world; what these things are, is explained in the ARCANA CŒLESTIA, and a collection of passages on the subject may be seen below.[8] But as for the state of the church, this it is which will be dissimilar hereafter; it will be similar indeed in the outward form, but dissimilar in the inward. To outward appearance divided churches will exist as heretofore, their doctrines will be taught as heretofore; and the same religions as now, will exist among the Gentiles. But henceforth the man of the church will be in a more free state of thinking on matters of faith, that is, on spiritual things which relate to heaven, because spiritual liberty has been restored to him. For all things in the heavens and in the hells are now reduced into order, and all thinking which entertains or opposes Divine things inflows from thence,—from

[8] FROM THE ARCANA CŒLESTIA. That wars in the Word signify spiritual combats, n. 1659, 1664, 8295, 10,455. That hence all the arms of war, as the bow, the sword, the shield, signify something of spiritual combat, n. 1788, 2686. That kingdoms signify churches as to truths and as to falses, n. 1672, 2547. That nations signify those in the church who are in goods and who are in evils, n. 1059, 1159, 1205, 1258, 1260, 1416, 1849, 4574, 6005, 6306, 7830, 8054, 8317, 9320, 9327. That famine signifies a defect of the knowledges of good and truth, n. 1460, 3364, 5277, 5279, 5281, 5300, 5360, 5376, 5893. That it also signifies the desolation of the church, n. 5279, 5415, 5576, 6110, 6144, 7102. That pestilence signifies the vastation and consummation of good and truth, n. 7102, 7505, 7507, 7511. That earth quakes signify changes of the state of the church, n. 3355.

the heavens, all which is in harmony with Divine things, and from the hells all which is opposed to them. But man does not observe this change of state in himself, because he does not reflect upon it, and because he knows nothing of spiritual liberty or of influx: nevertheless it is perceived in heaven, and also by man himself when he dies. Since spiritual liberty has been restored to man, the spiritual sense of the Word is now unveiled, and interior Divine Truths are revealed by means of it; for man in his former state would not have understood them, and he who would have understood them, would have profaned them. That liberty is given to man by means of an equilibrium between heaven and hell, and, that man cannot be reformed except in freedom, may be seen in the work on HEAVEN AND HELL, n. 597 to the end.

74. I have had various converse with the angels, concerning the state of the church hereafter. They said, that things to come they knew not, for that the knowledge of things to come belongs to the Lord alone, but that they do know that the slavery and captivity in which the man of the church was formerly, is removed, and that now, from restored liberty, he can better perceive interior truths, if he wills to perceive them, and thus be made more internal, if he wills it; but that still they have slender hope of the men of the Christian church, but much of some nation far distant from the Christian world, and therefore removed from infesters [infestatores], which nation is such that it is capable of receiving spiritual light, and of being made a celestial-spiritual man, and they said, that at this day interior Divine Truths are revealed in that nation, and are also received in spiritual faith, that is, in life and in heart, and that it worships the Lord.

THE END.

A CONTINUATION

CONCERNING

THE LAST JUDGMENT.

A

CONTINUATION

CONCERNING

THE LAST JUDGMENT,

AND

CONCERNING THE

SPIRITUAL WORLD.

From the Latin of

EMANUEL SWEDENBORG,

Servant of the Lord Jesus Christ.

NEW YORK:

AMERICAN SWEDENBORG PRINTING AND PUBLISHING SOCIETY,

CONTENTS

A CONTINUATION

CONCERNING

THE LAST JUDGMENT.

THAT THE LAST JUDGMENT HAS BEEN ACCOMPLISHED.

1. In the former small work on the Last Judgment, the following subjects were treated of: That the day of the last judgment does not mean the destruction of the world, n. 1 to 5. That the procreations of mankind will never cease, n. 6 to 13. That heaven and hell are from mankind, n. 14 to 22. That all who have ever been born men from the beginning of creation, and are deceased, are either in heaven or in hell, n. 23 to 27. That the last judgment must be, where all are together; therefore in the spiritual world, and not on the earth, n. 28 to 32. That the last judgment exists, when the end of the church is; and that the end of the church is, when faith is not, because charity is not, n. 33 to 39. That all the things, which are predicted in the Apocalypse, are at this day fulfilled, n. 40 to 44. That the last judgment has been accomplished, n. 45 to 52. Of the Babylon, and of its destruction, n. 53 to 64. Of the former heaven, and of its abolition, n. 65 to 72. Of the state of the world and of the church hereafter, n. 73, 74.

2. The subject of the last judgment is continued, principally that it may be known what the state of the world and the church was before the last judgment, and what the state of the world and the church has become since; also, how the last judgment was accomplished upon the Reformed.

3. It is a common opinion in the Christian world, that the universal heaven we see, and the universal earth we inhabit, will perish at the day of the last judgment, and that a new heaven and a new earth will become extant in their places; that the souls of men will then regain their bodies, and that man will thus again be man as he was before. This opinion has become matter of faith, because the Word has not been understood otherwise than according to the sense of its letter; (and it could not be understood otherwise, until its spiritual sense was discovered), also, because there is a wide-spread belief, that the soul is the mere breath exhaled by man, and that spirits, as well as angels are as unsubstantial as the wind.

While there was such a deficiency of understanding concerning souls, and concerning spirits and angels, the last judgment could not be thought of in any other manner. But when it comes to be understood, that a man is a man after death, just as he was a man in the world, with the sole difference that then he is clothed with a spiritual, and not as before with a natural body; and further, that the spiritual body appears before those who are spiritual, even as the natural body appears before those who are natural, it may then also be understood, that the last judgment will not be in the natural, but in the spiritual world; for all the men who were ever born and have died, are altogether there.

4. When this is understood, then may the paradoxes be dissipated, which man would otherwise entertain on the state of souls after death, and their reunion with putrid corpses, and on the destruction of the created universe; in other words, on the last judgment. The paradoxes he would entertain on the state of souls after death, are these: that man was then like an exhalation, or like wind, or like ether; either that he was floating in the air, or permanent in no place, but in a somewhere, (in Ubi) which they call Pu; and that he saw nothing, because he had no eyes; heard nothing, because he had no ears; spoke nothing, because he had no mouth; and was therefore blind, deaf, and dumb; and that he was continually, and, it must be, sorrowfully, longing to retain those functions of the soul, from which all the joyousness of life proceeds, at the day of the last judgment: also, that the souls of all who have lived since the first creation, were in the same wretched state, and that the men of fifty or sixty ages ago, were likewise still floating in the air, or remaining in Pu, and awaiting the judgment; with other lamentable things.

5. I pass over paradoxes, similar to, and equally numerous with these, which the man who knows not that he is a man after death, as before it, must entertain concerning the destruction of the universe. But he who does know, that a man, after death, is not an exhalation, or a wind, but a spirit, and, if he has lived well, an angel in heaven, and that spirits and angels are men in a perfect form, may think from his intellect, of the future state, and the last judgment; rejecting the non-intellectual faith which harbors mere traditions: and may also with certainty conclude from his intellect, that the last judgment, which is predicted in the Word, will not exist in the natural world, but in the spiritual world, where all are together: and furthermore, that whenever it does exist, it must be revealed, for the sake of the fidelity of the Word, [propter fidem Verbi.]

6. Put away from you the idea of the soul being an exhalation, and then think of your own state, or of the state of

your friends, or of the state of your infants after death. Shall you not think you will be a living man, [quod victurus sis homo] and they likewise? And since there is no proper life without the senses, you cannot think otherwise than that they also see, hear, and speak; which also accords with the inscriptions of those who erect monuments over deceased relations, and place them in heaven among the angels, in white garments, and in paradises. But if afterwards you relapse into the idea, that the soul is an exhalation, and has no sensitive life until after the last judgment, can you help being distracted when you think, "What, and where shall I be in the meantime? Shall I float in the air, or remain in Pu? Yet the preacher teaches me that after death I shall come among the blessed, if I have believed well, and lived well." You may believe then, as the truth is, that you are a man after death as well as before it, differing only, as spiritual differs from natural. Thus also, think all those who are believers in eternal life, without knowing anything of this hypothetic tradition on the soul.

7. From what has been said already, it may appear, that the last judgment cannot exist in the natural world, but may exist in the spiritual world. That it also has existed there, may be seen from the things related of it from sight, in the former small work ON THE LAST JUDGMENT, n. 45 to 72, and will appear still further, from the particulars about to be related from sight, of the last judgment upon the Reformed. He who attends, may also see it, from the new things which are now revealed concerning heaven, the Word, and the church. What man can draw such things from himself?

OF THE STATE OF THE WORLD AND OF THE CHURCH BEFORE THE LAST JUDGMENT, AND AFTER IT.

8. THAT the last judgment has been accomplished in the spiritual world, may appear from what has just been said: nevertheless, in order to know anything of the state of the world and the church before and after it, a thorough knowledge of the following subjects is necessary.

I. What is understood by the former heaven and the former land which passed away. Apoc. xxi. 1.

II. Who, and what manner of men, those in the former heaven, and in the former land, were.

III. That before the last judgment was effected upon them, much of the communication between heaven and the world, therefore also between the Lord and the church, was intercepted.

IV. That after the last judgment the communication was restored.

V. That hence it is, that after the last judgment, and not sooner, revelations were made for the new church.

VI. That the state of the world and of the church before the last judgment was as evening and night, but after it, as morning and day.

9. I. *What is understood by the former heaven and the former land which passed away, mentioned in the Apocalypse* xxi. 1. The former heaven and the former land there mentioned, neither mean a heaven visible to the eyes of men in the world, and a land inhabited by men; nor the former heaven, which is the abode of all those, since the first creation, who have lived well. But congregations of spirits are understood, who, between heaven and hell, had made seeming heavens [tanquam cælos] for themselves: and inasmuch as all spirits and angels inhabit lands, as well as men, therefore, by the former heaven and the former land, these *seeming heavens themselves* are understood. The passing away of that heaven and that land was a thing seen, and it has been described from sight in the work ON THE LAST JUDGMENT, n. 45 to 72.

10. II. *Who, and what manner of men, those in the former heaven, and in the former land, were*, was described in the work ON THE LAST JUDGMENT; but inasmuch as on a knowledge of this subject, depends the understanding of what follows, who and what they were, shall again be told. All those who gathered themselves together underneath heaven, and in various places formed seeming heavens for themselves, and also called them heavens, were conjoined with the angels of the ultimate heaven, but only as to externals, not as to internals. For the most part they were the goats and those akin to them, who are named in Matthew xxv. 41 to 46; who, indeed, in the world had not done evils, for, morally, they had lived well; but they had not done goods from a good origin, for they had separated faith from charity, and hence, had not regarded evils as sins. Now, because in externals they had lived as Christians, they were conjoined with the angels of the ultimate heaven, who were like them in externals, but unlike them in internals; they being the sheep, and in faith, yet in the faith of charity. On account of this conjunction they were necessarily tolerated; for the act of separating them, before the last judgment, would have brought ruin upon those who were in the ultimate heaven, who would have been drawn into destruction with them. This is what the Lord foretold in Matthew: "*Jesus spake a parable; the kingdom of the heavens is like unto a man who sowed good seed in his field; but while men slept, his enemy came, and sowed tares, and went away: when the blade was sprung up, and brought forth fruit, then appeared the tares also; so the*

servants of the householder coming, said unto him, Sir, didst not thou sow good seed in thy field? Whence then are the tares? Wilt thou then that we go and gather them up? But he said, Nay, lest, while ye gather up the tares, ye root up also the wheat with them: let both grow together until the harvest; and in the time of harvest I will say to the reapers, Gather ye together first the tares, and bind them in bundles to burn them; but gather the wheat into my barn. He who hath sown the good seed, is the Son of Man; the field is the world; the seed are the sons of the kingdom; the tares are the sons of evil; the harvest is the consummation of the age: as therefore the tares are gathered together, and burned, so shall it be in the consummation of the age," xiii. 24 to 30, 37 to 40; the consummation of the age is the last time of the church; the tares are those who are inwardly evil; the wheat are those who are inwardly good; the gathering the tares together to burn, is the last judgment upon the evil; *the care* lest a separation before the last judgment should bring ruin upon the good, is signified by "lest in collecting the tares you should at the same time root up the wheat with them: suffer them both to grow till the harvest."

11. III. *That before the last judgment was effected upon them, much of the communication between heaven and the world, therefore between the Lord and the church, was intercepted.* All enlightenment comes to man from the Lord through heaven, and enters by an internal way. So long as there were congregations of such spirits between heaven and the world, or between the Lord and the church, man was unable to be enlightened. It was as when a sunbeam is cut off by a black interposing cloud, or as when the sun is eclipsed, and its light arrested, by the interjacent moon. Wherefore, if anything had been then revealed by the Lord, either it would not have been understood, or if understood, still it would not have been received, or if received, still it would afterwards have been suffocated. Now since all these interposing congregations were dissipated by the last judgment, it is plain, IV. *That the communication between heaven and the world, or between the Lord and the church, has been restored.*

12. V. *Hence it is, that after the last judgment, and not sooner, revelations were made for the New Church.* For since communication has been restored by the last judgment, man is able to be enlightened and reformed; that is, to understand the Divine Truth of the Word, to receive it when understood, and to retain it when received, for the interposing obstacles are removed; and therefore John, after the former heaven and the former land passed away, said that he "*saw a new heaven and a new land, and then, the holy city Jerusalem, descending from God out of heaven, prepared as a bride adorned for her husband; and heard One sitting upon the throne, say, Behold*

I make all things new," Apoc. xxi. 1, 2, 5. That the church is understood by Jerusalem may be seen in the DOCTRINE CONCERNING THE LORD, n. 62 to 64. Concerning its new *revelations* see n. 65 of the same work.

13. VI. *That the state of the world and of the church before the last judgment was as evening and night, but after it, as morning and day.* When the light of truth does not appear, there is a state of the church in the world like evening and night; (that there was such a state before the last judgment, may appear from what is said in n. 11); but when the light of truth appears, and the truth is received, there is a state of the church in the world like morning and day. Hence it is, that these two states of the church are called evening and morning, and night and day, in the Word; as in the following passages: "*The Holy One said unto me. Until the evening* (*and*) *the morning* (*be*) *two thousand three hundred; then the holy thing shall be justified*," Dan. viii. 14. "*The vision of the evening and the morning is truth*," Dan. viii. 26. "*There shall be one day, which is known to Jehovah, neither day nor night, for about the time of evening there shall be light*," Zech. xiv. 7. "*One crying unto me out of Seir, Watchman, what of the night? The watchman said, The morning cometh, and also the night*," Isaiah xxi. 11, 12. Concerning the last time of the church, Jesus said, "*Watch, for ye know not when the Lord of the house will come, whether at evening, at midnight, at cock-crowing, or in the morning*," Mark xiii. 35. "*Jesus said, I must workwhile it is day; the night cometh, when no one can work*," John ix. 4; and elsewhere, as in Isaiah xvii. 14; Jer. vi. 4, 5; Psalm xxx. 6; Psalm lxv. 9; Psalm xc. 6. Since such things are understood by evening and morning, therefore the Lord, in order to fulfil the Word, also was buried in the evening and rose again in the morning.

OF THE LAST JUDGMENT UPON THE REFORMED.

14. THE former work ON THE LAST JUDGMENT treated of the judgment upon those who are understood by the Babylon; and somewhat of the judgment upon the Mahometans, and upon the Gentiles; but not of the judgment upon the Reformed. It was said only, that the Reformed were in the middle, arranged there according to countries; the Papists around them; the Mahometans around the Papists, and the Gentiles, and peoples of various religions in the circumferences. The Reformed constituted the middle, or central region, because they read the Word, and worshiped the Lord, and hence had the greatest light: and spiritual light, proceeding from the Lord as a sun, which *sun* in its essence is Divine Love, extends itself

in all possible directions, and enlightens even those who are in the extreme circumferences, opening *in them* the faculty of understanding truths, in as far as their religions allow them to be receptive. For spiritual light in its essence is Divine Wisdom, and it enters the intellect in man, in as far as, from knowedges received, he has the faculty of perceiving it; and does not pass through spaces, like the light of the world, but through the affections and perceptions of truth, therefore, in an instant, to the last limits of the heavens. From these *affections and perceptions*, arise the appearances of spaces in the spiritual world. On this subject much may be seen in THE DOCTRINE CONCERNING THE SACRED SCRIPTURE, n. 104 to 113.

15. The last judgment upon the Reformed shall be described in the following order.

I. Upon whom among the Reformed the last judgment was effected.

II. Of the signs and visitations preceding the last judgment.

III. How the universal judgment was effected.

IV. Of the salvation of the sheep.

16. I. *Upon whom among the Reformed the last judgment was effected.* The last judgment was effected upon those only of the Reformed, who professed a *belief in* God, read the Word, heard sermons, partook of the sacrament of the supper, and did not neglect the solemnities of church-worship, in the world; and yet thought that adulteries, various kinds of theft, lying, revenge, hatred, and the like, were allowable. These, although they profesed *a belief* in God, still made no account of sins against Him; though they read the Word, still they made no account of the precepts of life in it; though they heard sermons, still they paid no attention to them; though they partook of the sacrament of the supper, still they desisted not from the evils of their former lives; and though they did not neglect the solemnities of worship, still they amended their lives in nothing. Thus they lived as if from religion in their externals, yet were totally destitute of it in their internals. These are they who are understood by the Dragon in the Apocalypse xii.; for it is there said of the Dragon, that it was seen in heaven, that it fought with Michael in heaven, and that it drew down the third part of the stars from heaven; which things are said, because these spirits, by means of the profession of a belief in God, by reading the Word, and by outward worship, communicated with heaven. These same spirits are understood by the goats in Matthew xxiv.; to whom it is not said that they did evils, but that they omitted to do goods; and all such omit to do goods which are goods, because they do not shun evils as sins, and because, although they do not commit them, they think them allowable, and therefore commit them in spirit, and in body, too, when they can.

17. Upon all such among the Reformed the last judgment was effected, but not upon those who did not believe in God, who contemned the Word, and rejected from their hearts the holy things of the church, for all these, so soon as ever they went from the natural into the spiritual world, were cast into hell.

18. All who lived like Christians in externals, and made no account of a Christian life, were outwardly in unity with the heavens, but inwardly with the hells, and since they could not be torn away instantaneously from their conjunction with heaven, they were detained in the world of spirits, which is mediate between heaven and hell, and it was there permitted them to form societies, and to live together as in the world; and by arts unknown in the world, to cause splendid appearances, and by this means to persuade themselves and others, that they were in heaven; from the outward appearance, therefore, they called their societies heavens The heavens and the lands in which they dwelt, are understood by the former heaven, and the former land which passed away, Apoc. xxi. 1.

19. In the meantime, so long as they remained there, the interiors of their minds were closed over, and the exteriors were opened; by which means, their evils, which united them with the hells, were not apparent. But on the approach of the last judgment, their interiors were unclosed, and they then appeared before all, such as they really were; and since they then acted in unity with the hells, they were no longer able to simulate Christian lives, but rushed with delight into evils and crimes of every description, and were turned into devils, and, moreover, were seen as such, some black, some fiery, and some livid like corpses; those who were in the pride of self-intelligence, appearing black; those who were in the furious love of ruling over all, appearing fiery; and those who were in the neglect and contempt of truth, appearing livid like corpses. Thus were the scenes of those theatres changed.

20. The Reformed constitute the inmost part or middle region of the world of spirits, which is mediate between heaven and hell, and are there arranged according to countries. In the centre of this middle region are the English; towards the south and the east of it are the Dutch; towards the north, the Germans; towards the west and the north, the Swedes; and towards the west, the Danes. But those only who have led lives of charity, and its faith, are in that middle region: many societies of them dwell there. Surrounding them are those of the Reformed, who have not led lives of faith and charity: these are they who made seeming heavens to themselves. But there is a different arrangement of all in heaven, as well as of all in hell. The reason why the Reformed constitute the middle is, because the Word is read, and the Lord is worshiped among

them, in consequence of which, the light is greatest where they are; and thence, as from a centre, this light is propagated to, and enlightens, all the circumferences. For the light in which spirits and angels are, proceeds from the Lord as a Sun, and this Sun, in its essence, is Divine Love, and the light which proceeds from it, in its essence, is Divine Wisdom: all the spirituality [omne spirituale] of that world is derived from it. Concerning the Lord as the Sun of the spiritual world, and concerning the light and heat of that Sun, see the work on HEAVEN AND HELL, n. 116 to 140.

21. Every arrangement of the societies in that world, is an arrangement according to the differences of love; the reason of which is, that love is the life of man, and the Lord, who is Divine Love Itself, arranges them according to receptions of it; and the differences of loves are innumerable, and known to no one, but the Lord alone. He so conjoins the societies, that they all lead, as it were, one life of man; the societies of the heavens, one life of celestial and spiritual love; the societies of the hells, one life of diabolical and infernal love; the heavens and the hells He conjoins by oppositions. On account of this arrangement, every man after death goes into the society of his own love, and cannot go into any other, for his love opposes it. Hence it is that they who are in spiritual love are in heaven, but that they who are in mere natural love are in hell. Spiritual love is entirely and only implanted [unice inditur] by a life of charity, and natural love remains natural, if a life of charity is omitted; and natural love, if it is not subjected to spiritual love, is opposed to it.

22. From these particulars it may appear, upon whom of the Reformed the last judgment was effected;—that it was not upon those who were in the centre, but upon those who were around it: whose external morality, as was said above, gave them the outward appearance of Christians, while inwardly they were not Christians, because they were destitute of spiritual life.

23. *Of the signs and visitations preceding the last judgment.* There was seen, as it were, a stormy cloud upon those who had formed to themselves seeming heavens, which appearance resulted from the presence of the Lord in the angelic heavens above them, especially from His presence in the ultimate heaven, lest any of the *angels* of that heaven, in consequence of conjunction with these spirits, should be carried away, and perish with them. The superior heavens moreover were brought down nearer to them, by means of which, the interiors of those upon whom the judgment was about to come were disclosed; on which disclosure, they appeared no longer like moral Christians, as before, but like demons; in tumults, and in mutual strife, about God, the Lord, the Word, faith, and the church; and because their concupiscences to evils were then let loose, they

rejected all these subjects with contempt and ridicule, and rushed into every kind of enormity. Thus the state of those heavenly inhabitants was changed. Then at the same time, all their splendid appearances, which they had made to themselves by arts unknown in the world, vanished away; their palaces were turned into vile huts; their gardens into stagnant pools; their temples into heaps of rubbish; and the very hills they inhabited into mounds of gravel, and into other similar things, which corresponded to their depraved dispositions and lusts. For all the visible things of the spiritual world, are the correspondences of the affections of spirits and angels. These were the signs of the coming judgment.

24. As the disclosure of the interiors increased, so the order among the inhabitants was changed and inverted. Those who were most potent in reasonings against the holy things of the church, rushed into the middle, and assumed the dominion; and the rest, who were less potent in reasonings, receded to the circumferences, and acknowledged those who were in the middle, as their tutor-angels. Thus they banded themselves into the form (facies) of hell.

25. These changes of their state were accompanied by various concussions of their dwellings and lands; which were followed by earthquakes, mighty according to their perversities. Here and there, too, gaps were made towards the hells which were under them, and a communication was thus opened with these hells: there were then seen exhalations ascending, as of smoke mingled with sparks of fire. These also were signs which preceded, and they are understood by the Lord's words on the consummation of the age, and afterwards on the last judgment, in the Evangelists, "*Nation shall be stirred up against nation; there shall be great earthquakes in divers places; signs also from heaven, terrible and great. And there shall be distress of nations, the sea and the salt water roaring.*"

26. VISITATIONS also were made by angels; for before any ill-constituted [mala sarta] society perishes, visitation always precedes. The angels exhorted them to desist, and denounced destruction upon them if they did not. At the same time they sought out, and separated, any good spirits who were intermingled with them. But the multitude, excited by their leaders, reviled the angels, and rushed in upon them, for the purpose of dragging them into some public place, and treating them in an abominable manner; just indeed as was done in Sodom. The most of these spirits were *professors* of faith separated from charity; and there were even some among them, who professed charity, and yet led wicked lives.

27. III. *How the universal judgment was effected.* Since the visitations and premonitory signs of the coming judgment could not deter their minds from abominable practices, and

from seditious plottings against those who acknowledged the Lord as the God of heaven and earth, held the Word sacred, and led a life of charity, therefore the last judgment came upon them. It was thus effected.

28. The Lord was seen in a bright cloud with angels, and a sound as of trumpets was heard from it; which was a sign representative of the protection of the angels of heaven by the Lord, and of the gathering of the good from every quarter. For the Lord does not bring destruction upon any, but only protects His own, and draws them away from communication with the wicked; whereupon, the wicked come into their own concupiscences, by which they are impelled into every kind of abomination. Then all who were about to perish, were seen together in the likeness of a great dragon, with its tail extended in a curve, and elevated towards heaven, bending itself about on high in various directions, as though it would destroy heaven, and draw it down: but the attempt was vain, for the tail was cast down, and the dragon, which also appeared elevated, sank beneath. It was granted me to see this representation, that I might know and make known who are understood by the dragon in the Apocalypse; namely, that the dragon means all who read the Word, hear sermons, and perform the rites of the church, making no account of the concupiscences of evil which beset them, and inwardly meditating thefts and frauds, adulteries and obscenities, hatred and revenge, lies and blasphemies; and who thus live like devils in spirit, and like angels in body. These constituted the body of the dragon, but the tail was composed of those who, when in the world, lived in faith separated from charity, and were like the former in regard to thoughts and intentions.

29. Then I saw some of the rocks they inhabited subsiding to the lowest depths [ima]; some transported to a great distance; some cleft in the middle, and those who were on them cast down through the openings; and others inundated as with a deluge. And I saw many spirits collected into companies, as into bundles, according to the genera and species of evil, and cast hither and thither into whirlpools, marshes, stagnant waters, and deserts, which were so many hells. The rest who were not on rocks, but scattered here and there, and who yet were in similar evils, fled affrighted to the Papists, Mahometans, and Gentiles, and professed their religions, which they could do without any disturbance of mind, inasmuch as they themselves had no religion at all; but still, lest they should seduce these *spirits* also, they were driven away, and thrust down to their own companions in the hells. This is a general description of their destruction; the particulars I saw, are too numerous to be here described.

30. *Of the salvation of the sheep.* After the last judgment

was accomplished, there was then joy in heaven, and also light in the world of spirits, such as was not before. The kind of joy there was in heaven, after the dragon was cast down, is described in the Apocalypse xii. 10, 11, 12; and there was light in the world of spirits, because the infernal societies *which were removed*, had been interposed, like clouds which darken the earth. A similar light also then arose in men in the world, giving them new enlightenment.

31. I then saw angelic spirits, in great numbers, rising from below, [ex Inferis] and elevated into heaven. They were the sheep, there reserved, and guarded by the Lord for ages back, lest they should come into the malignant sphere of the influence of the dragonists, and their charity be suffocated. These are they, who are understood in the Word, by those who went forth from the sepulchres; also, by the souls of those slain for the testimony of Jesus, who were watching; and by those who are of the first resurrection.

A CONTINUATION

CONCERNING

THE SPIRITUAL WORLD.

OF THE SPIRITUAL WORLD.

32. The spiritual world has been treated of in a special work on Heaven and Hell, in which many particulars of that world are described; and since every man enters that world after death, his state then is also described there. It has been commonly known, that man will live after death, because he is born a man, and created in the image of God, and because the Lord, in His Word, teaches it; but the manner of his future life has hitherto been unknown. It has been believed that he was then a soul, of which the only idea conceived was, that it resembled air, or ether, with some cogitativeness residing in it, and without such sight as belongs to the eye, without such hearing as belongs to the ear, and without such speech as belongs to the mouth. And yet man is equally a man after death; and so much a man, that he knows no other than that he is still in the former world; he sees, hears, and speaks, as in the former world; he walks, runs, and sits, as in the former world; he eats and drinks, as in the former world; he sleeps and awakens, as in the former world; he enjoys the conjugial delight, as in the former world; in a word, is a man, in the general, and in every particular; from which it is plain, that death is but a continuation of life, and a mere transit.

33. There are many causes of man's ignorance of this, his state after death; one of which is, that he could not be enlightened, so little faith had he in the immortality of the soul; as may appear from many even of the learned, who believe themselves to be similar to beasts, and only more perfect than they, in having the faculty of speech; thus denying the life after death in their hearts, although they admit it with their mouths. This way of thinking of theirs has made them so sensual, that they cannot believe that a man is a man after death, because they do not see him with their eyes, for they say, how can a soul be a man? It is not so with those who believe they will live after death; their interior thought is, that they shall go to heaven, enjoy delights with the angels, see heavenly paradises, and stand before the Lord in white gar-

ments, besides other things. This is their interior thought; their exterior thought may possibly wander from it, when they think of the soul, from the hypothesis of the learned.

34. That a man is equally a man after death, although he is not apparent to the eyes, may appear from the angels seen by Abraham, by Gideon, by Daniel, and other prophets; from the angels seen in the Lord's sepulchre, and afterwards, oftentimes, by John in the Apocalypse; especially from the Lord Himself, who showed his disciples that He was a man, by touch, and by eating, and yet became invisible to their eyes. The reason why they saw Him was, because the eyes of their spirits were then opened; and when these eyes are opened, the things in the spiritual world appear as clearly as the things in the natural world.

35. Since it has pleased the Lord to open for me the eyes of my spirit, and to keep them open now for nineteen years, it has been given me to see the things which are in the spiritual world, as well as to describe them. I can asseverate, that they are not visions, but THINGS SEEN in all wakefulness.

36. The difference between a man in the natural world, and a man in the spiritual world, is, that the one man is clothed in a spiritual body, but the other in a natural body; and the spiritual man sees the spiritual man, as clearly as the natural man sees the natural man; but the natural man cannot see the spiritual man, and the spiritual man cannot see the natural man, on account of the difference between natural and spiritual; what kind of difference this is, may be described, but not in a few words.

37. From the visual experience of so many years, I am enabled to relate the following: that there are lands in the spiritual world, just as in the natural world; and that there are hills and mountains, and plains and valleys, also fountains and rivers, lakes and seas; that there are paradises and gardens, and groves and woods, and palaces and houses; also that there are writings and books, professions and trades; and that there are precious stones, gold and silver; in short, that there are all the things, in general and in particular, which exist in the natural world, and that these things are infinitely more perfect in the heavens.

38. But the difference in general is this; that all things in the spiritual world, are from a spiritual origin, and hence, as to their essence, are spiritual, for they are from the sun there, which is pure love; and that all things in the natural world, are from a natural origin, and hence, as to their essence, are natural, for they are from the sun there, which is pure fire. Hence it is, that the spiritual man must be nourished with food from a spiritual origin, as the natural man is with food from a natural origin. More may be seen in the work on HEAVEN AND HELL.

OF THE ENGLISH IN THE SPIRITUAL WORLD.

39. There are two states of thought in man, an external and an internal state; man is in the external state in the natural world; in the internal state in the spiritual world: these states with the good, are united, but not with the wicked. What a man is, as regards his internal state, is rarely manifest in the natural world, because, from his infancy, he has chosen to be moral, and has learned to seem. But what he is, clearly appears in the spiritual world, for spiritual light reveals it, and besides, man is then a spirit, and the spirit is the internal man. Now, since it has been given me to be in that light, and from it, to see what the internal is, in the men of various kingdoms, by an intercourse of many years with angels and spirits, it behoves me, from the importance of the subject, to declare what I have seen. I shall here confine myself to saying something of the noble English nation.

40. The more excellent of the English nation, are in the centre of all Christians, (see above, n. 20), and the reason why they are in the centre is, because they have interior intellectual light. This is not apparent to any one in the natural world, yet it is conspicuously so in the spiritual world. This light they derive from the liberty they enjoy of thinking, and thence of speaking and of writing. Among the people of other nations, who have not such liberty, intellectual light is buried, because it has no outlet. This light, however, of itself, is not active, but is rendered active by others, especially by men of reputation and authority among them. As soon as anything is said by these men, or as soon as anything they approve, is read, that light shines forth; and seldom sooner. On this account the English have governors placed over them in the spiritual world, and priests of great name for learning and powerful ability given them, whose commands and monitions, from this their natural disposition, they cheerfully obey.

41. They rarely go out of their own society, because they love it, even as, in the world, they love their country. Moreover, there is a similarity of disposition among them, in consequence of which, they contract intimacy with friends of their own country, and seldom with others: and they mutually minister to each others' wants, and love sincerity.

42. There are two great cities similar to London, into which many of the English enter after death: these cities it was given me to see, as well as to walk through. The middle of the one city answers to that part of the English London where there is a meeting of merchants, called the Exchange; there dwell the governors. Above that middle is the east; below it is the west; on the right side of it is the south; on the left side of it is the north. They who pre-eminently have led

life of charity, dwell in the eastern quarter, where there are a magnificent palaces. The wise, among whom there is much splendor, dwell in the southern quarter. They who foremostly love the liberty of speaking and of writing, dwell in the northern quarter. They who make profession of faith, dwell in the western quarter; to the right in this quarter, there is an entrance into, and an exit from the city; they who live wickedly are there sent out of it. The priests, who are in the west, and profess faith (as was said above), dare not enter the city through the broad ways, but only through the narrow streets, because they who are in the faith of charity, are the only inhabitants who are tolerated in the city. I have heard persons complaining, that the preachers in the west make up their discourses with such mingled art and eloquence, inter weaving the strange doctrine of justification by faith, that they leave it doubtful whether good is to be done or not; they preach intrinsic good, and separate it from extrinsic good, which they sometimes say is meritorious, and therefore not acceptable to God; yet still they call it good, because it is useful. But when those who dwell in the eastern and southern quarters, hear such mystical discourses, they walk out of the churches, and the preachers are afterwards deprived of the priestly office.

43. The other great city similar to London, is not in the Christian centre, (see n. 20) but lies beyond it in the north. They who are inwardly wicked, enter it after death. In the middle of it there is an open communication with hell, by which the inhabitants are absorbed in their turns.

44. I once heard some of the English clergy conversing together concerning faith alone, and I saw them form a certain image, which represented solitary faith. It appeared in obscure lumen like a great giant, and in their eyes like a handsome man; but when the light of heaven was let in upon it the upper part of it appeared like a monster, and the lower like a serpent, not unlike the description which is given of Dagon, the idol of the Philistines. When they saw this they left it, and the bystanders cast it into a stagnant pond.

45. It was perceptible to me, from those of the English who are in the spiritual world, that this nation has, as it were, a twofold theology, derived on the one hand, from the doctrine of faith, and on the other, from the doctrine of life; from the doctrine of faith, with those who are initiated into the priesthood: from the doctrine of life, with those who are not initiated into the priesthood, and who are commonly called the laity. This doctrine of life is avowed in an exhortation which is read in the churches on certain Sabbath-days, to those who take the sacrament of the supper; and it is there openly declared, that if they do not shun evils as sins, they cast themselves into

eternal damnation, and that if they then attend the holy communion the devil will enter into them, as he entered into Judas. I have sometimes told the clergy, that this doctrine of life does not agree with their doctrine of faith: they made no reply, but entertained thoughts they dared not utter. You may see that exhortation in THE DOCTRINE OF LIFE FOR THE NEW JERUSALEM, n. 5, 6, 7.

46. I have often seen a certain Englishman, who became celebrated by a book he published some years ago, in which he attempted to establish *the doctrine of* a conjunction of faith and charity, by an influx, and interior operation of the Holy Spirit. He gave out, that this influx affected man in an inexpressible manner, and without his being conscious of it, but did not touch, much less manifestly move his will, or excite his thought, to do anything as of himself, except permissively; the reason being, that nothing of man might enter into union with the Divine Providence; also, that thus evils might not appear in the sight of God. He therefore excluded the external exercises of charity from having any concern in salvation, but admitted them for the sake of the public good. Since his arguments were ingenious, and the snake in the grass was not seen, his book was received as most orthodox. This author retained the same dogma after his departure from the world, nor could he recede from it, because it was confirmed in him. The angels conversed with him, and told him that his dogma was not truth, but mere ingeniosity, aided by eloquence, and that the truth is, that man ought to shun evil, and do good, as from himself, yet with an acknowledgment that it is from the Lord, and that there is no faith before this is done,—still less, they said, is the mere thought, faith, which is called so. And since this was opposed to his dogma, it was permitted him, of his own sagacity, to inquire further, whether any such unknown influx, and internal operation, apart from the external operation of man, is possible. He was then seen to strain his mind, and to wander about (pervagari vias) in thought, always in the persuasion, that man was no otherwise renewed and saved; but as often as he came to the end of his journey, his eyes were opened, and he saw that he was wandering, and even confessed it to those who were present. I saw him wandering thus for two years, and in the end of his journeyings, *I heard* him confess, that no such influx is given, unless evil in the external man be removed, which is effected by shunning evils as sins, as if from one's self; and I heard him at length declaring, that all who confirm themselves in that heresy, will be insane from the pride of self-intelligence.

47. I have conversed with Melancthon, and questioned him concerning his state; but he was not willing to make any reply: wherefore, I was informed of his lot by others. They

told me, that he is in a fretted stone chamber, and in hell, alternately, and that, in his chamber, he appears clad in a bear's skin on account of the cold, and that such is the filth there, that he does not admit those visitors from the world, whom the repute of his name inspires with a desire of seeing him. He still speaks of faith alone, which, in the world, he was foremost in establishing.

OF THE DUTCH IN THE SPIRITUAL WORLD.

48. It was said above, n. 20, that Christians, among whom the Word is read, and the Lord worshiped, are in the middle of the whole spiritual circle of nations and peoples, because spiritual light is greatest among them, and thence, as from a centre, is propagated to, and enlightens, all, even the remotest circumferences: in accordance with what has been said in THE DOCTRINE OF THE NEW JERUSALEM CONCERNING THE SACRED SCRIPTURE, n. 104 to 113. In this middle, the Reformed Christians have places allotted them, according to their reception of spiritual light from the Lord; and since among the English, that light is treasured up in the intellectual part, they, therefore, are in the very centre of the middle region; and since the Dutch keep that light more nearly conjoined to natural lumen, and hence, there is no such brightness of light apparent among them, but in its place a certain opacity, which is receptive of rationality from spiritual light, and at the same time from spiritual heat, they, therefore, in the Christian middle region have obtained dwellings in the east, and in the south; in the east, from the faculty of receiving spiritual heat, which in them is charity, and in the south, from the faculty of receiving spiritual light, which in them is faith. That the quarters in the spiritual world are not like the quarters in the natural world, and that dwellings according to quarters, are dwellings according to the reception of faith and love, and that they who excel in love and charity, are in the east, and they who excel in intelligence and faith, are in the south, may be seen in the work on HEAVEN AND HELL, n. 141 to 153. Another reason why the Dutch are in these quarters of the Christian middle region is, that trade is their final love, and money is the mediate subservient love, and such love is spiritual; but where money is the final love, and trade the mediate subservient love, such love is natural, and originates in avarice. In the before-mentioned spiritual love, which, regarded in itself, is the common good, in which and from which is the good of country, the Dutch excel other nations.

49. The Dutch adhere more firmly than others to the prin-

ciples of their religion, and do not give them up, and if they are convinced that one or the other of them is erroneous, still, they do not confess it, but relapse into their former opinion, and remain where they were : thus they remove themselves from an interior intuition of truth, by keeping their reason under obedience on spiritual subjects. In consequence of this their nature, when they enter the spiritual world after death, they are prepared for receiving the Spiritual of heaven, which is Divine Truth, quite differently from other nations. They are not taught, because they are not receptive *of instruction*, but what heaven is, is described to them, and afterwards it is granted them to ascend there, and to see it, and then, whatever agrees with their genius is infused into them, which being done, they are sent down, and return to their companions, with a strong desire for heaven. If then they do not receive this truth, that God is One in Person, and in Essence, and that that God is the Lord, and that in Him is the Trinity ; and also this truth, that faith and charity as matters of knowledge and discourse, are of no avail apart from the life of faith and charity, and that faith and charity are given by the Lord, when evils are avoided as sins ;—if when they are taught these truths, they turn themselves away, and still think of God as existing in three persons, and of religion, merely that there is such a thing, they are reduced to misery, and their trade is taken away, until they are brought to the greatest extremities. They are then led to those who have abundance of everything, and a flourishing trade, and when there, it is insinuated into them from heaven, to think of the reason of their own condition, and at the same time to reflect on the faith of these persons concerning the Lord, and upon their life,—in that they shun evils as sins. In a little time they make inquiries, and perceive an agreement *of what they hear*, with their own thought and reflection : this is done repeatedly. At length, they think of themselves, that in order to be relieved from their miseries, they must believe, and do the same. Then, as they receive that faith, and live that life of charity, opulence and joyousness of life are conferred upon them. In this manner, those of them who have led anything of a life of charity in the world, are amended by themselves, and not by others, and are prepared for heaven. They afterwards become more constant than others, so that they may be fitly called constancies ; and they do not allow themselves to be led away by any reasoning, or fallacy, or obscurity brought on by sophistries, or by any preposterous view, deduced from mere confirmatory appearances.

50. The Dutch are easily distinguished from others in the spiritual world, because they appear in the same kind of garments as in the natural world, excepting that the dress is neater among those who have received faith and spiritual

life. They appear in similar garments, because they remain steadfastly in the principles of their own religion; and all in the spiritual world are clothed according to their religious principles; whence it is, that they who are in Divine Truths, have garments of white and of fine linen.

51. The cities which the Dutch inhabit, are guarded in a peculiar manner, all their streets being covered in, and provided with gates, in order that they may not be overlooked from the surrounding rocks and hills. This the inhabitants do, from their inherent prudence in concealing their designs, and not divulging their intentions; for these things in the spiritual world are portrayed by inspection. If any one enters a city with the animus of exploring their state, when he is about departing, he is led to the closed gates of the streets, backwards and forwards from one to another, and this to the most wearisome extent, and he is then let out: all this being done, to prevent him from returning. Wives who affect authority over their husbands, dwell on one side of the city, and only meet them by invitation, given formally; and the husbands then lead them to houses, where married pairs are living, without there being any dominion of the one over the other, and show them how ornamental and how neat their houses are, and how joyous their life is, and that these are the results of mutual and conjugial love. Those wives who attend to, and are affected with these things, cease to domineer, and they live with their husbands, and they then obtain a dwelling nearer to the middle, and are called angels. The reason is, that conjugial love is a celestial love, which is free from imperiousness.

53. In the days of the last judgment, I saw many thousands of that nation cast out of the cities in the spiritual world, and out of the villages, and surrounding country. They were those who, when in the world, had done nothing of good from any religion or conscience, but merely to preserve reputation, that they might appear sincere for the sake of gain; for such persons, when they no longer have the prospect of fame and gain, as is the case in the spiritual world, then rush into every abomination; and when they are in the fields, and without the cities, they rob every one they encounter. I saw them cast into a fiery gulf stretching under the eastern tract, and into a dark cavern stretching under the southern tract. This I saw on the 9th day of January, 1757. Those only were left, among whom there was religion, and a conscience derived from religion.

54. I have spoken, but only once, with Calvin; he was in a society of heaven, which appears in front, above the head; and he said, that he did not agree with Luther and Melancthon, about faith alone, because works are so often named in the Word, and the doing of them commanded, and that, there-

fore, faith and works ought to be conjoined. I was told by one of the governors of that society, that Calvin was accepted in his society, because he has honest (probus,) and made no disturbance.

55. What Luther's lot is, shall be told elsewhere, for I have often seen and heard him. Here, I shall only say, that he has often wished to recede from his faith alone, but in vain; and that therefore, he is still in the world of spirits, which is mediate between heaven and hell; where he sometimes undergoes great sufferings.

OF THE PAPISTS IN THE SPIRITUAL WORLD.

56. The Papists, and the last judgment upon them, were treated of in the small work On the Last Judgment, n. 53 to 64. The Papists in the spiritual world appear encircling the Reformed, and are separated from them by an interval, which they are not permitted to pass. Nevertheless, those who are of the order of Jesuits, contrive, by clandestine arts, to communicate with them, and send out emissaries, too, by unknown paths, for the purpose of seducing them. But they are discovered, and after being punished, they are either sent back to their companions, or are cast into hell.

57. After the last judgment, their state was so changed, that they were not allowed to gather together in companies, as they had done; but ways were appointed to every love, both good and evil, which those who come from the world immediately enter, and go to a society correspondent to their love. Thus the wicked aro borne away to a society in conjunction with the hells, and the good to a society in conjunction with the heavens; and, in this manner, the future formation of artificial heavens is provided against. Such societies in the world of spirits, which is mediate between heaven and hell, are innumerable; being as many as there are genera and species of good and evil affections: and in the meantime, before spirits are either elevated into heaven, or cast down into hell, they are in spiritual conjunction with men in the world, because they, too, are in the midst between heaven and hell.

58. All those of the Papists, who have not been complete idolaters, and who, from their religious principles, have performed good *works*, out of a sincere heart, and have looked to the Lord, are led to societies which are instituted in the confines nearest to the Reformed, and are instructed there, the Word being read, and the Lord preached to them, and they who receive truths, and apply them to life, are elevated into heaven,

and are made angels. There are many such societies of them in every quarter, and they are guarded on all sides from the treacheries and cunning devices of the monks, and from the Babylonish leaven. Moreover, all their infants are in heaven, because, being educated by the angels under the guidance of the Lord, they know nothing of the falses of their parents' religion.

59. All who go from the countries of the earth into the spiritual world, are at first kept in the confession of faith, and in the religion of their country; and so therefore are the Papists. On this account, they always have some representative Pontiff set over them, whom moreover they adore with the same ceremony as in the world. Seldom does any Pope from the world act the Pontiff there; yet he who was Pope twenty years ago, was appointed over the Papists, because he loved to think that the Word was more sacred than is believed, and that the Lord ought to be worshiped. But, after filling the office of Pope for some years, he abdicated it of his own accord, and betook himself to the Reformed Christians, among whom he still is, and enjoys a blessed life. It was granted me to speak with him, and he said, that he adores the Lord alone, because He is God, who has power over heaven and earth, and that the invocations of saints, and their masses, too, are absurdities; and that when he was in the world, he intended to restore his church, but that for reasons, which he mentioned, he found it impossible to do so. When the great northern city of the Papists was destroyed, on the day of the last judgment, I saw him carried out of it on a couch, and taken to a place of safety. A widely different event overtook his successor.

60. Here I am allowed to add a certain memorable circumstance. It was granted me to speak with Louis the XIV., grandfather of the reigning King of France, who, whilst he lived in the world, worshiped the Lord, read the Word, and acknowledged the Pope only as the head of the church; in consequence of which, he has great dignity in the spiritual world, and governs the best society of the French nation. Once I saw him as it were descending by ladders, and after he descended, I heard him saying, that he seemed to himself as if at Versailles, and then there was silence for about half an hour; at the end of that time, he said, that he had spoken with the King of France, his grandson, concerning the Bull Unigenitus, advising him to desist from his former design, and not to accept it, because it was detrimental to the French nation; he said, that he insinuated this into his thought profoundly. This happened in the year 1759, on the 13th day of December, about eight o'clock in the evening.

OF THE POPISH SAINTS IN THE SPIRITUAL WORLD.

61. It is known that man derives implanted or hereditary evil from his parents, but in what it consists is known to few. It consists in the love of ruling, which is such, that in as far as the reins are given it, in so far it bursts forth, until it even burns with the lust of ruling over all, and at length of wishing to be invoked and worshiped as God. This love is the serpent, which deceived Eve and Adam, for it said to the woman, "*God knows, that in the day ye eat of the fruit of the tree, your eyes shall be opened*, AND THEN YE SHALL BE AS GOD," Genesis iii. 4, 5. In the same proportion therefore as man rushes with loosened reins into this love, in the same proportion he averts himself from God, and turns towards himself, and becomes an atheist; and then the Divine Truths which belong to the Word, may possibly serve as means, but inasmuch as dominion is the end, the means are only loved in the ratio of their subserviency. This is the cause, why those who are in the mediate and in the ultimate degree of the love of ruling, are all in hell, for that love is the devil there; and in hell there are some of such a nature, that they cannot bear to hear any one mention God.

62. This love possesses those of the Papal nation, who have been dominant from the stimulus of its delight, and have despised the Word, and preferred before it the dictates of the Pope. They are utterly devastated as regards externals, until they no longer know anything of the church, and then they are cast down into hell and become devils. There is a certain separate hell for those who wish to be invoked as Gods, where such is their fantasy, that they do not see what is, but what is not. Their delirium is of the kind which affects persons in a malignant fever, who see things floating in the air and in the chamber, and on the covering of the bed,—things which are not. This most dreadful evil, is understood by "*the head of the serpent, which is bruised by the Seed of the woman, and which wounded His heel*," Genesis iii. 15. The heel of the Lord, who is the Seed of the woman, is the Divine proceeding in ultimates, which is the Word in the sense of the letter.

63. Because man's hereditary nature consists in the desire of ruling, and of ruling, as the reins are loosened, successively over more and more, and at length over all, and because the wish to be invoked and worshiped as God, is the inmost of this love of ruling, therefore all who have been canonized by the Papal Bulls, are removed from the sight of others and hidden, and are deprived of all intercourse with their worshipers. This is done, lest that worst root of evils should be excited in them, and they should be hurried into such fantastic deliriums, as prevail in the above-mentioned hell. In such deliriums are those, who, during their lives in the world, have

studiously sought to be made saints after death, for the purpose of being invoked.

64. Many of the Papal nation, especially the monks, when they enter the spiritual world, seek the saints, each the saint of his own order; yet do not find them, and marvel that they do not; but are afterwards instructed by others, that their saints are either intermingled with those who are in the heavens, or with those who are in the hells, every one of them according to his life in the world; and that in whichsoever they be, they know nothing of the worship and invocation which is paid them, and that they who do know it, and wish to be invoked, are in that separate and delirious hell. The worship of saints is such an abomination in heaven, that the bare hearing of it causes horror, because in as far as worship is paid to any man, in so far it is withheld from the Lord, for in this case He alone cannot be worshiped; and if the Lord is not alone worshiped, a discrimination is made, which destroys communion, and the felicity of life which flows from it.

65. That I might know, for the sake of informing others, what manner of men the Popish saints are, as many as an hundred of them, who were aware of their canonization, were brought up from the region below, [inferiori terrâ.] The greater part ascended from behind, and only a few in front, and I spoke with one of them, who they said was Xavier. During our conversation he was quite idiotic, yet he was able to tell me, that in his place, where he remains confined, he is not so; but that he becomes idiotic, as often as he thinks himself a saint. I heard the same thing murmured by those who were behind.

66. It is otherwise with the so-called saints who are in heaven: they are utterly ignorant of what is doing upon earth, nor have I conversed with them, lest any idea of the matter should enter their minds. On one occasion only, Mary, the mother of the Lord, passed by, and appeared over head in white raiment, and then, stopping awhile, she said, that she had been the mother of the Lord, and that He was indeed born of her, but that he became God, and put off all the human He derived from her, and that therefore she now adores Him as her God, and is unwilling that any one should acknowledge Him as her son, because in Him all is Divine.

67. I shall here add a certain memorable circumstance. A certain woman with glittering raiment and saint-like countenance, occasionally appears in a middle altitude, to the Parisians who are associated in the spiritual world, and tells them she is Genevieve. But as soon as any of them begin to worship her, then instantly her countenance is changed, and her raiment too, and she becomes like an ordinary woman, and chides them for wishing to adore a female, who, among her companions, is in no more repute than a servant-maid; and ex-

presses her wonder that men in the world are caught by such absurdities. The angels said, that she appears for the purpose of separating those who worship man from those who worship the Lord.

OF THE MAHOMETANS IN THE SPIRITUAL WORLD; AND OF MAHOMET.

68. THE Mahometans in the spiritual world appear behind the Papists in the west, and form as it were a circle around them. The principal reason why they appear in this situation is, because they acknowledge the Lord as the grand Prophet, as the Son of God, and the Wisest of all, who was sent into the world to instruct mankind. Every one, in that world, dwells at a distance from the Christian centre, where the Reformed are, according to his confession of the Lord, and of one God; for that confession conjoins the animus with heaven, and determines distance from the east, above which the Lord is. They who, in consequence of evil lives, do not from the heart make that confession, are in the hells beneath them.

69. Since religion constitutes man's inmost, and all else proceeds from the inmost, and since Mahomet with Mahometans is closely connected with religion, therefore some Mahomet is always placed in their sight; and in order that they may turn their faces to the east, above which the Lord is, he is placed beneath in the Christian centre. It is not the Mahomet who wrote the Alcoran, but another who fills his office; nor is it always the same, but the person is changed. One Mahomet was a native of Saxony, who had been taken by the Algerines, and became a Mahometan; and who, having been also a Christian, was actuated to speak to the Mahometans concerning the Lord, that He was not the Son of Joseph, as they believed in the world, but the Son of God Himself, by which he insinuated into them an idea of the unity of the Lord's Person and Essence with the Father. To this Mahomet, others afterwards succeeded, who were actuated to declare the same. By this means, many of the Mahometans accede to a truly Christian faith concerning the Lord, and they who do so accede, are carried to a society nearer to the east, where it is granted them to communicate with heaven, into which they are afterwards elevated. In the place where the seat of that Mahomet is, there appears a flame, as of a small torch, to distinguish him, but it is invisible to all but Mahometans.

70. Mahomet himself, who wrote the Alcoran, is not to be seen at the present day. I was told, that in early times he presided over the Mahometans, but that he desired to domineer over all things of their religion as a God, and that therefore he

was cast out of the seat he held beneath the Papists, and was sent downwards, to the right side, near the south. Certain societies of Mahometans were once excited by evil spirits to acknowledge Mahomet as their God. To quell the sedition, Mahomet was raised up from below [ex inferis], and shown to them, and I, too, then saw him. He appeared like corporeal spirits, who have no interior perception, his face of a hue approaching to black; and the only words I heard him say, were, "I am your Mahomet;" and shortly afterwards, he subsided, as it were, and returned to his place.

71. As regards their religion, it was permitted in its present form, because of its agreement with the genius of the Orientals, (on which account, too, it became the received religion of so many kingdoms;) and because, at the same time, it made the precepts of the Decalogue a matter of religion, and contained some particulars of the Word, and especially, because it acknowledged the Lord as the Son of God, and the Wisest of all. And besides, it superseded the idolatries of many nations. The reason why Mahomet was not made the means of opening to his followers a more internal religion, was their polygamy, which exhales uncleanness towards heaven; for the marriage of a husband with one wife, corresponds to the Marriage of the Lord and the Church.

72. Many of the Mahometans are capable of receiving truth, and of seeing justice in reasons, as I was enabled to observe, from conversations with them in the spiritual world. I conversed with them on the One God, on the Resurrection, and on Marriage. On the One God they said, that they do not comprehend the Christians when speaking of the Trinity, and saying that there are three persons, and that each person is God, and still asserting that God is One. But I replied, that the angels in the heaven which is composed of Christians, do not speak thus, but say, that God is One in Essence and in Person, and that in Him there is a Trine, and that men on earth call this Trine three persons, and that this Trine is in the Lord. In confirmation, I read before them out of Matthew and Luke, all which is said of the conception of the Lord by God the Father, as well as the passages in which the Lord Himself teaches, that He and the Father are one. On hearing this, they had a perception of the truth, and said, that of consequence, the Divine Essence belongs to Him. On the RESURRECTION they said, that they do not comprehend Christians when they speak of the state of man after death, making out that the soul is like wind or air, and hence is deprived of all delight before its reunion with the body at the day of the last judgment. But I replied, that only some talk thus, but that they who are not of that class, believe they are to go to heaven after death, to speak with the angels, and to enter upon the fruition of heavenly joy,

which they do not conceive to be dissimilar to their joy in the world, although they do not describe it; and I told them, that at the present day, many particulars of the state after death are revealed to Christians, which they did not know before. On MARRIAGE, I have had many conversations with them, and have told them, among other things, that conjugial love is a celestial love, which can only exist between two, and that a conjunction with more wives than one, is incompatible with the heavenliness of that love. They heard my reasons, and perceived their justice; as also this, that polygamy was permitted them, because they are Orientals, who without this permission would have burned for foul adulteries more than Europeans, and would thus have perished.

OF THE AFRICANS AND OF THE GENTILES IN THE SPIRITUAL WORLD.

73. THOSE Gentiles, who have any knowledge concerning the Lord, appear encircled by those who have none; so that, at length, the extreme circumferences are composed of those only who are complete idolaters, and have been adorers of the sun and moon. But they who acknowledge one God, and make precepts, like those of the Decalogue, a part of religion and of life, are seen in a superior region, and thus communicate more immediately with the Christians in the centre; the communication not being intercepted by the Mahometans and Papists. The Gentiles, moreover, are distinguished according to each one's genius and faculty of receiving light through the heavens from the Lord; for there are some of them who are more internal, and some who are more external; and these diversities are not caused by their place of birth, but by their religion. The Africans are more internal than the rest of the Gentiles.

74. All who acknowledge and worship one God, the Creator of the universe, entertain concerning Him the idea of a Man; they say, that concerning God, no one can possibly have any other idea. When they hear, that many think of Him as of a small cloud, they inquire where they are, and on being told that they are among Christians, they deny the possibility of it. But it is replied, that Christians have this idea, because God in the Word is called a spirit, and of a spirit, they are accustomed to think that it is like a particle of cloud, not knowing, that every spirit and every angel is a man. Yet when they were explored, to discover whether their spiritual and natural idea were alike, it was found that they were not alike with those who inwardly acknowledge the Lord as the God of

heaven and earth. I heard a certain Christian minister declare, that no one can have an idea of a Divine Human, and I saw him led about to various Gentiles, in succession to those who were more and more internal, and from them to their heavens, and at length to the Christian heaven, and the interior perception of all concerning God was communicated to him, and he perceived that their idea of God was no other than the idea of a Man, which is the same as the idea of a Divine Human.

75. There are many societies of Gentiles, especially from among the Africans, who, on being instructed by the angels concerning the Lord, say that it is impossible but that God, the Creator of the universe, should appear in the world, because He created them, and loves them; and that the appearance must be made before the very eyes in a Human Form. When they are told, that He did not appear as the angels are wont, but that He was born a Man, and thus became visible, they hesitate awhile, and inquire, whether He was born from a human father, and on hearing that He was conceived by the God of the universe, and born of a virgin, they say, that the Divine Essence of consequence belongs to Him, and, that inasmuch as It is Infinite and Essential Life, He was not such a man as others are. They are afterwards informed by the angels, that in aspect He was like another man, but that when He was in the world, His Divine Essence, which in Itself is Infinite and Essential Life, rejected the finite nature, and its life derived from the mother, and thus made His Human, which was conceived and born in the world, Divine. The Africans comprehended and received these truths, because they think more internally and spiritually than other nations.

76. Such being the character of the Africans even in the world, there is, at the present day, a revelation among them, which commencing in the centre of their continent, is communicated around, but does not reach their coasts. They acknowledge our Lord as the God of heaven and earth, and laugh at the monks in those parts they visit, and at the Christians who talk of a three-fold Divinity, and of salvation by mere thinking, saying, that there is no man who worships at all, who does not live according to his religion, and that whosoever does not, must become stupid and wicked, because, in such case, he receives nothing from heaven. Ingenious wickedness, too, they call stupidity, because there is not life, but death, in it. I have heard the angels rejoicing over this revelation, because, by means of it, a communication is opened for them with the human rational, hitherto closed up, by the blind which has been drawn over the things of faith. It was told me from heaven, that the truths now published in the Doctrine of the New Jerusalem concerning the Lord, concerning the Word, and in the Doctrine of Life for the New Jerusalem, are orally

dictated by angelic spirits to the inhabitants of this portion of the globe.

77. When I conversed with the Africans in the spiritual world, they appeared in garments of striped linen: they told me, that such garments correspond to them, and that their women wear garments of striped silk. Of their little children, they related, that they frequently ask their nurses for food, saying that they are hungry, and when food is set before them, they examine and taste whether it be wholesome, and eat but little; whence it is evident, that spiritual hunger, which is a desire of knowing genuine truths, produces this effect; for it is a correspondence. When the Africans wish to be informed of their state, as regards the affection and perception of truth, they draw their swords; and if these shine, they then know that they are in genuine truths, in a degree according to the brightness of the shining: this, too, is from correspondence. Of marriage they said, that it is indeed permitted them by law to have a plurality of wives, but that still they take but one, because love truly conjugial cannot be divided; and that if it is divided, its essence, which is heavenly, perishes, and it becomes external and thence lascivious, and in a short time grows vile, as its potency diminishes, and at length disgusts, when the potency is lost; but that love truly conjugial, which is internal, and quite distinct from lasciviousness, remains eternally, and increases in potency, and in the same degree in delight.

78. Strangers from Europe they said, are not admitted among them, and that if any such penetrate into their country, especially if they be monks, they ask them what they know, and when they relate any particulars of their religion [religiosa], they call them trifles, which offend their very ears, and they then send them out of the way to work, in order that they may do something useful; and in case they refuse to work, they sell them for slaves, whom their law allows them to chastise at pleasure; and should it be found impossible to drive them to do anything useful, they are at last sold, for a small sum, to the lowest class of the people.

OF THE JEWS IN THE SPIRITUAL WORLD.

79. Before the last judgment, the Jews appeared in a valley in the spiritual world, at the left side of the Christian centre; but after it, they were translated into the north, and forbidden to hold intercourse with Christians, except with those who wandered without the cities. In the northern quarter, there are two great cities, into which the Jews are led after death,

and which, before the judgment, were called Jerusalems, but since, by another name, because Jerusalem, after the judgment, signifies the church, in which the Lord alone is worshiped. In these cities, converted Jews are appointed over them, who admonish them not to speak disrespectfully of Christ; and punish those who persist in doing so. The streets of their cities are filled with mire up to the ankles, and their houses are full of filth, and are so offensive to the smell, that none can approach them.

80. An angel occasionally appears to the Jews in a middle altitude above them, with a rod in his hand, and gives them to believe that he is Moses, and exhorts them to desist from the madness of expecting the Messiah even there, since Christ, who governs them and all other men, is the Messiah: he says, that he knows it to be so, and also, that when he was in the world, he had some knowledge concerning Christ. On hearing this, they retire; the chief part of them forgetting, and only a few retaining it. They who do retain it are sent to synagogues, which are composed of converted Jews, and are there instructed; and if they receive instruction, they have new garments given them in place of their old tattered ones, and are presented with a neatly-written copy of the Word, and with a dwelling in a not unbeautiful city. But they who are not receptive, are cast down into the hells, beneath the great tract which the Jews inhabit; many also are cast into forests and into deserts, where they live in the commission of mutual robberies.

81. In the spiritual world, as in the natural, they traffic with various articles, especially with precious stones, which, by unknown ways, they procure for themselves from heaven, where precious stones exist in abundance. The reason of their trade in precious stones is, that they read the Word in its original language, and hold the sense of its letter sacred, and precious stones correspond to the sense of the letter of the Word. On the subject of this correspondence, see THE DOCTRINE OF THE NEW JERUSALEM CONCERNING THE SACRED SCRIPTURE, n. 42 to 45. They sell their precious stones to the Gentiles who encircle them in the northern quarter. They have the art, too, of producing imitations, and of making others fancy them genuine; but they who do so, are heavily fined by their governors.

82. The Jews are less aware than any other people of their being in the spiritual world, believing, that they are still in the natural world. The reason is, that they are wholly external men, and do not think at all of their religion from the inward. On this account, moreover, they speak of the Messiah just as they did in the world, saying, for example, that he will come with David, and will go before them glittering with diadems,

and introduce them into the land of Canaan; and that in the way, by lifting his rod, he will dry up the rivers they are to pass; and that Christians, whom privately they call Gentiles, will then lay hold of the skirts of their garments, and humbly entreat to be allowed to accompany them, and that they will receive the rich according to their wealth, and that even the rich are to serve them. For they are unwilling to know, that the land of Canaan in the Word, means the church, and Jerusalem, the church as to doctrine; and hence, that Jews mean all those who will be of the Lord's church. That such is the meaning of Jews in the Word, may be seen in THE DOCTRINE CONCERNING THE SACRED SCRIPTURE, n. 51. When they are asked, whether they believe that they, too, are to enter the land of Canaan, they reply, that they shall then descend into it. When it is observed, that this land cannot possibly hold them all, they reply, that it will then be enlarged. When they are told, that they know neither the site of Bethlehem, nor who the stock of David is, they say, that it is known to the Messiah who is to come. When asked, how the Messiah, the Son of Jehovah, can dwell with such wicked people, they reply, that they are not wicked. When they are reminded, that Moses describes them in his song (Deuteronomy xxxii.) as the worst of nations, they answer, that Moses at that time was angry, because of his approaching decease. But when they are told, that Moses wrote it by the command of Jehovah, they are silent, and go away to consult about the matter. When it is said, that they took their origin from a Canaanite, and from the whoredom of Judah with his daughter-in-law, (Genesis xxxviii.), they are enraged, and say, that it suffices them to be descended from Abraham. When they are told that within the Word there is a spiritual sense, which treats of Christ alone, they reply, that it is not so, but that within the Word there is nothing but gold; not to mention other particulars.

OF THE QUAKERS IN THE SPIRITUAL WORLD.

83. SEPARATED from all others, there are enthusiastic spirits, who are so grossly stupid, as to believe themselves to be the Holy Spirit. When Quakerism commenced, these spirits, being drawn out as it were from encircling forests where they were wandering, obsessed many, infusing into the persons thus obsessed a persuasion that they were moved by the holy spirit; and forasmuch as they had sensible perception of an influx, they became so completely filled with this kind of religiosity, that they believed themselves more enlightened and holier than the rest of mankind; on which account, moreover, it was impossible to induce them to relinquish their persuasion. They

who have confirmed themselves therein, enter on a similar enthusiasm after death, and are separated from the rest, and sent away to their like in forests, where, at a distance, they have the appearance of wild swine. But they who have not so confirmed themselves, are bound, separately from the others, to a place like a desert, in the extreme borders of the southern quarter, where they have caves for their places of worship.

84. When the former enthusiastic spirits were removed from them, the quaking of their bodies, which these spirits had occasioned, ceased, and they now feel a motion to the left. It was shown me, that ever since the rise of Quakerism, they have gone on successively from bad to worse, and at length, by command of their holy spirit, into abominations, which they divulge to no one. I conversed with the founder of their persuasion, as well as with Penn, who told me, that they had no part in such things. But they who perpetrate them, are sent down after death into a dark place, where they sit in corners, appearing like the dregs of oil.

85. Inasmuch as they have rejected the two Sacraments, of Baptism and the Holy Supper, and still read the Word, and preach the Lord, and speak from the obsession of enthusiastic spirits, and thus commix the sanctities of the Word with truths profaned, therefore no society is formed of them in the spiritual world, but after being divided from their companions, and roaming hither and thither, they are dispersed, and are gathered into the before-mentioned desert.

OF THE MORAVIANS IN THE SPIRITUAL WORLD.

86. I HAVE had much conversation with the people called Moravians, or Heernhutters. They appeared, at first, in a valley not far from the Jews; but after being examined and detected, were conveyed away to uninhabited places. On examining them, *it was found*, that they were cunning in the art of conciliation, saying, that they were the remains of the Apostolic Church, and that therefore they salute each other as brethren, and those who receive the more internal of their mysteries, as mothers; also, that they teach faith better than the rest of mankind, and love the Lord, because He endured the cross, calling Him the Lamb, and the Throne of Grace; with other the like expressions, by the use of which they lead men to believe, that the true Christian church is among them. They examine those who listen to their smooth harangues, as to whether they may safely entrust them with their mysteries; which they conceal or reveal accordingly; endeavoring in the latter case, by admonitions, and even by threats, to prevent the betrayal of their secret doctrine concerning the Lord.

87. The Moravians having acted in a similar manner in the spiritual world, when yet it was perceptible that their inward thoughts were contrary to their actions; therefore, in order to make this apparent, they were admitted into the ultimate heaven; but not sustaining the sphere of the charity and derivative faith of the angels there, they fled away. Afterwards, because in the world they believed that they alone would be alive, and would enter the third heaven, they were carried up into this heaven also, but on perceiving its sphere of love to the Lord, they were seized with anguish of heart, and began to suffer inward tortures, and to move convulsively, like persons in the agony of death, and therefore cast themselves headlong thence. In this manner it was first made apparent, that inwardly, they had cherished nothing of charity to the neighbor, and nothing of love to the Lord. They were afterwards sent to those, whose duty it is to examine the interiors of the thoughts, and these spirits declared of them, that they slight the Lord, that their rejection of the life of charity amounts to abhorrence, and that they make out that the Word of the Old Testament is useless, and despise the Evangelists; only of their good pleasure, selecting from Paul, whatever is said of faith alone: and that these are their mysteries, which they conceal from the world.

88. As soon as it became apparent that they merely acknowledge the Lord as the Arians do, despise the Word of the Prophets and Evangelists, and hold a life of charity in abhorrence, when yet these three things are, as it were, the pillars on which the universal heaven is supported; then they, who at once had a knowledge of, and a belief in, their mysteries, were adjudged Anti-Christs, who reject the three essentials of the Christian church, namely, the Divinity of the Lord, the Word, and Charity, and were banished from the Christian world, into a desert in the confine of the southern quarter, near the region of the Quakers.

89. When Zinzendorf first entered the spiritual world after his decease, and was permitted to speak as he used to speak in the world, I heard him solemnly asserting, that he knew the mysteries of heaven, and that no one enters heaven who is not of his doctrine; and also, that they who do good works for the sake of salvation, are utterly damned, and that he would rather admit Atheists into his congregation than such. The Lord, he said, was adopted by God the Father as His Son, because he endured the cross, and that still he was a mere man. When it was observed to him, that the Lord was conceived by God the Father, he replied, that he thought of that matter as he chose: not daring to speak out as the Jews do. Moreover, I have perceived many scandals from his followers, when I have been reading the Evangelists.

90. They say, that they have a sensation, and, from this sensation, an interior confirmation of their dogmas. But it was shown them, that the sensation proceeds from visionary spirits, who confirm a man in all his religious notions, and enter into closer conjunction with those, who, like the Moravians, are fond of their religion, and frequently have it in their thoughts. These spirits, moreover, conversed with them, and they mutually recognized each other.

THE END.

www.ingramcontent.com/pod-product-compliance
Lightning Source LLC
LaVergne TN
LVHW021309110826
845150LV00003B/531

* 9 7 8 1 4 2 5 5 5 8 6 4 2 *